MW00605523

Let the Older Women Teach

Sis.
Krysteana
Tarver

Let the Older Women Teach

MIDGE VICE

CREATION
HOUSE
A STRANG COMPANY

LET THE OLDER WOMEN TEACH by Midge Vice
Published by Creation House
A Strang Company
600 Rinehart Road
Lake Mary, Florida 32746
www.creationhouse.com

This book or parts thereof may not be reproduced in any form, stored in a retrieval system, or transmitted in any form by any means—electronic, mechanical, photocopy, recording, or otherwise—without prior written permission of the publisher, except as provided by United States of America copyright law.

Unless otherwise noted, all Scripture quotations are from the New American Standard Bible. Copyright © 1960, 1962, 1963, 1968, 1971, 1972, 1973, 1975, 1977 by the Lockman Foundation. Used by permission. (www. Lockman.org)

Scripture quotations marked TLB are from The Living Bible. Copyright © 1971. Used by permission of Tyndale House Publishers, Inc., Wheaton, IL 60189. All rights reserved.

Scripture quotations marked KJV are from the King James Version of the Bible.

Scripture quotations marked NIV are from the Holy Bible, New International Version of the Bible. Copyright © 1973, 1978, 1984, International Bible Society. Used by permission.

Scripture quotations marked NKJV are from the New King James Version of the Bible. Copyright © 1979, 1980, 1982 by Thomas Nelson, Inc., publishers. Used by permission.

Scripture quotations marked MOFFATT are from The Bible: A New Translation by James Moffatt. Copyright © 1954 by Harper & Row, New York.

Scripture quotations marked NLT are from the Holy Bible, New Living Translation, copyright 1996, 2004. Used by permission of Tyndale House Publishers, Inc., Wheaton, Illinois 60189. All rights reserved.

Scripture quotations marked GNB are from the Good News Bible: The Bible in Today's English Version, Robert G. Bratcher, ed., New York: American Bible Society, 1976.

Unless otherwise noted, all Greek and Hebrew terms and definitions are from Herb Jahn, ed., Exegeses Ready Research Bible, second edition (Nashville, TN: World Bible Publishers, 1993).

Design Director: Bill Johnson
Cover design by Amanda Potter

Copyright © 2008 by Midge Vice
All rights reserved

Library of Congress Control Number: 2008926037
International Standard Book Number: 978-1-59979-388-7

First Edition

08 09 10 11 12 —987654321

Printed in the United States of America

Dedication

I DEDICATE THIS BOOK TO Emily, Desiree', Sarah, Meghan, Savannah, and Victoria, my very special grandgirls, and my grandson, Kody, who is just as special. I want to thank them for being so patient and giving up so much precious time for me to work on "the book."

And a special thanks to my daughters-in-law: Trudy, who read the initial manuscript and was such a wonderful source of input and encouragement; Kimi, who helped with the scripture and questions I had; and Dionna for being there when times were tough. And to my sons: Grant, Matt, and Spencer, my joys, who made our lives together worth it all.

And how could I leave out Lamar? For without him, there would be no book. We have surely fought the good fight of faith and won. He has loved me as no other and he too has given up so much of my time for this project. Thanks, hon.

Contents

Preface

THIS BOOK IS FOR women—married or unmarried. It is for the woman who wishes she were married, and for the one who wishes she wasn't, and even for the already divorced trying to understand what went wrong. It is for anyone that wants real answers. My goal is to help you gain a better understanding of what God intended for marriage in general, as well as what He wants for your marriage in particular.

This is my attempt to tell how Lamar and I went from defeat to victory in our marriage. I have to admit for the first ten years we weren't in very good shape and it wasn't getting any better. In fact, it was getting a whole lot worse. I was having a wonderful experience as a Christian with significant changes in my life, but my marriage remained virtually untouched. In my frustration I prayed, "God, how can I recommend Christianity to someone if it isn't working for me?"

I didn't blame God. I knew I was the one who wasn't getting it. "Help me understand. Help me make it work!" What I didn't realize was this very determination was what it was going to take to make it work. This prayer, this attitude, is what made the difference. I was not giving up. It had to work. It does work. But God had a lot to teach me before I would get the victory. I didn't do anything extraordinary except throw myself at the feet of Jesus again and again seeking for answers. If I did anything right, it was not giving up.

I must stress the stories I tell about Lamar and myself are of a time long ago. I tell them not to make him look bad or me, but to help those who are in similar straits to see, not only where we have come from, but also the revelation God gave me in the middle of it all. That is the important thing—the revelation. As our story unfolds, you will understand why he was the way he was and I was the way I was. Thanks be to God, we didn't have to stay that way. Today we have one of those "kindred spirit" relationships. "All things become new." Only through the grace of God. Nothing in me. All in Him.

Anecdotes, scripture and movie references pepper this book. God used all three as a means of giving me the revelation I needed, and I believe each will hold relevance for your situation as well. I encourage you to pray along with me when you encounter italicized prayers in each chapter. I do want you to develop confidence in praying to God in your own words, but I hope mine will inspire you in some way. I also suggest you watch the movies I mention in this book. Perhaps they will inspire discussion between you and your spouse.

And so we begin on this journey together.

Introduction

S OMETIMES WE KNOW THINGS aren't right in our family, but when it comes to doing something about it we hate to face reality. Instead, we continue to delude ourselves, and the problems escalate. If you are unwilling to face the truth, the devil will force the issue—and God will let him. Let's face things early and spare ourselves the pain. I would advise you to opt for an easier way, but one thing is for sure: once you've taken the hard way, you have it down pat after that. At least I do. Some people seem to need more than a brick wall to fall on them. I may be dense, but I have my limit. Having to jump out of a burning van provided my impetus to change but also became a memory that haunted me for a long time.

I was coming home from substitute teaching absolutely worn out. After stopping at a local grocery store, I looked in my rearview mirror and saw flames flickering from the road to the van. My first reaction was to try to drive away from the flames, but wouldn't you know, the van stalled! I jumped out and tried to push the van. I wasn't getting very far when up in my spirit came the warning, "You'd better get out of here, girl." I ran to the door of the closest store muttering, "Lord, help me!" I expected the fire to go out, but His ways are not our ways. It wasn't to be.

The owner of the store was standing in the door watching the whole thing unfold. I asked if he had a fire extinguisher, but he replied that he didn't have one. I couldn't believe it. I thought a business was required by law to have a fire extinguisher. It was only a moment or so after my exchange with the store owner when the firemen arrived and swarmed all over our Volkswagen bus. You would think I would have been glad, but I wasn't; I was afraid the van would explode and didn't want one of the firemen to get injured or killed. I expressed my concern to the head firefighter, and he assured me they had everything under control. They know these things. I had to trust his judgment and trust God to give him wisdom.

Everybody standing around couldn't believe all the fire, smoke, and popping, yet there was no explosion. It was a miracle that no one was killed. After the fire was out, I went over to the bus to see what I could recover from the damage. My groceries and a box of Christian comic books with my Bible inside were sitting right over the motor, the source of the fire, but they didn't even smell of smoke. The box had a scorched place, but that's all.

That night after supper as the boys cleaned up the kitchen, I needed some private time to ponder the events of the day. I couldn't believe we had lost our beloved bus. It was so handy and such a gas saver. Plus, we only had a few more payments. I was finding it hard to give it up, but didn't have much choice. All of a sudden I remembered that when I got out of the van at the grocery store a lady pointed to a stream of gas coming from the back of the vehicle and warned me how dangerous it was. Another lady stopped and agreed.

I had been warned the gas line was broke, and I drove it anyway! Why would I drive it knowing how dangerous it was? Why do we do a lot of stupid things we do? There was a moment when I came out of the store that I remembered the ladies' warning but decided to drive the van anyway. Why? I was trying to get home, and I didn't want to bother Lamar. I thought I could make it, and I didn't want to listen to him complain. My mind was so warped by what he might say that I couldn't function normally. I had allowed his temper and attitude to warp my ability to think straight. My foolishness put my life at risk and caused us to lose our bus.

Looking back, I realized that I should have gone back and tried to smother the fire instead of trying to move the van. At that point, the gas that had dripped on the road was on fire, not my van. Why did I think the fire was on the road if I knew the gas line was broken? Because, it was on the road. At this point it wasn't all that bad and could have been easily put out. If the man in the furniture store had had a fire extinguisher it would have been all over. But it was not to be.

I couldn't understand until that night why God hadn't just put the fire out when I prayed for His help. I thought the bus was the important thing and that losing it signaled some sort of defeat. But it was really me, not the bus, that God threw into the fire—the Refiner's fire. God had something bigger in mind: the maturing of a saint and the healing of a marriage. The bus was just the sacrifice.

I didn't want to act so foolishly, but I didn't know how to turn things around either. I repented and determined that I would do whatever God showed me to do to change things and then added, "I can't tell this to Lamar Vice right now. He's just lost his bus. It would push him over the edge. You are going to have to show me when to tell him."

About a month later, I had taken our oldest son Grant out on some errands and arrived home a little late to start supper. Lamar was hungry and didn't appreciate the delay. Grant was outside working on building a rabbit hutch and Lamar was mad about the noise. Grant needed help but wouldn't ask for it because he didn't want to have to deal with his father's attitude and temper. He preferred to do it himself and risk having a bad job. My kids were reacting that same as I was.

I knew then it was time to tell Lamar about the broken gas line. I stepped into the living room doorway and said I had something to tell him when he was done watching his program. "Oh I'm not watching this. Just turn it off," he said. He knew how I felt about competing with the television when we had something important to discuss.

I proceeded to explain that his temper and the way he talked to his family made us reluctant to seek his help. I had considered that maybe his reactions were really his way of getting off the hook, but rather than make that assumption or be accusatory, I asked him to think carefully about how his actions were hurting his family. I didn't talk long and didn't scream or yell. I just made my point and stood there hoping it was God's point too.

Lamar was not thrilled with the revelation. It was really a shocker for him to find out I knew the gas line was broken. After a few moments he said, "Well if that's the case, I'll just stay on the road more." (He traveled quite a bit for our business.) "Now there's your good godly answer," I retorted. And with that he got his keys and left. I knew he needed to be alone, and I chose to trust that if I had spoken what God gave me to speak, He would anoint it. It was between Lamar and God.

When Lamar came back, he apologized and said God had helped him see that losing the van was partly his fault. He understood that he could have lost me, too, and said that was the worst part. Just as God used the loss of our van to show me how negative my thought patterns had become, God used the situation to help Lamar see the reality of what his ugly and ungodly words were doing to his family. Since then I have seen a gradual but significant change in Lamar, and I believe it started with that situation.

DRUNK SPIDERS

In college we read a study on the effects of alcohol on spider families. The researcher gave spiders alcohol so they became drunk. The drunken spiders proceeded to weave misshapen webs. The poor spiders then tried to make a life for themselves and their families. However, drunk spiders do not do a good job weaving webs. When the webs are warped, they don't catch food properly, which causes the baby spiders' diet to suffer. With a faulty diet, the little spiders don't grow up to be healthy, normal spiders, if they grow up at all.

Some time after the burning of the van and the revelation that our actions and perceptions were causing us to make bad decisions, I had a second revelation. Lamar and I were in the middle of one of our typical arguments when up in my spirit came the reminder, "Drunk spiders don't raise normal spiders." I hadn't thought of this study for years, but now I understood the message: Lamar and I couldn't continue interacting the way we were and raise normal adults. We had not consumed even a drop of liquor for years, but this was not about alcohol, any more than lust is about sex. I had to get my act together (with God's help), if I really loved my children.

We say we love our children, but if we don't discipline ourselves to do what we should so they will grow up to be healthy and whole, how can this be true? How can it be if we don't nurture or provide for them, or if we choose to remain ignorant as to what their real needs are? What if we discipline them too harshly or incorrectly—or not at all? Many parents are not age-appropriate in handling matters of discipline with their children. Wanting our children to be happy should not be the highest goal of a parent. A spoiled brat is happy. Love is disciplining yourself as a parent to do what is best for your child.

If disciplining ourselves for the betterment of our children means working harder to get along with our spouse, we need to be willing to do so. When one spouse is warped like the drunk spider, he or she inevitably does the wrong thing. The other responds poorly. The first one responds back improperly, and the spouse responds in kind. If neither responds properly, the confrontation goes on until it gets vicious. Heaven knows many marriages are in some phase of this cycle, but they don't have to be. There are proper responses and attitudes that diffuse instead of empower the cycle. However, if we don't learn and implement them, the cycle will keep building up steam until *Pow!* Our home and marriage became wreckage on the ash heap of life.

I call these cycle-inducing responses "gut level reactions"—GLRs. They are our natural responses. The problem is they are usually wrong and only make the situation worse. What comes naturally is not usually God's answer. We need to remember that God's ways are not our ways; they are higher than our ways. (See Isaiah 55:8–9.) So why do we think our GLRs are the right response? When we finally see the mess we've made, why do we blame everyone but ourselves? We need to try to understand the proper, scriptural response to confrontational circumstances. Until then, we will only continue making things worse.

People assume God knows their problems and will do something about them *when He gets around to it.* That's not faith. That's presumption. Faith is asking and believing He hears and answers. God does know our problems, but He doesn't act on them until we invite Him to get involved. Problems like sin and unforgiveness can also keep Him from acting. We need to know what those problems are and deal with them.

Amazingly, some people choose to keep their bitterness or sin rather than have the victory in their life. I want to be healthy, prosperous, and blessed more than I want to blame someone else. God has the answers. We just need to have ears that hear.

God can and will guide us into all truth, but He doesn't lead people kicking and screaming into it. Nor does He lead somebody who has her fingers in her ears humming a worship song to drown out the sound of His voice. God needs someone who is teachable, open, and willing to be led. As I said at the beginning, God can and will give you the impetus to change. He is the author and the finisher of your faith, and He is bound by His Word to accomplish your "finishing."

One beaten-down friend of mine jokingly said one day, "I hear what I want to hear." It was truer than she realized. What a messed up life this thinking caused for her and her children, and all just so she could play her games. Are you playing games with your own mind? If so, please stop. The truth—and the truth alone—will set you free. Say a prayer right now to ask that God expose your wrong thought patterns so that He can begin to heal them and replace them with His truth.

FEAR

Shortly after the van incident, Lamar got upset about something and jerked out the television cord, rendering the TV unworkable. I hate waste and destruction and normally would have tried to stop him, but I had learned my lesson. This sobered-up spider was determined to respond constructively. After all, no television for two weeks was no biggie for me. Lamar didn't have to replace too many items that he had destroyed in his anger before he came to see he was only hurting himself.

The scripture God gave me to stand on was 1 Peter 3:6 (NIV):

For this is the way the holy women of the past who put their hope in God used to make themselves beautiful. They were submissive to their own husbands, like Sarah, who obeyed Abraham and called him her master. You are her daughters if you do what is right and do not give way to fear.

Notice that last little phrase: "If you do what is right and do not give way to fear." The first part of the phrase means that if your husband asks you to sin, you have every right to refuse. Lovingly, gently, you may refuse. The latter part admonishes us to have a healthy respect for dangers. However, fear must not keep you from hearing and obeying God.

This verse showed me that if I wanted things to change in my family, I had to change first. Most of us get it backwards. We want our husbands to change before we will. If we can't or won't change, then why shouldn't our husband have the same right to stay the same? If you have been trying to get him to change and it hasn't worked, you should probably try something else. Let's put our hope in God and do everything we can to change ourselves. Then we can see if he doesn't change as a result.

I have learned to keep my mouth shut until I change. I still keep my mouth shut while I wait until Lamar changes. When he does, I let him bask in his own glory for a while. Eventually he comes to see I played a part in it and he says something. Learning to keep your mouth shut is one of the best things you will ever do for your marriage.

Watch and listen when things are happening in your life that you don't understand. God may not intervene when you think He should, but that might be your miracle. Your miracle may consist of the things you learn as you go through difficult experiences in life. It's sad to think the mess in our lives is because of our bad choices, but it's nice to know today we can choose better. It's time for you to decide what your choice will be. I am now going to tell my story, and please allow me to start at the beginning. My beginning.

ONE

Ken and Marion O.

I HAD A WISE MOTHER named Marion and a wonderful father named Kenny O. They were very special people, both nurturing and supportive. We had a peaceful, happy home with a great deal of humor in it. Respect came easy for us kids, maybe because they respected us. My parents respected their neighbors, too, so there was no gossip in our home. My parents weren't particularly talkative, and yet we had plenty of pleasant conversation. I was the big talker then, just as I am now. There was a lot of space to fill, and they always seemed glad to have me fill it.

I was the youngest of three children born two years apart, and I was the only girl. My brothers, Grant and Dick, were compliant children. Mother was great at encouraging children to be good; she very rarely spanked and when she did it was never more than a swat. Mother was very wise, and part of being wise is being a good parent.

Mom and Dad had their relationship all worked out: she generally ran things and Dad got his way. Everybody loved Daddy, so it was easy to give him what he wanted. I remember pointing out to Mom, "Daddy always gets his way because he says he never gets his way." She laughed because it was so true. She repeated this story for years.

Mom would come into my bedroom and warn me that Dad would be getting me and the boys up early to work at Gram's the next day. "Be sure to jump right up on the first call and get dressed without a fuss," she'd say. Mom was always defending Dad in this way, not that it was necessary. He was no pushover. If we were doing something wrong, he would let us know. If he found out that one of us used a tool and didn't put it back, he would line up the three of us and ask who used it last.

One-by-one we would either say we didn't use it or we did, and then he would ask when and where we left it when we were finished with it. There were no repercussions. We didn't get "licks" or extra chores, just admonished to be more careful. His demeanor, which communicated how important it was that we take proper care of things, made the point sufficiently. That was enough to make us not want to disappoint him or be lined up again.

Everybody loved Kenny Osborne. He was a city bus driver. He loved his job because it got him out with people and allowed him to work around the house in the mornings and still be there for us when we came home from school for lunch, like kids did in those days. He even took split shifts so he could be home in the evening for a while.

Daddy and I were kindred spirits. He probably made my brothers feel that way, too, but he and I had a special bond. Mom said of Daddy and me that if you met one of us, you met the other. I was a lot like his sister, Madge, who died at the age of twenty-six. My dad was sixteen at the time, and her son, Dean, was just six. The loss of his sister had a huge impact on Dad's life.

Contrary to popular opinion, I was not spoiled. I was, however, expected to do the right thing and to be responsible. I felt like Joanie on *Happy Days*. I had two brothers, great parents, and a near-perfect life. Then in October 1963, my senior year of college, my brother Grant was killed in an Army accident. Everything changed that day. Joanie had an older brother on the show that somehow wasn't carried over the second year, but it's not as easy to write someone out of your story in real life.

Grant's death was a defining moment in my life, just as November of that same year was a defining moment for the country. I remember sitting in the student lounge after Kennedy was killed watching all the pomp and ceremony of the funeral, feeling like I was in instant replay. My brother's funeral had also been a Catholic military affair. Little did our country realize at the time how deeply we would be affected by President Kennedy's death. We lost our innocence when JFK was killed. America would never be the same again. My wake-up call had just come a month earlier than everybody else's.

The next June I graduated with a bachelor's degree in Home Economics, majoring in Family Studies and Home Art. I wanted to be an interior decorator, but ended up a jane-of-all-trades. Since my fiancé was going to go to graduate school on Long Island, I got a job in New York City working the West Side Terminal of American Airlines. It was quite a commute, and we ended up not seeing much of each other. I decided it was just as well and ended the relationship. There was no use moving back home because the job market was so bad in Erie.

I found an apartment just outside the city in Jackson Heights. Couples in the area would buy a section of apartments and rent them out to either all girls or all guys that needed a place to live, four to a two-bedroom apartment. I didn't know any of my roommates when I moved in. Boy, what an eye-opener that was. One of my roommates was quite promiscuous and drank too much. I later found out that her behavior was the result of emotional trauma she experienced after having an abortion. Though this is typical of girls that have abortions, I didn't know that at the time.

I was into all this when Lamar waltzed into my life that New Year's Eve. He was in the Navy and had just been transferred to Pensacola, Florida, where he thought he was headed. Instead, the ship he was assigned to was dry-docked at the Brooklyn Naval Shipyards. The last place he wanted to go was New York City in the dead of winter. There were not many men on the ship when he arrived, so he asked one of the guys where he could go to meet up with some of his shipmates. He was given my address! When he got to the apartment, everyone had a date but him.

New Year's Eve was my last night on the night shift. It was eleven o'clock at night when I got off work, and I was just a few blocks from Times Square. It would have been so easy to go and watch the famous ball drop. Not being much for mob scenes, I opted to go home instead. I knew they were having a party and really didn't want to get involved in that, but I was tired and hoped for the best. When I walked through the door, it was as if Lamar were connected to the door—he travelled almost instantly from one side of the room to the other to introduce himself. Evidently I made quite an impression on him with my long brown hair, raccoon collar, and camel colored coat. I thought he was nice enough, but it was not love at first sight for me. I was just getting over one relationship and was not looking for another.

Early the next morning, I left to get my brother Grant's car in Washington, D.C. Mom and Dad had gone to Texas to get it and left it with Dick, my other brother, until I could get it. I was long gone when Lamar returned to the apartment that afternoon anxious to see me again. He was devastated and went to the apartment below to find out where I went. The girls assured him I would be back. He was inconsolable, and he couldn't even remember my name. It was like I was a mirage.

When I got back to my apartment from D.C., they told me Lamar had been there every day looking for me. Within a few days we got together and started dating. He loved me, but I didn't feel that way about him. He was a nice enough guy, but though I enjoyed his company, I wasn't ready to commit to anything. When we had a fight early on, he left saying it was over. Lamar came back eventually, but in the meantime I accepted another date.

Lamar thought he could pick up where he left off. When he started talking about what we were going to do Friday night, I said, "I don't remember you asking me about Friday night." Sheepishly, he asked and I told him I already had plans with someone else. He was livid and insisted I cancel it, but I refused. I don't cancel dates once I make them. It should have given him a clue as to what kind of girl I was: a girl of her word. It also should have given me a clue of what kind of guy he was. It's important that you let someone you are dating know early on that you don't play games and that if they choose to, they will lose out.

Ours is a wonderful love story. It starts out with Lamar's great love for me. I like that part, but I had misgivings. I wasn't one of those girls that got terrible crushes on guys and couldn't stand it. No, I wanted to be pursued, and if a guy didn't care enough to pursue me, he didn't care enough. Lamar fit the part. He liked the pursuit. It took me a while to jump in, but Lamar, being the optimist he is, ignored all that. I did come to love him, but I just don't go *ga-ga* over anyone. My mother helped my brother and me keep control of our hearts, which is scriptural, but I think she went a little overboard. We are very independent people.

> *Guard thy heart with all diligence for out of it are the issues of life.*
> —PROVERBS 4:23

A BABY!

We almost married that summer but I still didn't feel at peace about it. Religion was one of the issues. I was Catholic, and Lamar was Baptist. Catholicism was a very important part of who I was, and I had no intention of changing. It was very important to me that my kids be raised Catholic. Lamar assured me this was no problem. I could raise the children Catholic, and he would go to church with me. When we got to Lamar's hometown of Gadsden, Alabama, to get married, he wanted a local pastor to do the honors. That was not acceptable. Catholics aren't supposed to have someone of another denomination perform such an important spiritual task. When I balked at the idea of having a Protestant perform the ceremony, Lamar got angry and sent me back to Pensacola on the bus. I was in a state of shock, and as far as I was concerned, it was over. To be honest, I was glad. It was a high-maintenance relationship that I didn't need. The only problem was that a few days later I missed my period!

Now you must remember young people didn't know much about contraceptives in those days. We were just supposed to abstain, and I had until Lamar and I became serious. As a Catholic, I just wasn't prepared to be sexually active before marriage. Looking back I now realize how dumb I was. I was normally a very levelheaded, responsible young person. I understand we think kids are a lot smarter about these things today, but that knowledge doesn't mean they're mature enough to make wise choices.

By this time I was twenty-two years old and capable of raising the child by myself, but in those days there were few single parents. Most girls married the father or gave the baby up for adoption, which I feel is often the most loving choice a young mother can make. Abortion never entered my mind. I had not even heard about abortion until I got to college. I was horrified, which should be the natural response to the thought of killing a baby. No, neither my emotions nor my Catholic sensibilities would have allowed me to even consider aborting the baby.

I knew Lamar loved me dearly and desperately wanted to marry me. I loved him, even though I didn't like some of his ways. It just seemed like the logical thing to get married. Besides, I knew I needed to tell him about the pregnancy, not for support, but just because I wouldn't keep a child from knowing his father, or vice-versa. When I called Lamar, he was thrilled. He never thought our relationship was over. To him, sending me back to Pensacola was just his way of getting me to cooperate. His manipulation was the least of my worries, but it would be a long time before I faced it.

Being pregnant before we married was never known by anyone but our closest friends at the time, and we moved immediately. Mathematically, it was impossible to know because we married so quickly. Why bother to bring it up? Because when I started testifying, I just naturally had to tell the truth. I was not better than the ones I was speaking to. The truth sets us free. How could I continue to lie when God had done so much?

Lamar was in and out with the ship, so I had to make all the preparations to get married. I even had to pay the two dollars for the license. I have often kidded Lamar that I kept him all those years so I could get my money's worth.

The night before we married, Lamar was snotty to me on the phone, and I once again had serious misgivings. My roommate assured me I was just feeling the typical pre-nuptial jitters. We should have backed off, but

I was pregnant. That's just one reason why God tells us not to have sex before we marry.

Our Love Story

Perhaps you're wondering why I said Lamar and I had a wonderful love story. It is, but it wasn't either of our love made it wonderful. What we had soon ran out. If it had been our love story alone, it would have been awfully short. Instead, this is a story of agape love—God's love—that eventually brought beauty out of ashes, peace out of war, and joy out of grief. He saw a potential in our relationship that I couldn't see, but it was a long time before God got our attention.

When we were dating, Lamar seemed like such a nice guy. He was one of the Navy "swabbies" that started coming around our apartment because there were so many single girls in New York City. Everyone liked "Vice." He was dynamic, a "good-time Charlie." Two weeks after we married, much to my chagrin, Lamar changed almost completely. He was still dynamic, but he lost his good-time Charlie ways. Little did I realize how much his drinking had been affecting him. When he sobered up, all of a sudden I found myself married to a grumpy, serious, easily depressed young man on a mission to make it big.

I like to live comfortably, but I wasn't worried about it. After all, I believed in the American dream. I always felt Lamar and I would do just fine thanks to our talents and training. But Lamar didn't want to live *comfortably*. He wanted more, and he was singly motivated in that direction. It complicated things when we had one, then two, and finally three children in the first four years of our marriage. The situation really didn't lend itself to becoming quick millionaires, but Lamar wasn't dissuaded.

Because Lamar was often working, a lot of the work and responsibility at home fell on me. When you are pregnant and a new mother and move frequently, which we did because Lamar was in the Navy, it's hard to be anything else. I loved my babies and could have managed if Lamar had been satisfied. A satisfied mind is a wonderful thing. I praise God for mine. If there is always something that keeps you from being satisfied, how will you ever know peace? God wants to give you peace in spite of your circumstances. Receive it. Rest in Him and quit struggling.

> *Oh, Lord! Help me to have a satisfied mind and to accept circumstances with dignity and grace, not fighting and struggling against what I can never change. Help me to recognize what I can change and do what it will take. Help me to stand in faith that things won't always be like this, or worse. Surely, with You in my life the circumstances will get better. I believe that You are working all things to my good. Help me to quit struggling so much and just rest in You. I thank You, Lord; that I do have a satisfied mind. I claim it in Jesus' name. Amen.*

Back then I allowed a lot of things to bother me. During the first Christmas season as a married couple, our friends were having a New Year's Eve party and I wanted to go. I told Lamar a few weeks before Christmas about it and said, "If you are going to want to go to your parents over the holidays, we need to go for Christmas because I want to be here for New Year's." I thought I had been clear enough, and he assured me that he didn't want to go home at all.

After Christmas, however, Lamar informed me he wanted to go home the next weekend, which was New Year's. I was aghast. After going back and forth a while, Lamar walked out. It was late in the evening when he left, and he didn't come home until 5 a.m.—with a hangover. I stayed up all night worrying. He apologized profusely, and I assumed that meant we would stay in town. I was wrong. He may have been sorry he stayed out all night and worried me, but he still intended to go home that weekend. That was preposterous to me. I eventually gave in, which reinforced a terrible precedent set by his parents.

In my home, if my parents said no, they meant no. We never even considered trying to beg them out of it. Actually, my parents rarely had to say no because we knew not to ask for certain things. His parents, on the other hand, said no to just about everything and then let the kids beg them into a yes. They gauged how important a request was by how much the child fought for it. Lamar had been taught from an early age to verbally spar, and I was no match for what I was about to encounter. Of course, I didn't know all this that day.

We moved to Gadsden, Alabama, the day Lamar was discharged from the Navy, and I was released from the hospital with our new baby, Kenneth Grant, named after my father and brother. It was late when we arrived, and much to my dismay, Lamar's father had a terrible cold. By the next day baby Grant had a runny nose and a cough, and he was only six days old.

The Vice's argued frequently, and each one wanted me on their side. I didn't want to take sides. I didn't want to hear their problems, so I stayed in my room with the baby. It was just easier, but this didn't set well with Mrs. Vice. It was a hard time for all of us. It is difficult for two families to live together in one house, especially when not everyone knows each other. I finally insisted Lamar find a place for us, even though he didn't have a job yet.

Lamar found a little rental house and painted it inside. Friends and relatives gave or loaned us some furniture, and we were able to fix up the house really nice. We were soon out of money. One night he was going out and wanted some money "just in case," he told me. I gave him a twenty dollar bill and told him that was the last of the money. When he came home I asked if he needed it, and he said he hadn't. When pressed, he sheepishly admitted that he lost it gambling. I was appalled.

He was trying to turn twenty dollars into more money and ended up losing it in the process. He was kind of dumbfounded because he had always done so well when he was in the Navy. I told him not to ever do that again, and he never did, thank God. However, that night we were in a real pickle: neither of us had a job and suddenly we were out of money, too.

In Lamar's defense, it was typical for Lamar's mother to tell the kids that she had no money, only to produce some if needed. She kept some money back, so Lamar expected me to do it, too. It took him years to understand that I said what I meant.

The Jewelry Business

Having no money forced Lamar to try all the harder to get a job, which he did immediately. Even though everybody and their brother was helping him, no one was hiring. We knew it would just be a matter of time until one came through. In the meantime, he talked to the woman at the employment office. The only thing she had available was a sales job at the new jewelry store in town.

It was meant to be. God guides, or attempts to guide us, even in the hard times; we just don't always see it. The manager Lamar worked for was a wonderful mentor who taught Lamar much of what has made him the success he is today. Lamar not only started the job, but he became a workaholic. Grant and I were left alone night after night and on many weekends, too. This was not unusual in that time period, so Lamar couldn't understand why I had a problem with the hours he was working. Arguing didn't change his actions; it just made our times together more difficult. I was in a no-win situation. When he was home, he was no help. He was exhausted, uncooperative, grumpy, and depressed. When he was at work, I was all alone. My family was twelve hours away in Erie, and none of the women in our neighborhood were home during the day. Even if I had found somebody, they wouldn't have understood me. We may have both spoken English, but I was northern and they were southern; the cultural barrier was too great. It's amazing how isolated a young mother can be.

As money pressures and life demands increased, Lamar got more demanding. His answer for problems was to put down more rules, which just meant there were more rules to break, making him angrier and angrier. We were beginning a vicious cycle with no clue as to how to slow it down or stop it.

Lamar was not Ken Osborne, but I was constantly comparing the two. My daddy was so sweet and patient. He would take his time and tell us why he was doing something and explain things. He didn't mind answering the questions of a curious young mind. Not Lamar. Daddy knew realistically how much you could get done and that's all he expected. Not Lamar. Daddy didn't expect perfection. Not Lamar. It was obvious, Lamar was losing badly in the comparison. It didn't help that Daddy and I were kindred spirits, while Lamar and I are complete opposites. Of course, my father had been foolish in his early years, too, but I didn't know him then.

Oh, how I struggled to figure it all out. The Catholic Church had a stand against divorce that I wanted to honor, but I didn't see how I could. Lamar and I were obviously headed for a split, but I was determined to stay together. The message of the gospel had yet to reach me, so I thought I would be doomed for all eternity if we divorced. I just didn't see any good answers.

After working in our local jewelry store chain for a while, Lamar went into business for himself, first in the jewelry business and then in a discount salvage store. We took out a small business loan, but found ourselves among a long list of businesses that a local bank did wrong. The scam was happening all over the country. In our case, they didn't even do the usual paper work, but rather took illegal possession of our store. The Small Business Association took them to court, but it was too late; our business had been destroyed.

DADRA'S DEATH

Shortly after the loss of our store and the sale of our home in September, 1971, our three and a half-year-old daughter, Dadra, was fatally hit by a car as she darted across the street while we were out for a walk. By the time we arrived at the hospital, she had passed. Lamar caught a glimpse of us in the ambulance as he was coming home. He later told how he knew he needed to pray, but he was in no shape to ask God for anything. He determined never to find himself in a place again where he couldn't pray, but it's one thing to say it and it's another to do it.

As we left the hospital, I was struck by the fact that nothing outside had changed: the traffic lights still worked; cars were moving as usual;

everybody was going about their business as if nothing had happened. Nothing in the world around me reflected the catastrophic event that had just taken place in our lives.

When we got home, the people started coming. All those years when I desperately needed help, nobody came by. Suddenly—when all I wanted was to be left alone—everybody was there to see what they could do. It was too late. The most precious thing in my life was gone, and there was nothing anyone could do to change it. I wanted them to leave me alone to try and comprehend the incomprehensible.

I went in the bathroom and started cleaning because I didn't want our guests to see it the way it was and I didn't want to be out there with them. I thought maybe if I kept busy I wouldn't have to think. I remember Lamar trying to get me to stop. "This isn't the time," he said. I wondered what is a person supposed to do at a time like this?

We went in the bedroom and Lamar asked, "Why couldn't it have been me?" I didn't say it, but in my mind I agreed. "Yeah, why couldn't it have been you?" Our relationship was that bad, and my baby girl was gone.

People were making plans to stay the night, and I asked Lamar why. "What do they think I am going to do? Kill myself?" He knew I wouldn't do that to my family. After Lamar convinced them I wouldn't do anything rash and we that wouldn't need them, all our guests left and we eventually went to bed. I don't remember who took our sons Grant and Matt, but I do remember staying awake all night in a state of mental anguish. I was so numb that I don't even recall crying. I finally did cry, but privately; I didn't want to in front of the others. At some point I couldn't cry any more. Sleep eventually came, but I always woke with the reminder that she was gone smacking me square in the face. It was the first thought I had every day for I don't know how long.

It was as if someone had looked my whole life over and taken out the best part. I loved Grant dearly and never thought I could love another child as much, but Dadra was my little girl. She was a compliant child, a sweet little nurturer with blonde hair and eyes so dark you couldn't tell the pupil from the color. I couldn't imagine a more beautiful child inside or out—and she was gone!

Matt, our youngest, was one year old at the time of the accident. He was a lot like Dadra: blonde hair, brown eyes, a turned-up nose, and a sweet disposition. He was all boy, but he became more like her in personality as time went on. They were both the type to potty train and dress themselves early. They weren't verbally advanced. In fact, they both had a slight speech impediment. Their similarity was a comfort to me in some small way. All the boys were. My boys forced me to go on when I wouldn't have if I had been given a choice.

One special friend of mine, Valerie, came regularly and took Grant to preschool, but then we moved away and I was once again without help. Life kicks you when you are down and it seems that nobody cares. It would be years before Lamar was able to be much comfort, and my family was far, far away. I did have friends that would have been there for me, but they lived too far away. When I would write letters, they would seem so sad that I just couldn't send them; I didn't want to burden anyone, and I didn't think anyone could really help.

We did not settle down there and moved twice in Gadsden and then to Chattanooga, leaving what few friends I had behind. My best friend, Jean, decided since she couldn't stop by and check on me and since I wasn't good at writing, she would write me every day whether I wrote her or not. What an inexpressible blessing! It got to be a joke because I could tell when she was in a hurry and running out of something to say and using bigger script, etc. But I had something to look forward to. It was a little light in a very dark world. We soon moved back to Alabama from Chattanooga, but I didn't know anyone in the new town.

OFF TO ALTOONA

I had just decided not to get pregnant again when I realized I was going to have another baby. Lamar didn't know I had changed my mind and was confused when I was upset because he thought I wanted to be pregnant. In August, 1973, I went on to have another little boy, a sweet, affectionate little boy named Spencer. When I was pregnant people would ask me what I wanted, and I would say, "A girl, naturally." They would always counter, "Well, I guess the important thing is that the baby is healthy," afraid that if I had a boy I wouldn't accept him. But there is something that happens once you have a baby; I was instantly in love, and he was especially cute and sweet. I enjoyed my new baby, and Lamar was thrilled. You would have thought it was his first son.

Meanwhile, Lamar wasn't getting along all that well with Grant and Matt. They all loved me, but they didn't like each other. It put a lot of strain on our family.

Lamar quit going to church after we left Guntersville. I tried to go even as we moved around, but it was too painful to sit there when I had so many unanswered questions about why Dadra died. It was just easier not to go. When we moved back to Altoona, I decided if Grant was going to love the Catholic Church like I did, I had better start taking him to mass. This was quite the undertaking because the only Catholic Church was all the way down the mountain in Gadsden, forty-five minutes away. In order to get him into Catechism Class, we had to be there by 9 a.m., which meant I had to wake up at 7 a.m. Why I didn't leave the two youngest with Lamar, I don't know, but I took them, too. Matt was about three and one-half years old and Spencer was in a carrier.

My plan to encourage Grant to love the Catholic Church wasn't working. He hated it and wanted to stay in the nursery with Matt and Spencer. Sometimes I let him, figuring that in time he would change his mind. Going home was a problem because Lamar had by this time stopped at his parents' house to eat lunch. The boys and I passed by on the way home and would stop to say hello, but we wouldn't stay to eat because I wouldn't just plunk myself down unexpectedly at their table. Mrs. Vice would ask us to join them but wouldn't really insist, if she invited us at all. For the first two years after Dadra died, I wouldn't go to the Vice's at all. My feelings were too raw, and they weren't always sensitive to my grief. After that, sometimes I wouldn't stop at their house just so the boys wouldn't see that wonderful spread on the table and ask to stay.

I later came to understand it wasn't that she didn't have enough, but rather that she was humble. She never dreamed how much we desperately wanted to join her. She wasn't sure about what we wanted, how much she had, etc. It was just easier not to be insistent. Years later when we lived with her, I learned that if another family stopped by and she had a meal ready, she would tell us to act like we weren't about to eat. When I saw how much food she had prepared, it was ridiculous not to invite them. She was inhibited by her fear that there wasn't enough or that they wouldn't like what she had made. How I wish I had known that all those years earlier when the boys were young.

After four years, instead of getting better, I was just about suicidal! I remember going through our big, old house asking myself, "What is it all for? Is it to see how much I can take? To see if I can cope?" I didn't know if I was talking to the walls or if God could hear me. I hoped it was God.

One morning Lamar and I had a fight before he left for work. I was crying in my dishwater as I listened to Jim Bakker on *The PTL Club* in the background. He told me to say a prayer with him. I didn't think anything would help, but I wasn't too proud to say it while I was doing the dishes. Three days later I realized I was a different person. That pit of despair inside was gone. I had experienced a supernatural work of the Holy Spirit deep within my very inner being. I knew without a doubt that Jesus was the Son of God and the Bible was the Word of God. They say Christians work this stuff up, but there couldn't have been less exaggeration. After all, I never stopped washing the dishes while I was praying.

When Bakker talked about being saved or born again on another show, I thought, "That's what's happened to me." From then on I started getting answers. My best friend had just gotten divorced, and I wanted to tell her what happened but didn't want to say anything wrong. I prayed for an answer on divorce because the Catholic Church was so strict about it, and God showed me that He hates divorce, but loves the divorced. It was like someone plugged me in to an inner knowing. I didn't know everything, but I knew a lot more than I had before.

Another friend said something to me about cherishing Dadra's memory, but I couldn't say that I did. It was too painful. The truth was that my life *wasn't* better for having had her, and that was the worst part of all, for someone so sweet to cause such pain. I didn't want that to be true about Dadra. "Oh, God! Let it not be so!"

Looking back I can remember strange things that happened before Dadra died that, if I had been spiritually astute enough to pick up on them, things might have been different. I don't believe Dadra had to die. The devil has a plan for your life every day, just as God has a plan. Sometimes, though, God takes His hand of protection away. I was in a runaway cart going headlong toward the precipice, and Dadra's death was God sticking His foot out and stopping my cart. Could it have been done in an easier fashion? I doubt it. I wasn't looking for answers, at least not about God. I thought I had them. It wasn't until I lost Dadra that I realized how feeble my answers were.

There was a real move of God in our little town. We got connected with a wonderful group of Christians, and we all grew in the Lord together—just a bunch of crazy Methodists that wanted more of God. What a special time. This is how the spiritual aspect came into our lives. But I don't want you to think it was an easy time in our lives just because Lamar rededicated his life and I had finally found God. God's hand was over us again, but there was a great deal of pressure from the other side, too. The spiritual battle that raged was almost palpable, still, somehow I knew I had gone through too much to turn back. I stood determinedly on Romans 8:38–39:

> *For I am convinced that neither life, nor death, nor angels, nor principalities, nor things present, nor things to come, nor powers, nor height, nor depth, nor any other created thing, will be able to separate us from the love of God, which is in Christ Jesus our Lord.*

THE FORCE

Sometimes the best motivation to seek after God comes when we are able to look back at painful experiences and see God's hand in the circumstance or in our healing from a hurtful situation. Reverend T.D. Jakes shared how the long string of problems he experienced growing up in his adult life brought him to where he is today. It is these things from which we draw our strength. He called the effect of these problems "the force."

The force behind me is my little girl. My determination to see her again still helps me get over trepidation when God puts something in my spirit for me to do. When I think of Dadra, it gives me the joy I need to get through hard times that lie ahead. The thought of seeing her in heaven gives me the encouragement I need to persevere. The force behind Lamar is his childhood; the loss of his little girl; the years playing football for a coach that didn't particularly like him; the years in the Navy; and losing everything he had worked for at the hand of an unscrupulous banker.

Even if you haven't experienced great hardship or tragedy, it's important to reflect upon the experiences of your life and thank God for providing you with the opportunity for salvation through His Son and for blessing you in other ways.

> *God causes all things to work together for good to those who love God, to those who are called according to His purpose.*
> —ROMANS 8:28

While the Scriptures make it clear that salvation is by faith through grace, not by our own work or effort, it's important to remember that obedience to God and spiritual maturity go hand in hand. Obedience is an outgrowth of our love and devotion for Him, but adhering to His requests will also produce the fruit of love for God and greater anointing.

One evening my pastor preached on the anointing. He held up a bunch of beautiful grapes as we all admired them. Each one was so perfect. Then he squeezed them, ruining their beautiful form. Speaking as though he were one of the crushed grapes, my pastor cried, "God! Why did you do this? Why did You let this happen? Why would a loving God allow this to happen?" He explained that the point of grapes is not just to be beautiful. They are also food, used to nourish and refresh. For a grape to be what it was created to be, it must be crushed. Rather than ruination, its own destruction is the fulfillment of the grape's purpose.

We are like those grapes sometimes. We admire our own beauty and easily become caught up in appearances or circumstances. However, we must not forget that it's not until our willfulness is surrendered to the Lord that we are finally ready to be what we were created to be: a tool in the Master's hands. We must die to self to fulfill the purpose for which we were created.

> *When you put a seed into the ground it doesn't grow into a plant unless it "dies" first.*
> —1 Corinthians 15:36, TLB

Obedience brings the anointing, and the anointing comes not to be used for ourselves but for others. As we use what we are given to help others, we will have joy. We are each blessed to have a purpose, and we will be even more blessed when we walk in that purpose.

With that reminder, I send you forth. Now, go and do a good thing. There is nothing that you and God can't face together and get the victory over.

> *Oh, to be obedient as You would have me be, Lord. Help me to relinquish my own thoughts and ideas to You, and let me have Your thoughts and ideas. You promised me that I would have the mind of Christ (1 Cor. 2:16), and I ask You for it now. How very special to think like Jesus; never to succumb to the tyranny of the urgent; to know implicitly what You would have me do; to know You better. I pray this in the precious name of Jesus. Amen.*

Do your best today. That's all God expects.

Two

And ye shall know the truth, and the truth shall make you free.
—JOHN 8:32, KJV

My Personal Search for Truth

MARRIAGE IS SUPPOSED TO be a triangular relationship with God at the top. The closer a couple gets to Him, the closer they get to each other. It is His desire that we walk with Him, fellowship with Him, and include Him in our marriages, because without God no marriage will be what He intends it to be. It is never too late for a couple to apply His precepts to their relationship in order to have a great marriage, and an already-great marriage can be better with Him included.

Christian marriages should be happier and more successful than other marriages because of Jesus living in and through our lives, but the statistics don't seem to bear this out. Christian couples divorce at the same rate as other couples. Why is this? There are many factors that contribute to this sad statistic, among them that we have an enemy that works overtime to defeat us, we do not always walk in the Spirit, we often do not do what we should to get answers from God, and not everyone who espouses to be a Christian is one.

During the time I was desperate for answers about my troubled marriage to Lamar, I happened upon a Christian television program about alcoholism hosted by Rev. Richard Hogue, with a guest Christian psychologist, Dr. Andre Bustanoby. To my surprise, much of what they were saying applied to Lamar and me, even though alcoholism was not our problem. They talked about the two kinds of marriage: those in right relationship with God and with each other, and the rest of us. The pastor called the former Plan A and the latter Plan B. Plan A is when two mutually supportive, loving people share their lives together in a fulfilling relationship. Though it's what God intended, most of us struggle to create and maintain it. Plan B is neither fulfilling, mutually supportive, nor nurturing. If your relationship feels like Plan B, don't fret. Plan B is OK if God is in it with you. He will do everything in His power to get you to Plan A. Just don't rush Him. Give Him time and cooperate with His instruction. I realized that alcoholic or not, Christian or not, Lamar and I were in a Plan B marriage, and the principles that worked for the couples on the program would work for us. I finally had answers.

Watching the show I learned I was doing some things wrong. I was an enabler. I allowed myself to become a doormat, which made me just another part of the problem. There's nothing wrong with being nice, but there is something wrong with allowing what we call *nice* to escalate to co-dependency. When we have reached that point, it's no longer love. Repentance is in order. Repentance is not just regret, but determining to change the direction of one's behavior.

I can't tell you if you are an enabler or have other attitudes and actions that God is not pleased with. That is your job to discern through prayer and study of God's Word and other Christian resources. However, I will say this: if you are acting like a doormat, pray for the courage to stand up for what is right; if you're mouthy, be mindful of what you say and whether or not you're saying it with love.

God wants you and your family healed. That's a given. There is a great deal of help for women and marriages in trouble. If you aren't getting the help you need, keep reaching out to God and your church counselors until you receive direction and knowledge about how to proceed. Then hold onto God with all your might. If somehow you slip and fall, don't worry; He's holding onto you, too, and He won't let go. God will never withdraw His love from you.

For I am convinced that neither death, nor life, nor angels, nor principalities, nor things present, nor things to come, nor powers, nor height, nor depth, nor any other created thing, will be able to separate us from the love of God, which is in Christ Jesus our Lord.

—ROMANS 8:38

HOW DO YOU GET TO PLAN A?

No one who gets married expects it to be a Plan B relationship. Most marriages begin with two naïve people stumbling through life, doing the best they know to do, but nonetheless living ignorant of the things of God. They intend to be in Plan A but have no idea how to get there. Perhaps one or both individuals in the relationship are not Christians, or maybe he or she grew up in a dysfunctional household where proper marriage principles were not regularly modeled. Even if a couple is walking with the Lord, the church doesn't regularly address in specific terms how to have a Plan A marriage. Counseling isn't usually much better.

Often, when a couple marries, neither is a Christian. As time goes by, one of them gets saved, or born again—hopefully you. If so, you've probably found yourself asking, now what? Don't panic. I understand you are naturally worried about your other half, but don't be. Since you are now linked up with God, then he is linked up, too. That's why the Bible says the believing wife sanctifies her husband. *Sanctify* means "to set apart." You set him apart from the world. You cut the influence of the spirit of the world over him, but it takes time to see the effect of it.

Christians believe that when one member of a household is saved, the Holy Spirit has an inroad to that household. (See Acts 11:14.) If God can lead the animals to the ark, He can lead the unsaved person to the knowledge of Christ. As Proverbs 21:1 (NIV) says, *"The king's heart is in the hand of the LORD."* Even if your husband isn't a Christian, he can be led by the Lord. It is better when he has the Spirit of God in him, but all is not lost in the interim.

It's not perfect even when your husband has the Spirit of God in him. Your Christian spouse won't automatically be easy to get along with, either. There are things you should do whether your husband is a

Christian or not. You are to accept him, admire his God-given talents, edify him, support him in his acceptable endeavors, enjoy his company, laugh and fellowship with him, help him, and respect his space and belongings. It's nice when your mate shares in your relationship with God, the most wonderful relationship in your life, but when he doesn't, you must accept it and do your best with what you have. We can enjoy our half-empty glass and still believe faithfully that someday it will be full. It is important that you do your part to continue to mature spiritually, but it's also wise to avoid putting too much pressure on your husband to become a Christian. Your example and wisdom will have a positive effect on him, and you'll be able to stay out of God's way as He begins to work on your husband's heart.

How I Turned My Marriage Around

One thing above all others is responsible for turning my life and my marriage around: my desire for the truth. Without God, nothing would have been done, so I give Him all the credit for the radical changes I have seen. However, my desire for the truth gave Him free reign to do a makeover in me and in my relationship with Lamar.

> *Then said Jesus to those Jews which believed on him, If ye continue in my word, then are ye my disciples indeed; And ye shall know the truth, and the truth shall make you free.*
> —John 8:31–32, kjv

When we seek wholeheartedly after God and the truth, we will experience freedom. The first step is believing on Him, but after that we have to continue in His Word in order to see His freedom break through in some of the circumstances and situations of our lives.

People often say they believe, but their actions don't prove it. If you truly believe, you will do certain things and not others. I so often have to challenge my friends because they aren't acting in faith. They are acting in fear. Fear will stop freedom dead in its tracks. John 8:31–32 says that if you keep on responding according to what the Word tells you, then you are a disciple (a follower of Christ); then you shall know the truth; and then you will be free. It's a walk of faith, and it just gets better and better. If you find that your relationship with Christ isn't getting better or that you're no longer experiencing the same freedom you once did, take the time to examine your life and the Word of God. There is likely something in the Word you aren't understanding or doing. Perhaps you are harboring fear or unforgiveness, or maybe there is some habitual sin that you are still engaging in. Be willing to listen to the leading of the Spirit and get more familiar with God's Word. This is all part of the process of maturing as a believer.

Denial can be the greatest obstacle to turning a problem marriage around or making a good marriage better. The problem with denial is that it is self-perpetuating. It leads us to turn away the very answers that would help us, valuable information we desperately need to bring a positive change in our lives. Until we start taking every thought into captivity as the Word tells us to (2 Cor. 10:5), we will continue in defeat. Our worst enemy is ourselves. Pogo, the comic strip character, said it perfectly: "We have met the enemy and he is us."[1]

Our best friend in helping us to see the truth is usually our spouse. The only problem is most of us don't want to hear the truth, especially from someone we love and want to impress. It strikes at the very heart of a man's ego and a woman's pride. If anyone understands, it should be our beloved. However, when our spouse points out the areas in which we are in denial, we often interpret it as an attack. As a result, we lash out and then retreat to lick our wounds, telling anyone who will listen how "misunderstood" we are.

God showed me that the hand provides a visual example of the structure of the marriage relationship. On a human hand, the fingers are set opposite the thumb for grasping. If the fingers or the thumb is missing, crippled, or weakened, the hand doesn't function as it was meant to. The relationship of a man and a wife is similar to the way the thumb and fingers work together. By sitting next to her husband, a wife enables him to make proper evaluations. She may discern and help him see the full picture. The husband, in turn, supports the wife in her endeavors. Just as the thumb and the fingers work best when they are working in tandem, each spouse must be free to speak in a relationship. When a husband or wife has the other "backed off" so he or she can't or won't be honest, they have lost the beauty of the creation—two that live as one but seeing as two. Such a couple will not fully hear the truth, nor experience total freedom.

People in an emotional, defensive state can't hear from God. Their ears are shut to anyone, including the Father. After a while, if we still aren't listening, He stops talking. Some individuals take it so hard and pitch such a fit when we are honest with them and encourage them to see things clearly that it becomes easier to keep our mouth shut. This is not good, especially when it inhibits communication between spouses. It takes wisdom to know when to speak and when to be silent, but it also takes wisdom to learn what voice to listen to and trust.

When mankind began to reason on their own, their brains turned away from God. He never intended us to have to reason everything out. He intends us to take His word for things. That was the point of God's command for Adam and Eve not to eat from the tree of the knowledge of good and evil. They ate from it and became responsible for listening to their consciences and discerning good from evil. Until then, they didn't need the knowledge of evil. They only needed the knowledge of good, which they already had in knowing Him.

He wanted us to believe Him, not to rely on our own interpretation of circumstances. As soon as you start trusting your own perception of things instead of God and His Word, you get dumb. That doesn't mean you can't think; it's just that only those thoughts that agree with God are good thoughts, and we should reject all others. It takes some doing to know what His thoughts are, but this is why your Bible is so important to you. It tells you what God has thought from the beginning of this world.

WHEN WE DON'T WANT THE TRUTH

Perhaps you're wondering, "What if my husband won't listen to me?" There are some things he has to figure out by himself. If he doesn't receive what you are saying, pray about it and then give it fully to God. You may suffer loss because of it, but God will take care of that, too. God provides for a godly woman and her children. The Bible says so.

> *I was young and now I am old, yet I have never seen the righteous forsaken or their children begging bread.*
> —PSALM 37:25, NIV

Take those opportunities, when you are praying that God reveals something to your husband, to examine yourself. What is God trying to communicate to you that you won't receive? It is much easier to see how bad he is and what he is doing wrong, but while you are trusting God to take care of your husband, you need to hear what God is telling you about what you might be doing wrong.

It wasn't until I faced my own error that my marriage began to turn around. It's difficult for most of us to see the areas where we need improvement; that's why it's so important to listen to God. Job did a lot of things right and was a wonderful, godly man, but he struggled with fear. (See Job 3:25.) At the end of Job's trial, God spoke to Job, revealing Himself to him and giving him revelation that helped him overcome his shortcomings. Job 38–41 are some of my favorite chapters in the Bible because they remind me that God will speak to us when we need a word. It can be difficult to openly receive rebukes from God, but those chapters in Job and other scriptures remind us that God is just and that He only corrects us because He loves us.

> *Do not resent it when God chastens and corrects you, for his punishment is proof of love. Just as a father punishes a son he delights in to make him better, so the Lord corrects you.*
> —PROVERBS 3:11–12, TLB

This is what I call a *ponderable*—something to think about. God knows when we don't want the truth. We aren't kidding Him, and we usually aren't kidding all that many other people, either. The one we fool the most is ourselves. Sometimes we can maintain a façade to fool our husband and kids for a short while, but inevitably they catch on. If they don't, it's a sign that they are kidding themselves, too. Neither of you want the truth, and God knows it; He is not beholden to act on your behalf if you are playing games. This is one reason why some people never get the victory, in spite of their prayers. God will let you have the fruit of your own making.

A former lesbian transvestite lived as a man for a number of years, even going so far as to force her two older children to accept the fact that she would no longer be their mother, but rather their father. Her youngest son never knew her as his mother. After years of living this way, one day she asked God for the truth. She expected God to confirm the way she was living. He didn't. Suddenly, she saw how grotesque her behavior was. She had no other choice but to return to the way God created her, much to the dismay of her closest friends and her youngest son, who thought he was losing his father.

Up until the moment she asked God for revelation, this woman thought she had the truth. She never dreamed she was living a lie. She was doing what she felt she had to do because of the turmoil inside her. She had accepted her feelings as the truth, and it was years before she was ready to hear otherwise. Despite the assertion of modern humanists, there is only one truth. When we add our brains to the mix, somehow the truth can get perverted along the way. But we never quit calling it the truth. We should regularly ask ourselves whose truth we are serving, ours or God's?

We who want so desperately for our husbands to change need to check our own lives. I do believe in a word well spoken and at the right time (Prov. 25:11), but the best way of challenging our husband's behavior is to be more like Jesus and allow Him to live through us. The Bible says that a man will be affected by living with a godly, loving woman.

> *You wives, be submissive to your own husbands so that if even any one of them are disobedient to the word, they may be won without a word by the behavior of their wives, as they observe your chaste and respectful behavior.*
>
> —1 PETER 3:1–2

Excuses may work with others, but don't work with God—and they don't work with our husbands either. For example, if your husband won't tithe, stop complaining and find a way to tithe on the money you earn. If he won't allow you to tithe from your paycheck, tithe on your spending money each month. Give your husband the opportunity to see how tithing blesses God and, in turn, blesses you.

Some women struggle with feeling like their husband no longer desires them. It's important to remember that God loves you for who you are and how He made you. However, it's also important to remember your body is not your own. It is the temple of the living God (1 Cor. 6:19), and it belongs to your husband as well (1 Cor. 7:4). If you are continuing to eat poorly and live a sedentary lifestyle, you need to pray about what is stopping you from walking in freedom from those bad eating habits and lifestyle choices. When you are committed to something, you will prayerfully seek a solution or seek help to get to the bottom of why you haven't dealt with destructive, habitual behaviors. Your obedience will get his attention, and God can use your behavior as a means of holding a mirror up to your husband so that he can better identify the areas in which he needs improvement.

The Bible says, "*Iron sharpens iron, so one man sharpens another*" (Prov. 27:17). This passage is saying that two godly, strong people contending with each other develop and strengthen each other. I am strong, and Lamar is too. We are equals, and he respects my opinion. I am an invaluable asset to him—and he knows it. We sharpen each other. It's a good thing.

God never intended for you to be some puny, mealy-mouthed lackey just tagging along for the ride until your husband orders you to go somewhere else. Weakness is not godliness. Determine through prayer that you will be the complement your husband needs, not standing in opposition to him, but standing apart enough to help him see. Ask God to show you how to do this properly. A strong, silent woman, obedient to the voice of God in her life is powerful. She is set opposite to the husband to help and edify him daily, as he needs her to be there. Standing and waiting on God, especially when you are unsure of how to respond to your husband's behavior, is not weakness.

This is why it is needful to be open and see what God shows you. It will no doubt end up as a wonderfully woven picture that forms out of a grouping of experiences. God seems to bring many things together to make one revelation. "Of course!" bursts forth as you finally see, and then what has troubled you for days, weeks, or years dissipates. Your spirit soars because it finally knows the truth.

When God reveals something to you personally, it's not necessarily meant for you to act on it immediately or to tell anyone. It is for you to pray about and keep in mind as you go about your normal day. God will show you if and when to act on it or share with someone. After Mary gave birth to Jesus, the Scriptures say that *"Mary treasured up these things and pondered them in her heart"* (Luke 2:19). She was wise to be careful who she spoke to and when she spoke about it. If we want God to reveal things to us, we must show ourselves able to be trusted with the revelation He gives us.

Much is required from those to whom much is given.
—Luke 12:48, TLB

God doesn't take our position lightly, and neither should we. He is looking for clean hands to bless. If you have unconfessed, undealt-with sin in your life, you need to deal with that sin and put yourself in a position to hear from God. If you want your husband to change, be sure that you have repented and changed first. Let's live in faith and obedience so that we do not hinder God's desire to pour out a blessing on us.

Oh, dear Jesus, my life has been so full of lies. Mine and every-body else's. I repent of mine and forgive them for theirs. Help me, Lord, to turn around this web of lies and make it a net of victory that brings everyone up with it! I love you, Lord, and I know all this grieves Your heart. Help me do what I have to do to stop it!

The fields are ripe for harvesting, and your Father wants you out there helping!

THREE

The Search for My Personal Truth

THERE IS NO USE for God to send us the truth if we don't want it and won't listen. God knows our hearts and is ready to speak to us when the moment comes that we are ready to listen. In the Book of Revelation Jesus keeps saying through the Apostle John, "He who has an ear, let him hear what the Spirit says" (Rev. 2:7, 11, 17, 29; 3:6, 13, 22). Before I was born spiritually, I had no spiritual eyes to see with and no spiritual ears to hear with. After I received salvation and my eyes and ears were finally open, I wanted the truth. I was ready to see and hear. The question then was not only, How will God bring the truth to me? but, What truth will He bring?

We had a convenience store at the time and a friend named Theresa worked for us part time. We offered her the full-time position, but she turned it down because she didn't want to work that much. She had been an "at home" mom until she started working for us at the auctions where her husband was a ring man. She didn't mind the auctions because Bob worked there and it gave her something to do. She just didn't want to be tied down every day. We went to church together and were fairly close friends. Lamar and I had changed churches and closed down the auction when we opened the store, so Theresa and I weren't seeing each other regularly like we had been. But I knew she had to come to town once in a while and could have stopped by. There was no indication of a problem but, obviously, something was wrong. "Surely she should have stopped by now."

I was tormented by thoughts of what might have happened. My mind began to plant terrible ideas in my head to explain it. Although I had never known Lamar to say something inappropriate, I even began to wonder if he had said something to offend Theresa. "Instead of telling me she probably just quit coming around," I mused. I needed to know the truth. After praying about it, I felt led to go talk to Theresa. She didn't live very far away, so I decided to stop by the next day. As I approached her home, I told God I would face whatever she said straight-on and, with His help, deal with it.

It was so good to see her again. We had a nice visit, enjoying the closeness that being sisters in the Lord brings. Before I left, I asked her why she quit coming around. Theresa was not a woman easily caught off-guard, but my question seemed to leave her at a loss for words. "I just don't know how to say this without sounding unchristian," she agonized. "Just say it," I said; "I need to know." Finally, she said, "I couldn't stand the way Lamar treated you. I would get so mad I wanted to tell him off, but you didn't seem to mind. I knew unless you did something about it, I was just wasting my breath. Every time I go by, you are either both there or your car isn't there. I don't want to stop when he's there." I was speechless.

Theresa wasn't the only one that had said something about Lamar's way of speaking to me. "I wouldn't put up with what you do" was a typical remark from friends and family. This time, however, it hit home just how much it was affecting other people and our relationships with them. Not only did I have Lamar verbally abusing me, but my friends were making me out to be the bad guy for not doing something about it. Like Job's so-called comforters, they were more concerned with offering their opinion than understanding the situation and helping me get the victory. I could tell Theresa was truly concerned about me, though, which might have been the reason that her words affected me so deeply.

It was a wake-up call. I could finally see the situation clearly. I knew Lamar shouldn't have been talking to me the way he did, but I had ignored the problem rather than fight it. At that time in his life, Lamar was of the attitude that he would destroy everything—even our relationship—rather than lose an argument. Because of the way I was raised, I did not understand that people acted like this, especially toward someone they loved. I was wholly unprepared for such manipulative and confrontational behavior, so after we married, I continued to react in predictable ways that only made things worse. My tendency to be a peacemaker led me to put up with behavior I should have challenged. When I finally did challenge it, Lamar's reaction was so strong that I backed off, which just reinforced his behavior. His continued verbal abuse convinced me that I would never win, causing me to withdraw yet further. Instead of allowing him to hurt me more and more, I built a wall around myself. On top of the verbal abuse, things had recently gotten physical. He grabbed me one day, hurting me slightly. Another time we got in a shoving match and I slipped on a rug and fell, scaring our sons.

We were caught in a vicious cycle, and my GLR were part of what kept us spinning.[1] I thought my only other choice was to leave Lamar and get a divorce, and I wasn't ready to do that, though I considered it almost daily. I was putting up with garbage I shouldn't have and that many women wouldn't have because I didn't know how to handle the situation, other than divorce.

I am not saying being a peacemaker is inherently bad. It's just not always the answer. Some things should be challenged. Jesus turned over the tables in the temple when people were defiling His Father's house (Matt. 21:12; Mark 11:15). The guiding scripture is Ephesians 4:26 (NIV), which quotes Psalm 4:4: "*In your anger do not sin.*" Anger is the appropriate response to abusive behavior. Any other reaction would mean you don't comprehend the significance of what is happening. We can't help but be upset, but we can choose to respond properly. It is our responsibility to do the right thing, being careful to ensure that our anger doesn't lead us to sin.

I laughed and cried all the way home from Theresa's. On one hand, I realized how silly I had been for thinking perhaps Lamar had made improper advances toward my friend, while on the other hand I cried because what she said was so true. I kept my word to God and finally decided to face head-on the problem of how Lamar was treating me. Because he was such a strong personality and was used to fighting to get his way, when I began to try changing things, he balked. Everything in me told me to give up, but I knew this time I had to stand my ground. I wasn't really ready for a show-down but decided I couldn't back off now. I told him I was not the bad guy and he needed to see that and change his attitude. He responded that he couldn't see it and wasn't going to change his attitude. "What are you going to do about that?" he challenged.

I said, "Well, then I think you'd better pack your clothes." "Fine." he retorted, and he went home to put some of his stuff in the van. I told the girl that worked the day shift at the convenience store we owned that Lamar and I were having problems and I might not be working at the store any more. She was a close friend that I knew I could trust. I asked her to work as usual, but to please call me if there was anything she felt I needed to know. And then I asked her to pray for us. She assured me she would.

During my shift, God sent a friend to the store to talk to me. He ate snacks and talked for the longest time, which kept me from being alone and breaking down. I knew he had to have been God-sent because this man had never done it before or since. A short while later his wife called and said, "God just told me to call you. Are you OK?" I knew I could trust her, so I told her Lamar had just gone home to pack his things and leave. She said she would pray about it and asked, "Is he going to church?" I had to admit he wasn't. He had backslidden recently and hadn't yet come back to the Lord. She understood the gravity of the situation. What a blessing to have God send two friends to me at that difficult time. It reminded me He cared and that He was with me in it. I was learning how many friends I had and what a friend I had in Jesus. Even when the circumstance doesn't change, it's just nice to know God is there and has sent some good friends to be with you.

When I told Grant, who was about ten or eleven years old at the time, that his father might be leaving the home, he insisted we go tell his grandparents, Lamar's mom and dad. I hated to involve other people but knew Lamar would tell his side of the story; there was no telling what that would be. I wanted them to hear from me that there was no other man and that things had gotten bad enough that it was not healthy for the kids.

That night Lamar came home saying, "My mother told me I'd better come home and make things right." My response was, "Tell her not to do me any favors." I could have insisted he leave, but didn't feel led to. There was no rush. At the end of the night Lamar noticed I was crying and asked why. I explained, "I know you'd like me to say I love you, but to me it's a miracle that I don't hate you." Lamar understood and knew it was God. A few days later he told me he wondered what he would tell people. "It wouldn't have mattered because I would have told them the truth," I assured him. "That's what I was afraid of," he said and we both laughed, knowing people would believe me.

This is the point where many couples get it wrong. I could have taken a hard stand against Lamar and refused to budge out of hurt and anger, but this would have locked us into an adversarial relationship. I had not yet heard from God about what to do, and because I didn't feel that my life or the lives of my children were being put in greater danger by staying, I felt there was really no hurry to make a decision. I did know that another relationship was not what I needed; I needed my relationship with Lamar healed. If you're married and thinking of divorcing him so you can get a new relationship, first try adding more Jesus to your life and marriage before you work on finding another man.

I didn't know it that day, but continuing to be longsuffering and open to what God wanted me to do set big changes in motion. That decision paid off richly in the long run. Lamar's attitude began to change. He went back to church and attended the fellowship group. We still had a great deal of spiritual work to be done, but this was one of many steps that needed to be taken.

It is crucial to keep in mind that it's typical for things to get better and then worse again. People get complacent and fall back into old patterns, especially if they don't renew their minds regularly. Don't panic if this happens with your spouse. You can regain what you have lost. Each time, be more determined to pray and seek God and read your Bible to get spiritual answers. Resolve to stand firmly in faith on God's Word and His promise to give you wisdom and protection.

In the meantime, it's wise to seek a Christian counselor who will listen, pray with you, and provide godly advice. This will provide valuable help in examining your relationship—not an easy thing to do by yourself when you are in denial. The counselor will be able to help point out if you are missing something and can give insight you may be blind to in your relationship. If you disagree with what they say, don't debate with them or immediately discount their credibility. Thank them for being honest and take their opinion to God.

Be very discerning about who you open up to. It seemed that whenever I talked to someone about my problems with Lamar, he or she always diagnosed our relationship difficulties as stemming from my inability to submit. When I would try to get a Christian friend to help me lick my wounds, she would launch in on her testimony of how God helped her understand how she should submit to her husband. I did need to understand submission, but first I needed to take a stand.

Even if you are talking to someone in your inner circle, remember to choose your words carefully. Initially, I would talk to people and make jokes out of my life or the latest thing Lamar had said or done. Even though we would laugh about it, over time I realized that it really wasn't funny, and it definitely didn't help the situation. After all was said and done, I didn't feel any better. The only thing I had accomplished was that people thought less of Lamar and me. Making fun of your husband or the situation is a sign that you are likely harboring disrespect toward him in your heart. Jesus said that *"out of the overflow of the heart the mouth speaks"* (Matt. 12:34, NIV). Speaking positive words or telling stories of good things he did will reinforce the good aspects of your relationship. I'm not saying that you can't laugh at or retell funny things that happened between the two of you, and I am certainly not encouraging you to put on a façade that everything is perfect. I'm just saying that we need to remember that changes in our behavior and, ultimately, in how we view our relationships will begin in our heart and be evidenced in how we speak.

> *Look at the ships also, though they are so great and are driven by strong winds, are directed by a very small rudder wherever the inclination of the pilot desires. So also the tongue is a small part of the body, and yet it boasts of great things.*
>
> —JAMES 3:4

Not long after my talk with Theresa, I bought a book called *Do Yourself a Favor—Love Your Wife* by H. Page Williams for Lamar, but ended up reading it myself. I left it laying around for him, and he said he read some of it, but I was the one who was really impacted by it. Reading this book did something to me. It turned the guns on the guys and never took them off. I thought, "Any minute the author is going to turn on me and start talking about how women are the problem." But he never did. That book freed me from a lot of guilt that had been weighing me down. It let me know I wasn't all wrong and that, in fact, I was right about a lot of things.

Our marriage was in trouble, but we didn't talk about it. We just fought about superficial things. If Lamar had been so disposed, he would have fallen into the pit of adultery, and if I had been so disposed, I would have too. If either of us had been so disposed, we would have divorced. Lots of our friends did. Instead, we kept going.

The battle to reclaim and repair your marriage will require sacrifice on your part. The Bible says *"not [to] be weary in well doing"* (Gal. 6:9, KJV). Remind yourself regularly that your husband is as much a victim of uncontrollable forces as you are. True, he is responsible for his poor choices, but the truth is you made some wrong choices, too. Your husband is not the enemy. We have an enemy and we need to recognize him as such. Get in the Word and strengthen your relationship with Christ to find out how to fight the source of the problem, instead of fighting your husband. In the mean time, work on finding out more about God and who He says you are.

Pitiful but Powerful Prayers

I cannot stress enough how important prayer is to building a relationship with your husband. Couples that pray together are more likely to stay together. We always have to start with prayer: getting yourself right and getting things right between you and God.

I wish I could say I prayed wonderful, powerful, faith-filled prayers when Lamar and I began working on our relationship, but I can't. My prayers were just a reflection of how bad things were. Only too often I would come to God with the most pitiful prayers—prayers spoken in what sounded a lot like unbelief. However, they were honest prayers spoken from my heart. The fact that I was praying was proof I believed God could do something. They gave Him an opportunity to show me where I was wrong and to help me, and I was diligent to forgive others and repent to ensure that no sin or unforgiveness in my life could hinder me from receiving from God. Even though my prayers didn't sound very powerful, they turned out to be the impetus for a big change in our lives.

I determined that I would believe God, no matter how much my brain and body yelled to the contrary and no matter what proof might be put before my senses. I decided to be like the father of the demon-possessed boy who cried out to Jesus asking Him to heal his son and saying, "I do believe; help me overcome my unbelief" (Mark 9:24, NIV). Though simple, this is a powerful prayer. God appreciates our battle and our decision to fight the good fight of faith against such odds.

Prayers that start out pitiful don't often end that way. Somewhere along the line, faith rises up, along with righteous indignation against the devil for robbing you and your family. Somewhere the prayer switches and you ended up speaking faith and taking your authority in the situation in Jesus' name. Usually God shows me something or says something in my spirit that changes everything. Don't worry about how you sound. Just pray. Pray from your heart. Tell Him how bad it is. You can even tell Him you are disappointed with Him. Be honest. In the process, something will change in you and you will see things differently by the time you get done. And that's just the beginning. Pretty soon, you will have an experience that will make something crystal clear to you. Maybe you will begin to see the past differently. Perhaps God will give you wisdom and discernment for how to deal with a present circumstance. Whatever the Spirit reveals, you will gradually see that you are not just some poor, downtrodden worm but rather a child of the most high God. This is what I began experiencing not long after I started praying diligently about my marriage.

Why don't you try praying right now?

> *God, I am so tired of the garbage. It's obvious I've missed it some-where! I'm sorry, but I really can't see that I am the problem. If I am, I want You to show me. I've worked and tried and gone the second and third mile to no avail. I'm at the end of my rope. If You don't help me and do something or give me some answers, it won't get any better. In Jesus' name I pray. Amen.*

If you are the problem, try this one:

> *God, I know I'm the problem. But, he's the problem, too. Every-body is a mess and there doesn't seem to be any end to it. Help me find my way out of this. I do want the truth! I want Your truth! I know I'm wrong about a lot of things but, everything I try to do to help just makes things worse. Help me, God. I need wisdom. Your wisdom! I'm really going to try to hear this time with my spiritual ears. Help me with this, too! I pray this in Jesus' name, my Lord and Savior. I truly need His saving grace! Amen.*

CAT ON A HOT TIN ROOF

I have seen parts of *Cat on a Hot Tin Roof,* starring Paul Newman and Elizabeth Taylor, off and on for years, but I don't know if I have ever seen it all the way through. This time I intended to watch the whole thing, but even then was interrupted by an important phone call and the popcorn burning because the microwave went haywire and we had to air out the house! Here is what I gleaned from it that I think is significant to the discussion of marriage. It depicts three in painful detail. The sad thing is they are fairly typical.

Big Daddy and Big Momma somehow have managed to stay together in spite of his harshness. She seems to have made the mental transition necessary. However, it made for a very unhappy home, which she admits to, but they love each other. It is really a story of a lot of painful love. Typical.

Big Brother and his wife have tried to do what Daddy wanted but never managed to garner his favor. He has a passel of kids and one on the way. The sins of the father are visited to the third generation! You can see why. He and his wife want what they feel they are entitled to—the money.

Little Brother and his wife are Paul Newman at his moody best married to Elizabeth Taylor at her Southern best. She's beautiful and feisty and he can't stand her. She clings and crawls; he cringes and could care less. It is hard to sympathize with Elizabeth Taylor's character, but Paul Newman's manages to be so icy you can't help yourself. What will be the resolution of this loveless marriage? He even tells her to go get a boyfriend! She says she would just think of him, she loves him so. She's good! She carries on her duties in the family trying to make it work. At first you think she is just after the money, too, but as the movie progresses you see some depth to her.

Newman just generally hates life. He's a drunk and an ugly one at that. What hope is there for this poor group? You never heard such yelling and fighting. I guess that's why I never watched it. I couldn't stand all the fighting and figured they would all come to a no-good end. This one has tragedy written all over it. Big Daddy is dying, so right there is a lot of grief. Who needs it? Not anyone whose life is already grieved! But this time I was determined to understand its message and mark it down.

Paul may be a drunk, but he's sick of the lies, denials, and games. Now, there's hope—not much, but a seed. The fighting doesn't end, but at least they are fighting for truth and love. Paul in the end confronts his father for giving them stuff instead of love. Big Daddy, Burl Ives, tells the story of his daddy, a hobo who took Burl with him everywhere. He learned shame at an early age and, in the end, lost his dad before he was grown. At first you think he hated his father because he based his whole life on his contempt for poverty. But he admits his father died with a smile on his lips. Paul makes him admit he knew the love of his father. His father gave him something very precious. Something he hasn't given his wife or sons, Paul points out.

Elizabeth Taylor was a symbol of everything he wanted when Newman married her and everything he hated after a few years. He didn't hate *her*; he hated what she stood for. But once he came to terms with his father and himself, he came to terms with her. His father tells him to grow up! Father and son share some pretty harsh words, but honest words. Both recognize the truth and that they have hurt each other very much. Paul determines to quit drinking, and the father decides to show his love in his last days. Maggie (Taylor) announces she's pregnant. It ends happily with Liz and Paul embracing in the bedroom. There are miracles!

Maggie didn't run away or get a boyfriend. She admitted she didn't like what she was becoming. She forgave and was long-suffering. Moreover, she kept herself attractive and sensual even when he acted like he didn't care; and she never cut too deep. She never let him think she didn't love him. And yet, she had a strength about her. She didn't make a fool of herself. She didn't play games. She was herself. And it paid off. He did love her. She weathered her storm. "And they will rise up and call her blessed..."

Well, she did play a game temporarily and it backfired, and much of their fighting was a result of it. But I won't go there now. Watch the movie! Our games just make things worse.

Face the truth, act on it, and it will change your life. He didn't hate his wife! He hated himself, his life, so many things. She was just handy. How sad we don't understand we are handy and to keep doing what needs to be done until something changes. It is during this time we must be sure we don't get into sin, too. It's very easy to do. We get bitter, we get revenge, we lick our wounds, and then they do not rise up and call us blessed. We don't win the victory and then die, sad and embittered. UGH! Don't you know the next act in their marriage will be Paul Newman's and Elizabeth Taylor's characters cooing over their new baby and their newfound love? He will really love her now! He won't be able to do enough for her. I bet she sports a new diamond ring sometime soon.

Some people will say we must leave the marriage, and sometimes we have to, but I think verbal and emotional abuse is something we can fight in our own minds by finding out what God thinks. However, some people need a respite to find themselves and have a time of healing. Hopefully, during this time, the other person will start making some better choices, too. It is important if you get back together that things do not go back to the way they were. Old habits slide on like old slippers. If you are getting answers for yourself and changing your heart and your mind, things will change. It is in YOU that the change must start first! And that is why I will start with you.

FOUR

**He shall not be afraid of evil tidings: his heart
is fixed, trusting in the LORD.**

—PSALM 112:7, KJV

Trusting God

AFTER MY LITTLE GIRL'S death and the mess my marriage was in, you might be surprised I would be telling you to trust the Lord. In fact, I didn't trust the Lord at the beginning. I was still mad at God that He hadn't protected my daughter. I cried out to Him, asking why He protected other people's children but not my Dadra. I couldn't believe God would go to the trouble to create us and then just sit on high and watch our lives unfold like some awful soap opera.

I believed in God, but mere belief in God doesn't automatically put you in connection or relationship with Him. No, I knew *about* God, but I didn't know God. I just hoped He was there and that He would show Himself to me in some way. I even said, "Someday I will hear from God." On September 22, 1975, I did hear from Him. He and I got connected that day, and I've never looked back. My life took a phenomenal turn. All of a sudden I began to get answers, not just about heaven and my soul, but about divorce and things that were happening in my own life.

At this point you may be thinking, "But, Midge, how can I trust God now if He hasn't ever come through for me in the past?" I understand you may think God has let you down and that before you put your full weight on Him, you want to be convinced He won't fail you just when you need Him most. But you must trust your heavenly Father. Lean on Him. He will be there for you.

There are things you can do to ensure that you are not doing anything to hinder what God wants to do in your life. First, make sure that you have placed yourself fully under God's protection by making Him the Lord of your life. If you haven't done that yet, pray this with me:

> *Dear God, I acknowledge that I need You. I have tried to live according to the way that seemed right to me, and I have failed. Please come into my life and lead me. I believe that You sent your only Son, Jesus, to save me and give me the opportunity to have a personal relationship with You. In His name, I ask You to forgive me of my sins. I wish to repent of them and never repeat them. Teach me about Yourself and Your Word. Fill me with your Holy Spirit and cover me with Your protection. Help my life to be glorifying to You. I pray this in Jesus' name. Amen.*

If you have already asked the Lord to come into your life and repented of your sins, search your heart to determine if there is any unforgiveness that you are harboring toward an individual, ask the Lord to forgive you for it, and then let the bitterness and the blame go. Determine to walk in obedience to the best of your ability. There are probably things you should be doing but aren't. It is up to you to pray and figure out what God wants you to do. It's helpful to ask a friend if she sees anything that you're missing, but ultimately it's God who must show you areas you need to work on.

When my son was diagnosed with acute renal (kidney) failure, I prayed and sought God for a word from Him. Over and over again God confirmed the Word, that He heals, and I knew He was not a respecter of persons, but God never told me, "I will heal your son." After weeks of not hearing a specific word from God, my spirit was grieved because I felt like I was getting into unbelief. I cried out to God, "But I believe. Why am I never satisfied?" God answered as only He can, "Don't seek for the revelation that he will be healed; seek for the revelation of what is holding it up." This God-given advice applies to you, too, if you are asking God for things but haven't seen your breakthrough. In addition to standing in faith on His promises, begin to ask God to help you to understand what might be holding up your healing or victory.

GETTING TO KNOW HIM

After I got saved and realized I could hear from God and know Him personally, the next step was to see that I could trust Him in all situations. He was obviously willing to do His part. It was a very special time, getting to know Him better. The Bible was very relevant to my situation, especially in the early years. You need to see that it's relevant to yours, too.

My walk to wholeness personally and in my marriage falls into two time periods: the Alabama years, 1975 to 1979; and the Florida years, 1979 to the present. I was a citified northerner when we moved to Lamar's hometown of Gadsden, Alabama, less than a year after we married. It's not that people were mean to me; we were just from two different worlds. When I was saved nine years later and read the story of the Israelites in Egypt, it really spoke to my heart. I was wounded and broken when He reached down and picked me up out of the pit. He healed me emotionally and physically and began to lay a new, strong foundation in my heart. Lamar rededicated his life to the Lord and went through deliverance at the Friday night fellowship group we attended, and we both learned about and received the baptism of the Holy Spirit.

I learned about the faithfulness of God through seeing how He provided for our businesses and our family. I had to keep my hand in His, seeking Him daily for answers. He touched me in so many ways with discernment and wisdom in the midst of it all. It would be impossible for me to tell you all the stories I have that testify to God's faithfulness to me, but let me tell you a few.

NOT MINE, LORD!

On one of the many trips we took between Alabama and Florida while we were moving, I suddenly realized my purse wasn't in our van. I hoped it was stuck under a seat or under some of the inevitable mess of three boys and two adults traveling. When the reality hit me that we were not going to find it, I got physically ill. It wasn't that I had that much cash in it, but rather a combination of the hassle of canceling the credit cards, getting a new driver's license, and the frustration over losing the purse in the first place. "A woman just isn't supposed to lose her purse," I agonized.

I knew I had to pray about it. The first words that came out of my mouth were, "Well, God, You've lost Your purse." I figured that if I gave everything I had to Him, when I lost something, it was as though He had lost it, too. When I realized what I said, I laughed until I almost cried. I continued to pray, "I am so sorry that I have been careless. If You see fit to use the purse in some other way, I yield it; but if You don't, then I ask You to send it back to me."

When we got home, I called the Kentucky Fried Chicken restaurant, the last place we stopped, but it wasn't turned in if it was left there. That was the only place it could have been that I knew of. "Well, God, I tried." A little while later the phone rang and one of the boys handed it to me and said, "It's for Mrs. Lamar Vice." Nobody I knew would call me that. The call had to be about my purse. It turned out that one of the boys had drug it out of the car with his foot when we stopped at a payphone, and the man at the car lot across the street saw what happened. He was greatly concerned when we drove off without retrieving it. I thanked him for letting us know and asked him to use the cash in it to send my purse back, but he used his own money. What a blessing that experience has been.

You don't know how often I have repeated the phrase "Well, God, You've lost Your purse" when something awful would happen. I learned very early in my walk with the Lord to abandon myself and all my stuff to Him and not take it back.

What have you lost? Give it all to Him, and then it will ultimately be His responsibility to defend it and see that it gets returned, fixed, etc. The only way to learn to trust is to completely abandon yourself to God.

GOD MAKES A WAY

I had been saved nine months when a group of Church of God women who had been instrumental in the change in my life began talking about a camp meeting. They kept insisting that I had to go, but they didn't understand what they were asking. At the time, Lamar wouldn't let me go very far or for very long, and he certainly would not have let me out from noon until midnight or later. I had a babysitter for Matt and Spencer, so that wasn't the problem. He just wouldn't agree to it. I didn't really think that much about it and just prayed, "God, could it be possible?" I did not have faith for it at all; it was just beyond my thinking.

On the day of the first meeting I woke up with an especially strong desire to go that night. Lamar had been talking about going to Chicago to get tools for our auction business, so I reminded him that he needed to leave as early as possible to make sure that he would get there and back in time. Lamar decided to ask his mother to accompany him so she could visit his sister, who lived in the Chicago area. She agreed, and after a flurry of activity, they were in the truck and on their way by ten o'clock. I stood there stunned. God had wonderfully provided a miracle so that I could go to the meeting. I laughed and danced around praising God and shouting, "Camp meeting, here I come."

Before he left, I told Lamar I was thinking of going to the camp meetings, so if he couldn't get me by phone he shouldn't worry about it. He probably didn't realize how long I would be gone and didn't really think that much about it. Since he didn't say I couldn't go, I called my friend and we rejoiced.

That night at the camp meeting, Grant was saved and I was touched by the Spirit in a very special way. Shortly thereafter, I received the baptism of the Holy Spirit. I was delivered from watching daytime soap operas that week, too. Praise God. I just couldn't watch them knowing how good God had been to me, so I offered the habit up to the Lord. It was such a special week. I saw the power of God, heard powerful preaching, and enjoyed out-of-this-world singing that went deep into my inner being and watered my thirsty soul.

It may not seem like much of a testimony that I was able to attend the camp meeting, but to me it was a big thing. God made a way where there was no way. I didn't have to beg or carry on. I just gave it to Him. I'm a can-do girl, someone who always works hard to figure out how to get what she wants; but God showed me through this experience that all I had to do was back off and give Him room. I backed off and it was beautiful—a wonder to behold! My son was saved, I was delivered, and I got to go to camp meeting. Match that! I sure can't.

GRASSHOPPER LIVING

Lamar and I, like so many couples, lived from hand to mouth. Someone called it "grasshopper living." It worried me that we weren't saving for the boys' college education. I had had the opportunity to go to college and wanted to be able to send my sons, but Lamar didn't seem to have a burden for it. He managed without a college education for a number of years (he eventually got a two-year degree) and figured they could too.

One of the first things God told me after I made Him Lord of my life was to concern myself with the eternal things and let Him worry about the temporal things. This sounded like the reverse of what I thought He would want. I thought He would want me to be concerned with the everyday problems of life while He took care of eternal things. I worked hard to be a good steward and a responsible wife and mother, but He taught me that beyond that He wanted me to give the worry of it to Him. Just like the Bible says, I am to give Him my burden and take His, for His is light and mine is heavy (Matt. 11:30).

I had already tried to do things myself and made a mess of them all. Now it was my turn to step back and let God clean up the mess. This is not to say that He doesn't want our cooperation and for us to do our part. However, God wants us to let Him do His part while we do ours.

I had already started by receiving what Jesus did on the cross. After that, I just had to walk in it day by day as best I could, listening for His instruction and doing what He said to do. God, being a loving Father, would never put more on me than I could manage with His help. Without His help there was a lot I couldn't do. In the seeking and doing, the Father and I developed a very good relationship and my faith grew. The more it grew, the less I balked at what had formerly seemed so hard. Pretty soon I had a blessing cycle going instead of staying stuck in a web of tribulation.

SIZE 14 BAGS

One night as I worked the register, a young mother came in with a passel of little kids. She was a tiny thing to be a mother. She proceeded to load her basket full of groceries, which was very unusual for a convenience store. When she came to check out, I couldn't find any size 16 bags, the big ones, to put her groceries in. I felt awful having to bag her items up in the smaller size, but what else could I do? She was so sweet and insisted it was fine. I helped her out to her truck and asked God to go home with her and surround her with angels. I really prayed for her!

The next morning our pastor called to explain that he was sick and to ask Lamar to preach for him. I had it on my heart that God wanted Lamar to preach, but the pastor had never asked until now. I went on to church with the boys to do Lamar's duties as Sunday school superintendent and left Lamar home to prepare. As we went along the back roads early that Sunday, I saw smoke rising from an old house. The family had already run out and were standing there watching in horror as their home was consumed in flames. There were no fire hydrants and no way to put it out. Even if there had been, the house was too far gone. The woman standing there with the group that had gathered was the same lady whose groceries I had packed up the night before in the size 14 bags. She was having such a fit I thought someone was still in the house. I ran over and asked her if one of the kids was still inside. She assured me they were all out. "What about your husband?" I asked, thinking maybe he had gone back in for some reason. No, he was standing not too far away. I understood that she was very upset about the loss of their home, but I tried to ascertain why she was reacting so severely. She explained that they had just gotten a nice, new stereo TV. That was a shame, but she was acting like a woman who was losing her family. How blessed she was to be standing there with them all safe.

I shared with her that I had lost my little girl at three and one-half years old and that it was a miracle she wasn't suffering such a loss right then. It was as if I threw cold water on her. She stopped immediately. I could just see the revelation come over her of how blessed she was, and she thanked me for sharing it. Then she proceeded to say what a miracle it was that they woke up in time to get out because they had been up late and were all very tired. I now understood why I couldn't find the size 16 bags—so I would pray for her. That's how important a prayer can be. I saw it as a miracle that God had brought her into my path—and in such a memorable way, too—the day before the fire so that I could comfort her when she needed it.

How faithful God is. I went by a few days later to see how they were doing and was able to share with her husband and the rest of the family that I believed God had sent her to the store for prayer, not groceries. It was a shame they lost the groceries and their other possessions, but they sure got their money's worth in prayer. God had been actively involved with their survival.

If something has happened in your life and you don't feel God covered you in prayer, just give that situation up to Him. Trust that He had His reasons, and don't try to figure it out or compare what you went through with anyone else's experience. Don't assume He loved anyone else more than you. Just know that He loves you, and someday you will understand. Praise Him, not only when you are without problems but in the midst of them. God is not the author of strife and confusion or sickness and death. He is our healer and restorer. Let Him be that to you. Quit trying to figure everything out and agree to be open to a new thought, a "God thought."

Many times while counseling someone I find his or her whole life is dominated by a way of thinking that never occurred to me. Getting people out of thought patterns, however erroneous or illogical, is almost impossible. Childhood teaches us a lot of things, many of them wrong. As adults, we must reset our minds daily to conform to the Word of God. This is why a good devotional is needed. It turns your brain around every day. I recommend *My Utmost for His Highest* by Oswald Chambers.

Determine now to begin to discard the wrong thoughts and embrace the right ones. Ask God to show you the truth. Embrace Jesus and rely on His strength.

Lord, I really do want the truth. I recognize that if I don't embrace Your truth, I haven't really embraced You. I didn't realize until now how deep my desire was to justify myself rather than to see things as they really were. I feel victimized and mistreated; I am hurt, and the feeling is so real in my life that I can't seem to move on from it. I know that through You I am a victor, not a victim. Lord, help me to walk in that truth and to feel the effects of it. Greater are You in me than he that is in the world. I believe this, and because I believe this, I will move on. Your life and love and peace and power are working in this mortal body of mine. I believe they will do their work in me because You have promised if You begin a good work, You are faithful to finish it. Praise God. I can't wait to see Your plan for me and the woman You are making me to be. I praise You, Lord. In Jesus' name I pray. Amen.

FIVE

What God Intended

WHEN LAMAR WANTED TO get a dog to help corral his cattle, he chose a Blue Heeler, which we named Queenie. After many failed attempts at training Queenie, Lamar sent for a book on how to train cattle dogs.[1] I started reading the book, hoping to get to the part where they started training the dog, but the author just went on and on about choosing the dog. What I finally learned from the book was that some cattle dogs will never be able to corral cattle, in spite of training. You have to pick a dog that already has the tendencies you want. If you choose one that doesn't, your training will be in vain; conversely, if you choose a dog that does have the natural inclination to corral, or whatever you want in your dog, a little training is all he needs. In fact, if the dog has naturally good tendencies and the owner tries to over-train him, he can ruin the dog's ability to perform.

I think this is also a pretty good idea when you are choosing a mate. Choose a good man, a man whose heart is already turned toward God, and then don't ruin him. Don't pick a man who has no interest in the things of God and then push and prod him the rest of your lives to become a Christian. Choose a man whose interests you already share and who shares your interests. It saves a lot of heartache.

If you have already made your choice, does that mean you're stuck? Definitely not. I believe situations can be redeemed and men and women can change. God told John, *"Behold, I am making all things new"* (Rev. 21:5). This scripture says "all things" will be made new. Your man can be a new man—the man you want and need.

In the Beginning

What did God intend when He created marriage? After all, He didn't have to create the male-female relationship. (To be honest, there have been days I regretted His decision.) Whenever I attempt to make sense out of my own marriage, God just keeps bringing me back to Genesis.

Genesis begins with the creation of the earth and all living things on it. It doesn't say why God created them, at least not here. It just says, *"In the beginning God created the heaven and the earth. And the earth was formless and void, and darkness was over the surface of the deep. And the Spirit of God moved upon the face of the waters. Then God said, 'Let there be light'; and there was light"* (Gen. 1:1–3).

God doesn't create things without purpose; His method of creation is intentional and perfect. According to some theologians, the earth was in a suspended state at the time of Creation because of the rebellion of Lucifer and his cohorts. When Lucifer thought he could be like God, God immediately took His presence from him and the earth was plunged into darkness. But God devised a plan to redeem the earth. He needed a spiritual being to restore a right spirit to this world, His Spirit. That plan was man, and God created Adam.

> And then God said, *"Let us make man in our image, in our likeness, and let them rule over the fish of the sea and the birds of the air, over the livestock, over all the earth, and over all the creatures that move along the ground."*
> —Genesis 1:26, niv

Man was created in the image of God to fill the earth with his offspring, to rule, and to subdue it. He was created to be God's steward over creation. But man failed. I don't think God was surprised by Adam's fall, nor Lucifer's. God gave man the freedom of choice, but also set into motion a plan for redemption if he made the wrong one. I recently heard someone say we are a cheap image of God. We may have cheapened ourselves by making wrong choices, but the price God paid to buy us back—the life of

His Son—was anything but cheap. We are not a cheap copy. We are very expensive, indeed.

Satan knows this. He was created a spirit being, and didn't quit existing just because he fell. He just quit being beautiful and full of light because he lost his connection to God. When Adam sinned, humans lost our connection to God, too. With dead spirits, we are like dead men walking, even though our bodies and souls are living. To illustrate my point, allow me to quote what Jesus said: "Another of the disciples said unto him, Lord, suffer me first to go and bury my father. But Jesus said to Him, *"Follow Me, and allow the dead to bury their own dead"* (Matt. 8:21–22). Jesus told the young man to follow Him and to let the "dead" bury their own. Who were the dead? Since dead people can't do anything, much less dig a grave to bury someone in, he couldn't have been referring to corpses. He was referring to those individuals who were spiritually dead without the knowledge of Christ and the Father.

Here is further evidence: When God gave Adam life in the Garden, He gave him certain instructions. One of them was to abstain from eating the fruit of the tree of the knowledge of good and evil. *"For in the day you eat from it you will surely die,"* God told him (Gen. 2:17). However, after Adam and Eve succumbed to the serpent's temptation and ate the fruit, they were still alive. Since God doesn't lie, man must have died some other way than physically. Man and woman died spiritually that day. Real life is not walking around breathing; it is the life that we get from being in relationship with God.

Watchman Nee puts it this way:

> God's people not only must know they possess a spirit; they also must understand how this organ operates—its sensitivity, its work, its power, its laws. Only in this way can they walk according to their spirit and not the soul or body of their flesh....
>
> The spirit and soul of the unregenerate have become fused into one; therefore they do not know at all the presence of the

deadened spirit; on the other hand, they are very well aware of strong soulical sensation. This foolishness continues even after being saved. That is why believers sometimes walk after the spirit and sometimes after the flesh even though they have received spiritual life and have experienced to some degree victory of the things of the flesh....

Why must there be a regeneration of the spirit? Because man is a fallen spirit. A fallen spirit needs to be reborn that it may become a new one. Just as Satan is a fallen spirit, so is man; only he has a body. Satan's fall came before man's; we therefore can learn about our fallen state from Satan's plunge. Satan was created as a sprit that he might have direct communication with God. But he fell away and he became the head of the powers of darkness. He now is separated from God and from every godly virtue. This however doesn't signify that Satan is non-existent. His fall only took away his right relationship with God. Similarly, man in his fall also sank into darkness and separation from God. Man's spirit still exists but is separated from God, powerless to commune with Him and incapable of ruling. Spiritually speaking, man's spirit is dead. Nonetheless, as the spirit of the sinful archangel exists forever so the spirit of sinful man continues too. Because he has a body, his fall rendered him a man of the flesh (Gen. 6:3). No religion of this world, no ethics, culture or law can improve this fallen human spirit. Man has degenerated into a fleshly position: nothing from himself can return him to a spiritual state. Wherefore regeneration or regeneration of the spirit is absolutely necessary. The Son of God alone can restore us to God for He shed His blood to cleanse our sins and give us a new life.[2]

WHAT IS LIFE?

You might say man was, for all intents and purposes, dead on the day he first sinned, because death is separation from God. That's the bad news.

If you read the Bible, you will see there are two destinations after an individual's body dies: one with Him and the other without Him, heaven or hell. Without a plan for redemption, when Adam's body died, he would be separated permanently from God. God had a plan to redeem His creation, to buy us back before it was too late. That's the good news.

This plan of redemption begins to unfold early on in the Old Testament. First, man needed to understand that sin required a sacrifice, and God knew He couldn't just do it once, but rather over and over again (sin = sacrifice) so that when the final sacrifice, Jesus, came we would understand. It begins so early and there is never a first command to do it. We just know they start right after the Fall with Cain and Abel.

Since no man could manage to remain sinless, God decided to become a man and pay the penalty Himself. When God came to Earth, He took a human body and name; we know Him as Jesus of Nazareth. He lived on the earth for thirty-three years, teaching throughout a very small area in the Middle East. Though he worked as a humble carpenter for most of His life, Jesus had the greatest impact on this earth of any man. He suffered as the atoning sacrifice for our sins, and as He died He said in John 19:30, "It is finished." What was finished? Man was redeemed once and for all from his sentence of death.

Now all we have to do is receive what He has done. Therefore, *life is the period of time we have to accept what God, in His grace and mercy, has provided as payment for our sin.* This is why godly men for centuries have said, "*Choose you this day whom ye will serve*" (Josh. 24:15, KJV). This choice is fundamental to the course of our lives. In fact, the purpose of life is to gain eternal life with Him. (If you want to know more about this, I suggest you begin by reading the book of Romans.)

We are empty vessels. Without Jesus, when all is said and done—after you've tried everything to help yourself, to solve your problems, and get yourself fulfilled—you will still be empty, spiritually dead. Your fulfillment is in Him, whether or not you choose to acknowledge it. That is why we need to quit worrying about ourselves and instead focus on God and His Son, Jesus. It is not all about us.

Redemption is accomplished one person at a time. You, me, and everyone else has to be redeemed in our own hearts and minds. We must come to see we have a problem. In fact, we—more specifically, our sin nature—*are* the problem. If you haven't yet repented of your sin and asked Jesus to be your Savior, do it now. That is the first step in the healing of your heart and the healing of your marriage.

We cannot help anyone until we help ourselves. Once we have taken care of ourselves, we can begin to reach out to others. We can't redeem anyone, but we can do our part to show them the love of Christ and demonstrate the life-changing result of living in right relationship with God. The closer someone is to us, the more influence we can have on them. That's why we need to make good decisions.

Learn to recognize His voice and walk with Him on a daily basis. Even if you feel like God doesn't speak to you, keep listening. Romans 2:11 (TLB) says, "*God treats everyone the same*"; if He speaks to other people, that means He wants to speak to you, too.

> *Call to Me, and I will answer you, and I will tell you great and mighty things, which you do not know.*
> —Jeremiah 33:3

I really can't tell you how to know when God is speaking to you. I suggest that you get still and quiet all the voices and distractions down. Then listen. He never torments. He doesn't usually rush you or tell you it's too late.

The longer you walk with Him, the more you will know when it's Him and when it's not.

> *My sheep recognize My voice, and I know them, and they follow me.*
> —John 10:27, TLB

If you have spent time listening for God's voice and are still finding yourself unable to hear Him, there are a few possible reasons.

1. The connection has never been made. Since He is spirit, you must be spirit, too. Going to church is not enough. You must repent of your sin and make Jesus the Lord of your life, making you born again of His Spirit.

2. Something or someone is standing between you and God. Unforgiveness or sin will stop the flow between you and God. Ask Him to show you anything that might be wrong and if nothing comes to mind, assume things are OK between you, God, and man. If you think of something (you haven't been tithing fully; your brother is upset with you, etc.) then you must repent and determine to correct the situation as He would have you.

3. You aren't recognizing God. He is speaking and you are casting it off as something other than Him. He's that slight unction to do something good or nice, even and perhaps especially if it's difficult. Trust those little inklings and begin to act on them or at least be willing to act.

CHOICE

Decide today whom you will obey...But as for me and my family, we will serve the Lord.

—JOSHUA 24:15

My daughter-in-law, Kimi, recently shared something God said to her: "I took man out of the Garden, but I did not take the Garden out of man." The Garden of Eden is symbolic of the place of choice, and man continues to make choices. Day after day we decide if we are going to do this or that or, as Proverbs 4:27 puts it, *"swerve to the right or to the left."* It is in these small steps or choices that we choose our path in life. If we listen to God, we go down His path. If we don't, we go down our own path. His leads to life; ours always leads to death. It is really that simple.

Choice, whatever the choice is, takes a dynamic form. It doesn't remain unfruitful, dead, and without life, like a cardboard cut-out. Choices always have consequences. If we choose to follow God's path, we are choosing life, and the result will be salvation, health, prosperity, and joy. If we choose our own path, death is the result; that choice will bear the fruit of sickness, lack, and strife. Just as a plant cannot grow without the sun, our plans will not grow with out the life of the Spirit. Choices are spiritual factors that eventually become physical realities.

Sadly, Adam and Eve allowed a thought, a doubt, to enter their minds and pollute everything. They chose death. Sin always starts in the mind with a thought or a doubt, the culmination of which is a disobedient act. It is no different with us. Jesus came to do what Adam failed to do and what we fail to do: to bring us back to the original intention of God by restoring wholeness to our relationship with Him.

> For as by one man's disobedience [Adam's] many were made sinners, so by the obedience of one [Jesus] shall many be made righteous.
>
> —ROMANS 5:19, KJV

We are no different than Adam and Eve in the Garden of Eden. Like that first couple, we have been visited by the enemy of our souls and he has lied to us. We were placed in this world to watch over it, to guard and redeem it, but we have allowed Satan to enter into the garden of our lives and sow weeds there.

Our marriages are in disarray because we don't understand the fundamentals. Take me for example: my parents gave me a wonderful childhood and taught me proper morals. I had a good foundation by the world's standards. Still, I, like everyone else, failed. Why? Because I didn't understand the simple gospel message. I was in the unredeemed state and I didn't even know there was a problem. I was playing the game of life and losing because I didn't know the Source of real life.

It's because you don't understand the object of the game either. Have you ever noticed that when someone tries to explain a board game, even a simple one, it usually sounds confusing until they tell you the object of the game? Then it all falls in place. We mistakenly think the purpose of life is to be happy or to be successful or for our kids to turn out well. That's not the purpose of life at all. Even if you are happy all your life, which I highly doubt, you will still have missed the point of it all if you miss out on knowing Jesus. And you will lose the game. Have you been playing at the game of life all these years and losing, too?

LIFE

Thanks to Jesus, you and God can fellowship together day after day. He's there anytime you care to include Him. You are like a branch connected to a vine. *"I am the vine, you are the branches; he who abides in Me and I in him, he bears much fruit, for apart from Me you can do nothing"* (John 15:5). As the life of the Vine, Jesus, flows through you, it will nourish your spirit and produce fruit that will nurture those around you—your husband, children, friends, relatives, and even strangers. They will naturally want what you have and they will get connected.

> *The fruit of the Spirit is love, joy, peace, patience, kindness,*
> *goodness, faithfulness, gentleness, self-control.*
> —GALATIANS 5:22

We are a branch that gives forth fruit, and He is the vine to which we should be attached. Why all this garden talk? Because a garden is a place of life and beauty. When we are connected to Him, we are connected to life and beauty, and life and beauty will flow through us. We can't help but be productive. We are stewards properly caring for what He has put in our hands and using it for the furtherance of His plan and kingdom. This is the gospel, or the good news. It is good news to find out God forgives, redeems, and welcomes us back into His fold. And so the time comes to decide. Do you want to walk with God and produce good fruit? Make the decision today to be a sweet aroma to God. Pray with me:

Dear heavenly Father, I do want to be with You, not only when I die, but here on Earth. I understand You cannot have sin in Your presence, and I know I have sinned. I have heard that You came to Earth in the form of Your Son, Jesus, and He paid the penalty for me on the cross. It seems so gruesome and terrible that You would ask Christ to die that way, but I now see it was the only way to redeem man. The Bible says that because of Adam's sin, all men were condemned; so by another man, Jesus, all men have been justified. I receive that promise now. I ask You to cover me with Jesus' blood and put His righteousness on me. I do love You and want to feel Your love in my life. I thank You for it now and pray all this in the precious name of Jesus. Amen.

There! It is done. You are a child of the most high God! If that doesn't make your day, nothing will. You may not feel any different right now. It took me three days to realize I was a new person after I made Jesus the Lord of my life, but never fear—He has taken it very seriously.

Remember the dog story I told at the beginning? They said the hardest part of dog training is not ruining a good dog. God in your life is a good thing. Try not to ruin it with what you try to do on your own that does not come from Him. In your zeal, you can do more harm than good. It just helps if you back off as much as possible and allow God to do His thing.

Six

My Dark Hour

RELATIONSHIPS. PEOPLE. IT'S ALL about souls. I understand your life is a mess and the last thing you have on your mind is reaching out, at least not right this minute. But I am here to tell you, yes, in the midst of it all, you must minister. That's right. In spite of everything, you cannot get so caught up in your problems that you forget to be a part of the greater work. And even that won't be easy. You would think if you were helping, that God would cut you some slack, and He will. But not like you think He will! Just keep walking out your miracle. He's in it somewhere. Always assume He is there.

I wish I could say it was all grand and glorious in the early years, but I can't. In fact, I can guarantee you that if you have begun a walk with the Lord, you will encounter opposition. Every demon in hell will fight you every step of the way. Satan has plenty of people here on Earth that will cooperate, giving him hands, feet, and a voice. When Proverbs 1:16 says the evil run to do evil, it's talking about people. No, the devil doesn't have a tail and horns. In fact, you will very likely never actually see him. You will only see the evidence that he is there, just as we see the evidence the Holy Spirit is there, too, if we are astute enough to figure out how.

Even Jesus encountered opposition from evil people and the devil while He was on Earth. Why would Jesus, as wonderful as He is, have trouble with people? All He wanted to do was to love and bless them, yet they were always coming after Him. He walked away from the authorities over and over again, until the last time when He allowed them to take Him. The people who called for Jesus' crucifixion knew He was not a thief or murderer, but they voted to save Barabbas, a known criminal, in exchange for Jesus (Luke 23:18–19).

If this happened to Jesus, why should our lives be any different? Jesus confronted the evil forces that came against Him, and He gained the victory—a victory that was as much for us as it was for Him. In the process of becoming mature believers, there are a few things that we will be required to do.

I was always getting in trouble about something—mostly my witnessing. Some of it I deserved and some of it I didn't. God had to take care of both. I ran to Him time and time again to find out if I was right or if I was wrong.

The first time I heard someone quote the phrase, "It's out on the limb that the fruit grows," it ministered to me so much I put it on a card and stuck it on the refrigerator. Part of learning to live a Spirit-filled, Spirit-led life is being willing to trust God to direct—and then support—your endeavors. There is often, however, an awful period of time between when you go out on a limb in faith and when you see God begin to come through. This is when you are most likely to experience attacks from the devil and people who will try to discourage you and convince you that your faith is in vain. Many times I've cried out to the Lord saying, "Lord, help. I'm out on the limb, and they're sawing it off." Though the interim can be difficult, it's so important that we stand during this time and don't panic. I know it's hard, but it's possible. God will come through and prove that you were on the right track, after all.

> *Therefore put on the full armor of God, so that when the day of evil comes, you may be able to stand your ground, and after you have done everything, to stand.*
>
> —EPHESIANS 6:13, NIV

GO INTO ALL THE WORLD

I wish I could say that at least my mother and father understood, but I can't. A week after I was saved my parents were supposed to stay at our house for a few days before they went on to their home in Florida. I don't remember what I said about my salvation experience because I really didn't know how to express what happened to me, but whatever I said about being saved really bothered my mother. The next morning Mom got me up early to tell me they were going to go on home after only staying with us briefly. I was shocked. I walked them out to their car alone. We kissed good-bye and off they went. I sat down on the swing and prayed as the tears trickled down my face. I couldn't believe they were gone.

As I prayed and sought God, I knew this was the price of the gospel even though I didn't yet know what the Bible had to say about it (Matt. 10:35–38). Hearing from God at that moment helped. I felt He understood and affirmed that I wasn't wrong for believing what I did; I was right and this was the price. Still, my relationship with my parents would never be the same. We loved each other dearly, but something fundamental had come between us. God used the situation to help me mature, and I do feel He used me to help my mother come to understand the need for Jesus in her life just before she passed away over twenty-five years later. Dad understood, because his family were Christians, too, but sadly we didn't talk about it that day.

A Word Fitly Spoken

It was during this time that I came under attack by someone who was lying about me. I never knew who my accuser was or exactly what they were saying, but it was suggested that I was witnessing too much and running off business. Lamar took their word for it and wouldn't talk about it any more. I guess I could have pitched a fit, but with Lamar it wouldn't have done any good. It just would have made our so-called discussions worse.

Naturally, I tried all the more to be careful, making sure I wasn't obnoxious and that I was led by the Holy Spirit, but you have to understand how great the change in my life was. I was suicidal and suddenly I had joy unspeakable. I couldn't contain it, as much as I tried. I was saved and healed, and so much was happening, not just in my life, but in the town. There was a real move of the Spirit. It was hard not to share, and many of the people who came in the store were experiencing new spiritual things, too. And then there were the sick people that I prayed for that got well. Would they have complained? I didn't think so. They came in with a testimony. Still, no matter how careful I was, the accusations continued, and Lamar continued to be upset by them.

You probably understand what I am talking about. You could be telling your story as well. That's life: the good, the bad, and the ugly. Sometimes it's as if it all gets concentrated into an extra-strength dose of life. What's happening is either really good, really bad, or really ugly; sometimes they all come together. You just wonder what will be standing when the winds settle down. In these times we should remember Hebrews 12:27 (TLB): "*He [God] will sift out everything without solid foundations so that only unshakeable things will be left.*"

When I began to doubt whether I was doing the right thing by witnessing in the store, God reminded me that I was there not by accident, but by design, because I would speak what He gave me and others wouldn't. Every time there was some incident in town, like the death of a beloved slow-learner or a chainsaw fatality. He had given me a message, and I had faithfully delivered it to everyone who asked. "I put you there," He reminded me. I wasn't scheduled to be at the register when the Lord gave me the words so to speak, so if I was running the register, it was because somebody else couldn't. I believe He was behind those reasons. He was not displeased with me. Imperfect as I was, I was getting His Word out. What a humbling thought. "*Oh, God, that I may decrease so that You may increase*" (John 3:30).

The accusations continued and grew worse. I couldn't imagine who could be responsible or whom I could have offended. I checked again and again in my spirit, with no answer. One night things were so bad I couldn't sleep. I got back up and went in the living room to read my Bible and pray in the quiet, "What would you have me do, Lord? I don't want Lamar upset with me, and I certainly don't want to offend people. I'm trying to be sensitive to You in what I say and do. It seems to bless people. Should I stop? What should I do, God? I need your help."

I sat there not knowing the Bible well enough to look anything up.

So, I just sort of leafed through wondering where to stop. When I didn't feel I should go on, I stopped and started reading. "And the word of the LORD came to me, saying." I thought, "That's exactly what I want, a word from the Lord." I was hooked. The rest of the passage was just as powerful to me.

> *Son of man, speak to the sons of your people and say to them, "If I bring a sword upon a land, and the people of the land take one man from among them and make him their watchman; and he sees the sword coming upon the land and blows on the trumpet and warns the people, then he who hears the sound of the trumpet and does not take warning; his blood will be on himself. But had he taken warning, he would have delivered his life, But if the watchman sees the sword coming and does not blow the trumpet and the people are not warned, and a sword comes and takes a person from them, he is taken away in his iniquity; but his blood I will require from the watchman's hand."*
>
> —EZEKIEL 33:2–6

In this passage, God was telling Ezekiel that the people should pick a watchman to warn the community when he sees judgment coming from the Lord. If the people don't take the warning, then what befalls them is their own fault; the watchman isn't held responsible. But if the watchman doesn't blow his horn, then the blood of the people is on the watchman's hands. The watchman will be judged. As I read this verse, I knew God was talking to me. I was the watchman, and I was required to blow the horn warning of the danger. I knew if I didn't do what I felt led to do, their blood would be on my hands.

I sat there stunned. God was not saying I was wrong. He was confirming to me how very right I was—so right that I would be held accountable. If I was not obedient, I would pay a terrible price. What a revelation. I would never be the same. I wept as the reality of my calling, of our calling as Christians, sank in. We are all watchmen.

I was trying to tell people about the Lord. I was doing it by praying for their sicknesses, encouraging them, and giving them my testimony. Maybe I wasn't doing it the way they would, and I surely made mistakes. Still, I was doing my best, and I was learning a lot, too. I didn't keep making the same mistake all the time. I learned and did better the next time. As I sat there totally awed by the word I had just received from the Lord, the worry washed out of me. God had spoken to me in that moment as strongly as He ever has. I just knew I was doing what He wanted me to do. I laughed and cried and praised Him for a while and then went to bed to face another day. I don't know how long it was before all the mess was taken care of, but it really didn't matter any more after God showed me that passage in Ezekiel. I had heard from God. I continued to be sensitive to the Holy Spirit, but now I knew it was OK with God for me to share. That's all I needed to know.

I didn't want to be controversial. The last thing I wanted to be was a problem to Lamar, but I had to be true to what I was getting from God. We don't always know we are right. We have to keep taking these things to God. If Lamar would read this now and remember that episode in our lives, I'm sure he would say that it almost seems like it didn't happen. And I'm glad for that. We still encounter controversies and problems with people—there always will be—but Lamar now trusts me to do the right thing.

Not long after the revelation God gave me, a member of our fellowship group was caught embezzling from a rich elderly widow. When Lamar heard about it, he admitted to me it was this guy and his wife that had the problem with me. I never suspected that it was them because I thought they were some of the happy participants of the spiritual movement in our area. They acted like they were spiritual, but that was the problem; they were acting. It was real with me and I bothered them. I remember thinking something didn't ring true with the wife, but couldn't put my finger on it. After Lamar admitted that they were the source of the problem, I understood what it was that I sensed about her.

I felt a check in my spirit about another woman, a pastor's wife, who always seemed distant to me. We later found out she was having an affair.

One after another, the people that had a problem with me were exposed in their sin. Pretty soon, Lamar got the message. It wasn't me that was the problem, after all. I'm not saying I'm perfect, but other Christians should love me and be able to join me in my love for the Lord. The same is true of you and your enthusiasm for the things of God. When they can't, there is a problem. It's a spiritual problem.

Why was there such a battle over my witnessing? Because everything was at stake: my joy, my maturation, and my victory, not to mention the people that were blessed by my prayers. No wonder the devil fought so hard to stop me. Thank God, greater is He that is in me than he that is in the world. (See 1 John 4:4.) Without God's protection, I would've been toast.

YOUR PART

Many of you cringe at the thought of witnessing. If you have found an answer, then you have enough to share. People share when Weight Watchers helps them lose weight, or if Oprah's show really blessed them, and that journaling has been a real godsend. Is your answer any less special? I don't think so; not if it's Jesus. He's an especially good answer, the Answer above all answers. You surely have a right to share the best answer—the eternal answer. The question is, why would you keep it a secret?

You need to get the picture of the way things really are. To help some people do this, God gives them dreams or visions of people perishing. They are never the same after that. Benny Hinn loved the Lord and felt called into the ministry, but he had a speech defect. He thought that what he was getting in his spirit didn't make sense. Two nights later, God gave him a dream or vision of people perishing in hell. This is why he is so driven today. It is very real to him. It should be to all of us, you included.[1]

There is a precipice in front of every human being. At the bottom is eternal separation from God, the greatest of all pain. Eternal life doesn't start at death. It starts sometime in this life, before we die physically. If you have been born again, you will never die. You must believe this.

You have the answer to help people get past the precipice. It's Jesus. He died for all of them. The ones that think they are too bad are not too bad; and the ones that think they are too good, are not that good. The ones that are waiting don't need to wait any longer; and the ones that don't think they can live up to it need to be told God intends to do in them what needs to be done. It is not up to them to be strong or perfect. They all need to be told, so why are only a few of us willing to do it? God needs you to help Him. I know it may not seem like much, but every little bit helps. Don't you tell your husband or kids when you need them to help you keep the house clean or get a job done? Well, God is the original parent, and He requires your help.

As God does things for you and your family, you are supposed to share it. In fact, the Bible says we will overcome Satan by the blood of the Lamb and the word of our testimony (Rev. 12:11). We have to testify of God's greatness to experience the victory. You need to experience the joy that obedience and trusting God brings. In the midst of your mundane, dingy life, you need something to sparkle. Nothing will sparkle more than seeing God do things through you.

Don't wait for an unction. If you are standing in a checkout line, do you need a reason to start talking to someone and see where it leads? With me, it always leads to a good testimony. The Bible says He will give you the words to say (Luke 12:11). It should seem appropriate.

As I do for Him, He does for me. It is as you do what He would have you do that He will work on your problems. Why should He work on your problems if you aren't going to help Him with His? Yes, that's right: God has a problem. This unsaved, heathen world is His problem, and He has quite a few issues with the Christian world, too. He asks us to help with each. Are you willing?

You do not know joy until you have been obedient to share your testimony with someone and told them what Jesus has done for you. They might not say anything right then, and you might never see the person again, but you know He brought you together and enabled you to share. What a feeling.

COMPLETE THE WORK

I had a friend who felt God wanted her to stop by the doctor's office where she had an abortion years earlier. She was saved and had received forgiveness for her sins, and she felt she should share her testimony with the doctor. It was hard for her to do, so she procrastinated a long time. Finally, after months, she could stand it no longer. She went in and asked for the doctor, but was informed he had died a few days earlier. Oh, what regret when we know we have missed an opportunity. God knows all these missed opportunities; He saw them when He hung on the cross.

Don't let the devil rob you of your greatest joy. Nehemiah 8:10 reminds us that "*the joy of the LORD is your strength,*" and part of that joy will come from sharing what you have so freely received. Share His love, peace, and joy with anyone who will listen. Don't worry about troubling people if you're acting in love. Some individuals may think you are trouble, but that's because they can't see what real trouble is. The people that want to hear your testimony stand there and listen; the others excuse themselves and run off.

You can use this principle to get rid of people you don't want around you. People who are not receptive to the Spirit of the Lord don't stay around very long if you start talking about Jesus. Don't condemn them of their sin; just talk about how precious He has been to you. Act like they are a Christian, even when you know they aren't. They will either get right or get gone.

I will suggest that you be careful sharing your testimony repeatedly with unsaved family members. Take care not to talk too much to them because you don't want to run them off. Tell them the reason for your joy and don't be shy about sharing your faith, but remember to be sensitive to them.

Be sure your witnessing has the joy of the Lord. Don't linger in your description of the past, before you were saved, and as they share their problems, speak faith to them. Speak a blessing into their lives. Be bold and say that you don't receive the negative situation they are in. Tell them you are believing God will intervene because He has a plan for their lives. Speak a new future over them. We must not only break the cords of bondage and give them faith to believe for a resolution of their problem, but we must also give them a new life plan. I don't mean that you should tell them anything specific about their purpose or destiny right then, but just reinforce that you are believing God for good things for them—better things.

In some cases, you can and should pray right there for them. Let them hear the prayer. But for others, this would embarrass them. It is not necessary to pray right then if it's not the time. Just assure them you will pray, and ask others to pray, too. Ask their first name or the first name of the person they are concerned about. Assure them God is faithful and loves them and will work on their behalf. This chance meeting is not just for you to tell them about your life, but to help them with their life. God is the God of a new work.

When they leave, you know and they know that God goes with them. Why? Because you are asking Him to, and because if He began a work by bringing you together, He intends to finish it after you part. Philippians 1:6 (NKJV) says, "*He who has begun a good work in you will complete it.*" I have the faith He will be faithful and answer my prayer. I hope you do, too.

I am speaking to you about witnessing because it's such a vital part of your victory. Through it you will learn to trust the Lord and obey Him by doing what He gives you to do. Don't always think He is going to impress it on you. We are commanded to go to the highways and byways to compel the people to come. As you go, you will hear from Him, and as you do what He needs you to do, He will be working on your problems. It's just that simple. The victory in your marriage is tied directly to your sharing of the gospel to the lost. Is that a scary concept? It needn't be.

Maybe it seems like the wrong time for you to speak out about anything, but believe me, if that's how you feel, that probably means it's just the time to do it. I have found that oftentimes the worse a situation is, the more you need to take a stand. Believe me, I've been there. We should live like today is the only day we can do anything.

If you see a need or have a burden, that is what God is calling you to do. If you keep thinking, "Someone should do something about this," that someone is you. With and through the love of Christ, you just have to start doing what needs to be done.

GOD RAISES UP A STANDARD

I have found car trouble is one of the best ways to witness. Of course, you look terribly vulnerable and anything but victorious at the time, which is why it's so hard to speak in faith when you are in your mess—but you must. Romans 5:20 says, *"Where sin abounds, grace does much more abound."* In other words, if the devil is getting you and has raised the standard of evil in your life, God has promised to meet that standard. God is never trumped by the devil. God is never bested. You can say it a million ways, but get it in your head. Write it where you can see it and meditate on that principle until it soaks in your brain.

When I walk into the fix-it shop, they know I am a woman in trouble. "Having a bad day?" the guy at the counter asks. See. Right there somebody is willing to claim a bad day for me. He means well, but he is wrong. He doesn't know he is baiting me to sink into unbelief, but I don't take the bait. "Not me. I don't have bad days. The Bible says, 'Where evil abounds, grace does much more abound.' I'm about to see some grace come my way," I say with confidence. He and the other guys laugh and shake their heads like they know they have a nut on their hands. I'm used to that. We move on and discuss the business at hand. They are professionals, and I am respectful, too.

After an exchange like that, keep your religious statements as short as possible. Usually there is a Christian around, and he might respond with an "amen," but he's not going to step out any further because he knows he will still be there when I am long gone. I tell the men at the shop what my problem is, and they tell me what it will take to fix it. Whatever the scenario, I need my car fixed, so I tell them to go ahead with the work.

I might talk to someone in the waiting room, but I try not to be too pushy and to let the Holy Spirit guide. After I have done what I feel led to do and have waited a little while, my car is fixed. Inevitably, the same people who balked at my statement of faith tell me how lucky it was that this or that happened or didn't happen. The man that can fix it just happened to be there or they just happen to have the part or it really wasn't what they thought it was, etc. In the end, they are the ones that have to admit I am blessed and God did something special for me. (If a miracle doesn't take place, then I just know God has other plans. I am not the deciding factor. All I am is a steward.) I thank them profusely, pay my bill, and then tell them, "I told you God would raise up a standard." It's not my words that convince them; it's what God has done. I said just enough so that, when I was obviously blessed, they would know why.

God will raise up a standard for you. If the devil is attempting to give you a bad day or a lot of bad days, don't accept it. I didn't take that guy's assessment of my day; he just didn't know who my Daddy is, but he knows now. Do you know who your Daddy is? The Father you have in heaven? He owns the cattle of a thousand hills (Ps. 50:11), and He will sell them all to get you what you need. He stripped heaven of Jesus for you, didn't He? You must believe that. He has a million miracles for you. All you have to do is stand in faith, knowing *whose* you are.

MY BROKEN PIECE

When we had the convenience store, Lamar kept a few cars out front to sell. He found that people didn't want to pay very much, so he kept lower-priced cars, which meant they weren't in great condition. Somehow, I got in the loop. He sold the car I was driving, so I had to pick one from out front to drive. Lamar saw selling something at a profit as a way to move up; I just saw it as a big inconvenience. My car may not have been the best, but it was mine.

The car I ended up with had a problem overheating. It wasn't usually a problem because I didn't travel very far and stopped a lot. But one day I went into Gadsden, about thirty miles away, and was rushing to get home in time to greet the kids as they arrived from school. All of a sudden the light came on again. "Oh, God." I prayed as my heart sank. "You know my need. Help me get home." I stopped the car again, but when I got back on the road, it was obvious God was not intervening yet. I was going to have to pull over—fast.

"Help me get my car fixed." I pleaded to the Lord. Up in my spirit came, "It's not your car." I knew that was the enemy messing with my mind. "Well, half of it is." "Ya, but it's not your half that is broke," Satan countered. "God, I take the broke half." I prayed. "Help me get it fixed." I also reminded Him I didn't have much money and the boys would be arriving home soon. I didn't see how I could make it home in time. There was, however, a gas station ahead. I stopped, and the man inside knew who I was. He was related to the man who hosted our fellowship group. His cousin had changed so much since he came to know the Lord, so I looked forward to the opportunity to talk about that and share about the change that I had witnessed in my husband. Everybody knew Lamar from the auction business, so his testimony really struck a chord. It was really a special time.

The mechanic looked at the car and said it needed a new thermostat. That sounded expensive to me, but when I asked how much it would be, he said, "About $6.50." What a blessing. I told him to go ahead and fix it. While he was installing the new thermostat, he found it needed a new belt. "It's going to go any minute," he told me. Cars are always needing belts it seems, especially if you drive an old car. The problem this time was having the right size in stock. "I don't think I'll have the right one," he said, while I countered in my spirit, "I don't believe that." I had already prayed. The man looked through the belts hanging on the wall and exclaimed, "Oh, my goodness. Look-y here! I have it." I had already told him I was praying for the car, so I responded, "Of course you do. My kids need me to get home. Do you think my God would let me down?" We all had a good laugh, and I was soon on my way, praising God. The kids never missed me, but I needed to be home anyhow. Three boys in a house alone for very long can be a parent's worse nightmare.

So how does this help you in your relationship? Just as I had to accept responsibility for the broken-down car so that I could get it fixed, I had to take responsibility for the brokenness of my marriage so that I could ask God to fix it. Lamar's life was broken because of sin, and that, in turn, caused our marriage to be broken. As I came to understand that I was one with Lamar, I felt the need to intercede for my husband and ask God's forgiveness as though Lamar's sin were my own. I repented of our sin—Lamar's and mine together. I know this may sound ludicrous, but it was a significant step in our marriage when I became willing to stand in the gap for my husband, grieve over his sin, and assume responsibility for our brokenness together. I quit thinking of how his sin hurt me and started thinking about how our sin hurt God.

It brought me into a new dimension of intercession. It gave me a depth of prayer I never knew before. I truly grieved before the Lord for what sin did to our family and how much God hated it. I stood guilty before God. You can really pray when you have sin to deal with, and it really was my sin. I was a big part of our problems, for a long time a bigger part than I understood. I got involved with Lamar and didn't do the godly thing. I continued to date him after I knew there were problems. I was spiritually dumb and didn't have the answers. I may have repented, but there was more work yet for me to do. God needed me to be involved in the whole process.

This made us more fully one. We were no longer divided by Lamar's sin or mine. We were connected in it and, more importantly, in our deliverance from it. By embracing Lamar at his worst, I was doing what Jesus did. He embraced us at our worst and took upon Him our sin. He is One with us, just as we are one with our husband. We marry "for better or worse." The sin Lamar was dealing with was the "worse" part described in the marriage vows, and I chose to embrace it, take it to God, and leave it there. I felt a lot better when I didn't feel our sin was condemning our relationship.

The little book of Philemon describes this principle also. Evidently Onesimus, Philemon's slave, had run away and gotten saved through Paul's preaching. Paul writes to Philemon to ask that he take Onesimus back and promises to pay whatever debt Onesimus owes. Paul tells Philemon that he would like to keep him because he has been a big help to him and for that Philemon gets the credit. In fact, Paul actually puts their friendship on the line for Onesimus: *"If I am really your friend, give him the same welcome you would give to me if I were the one who was coming"* (v. 17, TLB). Paul wants Onesimus to have the same blessing Paul would be given, though he was Philemon's runaway slave. Paul continues, *"If he has harmed you in any way or stolen anything from you, charge me for it. I will pay it back (I, Paul, personally guarantee this by writing it here with my own hand) but I won't mention how much you owe me. The fact is, you even owe me your very soul."* (vv. 18–19, TLB). Don't you love that? Here is my paraphrase of these verses: "Oh, by the way, Philemon, you'd be on your way to hell if it weren't for me, ya know." How can Philemon deny Paul his request, as much as he might want to deal harshly with Onesimus? This is exactly what is required of us as Christians. We are to take on each other's burdens—and then some. Why? Because Christ, our model, did it for us.

I am not advocating you agree with your husband's sin. You know it's sin, and you should continue to stand in opposition to it, even if you do it silently. There is a difference between interceding for him and agreeing with his sin. Jesus didn't agree with our sin or participate in it; He took it on only to remove it from us and make us clean before God. That's what we want to happen to all the sin in our relationship.

This is my prayer for you:

> *Dear heavenly Father, my sister in Christ has come together with her husband, and things haven't worked out like she had hoped they would. I ask You to encourage her and give her peace and the joy that you will bring to her life in spite of the mess she is in. She wants to be obedient to what You would have her to do;*

she just doesn't always know what that is, and may feel that she lacks the strength to do what she knows she should do. Help her to see that she is forgiven and truly stands clean before You in Jesus' robe of righteousness. Speak to her spirit and let her know You are with her. Forgive her for any unbelief that has held back her victory. Help her to stand as You heal her and her family. I pray this in Jesus name. Amen.

SEVEN

God created the heavens and the earth.

—GENESIS 1:1

Authority

WHEN YOU CREATE SOMETHING, it is yours. You have authority over it, at least for a time. Because God created the world as we know it, God has authority over it. God's authority is the foundation on which the world is built. I cannot express how important it's that we understand the principle of authority and walk in this revelation. Man was created in His image, and since God has authority, He wanted man to have authority, too. Originally, He gave man dominion over the earth, an awesome responsibility. Unfortunately, we didn't have it very long before man gave it over to someone else—Satan. The earth was forever changed that day, and man with it. We lost our innocence and our godliness and gained instead a sin nature that works against what we know is right. Our flesh can make relationships difficult at best, but the Word of God offers crucial advice about dealing with this part of our nature.

Let every soul be subject unto the higher powers.

—ROMANS 13:1

The highest power is God Himself. Be subject to Him first and your submission to others will come naturally. If you don't acknowledge authority, you won't see your own rebellion. Watchman Nee explained this in *Spiritual Authority:*

God is working towards recovering the oneness of the body. But for this to be accomplished there must first be the life of the Head, followed next by the authority of the Head. Without the life of the Head there can be no body. Without the authority of the Head there can be no unity of the body. To maintain the oneness of the body we must let the life of the Head rule.

God wishes us to obey His delegated authority as well as Himself. All the members of the body should be subject to one another. When this is so, the body is one with itself and with the Head. As the authority of the Head prevails, the will of God is done. Thus does the church become the kingdom of God.[1]

God's authority is not ours to give away, even if it's entrusted to us personally. We may shirk our responsibility and somebody else may take it up, but that doesn't mean God gives it to them. No, they are in rebellion just as we are. If we take on responsibilities that are not ours, that doesn't mean we are walking in authority. It's rebellion.

Man abdicated his role, and the enemy stepped into the void. Satan was already in rebellion and brought rebellion into this world through man. The power and credibility he has is his only because we give it to him, and he works very hard at keeping it. How does he keep it? By convincing us that this is the way things have to be, that we have to be sick, poor, and beaten down, which is a bunch of garbage. He has no authority to do what he is doing. We are usually just too dumb to see it and call him on it. More of us need to wise up and finally putting a stop to his tactics.

I could have included the subject of authority in the "What God Intended" chapter, for truly, if He intended anything, He intended for a man or woman to represent Him properly when He places them in a position of authority. He never intended for man to use this authority to harm or abuse anyone or to be rebellious in any way. You can be sure He takes this kind of disobedience very seriously.

God intended for the world to be a beautiful place, and, actually, it has a great deal of beauty. He intended for the family to be a wonderful sanctuary where the fruit of our love—our children—would grow and mature. Most families do have a great deal of love expressed in them. However, even in the best of families, negative things happen, some mistakenly in the name of love. Human love leaves a lot to be desired. We all end up with problems that need to be worked out later on. Since things are no longer perfect because of the fall, it's up to us to do our part to help make this a better place. Our work must begin right in our home with our marriage and family. God will help us, but we must be willing to be obedient and follow the rules, His rules. Man brought into leadership the potential for error and abuse.

> *"Be quiet." Jesus said sternly [to the demon]. "Come out of him." Then the demon threw the man down before them and came out without injuring him. All the people were amazed and said to each other, "What is this teaching? With authority and power he gives orders to evil spirits and they come out." And the news about him spread throughout the surrounding area.*
>
> —LUKE 4:35, NIV

This is the authority God wants us to walk in.

> *One day Jesus called together his twelve apostles and gave them authority over all demons—power to cast them out—and to heal all diseases. Then he sent them away to tell everyone about the coming of the Kingdom of God and to heal the sick. "Don't even take along a walking stick," he instructed them, "nor a beggar's bag, nor food, nor money. Not even an extra coat. Be a guest in only one home at each village. If the people of a town won't listen to you when you enter it, turn around and leave, demonstrating God's anger against it by shaking its dust from your feet as you go." So they began their circuit of the villages, preaching the Good News and healing the sick.*
>
> —LUKE 9:1–6, TLB

This is same ministry He wants us to have, the same authority He wants us to walk in.

Authority is given to bring direction, to make the working of the plan a unified, cohesive effort to reach the goal. The leader is His representative and, as such, needs to pay attention. He or she needs spiritual eyes that can see and spiritual ears that can hear. It is not an enviable position. Rather, it's a position of grave responsibility. A follower needs spiritual eyes and ears, too (Luke 14:35; Rev. 2; 3; and 13:9).

The following scripture is one of the most quoted on the subject of authority and submission.

> *Everyone must submit himself to the governing authorities, for there is no authority except that which God has established. The authorities that exist have been established by God. Consequently, He who rebels against the authority is rebelling against what God has instituted, and those who do so will bring judgment on themselves. For rulers hold no terror for those who do right, but for those who do wrong. Do you want to be free from fear of the one in authority? Then do what is right and he will commend you. For he is God's servant to do you good. But if you do wrong, be afraid, for he doesn't bear the sword for nothing. He is God's servant, an agent of wrath to bring punishment on the wrongdoer. Therefore, it is necessary to submit to the authorities, not only because of possible punishment but also because of conscience.*
>
> —Romans 13:1, NIV

When we read this passage, it's natural to wonder how to respond to the bad authorities. I can almost hear you asking, "Does this mean I have to do everything someone says, even if it's wrong?" No, God doesn't expect us to do anything immoral. This scripture is talking about the laws that are set down by the governing authorities to bring order to the society. In other words, don't rob a bank, because if you do, you will face charges by the local authorities. They will be a terror to you.

Authority is meant to be a refuge, a protection for the people, never a harmful force in their lives. God instructs the leader, and he or she carries out His orders or instructs others to do so. If the authority figure gets it wrong, he answers to God.

It is an awesome responsibility that God takes very seriously. When you read your Bible, you will come to see leaders pay a very heavy price for their disobedience. It is a fearful thing to answer to God when He is angry, especially when He's upset with you. Hebrews 10:31 (KJV) says, "*It is a fearful thing to fall into the hands of the living God.*" It was for this reason that the Israelites preferred to answer to Moses than to answer to God themselves. "Let his hair turn white from the presence of the Lord." they said. God is merciful and just, but His presence demands respect and reverence.

When Isaiah was given a vision of God on His throne, Isaiah's response was, "*Woe is me, for I am ruined. Because I am a man of unclean lips*" (Isa. 6:5). Suddenly, Isaiah's sin was evident to him. In the presence of the Lord, things you couldn't see before are all at once crystal clear. Instead of looking at others and how sinful they are, you are painfully aware of what a problem you have been and still are, even if you have improved. Being with God is the greatest blessing in the world, but it's rarely comfortable to be made aware of your need to repent.

> *Oh, God. I am a man of unclean lips. Isaiah has nothing on me. Forgive me, Lord, for what I have said that You did not give me to say. Forgive me for the things I have done that You did not give me to do. Forgive me for the hurtful, careless things I've done, even those I meant for good that were not what You would have had me do. I want to do only what You would have me do. It's just so hard for me to know which is which. Help me hear You better. Stop the noise around me. I want to hear You more clearly so I can follow more closely. I start out following You and then don't realize when I get off track. I love You, Lord, more than anything, even when I have wandered out of Your plan.*

Forgive me for letting the world and its worries come between us, for surely it is me and not You that has let them in. Help me be a person of clean lips. I pray all this in the precious name of Jesus. Amen.

Just so we don't get full of ourselves with all this authority, Jesus also said, *"Among the heathen, kings are tyrants and each minor official lords it over those beneath him. But among you it's quite different. Anyone wanting to be a leader among you must be your servant. And if you want to be right at the top, you must serve like a slave. Your attitude must be like my own, for I, the Messiah, did not come to be served, but to serve, and to give my life as a ransom for many"* (Matt. 20:25, TLB). This should end the debate on how domineering someone in leadership should be.

Authority is a legal entity. In a world where everything you say and do can be challenged, you better have something or someone to back you up—something or someone bigger than your challenger. That is why we Christians quote 1 John 4:4 so often. It is so comforting to know that *"greater is He who is in you than he who is in the world."* We believe that. It is our only hope. If it isn't true, then we haven't anything. If Jesus hadn't risen from the dead, then He would have been no more help in this battle we are in than any other prophet. Paul put it this way: *"If there is no resurrection of the dead, then not even Christ has been raised. And if Christ has not been raised, our preaching is useless and so is your faith"* (1 Cor. 15:13, NIV). We need supernatural help. It all boils down to whether Jesus is God or not. If Jesus is not God, then He was a liar and nothing He said can be relied upon; we quote the scriptures in vain. Because He is God, He spoke the truth and we can count on what He said. I settled this question a long time ago. I was suicidal and now I sing. That's why I know that *"no weapon formed against [me] shall prosper"* (Isa. 54:17, NKJV). The same is true for you.

"But, Midge, the devil still has power."

That's right. But only because we gave it to him. He'll only keep having power if we continue to give it to him.

"I thought Jesus defeated him."

He did (Rev. 1:18).

"But, Satan still has it."

Yes, he does, but it's limited to what God and man allow.

"Then why doesn't God just take it all away?"

Because He gave that responsibility to us when He defeated the power of sin and death and gave us His authority. The better question would be: why don't we take his power away from him since we have the authority to do so? Too many Christians are walking around likes slaves to sin and temptation because they don't know they have the authority and freedom to resist Satan through Christ's work on the cross and His resurrection. Many of those that do know who they are in Christ still let something stand in the way: sin, fear, doubt, procrastination, legalism, a lack of repentence, etc. The believers who actually engage the enemy are few and far between.

Ignorance is every believer's enemy, and Satan knows that. In the book of Hosea, the Lord lamented, *"My people are destroyed for lack of knowledge"* (4:6). We can overcome this ignorance and learn to walk in our authority by staying close to God. Here on Earth we are facing a very formidable enemy, and we won't have a clue how to fight back if we don't read our Bibles. It is our manual to help us understand the rules of engagement. If you are going to take your authority and do what needs to be done, you have to know what is going on. You must renew your mind to the things of God. Living by the seat of your pants just gets you a sore you-know-what. It's time we learn to think ahead and know what we are doing and why we are doing it so that when something unexpected comes along, we will be ready.

Did you ever watch a Woody Allen movie? They provide a funny, beautiful depiction of the questions without providing answers: the dilemmas of life we all face. Humor has a great deal of truth to it. There are answers, but the popularity of Woody's movies suggests that many people don't have the answers and are content to appreciate that someone is asking the questions. They are as frustrated as he is. Christians have the unique opportunity to tell people the rest of the story, the answers to their questions. When I see one of his movies I just want to say, "Jesus died for your sins, Woody." It's just hard for some people to comprehend it because it seems too simple to accept.

God Puts Up and Pulls Down

It is a fearful thing to go against God-called authority. Numbers 12 records that the Lord chastised Aaron and Miriam because they were speaking against Moses. God was very displeased. God appeared to the three siblings in a pillar of cloud and spoke to them and said, "*Hear now My words…I speak with [Moses] face to face*" (v. 6, 8, NKJV). In other words, God was telling Aaron and Miriam to butt out. After that, "*The anger of the* Lord *was aroused against them, and He departed…suddenly Miriam became leprous, as white as snow*" (v. 9–10). Aaron admitted he and Miriam had been foolish and sinned, and asked Moses not to hold it against them. Moses intervened and God healed Miriam and lessened her punishment to a seven-day exile outside the camp.

Just as the person in authority should be in right relationship with God, giving proper instructions as God would have him or her, the person in submission must yield many of their everyday choices. They allow the authority figure to have a certain amount of control and power in their life. Woe to the parent or leader that asks an innocent child or follower to do something immoral. Matthew 18:6 records that Jesus said that a person that harms a child would be better off if he had a millstone around his neck. Over and over again people in authority are warned they will be held to a higher standard of accountability. Luke 12:48 (TLB) says, "*Much is required from those to whom much is given.*"

Have you ever been in a group where someone did not yield to the leader and not only had an attitude but outwardly fought many of the decisions he or she made? Or maybe that person just murmured, quietly sewing discord in the group. The leader can try to bring them around, but it's hard to convince a rebel. That is really a job for God. It is a challenge for the leader not to become part of the problem in his or her attempt to correct problems in the group.

Authority is a lonely place. That is not to say that an authority figure doesn't have people working closely with him or her or that they can't have friends and loved ones. It means they must stand alone before God. We may point to the fact that Moses had Aaron helping him in ministry, but it was still only Moses that God spoke to face to face. Aaron was a problem. Remember, he sided with the people against Moses much too often. God had originally told him to go alone.

The leader is the one that has to deal with the rebellious people and try to get them to cooperate. This puts leaders in a quandary. It's great to joke around and have a good time fellowshiping with our friends, but to be a leader requires a certain amount of distance. It doesn't mean you become unapproachable. It just means cultivating respect. Miriam and Aaron came against Moses improperly because they didn't respect his position. They thought they could speak to him as they always had, but Moses' position had changed. They needed to change with it. Wives must understand this principle, too, or God will deal with us just as harshly, even though it won't be leprosy. Wish it were sometimes. We have medication for it.

As a leader, we have to draw aside from the normal friendships, dearly as we love them, for their sake as much as our own. Maybe that's why husbands seem standoffish at times toward their wives. Even if he runs with his friends a lot, there is still a lonely place that he goes to that you can't come; things that he can't share with you because he can't express them. He doesn't even know himself what it is. There is a stirring, a discontent inside that nothing can fill. It takes time and even failing, maybe many times, before he gets the answer; before he sees and understands. During these years, he can be touchy and discontented and often without even knowing why. Your questions and your questioning just makes it worse. With his friends, he doesn't have the weight and responsibility of being "the head." He can just be one of the boys. It's so much easier than the struggle to lead.

If you are called to follow, you will need to draw aside and seek His face, too. Jesus was both a leader and a follower. He drew aside often to seek the face of His Father, just as we should. It takes time to see the wisdom of resignation to God-appointed authority, of not being your own man. This is especially hard for men.

If a man can't easily ask for directions to a city, how can he admit he needs help finding God? It is a response that men (and women) have to learn over time, and it helps to see other men and women do it. That's why a good church helps; it gives us access to godly men and women who have already learned how to surrender to God and are the better for it. As wives, we can have the same influence by preparing ourselves spiritually. If you surrender to God's authority, your husband will see your wonderful life and want to be a part of it. Your life should be a beautiful expression of God's love to him.

God accepts and loves your husband, and so should you. If we don't love our husbands, then we are not expressing what God wants expressed to them. We can grieve over our husband's sin and understand it's a problem, but we must love unconditionally. The Bible says the goodness of God brings men to repentance (Rom. 2:4). We should join in this goodness, not by cooperating with his sin, but by loving him in spite of it. I am not recommending you become an enabler. There is a difference.

A man or woman in a position of authority must be humble—no haughty attitude for God's man. That's why Moses and David did it so well. They learned humility early on. There can be no thinking you know best, like King Saul did. If you see a leader that is haughty and full of himself, back away. Never stand too close to a rebel or you might get swallowed up by the punishment they receive. God has special punishments for people in authority who stumble into sin, but He also has a merciful plan of redemption and healing for them.

WHAT A GREAT TARGET, ESPECIALLY THAT BIG HEAD

If you are in authority, taking you down is the goal of the enemy. The higher you go, the harder your enemy will try to topple you. Just because you won all those other battles doesn't mean you have convinced Satan to quit trying. No, no, no. It simply means you've retired the underlings. Now the big guy's coming on fresh just when you are worn out—and he's been watching and listening. He knows your soft spots. He knows just where to aim, and aim for the kill, he will. The devil has no sympathy for poor, pitiful people who are down. That's what he likes the best. He loves to hear us snivel and whine. That is why we must learn what it takes to win and do it.

You do not want to be the person that brings down the leader. There is judgment reserved for those that try (Luke 17:1). The Jezebel spirit seeks authority and gets in places she shouldn't be and wreaks havoc. Just because this spirit is named after a woman, the people who act in this spirit are not always female. It is an attitude and a mindset that can affect either gender. The Jezebel spirit seeks out an Ahab spirit—someone who will yield easily and completely.

If you are a strong woman and you are dating or married to a weak man, you will really have to fight against falling into these patterns. If you run the family, it is not a good sign. Repentance is in order for both of you. I understand it makes you mad if he acts like a wimp, but you're not any better when you get out of order. You can be strong, but you cannot be controlling and self-serving.

Leadership attracts friends that aren't really friends, wolves in sheep's clothing. Not every helpful person is your friend, nor does every person with a willingness to help possess a servant's heart. I learned this the hard way. Jezebels are willing to put years in establishing their credibility. Watch for little things they do or say that do not ring true. It's really hard to tell the difference between a true servant sent of God and someone sent by the enemy to steal, kill, and destroy. That's why we need our spirit to discern properly. God tells us these things in our inner man, and that's why we need a godly mate to help us discern when we might be fooled.

Do you see how a leader who shirks his responsibility and doesn't have faith in God to help him lends himself to accepting help that will be, in the end, harmful? Moses did this. He insisted that God send Aaron to accompany him, and God allowed it because Moses requested it. However, Aaron was not always a faithful partner in ministry. Just like Moses, we open ourselves up to problems when we don't listen and have faith in God to be there for us.

Let's face it; we have to be ever vigilant. Rebels can come in anywhere and when you least expect it. Then again, people can start in the spirit and end in the flesh. Just because a person is spiritual when they come in doesn't mean they are still in the right spirit, nor does it mean every hard worker or everyone with money has a Jezebel spirit and a goal to usurp leadership. This is why we must know those who labor among us and be open to what God is trying to show us. It is a wise thing to check a person's references. A Christian shouldn't have anything to hide. Don't be so committed and taken up with the ministry that you ignore the signs warning you of potential problems. Slow down. It's usually the enemy that gets us in such a hurry we swallow what we ordinarily would choke on. Learn to back off and wait until you are sure it's right.

> Behold, I send you out as sheep in the midst of wolves; so be
> shrewd as serpents and innocent as doves.
> —MATTHEW 10:16

One day God said to me, "I don't want you naïve." He wanted me to see what was happening, not to be mean or hateful, but to pray and be prepared to do the right thing. If you see something is not ringing true in the life of someone assisting you, beware. I don't want to make you paranoid, but we do need to be wise. Naïveté is disastrous in a leadership position.

If you are a follower, the enemy will do everything in his power to get you to cooperate with the taking down of the person in authority. Can you imagine being a tool of the enemy against the very person that God wants to use to bless you? Many people become unwitting accomplices to the plans of the enemy because they are not listening to God and seeking His will for their actions. This is true of husbands and wives. If you are not listening to God's will in your marriage, you could be your husband's biggest problem.

Spend some time looking at your actions and examining your heart. If you haven't been diligent to respect the leaders God has put in your life, whether it be a church leader or your husband, you need to repent and seek His will afresh for you. Feel free to pray the prayer below.

Oh, God. What have I done? I've not been the follower I should have been. I've not agreed with my leaders and have murmured against them and gone my own way. Even when I cooperated, I did it in a way that was not really helpful. Submission is so hard, and I've not done it very well. I am just realizing how far from the mark I have been all these years. God, forgive me for what I have done that has just made things harder for You and them. Cover my sin with the precious blood of Jesus so You see it no longer and will pass over it. I pray this in the precious name of Jesus. Amen.

ANNA AND THE KING OF SIAM

Anna and the King of Siam, starring Rex Harrison and Irene Dunne, is a black-and-white version of *The King and I*. It is about a widowed schoolteacher who is hired by the King of Siam to teach his children—all seventy-some of them. She and her ten-year old-son move to the faraway land and struggle to understand the customs and culture of the king and the people in his palace. Though the king loves his family and wants to do the right thing, what seems the right thing to him is too often very wrong to Anna. They match wits on many points, but the king assumes he should win all the time—especially because she is a woman.

In the midst of their attempts to understand one another, an issue arises over a slave girl. The young girl had been betrothed to another, but ended up in the king's harem with three thousand other wives and concubines.

Having lost the love of his life, the young man becomes a priest. Unbeknownst to him, his love sneaks out of the palace and pretends to be one of the monks just to be near him. She is caught and they are both hauled into court. He is brought into court on a stretcher because has already been beaten before the "trial" begins. It is obvious the judge doesn't intend to hear any of her witnesses and is going to force her to "confess" to save the priest's life. Anna gets wind of all this and appears at court in an attempt to intervene. When that doesn't work she goes to the king. He is tired of the whole thing.

She says some dreadful things to the king and wounds him deeply. He has the slave and the priest put to death right outside her room. She is mortified and makes plans to leave. The children are especially devastated. They have come to love her so much. Just before they are to leave, her son is killed in a riding accident. Anna is inconsolable. The king sends her a lovely letter. The prime minister tells her what he has said is very unusual and it's really an apology. She appreciates it, but is too devastated to think much of it.

The one child that stands out above all the others is the oldest boy, the same age as her son. It is obvious he will be next in line to the king. Anna appreciates the boy, but to her he is just one of many. He had become friends with her son, but had stopped coming around even before her son died and so had his mother, the first wife of the king. Anna stops to say good-bye. The woman asks if she can speak honestly. "Of course." Anna assures her. If she stands for anything, it's the truth. She has been trying to get the king to have laws instead of his ever changing decrees and whims. Truth stands above everything.

The first wife has her look at the pictures on her walls. Up until now they just looked like the usual Asian art. But, as she explains them, their significance becomes obvious. There is a huge tree to the right that dominates the first picture and a lovely small tree with lots of flowers on it. As the pictures go on, the big tree gets more and more grotesque and the little one more and more puny and the blossoms on it die. Other trees come in and take over. You can hardly see a smaller tree next to her tree.

That is her son, the oldest, the next in line, the mother explains. This is the one Anna has failed. The mother can do little to help him because of their strict rules. The king is too busy and doesn't take an interest in the boy. Only Anna has the power to influence his life in a positive way and she has not done it either. Not only has she failed the boy but the country, because he will be their next king and will be much like his father. Yes, the mother tells her, she has failed and as long as the mother lives she will never forget this. It is quite a poignant moment with no relief from the sorrow.

The king sends for Anna before she leaves. He doesn't want her to go. He needs her to be his secretary. She only cares about the children and stays to continue teaching. Eventually, she continues to do his correspondence. Years go by and she takes a great deal of interest in the oldest son. The king becomes sick and as he lays dying, he calls her in one last time to say what he has never said before. How much she has meant to him.

In the end, the young king stands before a sea of people, all crouching on their elbows and knees with their foreheads to the ground. The new king's first decree is to have them rise and face him. This is the first of many changes he is sure his father would approve. Through Anna, it's a new day in Siam.

WHERE WAS ANNA "GOING"? SHE WAS GOING TO SAVE A NATION

God can use anyone willing to be used; a simple teacher, changing the course of a nation. Just as a simple mother can. In the midst of our storm, we must not miss what we are sent to do. In her desire to save a slave girl, in hurt and anger over the unfairness of it all, Anna almost missed hers. It was a tragedy, but not worth sacrificing so many others. And the truth is she was as blind as the king. He wasn't doing what he should have, but neither was she. Their good points and bad were very much the same. He just had the position that carried the power and she didn't. His wasn't really an enviable place to be. His mistakes were obvious to all and he had such an ego.

The king was a male chauvinist pig of the worst kind. But, God was able to manipulate him at will. He was not the problem. She was. God gave her a great deal of favor in this country that was not her own. Actually, she was as big of a hot head as he was and as stubborn. These men aren't the only ones God is having to teach humility. What a lesson in authority and submission. And so marvelous to watch.

Why did Anna get into so much trouble? The clashing of truth and error was inevitable. She was naturally appalled. And she should have spoken out, but she went too far. She caused herself much of her own pain. She was going to have pain; that was the natural result of being in a godless country and the sin she found there. It is natural to feel bad about it. But, we are limited in what we can do and when. It was not in her hands to do much, at least not quickly. She should have spoken out and even put her safety on the line, but she went to far. She cut too deep. She became accusatory and judgmental. She should have challenged, but not condemned. And then she saw only his sin, not her own, and took matters into her own hands. She decided to leave. God brought her to Siam, but she was taking herself out when things did not go like she wanted. She became God's problem instead of His solution and He had to act to stop her or the whole plan would be scuttled. Only losing her son would humble her and hopefully cause her to listen. How terrible.

What about Anna's prayers for their safety? Surely she prayed them as they embarked on their journey. What about the prayers of the English Christians for Siam? When our prayers and someone else's collide, we had better be on God's side and not have switched somewhere along the line. She had switched. God would have kept the boy safe except that she took them outside of His covering. Disobedience and self-rule make us sitting ducks with no protection. Ignorance does, too. That was my problem.

"But, some lose their loved ones and haven't been disobedient and aren't ignorant. What about them?" God doesn't put us in a bubble. If what we have is the supernatural power of God and if He can give us peace that passes all understanding, then we must draw on that. Whatever happens in our lives; we must take to Him. We see through a glass darkly. Someday we will understand. Thirty years later, I see a lot more clearly.

The loss of her son made her realize how empty her life would be back "home." It would have been if she had gone back with her son, too. The regrets would have at some point kicked in, but she would have never faced the truth. She would have lied to herself and said it had to be. The woman that so wanted the truth would have stood on a lie as she reasoned away the loss of her greatest blessing and her destiny. How great her sorrow would have been, but she would have never allowed herself to grieve. She would have become a bitter, self-consumed old woman not much good to anyone, especially her son. The one relationship she cherished the most would have been marred irreparably. Because she did not sow to another woman; she would not have reaped in her own life. Oh, the pain of self-determination. It eventually destroys what we love the most.

And we are so worried about the oppressive king. No, the king would not have destroyed her life and taken away her destiny. The king was the one blessing her the most, stretching her, challenging her, asking great things of her, and giving her untold opportunities. The king is not her problem; he is the channel through which all her blessings will come. The king that is her greatest problem is her own mind: King Reason. King Self. Hers and ours. Don't worry about the authority in your life. Worry about you and your stubborn determination to do things your own way.

Her purpose was noble; her decision was ignoble.

> *I beseech you therefore, brethren, by the mercies of God, that ye present your bodies a living sacrifice, holy, acceptable unto God, which is your reasonable service. And be not conformed to this world: but be ye transformed by the renewing of your mind, that ye may prove what is that good, and acceptable, and perfect will of God.*
>
> —ROMANS 12:1–2

We are a living sacrifice to be used as God sees fit. If He sees fit to send a widow to Siam, then she should go and serve as best she can as long as He wants her there. She shouldn't have been concerned over her own feelings or reputation. Once she agreed to the plan, she agreed to it all. She did not have the choice to back out, although she didn't seem to know that. Her challenge was not to the king, but God Himself. Always remember, when you balk and refuse to cooperate, you balk against God. I understand sometimes we are fighting for noble causes. The death of two people is a noble cause. But, the battle was not hers. The battle was between God and the king and she should have left it there. Instead, she took action and kept acting wrongly opening herself up to being dealt with by God until she finally acquiesced and again became a living sacrifice, saddened forever at the loss of her son. I believe the plan was for them both, the mother and the son, to be living sacrifices. God sacrificed the son for the greater good, but it was Anna that brought it to that point. And once we have, we must go on, knowing even in this, He is faithful.

You probably won't get to go to Siam to teach the king's children, but you have a king right there in your home. How special God can make your life. Every bit as special as Anna's. Don't let the fact that you have an unworkable situation bother you. Anna's was pretty bad, too, but a special person in any situation changes it. There is something about grace and mercy, love and character that stand out in any place. The world has to make place for these things. Be the best person you can be, and your world will see Jesus in you. And that is enough to change it for the better.

EIGHT

The Lord God said, "It is not good for the man to be alone."
—Genesis 2:18

Man and Wo Man

As GOD CREATED THE other animals, it became more and more apparent that not one was going to fit the bill. Man was alone. How could he be alone? God was with him! Without a partner like himself, man stood apart, alone. That would have made him different than God, and that can't be if we are made in His image. Man was not made fully in His image until he was three in one. *"But if we are two in one, then isn't there still a discrepancy?"* There would be, but God tells us we are one *with Him* and until His place is filled there is a God-shaped vacuum that cannot be filled by anything else. He is the Third Person, the Spirit, in our trinity just as the Holy Spirit is the third person in His Trinity.

I don't think we appreciate what God did when He created man and woman. He could have just made another man, but He didn't want it to be a friendship; not that friends aren't wonderful. He didn't make two brothers, although brothers can be awfully close. The one to one relationship was the one He intended for Himself. For man He wanted something more.

Just as man is on a level all his own between God and the animals, marriage is a relationship unlike any other. He wanted that special spark, even tension that happens only between a man and a woman. I don't mean a negative tension but the tension as in working two muscles against each other to make them stronger. To achieve this He divided His divine attributes differently. We literally complete each other, not just physically, but mentally and emotionally. I don't think that we complete each other spiritually, but I know He completes us spiritually. We can be one with each other and one with Him, which is the ultimate.

It has been said that God had to create woman because something was wrong already. But it wasn't wrong. If it was, He would have said so. Nor was woman created to keep man in line. Man was supposed to do that for himself, just as God keeps Himself "in line." A person is not put in a leadership position to lead people who are *more* responsible than he or she is. That doesn't make sense.

We need to ask what God had in mind when He created man? I can't describe either man or woman without stepping on some toes, but I do know He had in mind someone godly, strong, disciplined, and moral; a person of character who would be led by the Holy Spirit and who would know when to lead and when to follow. A person like Jesus. No matter if you are a man or a woman, you should be a lot like Jesus.

What was Jesus like? He was all man. We think of Him as kind and gentle, but remember, He was coming to revolutionize the world. He was coming to change the natural order of things. He wasn't just kind and gentle; he was tough, tough enough to endure the cross. And not just tough physically, but tough minded. Nothing pulled Him from His goal. He was exciting and eccentric, not what we in America are trying to make out of men. I hate to tell you, but you would probably *not* be happy with Jesus. Remember, Jesus was very harsh to Peter when he wasn't agreeing with him. "Get thee behind me, Satan." He called Peter the worst name possible.

Do you honestly think He would fold when you pushed Him to give in like you want your husband to? I know you think you are right, but Jesus was doing some awfully outlandish things; things that were not culturally or politically correct and you do not want your husband to be out of step with your world, now do you? No, married to Jesus would be no piece of cake. Think of His mother, Mary. She's our example. Accepting, pondering, always graceful Mary. But she did prod him into His first miracle. She wasn't a wilting violet after all.

What is good? That special relationship between a man and a woman called marriage. When it is good, it is very good and when it is bad, it is awful. There is something inexplicable that happens between a man and a woman. The way she looks, moves, laughs, speaks, and thinks touches something deep inside a man, and something in a man touches a woman. It may not be immediate and it may not be physical, but it happens. We call it chemistry but it's more than that, although it probably is a physiological phenomenon that becomes emotional and spiritual. God intended this special love to exist within marriage. It can happen outside of marriage and it may never result in marriage, but when it does, it's special.

If we are called to marriage, we long for this special relationship; to be a soul-mate with one other person for a lifetime, to grow and share our lives together. And if we never marry or if our marriage doesn't live up to what God intended, we grieve over this loss. The man as well as the woman grieves when his marriage doesn't fulfill something deep within and God understands this grieving process. He has made provision, but it does mean we will have to draw continually on His grace. It is not poured out on just anyone. No, He reserves it for those who ask; so we ask daily, hourly, moment by moment, and in the end *our marriage is transformed* as we are fulfilled through Him.

The frustrations of love outside of marriage would never have existed if Adam and Eve hadn't spoiled everything. It's sad what men and women go through in the name of love. God never meant for us to suffer this way—unrequited love. A special love outside of marriage must be kept within your own heart and never acted on improperly. Love comes from God, and He can give you the proper love in your life. If it's not to be a special relationship with a mate, then it can be a special relationship with God. Plan A for a Christian, according to Paul, is singleness (1 Cor. 7:1–9). There are now two Plan As. We can't lose.

Above all else, guard your heart, for it is the wellspring of life.
—PROVERBS 4:23, NIV

"Male and Female Created He Them"

Man was made in His image. Therefore, man must have originally had feminine characteristics, too. When woman was separated out, I believe God removed certain attributes when He removed the rib and put not only the rib in the woman, but also these innate qualities. That is when certain attributes came to be considered masculine or feminine qualities. I don't believe men are more like God than women. We just have different attributes. We don't think of God as feminine but He does embody nurturing, gentleness, grace, and mercy, the more feminine qualities. One of God's names is El Shaddai, or "many breasted one." Sounds like a mother to me. In marriage we bring His attributes back together as one.

Adam and Eve's responsibility was to guard the garden. Adam first and then Eve. That's why she stepped forward when he didn't. She got out of order because he was out of order first. In his book *Marketplace Marriage & Revival*, Jack Serra makes a very important point about in the encounter between woman and serpent. It tells us how we are now supposed to "help."

> The term "revealer of the enemy" is one that is the Ancient Hebrew for helpmate. That's right. Your helpmate is considered, by God, to be the revealer of the enemy. What does that mean? To see how this works itself out we have to visit Genesis 3:13 where, when asked by God, "What is this you have done?" Eve replies, "The serpent deceived me, and I ate." In other words, *We were face to face and while we were talking the serpent convinced me to do it. I saw his face.*
>
> If she were that close there are two things she is saying here. First, I know his game now. He is a deceiver and a liar. You can't trust him. Second, Eve is saying I saw his face and I would recognize him anywhere.
>
> It is my impression that what we refer to as a woman's intuition and/or sixth sense is not that at all. What it really is, is God passing down the Spiritual DNA of Eve in recognizing

the enemy and his schemes. Now, I can't make a scientific case for this as easily as physical DNA, and I'm not going to try to do so. I will simply say that we have never been able to understand why a woman is so protective of her siblings and yes, even her husband. Much of it is covered by what we refer to as "Mother's instinct."[1]

To this I say: AMEN. Serra then goes on to talk about how a woman can help a man in all areas of life because of her "intuition," because she recognizes the enemy when she sees him in all of his many facets. The problem is most men don't trust their wives to help them. We have too often proven ourselves to be more of a problem than a help, like our grandmother Eve was.

It is very important who you are "face to face" with. Guard who you give your attention to and be sure you recognize the enemy when he enters. Guard your garden, guard your heart, guard your body, your family, your home. Guard everything God has allowed to come into your garden.

Many of the things we label male or female are not meant to be designated that way. I don't believe God meant for us to be so narrow-minded. He is far more creative when endowing each of us with our temperament, personality, and talents; making us all different, just as He does snowflakes. What is innately masculine and feminine? Certainly creativity is neither, nor is being loving and nurturing. In fact, being bossy or introverted falls to both depending on the individual. Not all women are the gossips or the mouthy ones either. If your husband is the one who works and brings in a paycheck, he should be respected and appreciated, but no more than the wife who stays home and takes care of the kids. She has as much right to their resources as he does. I hope I don't need to say this again. Just because a woman doesn't "work" (at a salaried job) doesn't mean she doesn't have as much right to benefit from "his" income as he does. As half of "one," she is entitled to as much as he is. Most of it should go toward mutual expenses such as a home and family needs. Her services are not free or cheap and should not be taken that way. Our part should *never* have a price put on it.

Some women are bad about putting themselves down and allow their husbands to get into a mode of selfishness that is as harmful to him as it is her. Something is wrong when he has guns, a boat, and goes hunting a few times each season when she doesn't have decent furniture.

If you are in this fix, before you challenge it and pitch a fit, pray and continue to strengthen your relationship with the Lord and watch what He does. I'm not saying he won't be challenged eventually, but let's pray about how we approach it and what to approach first. You have to be ready to stand up for yourself or you will just make things worse. Your husband will need some preparation for it, too. Be assured the changes will come if you are willing and obedient.

If one is unable to work or help around the house, they should still be respected and appreciated. This includes the kids. They should give and receive respect as much as anyone in the family, and share in the chores. I have a real problem with mothers that don't teach their daughters to cook or clean—sons too. Boys need these skills just as much as girls do. A child feels valuable when they contribute. Don't deny them this esteem-building experience. I taught mine as early as possible how to set the table and even do their own wash. I still did the lion's share, but they could do it, too. I didn't want my boys to marry just to have someone to do these things for them. I wanted them to marry because they just couldn't stand to be apart.

Who Is Supposed to Do What?

When you take into account that each person brings his or her own special gifts, talents, and personality into a relationship, there is no way we can dictate how these must work out in a marriage. There are the foundational gifts: prophet, teacher, exhorter, server, giver, mercy, and leader (actually about 28 in all); the four basic personalities: Choleric, Sanguine, Melancholy, and Phlegmatic and the mix of two or three in each person;

add to this, basic talents: artist, scientist, mathematician, those that are logical or common sense or are good organizers, etc. And finally consider environmental, biological, and physiological influences, to name a few, plus gender and the impact that being male or female makes on each of these things.

Give me a break! Let the two people who love each other work it out with fear and trembling, or should I say, with God's help. I'm certainly not going to try to tell them who does what. You really do need to understand the personality types when you are relating with people on a continuing basis. It colors everything they do. And if you don't understand them, you will frustrate both of you trying to get them to be or do what will never happen. Plan A doesn't make either spouse into something God never intended him or her to be. We should respect what God created when He created them. We destroy our children with our preconceived notions. Let them bloom, and nurture what comes forth. Well, stifle a little because there are weed tendencies that try to take over in their developing minds. We need to be very careful before we dictate what someone else should be, even our spouse. I must let Lamar work out how he handles his roles and callings with the Lord, and he must let me work out mine.

Think about the giftings in your family—spiritual gifts as well as physical and mental. We can only be fulfilled as we are fulfilling what we feel in our heart we were created to do and be. The foundational gifts (prophet, teacher, exhorter, server, giver, mercy, and leader) have the greatest influence on how the person thinks and relates. There are books that describe them in detail. I don't feel qualified to do it. I will point out when mercy is a woman's gift, it's the hardest thing to control because it makes her so "loving" that she is so busy extending mercy that she tends to overdo. The Bible gives a warning "with cheerfulness," to tell us not to get too burdened with it all. Mercy people are often very sad. Men can have this gift, too. It is not gender exclusive. None of them are.

Giver is another important one. My mother was a giver. She had a burden for the financial aspects of a project. Givers have a hard time being preached to about money because it comes so naturally to them, they don't understand why it's needed. If your husband has the foundational gift of giver, it's good to know so you can help him calm down and understand others don't have his gift. If the pastor doesn't teach on it, the offering goes down, and if the offering goes down, then the church can't do what it's called to do. But that isn't the important part. No, the important thing is to keep the channel of blessing open to the members from God. If they tighten up, He will tighten up. We don't want that. It's a vicious cycle many churches are in. So, for our sake, he preaches on the blessings and necessity of giving. And we are all blessed and the church does well. To be honest, if a person doesn't get the tithing and offering thing going in their life, they will never be the Christian God called them to be. It's so fundamental.

An exhorter has a burden for the spiritual development of the people around him or her. The prophet loves the Word for the Word's sake. And the server finds so many answers in his serving. Too many women push their man to do and be what God never created them to be.

Now for the personality traits: Choleric, Sanguine, Melancholy, and Phlegmatic. Sanguine is the friendly and "loves a party" person (Ronald Reagan and me). Choleric is the leader and likes to lead a project, but is not quick to jump in. They know how hard it is and count the cost. Ronald Reagan was probably part Choleric, too. Choleric and ruler is just a natural combination. People are usually a mix of two or three. Lamar is a Melancholy. They are detail people, artistic, loners, but do get "down." Everyone loves a Melancholy. And they love people, too. The Phlegmatic is the all-purpose person. They are the one everyone counts on to help, but they are so laid back, they aren't necessarily the best help. If you want a go-getter husband, don't marry a Phlegmatic. Marry a Choleric. But remember, you get something else, too. I got a Choleric/Melancholy. It's not easy to deal with depression when it comes. Being a Christian really has helped Lamar.

Men Are from Mars and Women Are from Venus by John Gray or *The Language of Love* by Gary Smalley and John Trent are two of many books to help us understand people better. The point of all this is: know your husband's natural, God-given tendencies and work within that framework to help him become what God meant him to be. Encourage him, don't put him down or frustrate him by trying to make him what he will never be.

Don't stifle everything God put in either of you. What a waste! Celebrate it! Just be sure to put it under the authority of the Lord so you don't get out of hand. God doesn't want wimps. He wants godly women who are graceful and merciful, but not wimpy. Celebrate your husband's gifts, too. A manly man is what God created him to be. Not muscular, but strong in soul and spirit. Be sure you do not join in the pack that has tried to emasculate men. The enemy not only wants to destroy you, he wants you to destroy your other half.

You are special! I hope you can begin to celebrate what you are instead of always bemoaning your negatives. There are times I can't stand myself. We all have those times. Even if we don't do something wrong, we can't be all things to all people. And the person we are married to has the same problem. There are empty places that in our humanness neither of us fill—raw, open, gaping wounds that no one else knows exist. We will always be missing something and some of it is important and needed. And don't we hate it? But what can we do? What else but take it to God. After we have done all we can do and it's not enough, what is left must be given to Him.

GET TO KNOW YOURSELF

There is a wonderful book that explains what a man wants so much better than I could: *Fascinating Womanhood* by Helen B. Andelin. She has such a way of putting things. Some women will find it to be a bit over the edge and some will absolutely reject it, but those that embrace its principles will be blessed. There is a great deal of truth and wisdom in it and we should consider it here.

One thing I like about the book is that she uses fictional examples like I use movies. It's such a great way to explain so perfectly what you are trying to say, and yet you don't lose a friend in the process of analyzing their choices. You are free to point out when the person was foolish or mean.

> Women are inclined to appreciate poise, talent, intellectual gifts and cleverness of personality, whereas men admire girlishness, tenderness, sweetness of character, vivacity, and the woman's ability to understand men. A marked difference is in regards to appearance. Women are inclined to be attracted to artistic beauty such as the shape of the face, the nose, and artistic clothes. Men, however, have a different interpretation of "what makes a woman beautiful." They place more stress on the sparkle in the eyes, smiles, freshness, radiance, and the feminine manner.
>
> The ideal woman from a man's point of view is divided into two parts. The one part is her spiritual qualification. We will call this side of her the Angelic. The other part relates to her human characteristics. We will call this side of her the Human.
>
> The Angelic side of a woman has to do with her basic good character, her ability to understand men, their feelings, needs, and sensitive nature. [This sensitive nature thing is VERY important.] It also includes her domestic skills and the ability to succeed in her feminine role in the home. It includes a quality of inner happiness or tranquility of spirit, which is a part of womanly beauty.
>
> The Human side refers to a woman's appearance, manner, and actions and includes the charms of femininity, radiance, and a quality of dependency upon men for their care, protection, and guidance. It also includes good health and a feminine dignity of spirit or spunk. The Angelic and the Human combine to make the perfect woman from the man's point of view. They are both essential in winning his genuine love.[2]

The following is a partial list that I have brought together as I understand it:

Angelic Qualities	Human Qualities
1. Understands men	1. Femininity
2. Has deep inner happiness	2. Radiates happiness
3. Has a worthy character	3. Fresh, radiant health
4. Is a domestic goddess	4. Childlikeness
5. Changefulness	5. Enchanting manner
6. Gentle	6. Inspires to protect
7. Has a fresh appearance	7. Amusing
8. Sensitive nature	8. Adorably human
9. Patient	9. Bright-eyed
10. Affable and courteous	10. Tender little ways
11. Has a deep inner wisdom	11. Grace
12. Sense of duty to her husband	12. Trustful

Take a look at the list and consider where you fit. Then try to add what you're missing. Why can't we be it all? *"I can do all things through Christ who strengthenth me"* (Phil. 4:13).

Some of these characteristics are confusing as to why they are on a particular side, but when you read the book, it all makes sense. I don't know about you, but I want to be *adored* by my husband. I want to be more than loved. I want me to be his compulsion, not liquor, the guys, or work. And I think you do, too. We aren't going to be if we don't need him; if he doesn't feel necessary and special in our lives. Not in a clingy, smothering way, but in a feminine, amusing, mysterious, fascinating way.

Since I was raised on a block of boys, understanding men came natural to me. My mother was so wise and had such a wonderful character, she role-modeled most of the angelic qualities. If she was lacking, it was on the human side. But we had a lot of humor in our home, and I would have to say, if anything comes naturally to me, it's the human side. So, I had the best of both worlds. But many don't. They've had poor role models and forced into a warped idea of what they need to be to protect themselves. You might have a lot of work to do, but it will be fun to discover a new you. And as you discover a new you, you will discover a new guy, too. If you want to be *adored*, you will have to find your other side—whatever that might be.

We have to quit being so independent and capable, and yet we need to do our job properly. Do not expect a lot of accolades. Just do it! Quit worrying so much and be sweetness and light. But be wise, too. You can do it. You can be all these things. You were made in the image of God, and when He told the Hebrew people who He was through Moses, He told him, *"I AM that I AM"* (Exod. 3:14). I am whatever you need. That means we must be whatever someone else needs. If we don't come by it naturally, then He is our source. He will provide. Just ask. (That's why we must pray continually.)

It is important that we be a woman of good character, but keep house and clean, too. And be something beyond that—mysterious, enchanting, funny, somebody he wants to be with every day for the rest of his life. Not someone to walk over. No, someone he admires and is proud of. Someone who fills up his senses.

Oh, God. Help me to be the fascinating woman you created me to be—bold and beautiful. At least as bold and beautiful as I can be right now. I know it will take a miracle, but then you are the God of miracles. I am already one!

Now, you fascinating woman: Go out there and face your world!

NINE

But for Adam no suitable helper was found.

—GENESIS 2:20, NIV

Suitable Helper

S O GOD CREATED ONE—ME! God has a Helper and He wanted man to have a helper, too; a proper special helper as He has a proper special Helper. And since we were created as a helper, we should ask how we are supposed to help. I do think Eve should have helped Adam keep the one rule instead of breaking it. That one incident shows the influence a woman can have on her man, her society, and the whole of creation. Everything we do has consequences, not only in our own life, but also in the lives of those around us. We should not take lightly the influence of a godly woman. There are people you are influencing for good or for bad each day. That alone should give you a good prayer life: *"God, help!"*

The original tenet was said in the negative: *No* suitable helper was found. Sadly, many a man has not found a suitable helper in the woman he is bound to in this life, and that is not what God wants for him or for her.

suitable: adjective; that suits a given purpose, appropriate

Appropriate. There is a lot to be said for being appropriate. If your husband needs you to represent your cause (his and yours), then he needs for you to be professional and well spoken. If he needs for you to sit there quietly while he does his thing, then sit there quietly. If he needs for you to attempt to do CPR on him, then that's what you have to do. He needs you to be appropriate, not sullen when you should be talking and talking when you should be listening.

To everything there is a season, a time for every purpose under heaven: a time to be born, and a time to die; a time to plant, and a time to pluck what is planted; a time to kill, and a time to heal; a time to break down, and a time to build up; a time to weep, and a time to laugh; a time to mourn, and a time to dance; a time to cast away stones, and a time to gather stones; a time to embrace, and a time to refrain from embracing; a time to gain, and a time to lose; a time to keep, and a time to throw away; a time to tear, and a time to sew; a time to keep silent, and a time to speak; a time to love, and a time to hate; a time of war, and a time of peace.

—Ecclesiastes 3, niv

That about covers it.

To be appropriate we need to know what time it is. I don't mean the physical time, but the time in our life and other people's, especially our husband. Is he struggling to get his career going? Or is he in grief over a lost opportunity? Is he just becoming aware of some tragic circumstance in his life? Or finally facing the truth of his past? Maybe he has finally arrived at a big goal and is ready to celebrate.

What time it is tells us what is appropriate. If it is time to fulfill his sexual needs, it's not time for a headache. And let me warn you: what seems appropriate to you is not always appropriate to him. And I can't say he will always be appropriate. I should also warn you: what is appropriate to you is not always appropriate to God. Sometimes He agrees with your husband.

One day I asked Lamar what he liked best about me. I thought he would say my beautiful green eyes or sparkling personality, but he didn't. He said that I let him do the things he wanted to do. I guess beautiful green eyes are not as precious as a cooperative helpmeet. Yes, you can take over and run the family, but I must warn you, when you do, you do it alone without your husband's blessing, or God's.

A suitable helper can be capable, enjoyable, talented. The list goes on;

but the one thing that a man must have in a woman, that without it all the others are rendered ineffective, is cooperation: yielding, listening, cheerfully doing what she is asked to do. You can have talent dripping from your fingertips, but if you aren't cooperative, if you don't listen and understand what he wants from you and do it, you are no help at all.

How Do You Prepare to Be a Suitable Helper?

Actually, parents and grandparents have been preparing granddaughters to be suitable helpers from a very early age. We make them cheerleaders. Nothing is more suitable for a man than his woman cheering him on and telling him he can do it. If he gets in a mess, instead of being negative, she can yell out, "Push 'em back. Push 'em back. Way back." That's about as negative as a cheerleader gets. You never hear them say, "You stupid incompetent fumbler." What kind of a cheer would that be? And don't you know, those boys get themselves bloodied and beaten, but stay out there until the game is over.

We must nurture our children and encourage them in the way they should go. Not only should we do the positives but we should also stay away from the negatives, not tearing them down with our words or actions: no bad labels, no boundary busting. Children have a right to set up certain boundaries and make choices that we respect. They do not have to receive affection when they don't want it. They are allowed to be angry, but they are not allowed to sin.

We program our children for failure when we raise them in dysfunctional families. We must nurture them and be their cheerleaders first, before they can be anybody else's. Once we have cheered them on, they will be ready to cheer on others whose lives they impact. Of course we need to help them hear the voice of God, to know what He is calling them to, and then encourage them in that. This is an assumed pre-requisite in any proper upbringing.

We need to let our children be children and be age appropriate with what we expect of them. This is why divorce and bad marriages are so devastating. It steals their innocence, their childhood. Suddenly the ugliness of the world floods in on them. They internalize everything and assume whatever is wrong is their fault. There is no way to convince them otherwise. It doesn't compute. Their little minds don't work that way. The world revolves around them, and, therefore, anything wrong in their world must be their fault. They are just learning Mommy is a separate person. When we do not discipline ourselves as adults to do the right thing, we make our children needy and neurotic; and once made that way, it's very hard to turn them around. The scars remain forever. If there is fighting and ugliness (strife and confusion) in the home, no amount of encouragement will convince a child he or she is OK. They know better. Nothing is OK, especially him or her.

It is very hard for a person to be suitable when he or she doesn't feel she is worthy. It makes us do things and react in ways that are not helpful We pull down our house, savage relationships, and walk in death and destruction, all because we don't feel good about ourselves.

It is very hard to be married to someone that doesn't respect him or herself. In fact, if they don't respect themselves, they can't give proper respect to anyone else. It throws everything out of whack. When others aren't showing us the proper respect, it is because we don't respect ourselves. We too are made in the image of God. When a girl or boy doesn't respect him or herself, they fall into bad relationships. The sicko needs of a boy picks a girl with sicko tendencies that fit his. Don't you know this leads to sicko kids an sicko relationships? The Bible says sin goes down to the third and fourth generation (Exod. 20:5).

You are worthy! Why? Because God says you are. If you don't believe that, you not only have a self-worth problem, but an unbelief problem—a faith problem. Now you have two things to deal with. I don't know why God wanted man and bothered with all this, but He does. He wants as many as will come to join the rest of us. He wants you to be one with Him. You must allow this to become a reality to you, to fill your very being. He loves you! I don't know why. I just know He loves me, too! (Heaven knows there are times when I don't!) And I'm glad He loves a lot of other people, too! Everybody! I'm glad He did all this, and it is only going to get better for both of us!

Say this: *"I am worthy. Jesus made me worthy! I am righteous. Jesus made me righteous! I am loved. Jesus loves me—this big! (Stretch your arms out wide with your palms wide open as if on a cross and feature the holes that nailed Him there!) I am forgiven and my sins no longer exist. God has put them in the Sea of Forgetfulness. He who has begun a good work in me is faithful to finish it! I am a branch abiding in the Vine, and His life-giving anointing flows through me. I am a child of the Most High God! No weapon formed against me shall prosper. I am healed. I am whole. I walk in peace and prosperity, and no one and nothing can pluck me out of His hands. When I am weary He carries me, and when I fail He is my Advocate. He forgives me seventy times seventy, or infinitely. Devil, you have done your best and I'm still standing. That just proves, greater is He that is in me than you! I command you to stop speaking to me and tormenting me, and I send you to the dry places. I thank You, Jesus, and praise You! You are worthy of all my praise!"*

Now don't you feel better? Keep saying it until you do!

If you have a problem esteeming yourself, you must allow God through the Holy Spirit, the Word, Christian friends, *something*, to help you appreciate yourself. You must be able to forgive yourself and others in order to move on and allow healing to come into your own life and those around you.

> *However, each one of you also must love his wife as he loves himself, and the wife must respect her husband.*
> —EPHESIANS 5:33, NIV

The Bible tells the husband to love his wife (probably because she's an emotional being) and it tells the wife to respect her husband. If there is anything that is suitable for a wife to do, it is to be respectful.

Years ago woman were accused of being too coy with their male counter-parts—batting their eyes and playing their flirty games. Well, people may laugh, but it worked, and I don't know that what we have now is any better. A man does have an ego and he does need to be admired and respected. If we don't play by the rules that he has written on his psyche, we will not have the happy marriage we hoped for.

ENOUGH

When a man is not showing his wife the proper respect, particularly if she has been respectful to him, it stifles their relationship. She withdraws into herself, which I had done. I wanted to be respectful, but Lamar was being so hurtful that I gave up. I tolerated it because I honestly didn't know what else to do. I tried everything: fighting, threats, silence; you name it and I tried it. Eventually I became disrespectful of Lamar.

After we had been in the mess for years, in spite of the fact that we were now Spirit-filled Christians, I kept getting the word "enough" in my spirit. I thought it was the devil. I kept fighting it in my mind and "rebuking" it, until I finally had to have an answer. Nothing seemed to come but that word. It was weighing heavily on my mind one Sunday when the kids and I decided to visit a local church. Lamar wasn't attending with us, so the boys and I decided to go to Mom Brook's church, the Altoona Church of God, which we were rarely able to attend. After the singing and preliminaries, the pastor got up and started preaching, "I have driven a stake in the ground with the word *enough* on it." And with that my whole mind, body and spirit yelled, "Amen!" (Thank God, they had an amen corner, so they didn't notice me.) That was all I needed to hear. What was in my spirit was from God. Knowing that, I could allow Him to lead me in what I should do next.

I came not only to see things were wrong in my home, but I must put a stop to them. Now that may sound like I was taking authority out of Lamar's hands, but I don't think so, any more than an employee might insist on certain things in the workplace. This revelation did not make me more aggressive or mouthy. I knew better than to go overboard. I had to continue to be led by the Holy Spirit. However, this revelation gave me a confidence that what I was thinking was right and that God was with me in whatever was going to come next. It was the beginning of a new day, not with me as boss, but God as Boss.

RESPECT IS NOT JUST SUITABLE, IT IS REQUIRED

I wish I could say things straightened out from then on, but we're human and Lamar wasn't perfect and neither was I. I did have a problem with my attitude sometimes. One day when I was complaining about Lamar to a friend, she saw I was being disrespectful to Lamar and challenged me about it. In my defense I countered, "He doesn't deserve respect."

"But you have to respect him. He's your husband and it's scriptural. Take a look at Ephesians 5:33," she explained. It was the last part that got me. I believe in being scriptural. "You need to get the book Gail loaned me: *Spiritual Authority* by Watchman Nee. I'm sure she'd be glad to lend it to you." The next day I just happened to be in Gail's area, so I stopped by to see her. When I asked her about the book, she insisted I take her copy. It should be required reading of every Christian. It sure puts things in perspective. *A Tale of Three Kings* by Gene Edwards is excellent, too. It's a really easy read. It, too, should be required reading, especially for someone that's not a good reader. I buy it and give it away because most people won't take the initiative.

As I was dealing with my own problems, Lamar was very involved at the church, and things were not going well. He did not like some of the decisions the pastor was making and was beginning to murmur. As God dealt with me and gave me some guidelines, I passed them on to Lamar. He seemed grateful for the help. One of the reasons he was so receptive was because I had apologized to him after I read the book and saw how wrong I was. I had been disrespectful and that was wrong. Boy! That really set him off! When he puffed up too big I countered, "I never said you were right!" We both laughed! Lamar was ready to listen because he knew I had heard from God.

This is what He seemed to reveal:

1. You can disagree, but you can't be disagreeable. You must do it respectfully.

2. You can speak, but you can't murmur. No bad-mouthing and certainly no screaming and yelling.

3. You are not a victim.

4. You cannot treat him like a naughty little boy. He is not your oldest son.

5. You cannot take over.

6. You cannot be uncooperative.

7. You cannot have a bad attitude.

8. You cannot revenge or pay back.

Show proper respect to everyone: Love the brotherhood of believers, fear God, honor the king.

—1 PETER 2:17, NIV

Respect for God.

Respect for God's creations.

Respect for their position.

Respect for their calling.

Respect for their gifts.

Respect for the anointing.

Respect for their opinions.

Respect for their emotions.

Respect for our differences.

Respect: regard / high valuation of worth / to feel or show honor or esteem for /consideration for/courtesy or consideration treatment/ to relate to.

God is our standard. He has shown a vast amount of respect for man, in spite of the fact that we don't deserve it. In response to this wonderful outpouring of love and grace, man not only turned his back on God, but treated Him shabbily. That is not to say God doesn't have His way of dealing with the rebellious and we must follow His lead, although turning someone into a pillar of salt is a bit beyond us. It's true people will turn their back on us and treat us shabbily. They may even involve us in their sin. We are allowed to turn away from them, but we must not be disrespectful, because it is sin, too. *"Anger and sin not"* (Eph 4:26).

Why does everyone deserve respect? Because we are made in the image of God. When we don't respect other people, it's a sign that we don't respect God. Ponder that for a minute. The Bible talks about people being the enemy of God. Could it be the disrespectful? If we can't respect God, how can we respect anyone else? Some people think they respect God, but they don't bide by the rules. And why is that? Because they aren't convinced that the rules in the Bible really are God's rules. So even if they try, they get all mixed up and end up making up their own rules. And then there are those that think they respect God and are in relationship with Him, but because they have a problem with obedience, hold their opinion above God's and therefore do not show Him the proper respect either. This too is unbelief. They don't really believe God means what He says. And they certainly don't believe He will judge them and find them wanting. These are the ones that don't attend church regularly or tithe fully or do the many things God has asked us to do. They do what they feel they should do, not what is scriptural.

Respect is not contingent on agreement. It's easy to show respect when you agree. It is not so easy when you don't. In fact, if you agree, it isn't respect at all. It's agreement. Respect is not based on the person being special or good either.

People are often disrespectful so that the person will get the message that they disagree with what they are doing. Maybe they will get the message and stay away or change. The only problem with this is again, it's unscriptural. It's a form of manipulation and that is the sin of witchcraft. The person being disrespectful becomes as sinful as the person they look down on.

God is grieved when someone doesn't receive the proper respect. However, He is more concerned about the one being disrespectful because it's a mindset, an attitude, that is very destructive and very hard to change. Not receiving respect is hurtful and makes things very difficult; not giving respect is sin. That's why God often looks upon the woman as bad as the man even though his mistakes are more obvious.

Respect First and Love Will Come

It does something to a man when he is respected and honored and it does something to him when he is not. One encourages him to do better and the other discourages him and makes him worse. Nothing takes the wind out of Lamar's sails more than me saying something negative to him or if I admire some other man. Lamar is a Melancholy, so it really gets him down. The worse part is it takes me a while to realize what I have done.

My mother honored, respected, and loved my father so very much it taught me to be respectful of him, too. When Lamar didn't live up to what I felt was a respectable standard, I stopped respecting him. When I stopped respecting him I began murmuring against him and became uncooperative. When I did that, he stopped valuing me and started bad mouthing and blaming me. I found him to be even more reprehensible and my attitude worsened. He, of course, found me to be less valuable and treated me even worse, in spite of the fact that he loved me dearly. Things went from bad to worse. We hated what was happening but were powerless to stop it because we didn't understand what was really happening, which is true of most couples. We got to the point of almost divorcing. That's a whole lot worse. It was at this point that Gail gave me the book and saved my marriage.

If anything will draw you up short, *Spiritual Authority* by Watchman Nee will. It gives many examples of rebellion in the Bible and what God does about it. The implication being, if He did it then, He will do it now—to me and you. It sure turned me around. It's not that I wasn't cooperative at all, it's just that I came to my limit too soon and then would act in a way that was not right (murmuring, etc.). I wasn't way off base, but it was enough that God couldn't defend me. I repented immediately and apologized to Lamar. It was the beginning of God showing me many things as I responded correctly to each revelation. If you show your husband respect long enough, I just believe eventually there will be something to admire.

DISRESPECT TEARS AT THE VERY FABRIC OF A FAMILY OR A GROUP

Disrespect strikes at the very heart of a marriage, or any relationship for that matter. In fact, lack of respect was one of the four deadly things that ruin a marriage. A marriage counseling clinic pointed out if they see a lack of respect on the part of either spouse, chances of the marriage succeeding are almost nil. If I remember correctly the other three are rigidity (inability to adapt), disgust, and apathy.

We don't appreciate the gravity of our offense, even more so if it is disrespect.

"But how do I esteem my husband when he's such a turkey?"

This is as good a time as any to talk about shallow, insensitive, selfish, stupid, sarcastic, stick-in-the-mud, manipulative, lyin', cheatin' men.

"Are you asking me to respect him?"

I'm not asking you, I'm telling you.

"How do I do that?"

You just do it.

"But he's such a mess, I can't do it."

You are not understanding respect. Respect is not a feeling; it's a decision.

"I don't feel I made the decision to act disrespectfully. It just comes naturally in response to the way he acts."

I'm sure that's true. Now that you know you should act respectfully, if you find you cannot do it and keep reacting in your same old patterns, *you* are out of control.

"How do you change a compulsive behavior?"

You get help. There are people who have traveled this road before you.

Why risk the pitfalls when you don't have to? Stay open to how God wants this to unfold. He loves your husband and wants you to, too.

"But, He isn't married to him. Anyhow, I've been praying for years. Why doesn't God do something about him?"

Because there is something holding up the works. Maybe you.

"Me? It can't be me. Anyone will tell you how hard I've tried and what I've put up with."

Anyone would tell you how hard I tried and yet God kept dealing with me. That's why I figure He will deal with you, too. If you have compulsions (shopping, Internet problems, eating, cleanliness, exercise, anger, revenge, bitterness) then you need to work on getting that area under control and don't blame him for you being out of control.

THE FIRST DRUNK

You need to understand if you aren't being respected it's because you accepted being disrespected. There is a history of ever increasing disrespect in your relationship and it will not be easy to turn it around because the person being disrespectful feels they have this right, and it's hard to talk them out of it, especially by the very person that allowed it. Dr. Phil had a couple on this past week that was especially problematic. The husband was so verbally abusive and even included the young children in it. The wife was very defeated. Naturally everyone wanted her to get away from him. Everyone but me. He loved her. She knew it better than the rest of us. And she loved him.

He was trying to motivate her to do better, but it had the opposite affect. It shut her down emotionally. Actually, this is where she got her power from. That he cared. So, she was trying to get him to back off. He didn't want anything that wasn't best for her and the family: to lose weight, to have a cleaner home, etc. And he was helping. It's not like he did nothing. Yes, he was expecting too much, but backing off and doing less and less just made things worse. Him worse.

Always be prepared to give an answer to everyone who asks you to give the reason for the hope that you have. But do this with gentleness and respect, keeping a clear conscience, so that those who speak maliciously against your good behavior in Christ may be ashamed of their slander. It is better, if it is God's will, to suffer for doing good than for doing evil.

—1 PETER 3:15

Maybe it's you, like this woman, that is not being respected. What then? You can't force someone to respect you, but you can require minimums. Verbal or physical abuse is not acceptable. This is why counseling is so important. Suddenly what the person is doing is looked at by a third party and looks completely different.

One important answer is to act respectfully. Take away his ammunition. Keep a clean house. Watch your diet. Take care of the kids. Don't flirt or have inappropriate relationships. Do not spend too much money. I understand you won't be perfect, but keep getting better. And don't let him get you down. Consider the source.

DISRESPECT PERSONIFIED

On another Dr. Phil program about divorcing couples, one man said his wife said things to him that he wouldn't say to his worst enemy. Their little boy would put his hands over his ears so he wouldn't have to hear it. The wife didn't disagree that she had done it, but said she was working on doing better. When Dr. Phil asked if this were true, the husband didn't seem to think so.

She seemed to think love would keep him there and he would be committed enough to work this through no matter what, but to him he had given it his best and it was too late. His love was dead and they just needed to move on. She couldn't move on. She couldn't accept that it was over. Dr. Phil pointed out in the letter explaining their situation that she talked more about losing her way of life and her stuff than of love for her husband.

I don't know if this woman really knows how to love. So then how is she going to show love? She evidently did the right things to get him to marry her, but wearied and the real person came out. If you saw the look on her face and in her eyes, you would understand what we're talking about when we say people who are not "born again" are dead men walking. She was death warmed over. The marriage was a living hell and her husband was tired of living there.

She was using ugly words to try to manipulate him. Maybe it worked in the past, but it doesn't work forever. Eventually the person decides they don't need it. And that time comes long before they take legal steps to end the marriage. This is why it's so important that we start today to try to find the truth in our life and begin to do what the Scripture says early—to give our husbands some hope that things will change because he sees it changing.

If this woman had forced herself to act respectfully, it could have changed everything. Her husband probably would have worked with her longer and they would have been able to have a decent home life even though they disagree on some points. But, sadly, reconciliation was not the topic of the day. Moving on was.

I'm all for moving on, but I'm tired of moving on with bad answers. A difficult wife is even worse as an ex with the kids as her pawn (or his). If someone is selfish and disrespectful in the marriage, they will be selfish and disrespectful out of it. If you see yourself unable to show love and respect to your husband after all I have said, then you need help. Especially if you have kids. You need to become accountable to a mature Christian friend or counselor. You cannot subject kids to a marriage filled with disrespect, anger, and lack of love. Something is terribly wrong and much of it is in you. Fix you first and your husband will automatically respond differently.

Dear God, I want to say "Yes, Sir" and be a suitable helper. I meant to be when I married my husband. Now the task seems to be more than I can do. He wants from me things I don't think

I should do and more than humanly possible to do. This help-meet thing isn't working out very well. How do I get us working together, God, instead of pulling against each other all the time? I take my authority over all this strife and confusion and ask You, Father, to come in with Your peace and joy. I loose the spirits of discipline and faith and faithfulness and obedience and any other good spirit we need and don't have. I bind the spirits of revenge and bitterness and lust and lying (and any other spirit you think of, murder even. Yes, people have the spirit of murder. It could be a deep, uncontrollable frustration, etc.) and loose long-suffering, forgiveness, truthfulness, etc. (Again, loose the spirit alternate to what you are binding. Jesus said what you bind on Earth shall be bound and what you loose on Earth shall be loosed. We should not only bind, but loose.) "I take my authority over my home and tell you, devil, you have no place here. I am a child of the Most High God and as His child have dominion over you. You must leave. You must cease and desist from all your torment. We are His now because I have placed me and my family in His hands. I thank You, God, that You are doing this for me and give You praise for all You have done and are doing in our lives.

ENCHANTED APRIL

Enchanted April, starring Miranda Richardson and Joan Plowright, is about two English women, lonely in their marriages, who have the big idea to rent a castle in Italy for a month. They let two other women go with them, to defray expenses. Lottie's husband wants her to go with him to Italy at the same time, but she opts to go to the castle instead, which really angers him. Rose detests that her husband writes cheap novels for a living. She reeks of disrespect for him, but he is evidently quite good at it and makes a lot of money.

The two women arrive at the castle, and it is more than they could have ever dreamed. The other two ladies aren't quite so mystified. One is an older, grumpy woman, and the other a beautiful, wealthy "lady." We don't know much about her because she stays off to herself all the time. In less than a day, Lottie feels guilty for not inviting her husband, much to Rose's chagrin, so she writes him and just knows he will come.

Lottie's husband arrives and somehow she realizes that their problems are not just because he is a greedy, manipulative, insensitive, selfish boob. She is part of the problem, too. She has withdrawn her love from him and has not been very responsive. In this wonderful atmosphere, they both apologize and are transformed.

Rose's husband arrives and we find out he has had a thing with the rich woman, but that is not spoken of to Rose. Somehow they manage to resurrect their love for each other. There is enough love to go around, and the rich beauty finds love with the owner, a younger man who inherited the castle.

I chose this movie because it so beautifully depicts cold marriages and how bad things can get and still be transformable. I assume these two women loved their husbands when they married. But love turned into tolerance, and that's a killer. It's wonderful that something was able to shake up their world and make them rethink things in love.

Edify. God never intended for us to fight and tear down.

TEN

She shall be called woman, because she was taken out of man.
—GENESIS 2:23

Men Are Not the Problem

C AN YOU IMAGINE A Fonzie-type guy seeing this beautiful creature for the first time and saying, "Wo! Man!" and then, "Praise
God, He sent somebody to help. And isn't she a good looker?"

Did you realize Adam was created outside of the garden and Eve was
created inside the garden? (See Genesis 2:7–8, 18.) Things like this are
significant because it tells us not only that we are different, but why. A
man's view looks outward toward the world and a woman looks inward
toward the family. He has yearnings we don't have. We yearn to have children; he yearns to conquer the unknown. If a woman doesn't understand
her man's heart, there will be a disconnect between them. Now don't get
me wrong, by the time you get your man it may not seem like he ever
had this adventurous side, but it's there in some form. If you don't see it
then it's been perverted, the result of continual wounding, as he clings to
what is safe and secure. But he will never be fully satisfied if he doesn't
put aside his fear and reach out for what he longs to do in the recesses of
his inner man.

It is up to us to encourage this inner life so that at some point it will
be expressed and he will feel fulfilled. Just know it's there and keep that
in mind as you observe your man over the years. It's not something to
talk about, at least not by you. It's something to listen and watch for and
eventually encourage. And even be willing to sacrifice for. Our need for
security has squelched many a good man and kept him bound for his
entire lifetime. I for one don't want to be the one that ends up with a

grumpy unfulfilled man when we are old. I talk about Lamar's "Ralph Kramden" ideas, but those ideas are the musings of his mind as he tries to figure out the best way to get to his goal. And in the end, it was a "Ralph Kramden" idea that got us there.

My job? Help! Help at what, I sure didn't know. Mostly, it's to do the day-to-day routine things that must be done: cooking, cleaning, child care, bills, etc. That's why I've been created a helpmeet. It is a very special role. I mustn't regret it or run from it. Instead I need to ask, "What does my man need help with?" Making a good place to lay his head, feeding his body, taking care of his offspring, and much more. Maybe that's why Eve answered the serpent—because she had to get supper. The fruit, if it satisfied, would solve her problem.

Women are "nesters" because we were sent to help and God gives a person the desire to do what they are sent to do. If He gave women the tendency to nest what did He give man? His ego! I know we hate it, but it was put there for a reason. God wanted the men to take care of us, and He wanted him to do a good job of it. His ego makes him work hard to provide and protect, or it should. Of course, like everything else, it gets perverted.

Why do you think the bachelor pad is notorious, not only for being so messy, but for its lack of décor and basic essentials of life. Why? Because that isn't what God created him to do. That's our job. Their job is to go out and conquer, to defend and provide, not only for himself but for his woman. Lamar loves to give me nice things. Why do you think God made man bigger and stronger? To protect and provide. He's supposed to get all sweaty for me—and want to do it. He likes to show off his big muscles, and I like admiring them. (A man my size and weight is normally 40 percent stronger than I am.) Did you see that commercial of the blue collar worker without a shirt, drinking a cold drink, with the sweat glistening on his stupendous physique and all the girls swooning? I don't care what anyone says, we love to see a great body. Men are just naturally virile and manly, and competitive.

I understand not all men are great physical specimens, but they still want and need to be admired, even the smallest boy. If he's yours, you better find things to admire, and not just your kids. Your husband needs to see balance in your attitude toward him, weighted heavily toward the positive. When a man becomes a Christian he should change his ungodly ways, but that takes time and maturity. I know it's hard to wait, but we all have our developmental problems and this is a man's. Bear with him (and God).

EGO: EDGING GOD OUT

Don't denigrate men because God created them with an ego. If it weren't for their ego and sexual desires, we would never get them to the altar. It's his ego that sends him out to conquer the world and bring the spoils back to us. He wants to and needs to be admired, not just by you but by the community. That's why he wants the best house and the best car, and, yes, the best wife and kids in the neighborhood. This all works for us if we help him. But we have to be careful that we don't get caught up in it and help it get out of hand. And then he blames us for putting too much pressure on him and that's what he doesn't want. The pressure should come from himself, not us. If his ego doesn't lead him in this direction, it leads him astray and that's what we don't want.

With three boys and Lamar and his projects that require so many extra hands, there is a lot of "male bonding" that goes on at our house, even though our sons have moved out. Men are no worse than women when they get together, just different. I don't have a problem with the difference but a lot of women do. They have had such bad experiences in their lives that they find it hard to appreciate men and that is especially sad because they want a family. They are angry at men yet desire a family; how does that work? Not very well. And it makes for some very hurt, angry guys. It's not always the men's fault in these failing marriages.

Men have a lot to cope with in a day. They have the baggage they bring with them (their past, family and health problems, finances, etc.), plus the stress of their job, the nagging realization of what isn't happening in their lives and may never happen, and their addictions. The devil fights them every step of the way and whose side do we take? The enemy's.

I will never forget the scene outside my front window one day when the city truck that picks up debris got struck across the road. They worked on it for hours but things just got worse. I watched as men and trucks came and left. At one point a waterline broke. They brought in heavy equipment and everything. I wondered would happen when these guys got home. Would they be met with love and support or would it be just one more mess that just seems to get worse (the kids and the wife)?

I started to pray and bind the devil from doing any more damage than he already had done; eternal damage that damages the soul. And we're not talking about just one soul. It's one multiplied by two and then by four and so many more.

I understand women have hard days too and that just makes it all the harder, but we can't expect much out of him until he gets himself unwound. The truth is our husband and kids are wound much too tight most of the time. We need know our own limits, too, and allow each enough space to unwind and heal. What a luxury in our hectic lives. Maybe God doesn't mean for us to do so much. Take care of the home better and let some of the outside stuff go.

> *God, my husband and I are so different. It seems like all we do is pull at each other and misunderstand. Help me, God, to appreciate my husband rather than to be continually hurt and frustrated. And help him to understand me so he isn't so hurt and frustrated. Bring us together not only in body, but in mind and spirit. I do want to love him as You love him through me. I pray this in the precious name of Jesus.*

Men Are Not the Problem, Sin Is, and Both Sexes Participate

America has done a good job of putting down men and masculine qualities. That's because they don't understand God and don't appreciate how

He thinks, not that He is a man. They think He is being too hard on people and they don't understand grace. It's time we begin to understand God and maybe someday we will understand men. And maybe if we understand them, we can appreciate them. And if we understand and appreciate men in general, maybe we can understand and appreciate our man specifically.

If you are the mother of a boy, you need to realize he is being harmed by this mentality and ignorance. If you have a bad attitude toward men, you first need to be honest and face it because a bad attitude has tentacles. If you are the mother of a girl, she is going to be harmed by it, too. She will catch your attitude and harm her own family. Or she will marry one of these damaged boys. He will be the person she turns to emotionally, but he will not be able to give her what she needs. He will be the father of her children, your grandchildren, and unable to give them what they need. We need to break these destructive cycles. First, we need to repent, then work to restore the damage we have done.

If you were neglected or abused by your father, ask God to become your father. He says He will. (See Psalm 68:5.) Begin to see the little ways He helps you and be sure to include Him in every aspect of your day. Don't be falsely humble and think you are doing Him a favor by doing it all for yourself. There are times when we need to be a child and climb up in His loving arms and have a good cry. Get quiet and study your Bible, and let Him speak to you and reveal things that will help you deal with the deep hurts so you can let go and move on. There are some things that will never be, and for those things we have a Savior, Comforter, and Teacher; but if we never let Him be that to us, then we won't be saved, comforted or wise.

It is our job to bring healing to our families, whatever their challenges, to help them bring healing to their friends and eventually their own families, to help them forgive the people who have hurt them, and encourage them to release them to the Lord. Our children need to understand that just as they make mistakes, other people do, too. Being a mother or a mother-in-law is a ministry and not always an easy one. So is being a neighbor and a stranger. We mustn't take the burdens on ourselves and think we are the Savior of the world, but we must try to introduce people to Him. It's really not all that hard if we do it right. If it becomes a burden, then you have taken too much on yourself. Cast it back on Him again.

I need to point out the harm to our children won't come in the form of a slap on the face. It is insidious, such as the need to medically calm boys down. I was a first grade teacher before the numbing of our children and none of them needed medication. I had thirty-two first graders. How all of a sudden do large numbers seem to need it? And why mostly boys? It is another sign too many people don't understand and appreciate boys. Take some of the sugar away and they will be back to where my students were. And could you please tell me why they eliminated PE? Kids need to let off some steam once in a while.

I didn't mean to get off into a discussion about food and exercise, but it is important. It is in these practical areas that we can see what kind of a wife and mother we are. We don't realize the toll it takes on our husbands and kids when they are out of balance. We think he's a big, tough, determined guy, and he may be, but there's a place in him that isn't big and tough and he isn't OK. There are places that are sick physically and some that hurt emotionally and spiritually. He needs help. Start with the physical, but don't stop there. Say things that soothe his needy ego and make him feel appreciated and respected. Be sure that you understand how he is thinking, where he's coming from. Then do the spiritual. But if you aren't doing the others, the spiritual will just irritate him. We have to do the others to have a right to minister to him spiritually.

Only too often we blame our husband and criticize him when he is really a victim. We look at the end result—his behavior—and react without taking into consideration what has brought him to this point. I didn't know for years that my husband had an abusive childhood. He told me how wonderful his family was. The dirty little secret was that he and his father never bonded.

God intended family to be a port in the storm, a shoulder to cry on, somebody to believe in you and edify you. But even more than that, He intended for us to care enough to say what needs to be said. When our home is not a port in the storm, then we must allow Him to be. There are some times that God is our only port in the storm, and when that happens, He is enough. He is our final port in the storm.

Our fears and marital problems tend to make us eat too much, spend too much, have an unnatural need for other relationships, and generally mess up our lives. Fear is a self-fulfilling way of life. Nothing makes a woman less desirable than being fearful and weak, except maybe being mouthy! Men don't admire someone they can manipulate, and they certainly don't admire a woman who doesn't stand up for what is right. Don't regret what's going on in your life so much. You will never have it all; but if you enjoy what you have, you will always have something to celebrate. Learn to enjoy your loved ones in their imperfect state. It's the only way you will ever enjoy them.

Years ago God helped me to see that I can be a friend to lots of people and help many more through this book than the few I could minister to personally. I do love you. I do care. I do understand. I've been to the dark places and God has come and shown the light and dispelled the darkness. He has told me to turn around and show those behind me how to come through it, too. He doesn't want you powerless and defeated; He wants to give you the tools in this book and for this to be the beginning of many good things. It's a wonderful life.

> *God, I lift up my friend and ask that what I say here ministers to her in a special, powerful way. I do not receive the loss she is experiencing in her life and I ask you to restore unto her the years that the locust has eaten. In the meantime give her peace and joy that passes all understanding and give her a hunger for the Word and your Holy Spirit in power and in grace. I pray this in Jesus' name. Amen.*

My Fair Lady

I'm going to assume you know *My Fair Lady*, the story of the professor and the flower girl played by Rex Harrison and Audrey Hepburn. Men love saving some poor wretch from the gutter.

After Liza succeeds and it's all over, she naturally wonders what will happen to her how and blames the professor for the mess she's in. He is totally baffled. Reaching the goal means she will be able to be gainfully employed at a much better job than if he hadn't taken her in. He sees her as ungrateful. I think theirs is a typical problem: they both feel unappreciated, when nothing could be further from the truth.

At one point Liza wanders around where she used to sell flowers and realizes she can't go back. Actually, Liza never wanted all that much. I was like that. I never expected the house on the lake or a lodge in Alabama. Just a primitive cabin. Forget that! God does things right as, Liza was soon to find out. Liza may move up to the big house, but she will always be a flower girl in her heart and head. It is possible to transform a person's speech, but it takes time for the coin to drop that they are no longer poor, fat, stupid, ugly, sick, a victim, etc.

A main thread of this movie is the power of words. They can transform us an the world around us. It did mine.

Professor Higgins doesn't think very highly of women. And yet, he comes to love and admire Liza. Maybe we should take a page from his book and come to love and appreciate our man, beastly as he may be. And to appreciate ourselves, too. Just because our man is not treating us the way we think he should does not mean he doesn't love us or think a great deal of us. It is just the way he is.

In the end, Liza brings the professor his slippers and they both savor the moment. Not because he is better than her, but because their love allows them both to serve teh other. He does care and it doesn't hurt her to serve him because she has come to care about him, very deeply indeed.

ELEVEN

... and there (in the garden) he put the man whom he had formed.
—GENESIS 2:8

One Vision and One Visionary

THE GARDEN WAS WHERE God decided to begin the plan. God has always had a plan. To have a people that look like Him and reflect Him. Just because He has had to adjust the plan doesn't mean the goal changed. It is a vast plan that encompasses the whole world, but because each person has to be reached personally, it takes countless men and women to carry it out. He calls us each individually, some to lead and some to follow. He doesn't call two or three people and show them the same thing and bring them together as a committee. Nor does He show the whole group simultaneously and expect them to collaborate. No, there is one vision and one visionary.

This visionary tells the rest of us what he feels God is calling us to do corporately. As we assist him in the greater vision, we keep in mind our own personal calling and goals. We are being led in our own way to join or not join the group, what our gifts and callings are, who He wants us to marry and where we should go. And when we don't feel especially "called" and there doesn't seem to be a vision, then we do what our hands know to do, keep walking and abiding, and eventually, we will see that things are coming together into a plan. If you don't walk and you don't keep on keeping on rightly, then the plan won't ever come together. Don't ever despise taking care of your husband and kids—them and you first and the world next.

Just when I think I have at least one sentence figured out, God reveals something new. That's what I love about the Bible. I was hearing two

141

different messages: that God has the plan and that man should have a plan. "God. Who is supposed to have the plan? You or me?" Then I read this sentence: "*The Lord God took the man and put him in the Garden of Eden to work it*" (Gen. 2:15). This solved my dilemma. The garden and the man were God's plan. The whole thing was God's plan. However, man had to at some point do what he was called to do, to work it, and he couldn't do that without giving it some thought and getting a plan. Then, as the man does what he feels God would have him to do, God directs his steps. So, both God and man will have a plan. God gives the vision; we get a plan and work it as He guides. God and man working together; that's the plan.

> *Without a vision, the people perish.*
> —PROVERBS 29:18

Man was not created to merely have a job or to be a watchman; he was created to be a visionary. If he doesn't have a vision, we will perish. If you and your husband are not part of something bigger than yourselves, you are on dangerous ground. I understand that right now your husband may seem to be anything but a visionary, but that doesn't mean he wasn't created to be one. If God gets His way, and He will do everything in His power to get it, your husband will come to that point.

Because Christians feel they should have a "vision," we often misunderstand that we are called to be a part of the body of Christ and part of a greater vision. Our giftings are not to be used exclusively for our calling. "Without a vision the people perish." It is a big work by a group. Don't overlook your place in the greater Christian body.

Take for example a local church. He calls a pastor to lead the congregation. As the pastor prays and seeks the Lord, he receives a word or a vision for that particular church. From that vision, the pastor makes decisions to accomplish what he feels God would have them do. The people will need training and there needs to be programs for the new converts and the children. This vision isn't going to die or leave with the pastor. No, it must be passed on so that the work can continue indefinitely. If the church is part of a denomination, the hierarchy should have an even greater vision and should be aiding the local pastors reach their full potential as well as their local church. This is why the New Testament gets so specific about who should lead and how, because it is so crucial in implementing the plan. The church is God's, or more specifically, Jesus' body on this earth.

One day I was really burdened with the state of the church. .As I pondered, God gave me a vision of a fisherman's net with all of its holes and patches. It looked bad after years of being used almost daily. The fisherman had tried to keep it up, but couldn't get to all the rips and tears. God seemed to say don't worry. It serves His purpose for the net to look this way. When the time comes to draw it in, it will hold. It will be ready.

God gifts every man and woman. But when you are in relationship with God using your gift as He guides, it is especially powerful. We are all gifted to serve. That in itself is a gift. As you serve, God will reveal things to you. In serving your relationship will grow. The important thing is the communication, the relationship, more than what He calls you to do. Your obedience enables you to continue the communication. I heard someone say the communication is the message. Just hearing is the important thing. But communication without a response is a travesty. The appropriate response completes what was said and keeps us open for the next communication. Man can do wonderful things on his own, though it's not really on his own because even then it is God that sustains and provides even the breath we breathe.

It is my understanding the word *vision* in the Bible could be translated as any communication, which is a good point. Without any communication from God, the people perish. And don't you know that is true. Look around at the people in the world that don't have any communication with God and how pitiful their lives are.

We now use the word *vision* to mean those special things God chooses to show us that He has planned for the future. Knowing where we are going and why we are doing some of the things He asks us to do helps, but it's not required. Sometimes we have to work "blind" because if we knew why, we wouldn't do it. Either way, hearing from God is still the most important thing.

The following is a concept that I want to share with you. It could be that you are beyond this and won't ever enter into anything so life altering, but I must share it for all who need it, and who knows? It may not be as late as you think. The least you can do is encourage others.

PARADIGM SHIFTER

Did you ever hear of a paradigm? It is a word they are throwing around a great deal lately; so let me tell you what the dictionary says: an example or model. Lamar and I were at a seminar where the speaker talked about a "paradigm shifter." That's the person that shifts or changes the model or the way things are being done now. It's the person that first catches the vision for a new way of doing something, like Ray Kroc, the man that took the McDonald's idea world-wide. You may not remember it, but years ago the hamburger places were like Arnold's on *Happy Days* or the local Dairy Queen. When Kroc worked at Richard and Maurice McDonald's hamburger place in California, he knew they had a better idea. He took their idea with their blessing (and a piece of the action) and soon a big change took place in America. Now we're exporting it to the world. I don't know if it's a good thing, but that's not my point. Maybe it was a needed change since the world was changing so much. It was inevitable because the Bible promises that knowledge will be increased in the last days. You can't have cars and women in the workforce without a place to eat that's clean and quick. It's a piece to the puzzle, and even though we may have a problem with American's eating so much fat and sugar, that's really not the point.

Being a paradigm shifter is not easy. You are going against conventional wisdom and conventional wisdom rules the day. Financing is hard to get; government agencies are not set up to handle new things and people are skeptical. The only one that makes things succeed are the customers. Word of mouth. Plodding along day after day with no end in sight until you either fold or flourish. A paradigm shifter has only his dream for a long time, but it's enough. It takes a special person that God chooses (or the devil) to tough it out to the end, the victory. Many men begin the process, but few are there to the end. And that is where the joy is: at the end, or at least the culmination of his dream.

After the paradigm shifter begins to finally make some headway, others realize it's a good idea and catch the vision. These people are called paradigm pioneers. At this point, this new thing is still thought of as a goofy idea. Naysayers are everywhere, reminding you, "You could lose your shirt." This is the point where I call it a Ralph Kramden idea. Lamar had lots of them. It's hard to tell the difference between a good one and a bad one. They both require that you risk what little you have. I guess I just figured, we had so little why not go for it? Who knows; he might make it. A paradigm pioneer needs a woman with this attitude, "Let's go for it honey," knowing full well it's going to cost everything and won't be easy on the kids either. And if it doesn't work, she will have to sympathize and not criticize or lick her wounds. No, she will just pick herself up, brush herself off, and be willing to go again the next time. Let me tell you something: your husband will learn with each fall. Every time he goes down, he gets up a little wiser and you do, too—not wiser never to stick your neck out again, but wiser not to make the same mistakes, learning what works and what doesn't.

Maybe there doesn't seem to be any new horizons on your landscape and maybe there never will be, but your church may have potential or your community or your country or your son or daughter or neighbor or friend. Maybe it will just be your job not to stifle that dream.

After the pioneers have gone forth and fought the battles and it's finally safe, then the settlers come on. The settlers do OK, but rarely as well as a shifter or a pioneer. That's why the Bible is not for the faint of heart. God loves the settlers, but He calls us to move before we know it's safe, when we only have that strange unction within that we follow, like Abraham and Sarah did, and He appreciates when we do.

Jesus was a paradigm shifter. He shifted us from one kingdom to another, from one destination to another, one destiny to another. After we begin to follow Him, He will ask us to follow our men when all he has is a still small voice, with no promise of security or anything but a hard row to hoe. Pioneer women built this country with their men and their families. It was never meant for the men to go it alone for very long. Once the course was set, the women had to be involved. I believe they knew even before their man did that something new was in the air, and when he told her, she was already ready at least in her heart and mind. Maybe it was that she saw the stirring in him, the dissatisfaction, the longing for something better. And she knew he would have to follow it or wither and die within. So she did what she knew she had to do, help him follow his dream.

If you don't feel you have reached your full potential or ever will, don't despair. Many will be a picker of the late hour. (See Matthew 20:1–16.) The point of that story is that they got paid. They made it, and that's the whole point of life. If you are worried about loved ones, pray for them and trust God to work in their lives just as He has yours. God understands the struggles of this life. Even if you are at the end of your days, that doesn't mean God won't do a new work. We don't know what lies ahead. We just know one thing and that is that God continues to call us to be willing to follow when He shifts. That's all He asks: whosoever will.

Called, chosen, elected, selected, handpicked, anointed, to do what? Park cars? Work in the nursery? Yes, that's right. We are chosen to serve! Do you feel called to do more than serve? You might have a beautiful voice or a gift to teach, but before you get to use your gifts, you will get to use your hands and feet! There's a lot to learn and a lot to unlearn between here and there, and there is no guarantee you will get there. So, do what your hands find to do. Let God decide if it's time and if you are ready for more.

You are called! We are all called. Called to love. Walk ye in it. Called to peace. Walk in that, too. Called to forgive. Walk it out. Called to victory. Walk until you have it. Called to do miracles. As you walk, the miracles will be as natural as fruit on an apple tree. Called to be a child of God! That's the best calling of all!

"Oh, God! I so often don't feel like I'm truly your child. Help that sink into my very being. Help me get the mind-set of being Your child!"

Allow me now to speak to those times when it appears that no one will see his or her dreams come true. As Christians we don't go by how things look. We serve an impossible God—impossibly able to bless. If you have a dream, or your husband does, don't give it up because it looks impossible. Don't be the "realist" in your home. Be the optimist. Stand for their dreams. I don't care what it looks like. If my God gave you a dream, my God will bring it to pass.

The truth is women do get in the flesh. We want security, and we want it so bad we try to force our husbands to provide it for us. He gets in the flesh if he yields. A man can yield many things, but he must not yield his dream. And the wife must be careful not to require it. She is the deciding factor, as is he. If she allows her spirit to dictate and not her flesh, it does a great deal to help him to fulfill his dream. She can't stop him from yielding to the flesh, but she can do a lot. She can't force him to be spiritual, but she can encourage him and at least not pull him down.

B.G., Sr.

Lamar's father had a wonderful gift as a salesman. He ran a drink route in the early days and loved it. We didn't always have drink routes like we do today. In the early days of carbonated drinks, the local drug store mixed them for you at the fountain. They would use the fountain syrups and squirt in the phosphate. We called them "phosphates," as in "let me have a vanilla phosphate," my favorite, now known as cream soda. They were a dime. Those were the wonderful, special, "Happy Days." It gave you a reason to take a walk with a friend.

B.G. was especially good at placing the product in convenience stores and expanding the routes. Actually, they weren't convenience stores, yet. They were the little corner stores that dotted every neighborhood. He had a wonderful opportunity open up to him to be in the corporate office, but his wife Mary didn't want him to do it. She wanted him to have a regular job. He honored her request and became a millwright at a local plant. He made a good salary and they did OK, but when he told his story years later, I could see the disappointment that he wasn't able to follow his dream. We cost our families the best when we insist on having our way. We have every right to expect our husbands to be moral, godly men, but we shouldn't insist they fit into our mold because we aren't the mold-maker.

God places a dream in a person bigger than they can attain without Him. We need to let our loved one hang on to Him and follow their dream. If your husband follows your wishes and isn't challenged in life, he won't have to hang onto to God. You want him to need God. We need our husbands to have to be carried by Jesus once in a while. If he listens to us, he won't need to be. He won't get to be. How sad.

I understand we hate to see our loved ones struggle, but it's in the struggling that they get to know God, His provision and His faithfulness. We mean well, but that doesn't make us right. In the end Mary died from a sickness that she contracted from tending the chickens they raised because B.G. wanted to earn a little more money than he could at the plant. I believe she was killed by something God never wanted her to do. She was doing her own thing not His.

Pray that your husband doesn't listen when your fears and your need for security are speaking. We aren't always right, and we can be very wrong.

Lamar's List

When we began our insurance agency and finally got in a real office, God had shown me to go to work with him full time. Lamar was very frustrated, and we ended up fighting a lot about things I didn't think were my fault. When I thought about what Lamar was saying, I realized he was frustrated because things weren't getting done. I was doing all I knew to do. The problem wasn't what was on the list; it was the things not on the list. Lamar wanted things done that weren't on the list. How can I do stuff I don't even know to do?

I came to realize Lamar was saying things, but we weren't listening.

We (me and the other girl) were so busy and Lamar talks so much, it just went over our heads. Instead of saying "Put this on the list," he just kept talking. When I finally saw that he really meant what he was saying, I took it seriously. These were big projects, huge mail-outs. I had to get some specifics.

I had to get mailing permits, learn how to use the computer for mail lists, get high school girls to come in and type them in, etc. That was the way Lamar wanted to increase our business. He was a mass marketer before we ever heard the term. It was his vision that has brought us a marvelous income and my cooperation that helped bring it to pass.

Many women would have stomped out in anger and sworn to never return, thus cutting off the very miracle that was going to bless her. I need to point out that I am not gifted at office work. This was not something easy for me. I'm an artist and find repetitive work difficult. I am not organized, but I was raised to be responsible and that makes the difference. Therefore, under very difficult circumstances, with no natural talent of my own, I was able to forge a wonderful work in our lives. I do not mean to denigrate Lamar or his importance because he was the guiding force, but I was instrumental too. Not that a man can't do it without our help, but it's very difficult; in fact, nearly impossible. If Lamar would have had to pay my salary, I don't know how he could have afforded it. Also, I just don't know how a person you hire has the insight to do what I did. I cannot fully express all it took on my part. It took the marriage of all that I could do and all that my husband could do to bring if off.

Do you see how vulnerable Lamar was? How much he needed me? He didn't look like it. He certainly didn't act like it. But, he was. It was up to me not to point out his need, but to cooperate and do what only I could do. Do you know what that gave me? The love of a man who has lived the plan of God for his life, a man who has reached his goal and seen his vision come to fruition. There is no way for me to have this special love any other way. But you must remember, I had to work through the fighting and misunderstandings. It did look ugly, but in the ugliness was a kernel of truth Lamar was trying to express but wasn't doing a very good job of it. You may be at this place today. Seek God for the answers. It is probably both of you that are wrong and both of you that are right. You just need a further truth. There is something you are missing. Only God can tell you what.

God expects man to have a plan. And He will help us accomplish it.

TWELVE

And God blessed them, and God said unto them, Be fruitful, and multiply, and replenish the earth, and subdue it: and have dominion over the fish of the sea, and over the fowl of the air, and over every living thing that moveth upon the earth.

—GENESIS 1:26-28, KJV

Ruling and Reigning

GOD INTENDS FOR MAN to rule and reign on the Earth. We may not be a king or queen in the usual sense, but we are part of a kingdom and that kingdom has influence in this world. We preside over a home and ourselves and that's important at least to us. Bad housekeeping is not ruling and reigning in your home. Being overweight is not ruling and reigning in your physical temple. Having discipline problems is not ruling and reigning in your family. Having a bad marriage is not ruling and reigning in your relationship. Being oppressive or abusive is just another way of not ruling or reigning properly. Jesus didn't rule and reign by being mean or ugly. He ruled by knowing who He was and the power behind His words.

In the New Testament it tells the converts that if they cannot rule and reign in their own homes, they cannot take a leadership role in the church. (See 1 Timothy 3.) If a person cannot rule and reign over themselves or their home, they need to do that first before they try to lead anyone else. This is not a license to dominate your family. Jesus told us we must be the greatest servant of all, but it does mean that you stand against what the enemy is trying to do. If your children are unruly, the enemy is trying to destroy their lives. Unruly children become unruly adults, and even if they are saved, they have a hard time walking the walk.

DOMINION

Dominion: sovereign or supreme authority; the power of ruling or governing; domination.

Subdue: to bring under control by influence, training, persuasion, or force.

Dominion is a very important concept. God intended for man to be the supreme authority in the earth, in obedience to Him of course. If you are to subdue something, evidently there is something to rise up. There is no sign that the animals were a problem at this point. Eventually one did come and challenge what God had said, but we have come to understand it was not the animal but the spirit in the animal that was and is the problem. Spirits for some reason want to take a physical form on the earth. As I pointed out earlier, there was already a negative force in this world and God was fully aware of its potential. Adam and Eve were not. They were created naïve. I speak of all this in chapter five. Jesus did take back what was lost, but He did not come to do the job for us. It is still ours to do, but it won't be easy. Dominion is a state of mind before it's anything else. *"For as [a man] thinketh in his heart, so is he"* (Prov. 23:7, KJV).

"I will give you the keys of the kingdom of heaven; and whatever you shall bind on earth shall have been bound in heaven, and whatever you shall loose on earth shall have been loosed in heaven" (Matt. 16:19, NCV). Jesus is speaking to His disciples, but remember, we were included in His prayer in John 17. We are included in the "whosoever" may come. We have all that comes with the coming.

This is not talking about physical binding. It is talking about spiritual binding, although eventually the spiritual will become obvious in the physical world. We must bind the spirits in our homes: spirits of unbelief, rebellion, control, lying, stealing, anger, bitterness, envy, unworthiness, revenge, cheating, gambling, astrology, smoking, alcohol, drugs, lust, pornography, victim-hood, self-pity, and yes, even murder. This may seem a bit far-fetched, but a spirit of murder enters when we participate in an abortion. It also enters when someone hates: *"Everyone who hates a brother or sister is a murderer"* (1 John 3:15, NCV). And there are many more. They travel in groups and the more the better in their minds. The Bible tells us one man had a legion of them. When we talk about stopping the garbage in our home and the resulting furor, there are spirits involved in the uncontrolled appetites we find there.

(The words in parentheses are the Exegeses interpretation.)

> *Who hath believed (trusted) our report? And to whom is the arm of the Lord (Yah Veh) revealed (exposed)? For he shall grow up before him (ascend at his face) as a tender plant (sprout), and as a root out of dry ground (parched earth): he hath no form nor comeliness (majesty); and when we shall see him, there is no beauty (vistage) that we should desire him. He is despised and abandoned of men; a man of sorrows, and acquainted with grief (knowing sickness): and we hid as it were our faces from him; he was despised and we esteem (machinated) him not. Surely he hath borne our grief (sicknesses), and carried (borne) our sorrows: yet we did esteem (machinated) him stricken (plagued), smitten of God (Elohim), and afflicted (abased). But he was pierced for our transgressions (rebellions), bruised (crushed) for our iniquities (perversities): and the chastisement of our peace (shalom) was upon him; and with his stripes (lashes) we are healed.*
>
> —ISAIAH 53:1–3, KJV

Notice the King James version uses "grief" and the Exegeses uses "sickness". Also note that it uses "ascend at his face" where the King James version uses "shall grow up." I love the way things weave their way through the Bible. I hope you have heard this scripture enough that this doesn't take away from the impact. Is there a difference between trusted and believed? Believe: to accept as true. Trust: confidence or faith in a person or thing. Trusted seems to be a bit more powerful. God seems to prefer the more powerful.

The important thing is that this scripture is telling of a person who comes, that has no outward beauty, but one that is acquainted with grief and suffering. So much so that He bore our sicknesses, sorrows, and sin upon Himself. "The chastisement of our peace was upon Him" (Isa. 53:5). Do you know how easy it is to lose your peace? Jesus didn't just take the big things; He took the little things, too. He took everything that is not acceptable. It's His now.

Let's see now; what is His? We already know that He is all things good, but since He purchased all the bad things as well, let's make at least a partial list of the bad things He now claims: sickness, disease, sorrow, grief, sadness, poverty, eternal death, and guilt. If sickness starts to come into your life, how can that be? I thought Jesus owned it. If sickness comes, it's a lie. It's illegal God is a God of law. Satan understands this. But he knows he can fool us into thinking it's ours anyhow.

If we are sick, how do we get rid of it? It is never too late to start refusing it. If you haven't done it from the beginning, do it as soon as you realize what you have done. Repent and start doing it right. It's easier to refuse it than to get rid of it. But it does take standing against it for a while. "I don't receive this. Go back to the dry places." Keep saying it no matter how much "proof" you receive. If the proof doesn't agree with scripture or what God says, then the "proof" must be wrong. The Bible says if you sign on a loan and then realize you have made a mistake, you should run and get out of it. (See Proverbs 6:1–3.) I feel the same about a sickness you've signed onto. Run and take your name off. Then, receive your healing and begin to thank Him for it in anticipation of the manifestation (feeling better).

Why does the devil have a right to write your name on anything? He does only when you don't tell him otherwise! If UPS delivered something you didn't want, would you accept it anyhow, especially if you would have to pay for it? Well, believe me, we pay for these things in our precious time, energy, emotions, and wherewithal. So why not refuse it? I do, especially when someone else tries to accept it for me. I say, "I put a hedge on those words!" I put a hedge around about a third of what I say and about half of what Lamar's says. Not really, but it seems like it. You can stop the effect of what has already been spoken! Just because you see the evidence that it has already arrived does not mean that you cannot still reject it. Say, "I don't receive that!" Speak it out: "Don't write my name on that!"

Jesus commanded an unclean spirit with His words. You will receive your healing through your words, and you will keep it through your words. This is why it's essential that you beginning speaking properly. "My heart works properly, my immune system keeps me healthy...." When my heart gets to racing, I command it to stop racing and beat properly. Never speak negatively about your body. Appreciate it and speak to yourself in a loving way. Speak this way to your husband and kids, too. Never accept their negative talking and encourage them to speak positively and thankfully for what they have. You can't live in the realm of life talking death all the time.

I understand they'll get irritated with this sometimes because they think you aren't being realistic. We are allowed to speak the truth. Right now the person may have a problem. We just disagree that it won't get better. Let them cry on your shoulder. Listen and empathize. Be real. And then be scriptural. And let them hear a prayer you say on their behalf.

God only heals what we give to Him. In salvation we ask Him to forgive our sin, but we actually say we receive the forgiveness and ask Him to take our sin. Heal my sickness is really take my sickness. We must continually surrender things to Him. The question then becomes how do you "abide in Him"? You meditate on what He said, the attitude He maintained. You watch for ways that He is manipulating your world. You begin to see Him where others miss Him. You continue to live your life, but you begin to see your life in a totally new way. Where you were blind; now you see. Where you were dead; now you live.

I think the greatest way that we begin to show the new life in us is that we quit striving so much. We can begin to allow God work out the problems in our lives. Rest in Him (Psalm 91).

I was born with allergies. I thought I would always have them until one day a woman on television told how she was delivered of allergies and then prayed for the people watching to be delivered of them, too. I was amazed, but I had enough faith and understanding of the Word that I knew she was right. So, I received it. That doesn't mean anything changed. I probably wasn't having any problems at the time, so I didn't really think about it until I had an attack and started sneezing weeks later. My nose and eyes started running like they always do with one of these attacks. Indignation rose up in me and I said, "Satan, you're a liar." I was tired of being tormented in this way. Every time I sneezed I said, "Satan, you're a liar." And I kept sneezing. Finally the thought came to me, "If you'd quit saying that, you would quit sneezing." I knew that wasn't God. "If I never quit sneezing, devil, I'm going to keep saying it." I must have sneezed thirty-five times. It sure didn't look like I won that day. About a month later, I realized I hadn't had an attack since. That was the last attack of allergies I ever had.

I'm telling you, you don't have to have this garbage. God did not give it to you. We don't have to pray about what God's will is in this instance. Would you want your child sick? In poverty? Certainly not! And God doesn't want His kids sick or poor either. He wants you blessed.

Now that you know He doesn't want you to have _____(fill in the blank with your own problem), learn to use your mouth to rebuke it and send it back where it came from. And not only reject what the enemy sends but construct a better life for yourself and your family. God has promised to create the fruit of your lips. So create! That is how you take your authority over the enemy—with your mouth, with the Word in your mouth. This stuff is not really hard once you know it can be done. God made it simple enough for a little child. You are a child. You are His child. Have a teachable spirit so you can pick up these teachings and do what you have to do.

Father God, I need healing of so many things in my life: my body, my immune system, my emotions, my mind, my finances, my marriage, other relationships. I guess I accepted more that I needed to when I didn't know that I could refuse them. I ask You now to take them and send them to wherever You think they should go. I ask You to restore unto me the years that the locust have eaten. Help me to keep my relationship with You fresh and to be a conduit through which Your blessing can flow freely. I bind Satan from working in my life any longer, and I ask you to begin to turn around the situation I am now living in. I pray this in the precious name of Jesus.

There is a spiritual basis at the core of your problems. Let me share one of my experiences. Things were really bad after we moved to Florida. Nothing was going our way. Financially things were a mess. The boys weren't happy in their schools. Lamar was so depressed he couldn't function. Just when I needed him to get going, he got "down" and moped around for weeks. Since he was self-employed, no money was coming in. You can imagine how concerned I was. I desperately needed him up off the couch.

We were both selling insurance, but I wasn't very good at it. In fact, it made me physically ill. He felt I should go out and sell and I felt he should; he's the salesman in the family. When I tried to encourage him, he put it back on me. Somehow, he thought I could do what he couldn't. I knew better, but he couldn't see it. "Yes, one of us doesn't need to be here," I murmured. If one of us was going to stay home, I felt is should be me since I was cooking, cleaning, and taking care of the kids and he was on the couch.

Once, after one such session of me trying to encourage him to go to work and him not receiving it, the word came to me, "Why are you fighting with him?" I knew it was God. "Because we need to eat?" was my honest answer. "You are in a spiritual battle. You must fight it spiritually." I had never heard of a spiritual battle before. I had been a Christian a few years by then. "How do you do that?" I wondered. God had nothing more to say. I guess He wanted me to figure it out for myself. And I did. Once you know to do something, it's usually not that hard to figure out how to do it.

You really must know who you are in Christ before you even start fighting a spiritual battle. Because if you don't, when you face the enemy, he will eat you alive. You must believe the Bible and know the promises, at least enough to have your armor on and your weapons of warfare. No warrior goes into battle unprepared, not knowing the enemy he faces. This is the list I came up with rather quickly. The list is in no special order, except Jesus. He's always first.

How to Fight a Spiritual Battle

- With Jesus. Literally by speaking His Name. (John 14:13). He said to use His name. It's powerful. Every knee must bow when it is spoken.
- With the keys. Jesus gave us the keys. Learn what He wants you to lock and unlock. "Whatever you bind on earth..."
- With the Word. Learn the scriptures and stand on them. They are your sword.
- With forgiveness. Revenge, bitterness, and unforgiveness render you helpless, defenseless.
- With prayer. Talk to God.
- With praise. Praise your way out of your problems, for He is worthy of our praise.
- With joy. Joy is the proof of your faith.
- With your mouth. "I create the fruit of your lips." Create your way out of your problems. Your mouth can defeat you in a heartbeat. I still bind about half of what I speak. "I put a hedge around that." I say it because what I just uttered is contrary to the Word of God or what I want to happen.

Just because it's true doesn't mean I have to agree with it.
God has a better truth. And the last Word.

- With the Blood. The work of the Cross and Jesus' blood
that was spilled for our sin is the basis of our redemption
and faith. Referring to the blood is our way of telling God
we are fully aware of how precious it is and applying its
authority.

Maybe you can think of a few more. Bind the devil verbally. Tell him to get out of your life; you are child of the most high God, etc. I understand this is not a full list and not a complete teaching. Just like God did with me, I want you to dig out the answers for yourself. If you think about it, it's the things you dig out for yourself that you appreciate the most. I want things that I say to you to minister to you and go down deep, but I also want you to figure out some of it for yourself.

Here is another big revelation in my life: I had been in a bad mood for weeks. Nothing Lamar did was right. I was upset with my mother, too. We lived about five blocks from her, and she was doing things that hurt me. We had always had a good relationship, but when I got saved everything changed, just like it says in Matthew 10:35.

As I worked around the house, doing the wash and all the stuff a mother does, the harder I worked, the more agitated I got. "I am so tired of having to go somewhere else for the love and fellowship I need," I thought. I was so upset that Lamar and my mother were not being there for me. I got angrier and angrier until finally, pounding on the table, I finished with, "I am so lonely!" "I didn't know that!" I thought. I didn't know I was lonely. If my best friend had told me this, I would have told her she was crazy. I'm the friendliest person around. But when it came from within, I had to rethink things. It was true. I was expecting Lamar and my mother to fill those empty spaces that we all have, and they weren't able to for whatever reason. We all have gaping holes we are trying to fill, and when they are left empty for too long, we start looking in all the wrong places. Well, maybe I wasn't looking in the wrong places, because

Mom and Lamar probably should have done better, but they evidently weren't going to. I have since found out it really wasn't their fault. Their childhoods predisposed them to their own empty places. It comes down the generations. When they didn't fulfill what I needed, I should have gone to God, because He is the only one that can fill them. We all have God-shaped vacuums that only He can fill.

It's when we go to the wrong places to be filled that we get into problems: men, women, money, alcohol, prestige, attention, sex, drugs, gambling, some Internet sites; all these things and more have a "hook" in them. They hook you and then tie you up, binding you tighter and tighter. The longer you are involved with any one of them, the harder it is to get out. This is why the Bible says to flee evil. Don't get hooked in and bound. Don't even start. This is why we should not smoke our first cigarette or take our first drink. I remember at college, most of the girls had no intention of smoking. We knew it wasn't a good thing, although we didn't know it was as bad as it turned out to be. We didn't like it, but it was so cool. And so the girls would practice holding a cigarette and puffing on it so they wouldn't look awkward if they were offered one by their date. I protested. It didn't make sense to me. Do you know they all ended up smoking? And drinking. Not me. Being cool never was my thing.

If it's bad, there is a spirit behind it. Everybody's list will be different. We are told to bind the bad spirits and loose the good ones. (See Matthew 16:18; 18:18.) Think of what is opposite of all those bad things I have listed: discipline, generosity, chastity, faith, love, grace, mercy, peace, joy, laughter. Do you want your laughter back? Loose it. But be sure you bind all those bad ones because until you do, or somebody else does, your peace, joy, and laughter will be severely limited. Binding spirits takes someone who is secure in their faith to do it.

A person can be oppressed or possessed by a spirit or spirits. There is a controversy in Christian circles as to whether a Christian can be possessed and not just oppressed. I don't want to get into this debate right now. Just know that you are not dealing with your husband or child alone. You are dealing with a spirit entity that is influencing or controlling what they say and do. That is why we find it difficult to make them stop doing certain things. Love is not the issue if it's an addiction or a compulsion.

If you feel your husband, child or someone close to you is "possessed" or "oppressed" with a demonic spirit or spirits, it's not something to take lightly. Ministering to this problem takes a maturity in the Lord that not many people have. You can take your authority over them and they do have to obey you in Jesus' name, but you must know your authority in Him. Better to continue to learn and grow and find out who in your area deals with these things for a while and see where God leads you. Satan is a spirit; yelling at him is inappropriate especially in front of non-believers or immature believers. Sometimes in taking your authority you will get a little dramatic and that's OK if you are only scaring the devil. You must have the agreement of everyone in the room before you can do anything spiritual.

A word of caution: there are some people that see demons behind every bush. It's their answer to all of our problems and that is simply not true. Very seldom does a child need deliverance. Most of the time just making them behave and giving them proper discipline such as Nanny Deborah would give, is enough.

You can take your authority over the spirits in your home without people being aware that you are doing it. Pray as you go about your day binding spirits and loosing spirits. Speak peace and healing over your home. These spiritual things don't have to be done necessarily in big obvious ways. It will often be the little things, your loving influence and God's through you that will send them away. Celery is supposed to be a calming food. There are physical things you can do to help calm down your home, like limiting the sugar intake. The things that keep us tormented are not always spiritual.

Some counselors like to do a few sessions of teaching and ministry before they begin to try to loose the person of whatever it is that's bothering them. They want the person to be grounded in the faith somewhat or they will not keep their deliverance. I would say it would be a good thing to keep touch with them afterwards to be sure they are doing OK.

NOW THAT YOU ARE BOUND

Once bound, it will take some doing to get free. It wouldn't have to take so long if it didn't take so long for us to get sick of the garbage and do something about it. Every situation is different. Some are easier than others. I have heard of people that decide they are sick of smoking and put down the cigarette and never miss it. And then I have heard of others that try time and time again only to return again and again. I have heard of people praying or being prayed for and being freed immediately and others that take longer. We can't get discouraged just because it doesn't happen the way we want it to.

Because Lamar and I are one, what binds him, binds me. However, when the cord comes around me, it takes on a different name. Let me explain. I had the spirit of loneliness and Lamar had the spirit of jealousy. When I cut the spirit of loneliness, Lamar's jealousy dropped away. Why? Lamar's jealousy was coming out of my unnatural reaching out for fulfillment. When I was no longer lonely because I repented and went to God with these frustrations, Lamar saw that and it changed things in him. He had no reason to be jealous any longer. It doesn't happen immediately, but eventually things will change because one changes.

If a man is an alcoholic, his wife becomes bitter or she has a victim mentality. She may become a shopaholic, etc. An alcoholic usually smokes. They are selfish. The more spirits a person has, the more they accept. And the more the one spouse has, the more that try to bind the other. This is how we end up in a bigger and bigger mess with tentacles going deeper and deeper into our lives. If Daddy is an alcoholic and Mommy is bitter, then the kids are fearful. If Mommy is controlling and Daddy is wimpy, there's strife and confusion in their home. Cut off what binds you and you free more than yourself. It's difficult not to be bitter if your husband is an alcoholic or an adulterer, but you can do it. You must forgive him and deal with what is controlling *your* thinking and actions. As you walk in the principles of God, your family will change.

The spirit of the Lord God is upon me; because the Lord hath anointed me to preach good tidings unto the meek; he hath sent me to bind up the broken-hearted, to proclaim liberty to the captives, and the opening of the prison to them that are bound; to proclaim the acceptable year of the Lord, and the day of vengeance of our God; to comfort all that mourn; to appoint unto them that mourn in Zion, to give unto them beauty for ashes, the oil of joy for mourning, the garment of praise for the spirit of heaviness; that they might be called trees of righteousness, the planting of the Lord, that he might be glorified.

—Isaiah 61:1–3

Remember, demonic spirits can return. This is why we are warned not to leave the person without an infilling of the Holy Spirit, so their "house" is not empty when the spirits try to come back and re-inhabit their dwelling. If the person doesn't act happy and free, you aren't finished; but too often the people doing the ministry aren't prepared to finish it. Sad, but true. Let's learn so that when we do have the opportunity, we can take the person all the way through to freedom and infilling. That's why Jesus sent them out in twos and more, because it takes working together in this ministry. I'm not saying it can't be done one on one, but more is better, and they need to be mature in the faith. Freedom, complete freedom, takes more than a day. It's a walk.

DELIVERANCE

Not everyone will cooperate with what needs to be done to rid them of these evil influences. Some actually like their demons. They like to smoke and drink and do stupid stuff. It's the rest of us that hate it. They are happy in their decadence. In their mind, you are the problem. And because they have an attitude, you really need to fight this spiritually through prayer, discernment, the Word, and maybe even fasting. Remember what I said about knowing when to keep your mouth shut. Getting more irritated about their habits is not helpful, at least not until you are led by the Holy Spirit to say or do something. The person needs to get saved first or be ministered to spiritually before they will change. However, it might be appropriate for you to stop your participation in their sin before they are saved or delivered. I had to face the fact that I was an enabler. You don't *have* to buy his beer and cigarettes (unless he is abusive and then you have bigger issues).

> *God used Paul to do some very special miracles. Some people took handkerchiefs and clothes that Paul had used and put them on the sick. When they did this, the sick were healed, and evil spirits left them.* [Some churches still do this and with very good results.] *But some people also were traveling around and making evil spirits go out of people. They tried to use the name of the Lord Jesus to force the evil spirits out. They would say, "By the same Jesus that Paul talks about, I order you to come out." Seven sons of Sceva, a leading priest, were doing this. But one time an evil spirit said to them, "I know Jesus, and I know about Paul, but who are you?" Then the man who had the evil spirit jumped on them. Because he was so much stronger than all of them, they ran away from the house naked and hurt. All the people in Ephesus—Jews and Greeks—learned about this and were filled with fear and gave great honor to the Lord Jesus.*
>
> —ACTS 19:15

Does the devil know who you are? When you wake up in the morning or if you are brought into a situation, the devil should quake in his boots knowing he is done. His plans have just been sabotaged.

God doesn't want novices doing the things that a mature Christian should be doing. You should have around you people that understand spiritual things, and by this I mean such things as deliverance. Jesus said we would do greater things than He did and this is what He meant. He only had three years and was only able to begin. He intended for us to do it from then on and more. Deliverance is a valid ministry, but you must be careful (prayerful and discerning) as you proceed. Things must be done decently and in order. Good counselors will spend a certain amount of time giving the scripture references before they begin to minister. The person receiving the ministry must understand and believe or it will not work. We can free a person only to have them bound again as the scripture warns. Most Christians stay away from all this and that is just as wrong. To leave people in their bondage because you think you might make a mistake is ludicrous. You can find people that have experience in this area. There is no reason not to get help for yourself or anyone else that needs it.

This ministry is done in the authority of the believer. I am a believer. You are a believer. Jesus had the authority given to Him by His Father and He gave it to us. Now, it's just a matter of learning how and using it. We speak forth our intentions, binding the spirits we feel are present and loosing the ones we want to be loosed. God has His spirits helping Him, and the devil has his spirits helping him. It's a war. And if you think the devil is going to back down just because you stand and face him, you are wrong. He will challenge you every inch of the way. That is why you must know your word carries with it the weight of almighty God. And to know this, you must know you are in right standing with Him. This is why holiness is important. Not that you are perfect, but you have kept things up to date. You have repented and stand clean before the Lord.

You should be as right as you can be when you minister—having repented of your own sins, forgiven others for what they have done to you, and asking Him to help you in areas you are weak. Once you have done that, you can stand and face down the devil. But again, unless it's something personal, don't try to do it alone and even then sometimes we need help. Of course if you are alone when the enemy comes at you, God will be enough to ward off any demonic attack. The name of Jesus is enough. And the blood is, too. Plead the blood of Jesus over yourself, your home and family, and anything you want spared from the ravages of the enemy.

Lord, I want to rule and reign over my own life and my home properly. I am sick of living in defeat. Help me to put a watch on my lips so I will stop saying things that are contrary to Your Word and Your thoughts. Forgive me for all the things I have said and done that have hindered Your work in our lives. I am so sorry that I am one of the biggest problems in my home instead of the one standing in the gap and saying and believing the right things. I love my family. I want them to succeed and be mature Christians. I want to be a mature Christian. I resolve this day to do my best to read my Bible and pray and seek You for answers, and when I get them, act on what You show me to do. I pray all this in the precious name of Jesus. Amen.

If you are not sure what you are supposed to do, here a few things to consider. Do you have a good church you attend? Do you have a Bible to read? Do you have a spiritual mother? Sister? Look around and see who God would have you relate closely with. Be open to new relationships in the body of Christ. Don't run before you can walk.

Remember, Jesus said He would send us a teacher, the Holy Spirit. (See Luke 12:12.) You are no doubt "getting" things in your spirit and are probably ignoring more than you realize. You should be learning what the Bible tells you. Today is the best day to start. Ask mature Christians to help. I'm sure they know lots of good scriptures. The Bible says to get saved. Do it. It says to get baptized. Do it. It says to tarry and receive the Holy Spirit. Do it. It says to forgive anyone who has offended you. Do it. It says to provide for your children. Do it. It says to come under authority. Do it. It says attend church. Do it. It says walk in love. Do it. It says work and pay your bills. Do it. It says pray continually. Do it. It says to study the Word. Do it. It says to pray in Jesus name. Do it.

Being a Christian is not jerking and shaking in the Spirit; although you may do that and I hope you do have powerful manifestations of the Spirit. Being a Christian is practicing the presence of God, watching for what He is doing and where He is leading, listening for what He is saying, responding to these things, and then watching the changes in your own inner being that comes from your willingness to turn toward Him. Don't be in a hurry and don't be fearful or quarrelsome. Try to cooperate with what God is showing you. Learn to listen and respond. He wants the best for you. You can trust Him even when you can't trust yourself. He loves you very, very much. He has already proven it in so many ways. All you have to do is receive. Just take it in. Be a little sponge. He thinks you are special. You are the one that has a problem with you, not Him. What needs to be done isn't that hard if He can get you to cooperate. It's Him that lives now in you. You must die to self so that He may live through you. Just walk it as best you can and He will do the rest.

> *Brothers and sisters, God loves you, and we know he has chosen you, because the Good News we brought to you came not only with words, but with power, with the Holy Spirit, and with sure knowledge that it's true. Also you know how we lived when we were with you in order to help you. And you became like us and like the Lord. You suffered much, but still you accepted the teaching with the joy that comes from the Holy Spirit. So you became an example to all the believers in Macedonia and Southern Greece. And the Lord's teaching spread from you not only into Macedonia and Southern Greece, but now your faith in God has become known everywhere. So we do not need to say anything about it. People everywhere are telling about the way you accepted us when we were there with you. They tell how you stopped worshiping idols and began serving the living and true God. And you wait for God's Son, whom God raised from the dead, to come from heaven. He is Jesus, who saves us from God's angry judgment that is sure to come.*
>
> —1 THESSALONIANS 1:4–10, NCV

Be like the Thessalonians that Paul is speaking to, so your faith and accomplishments are spoken of far and wide. You have the authority, but if you don't know it and you don't act on it, and you don't stand when he challenges, then it's the same thing as not having it. You will fold.

God understands that coming to Him initially seems to bring more problems into your life. He knows He is going to have to redeem the whole thing and He is up to the task. Stick in there. Don't weary. Just know it's typical. If you share what you are going through, I'm sure your Christian friends will share their struggles, as well as the victories. Just be sure that you share with victorious Christians and not the defeated ones. There is a difference. If someone doesn't have a testimony of what God has done recently, something is wrong. This is supposed to be a victory celebration not a pity party.

Rebuke the storm when it tries to come and destroy your home. Rebuke the disease that tries to destroy your body or your loved ones. If it's not from God, then we don't have to have it. But you do have to say it. If someone says something negative but you don't want to get into an argument with them about it, say it under your breath. It's a spirit. It will hear you. Say, "I don't receive that! I take my authority over this spirit of fear (or sickness, whatever) and send it to the dry places."

Please allow me to pray for you:

> *Father, I ask that You guide my friend to the people that can help her or him to get the help she or he needs. I bind Satan from interfering with their victory over the demonic influences in their lives. I can't be there, but You can, and I ask it right now and agree with their prayers for the healing and deliverance of their family. I pray this in Jesus' name. Amen.*

THIRTEEN

**Now the serpent was cunning, more cunning than
any creature that God, the Eternal had made.**

—GENESIS 3:1

One Spirit

LEAVING YOUR GARDEN UNCOVERED

SATAN STILL HAS ACCESS to man. He's in our marriages and communities. Just as Adam and Eve could've sent him packing; we have the same option. But do we?

In Romans 7 Paul talks about the problem. *"Oh, wretched man that I am."* Then we read on to Romans 8:11 (KJV) from where we get our hope, *"But if the Spirit of him that raised up Jesus from the dead dwells in you, he that raised up Christ from the dead shall also quicken your mortal bodies by his Spirit that dwelleth in you."* I understand he is talking about the resurrection and our adoption and, yes, our suffering, but listen to this: *"He that spared not his own Son, but delivered him up for us all, how shall he not with him also freely give us all things?"* (Rom. 8:32).

Here it's the same sentiment said in another way:

> *We also pray that you will be strengthened with his glorious power so that you will have all the patience and endurance you need. May you be filled with joy, always thanking the Father, who has enabled you to share the inheritance that belongs to God's holy people, who live in the light. For he has rescued us from the one who rules in the kingdom of darkness, and he has*

*brought us into the Kingdom of his dear Son. God has purchased
our freedom with his blood and has forgiven all our sins.*

—COLOSSIANS 1:11

It's plain that God doesn't mean for this power to just take us to heaven, but to take us to the end, *"so that you will have all the patience and endurance you need"*—not only patience and endurance, but joy. Be thankful always because the Father has allowed you to be a part of this inheritance and has rescued you from the enemy and put you in His kingdom. His kingdom starts here and now. We don't have to wait.

JESUS IN ME, THE HOPE OF GLORY

"I no longer live, but Christ lives in me"—Jesus in us and through us. *"I have been crucified with Christ and I no longer live, but Christ lives in me. The life I live in the body, I live by faith in the Son of God, (by faith in Jesus) who loved me and gave himself for me"* (Gal 2:20, NIV).

We die so that that He may live through us—His power in us. Don't you know, if we really believed Jesus was living in us, we could believe for anything, even the salvation of our husband and kids. *"The life I live in the body, I live by faith in the Son of God, who gave Himself up for me, for we are the temple of the living God."* I live by faith. Only in Jesus do I now live, and you must do the same. You can no longer live in your flesh; you must die to it and live only in Him. You might wonder why you feel so hurt and frustrated. Evidently you forgot to die. Or nobody told you that you were supposed to be dead.

Is it possible to fail with all this love and power, with Jesus living through us? Yes, it's possible. People do it all the time. But we can choose to fight this unbelieving nature that permeates our brains. Don't get discouraged because you struggle to understand and then have to fight to stand. I know it's a battle every step of the way. God does, too. That's why He tells us not to weary in well doing. Keep fighting the good fight of faith and eventually you will win. You will eventually get sick and tired of being sick and tired. I did. And Lamar did. And you will, too.

If we are dead to ourselves, how can we be alive to hurts and bitterness? I am no longer married to Lamar, but Jesus in me is married to him. Now that's a real mind-bender. And even if your husband is not a Christian yet, that same power resides in you, enough to raise him from the dead. Jesus considers him dead until he gets born of His Spirit. He will lead you in the way you should go. You are on a path and must not turn to the right or the left. Keep walking and you will walk out your miracle.

THE BAPTISM OF THE HOLY SPIRIT

There is great deal of controversy in the body of Christ as to whether it's necessary to receive the Holy Spirit after you have received Jesus' atoning blood and have been born again of the Spirit. If you are like me, you want to stay out of as much controversy as possible. I used to avoid visiting my in-laws to avoid controversy. The only problem was it robbed us of precious time together, but it wasn't something I couldn't live without. However, if you avoid the things of God, you very likely will miss something you can't afford to live without.

God is controversial. Jesus is even more controversial. And the Holy Spirit is the most controversial of all, but God doesn't allow us the luxury to pick and choose, "I like the Father and I like Jesus, but the Holy Spirit...I don't know about Him." This just won't cut it. I don't know that we can stay away from any One of them and still have eternal life. He expects us to grow up and face things head on. So, let's do it.

Yes, you are born of the Spirit when you are saved, which was true of the people in Acts, the disciples, and others at the time. However, Scripture reports they were told they needed to receive the Holy Spirit after their initial salvation. Remember when Jesus breathed on them in John 20:22? It was after this that the Holy Spirit came down at Pentecost. We receive the Holy Spirit when we are born again and we receive Him without measure when we are baptized in the Holy Spirit. It was and is a separate work.

Jesus Himself commanded His followers to go and tarry until they were endued with power, which was accomplished when the Holy Spirit came upon them in the Upper Room (Acts 2). Jesus did not begin His ministry until the Holy Spirit descended on Him in the form of a dove after John the Baptist baptized him in water. He was always born of the Spirit because the Holy Spirit came upon Mary at conception. However, the Holy Spirit descended upon Him in His fullness that day with John because it was after that that He would start His full-time ministry. We should do likewise and not begin our ministry until the Holy Spirit comes upon us. It's not a suggestion; it's a command.

The disciples and the people in the area had this second experience of receiving the Holy Spirit after they believed in Him. Then they went around helping others receive it as well. It also was assumed the Christians of their day would *"speak in other tongues as the Spirit gave them utterance."* Has it continued to today in Christians who have received this "Baptism of the Holy Spirit"? Yes, it has. I have received the baptism of the Holy Spirit and speak in tongues. Do you need power in your life? This is the only question you need to answer. If the answer is "no thank you, I am doing just fine," I should warn you: if you choose not to have power in your life, there is no telling where this will lead because there is a big devil out there that looks at you very differently now that you are a Christian. The reason someone would think they were fine without the power is because the enemy doesn't look upon them as much of a threat, which isn't good. He's already getting away with murder, so why bother? But, I must warn you; this won't last. Eventually the enemy will take you on, if for no other reason than to check you out, and God has a history of letting him do it.

I'm sorry if someone has told you that you don't have to have a special "infilling" of the Holy Spirit after praying to receive Jesus. Jesus never said that. He said just the opposite. I have heard of a person having the whole experience in one stupendous evening, but even then the people pray for it to happen. The person comes forward for salvation and they ask him or her if he wants to receive the Holy Spirit and he or she says yes. They include the Holy Spirit when they are praying. If we have received, there will be evidence. One evidence is boldness. The same cowering disciples when Jesus was taken away became fearless witnesses for Him after they left the Upper Room. Are you still too shy to witness? Get endued with power and you won't be. The "rivers of living water" is not just a prayer language. It's the life itself that manifests itself in what we say and do in response to the Spirit within. Sharing Life with a friend is part of that river. You can't help yourself.

I advise anyone with questions to read the passages at the end of the four gospels where Jesus tells them He will send them Someone after He leaves. After you are done checking out the end of the four gospels, you need to read Acts as if you were reading a newspaper at the time. It tells of the poor confused followers going to the Upper Room after Jesus has ascended and waiting there as Jesus instructed them to do. The Spirit descends like a mighty, rushing wind and they all speak in languages they didn't know. Peter gets up and preaches the first of many messages proclaiming what Jesus has done. Three thousand new converts were added to the church that day.

You must understand how important Jesus' last instructions were to His followers. He wasn't playing games or wasting time. It was of utmost importance. You must tarry. And tarry they did. And they were endued with power. How can we do any less? In fact, until you do, He doesn't want you to go out in the world. Do not got out until you have been endued with power. You are dangerous without the indwelling of the Holy Spirit. He doesn't just want your spirit born again; He wants a constant flow of anointed life coming out of you.

If God mentions something once, it is important. There are many of our Christian tenets that are mentioned only once and we feel we should hold onto them and practice them. Water baptism is handled, I feel similarly in the Bible. Jesus participated and recommended it. We saw it done how many times? Once? Twice? A few times? So, we do it. It's the same with the baptism of the Holy Spirit. Jesus participated in it, recommended it, and we saw it done over and over again. Why should we do anything else but do it? I just don't understand quibbling. To me, it is no different than quibbling about water baptism, salvation, Jesus, God, etc. There will always be these controversies and for me they end at the Scriptures. For others, they end in their own minds.

I have never understood why people who say they are the most humble are the ones that snub their nose at what they consider the least gift—speaking in tongues. I think this is a misinterpretation of the Scripture, but that is not the point right now. What they think is important because it can inhibit their faith. I think the best gift is the one needed at that moment. But if tongues is the least and they are so 'umble, why don't they grab it immediately and say, "This must be for me. Praise God, this is my gift!" But, no, they say they don't want it because it's the least.

"Tongues," in case you never heard of it, is one of the evidences of being baptized or immersed in the Holy Spirit. It's the Holy Spirit speaking through you to the Father. You yielding yourself to be used by the Spirit. It's important because God gave us authority in this world and He needs us to verbally agree with what He wants to do. That is a limitation He has put on Himself. He works within a set of rules, and since we don't usually know what needs to be done, He needs our cooperation even before we understand. It can be speaking a language you have never learned like French or Spanish or even a little known dialect, or it can be nonsense syllables or groanings. It changes depending on the situation and how the Holy Spirit is speaking through you.

Allow me to share a typical story of God trying to help people understand the need for the baptism with the Holy Spirit. We were on our first cruise with the top producers and management of our main insurance carrier. Two of our tablemates were the elderly founder of the company and his wife. One night he asked Lamar and me about our church. When we explained that it was a Pentecostal church, he said he had heard of them but didn't know much about them. Lamar explained as well as he could in a few minutes and even gave a little of his testimony, but it's hard with all the interruptions of a first class meal. Also, people are uncomfortable talking too much about religion in these settings, which we understand. I was a little concerned when Lamar said something to the effect that tongues worked for him but it may not for others. He didn't quite say that, but he was getting close, and I feel this is dangerous. It does work for him, just as it will work for anyone. No one is better off without the power of the Holy Spirit in their lives. And we shouldn't even hint anything other than that. Jesus never said it was optional, anymore than He is optional. He didn't die on a cross because it was an option.

I had brought two or three magazines with me in case I wanted to read. As we talked, I remembered that one of them dealt with this very subject, but I didn't want to say anything until I checked. Sure enough, it was the most in-depth study I have ever seen on the baptism of the Holy Spirit. I gave it to this precious man the next morning, and he was extremely thankful because he later taught a class on this subject at his church.

OUR TESTIMONY

We had friends God was dealing with at the same time He was dealing with Lamar and me. We were all in the auction/salvage business. Bill was an intellectual trying to figure out what was happening to his wife, Joyce, spiritually. Lamar was backslidden, but he knew the answers because he was saved at fourteen and had attended Sunday school and Royal Ambassadors as a child. Lamar likes to play with someone's mind and Bill's questions were perfect for that. This went on over a period of months. Eventually Bill got saved, I got saved, and Lamar rededicated his life. I don't know in what order. It was all going on simultaneously.

Bill and Joyce bought an old house we were interested in, but they did a better job of fixing it up than we could have at the time. It really turned out nice. They took down walls and opened it up so much. When they started their Friday night fellowship group, I was anxious to go, if for no other reason than to see the house and have some good fellowship. Bill knew a pastor that had received the left foot of fellowship from another denomination because he had received "the baptism." Earl and his wife had such a wonderful spirit about them—the Holy Spirit. I cannot express what these meetings meant to our spiritual growth. We would bring the kids and they would run and play for a while, but by the end of the evening they would end up around us watching what was going on and finally fall asleep. Earl taught on salvation and the Holy Spirit, all the fundamentals that we needed to know. He made us stand on the Scripture. We couldn't just say we were believing for something. We had to have the Word to back it up, and he would help you if you didn't have anything.

One night he prayed for a few people to receive the baptism in the Holy Spirit and then asked Lamar if he wanted to receive. I had already received at a church meeting a few months earlier. When we prayed for Lamar, he acted like he was in pain. Earl stopped and asked if he had ever played with a Ouija board or got involved in the occult. Lamar said no. He asked him a few more questions and then if he had ever wished the devil would get anyone? Lamar had to admit he had. Earl explained this was not right, even though the person had done Lamar dirty. It had opened the door to Lamar's spirit for the wrong kind of spirits. Earl proceeded to pray and cast them out. Lamar made a few sounds but nothing terrible, almost like a woman in labor. We could tell something was happening, and Lamar said he could tell a big difference. We were all standing around talking when Earl stopped and approached Lamar again. He said he needed to do something more. He prayed to cast out "companion demons." Lamar felt even better. We all praised God and eventually went home. Everybody rejoiced over our victory, but what they didn't know was that it wasn't to last long.

> *Now when the unclean spirit goes out of a man, it passes through dry places, seeking rest, and does not find it. Then it says, 'I will return to my house from which I came;' and when it comes, it finds it unoccupied, swept, and put in order. Then it goes, and takes along with it seven other spirits more wicked than itself, and they go in and live there; and the last state of that man become worse than the first. That is the way it will also be with this evil generation.*
>
> —MATTHEW 12:43–45

What we didn't know that night was that we should have completed the job and prayed for Lamar to receive the Holy Spirit (Matt. 11:24; Luke 12:25) like we had started to do. Because we didn't, Lamar eventually got worse. This is when we almost separated. Lamar never hit me, but we did get in a shoving match. Things couldn't go on like they were, so I asked Lamar to leave, but never felt led to insist. God was working things out.

I should explain we also made the mistake of not understanding how important it was to testify to what happened. Lamar was embarrassed and didn't want anyone to know. Our friends spread it around town, but that just made it worse. They weren't to blame because it shouldn't have been a secret. Lamar should have been the one to tell, and he should have understood the need for testifying, but without "the baptism" he didn't have the boldness to tell it. This is how we become self-defeating. Our ignorance and unbelief breeds fear and defeat. We were all such a bunch of novices. It would have been nice if we hadn't been so ignorant, but God is faithful to people whose hearts are in the right place. Eventually, He helps you do what you need to do, if you stay open to His leading.

Our wonderful victory soon turned sour. We discovered some of the people at the fellowship group were defrauding people in their business dealings. Lamar lost a small sum of money. Things were going wrong at church, too. The devil sure made a play for what we had and Lamar backslid again. But I just couldn't go back to the old way. There was nothing there but defeat and heartache. I kept on even though Lamar didn't.

It was hard to get Lamar back to the fellowship group, but he did agree to go the night another couple was coming to teach on the baptism of the Holy Spirit. Well, that night he received. When we got home, it was late and we went right to bed. Lamar wanted to pray and asked me to pray in my prayer language first. I didn't feel I could just do it on command and I told him so. Since he supposedly received, I said, "You do it." Lamar understood my dilemma. So, he said, "Well, then, I'll pray in English and then you pray in English and we'll see what happens." That sounded good to me. Lamar prayed and when he finished, I took over. As I started to pray, Lamar sounded like a Jew preaching. It was so powerful and went on for quite a while. I prayed silently. It was a very special experience.

Lamar has never really backslidden since. He may have gotten careless a time or two, but he has quickly come back to his First Love. Don't tell me it's not real, or that it's not for today. If anyone needs the power, we do. And Jesus knew it. That's why He sent the Holy Spirit and told them to go and tarry. That admonition still stands today. Don't start your ministry until you do. Oh, you might be able to tough it out without it, but why would you want to? Don't reason it away. Be obedient.

The baptism of the Holy Spirit is not just for miracles, but to help us in the long haul. It's first and foremost to help us witness, to help us go into all the world and tell what He has done for us, to give us the boldness we need. I know we want help in our marriage and healing and deliverance, but God's heart beats for souls. If we will help Him in this work, the marriage, healings, and deliverances will work out. Remember, when we take on His burden (souls), He will take on ours.

RECEIVING THE BAPTISM OF THE HOLY SPIRIT

Receiving the baptism of the Holy Spirit is like anything else you get from God. Talk to Him about it, and if it's something that has already dispensated to us, then you can tell Him you want to receive it. I should first explain, I go back and forth between using the word "it" the word "Him." He is a person, the Third Person in the Trinity, the Godhead. "It" is the experience you have with Him. I don't ever want you to think I am referring to the Holy Spirit as anything but a person.

The baptism in the Holy Spirit, as we have come to refer to this experience, is received like salvation. You don't work it up or conjure up anything. It's been provided; you receive it. Therefore, all that is necessary is a simple prayer telling God you want it and receive it in faith. Just ask your Heavenly Father for His Holy Spirit and He will send Him to you (John 7:37).

The "manifestations" such as speaking in tongues may not be immediately evident, but they will come just as turning the electricity on in a

house will eventually have outward signs. The lights don't go on immediately, but, eventually, they should if someone lives there. You got the
power when you prayed to receive. Eventually you will "do" something.
Some people notice a new boldness, or love for people they never had
before, or a burden for souls. Jesus will seem more real to you. And you
will have a new hunger for the Word and the things of God. There is
plenty of evidence. It may be simply greater joy. I really don't know why
some people have a problem "receiving." Usually it's because we are too
self-conscious. Don't worry about all this. Just pray and receive and let
Him worry about what form it takes. Just don't stifle Him (which is what
we do when we say we don't need it or it isn't meant for today). Let Him
make these choices. Just be open to what He will do. Be a yielded vessel
(1 Corinthians 14:22).

If you want the Holy Spirit with all of His many gifts, pray a prayer
something like this:

> *Father, I have heard about the baptism of the Holy Spirit and*
> *thought it wasn't for me. But now I realize it is and I want it. If*
> *it gives me power, I want it. If it makes me more loving, then it's*
> *for me. I want everything You have for me. I don't want to be*
> *the hold-up any longer. I ask you to baptize me now in the Holy*
> *Spirit. I receive You, Holy Spirit, and I thank You for coming*
> *into my life. I pray this in the precious name of Jesus, my Savior.*
> *Amen."*

Now just praise Him and tell Him you love Him. And if you find yourself hearing or speaking something other than English, go ahead and let
it out. Don't speak in English. You can't speak two languages at once. Just
allow Him to speak through you.

Don't get caught up in listening to what you are saying. That is not
important. What is important is that you are yielded and that He is
in you. An utterance is only needed to show I am yielding myself and
coming in agreement with whatever God wants to do in my life and on
this earth. The sounds I make may just be groanings or syllables until

God needs them to be something else, not for His sake, but for a person or maybe even another spirit. Scripture backs this up: *"Likewise, the Spirit also helpeth our infirmities: for we know not what we should pray for as we ought: but the Spirit itself maketh intercession for us with groanings which cannot be uttered"* (Rom. 8:26, KJV).

Don't worry about your prayer language. Just speak forth whatever, and if God needs it to be a specific language, He will make it happen. There are actually three forms of tongues. One is for a sign to unbelievers, another as the Holy Spirit prays mysteries through us, and a third is for public use. This should be interpreted and limited to no more than three in a service (1 Corinthians 14:27).

Don't ever forget how important these deep spiritual experiences are for they are truly the stuff of eternal life. However, I want you to keep in mind that you cannot live on this plane all the time. People need to do normal, needful things. God wants us to have good times and laugh together. We have to enjoy the people around us, whether they are where they should be spiritually or not, even before they are saved and on fire for the Lord. Heaviness is not helpful in winning the lost. It's God's to do, not yours. You get the easy job. You get to go to the beach or shop, hug or share a funny story, make something good to eat or eat what someone else makes. Do the everyday things that make up your life and woven in it all will be the spiritual part. And if you do your best, and leave the rest up to Him, the spiritual will get done. A step at a time, or at some special time, God will do something. Just do your part and He will do His.

Romans 14:21 tells us not to get into disputings, so after I have said what I have to say, I have to leave it between the person and God. It's His job now.

FOURTEEN

...and the two shall become one.

—GENESIS 2:24

One Mind

ONE? HOW CAN THAT be? In the fallen state in which we find ourselves, our thoughts are so contrary to each other we find it difficult to feel like one. It is impossible to comprehend that God meant us to be one as they are One. Jesus and the Holy Spirit are different expressions, manifestations, of God the Father. I guess you could say Lamar and I are different expressions or aspects of this one person God intends us to be. Can that really be? We sure didn't look like it. If any couple started out incompatible, it was Lamar and me. We couldn't be together ten minutes without fighting. Then I was "saved" and Lamar rededicated his life. Slowly things changed until now we are truly one.

Lamar and I didn't fully comprehend the dynamics of our birth families growing up until years later. We are just now discovering the meaning of some of the things we experienced and seeing them in a different light. As we share and experience things together, we change together, coming together more in our hearts and minds, seeing these experiences through each other's eyes. If we never get out of our own sphere of thinking, we will never understand or become one. Maturity and experience causes us to rethink many things, but nothing like becoming a Christian does.

I have heard people debate ad nauseum why Adam ate the fruit after Eve had taken a bite, when the only answer that's necessary is: they were one. There is no indication scripturally that there was a debate between the two of them. Some people seem to think he wasn't there and walked up after she had eaten and told him to take a bite, but that's simply not true. He was with her the whole time. Read what it says: "She also gave some to her husband, who was with her, and he ate it." He did not have a problem with what she was doing or he would have intervened. To say otherwise is to misunderstand what God created—our lack of understanding of what it means to be one.

I once heard Diane Hagee, wife of John Hagee, pastor of Cornerstone Church in San Antonio, Texas, tell this story: "One day John fumed, 'When I get to heaven I'm really going to give it to Adam.' I was peeling fruit for a salad and instead of correcting him, walked over and held the fruit in front of his mouth, at which he promptly opened his mouth and took the bite. 'If it hadn't been Adam, it would have been you.'"[1]

ONE IN THE BOND OF LOVE

The concept of being one is not limited to the married couple. God wants us all to be one. Let's go to Jesus' prayer recorded in John 17. I cannot express the impact this prayer had on me personally. I had come under a great deal of persecution when someone told me I needed to read John 17. It was as if Jesus was speaking directly to me. I guess it meant so much at the time because I was hanging on for dear life. My thread had gotten very thin and I felt like everyone had a pair of scissors. His precious words were all I had that kept me from losing it completely. Surely by now you know what I mean. I don't care how "lucky" we are; we still have low points—lots of them.

The prayer begins in John 17:1, *"These things Jesus spoke; and lifting up His eyes to heaven, He said, "Father, the hour has come; glorify Thy Son, that the Son may glorify Thee, even as Thou gavest Him authority over all mankind, that to all whom Thou hast given Him He may give eternal life."*

Jesus is reminding Him the hour has come for His glorification, that He may glorify the Father. Remember, Jesus was a man. He would therefore be glorified while He was a man, and through His glorification, God would be glorified. I believe this was the original intent when we were made in God's image and likeness. This was the beginning and we are to continue it. We are now to be God's glorification, and it will be as members of His glorious church. It is all coming together, and He has given us a chance to be a part of it. Don't let Him down.

Notice Jesus speaks of the authority God has given Him over all mankind. And the reason for this authority is so that He may give to us eternal life. We aren't given authority to heap upon us power and privilege. No, it's to continue the blessing God has begun, to spread the good news to whosoever will listen and believe.

John 17:11: *"And now I am no more in the world, but these are in the world, and I come to thee. Holy Father, keep through thine own name those whom thou hast given me, that they may be one, as we are."* Jesus never says He is of the world and He doesn't want us to be of the world, either. We are in the world, but not of it. There is a big difference. Then He asks the Father to keep *"through thine own name"* those He has given Him. There are four important points here:

1. The importance of His name. Jesus tells us to use His name when we pray. There is power in the name of Jesus—the name the Father has given Him.

2. There are certain ones that God the Father has given Jesus. Now I don't want you to misunderstand this. Jesus says whosoever may come and this never changes. The ones God gives Him are the ones who choose to come. You decide; God gives. It's a very important point that you are God's first and then Jesus'. And then Jesus passes you that Jesus' followers will be one as God the Father, the Holy Spirit, and Jesus are one. Remember, without oneness we have no right to speak. We have no credibility.

3. He is asking His father to "keep" us. Jesus' concern is for His followers because we are left here on this earth. The world is a cold, cruel place, and He knows it will take the power and intervention of God to keep us from being devoured.

Christ means "Messiah, anointed, sent one." If we are called Christian, or a follower of Christ, we are to be the anointed sent ones to bless and deliver, too.

Now listen to this next phrase (verse 21): *"that they all may be one: as You, Father, are in Me, and I in You, [here comes the best part] that they also may be one in Us."*

Let this sink into your inner man: We are one with the most high God—ONE WITH THE MOST HIGH GOD! You are His son or daughter just as Jesus is (Romans 1:8). This is why Jesus said we would do greater things; because greater things were planned and we are the ones to carry them out.

This next part tells you the reason for all this oneness: *"that the world may believe that You sent Me."* We are made one with God so that we can be a good witness to the world. Why? So we can win them. The good news goes forth so you can be saved from your sin, sickness, poverty, and distress; saved from eternal hell.

No use stopping now. *"And the glory which You gave Me I have given them..."* Gee, we keep praying for Him to send down the glory. We always seem to be asking God to do what He has already done.

Up until now Jesus was speaking to the disciples with Him, but now He includes us. Did you know Jesus prayed for you specifically? Jesus asks His Father: *"Neither pray I for these alone [the disciples and believers right there with Him], but for them also which shall believe on me through their word..."* My version is: "Neither pray I for these alone, but for __Midge Vice__, who testifies of Me." You can put your name in there, too.

You are not less than Peter or Paul. Remember, Paul did not travel with Jesus. I feel this is a very significant point. The fact that Paul was thought of as equal with Peter, and yet was not one of the twelve, means a great deal to those of us who have come after. Their ministry was based on the anointing, and we can have that same anointing. Each generation needs their anointed ones, and when we look at church history, we find this is true. Each generation has had their powerful, anointed men of

God. We only have to walk in obedience and do what He sends us to do. The devil hasn't changed, so why would God change His approach for defeating him?

You really must read this prayer for yourself. Don't rush. Sit and ponder as you read. Absorb it while you bask in His presence, for surely He will inhabit where a humble follower reads His Words. Take some precious time alone with Him, just you and His Words. That is Jesus praying for *you* when He walked on this earth.

To become "one," you need get to know each other better. To do this you must talk with your partner about his past, his childhood, the teen years, and beyond. I don't mean delving into his past sexual exploits. That is not helpful. Nor should he delve into yours. A blanket statement should do, "You are not my first..." You do need to know the basics, not names and places. Talk about how many friends he had, if he played on a baseball team, what moving to the farm meant in his life. For Lamar it ended his budding baseball career, in spite of the fact his parents *promised* he would be able to continue. That was a very important milestone in his life, but not a good one. We need to know the good and the bad ones.

It amazes me that Lamar and I are still discovering things about each other after forty years. He is just now hearing some of my stories. Because he was so verbal about his, I never got to tell mine. This has since changed. A few years ago I decided whoever was doing the driving got to pick the music or the topic. Since Lamar drives most of the time, that was great with him. Little did he realize what it would mean when I got behind the wheel. It was down I-75 for him and down memory lane for me. I thoroughly enjoyed it and hope he did, too. He was surprised that he was just now hearing some things.

Since the first few years are the most important in a child's development, it's very important you understand who nurtured him during this time. Was he properly nurtured? What was his mother like? What about his father? And the other people that were around on a daily basis? Did he bond properly? Was he made to feel safe and secure and loved? Or did he languish unattended for hours and suffer abuse at the hand of a parent or caretaker? Until you have a picture of his early years, you don't have a true picture of your husband. How can you mentally feel as one if you have no idea what is going on in his head? You can't. If he wasn't nurtured properly in the first two years, he will have a problem nurturing you and the kids.

I don't know that I was all that good as a mother. I've heard my boys talk and it isn't always sweetness and light. They may rise up and call me blessed, but they will sit down eventually and tell the rest of the story. How about you? Do you have regrets? Big ones? Well, just know that God has already provided forgiveness through Jesus and restoration through the work of the Holy Spirit. Come to Him and allow Jesus to heal your wounds and forgive every trespass against Him. Now that you have received, extend that same grace to your husband because he has regrets, too.

Do you see how knowing the beginning helps us deal with today?

I grew up in a nice middle class neighborhood where we lived next door to a widow and three children. We didn't see the mother very much because she worked to provide for the family. Patty Anne was a bit older than the rest of us and Petey, the older boy, was the age of most of the boys on the block. This was just after WWII when there were lots of new neighborhoods with families much the same age.

Buddy, the youngest, was a year older than me. He was a *MESS*! I don't know how old he was when his father died, but he sure lacked adult supervision. Patty Anne and Petey tried their best, but a little boy is a bit much for older kids to control all day, day after day, year in and year out. They were not mean to him, at least not to our knowledge, but Buddy sure thought they were.

Every once in a while, Buddy would "run away," at least until his mom got home. Sometimes he would be out in the snow without any shoes or jacket, refusing their pleas to come back in. We would try to get him to come in our house, but he wouldn't. He said he wasn't allowed to and that was true, but his mom would have understood. I really think he wanted to torment them with his victim-hood.

The mother didn't seem to be sympathetic to his plight. Probably because she figured he deserved what he got. I remember a grandmother being there once in a while, but I don't think she lived there. She would use the crook in her cane to bring us closer to her, probably to see us better. I now understand, but at the time it scared me to death. She never did it to me because I stayed away from her!

I don't remember ever being in their house in all the years we lived next to them. Evidently that was one of the rules ("no other kids can come in the house while I'm not here"), which was the rule at our house, because our mom worked, too. But, we evidently didn't go in when the mother was home, either. How different Buddy's childhood was to mine! We all moved off and married. Mom and Dad sold their home and moved to Florida. I never saw any of them after high school.

When my mother-in-law was dying at the age of 77, I stopped by to see her best friend, the mother of Lamar's best friends growing up. I assumed she knew Mary was sick, but thought it was strange that she hadn't been by the hospital. When I asked her if she knew Mary was in the hospital, she was shocked! No one had called her, and if they had, she couldn't have gone anyway because she didn't drive any more. I told her if she wanted to see Mary, I was on my way and she could go with me. She hurried and got ready. What a wonderful time we had. Mary was able to muster enough energy to enjoy the visit and talk about old times. Later, she said, "Well, that was the best surprise ever!" I was glad I made the effort.

We intended to go out after the visit but stayed so long she said, "Oh, I can't eat this late! I'll just have a little cereal when I get home." I told her I'd get something and take it to her house and we would eat together. That was fine with her. We sat and talked for a long time. She told me lots of things I didn't know about Lamar's childhood. It really helped me understand so much more about Lamar. I knew, but I didn't know. I didn't really appreciate how hard it had been for him. She filled in a lot of the blanks.

When I got home I didn't turn on the television but rather sat there in the darkened room pondering things. Lamar was out of town and I knew he would call soon. As I thought about it, all of a sudden the thought hit me, "I married Buddy Bohanan!" I laughed and cried simultaneously. To me that said everything!

I knew my husband had a hard time growing up. He was your typical snaky, mean little boy that got in trouble and was picked on all the time. I knew it and kept it in mind as I tried to work out our problems. But I never understood like I did at that moment when I understood his experience was a lot like Buddy Bohanan's. If I had known, I may not have married him! That sounds terrible, but it sure would have made me ponder the implications of such a marriage. I do think we should count the cost of these decisions. And if I did, I sure would have treated him a lot differently. Not that I would have let him get away with more, but I might have been more understanding, more patient. Though, heaven knows, I have the patience of Job. But maybe there was an edge on my patience that wouldn't have been there. Maybe the bitterness wouldn't have crept in knowing what had led him to be that way. But maybe I would have been too soft and that would have been worse!

One day Lamar's sister and I were talking having the best time. Nancy and I have a lot in common. We are both artistic, friendly, athletic (well, we used to be!), *raised with all boys*, etc. The list seems to be endless. So when we get together, we quickly get on the same wavelength. All of a sudden Lamar went ballistic. "Oh, my goodness! I married my sister!" he exclaimed in horror as the color drained from his face. Nancy and I really laughed at that! But for him it was a terrible revelation because Nancy had been his bothersome little sister all those years. I'm somebody's bothersome little sister, too! To Lamar, marrying Nancy was his worst nightmare, just as marrying Buddy would be to me! Think of how this is true in your marriage, for him as well as you. The ironies in life are endless!

For years, I assumed Lamar had a happy childhood because he told me he did. I knew there were problems when we were at his parents, but nothing big and nothing I could put my finger on. It takes years for these things to come out. I didn't understand something crucial in my own family until I was in my late 40s. How can you tell somebody if you don't know yourself? That's why a marriage needs a lifetime.

I like to think I am a nice person and that I'm not mean, but there is a place of steel in me, like that of my mother. Lamar has faced it a time or two. I don't pitch a fit or scream or cry. I would say I set my jaw, but it really isn't physical at all. It's mental—totally mental. I set my mental jaw. When I finally see and decide what has to be, all emotion leaves me. I may cry later and I may be hurt deeply, but there is a place in me, a time when emotion doesn't rule. As a Christian I know I have to be careful when and how I set my jaw. I pray about it and allow God to guide me through it. I must stay tender to Him through the whole process and use my toughness in love, mercy, and obedience.

God doesn't need us to be strong in ourselves. *"Therefore I take pleasure in infirmities, in reproaches, in necessities, in persecutions, in distresses for Christ's sake: for when I am weak, then am I strong"* (2 Cor. 12:10, KJV). This is Paul praying about a physical condition that plagued him.

When the Bible says we are weak, it means too weak to do things our way. That by trusting in Him and letting His strength be our strength, then we are really strong because we are allowing Him to be strong in us. God doesn't need us to be strong, because He is strength personified. However, He does need us to be steadfast in what He has said. And if that gets us in trouble, so be it. He will be with us in persecutions, too. He needs for us to be obedient. God wants to be your all in all. He's not worried about your inabilities. He is more concerned about your wavering, listening to others, and running off to do your own thing. God can make you the person He needs you to be. His problem is getting you to do what He needs you to do. We worry about what is happening to us, when we should be worried about who we are. When we become men and women of character and godliness, what happens to us will change. And it will change because He will be in it. Your fruit won't fall early; a drought won't come to your fields. Sounds good to me. Be a woman of the Word and God will be able to help you be what you need to be and do what you need to do.

Another good scripture is Psalm 147:10–11: "*He delighteth not in the strength of the horse: he taketh not pleasure in the legs of a man. The Lord taketh pleasure in them that fear him, in those that hope in his mercy.*" By "fear" it means scared into being to be obedient. We should fear God (respect Him) enough to do what He tells us to do because if we don't, He is someone to be feared. If you do right He will do right by you, more than right.

I didn't start out tough, but I ended up there. Luckily I had wonderful parents and didn't use this place in me until I married. Then instead of being ugly, I withdrew and became unresponsive. When I became a Christian all this changed. God replaced my heart of stone with a heart of flesh, and now I have a strength in me that keeps me obedient and helps me stand in adversity, but I am also able to show my feelings and be a responsive wife.

It's not that God wants weak people. He appreciates strength, but He wants it to be in response to what He says. He wants us to be "strong in the Lord." He wants people who are "humble," and by humble I mean someone who doesn't put their thoughts and opinions over His.

He wants us to be determined to stand, to be obedient in the face of great opposition. It's not wrong to be tough. It's wrong not to be under His control when we are tough. Jesus was not the softy He is portrayed to be. There was a place of steel in Him, too. It took Him to the Cross, just as mine must help me to take up my cross daily. I am grateful that I can control my emotions and guard my heart. But I am also grateful that I have a heart of flesh that has compassion for everyone, including the worst among us. That doesn't come from me, but from Him and for that I am eternally grateful.

Too many women are emotionally driven. Their emotions rule everything they do and this is wrong. That place of steel in us fights too often for things God never intended us to fight for, insisting on our way when we are wrong in what we are insisting on. This is our compulsion speaking. But Christians do not have the luxury of allowing their compulsions to reign. God will allow us to suffer loss as long as we do. When we are strong outside of the Lord, we just make things worse and get into a bigger mess. Yuck. Say it isn't so.

We must keep our emotions in check if we are going to serve God. Our spirit must rule. We must do what Jesus would do. One day a friend was talking about a difficult situation, and said she was anxious to see what God was going to do because it was in His hands. I didn't know that this was true. She very likely has been doing what emotionally feels good and not what tough love would tell her to do. In that case, it's not in His hands. She may verbally put it there, but if God sees her as being disobedient, it's still in her hands and won't be in His until she gets obedient.

> *Dear God, I do want to be one with my husband, although that seems almost impossible. Help me to be tender to You so I can know what You would have to do to make it so. Amen.*

How do you become "one"? You are "one." Commit to each other to do what it takes to love, help, and heal the other—for better or worse, for richer, for poorer, in sickness and in health, as long as you both shall live. Hang in there and hang on to God. And when you can hang on no longer, you will find He is hanging on to you. He will carry you through. At some point, you will realize everything has changed for the good.

You become truly one by sharing one spirit. For goodness sake, don't let it be the wrong one.

FIFTEEN

And they shall become one flesh.

—GENESIS 2:24

One Flesh

ONE FLESH. NOW THAT'S something since we are two people walking around. However, marriage was created for fellowship first, not sex, nor to produce an heir apparent. But don't tell this to the guys. They are really into the physical aspect. Think recreation, not procreation—someone to enjoy and have fun with as you walk through life together. Knowing this should help put things in perspective. Not that sex and children aren't important, but they are not the basis of marriage. I really think sex is part of our fellowship—a very special part. If the sex isn't good, the fellowship suffers for at least one of the partners. And if fellowship suffers for one, it should suffer for the other, but some people are so dense they don't even notice.

Since you hope to be together a long time, you will need more than flaming passion or children to carry you through. Other things start out more important than fellowship; things like sex, money, personality, looks, etc., probably because the teenage male has such high hormone levels. However, because fellowship was the primary reason for creating a partner, it remains long after other things have fallen by the wayside. Hopefully, as these things fall off, the couple will have gained a shared life experience that proves to be a stronger bond than anything else. Therefore, it's best if the couple share a great deal of their lives together. We are not supposed to live totally separate lives. A couple who does is missing the point of marriage— the beauty of the creation.

We must not minimize the family aspect, for surely if God commanded anything it was to multiply and be fruitful. It's out of this special relationship that we have kids; or rather, it's into this special relationship we should bring children. Why? To fulfill God's plan here on Earth. This is why it's important that we train them up in the way they should go. And why He hates divorce (not the divorced person, He loves them) because it jeopardizes His plan. If you want emotionally healthy kids, they need to see a healthy relationship between their parents.

SEX

The most exhilarating and potentially the most problematic aspect of marriage is our sexuality. It's a problem because we are in such a close relationship and there are so many things to work out and so many points of contention. We have to be intimate in the midst of it all. Boy, there's a challenge.

Most women would like to be made to feel like a princess by the wonderful prince they have chosen for their lifetime partner and hopefully he does that now and again. But we must not let it get in the way of our love-making when he doesn't. The truth is a man is not all that considerate or mature when we marry him (unless he is older and more mature). If you neglect to fulfill his physical needs, you just force him to get worse.

Sex relieves his mind a little and makes him appreciate you more. Well, maybe not, but at least he won't be quite so upset. A young man is upset and angry a lot because of so many things: mistreatment on the job, past abuse, their own mistakes, etc. I hate to say this, but he takes a lot of it out at home and that is where you are. He can't punch out the boss, so he verbally punches you. He won't always be like this, but you will never become one in other ways if you refuse to become one this way. I know it seems like he doesn't love you at times, but the fact that he married you means he has given you the best he has to offer: himself. I don't know why this no longer looks like such a good deal, but it must have at one time. This is no time to change your mind. A deal's a deal. And to a guy, sex is very much a part of the "deal."

It's really fraud on our part to act like we want sex before we get married and then like we don't after we get him hooked. Could it be we are more manipulative that we would like to admit? Men feel they have been duped, and this is not a good basis for a marriage. It's not unheard of for a man to "punish" his wife because she no longer "puts out" on a regular basis (by not coming home after work, etc.). Maybe we need to sustain what we started. Your body is not your own. "Who said?" God did.

> *Now about the questions you asked in your letter. Yes, it's good to live a celibate life. But because there is so much sexual immorality, each man should have his own wife, and each woman should have her own husband. The husband should not deprive his wife of sexual intimacy, which is her right as a married woman, nor should the wife deprive her husband. The wife gives authority over her body to her husband and the husband also gives authority over his body to his wife. So do not deprive each other of sexual relations. The only exception to this rule would be the agreement of both husband and wife to refrain from sexual intimacy for a limited time, so they can give themselves more completely to prayer. Afterward they should come together again so Satan won't be able to tempt them because of their lack of self control. This is my only suggestion. It's not meant to be an absolute rule. I wish every one could get along without marrying, just as I do. But we are not all the same. God gives some the gift of marriage, and to others he gives the gift of singleness.*
> —1 CORINTHIANS 7:1–7, NLT

Your body is God's, and now He's saying it's your husband's, too. That's a pretty powerful statement. God is the one that created sex, and He wants you to satisfy your husband sexually. The only exception is for a short period of time when you are seeking God in a special way. It's not acceptable to do this if your husband is not a Christian. He will only resent your "spirituality" and that is not acceptable. You cannot be too spiritually minded to be any earthly good, especially if he is not a

Christian. That's being a bad witness and it's not suitable. Your Christianity should be a plus in his life not a minus. Please don't use your religion as an excuse not to satisfy your husband's physical needs. God created sex and wants your husband to enjoy his sex life.

Few people harm their own body, at least not willfully, so it's assumed a man will take care of his wife's body as he would his own, because it's his. Too many of us take care of ourselves and treat our mate shabbily. This is unscriptural. Then there are those that treat themselves shabbily and their mate well. This won't happen if the couple is being scriptural. All the problems we have in our lives are because we are being unscriptural. It's just a matter of finding it and correcting it.

Our relationship deteriorated and our sex life deteriorated with it. I tried, but I was so hurt and angry at Lamar it was hard to respond. I said to him, "I'm so upset with you; it would be easier to make love with a stranger." And he agreed. It really would've been easier to be with someone who hadn't hurt me so much. But we can't because God insists we satisfy this area within the bonds of marriage. *"Drink water from your own cistern..."* (Prov. 5:15). Of course God wanted sexual intimacy without all the issues. That's why we have to deal with them.

There are physical changes that take place that we cannot prevent or anticipate. Having a baby changes your internal chemistry for a while. It changes your energy level and your emotional level, too. It did mine! And Lamar felt left out and didn't like the changes a baby brought to our relationship. I tried to bring him in, but he just stayed at work longer instead. He did love Grant and played with him, but when they are so tiny, they seem so fragile. I was so good at handling the babies, I didn't realize I needed to step back more and not nag him into doing more, but just things where I needed Lamar's help so he could get past that clumsy stage.

Speaking of physical changes, if you want to have a good physical relationship with your husband, and you should, then work on getting yourself in good shape physically. Eat those veggies, watch the sugar and fat intake, exercise, watch the stress, get enough sleep, etc., and you will be surprised what it does for your libido. But don't do it just for the sex, do it for your life in general. Your sex life can't be great if you're run down. And if your life is out of control in this area, it's probably because you are putting everyone and everything else first. You simply must begin to prioritize your needs for everyone's sake.

When I speak of "sex," I don't just mean the sexual act itself. Becoming one is more than sex; it's *intimacy*. I know most men seem to forget this, but they need intimacy, too. They may not know it but they do. Hugging and being hugged is a necessary part of life and especially needful in marriage. After I understood the truth about Lamar's childhood, it brought a lot of things into perspective. He didn't have a problem with sex, but he did intimacy. And I needed intimacy to enjoy sex.

Families in those days generally didn't hug as much as we do today. Some people have been so abused or neglected they don't like to be touched. We need to respect someone's space, but you can slowly, over time, get your husband used to more physical intimacy. In fact, touching and hugging are probably more important than the act itself, because without the affectionate touches, sex will never satisfy. It may relieve some pressure, like a donut crammed in your mouth temporarily satisfies your hunger, but in the long run, sex will never take the place of true love and affection that comes through loving caresses.

A couple should not just touch, hug, and caress each other. They should go so far as to give each other a good neck and back massage. I am shocked at how many women don't know how to give their man a good deep massage. I don't mean to hurt him, but to take her hands and massage deep enough to stimulate the nodes in the back to give up their toxins. Take his feet in her hands and work her fingers on them as he moans in ecstasy. Lamar has a vibrator that he likes me to use on his back. We all have aches and pains that only a massage will help. That's one of the many reasons God put us together, because we can't reach all the places we need to reach on our own.

For years Lamar didn't ask me if I was "interested," he just started massaging my back. I'm not naïve. I knew he was hoping it would go on into something more. I may not have been in the mood when it started, but I was too sore to resist. If he had asked me if I was interested, I would have said, "No way." I was too tired, too stiff, too lots of things. But I melted in his loving arms. I won't say we always did it, because he was tired, too, but at least the potential was there.

Another thing that needs to be included in the word "sex" is playfulness, a sense of wonder and exploration, an appreciation for the other person. It's really a shame when a couple doesn't appreciate the other and are locked into a marriage that requires such an intimate sexual act. I would suggest, even if you don't really like your husband or appreciate him, that you make it your job to get him to really love you and appreciate you. Be so special, so supportive, so positive, and so appreciative that he thinks you're the greatest. This will be a turn on sexually to him and that's not bad.

I have found that when I appreciated Lamar more and was more supportive and accepting, that he didn't need as much sex. Men need a lot of sex when they are unsure of themselves. It's the best way they have of feeling like a man, feeling worthy, and needed. If he gets fired from his job, or is having trouble in his other relationships, he needs sex to tell him he's still OK. He hasn't lost his touch. It's going to work out. When it does work out and he feels better, he doesn't need the sex to tell him any more. Then he just wants it because he wants it, not because he needs it.

Although I am talking about the whole relationship, I never want you to think that your relationship can exclude the actual act itself. We love the touch and hugging and the togetherness. It's all great. But it must go on to the natural culmination of your love, and that is the sexual act itself. To stop midway is to sabotage the plan. I'm not saying your hugging and touching and talking and laughing always has to end that way, but it should quite often, or often enough to be satisfying to both of you. And he shouldn't be pressured into saying it's OK when it isn't, when he really doesn't mean it. Since we are a receptor, it really isn't that hard to receive. He's the one that has to "perform." And we should receive in a way that makes it special for him. Just as God doesn't want us to tithe grudgingly, He doesn't want us to do this grudgingly.

If he is the one that doesn't want to go all the way, something is wrong and should not be ignored. Some women are kind of glad this is true because she doesn't want it. But you are choosing to keep your man dysfunctional and that is not good and not loving. He needs healing and you need to figure out what's wrong, not necessarily to nag him about it, but just pray about it and see how God reveals it to you.

The sex act is about as intimate as some men want to get right now, even the ones that don't act like it is. They often act that way because they are afraid of being rejected or not measuring up. If you act like you aren't interested that just confirms what he has been thinking all along. Many women like it when their husbands don't want it very much, but that is a trap. Those are the men that are found at their computers doing what their wives don't want them to do. And there are wives that have even begged for more sex and he has refused only to sneak away and satisfy himself in some other way. It's very important if this happens that you work through it. Hopefully he's sorry and he does want to resolve the problem. It doesn't make sense and supports the fact that sex is more than sex. When things don't add up, that's a sign you need some help to find out why. A man needs a neutral party he trusts to tell his secrets to. You cannot always stand the truth. It's too painful. This is when a counselor is helpful.

A man needs a safe place to be vulnerable. If he knows you will go and tell everyone or anyone, he will not talk. When Lamar and I were having problems I didn't discuss them with even my closest friends for their sake as much as ours. It's a burden to know these things. I don't want them to think about it when they are with Lamar and me. My mother always warned me that I would get over it and my friends wouldn't. However, if things are really bad, you do need to confide in someone mature and helpful and who won't talk.

Women tend to equate intimacy with talking, sharing. Men don't. Just being together is enough. It takes time for her to pick up on the unspoken communication and appreciate the silent intimacy and for him to see her need for him to express himself verbally. Men have learned to stifle their emotions and aren't really interested in learning how to express them. It's just too private. This is why trust is necessary, coming to trust you with his innermost thoughts. If you respond improperly to what he says and does, you shut him down emotionally toward you. He will still be able to have sex, but he will not be able to emotionally relate with you and thereby not fulfill you so you can be turned on sexually. Therefore, you hold the key to your own sexuality more than you realize. Making fun of him, embarrassing him, telling him how dumb an idea was, are all things that can ruin your sex life.

If it's a problem (one person not wanting much physical togetherness), it might be good to sit down and discuss it, pointing out that everyone has needs and somehow you as a couple need to meet both of your needs. But before you sit down to talk, you both really need to see a doctor to be sure there isn't a physical problem. I wouldn't talk too long without professional help because the truth is, some things can't be talked out or toughed out. Sometimes it's bigger than both of you and there are answers. I have heard of women having this problem, too, so just reverse it if it's you with the problem receiving physical touching.

Due Benevolence

Let the husband render unto the wife due benevolence.
—1 Corinthians 7:3

Years ago Lamar was grumpy and difficult much of the time, even though he was a Christian. Knowing he was going to want "some" later, it really irritated me that he was acting so badly and then was going to expect me to be receptive. He needed to be realistic. This had been going on for years and I was tired of it. I decided to face it straight on. The scripture about rendering due benevolence came to mind, but I didn't even know what that meant. He had been a Christian for years and I figured he should know, but if I didn't, I figured he wouldn't either. It didn't matter; I figured it had to be better than what I was getting.

I asked him if he knew what due benevolence was and he admitted that he didn't. I told him, "If you are going to expect me to be in the mood later tonight, you had better figure out what it is if you are supposed to be rendering it to me." He just sat there unconcerned, so I rendered an ultimatum, "Don't come around at 11 if you haven't rendered due benevolence by 9!" He knew I was serious and laughed. It worked! He did sweeten his attitude. If it was going to make the difference, he could make the effort. The funny thing is, once he started doing it every once in a while, and because he was never quite sure if tonight might not be the night, he had to start acting better every night. Pretty soon it became a way of life. How sweet it is.

I hadn't actually gone to the Bible and read it. I was just repeating what I had heard, which is not a good idea. If I had gone to the Bible, I would have seen that wasn't the end of the admonition. What I didn't read was: *"and the wife unto the husband."* If Lamar had been reading his Bible at the time, he would have known this. See how we lose when we don't do our homework.

My exegeses uses the word *wellmindedness* for *benevolence*: "*The man is indebted to give back to the woman wellmindedness* [Don't you love it? That fits right in with being an emotional sexual being. Note it says indebted to give back. I like that—indebted to give back. I guess we need to be sure we have already given what he needs in order to receive back.] *and the wife should do the same for her husband; for a girl who marries no longer has full right to her own body, for her husband then has his rights to it, too; and in the same way the husband no longer has full right to his own body, for it belongs also to his wife. So do not refuse these rights to each other. The only exception to this rule would be the agreement* [exegeses: 'by sympathizing'; isn't that a nice term for agreement?] *of both husband and wife to refrain from the rights of marriage for a limited time, so that they can give themselves more completely to prayer.* [Note this is a mutual agreement.] *Afterwards, they should come together again so Satan won't be able to tempt them because of their lack of self-control*" (1 Cor. 7:3–5).

No Excuse Is Good Enough—Well, Almost None

It's very common for a woman not to be satisfied by her partner sexually. It's much more difficult than we thought to have a "normal" sex life. There's a happy thought. You just know the devil had a hand in that. There are many reasons for a man to be way out ahead of us. It's not his fault he thinks about it so much. It's hormonal, just as we are hormonal in other ways. It's a wonder they are able to do anything else. Actually, they learn in their teen years to do two things at once: think about sex and do everything else.

Women on the other hand have many interests, the least of which is sex. I have found many of the women who act like they are into sex are actually putting on a front to attract the guys and aren't as into it as they make out. It's a power thing or a self-image thing. I do think sex can be a compulsion or addiction just like alcohol or cigarettes and some women are hooked. I know it makes the guys happy, but it doesn't make for a good marriage because other issues make things unbearable. Men think they would love to be married to a nymphomaniac, but the truth is if he was, he wouldn't satisfy her. Even if he did, he'd be paranoid wondering if she was looking elsewhere.

There are many things that affect a person's libido, and if we are having problems working up a desire, we need to look into them: medications, physical health, emotion health, spiritual health, problems from the past, etc. And let's face it; these guys can get pretty repulsive.

You probably think things will always be as they are, but that's not true. Your physical relationship changes just like everything else. Now that Lamar and I are older, we have new challenges to our sex life: diabetes, cancer, hormones, and so on. So we keep finding new answers to our challenges. Lamar appreciates that I care and am willing to stick in there as we work it out.

Soul Ties

What? Know ye not that he which is joined to an harlot is one body? For two, saith he, shall be one flesh, But he that is joined unto the Lord is one spirit.

—1 Corinthians 6:16

God created us to be one in marriage. Sex is an important part of this oneness. It creates what we call a soul tie. Because of this the Bible warns us not to join ourselves to a prostitute. If the two people remain two separate beings and yet become one, it must be something other than physical. It's mental and emotional, too. Even the most fleeting of sexual encounters register in your soul, your mind, and emotions. Sex brings with it a soul tie, and God wants that bond between a man and a woman in a covenant relationship.

If a relationship is godly, it's based on godly principles: giving not taking, loving not lusting, patience not impatience, edifying not tearing down, etc. A relationship that becomes sexual in nature before marriage is based on evil intent: selfishness, lust, taking rather than giving, risking another's health and well-being. We don't think in these terms, but God does. I understand we get involved when we are ignorant, but that doesn't change the results. That's why God wrote the rules on our hearts. Being a heathen doesn't excuse anyone.

I don't want you to think improper soul ties come about only through improper sexual relationships. Any relationship can develop a soul tie, good or bad. But sexual relationships always do because of their intimacy. And they are always bad if they are outside the bounds of the marriage covenant. And this means a proper marriage. Not just any marriage ceremony is acceptable. You may be married, but if it didn't happen in the proper way, then there is or was a problem. And let me say, this is not unusual. It's just that at some point we need to get our head on straight and realize how far off base we are and get back. We need to look at our lives in a whole new light and pray and continue to pray as God deals with the rat's nest we call our lives and let Him go into ALL the rooms and clean out those rats nests, too. Parents, relatives, and friends all have some type of tie with us and we need to make them right. Forgive, repent, and set up proper boundaries as you come to see the changes that need to be made in your life. No, you don't need another wedding ceremony, but you do need to do the spiritual work.

More and more people today are beginning marriage having had multiple partners, bringing into marriage sexual brokenness and soul ties that need to be properly dealt with. The problem is further complicated when they don't even recognize the problem, leaving it to continue to fester. Don't take my word for it. First Corinthians 6:13–20 of the Living Bible says:

> But sexual sin is never right: our bodies were not made for that, but for the Lord, and the Lord wants to fill our bodies with himself. And God is going to raise our bodies from the dead by his power just as he raised up the Lord Jesus Christ. Don't you realize that our bodies are actually parts and member of Christ? So should I take part of Christ and join him to a prostitute? Never. And don't you know that if a man joins himself to a prostitute she becomes a part of him and he becomes a part of her? For God tells us in the Scripture that in his sight the two become one person. But if you give yourself to the Lord, you and Christ are joined together as one person. That is why I say to run from sex sin. No other sin affects the body as this one does. When you sin this sin it is against your own body. Haven't you yet learned that your body is the home of the Holy Spirit God gave you, and that he lives within you? Your own body does not belong to you. For God has bought you with a great price. So use every part of your body to give glory back to God, because he owns it.

The scripture then talks about whether they should marry or remain single.

Where does that leave the pro-abortion Christians when they say her body is her own? They are being unscriptural and yet we have never called them on it in spite of the fact 80 percent of America claims to be Christian. Surely, if the scripture was pointed out, it would have an impact. Evidently we aren't in the Word enough to have even the most obvious points revealed to us. That is what is so amazing.

"No other sin affects the body as this does." There it is, right there in black and white put there by God, not me.

Because right and wrong are written on our hearts, there is a place in a woman that knows she should not have done what she did. She also knows he shouldn't have asked it of her, especially if they were truly in love. The very one that should have protected her exposed her to sin. And she's right. She is secretly upset with him and herself for going along with it. And in his heart, he knows he shouldn't have asked it and she shouldn't have gone along with it. Now don't get me wrong, we *never* admit it because we don't let ourselves go there. We think about everything but that. "We were young and dumb and didn't know any better." But somewhere in the deep recesses of our soul, we know the truth. The truth sets us free, but not if we don't face it. Sin has been swept under the rug, but somewhere in your spirit man where the candle of the Lord illuminates, it's there. I am just putting into words what I believe the Lord would say. Get it out and look at it. Admit it and be done with it. Until you have done this, you will never really be done with it.

"But Midge, I put all that 'under the blood' when I got saved," and that's true. We are forgiven for all of our sins when we are saved. Only what is placed at the foot of the cross is truly forgiven. Being a Christian means a growing awareness of sin. Yes, we are saved, but we at some point need to face the truth and see what our sin meant to our lives and the lives of others. It's not that we are digging things up as much as we are finally laying them to rest.

Allow me to share one of my big revelations. When I was saved, because of the emotional shape I was in from the loss of my little girl, I was not greatly convicted of my sin. The prayer included sin, but it didn't really mean that much to me. Two or three years later I was on my bed one afternoon pondering things (assuming my Best Friend was there with me). I always hated the thought of Jesus dying on the cross. "Lord, why couldn't I pay for my sins," I asked, wishing that He could have been spared all that suffering." "You could; it's called eternal death." Of course! That was the only other option. It hit me like a ton of bricks. I finally realized the true seriousness of my sin and I needed to. I needed to see things properly, and God, in His mercy, took His time to show it to me, until I was ready. Now you may be ready to see things in your past more realistically, as He sees them, and then you must proceed as He takes you through repentance and restoration to healing.

The best way to tell if you have already done it is if you testify of it. The Bible says we are saved by the blood of the Lamb *and* the word of our testimony. If you can't look at your past and won't talk about the sins of the past, then they are still there waiting for the day you do allow the light to be shown on them and for Him to help you face them, repent of your part in them, and then put them away forever. Don't ever think your testimony about every part of your life is not a necessary part of your new life. It's the only way the truth no longer hurts us.

One day Lamar and I were talking about the messes people get into because of being sexually active before marriage. I admitted that we fell into that trap, too, and Lamar agreed. I went on to share what God had shown me, that we needed to repent and apologize to each other, and he agreed. I told him I was sorry that I didn't maintain my part and he said he was sorry he didn't do his. It was a special moment. No biggy, but it really was. It was needed.

IMPOTENCE: HIS AND HERS

If a marriage goes on long enough, it will almost always have impotence problems, and I don't mean just the guy. Either sex can experience the inability to perform sexually. The reason this term is used so often for the male's dysfunction is because it means without strength or vigor or power. Since a woman is on the receiving side she is not considered impotent, but that's not true. I don't know that either is easier to correct, and we should not assume the woman's is not just as devastating.

I just happened upon a Dr. Laura radio program coming from choir one night. Once in a while I feel she misses it, but not usually. A woman called in that had gotten married a few weeks earlier. She and her husband both were virgins and looking forward to their honeymoon when they could have this wonderful consummation of the marriage. This woman even checked with a doctor to be sure her hymen was still intact, which is a shame because it's not uncommon for a girl, by the time she is married, to no longer have it intact. Sports and other things can rupture it without her ever knowing.

Going to all this trouble indicates to me there was a trust issue on somebody's part. Since this girl went to all this trouble, she should have had the doctor break it while she was there because I have known of the first time being a problem. Which it was. She was impenetrable. Of course it ruined their honeymoon. She came home and saw the doctor again and had to have surgery. Now she has stitches and still can't have sex. Talk about a nightmare.

Well, somewhere in it all, she has decided sex is not her thing. She will satisfy him, but she's really not into it. How noble! Don't you know that will get her a big jewel in her crown? Dr. Laura said the woman was punishing her husband because her fantasy was ruined. Dr. Laura insisted she was like a child having a tantrum. And she was right. "You have to allow him to give you pleasure."

Men love the female body and when a man marries a woman, he loves her body the most. He is thrilled that he can now share this wonderful thing he has fantasized about for so long with the person he loves and desires the most in the world. Even if he has had sex with others, he wants it most with someone he loves: you. You are the object of his affection, and he wants to actually feel his love in a physical way. And he wants and needs to know he is satisfying you and that you find him sexually appealing. This is a big way of satisfying his ego. It's the way God meant it to be.

If your husband has problems, he needs to know you will cooperate with whatever solution he or the doctors come up with (within reason, of course). They do have some great new solutions, but they may be a bit embarrassing if not met with your approval. If this aspect of your life together is over, you need to assure him that's OK. He needs to know you find him exciting and virile even if you are no longer sexually active. The stroking never ends, nor does our need for it. However, don't be too quick to take him at his word. Some men say it but don't mean it. They say it because they are having problems and feel they can't do it. Encourage him to go to the doctor. Very likely he is being premature. Be there for him during this most difficult time, and I can guarantee you will have a whole new husband. He will love you like you have never been loved before and I don't mean sexually.

> *Dear God, help me to fulfill, not only my husband's needs but mine. I just want to run away when he indicates he's "interested." I know this isn't right, but I feel he is as much or more of the problem than I am. How do I get him to change? To understand? He seems so selfish and so dense to my needs. I need someone to cherish me and love me in a way that makes me desire him. We're evidently both dysfunctional, but he doesn't seem that way. He seems so confident. How can it be that he is really needy? Help me to love him like You want and need me to. I need Your help to do this. Forgive me for my part in our problems. I really didn't mean to hurt him or me. I pray this in the precious name of Jesus.*

You know how Dr. Laura ends her segments with "Now, go and do the right thing"? That's what I would say to you.

SIXTEEN

...because thou has harkened to the voice of your wife...

—GENESIS 3:17

Why, God? Why?

BOY, THINGS SURE HAVE changed since the Fall. Maybe that's why men are so stubborn about doing what we want them to do. We get so frustrated because our men won't do what they are supposed to do. Even though they love us, they so often won't commit to marriage. Then, once married, they put off having a family. He doesn't work and provide like he should, doesn't keep the car in good condition, etc. It can get so frustrating.

God kept taking me back to Adam and Eve to help me understand our basic problem, so I'm going to take you there, too. Everything changes and nothing changes. Consider what happened in Genesis 3. The serpent came calling, and he and Eve got in a conversation and she tried to answer his question. Why? Because Adam didn't try. Isn't it typical for a woman to jump in when the man isn't doing his job? Yes, it is. And isn't it just as typical for the man not to answer when someone is talking to him. This scripture is not saying the man cannot listen to his wife. God simply has a problem when a man takes the word of his wife over what He has already said.

SIN #1 AND SIN #2

When God created Adam and Eve, He called each one to a different role or position—to do something different. Because their callings were different, their responsibility was different. Therefore, what would be considered sin for each would be different. The sin nature of a leader is to shirk responsibility that is rightfully his (Sin #1), and the sin nature of a follower is to take on responsibility that is not theirs (Sin #2). In the marriage relationship you see the result of this in the form of Deadbeat Dads and Super Moms. Why do you think they are so prevalent? Because it's in our sin nature. Don't you think it is kind of funny there are so few Super Dads and Deadbeat Moms? That's because men and women have different callings and our fleshly nature will be to not do what we are called to do.

Adam, in the position of leader, was responsible as the leader. He was the one God told personally not to eat of one specific tree (Genesis 2:16). It was his job to see that she didn't take that bite. Why didn't he knock the fruit out of her hand? Because he was wondering the same thing she was. When he allowed Eve to get into the debate with the serpent, it was because he didn't want to be the one to do it, but he was curious, too. Yielding to Eve, he no doubt surmised would take the responsibility off him and yet enable him to find out about this one special, forbidden, fruit. When nothing happened to Eve after she took the bite, I guess he figured it was safe. Just because nothing apparent happens doesn't mean we are safe. The day of reckoning finally arrives, for some a lot later than others.

Super Moms think they are better than Deadbeat Dads because they are working so hard and taking on his burden, but sin is sin whenever a person is "missing the mark" and not doing what they are supposed to do. When the man isn't doing his part, it puts the woman in a terrible position, but we can't assume we should be the one to take over. Eve did them no favors! She should have dealt with Adam first, and if that didn't work then taken her concerns to God, not entertained the serpent.

Adam should have put the serpent in his place and sent him packing. As far as I'm concerned, Eve was not the first to sin. Adam was. Well, it maybe wasn't an actual sin yet because no words had been spoken nor action taken, but it was the beginning of their sin. Since God sees the inner man, He knew. He also knew there was no need to judge him then because thought becomes action. Their initial failure was in their hearts and minds, not in their actions. Adam had stepped out of his place, leaving a void, which Eve jumped in to fill. Sins of omission are as bad as sins of commission.

MONEY IS NOT THE OBJECT

One day when I was in a huge financial mess, up in my spirit came, "Money is not the object." I countered, "Money *is* the object," because I thought money would solve my problems. God was saying my problems were bigger than money and I needed to figure out what they were. That was the beginning of a long process to figure out all the many ways we were getting it wrong. Much of the victory in my life came as I answered the question of what the real "object" is.

There is a dichotomy (double-mindedness) in most families. On one hand the woman wants to stay home and take care of her family, but on the other, she feels the pressure to help out because things are so tough and things are so tough because of the premise that set them up for failure (helping God—works instead of obedience and anointing). This premise is opposed to what God intended for the family. In other words, it's sin. Societies around the world are established on what men decide they should do, not what God says they should do.

That is not to say career women can't tackle motherhood successfully. We have a lot more doing both and doing them well. Society right- fully expects the husband to help more, and the grandparents, and the community. Because so many women are in the work force and because divorce is so prevalent, women are now approaching things differently and making career choices that take them out of the home permanently. They don't expect to be a stay-at-home mom. That doesn't mean women have changed all that much; it just takes them longer to realize their true nature. It's a big surprise to her when the baby comes along and she is all prepared to go back to work only to find the baby has recomputed her brain. Many career women find a new career as mommy.

To the women who want to have a career, I need to say: God doesn't mean for a woman to be only a stay-at-home-mom. If you read Proverbs

31, you see a godly woman very much a force in her community. You are not off base to want to be out there where the action is. You are just off base to do it in a way that leaves your children open to improper care and nurturing. Proverbs 29:15 says, *"Children left to themselves are a shame to the mother."* Why the mother? Because if it's her place she has abandoned, it's her that takes the shame of it. The father carries his responsibility, too, and shame comes to him for letting his family down in other ways.

So, what are we, as mothers and wives, to do? Mothers used to be able to stay home and American women were in the community through volunteerism. Everything changed during World War II and needs were so great after the war that women wanted to stay in the workforce. Actually, things changed because of the war. My mom was one of the ones that stayed in the workforce. The truth is my dad could have moved up in the company if he had wanted, but he didn't because he wanted and needed to be home during the day when Mom was at work. I really believe Dad could've made up for her salary and she could have entered the work force later when we were older. But I'm not sorry I had those years with Dad. It's not so much whether a woman works, but is it good for the family?

A woman can work out the problems and make the best of it; my mother did. But in my experience it's too often not done properly and the kids and the marriage suffers.

I don't want to give the impression that working mothers cannot do it successfully and for some women it might be the better choice. I now believe it was the better choice for my mother and our family, but I didn't at the time because it put so much of the burden on me. I had to wash the breakfast and lunch dishes when I got home from school. Dad would cook breakfast and lunch, but wouldn't wash dishes. It was a man thing. When I was old enough, I made supper three nights a week. I did a lot of the cleaning and ironing, a lot more than any of my friends. I guess that's why I am so against mothers working. Because I know how hard it was on me. But I lived and it probably made me a better person. I'm very responsible and independent, both very good traits. However, not every family can do what we did. My parents were very exceptional people.

In watching *Nanny 911* and *Swapping Wives*, I have come to see that many stay-at-home moms are not making it work for their kids, either. So, let's not put it all on the working mothers. These mothers are not using good parenting techniques. They don't schedule their days for work and play. It seems like mothers either let the kids strew their toys everywhere and give them way too much or they are too controlling and keep the house too neat. The fathers in either case are at a total loss. They love their wives and children, but have no clue how to get a handle on the problems. So, they just opt out. I don't know how many families had one of the parents that was absolutely emotionally shut-down; the last thing they needed.

If you have had a burden that working isn't for you, that doesn't necessarily mean you can quit immediately, but it can be a goal. I do believe we need to get our debts paid down. It's impossible to pay them off if you just pay the minimum balance each month. The problem when we are working is we make different choices because we do have the money. Just be sure you stop picking up food on the way home, getting a new car and a business wardrobe, etc. Stop spending so much and put that money on your bills so you can quit working and not be stressed about it.

Working part time may be an answer. I just feel if you are willing and doing the right things, like tithing, God will help you get better answers. However, I wouldn't assume God wants you to be a stay-at-home mom right now. There are some times it's not feasible and counter-productive. Going down the tubes financially is not a good testimony for a Christian and not good for the kids, either.

You may see yourself as an innocent victim of the system, or maybe your husband's foolishness, and by man's standards you may be; but you may have not listened to the warnings God sent. He was probably left out of the process and that's why you and your family are in a mess now. It may have been your parents that left God out and never taught you any different. It doesn't matter why He was left out, the consequences are the same. It's incumbent upon you to repent for your part in it, so you stand clean before the Lord, so He can finally start to solve the problems all this doing things your way has brought on.

It's terrible when we have to swim against the current, but sometimes we have to. Jesus did. That is why we have to study and learn, because the pressures are so great against us.

FINANCES

We need to get our own answers. Let's stop doing things because everyone else is doing it. The proof is in the pudding with the break-up of the American family.

Once sin is imbedded in the culture, it's almost impossible to get it out.

If obedience to God brings blessings that chase us down and overtake us, then conversely disobedience brings poverty and sorrow. What kind of disobedience? Let's be specific: (1) Not getting our relationships right. This includes our children. (2) Seeking other gods (putting people or things before God). How you can tell what it is: ask yourself what pulls you out of church? If it's not a reason Jesus would use, then it's something you shouldn't use either. You have put it before God and it has become a god. Things such as cooking, cleaning, some sicknesses (Church is a place to get healed, but sometimes we're too sick to go. Do you have someone anoint you with oil and pray for you like the Bible tells you to do?), and children. Yes, children can come before God. (3) Not tithing.

I believe in prosperity, and yes, that includes monetary prosperity, but Lamar and I always seemed to be at odds over money. I just wanted a good life, but Lamar wanted more. Getting more entails quite a bit of work and Daddy, and maybe even Mommy, to be away from home a lot. I didn't want that for my family. Since we struggled to make ends meet for years, it was a good thing that I wasn't dissatisfied. I just wished Lamar was more satisfied—and home more. It seems hard to believe, but I found it harder to be comfortable with money than I was with poverty. God had to show me that it was scriptural to have a lot of money. Once I got passed that, it was just a matter of being a good steward. I'm allowed to keep some of what goes through my hands for myself. God wants to bless me, too, not just others through me.

God let me know I shouldn't pray for prosperity because "the prosperity of the fool will destroy him." He then told me to put the things of life on a grid: things like taking good care of your kids, keeping your car up, paying your bills on time, etc.—all areas of life. Then He said to make two columns: one "yes" and one "no." The yes meaning you do feed your kids nutritious meals and no meaning you don't. The yes stands for being wise and the no stands for being foolish. Now go down the list and check off yes or no—wise or foolish. As I looked at the list, I saw I had quite a few foolish check marks. If the prosperity of the fool will destroy him, that's why my loving heavenly Father told me not to pray for prosperity. I needed to pray that my check marks get moved over.

I wasn't the best housekeeper. I had to get that dealt with. There is a spirit of poverty and bad housekeeping. I didn't have the spirit of filth, thank goodness, but some people have it. Procrastination and stinginess were a problem. I did have a problem putting money out on needed supplies and storage containers, etc. You can't have a neat house with no decent furniture or plans for storage. You have to learn to say no to some things and give up mementoes that crowd out your life. You can't keep everything to the detriment of your life today and your husband and kids. It's just not right. To live in such chaos is a form of child and husband abuse. It's not right to ask family members to live like this. We need to repent and ask for help and cooperate as they pry the stuff from our hands. Pick out a few items and then let them do the rest. If we try to do it, it won't get done. It's too painful.

If you want prosperity, be sure you are wise. Or, out of love, God won't give it to you. It's really sad when we can't be trusted to prosper.

THE TITHE

This may seem like a strange time to talk about tithing, when we are talking about the first two sins. That is until we realize Sin #3, Cain's sin, began as an "offering" issue. Since we no longer raise sheep, we bring a tenth of our increase. Tithing is foundational to your family's prosperity. Other than prayer, tithing is the first way a child can begin to participate as a Christian. When the teen or young adult moves out on their own, it's a stretch to tithe—a challenge to their faith. It's so tempting to say, "I can't do it," and because they don't do it, their finances seem to prove their decision to be the right one because there is no blessing of God or intervention on their behalf. And there won't be until they start tithing. It is a self-fulfilling prophesy, but if they will do it, it will undergird their faith.

We will never mature as Christians if we don't begin to tithe. Couples that don't tithe don't learn the faithfulness of God and how much He will come through for them in a pinch. When a real emergency rocks their life, because they haven't tithed and haven't seen that God can be trusted, they don't have the faith they need to carry them through. They may be healed by the doctors and the prayers of others, but they're still living on a grace level and not on the faith level they should be.

When things were at its worse, I posted a 3 John 2 (KJV) scripture on the inside wall of our house, *"Beloved, I wish above all things that thou mayest prosper and be in health, even as thy soul prospereth."* I put it there so I would be reminded to stand on it. After it was up there a while and things only got worse inside, I heard, "If you'd take that down, you'd be a lot better off." I knew it wasn't God. I said with every fiber of my being, "Satan, if the whole house falls down around me, that sign will stay on that wall." And it did stay and we did eventually come out of it. It was a wonderful walk, with many lessons I wouldn't trade for the world. It has made me the Christian I am today. These things we go through just make us stronger. It reminds me of the twenty-third Psalm, "Though I walk through the valley of the shadow of death I will fear no evil..."

Learn to enjoy the simple things in life and you will enjoy life a whole lot more. Be thankful for the simple things and God will give you a whole lot more. Teach your kids to appreciate them and they will enjoy life a whole lot more, too. Keep them away from the garbage so their appetites won't be tainted by the time they go to school. And fight to keep the schools untainted. It's a war-zone out there.

Families are not in a financial crunch just because of the system we have created in America or because of bad choices. We are in the crunch because we have the mentality that created the system and makes these choices. We need to go all the way to the root and deal with those things. We are frustrated and unfulfilled because our wants and desires are wrong, and they are wrong because our source is wrong. Just as Jesus said, He will give us a drink whereby we will never thirst again (John 4:13–14). Then why are we still thirsty? Simple, we've stopped drinking and have kept the mindset that created the financial crunch. Let me just list some of them:

1. That things will make us happy.
2. That we have to provide for ourselves.
3. That the answer is in us.
4. That we should be in control.
5. That we should take over.
6. That others are to blame.
7. That our husband is the problem.
8. That things will never change.
9. That we can solve our own problems.
10. That we deserve what we get.
11. That we didn't deserve what we got.
12. That God doesn't care.
13. That God will do it for others but not me/you.

I really think we should ponder this list a minute.

I don't want to put you under condemnation. That's the last thing you need. But you do need to begin to be scrupulously honest. Ask yourself: Do I have a gleaner's mentality? Do I have a hidden agenda like laziness? A victim mentality? Gluttony? Another compulsion? Am I playing games? There is something not adding up. What is the missing item? You would search high and low for a lost diamond, why not search high and low for what is defeating you. It's a cop-out to say it's God holding up our blessing. He wants to bless us, but out of love He won't until it's right. I know that was true in our life.

Bad finances are awful, but bad health is worse and bad family relationships are even worse than that. Actually, bad finances are the best mode of chastisement. I once told Lamar, "I do feel we will get the victory in our finances, but I want to learn the lessons now, because I sure don't want health or family problems." And we did get the victory in our finances. And we have had health and family problems. That's life and we have gotten and are getting the victory in those too. I've had cancer twice. Lamar had his gall bladder and thyroid removed. Matt had to have a kidney transplant. We aren't commanded not to have problems, only to get the victory.

> *Oh God, I know my thinking is all messed up. Help me to know what my spirit is telling me. My flesh has dominated me for so long, I don't know how to do that. Give me a hunger for the Word and the things of God. Send mentors, Christians fathers, and mothers my way so I can learn of You. I give You permission to speak into my life and adjust my steps. I pray all this in the precious name of Jesus. Amen.*

Since I brought it up, I should probably give the suggestions for getting out of debt:

1. Figure out how much you owe. There's a concept.
2. Run the numbers. Where are you spending your money? Keep up with your purchases and check your credit card bills. They will tell you most of what you need to know. One woman sent her family to school or work and then headed out for the mall every day. No wonder she owed so much. If

you can't afford to spend, you can't afford to shop. If I can't spend, I don't want to shop. Lamar will tell you that I shut down things if we couldn't afford them. I even shut off the cable. That really gets their attention.

3. Figure out how much interest you are paying and late payment charges. Pay off the high interest ones as soon as possible.

4. Try to get better rates. Call the credit card companies and negotiate.

5. Get a plan for paying them off. Use the low interest rate cards and pay off the high or even switch the balances to a low card. But remember, sometimes the new charges are at a higher rate. Know the rules of the game and play by them because if you don't, they will sock it to you.

6. Be blessable. Don't have sin in your life, such as bitterness, unforgiveness, laziness, gluttony, jealousy, etc.

7. Enjoy the freebies in life. There is no reason we can't enjoy each other and nature rather than things that cost a lot.

8. Watch your food bills. Change from highly processed foods to doing your own cooking and you will see a big difference. Get the kids involved. They can pack their lunches with supervision. Make your own snack packs. Stop dining out as much if this is a problem, too.

9. Volunteer and bless someone else. Nothing like seeing someone less fortunate to help put a perspective on your problems.

10. Speak positively, think positively and bind the devil.

Recently a friend paid off $22,000 of credit card debt with a portion of her inheritance. Most of it was buying things she didn't need and eating out all the time. Since she is renting, wouldn't it have been nice to pay $22,000 on a home and some new furniture? Some people can afford to eat out, but maybe we should be more frugal and give more to spread the gospel. Just because we have the money doesn't mean we have a right not to be a good steward with it. We don't need all the clothes and stuff we are buying. Use what you have. We are supposed to be consumers, not just buyers.

> We are the first nation in the history of the world to go to the poorhouse in an automobile.[1]
>
> —WILL ROGERS

Keep on keeping on, getting better as you go. Pay your tithes. Weed out problem areas. Do your best. Be obedient and you can't help but be blessed. The Bible says the blessings of the Lord chase us down and overtake us. We don't have to buy lottery tickets.

THE MISFITS

The Misfits, starring Clark Gable and Marilyn Monroe, is so powerful, it could be included anywhere. The Marilyn Monroe character, Roslyn, is the sweetest, prettiest thing around, and the guys all go ga-ga for her. Clarke Gable's character, Gay, tells her it's an honor just to sit next to her. He's in town for the rodeo. She came to get a divorce and befriends Isabelle, an older lady. They pick up another guy, Guido, and Gay talks Roslyn into staying in town. All four of them end up running around together.

Roslyn has never been in the country and loves Nevada's wide-open spaces. She's amazed and so appreciative of life, in spite of a deep sadness because of what life has brought her so far. I guess you could call her the eternal optimist.

She's been raised with both parents running off all the time and nobody caring about her. Somehow she knows this isn't right and that a family should love each other and stay together for life. It really strikes her how much Gay cares for her. He's so kind. There is no sex between them, just one kiss that he finally just has to steal. She doesn't think she feels this way for him, so he doesn't push it.

Perse, another friend, at one point asks, "Who do you depend on?" because his mother has betrayed him with his step-father. She answers, "Maybe all you have is the next thing...Maybe we aren't supposed to remember the promises." Earlier she says, "Maybe it's our fault if we trust them." Can't you just hear the hurt child in her? She's such a contradiction. So childlike and yet too old for her years.

It's as if she can't contain her questions anymore. Her inability to accept the unfairness and her desire for some answers just spew out of her as she attempts to make them palatable. She doesn't care anymore. She's tired of being what everyone wants her to be. She is so open for anything that will answer the gaping hole in her head, heart, and spirit. At one point, when they come back to Guido's house all drunk but her, she helps them and covers them up and then leans against the house, lifts her eyes and face to the heavens, and says, "Help." That small gesture shows that, in spite of it all, she believes in a God that hears, even though she has no reason to—yet. (I believe anyone who searches so honestly will find Him.)

Guido, Gay, and Perse decide to go mustanging. That's where the movie gets its name. At one point Gay calls the horses a bunch of misfits—not like what they used to catch. (Look whose calling who a bunch of misfits!) We all assume the horses will be sold to ranches but find out, along with Roslyn, they will be sold for dog food. She is mortified, and we are too. Gay tries to justify it and says it started out the other way but somehow it changed. Nobody wants horses anymore since there are other things to ride, like go-carts. So, it wasn't them that changed; it was other people that changed it. He makes a good point, but that doesn't change reality. The horses will be killed. "But that's how I make my living. I thought you liked me because of what I am," he yells. "No, I liked you because you were kind," she counters.

How he makes a living is a great deal of who a man is and how he sees himself.

What struck me was how hard it is to stop something once the momentum gets going. They were out there with the equipment, and they just kept doing what they had always done. I think the guys just hoped somehow it would be OK, and if she saw it their way, it would be. But she couldn't change her mind because nothing had changed. Once they were seeing through someone else's eyes, it looked different, but they couldn't stop it. And she couldn't either. Perse says, "It doesn't make much sense, for six horses." Originally they thought there were fifteen but only ended up with six. Gay says, "The fewer you kill, the worse it looks."

Gay and Roslyn were locked into a respect problem. He wanted her to respect him and she wanted him to respect her feelings. Typical of a man—he thought he could just talk her out of her feelings, tough it out, and worry about it later. I don't think it's so much that they don't respect our feelings; it's that they are just so sure they are right. Men and women think so differently, and we both think the other is wrong—when it's actually that both has a piece of the truth or wisdom and the other has a different piece. We also have different pieces of error. Therefore, we never get together.

Roslyn pitches a fit and calls them liars and murderers, yelling, "You call this God's country?" Gay was going to let her have the horses but changed his mind when she ran up trying to buy them. When asked why he responded that way, he said, "There wasn't nobody making up my mind for me." (Do you see the pride?) Perse finally went out and let them go, but Gay caught one and fought it down. It was really a fruitless effort for one. I guess it was just something he had to do. He needed to work off the tension some way.

After he cuts the horse loose and it's obvious Gay and Roslyn are going to get together, he says, "Bless you, girl." He was saying he wanted to be stopped. He wanted to do the right thing. He was sick of freedom that put him in bondage but he couldn't stop it. She helped him stop. She cared enough to do what it took to bring truth and sensibility back. Men appreciate what we bring to their lives.

They weren't fighting about six horses. It was over his very being, his way of life, his freedom, his right to make his own decisions—everything he stood for. And then this beautiful little wisp of a thing that he loved so much questioned the very thing he loved the most, demeaning it and asking him to give it up, to change so completely. It's no wonder he was as upset as she was. It is a fight for everything. And that's the way it is in marriages. Things seem so small and petty, but what they represent is a big chunk of the person. The other is asking us to go against everything we hold dear in these simple little skirmishes. We both want the other just to give in on this one, little point, but then neither understands it's the very fabric of our being cut into pieces.

Roslyn is a beautiful portrayal of all that is beautiful in a woman, so loving and caring and accepting. "When you smile the sun comes out," he says to her. She's so childlike and yet so wise. "You have the gift of life," one of them tells her, and you know it's true. We do carry the gift of life in us in so many ways.

"How do you find your way back in the dark?" she asks at the end. This is a very poignant thought because that is what she's been asking all her life. Of course, Clarke Gable has the answer. And somehow you feel their love will last.

When Gay is trying to explain how he feels to Roslyn, he uses her dancing as an example. She loved to dance, but the guys turned it into something ugly, just as they had his mustanging. "This is how I dance," she explains, and then reluctantly admits, "I'm just going to have to learn a new dance."

When you watch these movies, you get the impression these women are the equal of the men. In fact, you get the impression they are superior in many ways, and the men think it, too. They are idolized. They are amazed by them. Fascinated. Just being around them does something to the men. They love it and they hate it, but they can't stop it. It's like a train wreck in their head, a powerful thing.

Women need to understand the power they have and respect it. It can be frittered away. In truth, it isn't just defused; it turns like a boomerang and comes back on us. And, when it turns, it turns very ugly. The opposite of love is not apathy; it's hate. Did you ever hear a man or a group of men discuss a woman they feel does not live up to the standard they have in their mind for a woman? Such disgust. They almost spit the words out: "I can't stand to see a woman make a fool of herself." As if a man were any better. What's the difference? To men, it's all the difference in the world. They hate for one of their own to look bad and do dumb things, but a woman—that's a whole other thing. Men haven't changed their mind about what they want in a woman. They may have had to adjust it a little as society has changed, but men still want a godly woman.

Men have a natural power, but women have an innate power. A man's desire to please us and do for us puts him and his power at our disposal. We must respect the power we have by respecting him. We must not be careless with it or take it for granted. We must never be disrespectful of him. Disrespect distorts the beauty of all God created between a man and a woman. Even if you disagree, do it respectfully. He is not your little boy. Disrespect him enough, and you will kill your relationship. You might think you don't care, but it is never in your best interest to be disrespectful of anyone. Even if the person doesn't keep it in mind, God does.

SEVENTEEN

> "Blessed are you when men hate you, and ostracize you, and
> heap insults upon you, and spurn your name as evil, for
> the sake of the Son of Man. Be glad in that day, and leap
> for you, for behold, your reward is great in heaven; for in
> the same way their fathers used to treat the prophets."
>
> —LUKE 6:22

In the Workplace and at Home

I F YOU FIND YOURSELF in the workplace, you might find the devil got there before you. Like Gomer Pyle used to say, "Su'prise. Su'prise. Su'prise." If you aren't prepared for him, he will eat your lunch. You may come to see that your natural reactions to persecution are not that good. Licking wounds and murmuring are not Christian options. When you see yourself doing what you know you shouldn't, it can help you to see there are things in you that need correcting. God is putting you through a firing to get some dross out.

We will encounter problems wherever we are. We can either be part of the problem or part of the solution. We can either stay in the spirit or get in the flesh. And by "stay in the spirit," I don't mean not doing your work. I mean you don't get pulled into the gossip or petty squabbles, etc. You keep your mind connected to your spirit so God can help you discern things and understand how to react properly to the problems that arise. I don't mean talking the talk. I mean walking the walk. The workplace is not the place for your verbal testimony as much as your silent witness. I'm not saying you can't say anything, but keep it short, sweet, and anointed.

When you work closely with people, your actions speak louder than your words. They get to know the real you. It's better if you haven't sounded all high and mighty when they realize how human you really are. Saying "Praise God" all the time is not helpful. Too many people say "Praise the Lord" and then act like the rest of the heathens. We need to be consistent in our walk, day in and day out. I don't mean by just not swearing or wearing long hair and no make-up. I mean tolerance, patience, peace, and a good report. You should have joy and be blessed in spite of the dire circumstances, a positive in a world of negatives. And if you can't be, then you aren't being the woman God created you to be and the one He sent in to do a work there.

We are supposed to count it all joy when we go through persecutions. God wants you to learn to walk in love—the same love that took Him to the cross. I know you think you are there to make a little money to help your family get by and have a few extras, but God has more in mind for your life and the lives of these people. He uses these situations to bring us to maturity and to help others get saved or matured. He wants to bless us, but because man is fallen, it doesn't feel like a blessing for a while. He throws us into these messes, not to punish us, but to bless us and the people in the mess with us. We just have to keep going to Him for answers.

Because things are so goofy, we start doing things we were never meant to do. Our answers are not God's answers. Nurses are an adjunct to doctors and secretaries to bosses but, too often, the nurse, secretary, or other subordinates start making decisions they were never intended to make. We jump in and take over in ways we were never meant to and this leads to problems. If a person wants to make the decisions, then they should study and work to become the doctor, or the boss. They will find it's not that easy to get there and, once they arrive, they will not appreciate someone usurping their authority.

THE 9-TO-5 SYNDROME

I call this the nine-to-five syndrome. No, it's not working women. It's sin #2 in the workplace. The name comes from the movie *Nine to Five* with Dolly Parton, Lily Tomlin, and Jane Fonda. I loved the movie. It does speak to a lot of women's frustrations, and in such a funny way. Even though I question the moral of the story, I still enjoyed it on some level. It was so true.

The boss in the company they work for is awful. He is your typical obnoxious, domineering, abusive, male chauvinistic pig. The worst part is that he makes sexually harassing comments. In the process of dealing with him, the three women end up tying him up in his home to keep him from reporting them to the police for what they did to him in the process of defending themselves. Because he is not in the office and they are, they start making decisions for him, and naturally make the ones they would prefer. Of course, things get so much better: production is up, profits are up, and family needs are being taken care of. Isn't that what we want to teach our children: authority will use and abuse you, and if you take over, everything will be much better? The sad part is we believe it. It's the American way.

Let me give you a clue: it is through authority that your blessing will come. It may not come through this particular authority, but it will come through some authority.

What is the 9-to-5 syndrome? The assumption that rebellion is necessary and good. That we can do a better job than the person in authority; that authority figures are abusive, neglectful, stupid, irate, and we must defend ourselves against them. I fell into this trap like so many others. I just felt I had to do something. Don't we all? And I thought I was submitted.

What is wrong with this concept (that rebellion is necessary and helpful) is there a major flaw in it. First of all, these people would have you believe Christians and their God would have you put up with abuse and that is not true at all. Second, that there is no recourse other than drastic measures. No, the truth of the matter is we do have recourse and God will be a part of the resolution of these problems. Just like Haman, not Esther, ended up hanging, God has a plan to deliver you. They (the rebellious bosses and husbands) will wish they were dead, but He won't actually kill 'em. Remember Job. Just don't be like his wife and advise him to curse God and die (Job 2:9). Don't you become the problem. You know what happened to her don't you?

In the movie *9 to 5*, the main characters portrayed by Lily Tomlin, Dolly Parton, and Jane Fonda wanted the company to do well and the employees with it. That's a noble cause. And they did have a problem with the boss—a good reason to do something, but propping him up just made him the hero. Sometimes the best thing we can do for someone is let him or her fall on his or her face. By taking over, these women really made the boss look better and put him in line for a big promotion. Instead of allowing the natural consequences of what he was doing come about, they propped up a failure and made him a success. Don't do this. Let these people fail. God will take care of you. You have to trust Him.

They could have been honest and exposed what was going on. There were enough of them to get a group together eventually. Be careful, though, that you are not just murmuring and spreading rumors. Speak the truth in love and at the right time and to the right people. We can't just go around finding fault all the time. That is counter-productive. If we have been a good employee and always done our job, then we put ourselves in a position to speak when the time comes. Our life must speak for us as much as our words.

They had a choice. They had a lot of choices. Tying up your boss is not the best choice, but it made a great scene in the movie. Actually, I feel it ended in a way that is typical of God's intervention. Things are a mess, only to all of a sudden be turned around and not just be OK but wonderful. The boss got his comeuppance like Haman in Esther. And the office was now being run the way they wanted it to be. They left out the God element, which is bad, but it's a secular movie. I feel we could make a similar movie and put the God element in it.

DELEGATED OR RELEGATED

You might wonder why do things have to be so bad at work? Or at home? Why don't they listen to the workers? Those are all good questions. Why doesn't the boy, employee, or wife have any authority to make some of these decisions? Because the boss, the husband, or whoever doesn't delegate properly. He doesn't listen and he isn't open for suggestions. He's not a good leader. That is why subordinates take things into their own hands. Or at least, that is the excuse we give. God is not convinced, but we are. That doesn't mean God doesn't have an answer. There are times when the leader cannot explain and the followers don't understand, which was the case with Jesus, but not usually.

Why don't people in authority delegate more authority to their subordinates? Fear and doubt; fear of losing control and doubt that people will be able to do the job. The leader doesn't trust those under him not to mess things up, and he (or she) doesn't trust God to take care of things either. Possibly he has been burned in the past. That is a problem, but it doesn't give him the right to deny anyone their ability to grow because of the sins of another.

Some people have to do everything themselves to be sure they get done right. They say it saves them a lot of trouble. It probably does, but that's not why we are a wife, parent, or worker. What it does is keep a lot of people from developing their skills and talents—skills and talents they desperately need. It also limits what the person can attempt to do because they certainly can't do anything as big as what God has in mind all by themselves. Ultimately they are affecting God's plans and inhibiting Him from His goals and that is definitely not good. We are not talking about some small mistake here. We are talking about the whole ball of wax: the whole plan being scuttled, the gospel being stymied.

A Husband Needs to Develop Good Leadership Skills

Typically, there are two errors made by people in authority and Christians are especially bad to make them: (1) We don't delegate when we should; and (2) We are careless and don't oversee the project properly after we have delegated it to someone. Either one gets us in trouble. Subordinates need to have a certain amount of input. If they don't have it, they get frustrated, bitter, and are kept immature. God frowns on keeping people frustrated, bitter, and immature. And He also frowns on not checking back periodically to see how things are going. Repentance is the only answer for those in authority who have made these mistakes.

There are two ways to give a job to someone. You can delegate or you can relegate. To delegate: a person is sent with the authority to represent or act for another. Sounds ominous. To relegate is to refer for performance. (The authority remains with the other person.) So how does Jesus do it? He doesn't just tell us to do the job. He gives us the authority to go along with it. Matthew 16:19 (NIV) reads: *"I will give you the keys to the kingdom of heaven (the authority); whatever you bind on earth shall be bound in heaven, and whatever you loose on earth shall be loosed in heaven."* Sounds clear to me. We have the authority and He performs it. This is how a man should treat his wife. She should walk in his authority and he should even cooperate and help. She decides what color she wants the kitchen and he paints it. Works for me.

Remember the Proverbs 31 couple? If he doesn't like the color, then we should respect his input. Just as he should respect ours if we have a problem with something he has decided. But sometimes a man should yield in spite of the fact that he has a problem with it and wait until he sees the final result. Just as we have to trust an interior decorator to have a vision beyond what we can imagine. However, a good decorator wants our input and makes adjustments. When Lamar and I work together, that's when things work out the best.

When we do a job for a boss, husband, friend, etc., they should be pleased with the results. In fact, many times God has gifted us so that we go beyond their wildest imaginations. It's a blessing to them that they just hadn't even envisioned. Why? Because we know their heart and by knowing their heart, we can do what they want and do it in a way that goes even further. And yet we know what is too far, too much. They can trust us.

A wife, employees, and others should able to make some of the decisions. God wants us all to have some authority. Even a child has the right to make some decisions from the very earliest days. We must respect their "space" and their right to it. A good leader teaches the people He leads how to make good decisions and brings them into the process. Not to take over, but to relieve him so that they can all accomplish more and hopefully, someday, they will both be promoted.

God never meant for us to be a lackey doing all the work, never making any of the decisions. No. He meant for us to do the work and take on a certain amount of responsibility (authority). Sometimes all we do is respond to orders. And that's fine. Other times, we are left on our own and need to know why we are doing things a certain way, etc. Then we can make some decisions. That doesn't mean the husband or God won't have any input. It just means that is taken into consideration when we make the decision. God wants the people in authority to delegate some of this authority just as He does and He wants us to watch over it, just as He does.

Because the Leader Doesn't Delegate, We Take Things Into Our Own Hands

OK, so he doesn't delegate like God meant for him to do and you are in a mess, either because he didn't do what he was supposed to do, or because you did. I say this because I know taking over doesn't work. It may relieve a problem or two temporarily, but so many more take their place. It's literally a bottomless pit. Now what do you do?

First: allow him to fail. I know this sounds terrible, but it's the truth. Some people have to learn the hard way and we have to let them. God will restore the years that the locust has eaten (Joel 2:25). He has promised that. He has also promised His seed will not be begging bread (going hungry). So, you do have some wonderful promises, but there is nowhere in the Bible that is says God will carry you on a bed of ease in this life.

Second: we must cooperate to the best of our ability if what our husband or boss asks is not immoral or if God doesn't show us to refuse yet.

Third: pray, intercede, fight the spiritual battle.

Fourth: having done all, stand. One night the Lord spoke these words to me concerning a Christian I knew was making a big mistake in her life, "Because they would not stand, they were led into a delusion" (2 Thess. 2:11, paraphrased); or , *"For this reason God sends them a powerful delusion so that they will believe the lie."*) Imagine. Have you been deluded? If so, I hope you see it soon.

I don't think we should totally give over everything to a man we know is not qualified to carry the load. If you run the money and he can't run the money without getting things in a mess, then continue to handle the finances. I did. But I included him in the plans and problems every once in a while. Now he runs the money totally. We have to be reasonable in what we allow someone who is out of control take over. Our goal is to have him involved responsibly and I believe he will be. Just remember, as long as you are running everything and keeping everything afloat, this allows him to remain child-like. In the end, you are the bad guy. I have to ask, "Why are you doing it all?" You need to face the fact that somehow you were pulled in where other people wouldn't have been. They would have seen the signs much earlier. So, you are part of the problem and must determine, with God's help, to become part of the solution. But don't rush it. Timing is *very* important. Don't get ahead of God.

So what must you do? Pray. This should always be our first reaction, asking God for guidance, repenting of our part in the mess and forgiving the people that have hurt us. There is more than one kind of prayer: intercession, deliverance, taking your authority, creating, binding, etc. Don't keep taking it back either. That is a problem. Just because you forgive and even try to forget the sins of the past doesn't mean you ignore his sick tendencies. You can lovingly refuse the garbage. Forgiveness doesn't mean ignorance rules the day. It just means they must deal with God about their sins not you, while you deal with reality. You can still make him accountable and do things like getting his check from him so he doesn't spend it all. In fact, these are the things you will need to do and he should agree to it because he does need to be accountable. He does need some help if he has been compulsive about drinking, spending, etc., and he should welcome it. Add a little responsibility at a time. Don't overwhelm him.

Eventually you must move on from the "protecting yourself and your stuff" stage to the "proactive" stage. I don't mean arguing and nagging him. I don't mean licking your wounds, telling how sorry he is either. That isn't proactive. That's fruitless. By proactive I mean the speaking the Word over the situation (claiming favor, etc), speaking creatively, doing what needs to be done to win the victory. Taking every thought into captivity.

You may wonder how much do you have to cooperate with his rebellion?" Enough, but not too much. I can't tell you where that line is. You'll have to figure it out. Generally, you need to be his helpmeet unless you know it's wrong morally. There is no reason why at some time you can't look at him and say, "I'm sorry, but I can't in good conscience do this, hon." (Do you get the "hon" part? We must remain loving.) But, if it's not wrong, just foolish, you will have to pray about your part in it all. It's not up to us to second guess everything our husband asks us to do. He is in the leadership position, but even if he's not a Christian, we still expect him to act in a godly and moral manner.

If we have an attitude when our husband asks us to do something or if we balk and don't cooperate, then our husband will think it's our fault if his plan fails. Whereas, if we do our very best and it still fails, then he will know it was his fault. He can't blame you. And he will feel bad that you put all that effort in. He will learn something and rethink things—not necessarily to drop the project completely, but to modify it somewhat. I know you want him to drop it, but he feels called to do it. He has to figure out where he is wrong and doing it is the best way to figure these things out. I know it's painful to watch and even participate, but it is the best thing we can do if he won't listen and doesn't agree with what you have said as you tried to talk some sense into him.

BUT, WHAT IF HE FAILS?

There's the $64,000 question. Have you studied failure? It has a reputation it doesn't deserve. Good things come out of failure or at least they can (Romans 8:28). Some of the world's most successful people had colossal failures and often more than one before they ever succeeded. J.C. Penny, Thomas Jefferson, and Thomas Edison are just a few. Failure is a part of the maturation process. Does a baby walk without falling? Of course not. Why do we expect anyone to do anything for the first time without faltering? Because we are being unrealistic.

How can you deprive your husband of this rich experience? If you jump in and rescue the situation, then the whole plan has been thwarted. Don't you think maybe your husband will see the error of his ways? It's possible. And maybe it will teach him something in the process—lots of things. Will your children never fail? It will help them see their parent fail and live to move beyond it. Are we going to give them the mistaken idea that they fail and we don't? No, parents fail. Fathers fail. It happens to the best of us. And we must show them that just as we must brush ourselves off and try again, they must also. That is why how we handle failure is just as important as the failure itself. Will we withdraw our love from him when Daddy fails? Will we scream and shout and pout about? Or, will we be merciful, magnanimous, and loving? We must never give them the idea that their value is connected to their performance because our love for Daddy is.

"But the children will suffer." I would like to ask you, "How much will his failure harm them?" Will it keep them from eating or make them homeless? Won't somebody help you and take you in? "Oh, my goodness. I couldn't be homeless or ask others to feed my family!" Is that pride I detect in your voice? The Bible says pride leadeth the way to a fall. Maybe you should swallow your pride and let God work it out, and when it looks like He isn't, pray and wait some more. Fasting is a good way to break a spiritual bondage. If God doesn't provide a meal, assume you should fast!

It is a humbling experience to receive help from others and let people know you aren't managing your affairs very well, but your husband needs to see the consequences of what he is doing to his family. That is why God gave men such big egos—so they wouldn't want this to happen to their wife and kids.

If your children have a foolish father, I don't see how you can cushion them forever. Is it better to intervene now and avoid this consequence, allowing his foolishness to get worse and worse until it's bigger than you can cushion? You can't stop everything, and if he is on a destructive spiral getting progressively worse, the day will come when it will be huge. Why not let the consequences start early? And why not let him know you won't be a party to allowing his foolishness to continue. Step back and let him and his God work things out. For the children, allow it to come early instead of late. And if you have no children, do it for him.

GRACE

Why does God allow all this to go on? To enlarge our capacity for His grace. If we never had a problem, we would never need Him. Actually, there is no way we can have no problems in this lifetime. The Bible says there is enough evil in the day (Ephesians 5:16). We do need Him. We are just deluding ourselves when we think we can take care of things on our own.

Our problems bring us to Him and make us more like Jesus. He is taking us somewhere. And I don't mean heaven, I mean here on earth. God has a goal in mind. Many goals. Short-term, middle, and long-range goals. He just wants to make sure we're going the right place and we taking as many as possible with us. Any time things aren't turning out the way you thought they would, step back and tell God:

> *Evidently I don't understand the plan. I'm at a loss. You are going to have to help me see where I go from here because I sure don't know. Please help me to see if I am a part of the problem in any way because I sure can't see it. I know You are working all*

things for my good. I know You love me and I love You. I stand on that fact alone. If I haven't anything else, I have you. In Jesus name I pray.

PEARLS

I was watching a very interesting show on the production of cultured pearls. It was quite amazing. They have to surgically insert an artificial round pea into the oyster and then put it back into the ocean. It's two years before they see what the oyster has produced. Talk about trepidation. It's up to the oyster how it will handle this foreign object. They all do something with it. A few die, but those that live must cover the foreign object for their own preservation or comfort. Some make beautiful round pearls and others are lopsided. Some are white and others are off-white. Some are black. These are grown in a different area and have a wide range of color, too.

"It's up to the oyster what it will do with it," the caretaker of the oysters said. That's the one thing the caretakers cannot control. They monitor how long the oysters are out of the water, what is inserted and how. They are kept in a cloistered community all trussed up and moved and turned. It's all very controlled. But, not the oyster. They can't control the oyster. And that is how God looks at us. He has controlled a great deal, but He chooses not to control man, at least not very much. We are sovereign over our own lives. We will make out of it a thing of beauty or something ugly and worthless. It's up to each of us to decide. And if we choose correctly, they will rise up and call us blessed. Oh, how happy they are over the few perfect pearls. And oh how happy our Heavenly Father is over a few obedient, appreciative souls. Our worth is higher than rubies or pearls, even the biggest and the best.

EIGHTEEN

And the eyes of them both were opened, and they knew that they were naked; and the sewed fig leaves together, and made themselves aprons.

—GENESIS 3:7

Forever After

IN SPITE OF THE fall, Adam and Eve were still one. God's redeeming power had to start way back in the beginning with the first family. If you want to talk about shared experiences, Adam and Eve can top 'em all. It wouldn't do for them to marry someone else. Who could understand what they had gone through? How do you express the Garden of Eden? Walking with God in the cool of the day? The devil? Why you ate the fruit? And how everything changed? Oh, sure it's nice when the new husband or wife doesn't know how bad we've been in our former life, but is that good? Adam and Eve understood and could appreciate each other as they worked out their problems, even the ones with their sons.

Every marriage will have some bad memories and they might seem as bad as Adam and Eve's. We deal with the devil and get fooled, too. With sin in the world there is the possibility of every evil work and sometimes it seems as if we have it all right now. If you have never had much good in your marriage, take heart, God had a plan to redeem theirs and He has a plan to redeem yours. After that the shared memories won't be so painful. Mine aren't and they include the death of a child.

This is one of the saddest parts of death or divorce: family members literally ripped from the arms of their loved ones. They lose the life stream, the continuum that we are supposed to have with each other. New friends and relatives don't know them. I heard a man share this very thing. His first wife died when their two boys were quite young and he remained single to raise them. After they were grown, he fell in love with a younger woman and married again. He was in his forties and she was in her late twenties. They have three children together. He loved both wives deeply and all of his children. It was just sad that his second wife had no memories of his early ministry, the older boys when they were young, old friends, places they lived, etc. It wasn't her fault and she enjoyed hearing the stories, but it wasn't the same.

I had this experience with the loss of my brother Grant after he was killed in an army accident my senior year of college. Not only did I not have the privilege of growing old with my brother, but I also couldn't visit the past and my memories of him with my new family. They would never comprehend or appreciate all that my brother was to me. I couldn't even properly express what color his hair was. He was a redhead. Do you know how many colors there are of red hair? I have spent all these years pointing out redheads to Lamar and the boys to help them understand that one aspect. How can I ever begin to explain how funny he was and how he could recite Little Willie poems and Shakespeare at length?

The other day I called my son Grant "Grundoon," and when I did, he gave me the strangest look. Why would I call him that? He doesn't know anything about the name Grundoon. My brother was always calling me Midgeroonie, so I called him Grundoon or Graggadont. Nobody will ever again call me Midgeroonie. I lost not only my brother, but the one who knows my name. This is why my brother Dick is so precious to me and me to him, because he remembers the million things that we can't even begin to put into words. It brings a oneness to Dick and me and this is the oneness God wants us to experience with many people. But He doesn't want us to lose the ones we already have it with. That's not the plan at all. He wants us to keep adding to this number.

So why does God allow some, like Grant, to pass on early? First, let me make one thing perfectly clear; it was the devil that took my brother. Yes, God did allow it, but Grant was ready. Of all of us, he was the one that understood the gospel. The last time I saw him he explained to me about Jesus; why He came and what He did for mankind. I didn't understand then. I was a senior in college, but didn't have much spiritual education. He went to a Catholic college and must have had a priest or professor that had "a personal relationship" with God.

Losing a brother is *hard*. But losing a daughter is a whole lot worse; at least it was for me. Dadra was such a special, compliant child. I didn't love her more, but she sure was something. It was as if God looked my whole life over and took out the sun. I don't know if He would have allowed her death if I had gotten the answers earlier. Christians do suffer loss and I might still have lost her, but I would have had Him through it all. It would have been dark, but surely not as dark.

When Lamar and I married, it was just two years after my brother's death, not long enough to "get over it." Lamar said he understood, but to me that was ludicrous. He had only lost his grandparents—his father's mother and his mother's father. He never knew his paternal grandfather or his maternal grandmother. To me losing a grandparent was nothing compared to losing a brother. Although my grandmother, the only grandparent I remember, was still alive, we were not close. Mom never saw her father, and Dad's parents both had died by the time I was six. What I didn't realize was that Lamar had bonded with his grandfather, not his father. He lost probably the most significant person in his life other than his mother—a very great loss.

When Lamar was a toddler his father, B.G., was badly burned on his chest, arms, and hands when a gas stove exploded. His father couldn't hold him while he was all bandaged up. While still wearing bandages, he left for the World War II. So, his grandfather came to help Mary with the kids. Because of his absence during those formative years, Lamar and his father did not bond properly. When he came home, Lamar didn't even know who he was. The first time he remembers seeing his dad was when B.G. surprised the family with his return. When B.G. saw Mary, he ran and grabbed her, hugging her as she screamed and cried. Lamar thought some stranger was assaulting his mother! He didn't understand it was joy. Sadly, they never did bond. B.G. was a man with time to make up and a family to take care of, bonding with his son just slipped by unnoticed.

Lamar preferred Grampa, anyhow. He had been a widower since Mary was fourteen. She and her father had come to be very close in the years her mother was ill. B.G. was fond of him, too. He was a kind, wonderful man. I can see why Lamar preferred him.

Much to everyone's sorrow, Grampa died when Lamar was five. It was a very significant loss to Lamar. It wasn't like losing my grandmother that I saw only on rare occasions and with whom I wasn't especially close. Gram was OK, and I'm sure I loved her, but losing her was nothing compared to Lamar losing his grandfather. That was a wound that changed everything in his soul.

When Lamar said he understood my grief over losing my brother, I just waved it off as him kidding himself. It would be years before I understood. Communication at this stage was really not helpful because Lamar didn't understand very much either. He said he did, but I rejected what he said. The problem wasn't with him, it was in me. I wasn't ready. But it did elicit some discussion and any little bit helps.

We lost our little girl at a time when our marriage was falling apart. Why wouldn't it fall apart? Lamar didn't know how to relate or nurture. We surely would have divorced if we hadn't lost Dadra, not that the loss brought us closer. It didn't. In fact, it probably drove us further apart because we experienced it so differently. But I couldn't stand the thought of being married to someone who didn't know her. I had lost a brother and knew how hard it was when Lamar and the kids didn't appreciate what Grant was like. How do you explain a personality? A quirky smile? An attitude? A dimple? You don't. I didn't want that with my little girl. At least Lamar knew her and that meant a lot. I didn't have to explain Dadra to my husband. He knew how beautiful and special she was. Because of that, as much as anything else (because three boys aren't easy to raise alone or with a step-father), we didn't divorce, and eventually, with God's help, our relationship changed. I never dreamed Lamar and I could be as happy as we are today.

After we lost Dadra, Lamar didn't talk about her, nor did the Vices. We had just sold our home in one town and moved away from our close friends back to where he had grown up, close to his family. Suddenly, I had very few friends that had ever seen her. I naturally talked about her because she was still part of me. I was met with an immediate hush whether I was at the Vices or at home. Finally I asked Lamar, "Don't you ever think about her?" "Of course I do," he assured me. "You never talk about her," I countered. He thought a moment then answered, "She was the most beautiful thing in my life and now she's gone. What can I say?" How very much he cared. I had been perfect in his eyes, but had long ago fallen off my pedestal. Daddy's little girl was still perfect. She would now remain perfect as long as he lived. They had a very special relationship that only a daddy and daughter can have. I knew that all along. It just helped to hear it. I never asked again.

Even if your husband doesn't talk about the dark times, that doesn't mean he never will or that he doesn't feel them very deeply. Your husband needs to see it redeemed and the blood of Jesus applied over these terrible times of the past before he can go there mentally or verbally. Respect his right to his privacy. Healing will come. Give God time. Trying to rush this work only tears the scab off the wound and you don't need that. God will cleanse and anoint something, in His time.

This reminds me of Jeremiah 8:22: *"Is there no balm in Gilead?"* If you read the whole story the answer is yes, there is a balm in Gilead. They just weren't using it. The balm is God, His peace and provision. If your loved one is hurting or you are hurting, just apply Jesus. Apply praise and prayer and out of that will come peace that passes all understanding and joy unspeakable. *"Out of the ashes of mourning come joy"* (1 Pet. 1:8). That is a promise. Claim it for yourself, your husband, and loved ones. There is a balm in Gilead. Be sure you use it.

Often, at times like these, we are forced to admit we don't have all that close of a relationship with the Lord. We have been living off a past experience or maybe even the experience of our parents. God wants more and we should too. If you really don't hear Him or feel Him or know He's there, just know He wants you to hear and feel and know and He's just waiting for you to come and spend some time with Him. Watch for those special things that only God could have done or known. Knowing Him is getting still and seeing what is unseen to everyone else.

Nothing would make things better, so why divorce? Since I had no answers, I did what was best for the boys and Lamar and that was to keep things as they were.

There will be times in your life that you find you have no wiggle room. When you assess your options and none of them seem to work, at least not right now. When that happens, just know it could be God forcing you to stay put. It's not bad to stay when leaving makes no sense. It wouldn't make things better, if you are realistic and really think it out. Ask your-self: "If I leave, what is the worst-case scenario?" It just may come to pass. I am a very positive person, but if something isn't anointed, I know it can get that bad. It would be nice if I could say God spoke to me from on high or I got an infusion of love for Lamar, but I can't. I have to be honest and say, nothing looked all that good to me. So, I just waited and that was the best thing I could have done.

One holiday, years after Dadra died, I was running around upstairs trying to get everything done, frustrated because I had no help. Most boys don't help much around the house. I needed a girl. I had a girl and I lost my girl! I started to cry in my pain and frustration, but I didn't want to go there. What good would it do? And so I cried out to God for strength and for Him to take it away. I dried my eyes and went downstairs, never missing a beat. No one knew the dark place I had just gone, not even Lamar. I could have told him, but it was easier not to say the words and it passed. After the day was all over Lamar said, "Well, didn't you have a good time!" And I did have a wonderful time. He just never knew it was tinged with such pain. I eventually told him, but not that day.

The day of Dadra's thirty-third birthday I realized this was the age Jesus died, and the age I was saved. Maybe this is why this year it seems so much more significant. Maybe it's because relationships here are not what they should be. It is a lot of things that come together to produce our sadness. When it comes, we just have to steal away and let the tears come. Take it to the Lord and let Him sort it out. I'm just a branch. He's the vine. If I'm a branch, it's amazing that I feel so bad sometimes. I didn't know they had feelings. It's the heart of flesh He put in when He took out my heart of stone. A branch with a heart of flesh. There's something to ponder.

I am painfully aware that a big part of life is still mine to face alone. When Dadra's birthday was so difficult, I couldn't really share it with anyone. It was too deep. To express it would have made it worse. There was nothing Lamar could do and it would just frustrate him to know how sad I was. So I waited to tell him until I had taken it to God and we had dealt with it.

Sometimes I don't express things because he would tell me it's my own dumb fault. And it is. I should be able to get over it, but I don't need to hear it. It just makes it worse. There is nothing he or anyone can do. It's just something I have to work out. And as I take it to God, He sorts it out for me and in the end it's not a bad thing. Something is revealed to me that I never understood before. God is "going" somewhere with these dark times we go through. We just have to go through them.

During a revival one night, the evangelist talked about "movers and shakers" for God. When you have come to the place that you move in oneness with each other and with Him, there is no limit to what God can do through you. This is what God wants and this should be what you want. This is why I say: do everything you can in your power to bring it to pass. Your healing and the healing of your husband and marriage is the most powerful thing you have to offer.

> *Oh, dear God, to be a mover and shaker for You with my husband sounds impossible. But you are the God of the impossible. Oh, how I long to be truly one with my husband; to share the most important love of my life, You, with the next most important love of my life. God, I ask you to knit us together mentally, phys-ically, and spiritually. Help me to do my part to bring it to pass.*

I bind Satan from anything he would have planned to stop this. I come against every hindering spirit in the name of Jesus and render them powerless in our lives. I thank You and praise You God that I can come, that I am Your child and You hear my prayers. I ask You to take the blinders off of my eyes so I can see what You would have me see, so I can do what you would have me do toward the healing of my marriage. Take the blinders off husband's eyes, his mind's eye, and soften his heart to receive what You need and want him to hear and accept at this time. Soften his heart toward me. You say You give me favor with men and I am claiming it right now in my life. And I ask You to pour Your love for my husband through me. Forgive me, Lord, for not being the wife he needs and help me to do better. I've done the best I could, but help me to see how to do better, especially in his eyes. I pray all this in the precious name of Jesus. Amen.

PARADISE

I love kid movies and *Paradise*, starring Don Johnson and Melanie Griffith, has a boy and a girl that carry the movie, although it isn't a movie for kids. It's much too dark. I buy these movies hoping to watch them with my grand-girls and then find many aren't appropriate.

Becoming aware of problems in her marriage, a mother sends her young son to an old friend that lives in the perfect place, thus the name *Paradise*. It is a wonderful place for a boy to grow up, but it's just for the summer. The boy hits it off with both the man and wife, but they obviously aren't hitting it off with each other. A bad marriage can turn Paradise into Hell in a hurry! Their little boy died as an infant and she can't get passed it. Don is tired of being shut out of her life. The tension is palpable and it's no wonder.

All the while the young boy is relating fairly normally to these two people. And isn't that true in our crisis? We have kids! We could divorce and go our separate ways if it wasn't for the kids. And sometimes we do anyway and then it is a dark movie for them, too. There is a little neighbor girl in the movie whose mother is divorced. She is so cute and *so wise* in spite of the mess she is being dragged through. She's the only one with a clue.

After Don moves out, he comes back for something while Melanie is upstairs lingering over the memories. She tells him she heard the baby cry once the night he died but didn't go in to him. She was sewing and he didn't keep crying so she ignored it and later found him dead! If only she had responded. If only... This is why she cannot respond sexually. She can't stop the sound of his crying in her head. Don tells her no one can respond to every cry. She realizes that. But it doesn't matter. Her guilt overwhelms her. The little boy forces them to come out of their cocoon and heal. Somehow she allows Don in to become a part of the grieving and healing process.

We make mistakes. It is going to happen. The hardest thing to do is forgive ourselves. First, offer forgiveness if your husband has hurt you in some way. It is human to err. No one is more distressed over their own sin than the person himself. An adulterer hates that he or she is weak in this way. I don't know why these things happen. I just know they do.

We all have these battles to face, and if we are married, we are supposed to face them together. Don and Melanie in this movie could have divorced. He could have come around with his new wife and child and put on a face of complete joy. But there would always be something unfinished—a place inside that knew they missed the best. Wonderful as the new wife and child would be, it wouldn't be the same. And yet, he would know he did all he could. He would try to say it would never be. But the movie proved that wrong. She did begin to heal. Just think if he hadn't come back. She would have never healed. Her divorce would have just been one more thing that haunted her

I should point out she was attending church, but he was too skeptical to go. At least she was reaching out. I hope, with or without Don in her life, that she would have eventually found peace. I guess Don blamed God and Melanie knew better. It wasn't God at all!

The moral of the movie: forgive! And be sweet to boys, big and little.

Forgive yourself. No one is perfect. We all make mistakes. God can redeem even the worst of situations and bring new life out of the death of this relationship. God does not want you to walk forward grieved and broken, He wants you to come to His throne boldly and to face life that way. Tell the devil he's a liar and to get away from you. You are a child of the most high God and He has a plan for your life *this day*!

NINETEEN

I will greatly increase your pains in childbearing.

—GENESIS 3:16

To Be Content

AFTER THE FALL, GOD made a new covenant with man. Let me give you a tip: when it can't get any better, don't renegotiate. Sad to say, Adam and Eve didn't get this tip. They disobeyed and after that taking care of the garden became a great deal harder. Now we can call it work. God chastised the serpent, the woman, and the man.

To the serpent He said, "*Because you did this, a curse will be put on you. You will be cursed as no other animal, tame or wild, will ever be. You will crawl on your stomach, and you will eat dust all the days of your life. I will make you and the woman enemies to each other. Your descendants and her descendants will be enemies. One of her descendants will crush your head and you will bite his heel*" (Gen. 3:14–15, NCV).

To the man God said, "*You listened to what your wife said, and you ate fruit from the tree from which I commanded you not to eat. So I will put a curse on the ground, and you will have to work very hard for your food. In pain you will eat its food all the days of your life. The ground will produce thorns and weeds for you, and you will eat the plants of the field. You will sweat and work hard for your food. Later you will return to the ground, because you were taken from it. You are dust, and when you die, you will return to the dust*" (Gen. 3:17–19, NCV). I don't think He is saying you can never listen to your wife. I think He means, don't listen to your wife when she disagrees with Me!

Did you ever hear the story of a man admiring a beautiful garden to its owner, "My! Hasn't God blessed you with a wonderful garden!" To which the owner replies, "You should have seen it when God had it by Himself!" and everybody laughs! Proving we have a problem integrating into our thinking that it was man's fault and not God's that the garden was full of weeds and thorns when he found it.

Please note the serpent didn't crawl before the fall. Why then is he always depicted as a snake slithering up to Adam and Eve? If Satan is a spirit, why does God put this physical reprimand on him? Probably because Satan likes to have a physical body and inhabit living things. Since this animal was used by him to do such a dastardly thing, it was reduced to slithering. Notice how the scripture goes from the physical to the spiritual. This scripture prophesies of Jesus.

> To the woman He said, "I will greatly increase your pains in childbearing: with pain you will give birth to children. Your desire will be for your husband, and he will rule over you.
> —Genesis 3:16, TLB

This is the scripture that makes women cringe, and to a certain extent, rightfully so. It's the beginning of "the curse." Please keep in mind Jesus became a curse so we don't have to be cursed any longer (Galatians 3:13). He fulfilled the law and paid the price for sin (the curse), but He didn't change the fact that we must come under authority. He didn't come to change authority, but to show us how to do it: how to relate properly to God and man. He takes the sting out of submission. I can honestly say now, "How sweet it is." Not bondage, but proper relationships.

The curse brought about authority and submission, as we know it. At the moment Adam and Eve disobeyed, something changed; the critical element—the spirit—died. Although the man's headship, their love for each other, and children were all there in the original plan, virtually everything changed. The world was literally turned upside down where instead of blessings we have the curse, a negative aspect that affects everything we touch, do, and think. Man (including woman) now has a new nature. And with that new nature comes pain in childbirth, a woman's desire for a man, and his rulership over her; all as a result of their disobedience. Don't you know God had to give woman this desire toward her man or we would not continue the relationship very long!

Heaven knows the pain in childbearing part is true. Actually the word used is the word contortion. The contorting of childbirth is symbolic of what we did to the world. I should point out: other animals don't normally give birth in the pain we do. If the childbearing part is right, the rest is probably right, too. However, I have heard of Christians believing not to have terrible labor pains and their delivery was a wonderful experience, but it takes faith and standing for it. And if it doesn't happen, then we give it to God and the doctors.

Women do have a desire toward their man, to have someone special. When we don't receive his continued affection and admiration, everything is warped in our lives. This is why widowhood is so painful. We are supposed to help our husband. Yes, that's the plan. Did God tell them? Yes, I guess He did, because Lamar really does want my help, but oh, how he fights it. He welcomes it and hates it at the same time. I try my best, but it's rarely good enough. But I keep trying. I can't help myself. It's the way women are wired.

It's a control issue. He wants to control what happens in our lives and I'm a free spirit. Controlling me is like controlling a frog. There is no telling what I might do, at least that's how it seems to him. I think I'm very predictable. He still has to ask what kind of ice cream I would prefer. You'd think after all these years he would know since I'm a chocoholic, I want chocolate. When he can't control me, then in his mind he isn't in control at all. But he is in control. It's just that he's never really sure of it. It's tenuous. I guess the early years didn't help.

I found it hard to give over the control of my life. It's not that I didn't want to help Lamar; I did. I just didn't agree with many of the things he wanted to do. It's hard to help when you don't agree. God doesn't have this problem, at least not in the Godhead. Father God, Holy Spirit, and Jesus get along swimmingly. There is no disagreement because Father God is all-wise and they are, too. But Lamar isn't all-wise. In fact, at the time he wasn't wise at all. He was very foolish. And this was the basis of our problems: his foolishness and my fear. My fear that he would lead us into disaster, and wouldn't you know, he confirmed my worst fears and did just that. We lost everything: our business, our home; everything we had worked for. We were forced to declare bankruptcy; although, it wasn't entirely his fault. I tell the story in chapter one about getting a small business loan and having problems with the banker.

Lamar had a lot of fears, too, but he didn't talk that way. Men hide their fears. They are so busy hiding their fears, they can't seem to hear what we are saying or see what we need. That's why talking more doesn't seem to help and being needy really doesn't work into their plans.

Because I am writing about families, I like the reality shows. I am shocked at how many men are totally shut down where the family is concerned. The wife is struggling to make it all work on her own and it doesn't work. The more the family gets out of hand, the more he checks out. I have to admit our family got to this point. Wives and mothers shut down, too.

Men and women approach life so differently because our vantage points are so different. God presented the garden and all the animals to the man and He presented to man the woman. Women are focused inward toward the family and man is focused outward more toward the world. Women fight for the family and men try to get us to see things as the world sees them. This is the reason men and women are so frustrated, because we think the other "just doesn't get it." We were created for entirely different purposes and God Almighty is the creator of the difference. Since it's His fault, we evidently need to rethink things (renew our mind).

Man was created to rule the world. Woman was created to rule, too. We are supposed to be of one mind like the Father, Son, and Holy Spirit. We should be in agreement, and when we aren't we should pray about it and wait until we are. Love should take care of all of the problems that arise, but sadly selfishness rears its ugly head.

With his new willful nature, the male tends to be too domineering and insensitive to the woman's needs (abuse of his authority); and the willful nature in the female, tends to be rebellious, refusing to follow his lead, and to be critical of him (rejection of his authority). This is exactly what happened to Lamar and me. You will find it in your marriage, too, because it's a factor in both of you. None of us can escape it, much as we might like to. We can learn to subdue it and renew our minds to understand what we are facing, but the process will never end as long as we live in this body of flesh. Lamar and I still butt heads once in a while, but we have learned to back off and give God time to work it out.

When man "fell," we lost our spiritual relationship with God, which is the only way we can relate to God. If the husband isn't a spiritual man, there is nothing for the wife to submit to. She is not meant to submit to flesh, but to Christ (in him). Anything that is not Christ-like will cause her to rise up in dominion. When the woman sees the man acting in ways he shouldn't, expecting her to go along with ungodliness, dominion rises up in her against him and he has a fight on his hands. Suddenly there are two people attempting to be in dominion but not in agreement. This is not what God had in mind. One of them has to yield and God has already said it must be the woman. Therein lies the rub: submitting when we know in our heart something isn't right. And, the truth is, something may not be right in us either. Ungodliness on both sides is the norm, not the exception. Being a Christian helps, but it doesn't guarantee we are always right. It's in times like these that we need to know the Word and do the right thing.

Let's look at Paul's advice in 1 Corinthians 11:1–3 (NAS) regarding the authority of the husband. *"Be imitators of me, just as I also am of Christ. Now I praise you because you remember me in everything and hold firmly to the traditions, just as I delivered them to you. But I want you to understand that Christ is the head of every man, and the man is the head of a woman, and God is the head of Christ."*

There it is in black and white. The hierarchy of authority reiterated in the New Testament. God, through Paul, is reaffirming the chain of command that was set up so long ago. The man is responsible to Christ as He is responsible to God the Father and we are responsible to the man. Jesus isn't expecting us to do anything He hasn't already done. He was responsible to Someone, too, and He submitted to men and women when He walked this earth as a man. You need to continue in the hierarchy set up from the beginning. You need to answer to your husband as he answers to Christ and as Christ answers to the Father. God really doesn't need a bunch of loose cannons running around. And even if the husband is a loose cannon, it's a more workable situation than the wife being one, too. He will deal with the man in due time. It's all the more important that you are obedient when he isn't. (Remember Moses smiting the rock in Numbers 20:11?) In Ephesians 5:21, Paul is telling the Ephesians to walk in wisdom or circumspectly, in other words not as fools. Be a good witness to the world we are trying to reach with the gospel. There's a novel idea. Don't be drunk, etc., submitting one to another in the fear of God. Then he talks to the wives, husbands, and even bondservants in this same lesson on walking circumspectly. If you have been a Christian very long, you have heard or read this scripture:

> *Wives, submit to your own husbands, as to the Lord. For the husband is head of the wife, as also Christ is head of the church, and He is the Savior of the body. Therefore, just as the church is subject to Christ, so let the wives be to their own husbands in everything. Husbands, love your wives, just as Christ also loved the church and gave Himself for her, that He might sanctify and cleanse her with the washing of water by the word, that He might present her to Himself a glorious church, not having spot or wrinkle or any such thing, but that she should be holy and without blemish. So husbands ought to love their own wives as their own bodies; he who loves his wife loves himself. For no one ever hated his own flesh, but nourishes and cherishes it, just as the Lord does the church. For we are members of His body, of His flesh and of His bones. "For this reason a man shall leave his father and mother and be joined to his wife, and the two shall become one flesh." This is a great mystery, but I speak concerning Christ and the church. Nevertheless let each one of*

*you in particular so love his own wife as himself, and let the
wife see that she respects her husband.*

—Ephesians 5:22–32, niv

According to this scripture, she is to receive love and he is to receive
respect. This is the way we are made. Men need respect like they need
air. Women need love just as much. If a man does something that hurts
a woman, she reads it that he doesn't love her. She reacts in a way that
he interprets as disrespect, and reacts in a way that appears to her like
he doesn't love her by having a drink with the boys and comes home
late. She gets angrier and reacts more disrespectfully by spending more
money when he has told her not to. It becomes a vicious cycle. But he
does love her. And she loves him. In America, we feel a person should
deserve respect, but God shows us respect when we don't deserve it.

She should show him respect even when he is treating her in a way
that is unloving, but it takes maturity. She has to go against her natural
tendencies. Just as it takes a man to go against his nature to show her
love when she is showing him disrespect. However, we do have the right
and maybe even responsibility to set proper boundaries—doing it in the
proper way, naturally.

There is so much here to expound on in this scripture, and yet I feel it's
pretty straightforward. It's not that we don't understand what it's saying
that is the problem. It's that we don't like what it says. If you think about
it, it's a very special order that a man has been given: to love his wife as
Christ loved the church and gave Himself for it—for us. Everything He
did was for the church, His followers. We might have been told to submit,
but we were also told how special we are in this relationship. We are not
second-class citizens but gems to be appreciated and protected.

He then speaks to the children admonishing them to obey their
parents, honoring them so that it might be well with them. And then
he warns the fathers not to provoke their children to wrath, but to bring
them up in the discipline and instruction of the Lord. Then Paul speaks
to the extreme case—the slave in Ephesians 6:5 (nkjv):

Bondservants, be obedient to those who are your masters according to the flesh, with fear and trembling, in sincerity of heart, as to Christ; not with eyeservice, as men-pleasers, but as bondservants Of Christ, doing the will of God from the heart, with goodwill doing service, as to the Lord, and not to men, knowing that whatever good anyone does, he will receive the same from the Lord, whether he is a slave or free. And you, masters, do the same things to them, giving up threatening, knowing that your own Master also is in heaven, and there is no partiality with Him.

Have a sincere heart. Do the will of God from your heart and He will return the same good to you. God will be indebted to you even if you are a slave. Do you see how to ponder and claim for yourself the promises of God? Notice He speaks to masters, too. He tells them they aren't any better than their slave.

"But I thought you said Jesus brings us freedom! Why doesn't Paul try to free them?" But, he does free them. True freedom begins in the heart and mind and that he does give them. But he does not tell them to fight for their physical freedom because he does not have the authority to free a slave. They go after run away slaves, beat them severely, and bring them back, maybe even kill them! No, Paul must teach them to minister in the state they are in—as slaves. Just as he tells wives and husbands to minister in the situation we are in. We are not to run. We are to bring God in. We are the entry point. If we run, we ruin everything. God has lost His contact point; His legal right to be there. The Bible says having done all, stand—with the assumption that you are praying without ceasing.

Now godliness with contentment is great gain. *For we brought nothing into this world, and it is certain we can carry nothing out. And having food and clothing, with these we shall be content. But those who desire to be rich fall into temptation and a snare, and into many foolish and harmful lusts which drown men in destruction and perdition. For the love of money is a root of all kinds of evil, for which some have strayed from the faith in their greediness, and pierced themselves through with many sorrows.*

—1 TIMOTHY 6:6, EMPHASIS ADDED

Paul is encouraging them to be content with the simple things and not to get caught up in the desire for more, thereby losing sight of what is important: souls. By being the best possible worker, respectful and hardworking, he or she will bring honor to the One he calls Savior and thereby win some to "The Way." And once a slaveholder becomes a Christian, he or she can no longer stand to hold another in bondage. This same principle holds true to wives and anyone under authority. Please keep in mind, it is godliness first! Contentment without godliness is a whole 'nother matter! (That could be a drunk with his beer!) We must do what God tells us to do. Obedience will always be the key. Clarence Thomas, the Supreme Court judge, talking about his recent book quoted his grandfather as advising him to "play the hand you're dealt."[1]

The point is not slavery! The point is being a servant of His.

If there is one aspect of my being that has held me in good stead other than my desire for the truth, it's my ability to be content. I can go from grand to grungy and be just as happy. I hate waste and I especially hate when things harm children (and the earth they will inherit), but I am able to find peace in spite of it all. I can't fight all the battles and have to lay them down in the knowledge that Someone bigger than me is wrestling with them, too.

Dear Heavenly Father, I want to be a blessing. I feel like I have so little to give that it wouldn't make much of a dent in the needs I see around me. Help me to be sensitive to how You would have me help others. Help me to have the resources to do more. And help me most of all to have the faith to give in the first place, so that I will be a conduit for Your blessing and not a stagnant pool that grows ever more polluted because there is no outlet for what pours in. I thank You for all You have given me...But most of all, I thank You for the contentment I feel that I didn't always have... and never thought I would feel again. For peace and joy and all good things.

TWENTY

Timothy, guard what has been entrusted to your care. Turn away from godless chatter and the opposing ideas of what is falsely called knowledge, which some have professed and in so doing have wandered from the faith. Grace be with you.

—1 TIMOTHY 6:20

Hair and Hats

BEFORE WE PROCEED, LET'S make the first and overriding statement that will underlie everything else I say, and that is that Jesus has made us free and nothing He does from now on will be intended to send you into bondage again. No rule, no law, nothing He asks you to do should put you back into bondage. I don't believe it's God that asks an alcoholic to go back to the bar to witness. It's their own misguided zeal. The proof will be in the outcome. If you are doing God's thing, it will work out. If you are doing your own thing, then you will get in a mess.

God never expected people to accept abuse. However, I have heard women in very problematic marriages say they knew they could leave but chose to stay because they felt that is what God would have them do. They were usually telling this *after* their husbands were saved and serving the Lord. However, I do not believe we have to pray about removing ourselves from danger. The Bible says in 2 Timothy 2:22, "*Flee evil.*" It doesn't say pray about whether you should flee evil. If evil has taken over your husband, you have every right to flee. And you have a responsibility to do it in a manner that provides you the greatest protection. Do not be foolish at this time. Many people are hurt in the process of removing themselves from bad situations. We must be wise and have the help of professionals. Yes, I mean the police if necessary. And even they aren't enough. We need a prayer covering as we do what we feel we must do. Use wisdom. You need the help of friends and relatives to help you monitor the activities and intentions of your "loved one" that is right now not acting responsibly. Sometimes you have more control staying than leaving.

Continuing to stay often keeps our spouse from making the necessary changes. Any time he's not cooperating with the help he is being offered, he needs to feel loss. We don't expect perfection, but we do expect cooperation—real cooperation and not just words, promises of a better day or "next time." It's easy to spiritualize our sicko tendencies rather than deal with them. The truth sets you free. The easy part is seeing his sin, the hard part is seeing our own. Seek to know the truth in you first and then you can begin to find it in others. What is the truth?

1. God has brought you into freedom, not to be free to sin, but to be free to serve Him.

2. Once you are free, be sure no one puts you into bondage again—the bondage of legalism, of rules in place of a relationship with Him, or of producing your own fruit.

3. We not only serve our husband and loved ones; we serve as the hands, feet, mouth, and ears of the Lord. We are ministers of God to others and, as such, should minister to their needs as He asks us minister—the servant spirit.

4. We do not cooperate and submit because we agree; we cooperate and submit because God requires it. We should not get our brain involved deciding the wisdom of the plan. If we do, then *we* are in authority. A being with two heads is a monster not something created by God.

5. You may refuse to do anything you are asked to do. Just be sure it's for the right reason—because it's morally wrong, dangerous, harmful, unscriptural, etc. Trust mature Christians to help you, but remember, sometimes they are wrong. Trust yourself, too.

I need to clarify: I am speaking to Christians. I expect you, the reader, to pray and get answers from God, not just think up things on your own. I certainly don't want you to do what you think is best if it's not what God thinks is best. We don't need you doing your thing. You've been doing that long enough.

Now I am going to go from talking about slaves to the hat and hair issue. Why? Because it's in the scripture we've been talking about. I am not a proponent of "clothesline theology" (having oppressive rules on how we dress), and would prefer not getting into it, but since it's right here, I need to touch on it briefly. There is too much contention born out of this issue to ignore it.

Let's go back to our scripture 1 Corinthians 11:1: *"And you should follow my example, just as I follow Christ's."* There is one matter I want to remind you about, and since it's the first thing he mentions, consider it of utmost importance: a wife is responsible to her husband, her husband is responsible to Christ, and Christ is responsible to God. This is where I stopped in the last chapter, so now let's go on: *"that is why if a man refuses to remove his hat while praying or preaching, he dishonors Christ"* (v. 4).

Because the hat is symbolic of being under man's authority, a man would be indicating that he is not under Christ's authority, but under man's. This would be OK on the job, but not during the worship service. In other words, he should be under an open heaven, nothing between God and him.

Please note in the following scripture that the woman is allowed to pray and prophesy in the church, just not bareheaded. Gee, and I've heard it taught we shouldn't talk in church at all.

Verse 5 (TLB): *"And that is why a woman who publicly prays or prophesies without a covering on her head dishonors her husband* [for her covering is a sign of her subjection to him. Evidently, it's a sign of disrespect in that culture for a woman not to wear a covering over her head.] *Yes, if she refuses to wear a head covering, then she should cut off all her hair.* [In other words, if you're going to be rebellious, let it be obvious. Something he knows she isn't going to do.] *And if it's shameful for a woman to have her head shaved, then she should wear a covering. But a man should not wear anything on his head* [when worshiping, for his hat is a sign of subjection to men]."

The man is representing his headship of the family, answerable to God and God alone. This doesn't mean there is no authority in the church such as pastor, associate, etc. If you take a position in a church, you must submit to the pastor's authority and others' where necessary.

God is a God of symbols. He wants an outward show of an inward reality. I should point out these rules were already in place in the Jewish community. Paul used them as a point of reference to explain what the hat symbolized. Just as a parent needs a child to make some show of obedience when asked to do something, so should man make an outward show of his obedience. God instituted clothing and covering requirements especially during times of worship. If you remember the priest that went into the Holy of Holies had to cover his head. But this is a new day. Evidently God feels it's important enough to make a point of it. In that case, we should do what He asks.

There are some rules that cannot be changed and some that can and we must know the difference. Clothing and what is considered proper attire is constantly changing. Traditions change. One culture's idea of modesty and acceptable behavior is different than another's and changes from one generation to another. In the Middle East, because of the sun, it's necessary for people to cover themselves or they would be burned, especially me with my lily white, freckled skin. As the gospel moved into other cultures, the covering of the head by woman or men was no longer a sign of respect or proper modesty. Therefore, I feel Paul would tell them to do what is respectful in their culture. Respect is the criteria. We may no longer wear the outward sign of being under our husband's covering, but that doesn't mean we don't have the inward attitude of answering to and being responsible to our husband. We may not have the hat, but we still need to have a "hat" attitude.

A woman's hair and her appearance are of utmost importance. If you notice he does admit it's a matter of practice; therefore, I do feel we have some latitude, but one thing will remain constant and that is that a woman's appearance must be perceived as being respectful and appropriate.

Most denominations have a certain idea of what is modest and I have no problem with this. I do have a problem when it becomes bondage. When a woman can never wear a pair of slacks, especially working in the yard or on a cold day, then I feel we have lost our freedom and slipped into bondage. The woman, in her love for her precious Savior, may feel this is not too much to ask and I can agree with this if it keeps someone weak in the faith from falling. But when it's perceived as ridiculous and makes Christians looks silly, I have to question the wisdom of the sacrifice. Actually, the reverse of what she intended is what is happening. People reject our religion and therefore our Jesus because they see us in bondage. We're saying, "Come join us in our bondage" with our out-dated clothing and hair. Of course, they say, "No, thank you." People are trying to get free and our ignorance is keeping them from seeing ours is the way to freedom; that Jesus is the way. That makes the clothing and hair issue the most important matter of all (their salvation).

Then there are those that say, "It's what is in my heart that's important." I agree what is in their heart is what matters, but I can't agree how they dress doesn't matter. It's an outward expression of an inward reality. If you notice, it's usually a teen in baggy pants looking weird making this statement. It has been my experience that there are other things in their lives that are out of order.

People can tell a lot about us by the way we dress. I don't feel we should be legalistic, but I do feel we should be reasonable. And that goes for our kids, too. I don't like it when Christians make their kids weirdos or nerds because they make them look so out-of-style. But we can't let them set the standard either. They should dress like the kids we want them to hang around. And we should dress like the people we want to hang with, too. I am really shocked at the attire and make-up of some women today. Is that really the kind of attention they want to attract?

What is she lacking in her soul, her inner man, that makes her feel she has to dress this way to get attention or love? Many people blame her husband for not being attentive enough, and it may be a problem, but no person will ever fill this hole. All I can say at this point is the woman has a lot of work to do in her head and it can only be done as she reads her Word and seeks the Lord for help and discernment. I would recommend the place to start is to repent. She should grieve over how this has affected her life and those around her. We do not have the luxury of causing another to fall in order to dress any way we want.

A Man's Glory

A man wants to be admired and one of the most significant ways he needs to be admired is by his wife. Yes, by you. He wants to think he has the best wife in the world and he wants other people to think so, too. He wants the world in awe of you. He cares a great deal about how you look, how you sound, and what kind of an impression you make. If I am slovenly, it looks bad on Lamar. If our kids are a mess, it looks bad on both of us.

It's scriptural. A man can't help himself because God created him this way. First Corinthians 11:7 says, *"God's glory is man made in his image and man's glory is the woman."* I am Lamar's glory. That is amazing. The first time I read this it really had an impact on me. It helped me understand a lot of things and why Lamar cares so much how I look and appear to others. Why am I his glory? Because I reflect what kind of man he is, the kind of decisions he makes, how he takes care of someone he loves and how he provides. Evidently this scripture means man and woman generally, but the man personalizes it when he marries. I am a reflection of him, just as we are a reflection of our God. If I'm a mess, especially if I am mouthy, critical, and have an attitude toward him, it makes him look bad.

I don't mean to put undue pressure on you, but you need to know this. If he is embarrassed by you, he takes it especially hard. You may think it's no big deal or it's his fault, but that's very little consolation when he is rejecting you. He may not say it, but he's thinking it. We need to keep this in mind and slowly upgrade instead of continuing to degrade.

It's amazing to me how many women do not dress in a way that is satisfactory to their husband. It's to be comfortable, to save money, carelessness, etc. A man is a visual person. How we look matters to our husband and our kids and our parents and brothers and sisters in Christ, very, very much. It's the best investment you will ever make to make a good presentation of yourself to your family and your community. I would make the effort to put on make-up on Saturday for Lamar and the boys. I didn't care, but they did. And it helped my skin, too.

If his wife looks or acts badly, the only thing a man can do to counter-balance it is to act like he doesn't care. And sometimes he even convinces himself he doesn't. Men numb their feelings with alcohol or by going out with their buddies, but he is really mad at his wife that he has to do this. Then the wife gets an attitude and yells at him for not coming home and that just makes it worse. She gets more careless about herself, the house and kids, or spends money or does something destructive to soothe her feelings and get back at him or to get his attention. This is all contrary to scripture. We are not allowed to repay evil with evil (Romans 12:17).

I don't think a wife has to put up with bad behavior, but do it looking good, with the house and kids looking good. If he comes home late, have a great meal that he missed, not a bad one. Act like you are happy to see him; like you don't notice anything is wrong. Heap coals on his head. Be in a good mood. Laugh and have a good time while he is gone so that when he gets there he will have missed a good time not a bad one. Espe-cially if you have kids. They deserve to have a good time even if he has been irresponsible and thoughtless. Yes, the day may come that you have to get serious and make changes, but until that day comes, make today the best day you can. Then if you leave, he will realize he lost a good thing. And maybe, if he is lucky and if you are just as lucky, it won't be too late.

And in your magnanimous spirit your family will be all the better for the hard times. Just be sure you aren't denying his feelings about true concerns and are dealing with them. You can't be in the wrong and act like nothing is wrong. That doesn't work.

Be sure your kids are a joy to come home to. I know they get sick and grumpy once in a while, but I see too many spoiled, cranky kids today. It's not a good thing to be three years old and running the world. It's scary. Kids reject a parent's authority; be sure it's not yours. Of the four parenting types: neglectful, permissive, controlling, and balanced, only one is good. Be sure you are a good parent even if your husband isn't. Don't be so grieved about your marriage that you become a bad mother.

There was a time when God convicted me of being too mouthy. Lamar has very sensitive hearing and I have one ear that is almost deaf, so that makes things worse than they normally would be. But I can't just excuse myself and hurt Lamar. No, I have to make the adjustment. So I started watching how I sounded especially in public. By myself there is no problem. It was when I added my friends that things went down hill. I hadn't realized how bad we sounded when we got together. The only problem was when I wanted to quiet down, it just made them mad and that made them louder.

When God tells you that you are too mouthy, it does something to you. At least it did me. I just couldn't be as mouthy anymore. I still fight to be as quiet as I should be, but I'm a whole lot better. This glory thing isn't easy.

I should share the vision God gave me to help me because it was so powerful. I am often frustrated when we attend a church function because things are set up in a way that I feel is not conducive to serving the people quickly. As Lamar's right hand man for years, I set up numerous auctions and business meetings. We usually had a snack bar or food being served. I just hate it when everyone has to wait a long time when it could have been organized better. It's especially hard to be one of the workers setting things up when it could be rearranged so easily at this point.

Oh, how hard it was to stifle my frustration. That was until God gave me a vision of a snake striking out and let me know that was me! It's so easy to say something and get people on your side, because they want it to be better, too. But that doesn't make it right. God was saying, "It's not your day." The person has a right to do things the way they want to do them without my interference. There are times when we need to keep our opinion to ourselves and smile and work as hard as we can to help the other person do what they have planned. If it's where you can make a suggestion, do it quietly and if they reject it, let them learn a lesson or maybe you will. Don't ruin their day or yours by trying to push this on them. Let it go. Yes, even if they are wrong. It's not up to me to point it out or murmur.

Lamar's last addiction was projects. I usually cook lunch when he has people here working, even though I don't cook generally as much as I used to. One particular day, besides the sandwiches, I had made my latest favorite quickie soup, and it was quite good. As I scurried around, Lamar said proudly, "There goes my glory," which is scriptural. Evidently the pastor had shared this at the men's prayer breakfast that morning. I said it was funny that he didn't seem to believe me all those years when I said it. We all laughed.

The next day three men delivered our new gas stove. When they removed the old one, it was filthy behind it. I must have had something boil over and didn't realize it went so far. Yuck! The deliverymen took the new one out of the box, but since they couldn't hook up the gas, suggested they not put it where the old one was. "It's quite dirty," the man explained. "Oh, if you pick a good wife, you don't have to worry about that," Lamar assured him and then yelled out, "Do you have it clean yet?" I replied, "Almost!" A look of shock crossed the man's face. They all laughed, but with a tinge of admiration.

After they left, Lamar shared with me how nice it was to know that I would clean it up and what he had said to the men. I played my part perfectly. We kissed and I thanked him for the new stove. As he walked out, I wondered if he had shared the glory part, because it would have been nice if they understood this biblical principle. Then the thought crossed my mind, "Gee! It really puts the pressure on when someone's glory depends on what I do!" I was suddenly in awe of what that meant to me and what I do. Talk about pressure!

And the truth is… (Maybe we should keep saying this like a game show announcer so we feel the impact of it. Get out the trumpets. We're going to have some truth now.) And the truth is: we should want to be this wonderful woman that our man wants us to be. Or maybe I should say we should want to be the wonderful woman God wants us to be. Hopefully, it's one and the same. Our husband isn't the only one that doesn't want us to be a slovenly, lazy, good-for-nothing, mouthy woman, or any of the aforementioned. And I hate to tell you but God doesn't accept a lot of excuses either. He's the I-can-do-all-things-through-Christ-who-strengthens-me God.

Your Authority Figure Is Your Covering

This hat issue is really not an aberration in the Bible. The hat is symbolic of the man "covering" his mate. The woman is the weaker vessel; especially vulnerable when she is pregnant, nursing, and caring for the children. And as the weaker vessel must be protected, nurtured, and esteemed. Just as you as a mother cover your children and protect and nurture them, your man must protect and nurture you. That's the plan.

If we look closely we will find it was man, not God, that made her subservient. God has always upheld the honor and station of the woman. He included Sarah in the promise and when Hagar cried out for her son, He saved him and gave him a promise, too. God has always been on woman's side.

Right after this discussion of hair and hats, Paul talks about the problems arising in the church, 1 Corinthians 11:27–32 (NIV):

Therefore whoever eats this bread or drinks this cup of the Lord in an unworthy manner will be guilty of the body and blood of the Lord. But let a man examine himself, and so let him eat of the bread and drink of the cup. For he who eats and drinks in an unworthy manner eats and drinks judgment to himself not discerning the Lord's body. For this reason many are weak and sick among you, and many sleep. For if we would judge ourselves, we would not be judged. But when we are judged, we are chastened by the Lord, that we may not be condemned with the world.

Evidently they were coming together to eat and drink in the church and disputes were arising out of it. Don't you know if we get together very long, we will get tacky. What was happening was that some had more than others and were not sharing. Can you imagine? Good Christian people—people that may have even seen Jesus with their physical eyes. Unbelievable!

What is even worse is they are going from these church suppers to the Communion table leaving their brothers and sisters in the Lord hungry. Some even came in drunk because they drank so much wine. And then they participated in receiving the body and blood of Jesus. Needless to say, Paul was mortified. He tells them if they eat unworthily they will be guilty of the body and blood of the Lord—putting Him to death—something we have been forgiven of if we receive Him. Sounds like the "once saved always saved" message may be contradicted here.

We are told to receive Communion. So we can't refuse to receive, and yet if we receive with sin in our lives, we bring condemnation upon ourselves and become guilty of Jesus' suffering and death. Darned if you do and darned if you don't (1 Corinthians 11:27).

Those who do not properly judge themselves are guilty of not discerning the Lord's body. They are taking Jesus cheaply, and Jesus is not cheap. What He gives is free, but not cheap. Do not cheapen what He gives you with your sin.

Paul is telling them to be in proper relationship with each other before receiving the body and blood of Jesus in the form of Communion. Get it right or don't participate at all. You are not one of His if you are not in right relationship with each other. If you don't recognize your sin and participate anyhow, you will heap a whole lot of trouble on yourselves. Since he had just talked about the marriage relationship, he is saying we must be right in these relationships, too.

There are many people who, out of humility, refuse to partake of the Lord's Supper, and rightfully so if they are still living a life of sin. However, it's just as wrong not to understand what Jesus has done for you and receive it. We can repent and ask God to forgive us and sincerely want to stop. We are forgiven at that moment even though we may sin again. Not that we intend to. Certainly not. It takes God time to work out our fleshly tendencies. It is very important that we are in right relationship with not only the Christians close to us, but also with the people we meet in the market place. Our testimony rests in our relationships. Let's not be guilty of not properly discerning the body of Christ.

Oh, Jesus. The last thing I want to do is to bring reproach upon You. To make You a laughing stock or, worse yet, to be avoided. How sad that Your followers are Your biggest problem. Help me to see and understand how to relate properly with everyone I come in contact with. For truly, it is out of seeing and understanding that our relationship springs and that is what is most important to me.

Twenty-one

A man is responsible to Christ, a woman is responsible
to her husband, and Christ is responsible to God.
—1 Corinthians 11:3

Lamar Is My Covering

I N THIS CHAPTER I tell three stories that are typical of our confusion over the man as our covering. I have changed the names and details to protect their identities.

My Testimony

I never thought much about Lamar as my covering. So, just to prove I'm not above criticism I'm going to tell you one of my stories:

I'm a real can-do woman. I was raised to be very responsible and independent. Lamar is such a strong person it was obvious he was the head of the family. Head of the family doesn't mean everyone is submitted all the time. I had a problem submitting to some things and did my own thing once in a while, but I yielded most of the time. I didn't always think of Lamar as my covering. When I was little, people would accuse my brothers of teaching me some of the "precocious" things I did. My mother would counter, "Her brothers? They didn't teach her. She teaches them!" I'm really quite a toughie. I look feminine enough and I am an artist, but there is a place of steel in me.

I'd heard Lamar was my covering, but I never gave it much thought. He did his thing and I helped. It wasn't until a certain incident took place that I came to appreciate what this meant to me. Allow me first to me preface this by saying, I think a man needs a covering, too. (Jesus did send His disciples out in groups of twos.) Actually, his wife can be a covering to him in a slightly different way. We should both be accountable to others, and our spouse is one of these people. In the end, we are both accountable to God.

A few years ago I went through an experience that was somewhat traumatic to me. Lamar and I had already moved on from a ministry when they called and asked us to come back and help them with some problems they were having. Lamar was not able to attend and I did not intend to go either, but I prayed about it and felt led to go. I tried to walk in love and I didn't say anything wrong, but let's just say things did not go well. I left the meeting totally devastated.

On the way home all I could think was, "What was that?" I honestly didn't know if I should repent. "God, You have got to help me understand what just happened." When I got home, Lamar was working and there was no way to talk to him. I eventually told him, but I don't think he ever realized what it meant to me. How devastated I was. What bothered me was that I had prayed about it and felt led to go. I hadn't intended to go. I changed my mind in the process of seeking the Lord. I felt betrayed. How can I trust myself to know the next time if it is or isn't Him? Why did it happen?

God doesn't always answer our whys because sometimes there is no answer that is good enough, at least to our mind. We will just have another why and another. But we can answer our own questions if we will allow our mind to look over what happened and properly assess things without trying to defend ourselves or squeeze it into our narrow way of thinking, using the Word as our guide or maybe a Christian friend. And so I embarked on a journey to answer my own questions. And yes, I have arrived at some answers.

First of all, I have come to see I should not have been praying about whether to go or not. God had led us out and I don't know that He wanted us to get involved again—the "pillar of salt" principle. Knowing the situation was as bad as it was, I should haven't gone alone. I needed Lamar.

There was a point earlier when we were still in the group that Lamar went against my better judgment and met with leaders and he was hurt, proving again that it takes at least two in these spiritual battles. If either of us doesn't have peace, that should be enough to make the other stop, even if one is not a Christian. If this is the case (that your husband is not a Christian), you should keep it in mind. He could be wrong, but he could be right too. Find a brother or sister in Christ to ask.

Was I right or wrong in what I did? In my defense, let me say this: it's better to be wrong attempting to be obedient than to be willfully disobedient. I'm an improvement over some rebels but not enough not to be hurt. God is not obligated to tell us anything when we start doing our own thing, and that's really what I did, because in the end I don't feel I was led. I just wanted to go. He is not obligated to keep us from getting in a mess. We can spiritualize it all we want; the proof will be in the pudding. We can say it is everyone else's fault but ours, but if things are coming down around us, we are very likely missing something that He could have told us and would have told us if we had been open, or we ignored what His silence meant. If He says nothing, it is because He either wants us to do what He has already said to do and will not say it again or He does not want us to do what we are asking to do. Wait for orders. If you have orders, don't ask for more. And if you have no orders, do what your hands find to do not what your brain thinks up for you to do. And never go against Scripture.

I finally came to see I did break the rule of authority. Right or wrong, it was not mine to do alone. I was out of place and didn't stay there long. I would have loved to fight the good fight of faith; but sometimes it's not our battle to fight or not the time to fight it, and it is not the good fight of faith. So, it would have been better if I had just stayed home and cleaned my house. What I didn't know to do that day (repent) I did when finally I saw I was wrong. I was not wrong to help, but wrong to step out without a covering. That I should have known!

No Permission

I'm telling the following story because so many women work closely with their husband either in business or in ministry. When we are in a position of leadership, we must know how to handle it properly. The success of the endeavor rests on understanding when we are about to cross over the fine line of submission into rebellion. Leaders can be in rebellion, too.

Lamar and I were members of another group when the leader's wife, in his absence, made some rather harsh remarks at one of our meetings. We knew these remarks weren't on the agenda because she prefaced it with: "This may get me in trouble, but I feel I should say it." She proceeded to say something to the effect that if we, the group, couldn't get our act together, they had other things they could do with their time.

I couldn't imagine what she was talking about because everyone there was working very hard, doing everything we could to facilitate the ministry. The leader said later, "My wife figures it's easier to get forgiveness than permission." Everyone but me laughed. I had to pray about it for some much-needed answers. If they understood the gravity of it all, they wouldn't have been laughing. Although he maintained it was the beginning of good things, I feel it had a negative impact on the ministry. And I don't mean the members that left right after that, but the continuing absence of real growth.

He was saying that she couldn't have gotten permission, but now she had forgiveness and everything was just fine. We never saw repentance that she had done anything wrong. She had usurped his authority, acted in a way that he did not agree with, hurt their ministry, and everything is not just fine but better? It can't be, and it wasn't. They certainly were in denial.

I understand when a man is called into the ministry, they are both called. But they aren't both called to the same position. She has her own calling and has no right to jeopardize his ministry even if hers is tied to it. If someone hurts the ministry by such remarks, it should be him. It's true that sometimes someone else can say things that the leader can't and they need to be said, but they should be said only with his wholehearted approval. Not even a half-hearted nod will do.

Many leaders are not very good at confrontation. As his helper, your husband, boss or pastor, should totally endorse everything you say and do. If you know he wouldn't agree with what you are about to say, then you cannot not say it, and you certainly can't spiritualize it with, "I feel God would have me say this." If her husband wanted it said, but didn't want to say it and allowed it to come from her, then he was wrong. It isn't her place to be saying it.

She may have been frustrated and felt it needed to be said, but the meeting, with her husband absent, was not the time or place. Everything else she said that night was great and it should have been a wonderful meeting. Instead, we all left wounded and heavyhearted. We pollute everything when we "get in the flesh" just a little.

God will sometimes show us something that our husband doesn't see yet, but not to announce to the world. He gives it to us to pray about and to be involved in the spiritual battle. He will deal with our husband or leader until such time that it needs to be made public. And yes, we may suffer loss because of it and then he will get to learn a hard lesson. And yes, we have to have a good attitude as he learns it or we will be wrong again. I told you so's come at a very high price and a silent one at that.

This couple has continued to suffer loss in their ministry over the years, in spite of the fact they were praying and seeking the Lord and obviously anointed at some level.

I have a suspicion that her husband could have been there but wasn't because he knew she might say something. And that's probably why she said it. Because she knew deep down inside he agreed. But that still doesn't make it right. It should have come from him and until it comes from him, she should pray and fast, not take things into her own hands. Don't you see how this is like Adam and Eve? The man not willing to do what he's supposed to do and the woman stepping into the void.

The truth is the husband/leader was not right about so many things he was doing. He was a wonderful preacher of the Word, very anointed and gifted. He had a promising future as a minister of the gospel. But there was a flaw and every once in a while he would speak improperly and beat up the sheep and cause a division just when things were going good. I honestly think this is why she said what she did, because she knew what he was thinking and thought maybe if it came from her it would sound better. It didn't. It shouldn't have been said by either of them.

Beyond all this, I really feel the wife was not doing her job as a wife. She should have been able to see his error instead of sympathizing with him and agreeing with him. He was his own worst enemy and the things he was thinking were wrong, so the way he was handling things would not bear fruit. We are to edify, but sometimes we have to be honest and help them see the truth. It was as if he were two people and for the bad side, he needed intensive ministry to rid him of his demons (counseling).

ONE FINAL EXAMPLE

Lamar and I were at a leaders meeting for a teen ministry planning its annual convention when it was obvious there was a major problem. The kids had ideas they wanted to implement and every time they would mention something, some of the old-timers would shoot it down saying they had tried it before and it didn't work or it cost too much money. By old-timers I don't mean old in age. Lamar didn't want money to be the hold-up for having a good conference, so he assured them he would help financially. You might think that would make everyone happy, but it didn't. The negative group still had their objections.

Lamar is a can-do guy and we wanted to help the youth. The last thing we wanted was to take sides or to be a part of a controversy, but anything anyone said seemed to put them on one side or the other.

Most of us were praying silently and a few not so silently. One young woman got down between the seats and was really loud. What happened to "decently and in order?" About this time a young woman said the Lord would warn us not to commercialize the conference. Well, there was no way we would make any money on it. The event was free! We just wanted it promoted to bring in as many kids as possible.

I'm not one to tell someone they didn't hear from God, but she didn't hear this from God because it was not a concern. We have to be very careful that we don't take a thought and assume it's God and then justify it with everything we hear and see after that. And God will let it go on to its natural conclusion and that is failure. It cannot bear fruit, but sometimes the end is so far from the beginning that the person never understands none of it was God. They left God a long time before they realized He was gone.

This young woman could have gotten to know us better and seen our motives were pure, because that is what was in question. But instead, because she saw us as the problem, the enemy, she avoided us. She eventually came to see things weren't right and left the group, but I doubt that she ever questioned her part in any of it. That's sad because then she won't correct her own error.

I wish she would have asked herself why God didn't warn her about the things that did happen that hurt the conference? Why didn't He say, "Tell my people to go out into the neighborhoods and invite the teens to come to the conference?"

If there is sin in your life, you must question any "word" from the Lord as being suspect. Ask yourself: Is it scriptural? Is it true? Does it edify? Is it helpful?

A whole faction of the leaders were in rebellion. After the meeting the youth pastor admitted they resented him because they had hoped to be appointed to his position. They saw him as a usurper and had never cooperated with anything he wanted to do. The conflict was palpable. Needless to say the leaders made other grave errors such as being respecters of persons, which is especially grievous in a teen ministry.

What if these people were ministering to your precious son or daughter? Run don't walk to the nearest exit with your kids. Unfortunately, the parents of the kids in this group had no idea what was going on.

THANKS

In spite of the mess, we had a marvelous youth conference. The kids had been able to do the graphics they wanted with Lamar's help. It was held in the big church and a Christian rock group out of Tampa came over with all their equipment. It was glorious. The saddest part was that the youth didn't get out in the neighborhoods around the church or invite their friends. It was mostly church groups that came. Why? Because they didn't trust the ministry. And the leaders didn't have a vision or a burden for it either. Bad leadership is always a killer.

The next year the conference was held in the old smaller building and the leader was one of the rebels. Lamar and I stepped down shortly after the conference because of the confusion and that leader stepped down shortly after that. But we still attended the church, so I went to the conference.

The first night the youth pastor got up and graciously thanked the worship team for doing such a great job. He gave the glory to God for the instruments and the live music. They had evidently had to go to tapes for their worship which we had never done, but it's good to be thankful.

I stood there knowing that God had so much more for them. He had sent us to bless them and help them have what they needed to minister to the youth of our city. Neither youth pastor had a vision for what God wanted to do. "Let's strengthen what we have," and everybody said, "Amen." Wouldn't it "strengthen what you have" if they saw their friends and neighbors getting saved, delivered, healed, and on fire for God, too? I just don't know how effective it is to be such a pitiful, cliquish little group.

I looked around and saw a few from other churches and those few we had left. The ironic thing is the church is surrounded by low-cost housing filled with kids that desperately need this ministry. The "conference" was not even announced on the church marquis.

The visiting evangelist did such a good job preaching to the already reached. He preached his heart out. I'm sure he was glad to be invited.

It's not easy to even get the invite. Not many churches even do this much. Did we say we love the kids? Did we say we love God? I question how much we love the kids or God if we don't love their souls enough to tell them somebody is coming with good news and they need to hear it.

If it's true we reap what we sow and if, in this case they sowed rebellion, selfishness, and bigotry (because that is what it is when you esteem your own kids better than another's), then they will reap rebellion, selfishness, and bigotry. And they wonder why their kids are rebellious? So many Christian parents do not understand how important it is that they are open to what God is doing and be discerning about problems, too. Check out the teen ministry. Be involved. Let me say this about teen ministries. Notoriously they are led by young adults who have often spent years in rebellion and heard very little of what was taught to them at their parents' church from the age ten or twelve on, if they heard anything before that. I have three boys; I've taken a passel of little boys to church. They pay very little attention. It always astounds me when the worst one raises his hand to get saved. So, they are getting something, but very little.

When this guy rededicates his life or gets saved at twenty or twenty-five and is "called" into the ministry, guess where he starts? That's right. In the teen ministry. He still needs adult supervision, but most get very little. It's sad how little mentoring goes on in the normal church. The "normal church" is a dysfunctional church, just as the normal family is a dysfunctional family. Remember, rebellion and dysfunction are the normal human state and all of us return quickly to that state. This teen ministry is typical. I don't want you to think it's some special case.

I know this is a terrible indictment against the church, and I'm sorry, but it's the truth. It's still no reason not to attend church. That is not optional. God wants us to work these things out. He understands how hard it is. Life is hard. He wants us to struggle and work it out with His help. He said there was enough evil in the day and some of it's in our churches and *we* have to be a part of shooing it out.

What could we have done differently? The first youth pastor wasted too much time. He was careless with the ministry. It's a precious time for these kids. They are about to graduate and face the world alone for the first time. They need what the gospel teaches. They need the wisdom of God and they weren't getting it. They were getting games, clichés (a trite expression or idea—a simplistic version of the scriptures), and frustration at the very place that should be helping them the most. The parents were helpful and supportive, but the ministry let them down. Big time. And for that, he was responsible. He licked his wounds, but God saw him as part of the problem, not the solution. This is one reason I feel hearts were hardened against him. He left in defeat.

But beyond this his wife couldn't see it. She saw them as victims, too. And here is my point: Encourage your husband and think the best of him. Edify him, pray for him, help him in any way you can. But don't be blind. He doesn't need you to kid yourself or allow him to pull the wool over your eyes. He needs you to see and stand in the truth and to say it lovingly when necessary. Do not nag or beat him over the head with the Bible, but at least know when he is wrong. But because she couldn't see it there was no correcting influence in their lives. And that is what I regret. That he has never really gotten his act together. The potential was there, but as long as they see themselves as the victims, they will not reach their potential. Accountability is so important to a minister and I don't mean someone that doesn't see your life up close and personal on a daily basis.

Check your life and check it again. The proof is in the pudding. The gospel has life. Is there life in what you are doing? Or do you keep suffering loss? Or shooting yourself in the foot? Open yourself up to the prophets in your life, to your critics, to what you don't want to hear. Don't be so sure you are right all the time. Are you on your way up the mountain? (Like Aaron was, about to be stripped of his priestly robes and pay for coming against Moses.) Let's face it; there is always something we are missing, something that is displeasing to God. Ferret it out.

Oh, God. Let it not be so. Let me not be blind to my errors or my husband's. I want to walk in the light. I want to see things as You see them. Help me, Lord, to see. Open my eyes, open my ears, open my heart. Where am I missing it, kidding myself, playing games? Oh, God, let it not be so. Not in my life.

TWENTY-TWO

God sets the lonely in families, he leads forth the prisoners in singing; But the rebellious live in a sun-scorched earth.

—PSALM 68:6

Lonely

GOD NEVER GAVE UP the original idea of an intimate relationship with man, even though we are now two. He wants to be an integral part of every marriage, as close as we are to each other, assuming we are close. To do this He has to be included on the inside, in our souls. Actually, this is where man and woman relate, too, in our heads and hearts first—soul to soul.

The Bible says the candle of the Lord searches the inward parts (Proverbs 20:27). That's why we need to keep our heart pure. Because He sees what's there and it disturbs Him when He sees something that is not right. I experienced this when my son got one of those weird haircuts with lines cut in both sides. It was awful. Every time I looked at him, it took me back for a minute and I had to work at ignoring it. God is a parent, too. Just think how God feels when He sees revenge, bitterness, or selfishness cut into our very being.

The only way to be pure is to be pure in heart, constantly keeping up to date with our repentance—a repentant heart.

The Bible speaks of our relationship with God often in the same terms it uses for lovers. He wants us to pursue Him, long for Him, just as He pursues and longs for us. We all want this. I wanted a guy to pursue me. Didn't you?

When I was dating, if a guy made the slightest indication that he might be interested in someone else, that was it for me. If he wasn't so smitten with me that he was blind to other girls, he wasn't smitten enough. And I'm not talking about physically. I mean that innate something that attracts one to another—more than chemistry—a meeting of heart and mind. That is what I wanted, and I have to say God gave this special love to Lamar for me.

It's a shame kids today don't understand the wonderful bonding God meant to take place in the male-female relationship before marriage: the bonding of hearts *before* bodies. Then the sexual, when it happens, is especially powerful.

Not only does God want us to pursue Him, but once we come into a personal relationship with Him, He wants us to put Him first. He doesn't want to take second place to any guy or girl, let alone to a car, money, or our career. Is this so hard to understand? (Hebrews 11:6.)

It's amazing that God allowed us to have each other knowing we would naturally prefer each other over Him. That's unselfish, agape love—the God kind. God isn't jealous in a bad way. He just wants His due and if He doesn't get it, He gets very upset. Not because it's bad for Him, but because it is error. It's wrong thinking to not include Him in our love.

God must have known He would be second fiddle much of the time, but He still made the choice to go for it and even went so far as to fight and die for us. That's an amazing love. Of course, He doesn't weary or wear out like we do. It's the kind of love God wants us to have, even when our relationships go sour and our loved one goes their own way—enough love to fight for them until they are pulled from the clutches of the enemy. I don't mean we can stop them from filing for divorce or force them to stay in the home. That isn't always possible. I mean enough to fight the spiritual battle, to pray and intercede in spite of how much they have hurt us. We need to think more of them and their soul than we do our feelings. We may have to pray and love from afar, just as God has done for us.

I cannot promise that God will heal a particular marriage. I know some people stand for years for the restoration of their marriage and that is commendable. But I don't know that it will necessarily happen.

I encourage readers to do what it will take to heal their marriage but there are so many factors. I don't know that God is compelled to do what they so desperately wait for. I believe in miracles, but I can't guarantee what it will be or when. It's counter-productive to try to maintain the marriage or to bring it back together until some issues have been properly dealt with. If our spouse refuses to be respectful and do what is right, we must establish boundaries. And that includes separating and possibly divorcing. If something happens later, fine, if not, that must be fine, too. God is the God of a new day.

Numero Uno

We make a big mistake when in our loneliness, compulsion, or dysfunction, we make our spouse our all in all. When we give him the place intended for God alone. When we do, we are breaking the First Commandment. There's an ominous thought. We are putting something or someone ahead of God and that is the one thing He doesn't want us to do. It's not fair to God, it's not fair to the other person, and it's not fair to us. Everything is out of whack and won't be right until we recognize it and make it right.

The causes of loneliness are caring too much, having unrealistic expectations, or being deprived of the love and nurturing we should have and others aren't providing for one reason or another. The cures are just the opposite of a person's natural inclinations. "Like what?" you ask. Like withdrawing, grasping, and trying to control the other person, buying affection—not just through money but through what we do for others, using our beauty or talent improperly, etc. Once lonely, a person sabotages him or herself and makes things worse. Nothing is less attractive than a whiney, pitiful, or manipulative person. We end up driving away the very people we want to attract. When loneliness has made us compulsive, it has gone too far.

I think it's very important that we understand loneliness is a universal problem of all people. Loneliness will not be solved by answering your questions about your biological past or by finding someone to bond with. Those things are great and helpful, but the hole will always be there and only God can fill it. And there will be more than one hole; there will be many holes, and that's why we have to keep in touch daily with the great Filler of Holes: the Holy Spirit, or should I say, God Himself.

There is a book, *Women Who Love Too Much* by Robin Norwood. It's not a Christian book and doesn't give the Christian answer, but it sure does flesh out the problem in living color, which many women need before they will do something. There are meetings that can help you understand and change problem behaviors. If you attend a secular group, be sure to add the Christian perspective. They won't understand what we do, but it shouldn't go against our beliefs. Freeing yourself from one bondage to another is not freedom. Going from a compulsion for a man to drugs, alcohol, some weird religion, or cult is *not* an improvement. Go to God.

It's really best if you can find a Christian group rather than a secular one. If you can't find one, maybe you should look into starting one at your church. God will lead you to where He wants you to go. Pray about it and then listen and watch. There are so many people just like yourself. I just know God has a place for you. It's your job to find it. If you figure out you are in the wrong one, run, don't walk, to the nearest exit. Get away from people in error. They are dangerous. Even if they have a little truth, we can't mix truth and error and get anything but a mess.

MOVING ON

Once as I visited with a friend, she said doing what the Christians said to do didn't work for her. After ten years of a bad marriage, God showed her it was never going to work. As we discussed what happened, she said her husband cheated on her shortly after they were married. I hated to tell her, but he was probably never faithful.

Well, the Scripture plainly says you can leave in the case of adultery. God never said for her to endure his cheating, drinking, and abuse all those years. It's sad when Christians say otherwise, but the woman could have read the Bible for herself and gotten the answer much earlier. We can blame others if we have access to the same things they do: the Word, the Holy Spirit, and a personal inner witness, then it's our responsibility to do some of our own digging.

Something early on should have sent her to her Bible. When I pressed her why she didn't, she finally admitted, "I couldn't give him up." The truth is she didn't want to give up her man. He was her compulsion. She loved too much. She wasn't ready for the truth. Ten years is a long time. After he had done her dirty long enough, she was ready.

It took me ten years, too, but we didn't divorce. Lamar hadn't cheated on me. If he had, I wouldn't have waited ten years to do something about it. I do think you can get past adultery and your marriage can be more fulfilling than you ever thought possible. In her case, he didn't want to change.

A Nominal Christian Is Not a Normal Christian

Did your father abandon you? Maybe your mother wasn't even sure who he was. Even if it wasn't his fault he wasn't there for you, you still didn't have the advantage of having a father—a very special person in a girl's life. Or maybe he was in the home, but absent emotionally. It's important to understand there are places in him that grieve, too. He has gotten to the place where he is numb, where he can't cry any more. He's coped, as I did after losing my little girl. Things are so bad in his own heart and mind that he can't speak of them. He feels he can't let anyone in. It may have all taken place when he was very young. There are just so many mixed up ideas people latch onto and call them true when they are really lies. But it's hard to get them to see that. Forgive him and pray for him, your two most powerful weapons. He needs a hero. I was my dad's hero. Not that he was bad; he was a wonderful father, but he had back-slidden many years earlier. I helped him get back.

You can't allow your father's lie to become your lie. So, if he hasn't been there for you, then take God up on His promise to be a father to the fatherless. He loves you more than any earthly father ever could. You just have to give Him a chance. Tell Him you want Him to be that for you.

I have heard wonderful testimonies of children who had done this and been greatly blessed with a very special relationship with their heavenly Father.

Remember what it says in Proverbs 23:10 (NIV), "*Do not move an ancient boundary stone or encroach on the fields of the fatherless, for their Defender is strong; he will take up their case against you.*"

There's a promise for a bad day. I'm sure He means the devil, too, not just human enemies. Also, read Psalms 68:5, 82:3, and 146:9.

Separated Out

A few years ago, I went to a conference in Ohio with a group of ladies. Because I was a late entrant, I was split between two groups. During the day I rode in a car and at night I slept with the women in the van. It shouldn't have been a problem, but it was. The women in the car were very inhospitable, although I don't think they meant to be. They had been part of a singles group and had a lot of mutual friends. Two of them had since married and moved on, but it was fun to catch up on things and reminisce about old times. Fun for them, but not for me. They had a lot to talk about and a lot of time to kill. They made no attempt to include me. I think it was simply ignorance of common courtesy. I certainly wasn't rude enough to say anything. One of the ladies even mentioned they were leaving me out, but it was too compelling for them to stop. One woman was especially obtuse. Things got so bad, I regretted going on the trip. I kept asking God, "Why am I here? Why am I always the odd man out?"

I grew up the odd man out as the only girl on the block. And then in school things would happen that would make me the one left out. Mom worked and I was always by myself trying to find someone to play with. And being the only girl, I was always thrown in with Mom and that left me out, because I wanted to be with Dad and the boys. So, being the odd man out is very painful to me.

Help came in a most unlikely form. All the women in the group wanted to go shopping after the first part of the morning session. I didn't travel fifteen hours to shop. I wanted to attend one of the small morning classes, so I stayed at the church. To get back to the hotel I reached out to a group from another church and ended up having the best time, sharing and ministering to them. They seemed to think I was special. But the group I was with most of the time in the car didn't seem to care.

It just seemed so unnecessary—going through all this. I ended up further torn between groups, but it was good. I felt God wanted me with the new group, but on a limited basis because I would have to return with my original group in the car after the sessions. "Why, God, do I have to be the odd man out all the time?" As I prayed about it, He helped me understand that my loneliness had forced me to reach out and this was a good thing. I had been able to witness and minister to people I never would have if I had stayed with my group. And it also forced me to Him. My loneliness all these years has made me the person I am today. He was telling me, "Don't regret it. Be thankful for it. Embrace it. For it's out of your loneliness that many of the good things in your life have come." Praise God. It's out of my loneliness that my ministry has been birthed. This was reinforced recently by a man on television that testified God had said the same thing to him when he was betrayed by one of his closest friends.

Why do you think I am the woman of God I am? Because I had nobody else. Because He separated me out and forced me to get my answers from Him. Not that friends aren't wonderful, and godly friends are a big help, but nobody is as good a Help as God. Consider Abram and Sarah. And don't think Abraham was a great comfort to her. As usual the man is more trouble than he seems to be worth. But that's not true. Without him there would have been nothing but misery, no calling, no vision, no ministry. No, they were called together, but it didn't feel like a lot of togetherness when she was in the harem alone.

I didn't find Lamar much comfort either. I went through the loss of my little girl, a bad marriage, kids that didn't get along, bankruptcy, the loss of my home, all alone. My parents lived in Pennsylvania while I was in Alabama. We moved a few times and I lost what few friends I had.

God wasn't the cause of my loneliness, but He did allow it to separate me out. Why? To minister to me. To heal me and save me. And this is what you must see if you are separated out from all you love. Jesus walked His life very much alone. Abraham was told to leave his family and friends. Moses. You name the person, and I can show you how they were separated out. It's a very important concept with God. No, He didn't take these men and women to more godly places. He just took them to a place where they can't rely on Daddy or Momma or friends and relatives.

Finding yourself alone is not a sign that He doesn't love you; it's a sign He does. Problems arise when we start solving the problem of loneliness on our own, when we reach out in unnatural and ungodly ways. Then we end up in a bigger mess. God wants to be our all in all and He can't do it until He is all we have. Sound familiar?

We get married to have a special love and end up lonelier than ever. Even if we have a wonderful husband, children, parents, and friends, and even if we have a relationship with God and a vibrant church family, we still experience a great deal of loneliness. It doesn't make sense for us to feel this way, but we do. We all do. Everyone has these times of total separation. Take my word for it, it's a lie from the enemy, a spiritual thing, and we must fight it spiritually. Even Jesus experienced it. Just know it's a lie that nobody cares and nobody understands.

God doesn't always intervene when we think He should because there is a greater purpose to be served, and to accomplish it He must allow us to suffer through some things. Just trust, be still, and draw closer to Him. He does care. He cares very much. He is dealing with some very difficult circumstances and He wants as many saved as possible. His is a greater work and you are a part of it. You must be determined to be a part of the solution not a part of the problem. In Galatians 5 Paul tells us how to fight the good fight of faith.

Finally, be strong in the Lord and in his mighty power. Put on the full armor of God so that you can take your stand against the devil's schemes. For our struggle is not against flesh and

blood, but against the rulers, against the authorities, against the
powers of this dark world and against the spiritual forces of evil
in the heavenly realms. Therefore put on the full armor of God,
so that when the day of evil comes, you may be able to stand
your ground, and after you have done everything, to stand.

—Ephesians 6:10–13

The first thing Paul tells us to buckle on is truth for out of it will come righteousness, faith, peace, power and the readiness to go forth. You must fight this fight. You are an ambassador with all the privileges and responsibilities that position brings. It's up to you to figure out what all this means and walk in it. Your life will never be the same. Fight this good fight of faith so that at the end of the day you can say, "It's well with my soul."

Oh God. I want it to be well with my soul, every day and at the
end of all my days. Help me to fight this good fight of faith. Help
me to come to see the power of the weapons at my disposal, the
power of my prayers, the power of my words, the power of what
I do, the power of my choices, the power of my love, and the
power of my fear and doubt and unforgiveness. I know I am as
much of the problem as anyone in my life. I have made my bed
and now don't want to lie in it. Help me to remake it, so it's a
bed of peace and joy and I am the source of peace and joy for
others as I draw from You and make You my Source. I love You,
Lord, and give you the pieces of my life. Amen.

It can be difficult to know the difference between the good fight of faith and a compulsion. Be sure to figure it out.

A Home of Our Own

In the movie *A Home of Our Own*, a poor single mother loses her job because a pervert does something inappropriate and she over-reacts. How is it that she seems to attract perverts? Sounds like the inner peace point fits here. She packs up the family and lights out to who knows where. She is determined to find the right place. Needless to say, the oldest is not a happy camper. He sees lots of places he likes, but she turns them all down. We can't believe what she feels is acceptable and you know the kids feel the same way. It's a hull, not a house. The owner is a Chinese or Japanese widower who needs help in his business. So they take over the "unfinished" house and his life in the process.

She and the kids work in his business and on the house, sacrificing and making do with this make-shift dwelling. Let's face it, they are camping out. People give them stuff and they work for more of the things they need and eventually it's coming together to a limited extent. The boy cooperates but seethes. The mother is undaunted. Christmas brings about a crisis. Well, there were other crises, but this is a big one. The crisis is precipitated when she has the audacity to spend their Christmas money on tools and things for the house and nothing for the kids. The oldest boy explodes. It's so selfish of her not to give the kids something for Christmas. He about loses it. He is bitter for a long time.

They make up finally just before they both have their first dates—the same night. His turns out fine but hers is a bad scene. (I think her friend-liness misleads the guys. She thinks she just attracts problems, which could be true, too.) A few days later in a moment of celebration because they finally have real indoor plumbing, the middle boy ignites the out-house to burn it down. Horror of horrors! The fire jumps to the roof of the house and, try as they might, they can't save it. The mother comes home as it erupts its flames and is mortified. After all their hard work and sacrifice, it's GONE! The son screams at her to face facts. They haven't lost their home; they have lost a shack, a hopeless, endless, stupid hole that has sucked everything out of them. It would never have been a house. It was a joke. And he's right. But she can't see it.

The best thing that ever happens is the house burning down. As long as it's there they will keep trying, keep struggling to make it right. And it never would be right. With it out of the way, they can move on to the frui-tion of her dream: a home of their own. Against her better judgment, she is forced to accept the town's help and let them build her a proper home. Against her better judgment; keep this in mind. It happens to you and me too. We can't always see that we aren't the best judge in the middle of pursuing our dreams.

I'm not saying when your dream burns down that there was anything wrong with it or that it was on a bad foundation. How can I say my little girl dying was the ridding myself of something wrong? It wasn't. It was the loss of one of the most beautiful things in my life, my dream. The best would have been my life with Dadra *and* Jesus. But, I don't know if I hadn't lost Dadra if I would have ever found Jesus, and that's the truth. I can say having Jesus in my life has more than made up for it. Dadra wasn't a bad foundation, but building on *my* strength and what I could do for myself was.

At the time of her death, I had a beautiful little family. Somehow, going from boy, girl, boy, to boy, boy, boy made a big difference and it wasn't a good one. Not that anything was wrong with the boys; they just didn't relate like they did with Dadra in the middle. We went from barely getting along to a whole lot worse. And it kept getting worse for a while. It's at this point most people would have added the liquor or another man or relationship or something to fill that hole in their heart. I don't know why; I just couldn't. I couldn't jump from the frying pan into the fire.

God could have made something beautiful out of my first family, but He didn't have that choice. I was too strong and Lamar was too stubborn. We were too dysfunctional, so God allowed our house to burn down, so to speak. My dream of raising a little girl died that day, but my dream lives again in every woman I have ever ministered to. God is raising up spiritual daughters in the multiplied thousands to take her place. I just know it. Dadra did not die in vain. She was the first-fruit of which there are many more. It's the promise God made to me.

Sometimes we don't know where we are going or what we are doing. We are just following some inner something we don't understand. And it doesn't always work out. We go from bad to worse. All you can do at times like this is stand and not shut God out of your life. Listen and learn;

embrace people and life. Don't run from the people in your life. They are hurting, too. It doesn't help to get bitter and vengeful and critical. It just adds to your problems. Don't give up. This is no time to go off on your own. If you can't follow anyone else, follow Jesus.

I must warn you, if you run away, you will go around this mountain again. If you don't deal with things today, people and situations will come about in your life that will seem as bad as the ones you have now and maybe even worse. You will just be a little older and wiser and maybe that time do a little better, but it won't be any easier. I have to ask, if you can't do it today, how will you be able to do it later? When will you start, if not today? No matter who is in your life, you must treat them like you would Jesus or like Jesus would treat them. The Golden Rule tells us so.

> *In everything, therefore, treat people the same way you want them to treat you, for this is the Law and the Prophets.*
> —MATTHEW 7:12

Twenty-three

**In my distress I prayed to the Lord, and the Lord answered me
and rescued me. The Lord is for me, so I will not be afraid.
—Psalm 118:5–6**

Grateful

IN THOSE EARLY YEARS when God was doing so much, I was thankful
and full of praise. In spite of the difficulties, I was able to keep my
naturally positive attitude. However, no one is immune to negative
feelings and our problems were very real. We would get the victory
one day only to lose it the next. Friends would try to counsel me, but
it didn't seem to help. We probably needed professional help, but we
lived way out in the country and couldn't afford it. Lamar wouldn't
have gone anyway. They say the one that needs it most is the one that
refuses, although, it does help the better one to go. At least he or she is
getting help. But without both trying to make things better, it's hard,
but not impossible. I am proof that you can turn things around starting
with one.

I knew it wasn't right to have the attitude I did. I was so angry and
bitter toward Lamar. I couldn't change him; I had tried that. I had tried
meeting him with logic and anger; nothing seemed to work. I had to
somehow change things. But how? I was trying my best. Trying your best
only works if it's scriptural and sometimes we don't know the scripture
to apply. We are so confused and torn up emotionally that we can't even
think of scriptures. That's why it's good to have godly friends.

It took me a while to see that I had fallen into the trap of unthankful-
ness—being ungrateful. The "good confession" teaching was popular at the
time and I became aware of how negative I was speaking, especially about

293

Lamar. I knew I had to begin saying positive things, but what? How can you when things are such a mess? When he's such a mess. It seemed like I would be lying; but I was committed. I had to do this.

Every time Lamar upset me and I started to say something negative, I would stop and force myself to say through gritted teeth, "Praise God, Lamar Vice is a blessing to me." It was amazing how often I had to say it. I didn't realize how often I was thinking and speaking negatively about him. After six months or longer it suddenly hit me: Lamar Vice *is* a blessing to me. Who else is as strong in the things of the Lord as I am? A few, but not many. Because of Lamar, I have become the woman of faith I am. What a blessing! Finally, I meant what I said, shouting every word, "Praise God. Lamar Vice is a blessing to me!" I laughed and cried and praised God for a long time. I still laugh about it.

When we become Christians, our minds are all messed up. We have been thinking the other way so long that it takes a while to turn it around, and takes every day in the Word to keep it that way. Our thinking comes from "the pit", but we aren't destined for the pit. We are headed for the palace. We are King's kids. King Jesus is preparing a palace for us. In fact, we should have the beginning of regal living here on Earth, but we've haven't been raised to think like royalty. We don't expect the best and even when we get it, we think we don't deserve it and will lose it at any moment. We've been raised to think like street urchins: clutch, grab, fight for all you can, and hide what you get. Don't brag on it or you'll jinx it. All those *The Prince and the Pauper* movies are really true and we are the main character. The pauper and the prince all rolled into one. We have the brain of the pauper and the standing of the prince. Amazing.

But nobody knows we are royalty. We look just the same and sound the same. We live in the same place. My own mother said she liked the old Midge better. I assured her that "she won't be back." Our relationship was never quite the same. Dad was just bewildered.

We may be King's kids, but if nobody tells us, we won't know it either. If we are going to get to the palace, we are going to have to figure it out for ourselves and do it for ourselves. That's why we have to read and study on our own and find good mentors that understand who we are. We certainly don't need people who still think we are sinners saved by grace. We may be, but we are now saints—sons and daughters of the king. And we need to move on from the sinner concept and learn how to rule and reign. Because we will be doing a lot of it before we get promoted to our personal palace.

The question now is, "How do we get from the pit to the palace?" First, we have to change our brain. Our thinking must be totally revamped. So, it won't be a one-time thing. We will constantly have to check our thinking and our attitude against the Scriptures. And we will have to learn to listen to a new inner voice: the voice of our spirit man. He must now rule. Our flesh must be kept in it's place.

Second, it will be accomplished by our mouth. Just as Liza Doolittle had to learn how to speak properly in the movie *My Fair Lady*, we must learn to speak properly and to do that we first have to quit speaking improperly. If we have what we say, then we better bring our mouth into line. We will speak positive things and not negative. We will use words we haven't used much before and in a whole new way. There's a lot to learn.

And finally, we will get there by our actions. Our actions must match our new life. We have to leave the old haunts that feel so comfortable and start getting acquainted with our new digs. Yes, you have to stay away from people and places that pull you down and go to places that build you up. The Bible says to flee evil and to watch what we put before our eyes. This is not a suggestion it's a command. Maybe you aren't used to commands. Well, get used to them because you now serve a real King and He expects obedience.

It's a whole new life and we have to start at some point to speak and act in the new manner. That point is now if it hasn't already begun. All this will only happen as we determine to become the regal person we were born again to be. We are King's kids and we better start acting like it. And I don't mean like a spoiled brat. Don't you know a truly fine King is loving and magnanimous, and as His heir, we should be loving and magnanimous, too. A king is the servant of the people and you are to be, too.

Myles Munroe has a wonderful book on this concept, *Understanding the Kingdom*.

WHO'S AFRAID OF THE BIG BAD WOLF?

My son Grant loves animals and wanted to keep a few goats in a small pasture next to the house when he was about twelve, but it wasn't fenced. One day he was complaining about the fact he didn't have any animals and he probably never would because his father and grandfather never would get around to building the fence they had promised him. He was saying it this way for the impact it would have on his loving, sympathetic mother. But this day I realized his attitude was all wrong. Knowing the power of the tongue, I knew he was creating his own defeat. I wanted to change his attitude, but lecturing isn't very effective with kids or husbands. It just makes things worse. (Verbal is the least effective way to get someone to do something. That is a rule. Learn it.) I did try to talk him into speaking positively, but it didn't work. He was too upset.

Suddenly the melody to "Who's afraid of the big, bad wolf" came to mind with new words and I burst out in song, "Praise the Lord the fence is built, the fence is built, the fence is built. Praise the Lord the fence is built…tra la la la la la." Catchy isn't it? You can easily change the words to fit other problems. Praise the Lord, my marriage is healed, my marriage is healed, my marriage is healed, praise the Lord my marriage is healed, tra la la la la la…my house is clean, my husband is saved, etc. You could have lots of verses changing it each time for something else you are believing for. I was really getting into it. I couldn't help but laugh which made Grant frown all the more. He didn't appreciate my levity over such a serious subject.

"Grant, don't you understand? You are binding God's hands when you claim your dad will never build the fence? We have to talk faith—the fence *is* built." Faith is believing what you don't see (Heb. 11). He didn't understand this concept at all, and certainly wasn't going to sing my silly song. I was on a roll. I just knew the fence would be built. Faith may not have risen in Grant, but it sure did in me. That's enough for the victory. That man on the stretcher in the Bible that was let down through the roof was healed by his friends' faith. Where two or three are gathered in His name, there He is, too. Well, I'm one with Lamar and Jesus is there, so that's three. All we need.

The next day Lamar came in saying he was going to quit waiting on his father and go get the tractor and build the fence. I burst out singing and laughing all at the same time. Lamar didn't seem to appreciate my song, either. Grant could finally join me without reservation. And the fence was built. Praise God. These are the things that build faith in a boy and that's better than a new fence or animals to a mother.

THANK YOU, GOD

When we receive Jesus, we not only have the benefit of a new life, of being a new creation with joy, peace, favor, health, healing and all those good things, plus eternal life, but we also have smaller changes that in the end totally revolutionize our lives. Little things begin to change and eventually become big things. One thing that happened was that Lamar became a "handyman" around the house. Talk about a blessing and a miracle!

When we moved into the big old house, there was no kitchen sink or cabinets. The electricity was minimal and the plumbing pitiful. A dog could climb through the hole in the bathroom floor and I had a crawling baby. Erskin Pullen, a marvelous older man who helped everyone around town, agreed to help bring our handyman's dream up to par. A local furniture store had a big going out of business sale so we bought a metal sink unit, two base units, and a few top cabinets. I had never seen this kind of thing before, but they looked nice enough. Mom had built-in cabinets. Little did I know how soon they would be a problem. You would think if they could get a man to the moon, they could make a sink that wouldn't rust that fast. It started to leak and I had to use a bucket to catch the drips. I'd forget every once in a while and it would overflow. What a mess! There is something that will take away your thankful heart.

I was very upset with Lamar because he puts everything off. He does everything but what I need done. Finally, it got so bad I couldn't use the sink any longer. The dishes quickly piled up and I was at my wits end. The only other sink in the house was in the tiny bathroom right off the kitchen. The room was six-foot by six-foot with a tub, water heater, sink, and commode in it. The only thing I could do was to use it. I set the dish drainer in the tub because the sink was one of those round kind with no counter area. It was so handy, right there within easy reach. The plan was coming together.

I knew I couldn't keep this attitude and decided to praise God about something. I could at least be thankful for clean water. So I thanked God for that, and hot water. Not everybody has that. Then I thought about women of old that had to make their own soap. Praise God for soap. It's amazing what you can be thankful for if you think about it. I had hands that work and fingers. I had a roof over my head; lots more than people in India have. We take so much for granted. How dare I be upset about a leaky sink when I have so much. The more I thought and thanked God for, the happier I got. I was laughing and praising God having a big time when Lamar walked in. He suddenly realized that he needed to get on it, and he's been handy ever since. That's the way it is now.

About this time Lamar peeked in and asked, "What are you doing?" I must have been quite a sight in that tiny bathroom. "I guess I'm doing the dishes. What does it look like I'm doing?"

"Why are you doing them in there?"

"Because the other sink is broke?"

"Oh, that's right! Why didn't you remind me?" (I thought I had.) "I'll have to get on it and fix it," he said. Yeah, there's a concept. Praise God for a husband who can fix it. This was the beginning of a wonderful change in our lives. I truly believe if I hadn't changed my attitude, I would not have the helpful husband I have today. I learned to praise my way into a lot of blessings.

A Nice Visit

My mother was coming for a visit and the dishwasher she gave us was broke. I prayed about it and gave my relationship with my mother to God, knowing it would be a problem if we couldn't use it while she was there. I mentioned it to Lamar and reminded him my mother had given it to us and would be upset if it wasn't working. Lamar got right on it. I tried to help, but he found me distracting. Being the woman of faith I am, I left him alone in the kitchen and fell asleep on the couch. I woke up in time to praise God and thank Lamar for fixing it, and then went to bed.

One day I found everything defrosted in the side-by-side refrigerator/freezer. What a mess! "Just call Sears," was Lamar's answer. I replied, "I would, but they won't be out until Thursday, and then they will have to bring the part out next Thursday. The earliest I will get it fixed will be a week from Thursday. That's a long time for a family of five to live out of a cooler." He understood that and decided to stop at Sears while he was in town to see if they could help him. They figured out what it was, sold him the part, and he put it in. He was anointed. God can't anoint nothing, but He sure can anoint something.

I was not only being blessed with the stuff he was fixing, but by what this was doing for Lamar. Lamar was not a patient person, but after ten years of marriage, he was finally beginning to change.

"I Am a Very Patient Person"

Do you know how the Bible says we learn patience? Through tribulation. If you need patience, He brings tribulation into your life to help you learn it, because you won't learn patience if everything goes your way. So, what did Lamar get? The same thing he had been getting all along. More tribulation. (Romans 5:3.) One day the drier broke! It wouldn't tumble the clothes. He didn't even consider calling Sears that time. He took it apart and carefully laid the pieces in order so he could put it back together. Somehow, in all the maneuvering, the drum fell on his wrist, cutting him badly. I knew it hurt, but he didn't want any help. He wrapped it in a rag and went out under the big pecan trees. I could hear him out there yelling, so I continued to pray for him. One of the boys heard Lamar and asked what was wrong. I told him what happened and assured him, "He's OK. He's talking to God." Lamar was a lot better after that.

Howard

Do you know how the Bible says we learn patience? Through tribulation. That's right. If you need patience, He brings tribulation into your life to help you learn it. How are you going to learn patience if everything goes your way? You won't. You just expect everything to go your way and get impatient when it doesn't.

Permit me to tell you a cute story that exemplifies the difference between not panicking, keeping your mouth under control, and panicking. I don't mean just stifling, I mean having a good attitude. When we had the convenience store, Lamar asked me to go update the car tags. He was too busy and it was the last day before the tags expired. The only problem is Joyce needs me to get back quickly so she can leave to attend a funeral. The courthouse is way down the mountain at a nearby town. I pray for a good parking place and get it. What a miracle on such a busy day! God is with me.

Inside the people fill the big long hall leading to the double doors behind which are the counters I need to get to. This huge group of people is the line and it winds all the way back around to God only knows where on the other side of the building. Can I possibly stand in this line and get back in time for Joyce to go to her funeral? I whisper a prayer, "I'm not asking for me, Lord," standing there immobile trying to decide if I should just go back home and pay the fines. Lamar would have a problem with this decision.

A man from my town, the local "drifter," spots me and starts talking to me, but my mind is whirling about what to do now. I'm trying to be nice as I wait for an inspiration. All of a sudden someone from the middle of the line calls out to me, "Midge, Midge, come here." As I walk over to my friend she indicates with her eyes to jump in. I see the people eying me and they don't look too happy. I ask how fast it's moving and she says "It's not. It hasn't moved in forever." I don't know what to do. It's tempting and the people would let me if they understood about the funeral. But I certainly didn't want to get into a discussion. I wonder if I should just go home. Suddenly the double doors open and this huge wall of people starts moving in one huge swell. I probably could've backed out, but I really didn't think I would actually get into the room. But I did. The doors shut right behind me. If anyone had a problem with it, I couldn't hear them and the cop would have just shaken his head, unable to do anything about it.

I stand there stunned. Suddenly, I realize the lines at the windows are filling up fast and I need to pick one. Getting in so quickly, I could be magnanimous and be happy with the end spot. There is no hurry. I gather my thoughts and pick a window with a sign I figure applies to me. When it's my turn, the woman asks me for my decal number. I don't have that. I only have the tag receipt. She tells me, "Go out and get it off your car and tell the man at the door and he will let you back in."

I explain to her the vehicle is all the way up the mountain and I will not be able to go back and forth today. As I talk to her, again, I pray under my breath, "Lord, help." The woman behind the widow next to hers suddenly takes an interest in what we are saying and asks, "Where do you live?" I tell her. Then she asks me if I know when we bought the vehicle and from whom and I say yes. She proceeds to tell the lady waiting on me, "If somebody lives in a small town and knows the name of the person and the month they bought it, you can look it up in the book." My lady goes over and in a minute comes back with the number. We do our business and I move on to the next window. No fits, no panic, just anointing.

I move from one window to another doing what has to be done. As I stand in a line for a trailer tag, a local pastor passes by muttering disgustedly that he has to go home and get his decal number. I sympathize with him and tell him I almost had to, too. My solution doesn't fit his case; he's from the bigger town and didn't just buy his car. I knew when I left there I had witnessed a miracle. I laughed and praised the Lord all the way up the mountain. No fits, no carrying on, and if it hadn't worked out, I would have paid the fines and hopefully Lamar would have learned a lesson because he probably would have been the one to go next time, sheepishly knowing it was his fault. He was so thrilled I got it done and Joyce was shocked to see me back in time for her to go to the funeral. I gave them the wonderful praise report as I laughed joyfully.

> *And we know that all things work together for good to them that love God, to them who are the called according to him purpose. For whom he did foreknow, he also did predestine to be conformed to the image of his Son, that he might be the first born amongst many brethren.*
>
> —ROMANS 8:28

Let's pray.

> *All things will work together for my good and the good of my family. I believe this, Father, help my unbelief. I thank You God that You are working all things out for my good—not that they are easy, but in the end, it will be good. I claim it in the precious name of Jesus.*

Twenty-four

Bare Minimums

MARRIAGE IS THE WALK through life of a man and a woman. The Bible asks in Amos 3:3 (KJV), "*Can two walk together except they be agreed?*" In other words God is saying, and wisely so, that to walk together two people must be in agreement. He doesn't think you are really walking together if you are not agreed. You may live in the same house and have the same kids, but you are not really walking together. It's easier said than done—this agreement thing.

I call this chapter "Bare Minimums" because if you are going to make it as a couple, there are some basics that you must agree on. Although, heaven knows, many don't have this much. If it's you, don't panic. No matter how bad it gets, we serve a God of miracles.

AGREEMENT

Jesus in Matthew 18:19 gives a beautiful promise that agreement brings: "*Where two or three are gathered together in My Name, there I am also.*" This is powerful. Ponder what it means to have Jesus in your midst. Now you just have to find someone to agree with you—really agree. The sick will be healed, the dead shall be raised (this includes the spiritually dead), and demons will have to flee. Now let's bring this power of agreement to our marriage.

THE CONVENIENCE STORE

As I have mentioned before, when I was a new Christian we owned a convenience store. There is nothing like something so big and so needy to develop your faith. I couldn't do it. If God didn't do it, it wouldn't get done. And no place sees the needs of people like a convenience store. Some people would stop on the way to the hospital.

When someone would tell me their problem, I would have to say I would pray for them. I couldn't have someone stand there green with a virus and not say I would pray for them. I would pray after they left, never in front of them. It wasn't necessary. They would come back with a praise report. They didn't have to be admitted. They went home and cooked supper. It was amazing. Talk about building your faith. The more I prayed, the more victories I heard, the more faith I had to pray for more. It was in the convenience store that I came to see just exactly what I had in this Christianity thing.

I did have to have the person agree that it could work. Sometimes they would say something negative and that would stop me immediately. "Oh then there is no use me praying." I might as well not pray, if they don't think it would do any good. That sure changed their tune, "Oh! I believe God can do it…" Truth of the matter is, they didn't believe He would do it for them or that their case was too bad, etc. Finally, they would agree that, if it was done, it would be God. And it worked. I can't number the times people came back amazed at what God had done. And I was a brand new Christian. The Bible says these signs shall follow them that believe, and I was child-like enough, and my inner healing had been so great, that I believed.

Can you be a child? Can you believe like a child and find another child (of God) to believe with you? Yes, even your children can agree with you. Just be sure you phrase things in a way that doesn't burden them with worry. And be sure the ones you share your prayer requests with won't make it worse. Some people can't seem to be a child even with God. Don't include them. You need someone who really believes, who can believe with you (and won't spread rumors). If you can't find one, then just turn to Jesus and be two with Him and three with the Holy Spirit. They will agree with you. Send away the nay-sayers like He did. Better to pray alone than with someone thinking, "Well, I don't know if God will do it." Who needs a prayer partner like that? It's the prayer of agreement we are to pray, not disagreement.

Give the scriptures that say you have a right to ask and expect it. You need to be standing on solid ground with God when you do it. Repent if there is something between you and God, and then go for it and watch for the answer. Some people pray and then don't prepare for the answer. I prayed for a girl with a sprained foot and she was instantly healed. She whooped, "I knew He was going to heal me." She took off the bandage, threw down the crutches and ran around laughing and rejoicing. When she had to go to the car, she hobbled out in the cold because she had no shoe. "If you knew you were going to be healed, why didn't you bring your shoe?" I chided and we laughed together.

Maybe your husband doesn't agree with you spiritually right now, so praying together is not an option. That just means you pray and agree with friends or your best friend, Jesus. But you should tell them what you are praying for, so when they come to pass they will know your prayers are powerful. My mother once asked me to pray about something because "you seem to be closer to God." Now there's something that's nice to hear.

BEING SET APART

For the unbelieving husband is sanctified through his wife, and the unbelieving wife is sanctified through her believing husband; for otherwise your children are unclean, but now they are holy.
—1 CORINTHIANS 7:14, NAS

That's good news about the kids. Sanctification is the act of being set apart from the world by God. "The altar sanctifies the gift" is a wonderful concept. Maybe this is why we ask the couple to go to a form of the altar to get married—so they will understand this concept of being set apart. The world can be a hateful, harmful place, and it'll pull at this tender young couple until it succeeds at pulling them apart. That's why they need to be set apart from the world, so there is a certain protection against the enemy.

It doesn't say God sanctifies the gift, the gift being ourselves. No, the altar does the sanctifying. That seems odd since an altar is an inanimate object. Let me explain. When we get saved, this is a spiritual altar in our lives, a laying ourselves out as a sacrifice. Some people come forward to a real altar, but more often than not we come forward in our heart. In the Old Testament the altar was a very important and sacred place. The New Testament fulfilled the need for a real altar, but the concept is still there: the sacrificial lamb.

When we complete the act of our salvation by acknowledging our sin and our need for a Savior, this is our "altar"—the giving over the lordship of our lives. This sets in motion the power of the universe on our behalf. Not because of anything in us because we are the same incompetent that got us in the mess. No, the altar (the yielding our lordship), will put His protection (sanctify or set us apart) around us. This yielding, the altar, will not only redeem you, but deliver you and teach you, guide you and comfort you. The altar sets you apart and if you are set apart, your husband is too. How wonderful.

COMMITMENT

The first thing you have to do is to agree to stay together. This is what the marriage ceremony is all about: two people vowing in front of witnesses to stay together through thick and thin, in sickness and in health, as long as they live. I don't know why we don't kick up a bigger fuss when they break their vows. We used to and it helped couples get past some rocky times. It's a shame we have taken away most of the incentives that keep couples together, but kept everything that pulls them apart and added more.

You can't become one and walk in agreement if you don't work at it respectfully and cheerfully. I know that is asking a lot, but the Bible tells us not to let the sun go down on our anger. Therefore, holding onto things and making things worse is not only not helpful, it's against the rules. Commitment must have by its very definition the agreement to do it God's way. You may not be able to force your spouse to agree to that, but *you* have to. As much as it's up to *you*, do the right thing with the right attitude. It's called love.

Marriage is a covenant relationship in the same way God has made covenants with man for thousands of years. We have lost the whole concept, especially as it applies to marriage. This is a very solemn agreement and should not be broken. It's legally binding as God means legally binding. Since there are things worse than divorce and that is the mistreatment of women and children, and men, God has allowed us to separate. But that is the last resort. We're going for healing and restoration—the fulfillment of the covenant agreement.

Why is commitment so necessary? Because we will make mistakes and we need the time and space to heal, mature, and for things to change in both of us. All this can't be done in a day. It will take time. So many of the marriages today break up because of legitimate reasons only to have the partners move on and marry the person someone else divorced for the same legitimate reasons. The problem is we are dragging some special baggage (our kids) through it, as well as our family, friends, neighbors. Why not stay in the first marriage and redeem it? It's possible, you know. We can forgive "legitimate reasons."

We need commitment because we need to get to know each other. We both have separately formed ideas of what a home should be like, and it won't be easy bringing these two ideas together. Even if two people were raised very similarly, they will still have very different concepts of what their home should be like. We may love each other dearly, but we don't necessarily love his or her taste in furniture or drapes. I hate to be the bearer of bad news but all these preconceived notions are the grist for many difficult adjustments. This is probably the reason God placed in us the desire for each other physically and emotionally, so that we will be willing to work out all the kinks. We need commitment because each of us needs to say some hard things, not to be ugly or cruel, but to say what needs to be said—things the other person doesn't want to hear. There will be times when we tell it like it is, when we hurt the other very deeply, and we need to know he or she won't walk out. They need the security to speak honestly, too. It goes both ways.

It may not always be the truth in love that is spoken by our loved one, or by us for that matter. It might be a lie. It might be a lie they believe, or we believe. It might be cruel and hurtful. They might even know it's a lie. What do we do then? Our heart and head might say to leave. Commitment says to stay.

I remember one day Lamar accused me of turning the boys against him. Nothing could be further from the truth, but he believed it. I had defended him for years with the boys. All I could say was, "I'm sorry you believe that, because it's not true," and left it at that. He eventually discarded these thoughts as the lies they were, but he didn't that day and I couldn't force him to. All I could do was keep doing my best, because if I do, the Bible promises me he will rise up and call me blessed. And one day he did.

If you are not totally committed when these, the worst of all hurts, hit you broadside, you will fall. You will not achieve victory, and you will experience an even more painful loss, the failure of your marriage. For no matter how much you may tell yourself it wasn't your fault, there will be a place in you that will say it was. I am not saying the divorce will be your fault or that you didn't fight the good fight of faith well enough, only that somewhere inside you will have doubts. Therefore, the only answer is to commit and do everything in your power to stay that way. Then you will have peace no matter what happens.

ACCEPTANCE

Before we get started on some loftier ideals, I need to mention the lowly one, ground zero, acceptance. I know we want fiery love that drives us absolutely wild, or maybe even a joyful, or a peaceful love, but acceptance? Yes, we want more and God intended for more but there needs to be a level below which we refuse to go and that is acceptance. We may not always agree; we may not always flow together in this marvelous stream of oneness, but at least we can accept the other, faults and all. When all else fails, just accept him and hope he accepts you. Don't ask more of him than he is capable of giving at this point in his life. Accept him as he is and when you can't, ask God to make you a channel of His love. God accepts us the way we are. If He can, we can. Our job is to edify our mate, and you can't do that if you don't accept him.

DIBS

I have to tell this one powerful testimony of a little boy being emotionally healed by acceptance. Isn't there a little boy and little girl in each married couple? I think so, and an old man and woman, and two vibrant, romantic, young lovers. We bump around in our homes going from one to the other, sometimes appropriately and sometimes very inappropriately. Whoever we are, we all need to be healthy and happy.

His story is written in the book, *Dibs, The Discovery of Self* by Virginia M. Axline, a little boy so dysfunctional that he wouldn't or couldn't speak or interact with his pre-school class in any way. The teachers had to do everything for him, take off his coat, put on his shoes, etc. They never saw him smile. No one knew if he was retarded or disturbed because they couldn't get him to cooperate for the testing. So they just tried their best to work with him. All he would do all day long is crawl around the edges of the room and study each item he found at length. Finally they elicited the help of a child researcher/psychologist.

The parents agreed to allow Dr. Axline look into Dibs's problems. Because he was such a special little boy and his problems such as they were Dr. A. agreed to work with him. The parents refused to be interviewed by her. That was the stipulation for him going to the playroom at the research center for one hour a week for the rest of the school year—about eight months. Dr. A. is very busy and made no promises. She would merely observe him. Doesn't sound like much—one hour, one day a week.

The little boy, Dibs, came in and was pretty much like he was at school. He silently examined everything in the room item by item. Dr A. would comment slightly on what he said or ask a question to show she was listening. She didn't try to get information out of him or point him in any direction. He was told he could do whatever he wanted and that's what he did. She did not stop him if he threw paint on the floor or broke a toy, although he was not generally destructive. She did stop him from eating something harmful and that traumatized him until he realized she wasn't trying to harm him.

She didn't coddle or hug him or give him any sign of affection. The one thing she did give him was her undivided attention. There's a novel idea. Kids are so often surrounded by people, but get very little real attention, or they get too much. In spite of his lack of appropriate relating, Dibs didn't want to leave at the end of the hour, the same problem they had at the pre-school. Dr. A. told him he had to go and after the first day they had no more problems. He accepted it even if he would protest a while verbally.

A great deal came out in his play and the few words he spoke, although he did eventually get to be quite conversational in his own special way. He was very creative and very expressive, a very special little boy. It was obvious how disturbed he was by what he was saying mostly to himself. He drew locks on the doors of the playhouse and said he hated locks. It was obvious something bad had happened because of locked doors. He would talk very mean to the father, mother, and sister dolls, especially the father, burying him deep within the sand.

He did not use the pronoun I. He spoke in the third person, referring to himself as Dibs. He did not speak to people at all. When Dr. A., whom he called Miss A., talked with him, he was really not talking to her. He talked to inanimate objects, like the truck. Why? Because they won't hurt you. It was obvious things at home were not good. The mother finally did come in and talked to Miss A.

She had been an up-and-coming surgeon and her husband was a famous scientist. A baby was not in their plans. He must have felt the animosity and rejection in the womb because he came out very stiff and reactionary. Dibs's reaction was their worst nightmare and everything they did just made things worse. Dibs didn't seem to bond with his mother or his father. His mother tried her best, but she had too many issues. (I know it sounds awful to say, but sometimes a child is better off being put up for adoption. Adoption is preferable to abuse and some homes are truly abusive, not necessarily physically. It happens in the best of homes.)

It was the beginning of devastating changes in their lives. She gave up her career, but not without a deep regret for having to do it. The father regretted the changes, too. I never have understood her giving up her career, except they believed if you have children, you should raise them. However, when she saw it wasn't working, why didn't she reconsider and go back to work? The baby could have had a loving nanny and she could have come home and enjoyed him for a few hours.

They didn't feel comfortable socializing because it was obvious something was wrong with their baby. They were mortified and afraid their friends would think he was retarded. She began working with him and taught him letters and words at a very early age. He could read by the time he was two. But they didn't know because he didn't talk to anyone. His mother came to understand he wasn't retarded, but had no words for what he was. I guess you would call it emotionally disturbed. Since she was home anyhow, she decided to have another child. A year after Dibs was born she had little girl who was "the perfect child." Dibs's mother doted on his little sister and of course the sister ate it up and loved the mother all the more.

Miss A. did not tell Dibs he should forgive his father or that his parents really did love him. All she did was accept him and let him do what he wanted for an hour. If he drew a picture, she would say it was good, but nothing too ecstatic. There was very little input from his teachers at the school for a long time. It was an expensive private school. If it had been a public school, the situation would have had to be turned over to the authorities much earlier and no telling what would have happened then. The teachers let this go on for two years before they elicited help from Mrs. A. In the end, it wasn't necessary to remove him as Dibs came to accept his parents and gained the skills he needed to relate. He changed, and as he changed, his parents changed. Their love was finally able to be felt and expressed in their relationships.

The whole situation turned around in those few months. I know we tout the wonders of love, and it was truly love that Miss A. was giving, but she had to keep her distance. She was not in a position to become Dibs's source of emotional support. She did not want to create a dependent child knowing she couldn't continue the relationship indefinitely. People that try to "help" often cripple their subjects by taking too much on themselves, creating dependency when they won't be able to be there after a certain time.

Dibs had to come to terms with his family. Removing Dibs was not the solution. Helping Dibs through his problems to emotional maturity was the answer. He was a brilliant child intellectually but emotionally he was stunted. Telling his parents or teachers how smart he was would not help either if he was not ready to handle advanced classes emotionally. No, all she could do was show him acceptance. Dibs worked out the forgiveness and acceptance of his family on his own. What a story![1]

What a truth! If we accept the person, we can move on to a loving relationship. If we never accept them, we will never move on. Remember, God accepts us the way we are. You can, too.

Please, watch your tongue. Listen to yourself. So many of us don't realize how harsh, critical, judgmental, and totally rejecting we sound even when we love the person very much. Love doesn't help much if our criticism isn't tempered with it. Many wives have a lot of catching up to do because they have already backed their husband into a corner with their mouth.

Trust

On the short list of things needed in a relationship, I must put trust up there with those I have mentioned. In *Exegeses*, *unbelieving* means "trustless." Either a person is trustworthy or trustless. Have you heard of "Promise Keepers," the Christian men's ministry? They get their name because they preach and teach the need for keeping their promises to their God, their wife, children, community, country, church, etc. In other words, they teach men to be trustworthy. It works for women, too.

In Proverbs 31:10–12, after Lemuel's mother tells him some things he needs to do: do not spend your strength on women, your vigor on those who ruin kings, don't drink wine or beer, speak up for those who cannot speak for themselves, judge fairly, defend the rights of the poor and needy, etc., she talks about the importance of a good wife and how rare a really good one is: "*Who can find a virtuous woman? For her price is far above rubies. The heart of her husband doth safely trust in her, so that he shall have no need of spoil. She will do him good and not evil all the days of her life.*"

We tend to be more worried about whether we can trust our husband than if he can trust us, but trustworthiness is something God requires of wives, too. If we are not trustworthy, it will destroy the relationship. The godly parent, the author of Proverbs 31, was expressing the things that would help her son in his life. Writing down her advice, Lemuel described how precious a good woman is: "*The heart of her husband doth safely trust in her, so that he shall have no need of spoil*" (Prov. 31:11). We must never undercut his authority, hurt his reputation, or make him look bad. When we do this he suffers loss.

If a wife is virtuous, if she is trustworthy, her worth is far above rubies, which is one of the most expensive jewels. He doesn't tie her worth to rubies because values can change. It's just a reference point. To be trustworthy is to have a true servant spirit, to have his best interest in mind, to do things the way your husband wants them done, to know his heart.

Because women don't understand how important trust is to her man, she doesn't understand what happens to their relationship early on. Let me explain.

When a woman marries, she usually jumps in totally by giving her all. A man, on the other hand, withholds a little. He wants to see if he can really trust her, if she will respect him, if she has his best interest at heart. The problem is she is not perfect and she has her concerns, too. Just about the time he's convinced it's safe, she does something that indicates there's a problem. So, he holds off for a while. Something else comes up and again she proves he can't trust her. He holds off again, each time making him a little more leery. In the end he never does jump in totally and it leads to most of their problems. He is a double-minded man.

He's in the marriage, but he's not all the way in and don't think she doesn't notice. She does notice and it eats at her. She does everything in her power to get him to jump in totally, not realizing she failed the test or how important it (what she did) was to him. "It" may have been just a little disrespectful remark to one of his friends said in jest—nothing important. Or was it? It was *very* important to him and ultimately to her!

At this point, she needs to apologize for breaking his trust, but she doesn't apologize because she doesn't understand what she did or that what she did was so awful. They go round and round about it, getting nowhere.

My "it" was throwing away a box of paperbacks when we were moving. I still don't remember doing it. Somehow they didn't get moved and I was blamed for it. You know how you have a pile of stuff that he's supposed to go through, but as far as you're concerned it needs to go. When he eventually asked me about them, I told him they must have gotten thrown away. When he protested, I defended myself saying there was no use lugging them around since he didn't read them. Evidently he read them on the ship when he was in the Navy before we met. I never saw him read them and assumed he didn't like to read. Saying that if he wanted them, he should have taken care of them or he should have seen them in the "get rid of" pile and rescued them are not the right things to say to a hurting husband. Apologizing and showing actual sorrow for his loss would have been better. But I resented it being put on me. Resentment didn't help either. Everything I said just made it worse.

Isn't it funny that these disputes involve very painful connections in our lives. It's not about books. When my brother died, he left a small library of almost new paperbacks that Mom didn't want, so I took them and lugged them around for years. To me we didn't need one more box of paperbacks, especially if he had already read them. I don't read many books twice, especially cheap novels. He could have read some of Grant's books or mine. Heaven knows there were books in the house.

To me paperbacks were cheap and a nuisance. To Lamar his paperbacks were a symbol of a special time in his life and that I didn't care and wouldn't see to his things like I saw to my own. I honestly don't know what happened to the books. I don't remember throwing them away. Somebody did and I got blamed—for years. I can't even say you are to blame for what your husband holds against you, but it's good to know what it is. I finally told Lamar, if he had thrown my books away, I would still read. I think it's a cop-out.

Anger comes from fear. Fear comes from losing control. If you see anger in your husband toward you, it's his reaction to his loss of control. To you he is over-reacting and that's because you don't understand the gravity of what you have done. It's bad enough that you've done it, but it's even worse that you don't seem to comprehend what it means to him— that you didn't have his best interest in mind; that you couldn't even see how much "it" matters to him. Remember, this is the problem God had with Adam and Eve. They didn't understand the gravity of eating the fruit. They "just didn't get it." Your husband sees you "just don't get it" and that scares him, so he reacts in anger. He's not over-reacting as much as you are under-reacting.

HOPELESS

When the big revelation "Jesus" came into my life and I began this wonderful relationship with the Lord, I thought Lamar was hopeless. I'm serious. He rededicated his life that day in church, but it didn't last long. He backslid shortly after. He never went back to drinking, but he had an attitude. He wouldn't go to church and I didn't bother him about it. Eventually I stopped inviting him. "Why bother?" I thought. "He's hopeless."

I was in such a mess after the loss of my little girl and ten years of a bad marriage, I was just worried about getting myself healed. I had worked on Lamar for years and nothing changed. I finally saw some hope for myself and I was going for it. He was welcome to come with us. I just didn't make a big deal of it. He would do better for a while and then backslide again. Something was always discouraging him. This was *before* we did some spiritual work that we were too dumb to know needed to be done—deliverance, the baptism of the Holy Spirit and things like that. If you don't get these things done when they are needed, you will not keep the victory long. This is why it's so important that you attend church regularly and have a good, mature group of Christians around you that understand these things and move in the gifts of the Spirit.

Lamar's melancholy personality didn't help either. He tends to get "down" easily and can't get back up. Not everything is spiritual in nature. Some things are just the way we are created. We have to figure out how to handle our natural tendencies and not let the devil use them to defeat us.

As I prayed for Lamar one day, I had to admit I didn't think he would ever change. But that just didn't sit well in my mind as a woman of faith. I believed in God, but I didn't believe in Lamar. He was the weak link. Couldn't I believe God could work in Lamar? Again, I thought Lamar would be the problem, but the Bible says, *"He (God) who has begun a good work is faithful to finish it"* (Phil. 1:6). I had to agree God had begun a good work in Lamar. He had been saved at fourteen and rededicated his life when I got saved. He had done the right thing in the past so maybe I could trust him to do the right thing this time. I had to trust the Word, and it said God not only could do it but would do it. No matter how impossible it looked, I had to stand on what God said not what I felt.

I suddenly realized Lamar was going through the struggling a horse goes through when they try to put the bit in his mouth. Eventually the horse accepts it and learns to live with it. God was trying to put the bit in Lamar's mouth and he was resisting. I knew Lamar would fight it, but I also believed that he would at some point quit fighting and accept it. He had done the right thing in the past and would do it again. Finally I could have faith in God and Lamar—God in Lamar. What a glorious day that was! I didn't see the victory that day, but the battle was over in my mind. I was now able to stand in faith that Lamar would take the bit. I saw it spiritually weeks before I saw it physically. God couldn't begin until I was standing in faith. As usual, I was the hold up. Shortly after, Lamar took the bit.

Let me make it perfectly clear, it's wrong for the man not to jump in totally. He should. But we live in reality. Someday we hope he appreciates his error and repents of it. This will happen after you appreciate your error and repent of it. Right now you need to be aware of the problem: you jumped in totally and he didn't. He's checking you out so don't fail the test. If you have already failed the test, it will take a long time to convince him otherwise. You must not do him harm or embarrass him or in other ways prove you are not to be trusted for a while in order to regain his confidence. It's not something you can talk him into, although a heart felt apology is no doubt in order. It's something you must exemplify over time. *If you can't trust your husband, at least trust God.*

Maybe you haven't seen your husband do anything positive spiritually. I hope you have seen him do the right thing physically: work a job, pay his bills, take care of his family, etc. I don't mean perfectly. I mean generally he tries to do the right thing. If so, just know that when the gospel is presented in a way that strikes him as being the truth, he will accept it. God is the one who will orchestrate this presentation. Don't weary him ahead of time, kind of like some people start potty training before a child is ready and end up making it worse. That's what we wives do when we try to bring them to Jesus before it's time. There is a timing in all this and we don't have the clock. God does.

You need to understand how much of a problem this trust issue is in your marriage. He may love you and find you very attractive, but that doesn't mean he doesn't have trepidations about what you might do to trip him up. If you are worried about being able to trust him, he is just as worried about whether he can trust you.

I should mention that the wife may have a similar problem in that her new husband does something that hurts her deeply. She may tell him and he may apologize to her, but he doesn't understand the gravity of what he has done. She finds it impossible to get over. It might be something that happened at the wedding or on the honeymoon. These "its" in a marriage make it almost impossible for the couple to go forward. It's so important that we really try to understand what things mean to our mate and it's also important that we understand our mate will never truly comprehend some things and let it go.

Cleaving

Therefore shall a man leave his father and his mother, and shall cleave unto his wife: and they shall be one flesh. And they were both naked, the man and his wife, and were not ashamed.
—Genesis 2:23–25, kjv

Cleaving. There's a concept whose time has come. Sounds like a step beyond commitment. The dictionary says: adhere, cling. Stick to each other. Grab, clutch, cleave. That's pretty intimate to me, especially if a man and a woman are doing it for very long. That is why we must be very careful about our intimate contacts outside of marriage. Can someone get between two people who are cleaving to each other? I don't think so. I think the cleaving stops long before other inappropriate relationships begin. Maybe the cleaving never really began. Maybe one did and the other didn't.

I will say this: if he isn't cleaving, you need to back off too—at least temporarily. One person cleaving doesn't work. It's a "turn-off." It just makes the other uncomfortable and he withdraws all the more. Instead of trying to cleave to someone who is running away, cleave to God. He won't run or get turned off. Just continue to be a very special person in his life—his biggest fan. Too many women don't really hear what their husband is saying. They don't know his heart.

It's impossible to cleave to too many at once. Have you ever seen a family reunion after many years absence? At first they try to include three or four in this group attempt to hug. It's really quite clumsy. In the end they quit trying and do it one at a time and it works out much better. A hug is not cleaving. Cleaving is a hug extended indefinitely.

God not only tells us to cleave to each other but to leave our existing family of origin—leave and cleave. In order to cleave to your mate, you must cut all "ties" or apron strings to your mother and father, sister and brother, whoever. That doesn't mean you can't still visit and love your family. You just can't be tied to them in the same way you were. *Leave,* then cleave. Don't get it backwards: cleaving before leaving. You can date, but you can't cleave. Once you marry, then you can cleave.

Let me say this: your biological family or the family you grew up in doesn't have to be wonderful and nurturing to have holds on you that need to be severed. Children of alcoholics are notorious for trying to fix their first family while their new family comes in a very late second. It's a source of much of the maladjustment in marriage—the original (dysfunctional) family with tentacles into the new one. God knew it and made provision. It's man that is disobedient or ignorant and pays the price.

I need to put a caution in here. You must sever the ties with your old family, but not your relationships. Some spouses and religious cults insist we cut off all relationships with our family and this is wrong. We should always maintain a loving relationship with our parents and loved ones. It's just that we have to put our husband or wife first now. Our relationship changes, but it should be good.

I do not advise you to counsel too much with your parents or siblings, but if things are too bad, they do need to know. You need to get your pastor or a professional involved. It could be that your spouse is picking up on problems in your family. He may not be wrong. Sometimes we do need to heal and not being so close is good. The best thing that ever happened to Lamar was moving to Florida. He finally was able to get away from all the negatives. Now he goes back healed and whole and the garbage doesn't affect him like it did. He's fine. He doesn't need them to be.

Who is the biggest problem—your husband or your parent? Danged if I know. Sometimes it takes a while for this to be revealed. In the meantime, you must love them both. Usually, neither is innocent, which makes it all the harder to deal with.

FIDELITY

I really need to add fidelity to this list of minimums. This is scriptural—to add something after you have already made the list (Proverbs 6:16). God requires fidelity (faithfulness) in our relationship with Him and He intends it for marriage. I know the Israelites practiced polygamy but that was not what God intended. Just as unfaithfulness destroyed the foundations of Adam and Eve's world, unfaithfulness tears at the very fabric of a marriage. Fidelity is more than just sexual. The physical, mental, and spiritual run parallel. I will deal with it later in chapter 41. Just know it's on the list. I have four chapters on the physical side of marriage.

> *Dear God, without Your help I can't even do the minimums. And I know Midge is right; I do need to be doing at least this much. But it's so hard. Everything pulls at us. The enemy is good at what he does. Guide me, God, into what I need to know and into healing and wholeness so I can do these things and someday more. Without Your help there will be no victory here. I pray this in the precious name of Jesus, sweet Jesus, my Savior, strong Jesus, my Redeemer. Amen.*

TWENTY-FIVE

Sabotaging the Plan

LIFE IS NOT JUST about you having cute babies and cuddling them as long as you can and then when they run off and get lives, having the cutest grandbabies in the world and cuddling them for as long as you can. Life is more than this. God has a plan; the only problem is He can't always get it to us. We don't even know He wants to go somewhere. And even if He finally gets us to understand, that doesn't mean we will cooperate. It's a continual battle within the confines of our mind to get us to see and then do. Actually, there are many plans and, yes, one of them is to have a great family and enduring friendships. But beyond that, try to open your eyes and ears and see what God is attempting to do outside of your little circle, or at least cooperate when you don't know what He or your husband is trying to do. Trust God to work through him.

Think outside of the circle more and inside the circle will get better.

Women are very important to the plans of God. This is why we should not take any course without a great deal of prayer. We can sabotage the plan, too! I don't want you to ever think you are not as important as your husband. We are all important. We either help the plan or we hinder the plan. God is no respecter of persons and therefore, we must not sell ourselves short. I want you to consider your husband in all things, taking for granted that you have considered yourself since you are the one that will stand before God and answer for what you did with your life some day. If you don't consider yourself first, I doubt that anyone else will. As William Shakespeare wrote, "To thine own self be true, and…thou canst not then be false to any man."[1]

If you are married and your husband has no burden for your calling and in fact even sabotages it, fear not. He's not fighting you but almighty God, and God will defend you, even if He doesn't do it quickly. He may allow you to be persecuted for a while, but defend you He will. Just keep on keeping on, doing your best, keeping your spirit and attitude right, being obedient and learning. (*"Count it all joy..."* James 1:2) You are in the schoolhouse and God has allowed certain people to be there with you. They will teach you many things you will need when you get where God wants you to be. And when you get there, many of the people that fought you will be there, too, but not as they were. They will be changed. They were in the schoolhouse, too.

> *Young women of Jerusalem, I charge you, by the gazelles and the wild does of the field: do not stir up or awaken love until the appropriate time."*
>
> —SONG OF SOLOMON 2:7

Dating is the dance we do to choose our life's mate. A boy usually does the asking and the girl, the accepting. He leads; she follows. But, it doesn't always go smoothly. Some boys are better at leading than others and some girls are better at following than others. Sometimes they just dance the one dance; others last a little longer. And some choose to dance to the exclusion of all others.

If dating is a dance, marriage is too: giving and taking, submitting and leading as we sway through the obstacles. Only too often a sick dance has begun, but to change the dance now is to attempt to change a fundamental part of who we are. We might tire of dancing, but we don't want to change the tune and both rarely tire at the same time. One wants to keep on while the other wants to try something new for a while. At a real dance, we would merely walk off the floor and choose new partners. Once married, it's not that easy. Engaged couples hate to break it off, too. How then can we force our partner to accept a new dance? We really can't. We must somehow convince them a new dance would not jeopardize anything and actually add richness to their lives. This is our challenge:

not only to find a new dance, but to show both partners the new dance is actually better than the one that brought them together.

This dance should start with parent and child even in the early years. A child has a right to make certain decisions in their lives and we should respect them. We should know what is appropriate and yield to them. This dance should go on in the business world, yielding and taking authority. Sometimes it is mine to choose and sometimes it's the other person's. It should be a beautiful thing. But when it's not, it becomes a power struggle, a horrible power play that can destroy any relationship, any dream.

In my father's last few years, our dance changed. It was especially beautiful because it was so natural. Most of the time I would make the decisions and at other times he would, yielding back and forth as we danced through the health issues he faced. We would just know whose turn it was. I know they say the parent becomes the child and the child becomes the parent, but I don't feel this is true. He was still my father and I was still his daughter. It's just that at this time who made certain decisions switched around, and we knew this without even saying it. I guess it was so unusually smooth because there was such love and respect in our relationship. I trusted him and he trusted me. It was the trust God intends for dancing couples, especially if it's to last a lifetime.

When we get it wrong: when we do our own thing, go our own way, make the wrong choices, everything gets out of kilter: our marriages, our kids, our health, our finances—everything. The dance is no longer a wondrous thing to be hold. It's bizarre, pitiful, draining.

WHO CHANGES WHOM?

It has been said that a man marries a woman and expects her *not* to change; whereas, a woman marries a man and expects him *to* change. Sounds like a recipe for a lot of dissatisfaction to me. Because the truth is, a lot of her sweetness will drop off as life disappoints and a lot of his foolishness won't.

Actually, things do change. I know we think, "He will never change," but that's not true. Everybody and everything does change, just not like we think they should. I have found since I began serving the Lord, they change more often in a good way. Thank you, Jesus.

I know it happens a lot that she changes and he doesn't, but you can't make a steadfast rule. In our marriage, Lamar changed immediately and I guess I have changed, but not all that much even with me getting a Southern brain. Maybe I didn't change, but Lamar's perception of me changed, so to him I changed. (Perception is reality.) I know Lamar changed because he sobered up and became a totally different person. I didn't realize he was drunk. He doesn't like me saying that, because to him, he wasn't drunk. Let's just say he wasn't completely sober.

Why doesn't a man want his bride to change? Because he chose her for specific reasons and he wants things to stay the way he perceived them. He didn't change his mind as to what he wants and when we change, it throws him a curve. What does he do now? This isn't what he wanted; what he bargained for. He wants the girl he married. When she changes, he becomes frantic. He's sick about it. She is pregnant and permanently installed in his life. There are family and financial considerations. He figures he's been taken to the cleaners and she is the one that did it. No wonder he has little pity on her.

When a man doesn't change, he is doing exactly what he wants his woman to do. He doesn't think he needs to change and he doesn't think she needs to either. He picked her the way he wanted her. If anything changes, he figures she messed it up, not him. It's just not fair for these things to change. It's fraud. To enter into a contract leading a person to believe one thing, not intending to do it, is fraud. And yet we do it every day. Another word for it is *manipulation* and the Bible says it's the same as witchcraft (1 Samuel 15:23). Ponder that.

Why does a woman want a man to change? Because men have some very undesirable traits. They are often uncouth and uncivilized, except for the rare few that get civilized by their parents early on. Thank you, God, for good parents. The sad truth is we have limited options in our selection and that is partly because we are supposed to wait until we are asked. We are to be the pursued and too often the best are off pursuing someone else. There are better choices, but they may not come to our door because they have better choices. We have to choose from what we can get. So, again, it falls back on you and me personally. We are the problem as much as they are. If we would get our act together, maybe we would have better choices.

Too many people marry with the hopes that they agree with each other's plans (vision and calling) but without a clue as to what that is. Then they try to pull and prod their mate into things (callings and visions) they never had. We assume too much because we presume too much. We were talking when we should have been listening. It may be a little late but there is no time like the present. We need to hear what the person is telling us, all of it! Instead of kidding ourselves and thinking it will be OK (like Scarlet O'Hara, "I'll worry about that tomorrow." You bet you will.), we need to face the truth and turn away from relationships that are not compatible with God's plan for our lives or face the fact we missed the mark and made ourselves and God some extra work.

THE DATING PROCESS LEAVES A GREAT DEAL TO BE DESIRED

I think the seeds of problems are sewn early on when we don't really listen during the dating process. Not only don't we know God and therefore don't get His input, but we don't listen to each other and hear what we are saying either. We see a few things we like and ignore the ones we don't like. The day comes when all this is crystal clear. The only problem is it's after the ceremony. My mother always said the quickest way to cure a romance is to get married.

When we were dating, I told Lamar, "You like what you think I am." He wouldn't really listen and get to know me. He liked the "idea" of me. When I told him I was a Home Ec major in college, he assumed I would be a Home Ec teacher. He liked the thought of being married to a college graduate and a teacher. No one else in his family had a college degree.

No matter how many times I told him I was a Home Art major, intending to be an interior designer and not a teacher, he could never assimilate that thought. Every once in a while he would ask, "Now, tell me again, why can't you teach Home Ec?" I would explain it over and over again, "I did not major in education. I took *no* education courses. To teach, you must get an education degree, take all those special courses, and student teach. I did none of this. I don't want to teach. I can't imagine it." I may have said it, but it didn't compute.

Lamar always assumed I would continue working (teaching) after the children arrived. I was already pregnant and had no intention of working after the baby was born. I had a working mother and hated it. I knew the importance of a mother being home. He didn't. His mother made fried pies and all that good stuff. He should have known the importance of a mother being home. As a Family Studies major I knew the detrimental effect being in daycare from an early age can have on a child. When I grew up, women didn't have to work and I didn't want so much that we couldn't manage on one salary. I figured Lamar was go-getter enough to provide. I wanted to have three children two years apart and stay home at least until the youngest was in school. That's a total of ten years. He couldn't understand this concept. "Now, when do you think you will go back to work?" he would ask every once in a while. I would patiently reply, "I don't intend to go back to work until the youngest is in school." He would just shake his head in disbelief.

I know he thought it was a waste of a college education. His vision of me, his college educated wife, was teaching Home Ec. In fact, he eventually got me a job teaching. It was my worst nightmare because I was not prepared to do it. There was a teacher shortage that year, so they weren't so picky. I didn't think Lamar could get me a job teaching, but then I didn't understand what a good salesman he was either. I loved the students and did my best, but boy, was it hard. It was a typical example of a husband or wife being determined to put their spouse in the mold they have in their head rather than listening to what their mate is telling them. Hearing from God is a lost concept for some.

He wanted me to conform to his idea of me. And I have to say it caused both of us a great deal of grief just as a woman causes her husband grief when she tries to make her husband conform to her idea of what her husband should be.

WHOSE AGENDA?

Too many women marry for what they can get from a man. Oh, she doesn't think she is. If you think men are the only ones with a hidden agenda, think again. Teenagers don't think this far. They just want to date and have somebody. She doesn't know she needs him to complete her. That a man gives her significance. She doesn't know why she just has to have a man. She just does.

He is the means by which she can fulfill her desire for children and a family, or for power, money, name recognition, etc. I hate to tell you, but this is all wrong. It's backwards. You should be adding to him and what he feels called to do. The family and all the other things you want should come as a natural result of your relationship, but if you start out with the idea he is adding himself to your plans, you have the horse before the cart. You need to look first at his needs, his calling, and pray about whether to add yourself to that or not. If you've already done it—added yourself— then face the fact that you should be cooperating with his calling. If, as a Christian, you disagree with what he is doing, you need to take it to God and let Him sort it out. (If what he is doing is not what God wants him to do, it's not a calling. It's just what he is doing right now.) If it's not sin, you must cooperate with him as much as possible.

If the desires of your heart are not the desires of his heart, marrying will just frustrate both of you, because neither will give up your dream, nor should you. Just when it's time to do something involved with your calling, your partner will resist. And just when he feels led to do something, you will resist. Suddenly, you have a problem. Or should I say, suddenly you are aware of your problem. You had it all along.

We begin by trying to talk our mate into our agenda. He (or she) resists, so we talk some more and he resists more, so we talk even more and he resists more. We get ugly and he gets uglier. We get bitter and he stays away. We retaliate in various ways and he retaliates in kind. Things go from bad to worse. This is how we get a vicious circle going. You and your husband will be your own worst enemy. This is not what God intended.

About this time you start saying you need to "communicate" more because he has withdrawn into himself. No, you don't need to communicate. You needed to face reality a long time ago. There is a calling problem and you need to address it with God. Prayer helps. Communication should come only after you have communicated with God.

It's time we honor our husbands, their calling, and their authority. Men are wonderful people and should be appreciated and edified. They weary fighting the battles of life. We need to hold up their hands and sustain them. That's our job—helping. Instead of being negative and butting heads with them all the time, we need to back off and yield, turning it over to God. Let Him fight the battles. It's bad enough when these men have to fight the enemy, and the disgruntled in the congregation, but when they have to fight us, that's really hard on them. That does a real job on his head.

You have your time, energy, and talents to use to the best advantage of your family. We should help our husbands do what God has called him to do, just as he should help us in what we feel called to do. We have to take stock and re-evaluate every once in a while. Just as parents assess a child's talents and abilities and try to channel them in the right direction, I feel husbands and wives need to assess their own and their mate's, too. Things change. Realities change. Nothing is set in stone in this life. We must be willing to make adjustments in the light of the changes around us.

Many Are the Plans in a Man's Mind; It's the Plan in God's Hands That Will Stand

There were two men, one successful and the other struggling to make ends meet. The difference was not that one wife did things to scuttle her husband's dream and the other didn't because they both inadvertently sabotaged them, and by this I don't mean they did it on purpose. It was just the natural result of doing what each did for whatever reason. The difference is one man wouldn't let his dream be stolen and the other did.

Sometimes it does come down to choosing between what is best for the family or the dream and that is especially sad. There are wars and famine and times when there are no dreams. When our goal is to make it to tomorrow. I'm not talking about these times. I'm talking when it's possible, even though it will be very hard and require a sacrifice. Even then many men give up their dream for the sake of the family because his wife gives him no choice. And it probably looks to her like there is a choice. He no doubt made some mistakes and is to blame for her panic. There is enough blame to go around. The enemy makes sure about that.

The truth is women do get in the flesh. We want security and we want it so bad we try to force our husbands to provide it for us. He gets in the flesh if he yields. A man can yield many things, but he must not yield his dream. And she must be careful not to require it. She is a deciding factor, as is he. If she allows her spirit to dictate and not her flesh, it does a lot to help him reach his goal—to fulfill his dream. She can't push him if he insists on yielding to the flesh, but she can do a lot. She can't force him to be spiritual, but she can encourage him and at least not pull him down.

THE DEATH OF A DREAM

There is only one thing worse than to have no dream and that is to have a dream die. It's one thing to be Moses and at least know somebody got to go in to the Promise Land and it's another to have nobody go. That really hurts. But it is only too typical. Oprah had a show where a man talked about how women shut their men down and steal their dream from them.

IT'S NOT DEAD YET

You mustn't be too quick to despair. I once heard a man preach on the death of a dream twice. He gave scripture after scriptural reference of dreams that died twice and went on to live again. Abraham and Sarah were not only childless, but they were *old*. Her body had withered. I heard of a man that felt God wanted him to buy a certain piece of property. Not only did he not have the money, but it was sold to someone else. Talk about dead. The ministry stands on the property today. I won't say he got it the day he thought he would. He had to wait a few years, but what is that to God? Just because it looks impossible for a dream to come to pass, hold your tongue. Don't do as Job's wife and curse God and His promise. No. Do what Martha did when her brother was in the grave. "Even now?" Do you know how often I have to prop Lamar up with my faith? Lamar is a very faith-filled guy. He has a lot of faith. But there are times when things go too far and I have to be the one that says, "Even now, Lord Jesus. Even now." And don't you know he has to prop me up, too. That's why the Bible says two can prop each other up.

Lord, if I do a job on my husband's head, I want it to be a good one. I guess I haven't always been the helpmate he needed, like the Holy Spirit is for You. I ask You this day to help me do better. Put a watch on my lips and enlighten my brain to see and hear what I am saying and doing that defeats my husband and hurts our relationship. I want our marriage to be beautiful and have come to see that I am part of the reason that it's not what it should be. Forgive me, Lord. I will this moment to do better and ask You to use the power of this universe to bring it to pass. I bind every hindering spirit from interfering in this matter, and I pray all this in the precious name of Jesus. Amen.

I remember the time Lamar decided to move the auction to Rainbow City, Alabama, miles away from where it was located. He felt it was a good area that would respond well to having a local auction. His assistant auctioneer and I just shook our heads as we looked at the building and the prospects. It's a job to move a business and to forge a new work in an area. It takes a lot of promotion and extra work. Lamar was all enthused. We were realistic, but Lamar was making the decisions. Once the decision was made, we wholeheartedly pitched in.

We did OK, but inevitably had to move again because it was not profitable. We didn't starve and we had a good time. It was a good experience even if it wasn't all that good monetarily. Actually, Lamar was the one that had to do most of the work. It didn't hurt me to cooperate. That's what Lamar appreciated. I cooperated. I had my say and then once he made his decision I did everything in my power to make a go of it. If it didn't work out it wouldn't be because we didn't it give our best. And Lamar wouldn't have to deal with my attitude at the same time he was trying to make a go of the auction. He had a right to do what he felt he wanted to do. I didn't have the right to take that away from him. And he had a right to do it unencumbered.

What was so important that I should have insisted he not do it? Nothing. New furniture? For stuff I'm going to go against Lamar and his ideas for his career? I don't think so. For stuff I'm going to go against the plan in his head? I don't think so. For stuff I am going to bring the chastisement of God upon myself? I don't think so. No, I said my piece and then I kept my peace. Lamar never heard "I told you so" come out of my mouth. "Well, Hon, we gave it our best," was all I said. We walked away satisfied and happy. Lamar learned a lesson more than he made money. Lessons are worth a lot. The next time, he wasn't so quick to move and a lot quicker to listen to me and Bobby. He found another location; we moved there and did very well.

How does the enemy sabotage the plan?

1. Downright rebellion. We understand the rules and go ahead and do it anyway. Rebellion agrees with the enemy. That is why we must not take part in it. When we do, we become God's enemy. Rebellion is disobedience in action.

2. Ignorance or blindness. Remember how the enemy confused Eve? He tries to keep the person from knowing the plan, and if that doesn't work, he tries to put confusion in our minds, anything to keep us from being obedient.

3. Rushing. The enemy make us think we must hurry. Getting us ahead of God is a good way to scuttle the plan.

4. Rebellious helpers. He sends someone to help that acts like they agree but really has their own agenda. Once God gets us

past the other obstacles, the enemy regroups and tries to link us up with people that won't cooperate with the plan, people who will fight it, not because they want to be mean, but just because it interferes with their plan or they can't see how it's possible. This is where you and I come in. We will either help or hinder the plan.

5. Fear. Fear in the leader or in the followers, either one will stop us stone cold. Fear is unbelief in action.

6. A critical spirit. The enemy will point out each others' faults.

7. Accusations. The enemy will get you to blame each other—the blame game.

8. Self-pity. The enemy will hold a pity party, get you to lick your wounds, or lick your wounds for you—the poor-me game.

9. Chintziness. The evil eye is the stingy eye. There is always someone that says we can't afford it. If God calls you to do it, He will fund it.

10. Procrastination. How often have I waited, only to see the opportunity pass, never to come again?

Don't think this is the end of the list. It goes on endlessly. The devil always has a new plan. Let's be sure we aren't helping him!

Twenty-six

Esther

SOME WOMEN WILL FIND this chapter an anathema, a complete joke or worse, harmful to women. It is true we can lead our lives being the strong one, the one in control, defending ourselves at every turn, being sure we are not the victim, and it works at some level. These women stop much of the garbage and that is not bad. The problem is their solution does not solve the big problems in their lives and it doesn't answer the big questions in life.

Let me make it perfectly clear, God does not want little mealy-mouthed, weak women. He wants women to be strong, but He wants to be strong in us. A woman can only have true strength when she acts in agreement with her God, if it's in the one true God. It is in our weakness that He is strong. Not that He wants us to give in and just take everything dished out to us, but to let Him be our strength. I am not strong in myself. I thought I was. I did a good job of being strong until I was reduced to a whimpering lump and had to admit how powerless I really was. The Bible not only tells us the pitfalls so that we can avoid them, but it also gives us stories of triumph and we need to look at them as well.

Let's now look at Queen Esther, one of the most famous queens who ever lived. It's important to note that she had few choices in her life. Most of her life was dictated to her by others, and it was not an easy time or place to live. Sounds a lot like our lives. That's why I chose her. This chapter is not about choosing a good man. This is a chapter for the woman who has a man who, for whatever reason, isn't all that good, and for the woman who has a good man because we all need to be a lot like Esther.

A Woman Called Esther

King Xerxes was having a six-month party. After seven days of unlimited alcohol for him and his friends, he asked for Vashti, the queen, to be brought to him. Knowing what was going on, she refused. The king asked his friends what they thought he should do. They knew it was a big problem because now all the women will give them trouble and that the king had to defend his honor by demoting Vashti. So, he banished her.

Word was sent out that the king was looking for a new wife. Mordecai, a Jew, had an adopted niece, Esther, who was one of the women eventually brought to the palace for the king to consider and was chosen to be queen. The king's right hand man, Haman, didn't like Jews or Mordecai and plotted to get him in trouble. He tricks the king into sending forth an edict that he knows the Jews cannot obey and will get them killed. Mordecai sees what is happening and enlists Esther's help. She must go to the king without being summoned, at great risk to her own life. She does go in and ask the king and Haman to come to supper. During this time, Haman is caught in his evil scheme and is put to death instead of Mordecai and the Jews. Esther delivers her people and gets Haman's nice new mansion.

The Ultimate Make-Over: Orphan to Queen

One of the most important aspects is Esther's preparation to be queen. She did not start preparing when she was about to be crowned or when she got in trouble. She prepared early in order to be chosen, which is what you must do. If she hadn't prepared early, she would have never been queen. If you don't prepare, you will never be queen. You may be married, but you won't be a queen. You don't have to be married to be a queen. Jesus is the King of all the kings and if you are married to Him, you are queen. It's never too late to become royalty.

PRINCIPLE ONE: START EARLY

You don't just stumble into being queen. Or if you do, you end up in a mess like Vashti, the queen before Esther. The truth is some women have such outstanding physical beauty or something desirable that they do and literally stumble into being queen unprepared.

I believe God creates every man and woman a prince and princess. Life may turn us into some pretty undesirable beasts; however, my God redeems unworthy creatures. You can do principle number one now. You may think it's too late, but with God you can always start now and now will be early enough. Maybe not early enough to spare you and your family some of the pain, but early enough to stop much of it and redeem the rest. You can still see the redemptive power of God. "Restore unto me the years that the locusts have eaten" (Joel 2:25).

The king was not changed because Esther was sweet and loving or beautiful. She was chosen because she was beautiful. She succeeded because she was obedient and anointed. There is a big difference. You will not deliver your family by being sweet and loving or beautiful, although that is important. You will deliver your people because you are anointed and obedient to do what He shows you to do. Anointing comes when you are obedient.

The reason I picked Esther to speak about in this chapter is not because she became a queen but because hers is a story of taking a bad situation and turning it around. She is a woman under ungodly authority that she helps become a blessing not only to herself but to her people. Hers is a story of hope and inspiration. I tell it here because it's just what we need to hear. If you want to succeed at something, find someone who succeeded at it and do what they did. How did she do it? That's what we need to look into.

I don't ever want to give the impression a woman should manipulate a man with her wiles. This is not the point at all. My point is to be the best woman you can be, all that God created you to be, and don't be what He never intended you to be. Then all your relationships will be better. Your whole life will be better. I'm not telling you all this to help you land a man. I am just telling you if you want a relationship or are in a relationship, don't be lazy, sloppy or presumptive about it. God does not intend for us to take our relationships for granted and just hope the best happens or hope it heals. That is not how God does things. God is a planner. He anticipates problems and institutes measures to take care of them. He doesn't just hope for the best; He plans for the worst. Jesus was one such plan. He has a Plan A and a Plan B, knowing from the beginning when it will probably take Plan B. Naturally He wants us to pray before we act. Pray, plan, and work the plan as you pray without ceasing. God is a can do, hands on God, and He intends for us to be can do, hands on women. Hands in the symbolic sense, of course. By hands I mean mouth, ears, feet, attitude, etc.

Let me make it perfectly clear, you being a better woman and being more of what your man would like in a mate, although commendable, is not what will turn your marriage around. I don't want to lead you to believe the burden is on you and if you don't jump the hoops exactly right, your marriage is not going to change to be what you know it should be. After you have said and done everything perfectly, it won't be enough. The truth is you can never be good enough or perfect enough to satisfy him or anyone else. You will never be everything another person needs. That's because it's a spiritual problem more than anything. Your loved one has a God-shaped vacuum that only Jesus can fill. And even after Jesus has filled that empty space, there will still be a lot of work left to do. Yes, it will be a never-ending job. But I can guarantee it will be worth continuing because it's in doing it that your joy will come and your peace and your victory. You will be redeemed in your husband's eyes if you continue. "The heart of the king is in the hand of the Lord." Only God can change a heart.

I do want you to know that a lot does depend on you: not on your perfection but on your determination to hear from God and respond; not only to respond to Him properly but to respond to your loved one properly, too. You can't respond improperly to your husband and say you are responding properly to God. Part of responding properly to God is to respond properly to the people around you. God wants to love your husband through you.

Your preparation must be spiritual as well as mental and physical. You can do all three simultaneously. You *must* do all three simultaneously. The physical, mental, and the spiritual run parallel. It's hard to be very spiritual if your physical body is down, just as it's hard to be well physically if your spirit man is down. And if your thinking is down, everything is down.

You must do your part and God will do His. Too often we think the ball is in God's court when, in reality, it's in ours. We are waiting for God and He is waiting for us. Isn't that awful? To think of waiting twenty years for God to do something about our problem (our husband), only to find out God has been waiting twenty years for us to be respectful, or to forgive him, or to repent of a root of bitterness, etc. Just imagine how disappointed you will feel if you get to heaven and finally get to ask God why He never did such and such, and He answers, "I was waiting for you to do such and such."

DON'T START EARLY ON HIM

It's very important that you understand, although we would like you to have a recreated husband in the likeness God intended him to be, it's not up to you to change him. The only person you can change is yourself. That doesn't mean we won't do things that encourage him to change. The point of all this is not to see what he has done wrong, is doing wrong, and will probably do wrong in the future. The point is to get you to see what God intended, what He expects you to do now, and what you can do in the future.

The mind is renewed by learning how God thinks, and you do that through the Word of God helped by the Spirit of God. Your mind must never rule you. Every thought must be laid against the Word so that you know if it is truth or not. Anything that is at odds with the Word must be reconsidered. If you get confused, search further in the Word or find a mature Christian to help you understand the Word. We must no longer do things because our mind or our body wants to do them. We must now do what we know is right in our spirit and what agrees with Scripture.

PRINCIPLE TWO: TAKE TIME FOR YOURSELF FIRST

What does the oil of the Holy Spirit bring? The fruit of the spirit: love, joy, peace, longsuffering, gentleness, goodness, and faith, meekness, temperance: against such there is no law (Galatians 5:22). Sounds like what a man wants or at least needs in a wife. Believe me, you will need the fruit of the spirit in your marriage. God can give you love when the love has died, peace in the midst of a storm, peace that passes all understanding (Philippians 4:7), peace when it doesn't make sense to have peace, joy out of the ashes of mourning. It's hard for a man to fight against these things. He's down and you're up. In spite of everything, you are full of joy. Amazing. He will be stunned. Just be sure you are full of joy and peace and not judgment and condemnation.

If you are married and in a mess, the truth is you probably got caught without your oil. You probably married unprepared like Vashti, and me, and the lack of preparation is showing. When the Rapture comes you won't get a second chance to get ready, but in this marriage, you probably still have a chance to get your oil and get purified. I tell how to receive the Holy Spirit in chapter 13. It's a must if you are going to turn your marriage around.

A YEAR OF PURIFICATION

We need a year of purification. Let's take a year to become a new woman worthy of a king, a year of fixing ourselves up instead of our husbands. Let's get the debris out. "What's that?" you might ask. Let me give you a few examples. First, *murmuring*. Do you murmur and complain about your husband to everyone who will lend an ear? *Revenge*. Do you run out and spend money when he hurts your feelings? *Self-pity*. Do you throw yourself pity parties and invite your friends? *Slothfulness*. Do you neglect your home and children because of the mess in your marriage? *Control*.

Do you get your way much of the time because you are so insistent? *Fear.* Have you taken a job to relieve the stress when you should have prayed and left the situation between God and your husband? *Hypocrisy.* Have you been a spiritual shrew beating your husband over the head with the Bible or Jesus? *Immaturity.* Have you given too much time and attention to the things of God and neglected your home? Need I go on? Have you taken things into your own hands instead of leaving them in God's? *Disobedience. Unbelief.* The list goes on. What is the Holy Spirit putting on your list?

Repentance Is the Initial Bath

Don't you know they started with a bath for the girls that were to be considered. It's hot and dusty over there. No king wants a sweaty, dirty woman. Cleanliness is very important. We start there. God is looking for someone who is blameless (not dirty). He defends those with clean hands (1 Peter 3). I have to ask, are your hands clean? Let's not talk about your husband right now. Let's talk about you. Are you purified? I understand when you compare yourself to your husband and other people, you look pretty good. Or maybe you don't. It doesn't matter. Whether better or worse, never compare yourself to others. It's a quagmire of error sucking you into thinking in ways you ought not to think. As a Christian, Jesus is our standard. When we compare ourselves with Jesus, that's even worse. It's obvious we need some work. And not just work, but help. Where do we begin?

First in the purification process is a good scrubbing: the inner washing of true repentance, coming clean and admitting all we have done to hurt others. The truth is we have hurt them in so many ways and we need to be honest and admit it. If they had an "intervention" and each one got to say how they have been hurt by you, what would they say? We need to grieve over the things we have done or neglected to do and what they have meant in their lives, the loss and hurt they have experienced because of our choices.

Once it's all out in the light, then we should deal with it and not stick it back to be brought out again and again. Maybe you have already repented. Then today you only have to repent over what you haven't admitted to so far. The truth is it takes time to see some things. We must repent as the light is shown in the darkness and we see for the first time. We don't have to go back and remember what God has put in the sea of forgetfulness. He has a perfect memory; we don't. He can forget. If someone accuses you of something that you have taken to Him, it no longer exists. You need to know the difference between conviction and condemnation. One is from God, the other from the enemy.

Some things are so offensive to God they are a stench in His nostrils. We need to check our lives for these things: lack of respect for the authorities He has placed over us, bitterness and unforgiveness, malicious speaking, manipulating or controlling our lives or the lives of others, etc. We should not be putting perfume over something that is repugnant to God or our husband. Before they put oils and perfumes on the women, they got them good and clean. Did you ever see the nurse wash a newborn baby? I thought she was going to scrub our little grand-girls' skin off. We must first work on getting rid of these things before adding all those other things. Have you forgiven everyone that has ever hurt you?

The truth is we won't be perfect mentally or physically. But we can desire or "will" to do the right thing. Our attitude can be right. And once our attitude is right, our lives will begin to line up with our will. Often our attitude is holding up our victory over the things that so easily beset us. Give the hurts to God. The person has sinned against God, not you. You didn't make the rules, you don't have to maintain or defend them; He does. It's too hard to do all this. You have enough to do. Cast it all on Him. Just answer for yourself.

Pray, fast, and most of all, praise Him. Not because everything is great but because He is great. Be guileless. Have a sweet innocence about yourself. Have pity on others even if he or she is a spoiled brat. That is a form of abuse they didn't ask for or didn't mean to create in themselves. Don't be so hard on people. And most of all, don't be so hard on yourself. People that are hard on others are hardest on themselves. Jesus died for all this. Receive it. Cast the rest away, as God casts it away. He forgives for His sake as well as yours. You must forgive for your sake as well as theirs and His. Who can stand to live in this garbage all the time? It's a stench. He never intended you to live in it. He doesn't intend it now.

Christians talk about the washing of the mind by the Word. Get the old out by rinsing it with the new. Ephesians 5:26 says, *"And you husbands, show the same kind of love to your wives as Christ showed to the church when he died for her, to make her holy and clean, washed by baptism and God's Word; so that he could give her to himself as a glorious church without a single spot or wrinkle or any other blemish, being holy and without a single fault. That is how husbands should treat their wives, loving them as parts of themselves. For since a man and his wife are now one, a man is really doing himself a favor and loving himself when he loves his wife."* We are washed by Jesus, so that He can present us to Himself. His forgiveness washes us clean and the Word keeps us that way.

> *Oh, dear God, to have a bath in my mind. I have known the glorious feeling of a bath after getting all dirty and sweaty. I need to feel that same way in my dirty, sweaty brain. I have been doing too much of the work on all these problems. I am going to give them to You to let You tackle them. It's obvious I'm not doing them any favor. I ask You God to forgive me. I forgive him. I forgive everybody and will do anything in my power to make up for my mistakes to the people I have hurt. But, other than that, I ask You to help me put it behind me and walk on. I want to feel like a brand new creation. I receive it right now. I pray all this in the precious name of Jesus. Amen...* (You can say your own prayer, too.)

Are you finally clean? I hope so. Remember cleanliness is a daily ritual as is the applying of oils and perfumes. The longer you do it, the better you get at it. Just as your outer body responds to continual pampering, you inner man will, too. More and more will be sloughed off and your pores will get smaller and your skin softer. You will get softer and softer inside.

You may not think you are married to a king right now. King Xerxes didn't look like much either. He was coming off a six-month drunk. Now there's a real prize. Most women would have run the other way, and should have run the other way. Except in such a case when your uncle tells you must cooperate and prepare yourself to be chosen, then, for sacrificial reasons, you must do what you have to do. Maybe Esther carries less blame for getting into a problematic marriage than most of us, but the answers for turning it around are the same. Notice I didn't say the answer was getting her out of it. No, Esther can't get out of her marriage. And maybe we shouldn't either.

Don't ever make the mistake of thinking a problematic man can be dealt with easily. I don't blame Vashti. Heaven knows Xerxes was a mess, but it wasn't going to get solved by refusing to cooperate. I am not saying to cooperate with sin. He did not ask her to sin. He only asked Vashti to come to him. He was proud of her and wanted to show off his beautiful wife and the gifts he had bestowed on her. That brings us to another principle.

PRINCIPLE THREE: DON'T EMBARRASS HIM IN FRONT OF HIS FRIENDS

It may force him to do something he will regret later and you will, too. Just think, Xerxes's friends got to dictate what would happen to her. You may not like his friends, but they carry a great deal of weight. You might as well face this fact and be respectful of him in front of them. They may be the cause of your demise as queen. Hold your tongue and wait for the proper time to deal with problem people. If they are that bad, they will eventually hang themselves.

It should be pointed out fear of the rebellion of the other women was his friends' reason for taking action against Vashti. They aren't dumb.

Rebellion is catchy. Kids catch it from mothers who catch it from fathers. Or was it the fathers catching it from mothers? Whatever. Are your kids rebellious? If you haven't been a Christian, or an obedient Christian, then you have been rebellious. Nipping it in the bud is the answer. Beautiful as she may have been, her rebellion made her very undesirable. Your rebellion will do the same for you.

PRINCIPLE FOUR: DON'T THINK TOO HIGHLY OF YOURSELF

Vashti thought she had the right to choose whether or not to go when summoned by the king. She didn't. A wise woman knows when she doesn't have a choice. I am fully aware that they were all drunk and I can't honestly say that I blame her, but he was the king. It looked bad, but I don't think the king would have allowed anything to happen to her. I think she had too much pride to be gawked at by a bunch of drunks. Pride leadeth the way to destruction. She thought she was too special for the king to take the action he did. She was special but not so special that she could spit in the eye of a king in front of his friends and get away with it. It became a matter of his pride.

She should have cooperated until something immoral was asked of her. Like Sarah did when Abram said she was his sister and God shut up the wombs of every woman and animal in the country until she was out of danger. Then if Vashti had refused at that point, the king would have upheld her in front of his friends, as he later did Esther. She didn't want to get involved either, but she had a wise counselor in Mordecai. And she listened. You can have good counsel and not listen. King Xerxes's counsel wasn't wrong. The other women would have rebelled. Vashti just reacted too soon. She needed to stand and let God defend her (through her husband). We as wives should cooperate as far as it is in our power to cooperate; until it's immoral and we know that God would not have us do such a thing. Sometimes we have to say like Esther, "If I die, I die." We're not talking a simple little thing here. If you go in to the king when you are not summoned, you can be killed. I don't know how much her life would be worth if she hadn't done what she had to do and all the Jews had been killed, but her. There are things worse than death and doing nothing in this case, to me, would be one of those things. If you are on God's side, you probably won't die.

PRINCIPLE FIVE: HAVE GOOD COUNSEL AND LISTEN TO IT

"There is safety in the multitude of counselors." (See Proverbs 11:14 and Proverbs 24:6) Pick good friends. I cannot express strongly enough this principle. Most of us won't be lucky enough to have professional counselors and groomers and by the time we can afford them, it's too late. By this time we are begging, "God, restore unto me the years the locust have eaten." I guess it's never too late, but it's pretty far down the line. Get good advice early and listen to it. It will be your friends that will make or break you. Your choice in friends tells a lot about you. And by good advice and friends I mean Christians: mature fathers, mothers, sisters, and brothers in the faith, not some heathen that only has the wisdom of the world to offer. To be a successful queen, get good help. And there is no greater help than God.

PRINCIPLE SIX: GOD WILL GIVE YOU FAVOR

One thing that helped Esther was that God gave her favor with so many people. The eunuch that took care of the virgins took a liking to Esther and gave her extra handmaidens to help her prepare. God will give you give you the favor you need and the help you need. We just need to ask for it and expect it. "God, I need some help down here, in Jesus name I pray." It could be a little longer, but I've been known just to whisper "Jesus" and have that prayer answered. Once you walk in favor and anointing, you will never want to walk any other way.

Esther helped the king be a better man. That's the power of a good woman. Every man, I said. Every man needs a good woman. Even if he never marries, he still needs a good mother. It's hard to get over not having a good mother. You may say he doesn't deserve a good woman.

That man especially needs a good woman. No, he doesn't deserve her. Thank God when He doesn't give us what we deserve when He gives us what we need. And, Xerxes needs a good woman. She can be influential in turning a bad man around. If the head of your family is not a good man, all the more reason for you to be a good woman. Woe to the man who has a bad woman. A bad man doesn't need someone else pulling him down further. He has enough problems. Don't give him any more.

You may not think your husband is much, but if you want him to be a Christian, then he has the potential to be a King's kid. If he's not a prince now, there is no better way to make him a prince than to become a princess yourself. Prepare yourself and somehow, in preparing yourself, you will see a transformation in him, just as Esther transformed the king and the whole kingdom. Nothing was the same. The evil manipulator was exposed and hanged; her people were released from their bondage; she got a brand new palace; and she was revered. Sounds good to me. She risked death facing the king, and almost didn't do what had to be done—what only she could do. Mordecai said in Esther 4:14, "who can say but that God has brought you into the palace for such a time as this." Accept your calling. Nothing will be the same when you change.

PRINCIPLE SEVEN: A GOOD WOMAN CAN MAKE THE DIFFERENCE BETWEEN LIFE AND DEATH FOR THE PEOPLE SHE LOVES

This life will end for each of us someday and we will enter into another world. Life has challenges, challenges so great they can kill us. And not only do we have these problems, but then there is the question of where we will spend eternity; not only us, but the people around us. Women, as wives, mothers, friends, and citizens, figure heavily in the outcome of these life and death issues. We need answers. In order to help others make the right choices, we must first make them for ourselves. We must get the victory first and then teach them how to get it, too.

The story of Esther is the story, not only of a woman delivering her people from death, which every godly woman does for her family since we are all headed for death, but it's the story of a woman delivering her man from a ruinous reign and by doing that, delivering everybody else. Put yourself in the story. Are you Esther, Vashti, Xerxes, Haman, or Mordecai? Esther, was the godly woman; Vashti, beautiful but dumb; Xerxes, the one in authority but a victim of his own appetites and ignorance of the way things really are; Haman, the evil manipulator; and Mordecai, the wise guardian. Our goal is to be a combination of Esther and Mordecai: a godly, wise woman. It's wonderful that we can start out as Vashti, Xerxes, or Haman and end up Esther. That's the redemptive power of God.

Principle Eight: Don't Do Your Own Thing; Allow God to Do His Thing

Esther did not act on her own. Others determined the path she would walk. How do you decide who will tell you what to do? Look at who God has put over you. In this case it was Mordecai. Try to be as cooperative as possible, as long as possible. It's not our place to dictate to others except when we are called to lead. There are some very important things God needs to accomplish and He needs your cooperation. Be very careful not to be the wrench in the works. It's not always ours to understand for a while. Just do it.

Principle Nine: The Heart of the King Is in the Hand of the Lord

Don't worry about the king. God can take care of him. He will soften his heart and give you favor if you are going in for Him and not yourself.

Let me speak of Vashti a minute. She is a victim of this principle, too. God needed Vashti to step down, so He hardened her heart from going in and hardened the king's heart toward her. If the king's heart is hardened there is a reason for it. Seek God for the reason and if you get none, trust Him. If you are Vashti, you just have to give it to the Lord. He delivers the Ishmaels and the Vashtis as well as the Mordecais and the Esthers. Don't despair if you are not Esther and find yourself in Vashti's place. We

346

can all go to God and get wisdom, mercy, forgiveness, power, and all the things we need.

There are times when we are put in a place we don't deserve and shouldn't be. We have a right to challenge the people and institutions that do this to us. But when you have said all you can say and challenged the ignorance and sin and seem to get nowhere, sometimes you have to lay it down for a while. You can't fight every battle. We may be right and God may be on our side, but we have to let Him pick our fights. Right or not, sometimes it's best just to keep quiet and wait on God to deliver you. This is not a black/white, male/female, slave/free, Greek/Jew issue. It's sin and anointing issue. It's an issue that faces every man and woman in this lifetime, some more than others. We must wait for the anointing. When you are thought of as a second class citizen, don't move on your own. Remember, God puts up and God takes down. Don't be just one more Vashti, queen for a day. Be an Esther, queen for all eternity.

PRINCIPLE TEN: WAIT FOR THE RIGHT TIME; TIMING IS EVERYTHING

Let me say this about Esther. Hers wasn't really a big part. We hear about Haman, Mordecai, and the king throughout most of the book. I know we hear about her now and she is the main man. She's Queen Esther. Actually, most of the time was spent preparing and waiting. And that proportion is about right especially for a Christian wife. Spend most of your time preparing and waiting: First, because you must be ready when the time comes. If you aren't prepared, you will blow everything. People die when women aren't prepared. And second, because it takes time to bring all the elements together. Spend the time you wait wisely. Don't wile away the hours foolishly. You won't get them back. God doesn't choose women who are foolish for the big jobs. If you want to be used by God, you must learn how to wait constructively. No, Esther wasn't impulsive. She waited for the right time.

That is why what she did was anointed, because she was right on time. Act on your own and you get yourself in a world of hurt. Wait until the timing is right and things will turn out right. Remember, it's the usually the devil that is pushing you for a quick answer, telling you you've got to move now or it'll be too late.

PRINCIPLE ELEVEN: KNOW YOUR CALLING

Esther didn't come to bring the king his calling. King Xerxes already had his calling, but he was having problems. Esther was brought in to help him. These guys already have their calling. We are called to serve along side. She just had to pray about what God would have her do in a very difficult situation. That was her calling.

Why was the realm in a mess? As usual, it was because the king was a man of unrestrained appetites. Sound familiar? We get caught up with him before we know this and then try to save him from himself. Let me warn you: he doesn't want to be saved from himself. He likes himself just the way he is. He likes his friends. He likes his family, or at least there is a place in him that does. He will fight you, his friends will fight you, and his family will fight you. And, if you succeed, everybody will hate you, including him unless by some miracle God did it.

The question is will you be like Eve or Esther? Esther was Queen and a hero for all time. Eve will never be. The story of Esther is the story of being the woman you should be and respecting your man, no matter what he is.

PRINCIPLE TWELVE: GOD WILL COME THROUGH FOR YOU; GOD IS ENOUGH

Bleak as it looked when she said, "If I die, I die," it turned out wonderfully. Her people were spared. Haman was exposed for what he was and she got a big, new house. (See Esther 4:16.) God doesn't just help you squeak by. He gives you beyond your greatest expectations. Why do you think we have all these Christians running around giving their testimonies? Because what happened in their life is so special they have to tell people: "I was blind and now I see. I was deaf and I can hear. My husband was a drunk and now he is sober and loves the Lord."

There is no way I would have ever comprehended the change God had planned for my life. And He is no respecter of persons. He has a wonderful plan for any life that comes to Him and gives Him the pieces of her life to do with as He will. I have a wonderful life now, but it all pales in the light of His love. Our relationship is the best part, not just the power for the provision. I know if I lost the "stuff" I would miss it. I'm not foolish enough to say it doesn't matter at all. But, I must say, if I had the stuff and my old life, I wouldn't have much. Because I had my old life and nothing could dress it up enough to be very special. What I have is all brand new. A brand new me, a brand new Lamar, a brand new family, and a brand new life. Yes, I have problems and disappointments, but nothing matters all that much any more. Yes, I get down and can't seem to get passed it once in a while, but the sun comes out again and I win the battle to fight another day. It's sweet. It isn't easy, but the victories are so sweet.

The word from Esther is: prepare yourself.

Dear Lord, only You can prepare me properly for what I need to do. I yield myself to You to do as You see fit. Mold me, make me. I want to be a vessel of honor for You and for my husband.

PRINCIPLE THIRTEEN: PRAISE THE LORD IN THE PRESENCE OF YOUR ENEMIES

Prepare a table for your king. I recommend Tommy Tenney's book on Esther, *Hadassah: One Night with the King* (and the movie of the same name). Forget your enemies for a while. Give them to God and then put your attention on Him and spend some time with Him. Don't let your problems rob you of this most important relationship in your life and the time you so desperately need to spend with Him. If you will give Him time, your problems won't need so much of your time. I guarantee it.

Twenty-seven

What Does a Man Want?

WE TALK ABOUT A man being the king of his castle. That means we are a queen. We may think a queen has her way, being pampered and spoiled constantly. She may be pampered and have a lot of perks, but the truth is she serves the realm at the pleasure of the king. If you read your Bible, you will see how appropriate this discussion of kings and kingdoms is. If we appreciate what it means to be a royal priesthood, we might begin to act differently than we have so far. If he's not the king, then you can't be the queen. You are at the very least a princess and nothing is more unattractive than a princess that doesn't act like one.

Once Vashti had been rejected, the question became who would King Xerxes choose? What kind of woman will he find desirable? How special it is to be chosen by a king. Even if he has his faults. All men have faults, better to be a queen with all the perks than a peasant with none. Even more special to be chosen by the King of all kings. I don't want you to think we are just creating you to be the woman a man wants. I want you to be the woman He wants and then you will be the woman your man needs you to be. You can be cherished by the man in your life if you take the time and have help to pamper and prepare you properly. Everyone appreciates a beautiful woman who has taken the time and pains to present herself well.

WHAT DOES A MAN WANT IN A WOMAN?

"What does a man want?" Good sex, good food, and a happy wife.

This may sound simplistic, but there is a great deal of truth in it. If the good sex isn't there, everything else is canceled out. And if his stomach isn't satisfied, he isn't satisfied. But most of all, he wants you happy. It's very important to him that you are happy and he is the beneficiary of your happiness.

I think the one thing that soured our marriage more than anything was my dissatisfaction with Lamar and all its ramifications. He reacted poorly, which made me all the more dissatisfied. Sound familiar? What should a woman do when she is dissatisfied? She should become all the more desirable to him, and I don't mean just sexually. And that is what we are about to consider.

Here in America all the guys can take their pick or at least contemplate one. They can dream can't they? One thing about men: they try not to marry until they find the girl of their dreams. Not necessarily the most beautiful, but one with many special qualities. The guy that gets you should feel he's the luckiest guy in the world, not that he was tricked into marrying you. Most guys are thrilled that the girl they are attracted to actually likes them back. They aren't as self-assured as they put on.

Most men want serenity, peace, grace, and a gentle, tender spirit in his woman. A man needs a gentle touch in his life. But he also desires an inner spark or spunk; someone to meet him head on when needed, but not in a bad way. (See Proverbs 27:17.) Men may date someone tacky, but they tend to marry a woman with dignity and character, although not so much so that she is high flutin' or prideful. They want her to be down to earth, but someone people look up to.

They find especially appealing a spiritual woman, even if they aren't so inclined. He likes a childlike quality, especially one that looks up at him in awe. He doesn't want a woman that is untouchable or that won't touch him. He wants a special, physical relationship. Most men like a woman who will take charge of his domain and give him an heir apparent, seeing that he or she is properly raised. He also wants someone to see to his physical needs such as nourishing meals and a clean royal robe. I'm sure he appreciates her physical beauty, but that gets a bit passé when he is weary and needs nourishment. But most of all, he needs a woman to help him. We return to God's original reason for creating her, to be a suitable helper. He wants someone who will help him do what he wants to do without saying a whole lot. He doesn't need another opinion; he already has one. He just needs two hands, a good back, and a pleasant attitude to go with them. If he gets a joyful spirit or a special talent, that's all the better.

I am well aware a man marries a woman without all these qualities, but he will eventually wish she had them. In fact, men will stay away from home because too many of the qualities he desires are missing and something undesirable is in its place, such as the "b" word. I don't know if they were always missing or if she tricked him into thinking she had them when she didn't. I'm just saying, if for whatever reason they aren't there now and he wishes you had them, saying "too bad, you're no catch yourself" is really not going to bring him around. You may force him to accept you as you are, but force is not very effective over the long haul. Let's make him want to come around because you are the woman he wants and needs and God created you to be.

High Maintenance vs. Low Maintenance

As I perused the TV channels one day, I came across a lecture and stopped to listen. The woman was speaking about high-maintenance women as opposed to low-maintenance women. Which does a man want? He really wants a woman he wants to pamper. So, he really wants a high-maintenance woman. But if he ends up with a high-maintenance woman he doesn't want to pamper (and don't you know that's bound to happen) then he would rather have a low-maintenance woman or no woman at all. So, it's better to be a low-maintenance/high-performance woman, and he will treat you like a high-maintenance one.

I am not picky about how I eat, what I wear, or how I look most of the time. I cut and fix my own hair (or used to), do my own make-up, and I'm not hard to fit for clothes and shoes. I like to be around people, and even if I have a problem with someone, can manage to smile and be pleasant. I'm sturdy and can work hard, if necessary. I can cook and clean with the best of them and yet enjoy a book and being by myself. I think of myself as low maintenance, but I don't think Lamar thinks of me this way. Since he's always trying to please and he's goal oriented, he takes my requests as orders that must be done now. I never said it did, but I like to think that he likes doing for me and even though he thinks I am high-maintenance, I'm worth it.

WHAT A MAN REALLY WANTS IS A HIGH-PERFORMANCE/HIGH-MAINTENANCE WOMAN

What does a man want? A cooperative woman who yields to him with a good attitude and keeps a light heart in spite of the heaviness around her. A woman who can laugh at the right time and yet grieves when he has suffered loss. He wants an appropriate woman who properly reflects their life, his life. But most of all he wants a spiritual woman even if he's not very spiritual. I don't know why a non-Christian man would marry a Christian woman and even fain a relgious front to fool her until she's stuck. Well, if that's what he wants, that's what we should give him. Not a pseudo-Christian like he is. No, the real thing: a woman who hears from God and does the right thing, the loving thing. And I don't mean the weak thing because a real woman of God isn't weak. But she isn't shrill or judgemental either.

A real woman of God knows where to put the boundaries and how to lovingling, firmly maintain them. How to stand and pray. How to fight the good fight of faith and have joy in the face of the enemy when he has thrown his best at her. She doesn't panic when things look bad, because she doesn't look at the bad. She keeps her eyes on Jesus, on the good report. She believes all things, endures all things, and knows when to speak and when to be quiet. She is a channel of God's love, peace, and wisdom. She caresses and nurtures. She speaks encouragement to the downtrodden when they weary on their way. She has a cup of water ready and, if needed, a hot meal. She knows what people need before they need it and prepares ahead without being asked. She forgives quickly and takes on no offense. She's too busy to lick her wounds or to have a pity party.

But most of all she loves her God, her Savior, and seeks Him early, hears His voice. And, yes, her loved ones eventually rise up and call her blessed. But long before they do, she has the pleasure of His company and His favor and that's what matters most. What does a man want? A woman who obeys God first and him second.

Oh, God, I know I haven't accepted or appreciated my huband. I've criticized him and humiliated him to get him to be a better man and it's just made him worse and ruined our relationship. It's gotten to the point that I don't appreciate much about him things have gotten so bad. I am so sorry and ask You first to forgive me. Cover me with Jesus' righteousness and help me to do what it will take to make amends to my husband. Give me favor with him, so that when I approach him to make it up to him he won't reject me again. Help me to see where he was the victim and how he has hurt. Give me discernment of what I need to understand. Give me wisdom and understanding. I pray all this in the precious name of Your Son, Jesus. Amen

A DRUNK WOMAN

One day in our convenience store some men were talking about an incident that had happened in our little town. One of the men said disgustedly, "I hate a drunk woman." I had heard this all my life, but it just hit me wrong that day. I am very fond of women and have a love for the downtrodden. When he said this all I could think was, "I'm not too fond of a drunk man, either." And, of course, it came out of my mouth. He laughed and so did the rest of the guys standing around. Well, it's true. Sin is ugly any form it takes.

Men that put women on a pedestal mean it as a compliment, but they are really not doing us any favors. Men are especially hurt or disgusted when a woman fails to live up to their expectations. They expect more of a woman. Anyone that tries to put you up on a pedestal is setting you up for a fall. I should know; I fell. After I fell, Lamar would find someone else to put up there verbally to me. He especially admired women with children who worked and kept a good house. I do, too. I just know the other woman has her faults, too. If he got a real picky housekeeper, I don't know that he would be so thrilled with the hoops she would put him through.

Why get jealous and hate the other woman? Don't take the bait. Just keep it in mind and try to keep a better house or cook better meals, etc. If other women can do better, then I can, too. I don't want him wishing he had better. I want him to think I'm the best. So, I try a little harder. It won't kill me and he appreciates it. This is an opportunity, not a problem. Don't look at her and resent her. It's not her fault. There will be a lot of "other women" in your husband's life and by this, I don't mean sexual. I just mean a friendship or admiration. Don't wait until it becomes more than this before you correct things in your life. It's his way of telling you the two of you have a problem. You've wanted communication. It comes in many forms.

Of course, the women loved the adulation. All I could think was "Look out, honey, you are about to fall," because I knew she couldn't stay up there long. Nobody can. It's really not fair, because when she falls the poor thing wonders what happened. In fact, one friend said something to me about how Lamar's attitude had changed toward her. "Don't feel too bad. You just fell off your pedestal," I said. She was mortified. We were friends enough that I could assure her he'd get over it and then she could be human like the rest of us. We had a good laugh and were friends for years.

Oh, by the way, Lamar got over this tendency after a few rounds of it not working. I don't know that he ever knew he had the problem or that I had the solution. He's just happy. Happy he has wonderful me. It's nice to have a wife that is so intuitive that she gets you past the rough spots and you keep your friends and everybody is happy (and a little wiser). All that fighting and discontent is so unnecessary.

I did have to warn him a time or two of a pitfall before it became a problem. Men are so naïve about some women's tactics and they do appreciate our input, even if they don't believe us in the beginning. Just plant the seed and she will water it. It's wonderful when the light bulb goes off in his head. Who am I to talk? I was naïve, too, to another man's intentions. Lamar clued me in and I woke up. We are all naïve and need help at times.

You are allowed to point out something your husband likes to do and you've been especially helpful or patient about that she probably wouldn't be, like car shows or camping out or living in a weird house, whatever you do that she wouldn't. Help him to see that you have allowed him to be the man he wants to be and created for him a world that he enjoys. But you have to be careful. In his mind, she might have done a better job of creating a world he wants to live in and you haven't. You might find out that your husband would cooperate more than you thought he would to have the perk she would bring with her. He'd rather have ashes in his hand than a dirty house. In this case, clean house!

Be the woman he most admires. Just be sure you don't over-do your criticisms of another woman. You don't want to appear catty. You don't need another black eye, figuratively speaking of course. It's OK if he's pointing out her good points to maybe pick out one of her husband's. So he can understand they deserve each other because they are both wonderful. The point is to help him see reality, not to have a fight accusing and defending. If it begins to go this way, back off. That's why you should only make a one sentence statement.

The ironic thing is the man that is saying he hates a drunk woman is usually the one that leaves a lot to be desired as a man.

Serene. I want to be serene. I think of Grace Kelly as serene: graceful, peaceful, and reserved. For some reason the King James version of the Bible doesn't use the word *serene* or *serenity*. But it has a lot to say about peace. Since peace is so important, I think we should look into it.

The scripture speaks well of the peacemaker: "Blessed are the peace-makers for they shall be called the children of God" (Matt. 5:9, KJV). Sounds good to me. Women, with their loving, giving nature, take on the peacemaker role naturally.

I thought everyone wanted peace. You would think so, wouldn't you? Well, think again. Some people are raised with arguing and crisis as a way of life. If they don't have a crisis, they will make one. There's a happy thought. Here you are going along just fine and they throw a wrench in the works. You think they are as upset as you and they act like they are. And they really are, but somewhere in them is a place that the crisis satisfies. In fact, this is why some people marry one person and not another. They seek out a crisis waiting to happen. A nice guy or gal has no appeal to them. What they call love is really excitement. No wonder peace eludes them. And us too! We are the clueless out there dating and marrying these people.

I hated that Lamar and I disagreed as much as we did, if for no other reason than what it does to the kids. They needed to grow up in a happy, peaceful home. I tried to be a peacemaker, but the more I gave in, the more Lamar took advantage of my good nature. One day it dawned on me, "He doesn't want peace! He wants a fight!" I was stunned. What a revelation! Once I came to my senses, I wondered, "What should I do now?" because this changed everything. I decided, since he was so determined to have a fight, I would give him one! Well, maybe not a real fight, but maybe meet him halfway. Since I was a Christian, I had to be very careful how I did this.

I grew up in a very intelligent household and learned to debate with the best of them. It seemed like I was always verbally sparring with my oldest brother, Grant. He was four years older, a real stretch for me. So when I realized Lamar wanted a fight and decided to give him one, I was prepared. Not by yelling and screaming. Heavens no! I would just say what I felt needed to be said and in a way he couldn't deny it. But he was so hard to reach! Lamar has very sensitive hearing and a cement-block head, so it didn't seem to be doing much good at first. I think this was about the time God said to me, "I chip on stone, not you!" He helped me learn how to not say too much or be too hard on him but still do what I needed to do to stop the fighting. Lamar didn't want to fight and lose! The whole point was to win. He was the cat and I was the mouse he tormented. When I quit being the mouse and became a very competent cat (never catty though), everything changed. He decided he didn't want to fight and that peace is a good thing.

JUST BECAUSE YOU AREN'T VERBALLY FIGHTING DOESN'T MEAN YOU HAVE PEACE

But the wisdom that comes from heaven is first of all pure; then peace loving, considerate, submissive, full of mercy and good fruit, impartial and sincere.

—JAMES 3:15

Here I am talking about peace and He throws in submission. To have peace, somebody has to yield or "submit"—more than we might like. The wisdom that comes from heaven is first of all pure. Makes sense to me. Then it's peace loving. Wisdom loves peace. A wise person will love peace. Women are, for the most part, peace loving, considerate, full of mercy, impartial, and sincere and we try to be submissive. But it's not easy. Or, we think it isn't. That's because we don't understand how much God is going to help us and fight our battles.

We have married our counter-part, a member of the opposite sex. If we want to have a happy marriage, we must make some adjustments. Some men are very punctual and organized. Sometimes it's the woman. She wants to know what he is thinking about doing so she can get a baby sitter and make arrangements, and he doesn't want to say because he doesn't really know yet and isn't worried about it. He figures they'll make do. Instead of nagging him and being the bad guy, she should let him experience what lack of planning feels like when they have two, three, and more people to take care of. It's not like when he just had himself to think about. And who knows? She may find out they manage just fine and something very special comes out of it.

Peace is defined as "freedom from war, an agreement to end war, law and order, harmony, concord, serenity, calm or quiet."

A peacemaker is the person between two warring factions. It would behoove us, if we are being a peacemaker, to ask who is at war? Nobody should be. Maybe we aren't so much a peacemaker as "the other side," at least Lamar saw it that way. How did I get on the other side? I was trying to be helpful. But often in the process of being helpful, I began to see a problem and in trying to help Lamar see it or deal with it, somehow we were at odds with each other.

The battle is not so much between Lamar and me, as between Lamar and the Lord, or me and the Lord. Don't you know every demon around will rise up and take notice that your marriage is in discord. They will rally together and try to get you to solidify the wall between you and your husband. It's at this point that you need to back off and see what happens next. It may seem like there is no coming together, but that's not necessarily true. God can reveal (through people and circumstances, or a revelation) things to both of you that help you come together. Sometimes in being helpful, I get an opinion and it's hard to give up that opinion even when it's not Lamar's opinion.

I am not advocating you become a doormat. Being a doormat <u>doesn't</u> mean you are necessarily in submission. When I saw myself as a doormat, I wasn't submitted even though I was doing good things. That led me to believe I was in the right and Lamar was wrong. But I wasn't right at all, or at least not as much as I thought I was. I was being dishonest in our relationship because I thought I had to be. It took God a long time to turn my thinking around, to help me see that I was as wrong as Lamar was. That I was, in fact, in rebellion. Now how does that work? A peacemaker in rebellion? There's no serenity there.

God doesn't want me to do anything that requires me to be dishonest under normal conditions. (Abuse is different.) And I didn't have peace because things weren't right with Lamar. I finally saw that I had to wait until God did something to bring Lamar and my thinking together.

So often we are dealing with someone that is anything but peaceful.

That doesn't mean we can't have peace; peace that passes all understanding, peace in the mess, joy out of the ashes of mourning. Our peace and joy depend on our relationship with our God, not on our mate. Oh, thank God! Because for years, I thought it did. And the more peace I have, the more peace Lamar seems to have.

I keep thinking of this one example. When we were building the lodge, I wanted a certain kind of doorknob. Kind of a lever thing. I'm an artist, so these things are very important to me. Lamar isn't. He wants what he feels is handiest, but also cares about price and mine were a bit pricey. I was ready to go to the mat for my knobs, and if I had he would have given in, but somehow standing in that showroom, it just didn't seem that important any more and it wasn't. The knobs we got are fine. We have to allow our hearts to be softened. That is not being a doormat.

Jesus talks a lot about peace. He was and is and always will be the ultimate peacemaker.

THE PEACE OF GOD

Peace. What a special concept. In Hebrew it means nothing missing, nothing broken. Is there something missing in your life? Is there something broken? Then you don't have peace and you don't need me to tell you that you don't.

Jesus said He came to bring us peace: *"Peace I leave with you. My peace I give you. I do not give to you as the world gives. Do not let your hearts be troubled and do not be afraid"* (John 14:27); *"I have told you these things so that in me you may have peace. In this world you will have trouble. But take heart. I have overcome the world"* (John 16:33). In other words, He came to fix things and finish things. Really finish things. As in eternal things.

If God came to provide all the things we need to have peace, then why don't we have much? I know I didn't. I wanted it, but didn't know how to get it. Let's look at the progression of the peace teaching. Matthew 5:9 states, *"Blessed are the peacemakers for they shall be called the children of God"* (KJV). If you are a peacemaker, you shall be known as a child of

God. We are peacemakers; however, we are not always received well. In Matthew 10 Jesus deals with this problem. He tells the disciples if they are not received (as His representatives), they must shake the dust from their feet and move on. In other words, peace has its limits. Peace can be rejected, and we have to respect a person's right to refuse it for now, as we pray for God to ready their heart, assuming we won't be the only one He sends. He is so merciful, but His mercy does end.

When the peace we bring is rejected, it's just as important that we leave in peace. We Christians can get awfully snotty when we are rejected. Peace has its limits with others, but not in us.

I work hard at being a peacemaker, but the time comes when I have to quit. Why wasn't being a peacemaker working for me? Because there are two principles at work: peace vs. the sword. (Romans 12:18) As we read on in Matthew 10:32, Jesus explains further: *"All those who stand before others and say they believe in me, I will say before my Father in heaven that they belong to me* [you are His child]. *But all who stand before others and say they do not believe in me, I will say before my Father in heaven that they do not belong to me."* You do not want Jesus to deny you to the Father. Now here comes the part I want to emphasize in verse 34, *"Don't think that I came to bring peace to the earth, but a sword."* Why would Jesus say this when He keeps saying, *"Peace be with you"*? (See Luke 24:36.)

Jesus does want people to have peace, but that is not always possible. Some people covet what others have and will kill them to get it. Or they insist on forcing their religion on others and will even kill those that refuse. Then there are the demented that are cruel for no good reason. Evil has a million expressions. The recent war in Iraq exemplifies this scripture. We went to bring peace, but before we could bring peace, we had to bring a sword because there are cruel, evil, mean men we must defeat first. Hitler proved how fruitless negotiating with such a person is.

I understand war is not a good answer. When my son was being rebellious and things were going from bad to worse, I said to him, "You aren't giving us very good choices." We don't always have good choices. People force us to do the unthinkable, and God doesn't always intervene. I know He has His reasons, but He doesn't usually tell us. *"The days are evil,"* says Ephesians 5:16. *"I did not come to bring peace, but a sword.* [In Ephesians 6:17 the sword is the Word.] *I have come so that a son will be against his father, a daughter will be against her mother, a daughter-in-law will be against her mother-in-law"* (Matt. 10:34–35, NCV). This version uses the words "will be against;" the KJV uses "will be at variance with another." The exegeses reads "alienate a human." Jesus will alienate one human from another. Not because He wants to but because it's a natural result of the adversarial relationship between the two spirits in this world.

- Against: in opposition
- Alienation: to cause the transfer of ownership or affection.

It's the *"choose thee this day whom you will serve"* concept (Josh. 24:15). When we enter into this choice and take His side, we automatically put ourselves at variance with the people who, up until now, we have been in agreement. (This happened to my mother and me.) There will be by the very nature of things a division between those who accept and follow Jesus and those that don't. That is not to say they are bad people or aren't well meaning, but there is a big difference between meaning well and following. If you notice, He even goes so far as to say we cannot prefer our children over Him. Yes, it's true. The kids may be happy now (when we give in to their flesh or ours), but it will be at a price they will regret later because it will be awfully hard for those children not to continue to put themselves first ahead of God. This puts them at variance with God, the One they desperately need to help them in this devil infested world. His hand of protection has been withdrawn and by the very people who think love them the most.

I need to qualify my assertion that most women play the peacemaker role. I'm afraid this is changing. As women get more assertive, more and more men are being pushed into this role. So many women are now being so strong and unyielding that their husbands have been forced into giving in much of the time and that can be a problem. It's good that the man is being a peacemaker, but it's not good if his wife is not one, too.

On *Divorce Court* one day the man wanted a divorce because he was tired of the struggle. Nothing ever went his way and he was tired of it. Women feel this way, too. He didn't see it as wearying in well doing. He was just a man trying to make his way in the world. The woman was lucky to have him. She had children from another marriage and he had taken care of them as his own. It's a shame she didn't cut him some slack. He got his divorce, but it cost him dearly. He said it was worth it just to have peace in his life.

THE PEACE OF GOD OR PEACE IS YOUR GOD

There is the peace of God and then there is the other kind: the peace that we make by giving in when we shouldn't to keep the peace. Peace has come at the expense of the good, or the proper thing. I call it "peace is your God." When a person begins to allow sin to go on in their lives and their family in order to keep the peace, then peace becomes the door of destruction into their lives. It's not peace at all. It is bondage.

When peace is your god, it compromises your obedience to God. If what God asks you to do will be controversial and you can't find the wherewithal to do it, you are a double-minded man, unstable in all your ways (James 1:8). Until you repent and determine to do what He shows you must be done, you will continue to be a big contributor to your own problems.

Conviction is not pretty. It will no doubt take a certain amount of it for your husband or loved one to come to the point of surrender. However, with your continuing intervention as an enabler disguised as a peacemaker, it may never happen. We are talking about your husband's eternal life. If you don't stand, it may affect your children to such an extent that they don't come to God either. This is the most important thing in your lives (allowing conviction to go on in the lives of your loved ones) and your false "peacemaking" is not helping. Your family needs—deserves—someone willing to stand in the gap, not to be giving in all the time. Love asks you to do the difficult thing.

> *Behold, I send you forth as sheep in the midst of wolves: be ye therefore wise as serpents, and harmless as doves. But beware of men: for they will deliver you up to the councils, and they will scourge you in their synagogues;....But when they deliver you up, take no thought how or what ye shall speak: for it shall be given you in that same hour what ye shall speak. For it's not ye that speak, but the Spirit of you Father which speaketh in you.*
> —MATTHEW 10:16–20, KJV

Notice He doesn't tell us to punch 'em out or cuss at 'em. Just speak what He gives us to speak.

Jesus challenged the things going on around Him, going as far as overturning the tables in the synagogue (Mark 11:15; John 2:15) and calling the Pharisees a brood of vipers (Matthew 12:34; 23:33). Yet, we call Him the Prince of Peace. He didn't seem to be worried about being popular or hurting feelings, like so many of us do. Why do you think He was crucified? They were the top men in the church. Today, we don't think very much of the Pharisees, but in His day, they were highly esteemed.

As Christians we must stand against sin. Year after year, if we don't stand against sin in our own lives and in our home, community, and country, our friends and family will assume it's OK with us and maybe even our God. And it's not OK at all.

Problems ignored don't get better; they get worse and warp lives. Ignore them at your peril. As you continue to ignore things and excuse the things you do to compensate, you will move into a cycle of denial. But it won't stop there. Bitterness, revenge, self-pity, and worse are next. But you won't see it as that; you will see yourself as the victim. All this takes the form of bad attitudes and bad choices; overindulging yourself in some way, like overeating, over-spending, or even worse. You are playing a dangerous game allowing yourself to become hardened to sin, some of it your own.

Sin makes people ugly, selfish, and hard to live with. The sinful life is a turbulent, "unpeaceful" life, and you, in the midst of it, will be affected. The only peace you can have is when you know you stand clean before your God.

Having a peace that passes all understanding doesn't make sense, but you can have it in spite of how things look; in spite of what is going on around you; in spite of everything. Peace. Oh, blessed peace.

Oh, dear God, to be the peacemaker You would have me be, to know when to give in, when to stand, when to do even more. Oh, God, I need Your help, Your wisdom. Come into my heart and mind. Give me Your heart and Your mind in the circumstances I face, not only in my home and family but as I go about my day. I want to be a conduit for Your peace, Your love, Your grace, especially to those I love the most. Help me to love them as You love them. I pray all this in the precious name of Jesus, the greatest Peacemaker of them all. Amen.

Peacemakers who sow in peace raise a harvest of righteousness.

—JAMES 3:18

What a promise for a peacemaker to claim. When someone enters into His peace, which is the only true peace, they enter into His righteousness. When you sow in peace, you ultimately win souls to Jesus and in that way raise a harvest in righteousness. Go out there girl and tell someone in the fields to be harvested what He has done for you.

TWENTY-EIGHT

Peace I leave with you. My peace I give to you; not as the world gives do I give you. Let not your heart be troubled, neither let it be afraid.

—JOHN 14:27

No Peace

HOW CAN I HAVE *peace when there are so many pressures on my time?"*

Jesus didn't go running around like a nut healing everyone, in spite of the fact that so many were sick. Why didn't He just lay hands on the sick and say, "Be healed! Be healed! Be healed"? Or make a sweeping gesture and heal the multitudes? Or just take all sickness out of this world? Didn't He care? Surely He knew. He knew better than the rest of us what was going on and the desperate needs around Him, and yet, He was so calm and collected. He drew aside for hours and days at a time. It almost seems callous. But you know Jesus and God aren't callous or uncaring. There must be another answer.

Jesus was calm and collected because He knew what time it was; that He had brought into the world everything they would ever need. Healing was there. All they had to do was reach out. A few did: the woman with the issue of blood, the man whose daughter died. No one was stopping the rest from reaching out. No one but themselves. What kept them from reaching out was their lack of revelation of who Jesus was and what He had brought with Him. Until it was revealed to them, and it wouldn't be to most of them until after His death, they couldn't be healed. After His death, and after the gospel was preached, then they could receive, but only if they mixed what they heard with action (faith). The big "if." It was imperative for Adam and Eve. It's imperative for you and me; and it will be imperative for your loved ones. What is imperative? To mix what we hear with corresponding action.

You are the repository of the love of God in this world. You are God's hands and feet. You are the one that must tell them the good news: the news that they can be saved; that Jesus died for their sins, and they can now be forgiven and reconnected with God. What an awesome truth and so many don't know it. You can't get so involved with the chaos in life that you forget what your life is really about. Jesus now lives in you. He's not here any longer in person. You are! That's why God sent Holy Spirit, because Jesus went back home. You, like Jesus, must know who you are and be about the Father's business. Yes, you have to love and nurture your family. Jesus would. Yes, you have to take care of the concerns in your life. Jesus would. But He wouldn't get so bogged down with them that they would sink Him. He would rise above them because He would see the bigger picture. You must see the bigger picture, too.

We Are Pressured by Things That God Never Intended Us to Be Pressured By

After He died, the significance of Jesus and what He accomplished for them was preached throughout the land. People got saved, healed, and delivered. While He was here, His job was to disciple the few men God gave Him, teaching the principles of God, explaining what was about to happen so that when everything changed and He was physically gone, they would understand. Jesus couldn't let the needs of the few deflect Him from what He needed to do. He couldn't get pulled to the right or to the left to help the people He saw all around Him. If He didn't get His job done properly, then salvation, healing, and deliverance would never come to the whole world. If He didn't draw aside, allowing God to speak and minister to Him, Jesus would not have been able to do what He had to do.

You must do what you have to do. You have to prioritize and not let things around you pull you off task. One of the sayings that helped me so much that I put it on my frig in big letters was:

Lack of planning on your part does not constitute an emergency on my part.

Too much of our life is controlled by our own or others' foolishness, immaturity, or compulsions. We have to begin to wean people of expecting us to solve all their problems. When my kids missed the bus, I made sure I got them to school late. Why? Because the teacher didn't appreciate them being late and she had ways to make it a nuisance for them. Too many mothers run to get them there on time only to have them repeat it day after day. Not mine. And I didn't whine and scream either to get them dressed in the morning, though I have been known to dress the youngest. (You go by their room and if they aren't almost dressed say, "If you're not dressed by the next time I see you, I'm dressing you!" Normal children want to do things for themselves.)

After walking with the Lord a few years, things weren't changing in our marriage as I felt they should. I was getting better personally and Lamar was too, but together... I decided to look around and see how other women were fairing who had walked this way longer than I had. I was sowing love, and I wanted to be sure I would eventually reap love. There were ladies reaping love, but some were sowing with very little to show for it. Their families were as selfish as ever, or so it seemed. Oh, how I longed for the day that would change in my family. "God, why aren't they reaping yet? It seems like they should be bearing fruit by now. If I keep sowing love, I want to know I will eventually reap it. The Bible promises I will." I cried out more in desperation than faith.

"You aren't in the sowing and reaping cycle. You are in the feeding and growing cycle." Say what? "What do You mean I'm not in the sowing and reaping cycle, Lord? I'm sowing in love." I countered, but there was no answer. He had spoken and did not feel the need to explain Himself further. Actually, it's just as well. The second time might have turned my hair white or turned me into a pillar of salt. No, I had my answer. I just had to understand it.

I pondered, What was the feeding and the growing cycle? What do you feed—animals, people, flesh? I sure had enough flesh around me with a husband and three boys. I had to admit I was feeding flesh and it was getting bigger and I don't mean just physically. I mean appetites that must be satisfied. You can have an appetite for more than physical food: an appetite for too much television, laying around, controlling things and people, having your way, manipulating, money, power, maintaining your "front", to be loved, and yes, sex and drugs. Luckily my boys weren't of an age for that yet, but they were heading toward it. There are a lot of ungodly appetites possible, that's for sure. And yes, some of them are for physical food: sweets, fats, carbs, etc. The more you give into them, the more they require until something gives and you and your family are harmed in some way with sickness, disease, exhaustion, poverty, emotional or mental problems, etc.

I asked myself, "OK, so I have these four enormous 'fleshes.' What do I do now?" Stop feeding them was the obvious answer. Do you know what happens when you starve flesh? It cries out loud and clear. It tells you what it needs and how fast, and it doesn't quit until it's satisfied. Do you know what I was in for when I stopped? A whole lot of bellyaching. It was not pretty. Are you ready for this? Don't start until you are.

I'm not talking about food. It can be food, but it's more than food. It's spiritual. If the flesh wants to sit around and watch television most of the day, then feeding it is allowing yourself or your loved ones, to be a couch potato. If your kids or husband are used to not helping around the house, then feeding the flesh is allowing them to continue to not help. Giving up on having a prayer time or reading the Bible; any time you do what your flesh wants to do instead of doing what your spirit tells you to do is sowing to the flesh.

The first point I need to make is that your husband is not your oldest child. Your responsibility and way of dealing with him is different than it will be with your children. You can't tell your husband how to eat or act, but you can and should tell your children. But even children need to be handled properly and not pushed into rebellion. The more you can do without them noticing the changes the better. Slowly making changes as you learn new ways of doing things is the best way to do it. Confrontation is usually counterproductive. How would a "Super Nanny" do it? She makes big changes and makes it look like the biggest hoot in the world. But if you notice, before she starts, she has a plan.

Sowing to the flesh is sowing to corruption. God would never want us to do that. But He doesn't want us to be harmed or abused either and understands that sometimes we don't have a good choice. He also wants us to walk in love. Just because we shouldn't sow to the flesh, doesn't mean we can stop walking in love. And we must be obedient to our husbands, even if it's against our better judgment, within limits of course. We can't harp about how they eat and the habits we disagree with, and then feed them stupid meals. We should at some point refuse to participate in the stupidity, not to get a new dumbness.

Let's be reasonable. Our job is to put nourishing food on the table and to make it taste good. They don't always want it. They want junk or fattening foods. And we do, too. How we handle changing our tastes is between ourselves and God. There comes a time when He says enough and we have to lovingly refuse to do everything we are asked to do. If we continue to sow to the flesh, we will reap a whirlwind. It gets worse and worse until it there is no telling what it will destroy. I can't tell you when that is or how you should do it. I just know God will lead you to be loving and merciful when you do.

If we do it right, we will eventually get our husband's agreement and then our kids. It's so much easier when everyone is on board. In fact, I question whether it will work at all if they don't want to cooperate. We should present what we feel is best for them in a form that helps them reach their goals: more energy, looking better, losing weight, etc. These are good incentives. If we are the chubby one, they may cooperate if it's us that needs their help. We can also trick them by substituting something bad for them with something good that tastes as good. I hide a lot of vegetables in the food I cook. And I sometimes do add a little bit of sugar. If they aren't getting it everywhere else, a little sugar can be added to the food.

One thing I need to point out is that we didn't used to have juice boxes and sippy cups, snack packs, constantly at our fingertips. We took the bottle away at one, so the child knew how to drink out of a cup before that. Yes, they threw it in their face and over their head a few times, but they learned and didn't get many face-fulls. They don't need that much juice; it's very high in sugar. If you're going to bring something to drink, bring water. If you need something more add lemon and Stevia.

Give your kids a chance to get hungry. When they sit down to a nutritious meal, be sure they haven't had anything to eat for a few hours. The doctor even told me not to let have Grant milk or juice between meals if he didn't eat, just water. He ate his next meal. Don't beg your kids to eat. Let their body do its thing. Healthy hunger is a gift.

It won't be easy at first to make the changes. Try to make it interesting and fun. Work on the kids when your husband isn't around as much as possible. Men do not do well with a lot of bellyaching. I know you want him to help and may feel you need his help, but I feel you need to learn to do some of this on your own. You need to get a little tougher (most mother's do anyhow) and not be in a popularity contest all the time. I love *You're Killing Your Kids*. These programs are so good. Notice how she doesn't just deal with how they are eating. She deals with sleeping problems, the parents not having time for themselves, doing things together as a family, etc. If we are killing our kids and this needs to be changed, then you need to implement the changes. Get a plan.

My mother never forced us to eat, but she sure did have ways to trick us into cooperating. If she thought we wouldn't like something, she would tell us it wasn't for us. "You won't like this. It's 'adult food.'" Knowing full well we would be determined to prove we were old enough to eat it. Another was what I call, "three bites is a miracle." When a child sees a food they don't want to eat (and you know it's not that bad), tell him or her she must eat at least three bites. It's at this point the child usually balks. "Well, if you don't eat three bites, then don't ask for dessert." I don't dicker with how small the bite was, within reason. It has to be a bite. If kids eat three bites of something often enough, they usually get used to it.

I do not agree with making a child sit there too long. Keep only nutritious foods in your home and anything they eat is fine. What's to fight over? It's the processed stuff that is bad. Don't buy it. When they really get hungry, an apple will sound good, or green beans. Let hunger work for you.

We need to keep them acquainted with milk, eggs, tomatoes, onions, etc., when they are little because if we let too much time elapse, they are revolted by them. So many mothers of first-time eaters take their dislikes as gospel. Keep giving them green beans and eventually they will quit spitting them out. Mix them with the applesauce. I fed mine the meat, veggies, and fruits separately when we started their feeding as toddlers and by the end they were mixed together. I didn't like the chicken noodle dinners because I wanted to control how much protein they were getting. I thought the mixtures would be heavy on the noodles or rice and light on the protein and later the professionals said I was right. I remember when baby food was twenty jars for one dollar on sale with ten dollars of groceries. I would go every day for three days, breaking up my weeks' grocery shopping in order to stock up.

Mealtime should be a pleasant experience. It's rude to complain about the food and refuse to try things. It's also unsightly to pick huge quantities of ingredients out of the dish such as tomatoes and green peppers. Our children need to eat like they should eat out in public or if they were at someone else's home. Teach them to eat around such items. I cut tomatoes and green peppers up so small, they don't even know they are in there. Sometimes I puree objectionable veggies and add them that way. Spaghetti sauce is a good place to hide tiny shredded carrots, celery, green peppers, and onions.

One thing I had to do was to stop the denial. I had been nice to Lamar for years about his weight. I even believed him when he said he wasn't eating that much and maybe their was something wrong with his metabolism. Then one day when I said it to the lady that ran the lunch counter in his store, she laughed, "You believe that?" She saw how much he ate. Boy, did I feel stupid. If he was overweight, he came by it honest. He ate every bite. After that I started challenging the denial. Not in an ugly way, but firmly. "Hon, if you think there is something wrong, go get checked out. I really don't think there is. I think you are eating more than you realize; but if not, you need to know it." It wasn't too long until Lamar was losing weight because he finally faced the truth. Men can lose it so much easier than women. Years later, we did find out he had a thyroid problem. This is one thing they often don't check at annual physicals unless requested and it's very common to have thyroid problems. However, I don't think it was a problem at the time. Getting his medication did not bring his weight down, dieting did.

Where to begin? For our family it was the television and general selfishness. Control over the television was never much of a problem in our home because I didn't watch it that much and most of the time could do without. (Peace, if nobody is challenging the selfishness, isn't really peace or a good thing.) There was only one Christian station at the time and that was pretty much all I watched except a half hour of news each evening, which Lamar wanted to watch, too. I didn't like the boys watching much television and they didn't want to either. We are all fairly active. In the evening, it was usually Lamar's choice and they had homework. When he was home, he ran the remote. I retired to the bedroom and read a book. If you don't watch television, you don't see the commercials to know what you are missing. If I ever did have a choice, it was totally contrary to what Lamar and the boys wanted to watch, but I never made an issue out of it. Actually, the boys were fairly cooperative. Lamar was the problem.

After the "Drunk Spiders" episode, the Lord helped me see I had to start requiring my family yield a little and not just take all the time. We are creating selfishness in our family when we do all the giving and don't let them give some, too. I had to insist on having my choice of programs once in a while. A few days prior to the show, I would tell Lamar that I wanted to see "the Julie Andrews Special" or whatever and what day and time it was to be on. Well, you never heard such caterwauling. Lamar was so upset the first time I insisted, he took the boys to see a movie. It was awful. Not the movie, the transition. But we got through it. Slowly, painfully, step-by-step, instead of yielding to their selfish desires and by insisting on what was right, we came out of it. They had to see that I meant what I said when we had our little talk about sharing the television time.

Many parents, because they haven't disciplined themselves and done the right thing, feel sorry for their kids and don't discipline them properly, either. It's a vicious cycle that just gets worse and puts the burden on the kids to turn things around. "Gee thanks, Mom and Dad. Just what I wanted: to end up as an adult lazy, over-weight, and with a bunch of bad habits." Much of this is a result of divorce or having to work. You can't always avoid a divorce, a bad marriage, or having to work, but you must avoid spoiling your kids. Love them, be merciful, but be firm where it counts.

Lamar loves and appreciates me a lot more today than he did when he was getting his way most of the time. And he likes that our life and our testimony is better, too. We're not perfect but we are a lot better. Wives are to submit, but we don't have to submit to sin, to people's fleshly, ungodly appetites. We can refuse to go get their beer. But I wouldn't if he might hit me. I choose my battles and check it out with the Lord as to how necessary it is that I refuse. He will have to fight these battles. We cannot do it all by ourselves. We need to wait until we know now is the time. Some things He has already said enough about in the Bible. Don't wait for more because He may never speak personally. Abuse is never acceptable.

VERBAL ABUSE

It's easier said than done to stop verbal abuse, but it is possible. Since verbal abuse is so common, and I do think almost every relationship will have a certain amount of unnecessarily hurtful and ugly talk, we might as well talk about it now. I don't think it's a good idea to ignore it like I did. It actually just makes it get worse. Sin in any form should not be tolerated. It's just that it's so hard to confront. Often we are afraid it will make him get all the angrier and maybe even get physical. I don't think it's a good idea to start when tempers are hot. The time to start is when things are calm and you can talk reasonably. The only problem is we hate to disturb the peace, but disturb the peace we must, so that some other day will be better.

Many people are bad to say things they don't mean and then feel sorry about them later. He does love you and you love him. You both hate that it came to this. It's a good thing that at least he or she cares enough to come back and apologize. This is an especially good time to bring it up, because this is not acceptable, you are going to have to be more proactive if happens again.

If the person doesn't come back and apologize, that doesn't mean you don't broach the subject. That means it's all the more important that you do. That it has gone much too far. One woman that suffered extreme violence said that she should have stopped the verbal abuse earlier. And that is what I found to be true, too. Remember my story "Enough" in chapter 2, Truth. It took me ten years to have enough. But that didn't mean that we were too far gone to be turned around. It just meant we were finally ready to start. However, I don't think just stopping the abuse is enough. We do need to let them know that they will suffer consequences if they don't cooperate. But, I also think we need to give them hope back. But not just the hope of seeing their children, the hope that things can get better. They need to understand this is just a part of making the relationship better. They need to understand what they said in the heat of anger is not right and must be stopped.

A good scripture is "anger and sin not" (Eph. 4:26). It helps the person who does have a temper to know that Jesus got angry, too. He turned the tables over. It's ridiculous to think that a person is going to experience some terrible assault to their being or something they believe in with all their soul, or some such offense, and not react severely. That is asking too much, more than God asks, in fact. He allows us to anger, but then He asks us that in that anger, in the heat of the emotions, that we sin not. He does ask a father not to revenge and that's hard if his daughter has been raped or murdered. It takes something greater than our own restraint to do it. And to forgive takes even more. We won't even talk about that right now.

It's just not healthy in a family to have one member out of control to the extent they are abusive and they need to understand this. Whether they do or not, the new standard must be put in place and the consequences firmly established. I don't like consequences to be too harsh because then we tend not to carry them out—not a good thing. The more you move the line, the harder it is to convince them once you are strong enough to stop moving the line. These were my suggestions:

- Stop hiding the abuse. This is a hard one. But, I'm telling you, when I told Lamar's parents why I was having to ask him to leave, it made all the difference in the world. Be sure whoever you involve is up to the task, someone he cares if they know or not. And you could make this part of the talk. "If this abuse doesn't stop, I will have to take it beyond you and me and the kids."

- Refuse to stay in the room as soon as he starts being verbally abusive. You must stop him immediately so he understands exactly what he is saying that is inappropriate. This is what good counseling does. We can't talk in generalities like, "You always say I'm lazy." When he says you are lazy, stop him. (This becomes a problem if you have been lazy. Maybe he's not verbally abusive, but just trying to get you to do what you should be doing without him having to say it.) Men don't realize how hard it is to get it all done. We do need their help, but when we get it, it comes with their mouth and they will have an opinion on how you should do things. All this has to be worked out. And we need to consider their suggestions. I find Lamar's do help.

- Help him to understand how things he says are hurtful. Often men don't realize how harsh they sound. Say it back to him. If you have been wrong, then you should apologize and ask for his help. Engage him in the solution.

- Do not allow him to be verbally abusive to the children or other people. No labeling. Privately explain a label that could be put on him that he doesn't like. A parent cannot allow the other parent or anyone else to verbally abuse their child. However, it's true a father is a lot tougher than a mother and we must allow their toughness in the relationship. Many women try to emasculate their men and that's wrong and just as bad for the kids. There is a balance that can be found. "Come on, kid, try harder. You can do it."

- Be willing to give up your security to stop the abuse. Find out what the community provides in the way of shelters, police protection, etc.

- Have him checked out medically. There is often something physically wrong with the person.

- If you think it's necessary, take steps to have an intervention to get him the emotional and mental help he needs.

- Learn your rights. Know how to get into your bank accounts, etc. Be sure payments are being made properly. Get professional help in case you will have to take over your finances or other personal affairs. It may get worse before it gets better, and you have to allow it. Like that lady said, she wishes now she would have stopped it early on. The earlier the better, and there is no earlier day than today. At least pray about how to proceed because proceed

you must. First with the talk, but no talk until you are
ready.

I need to speak here to the debate we find in Christian circles: the use
and misuse of the tongue. There is the scripture that our husbands will
be won by our silence as we are a living epistle before them. (See 1 Peter
3:1.) Sounds good, but it seems to take forever. And, all the while I'm
being good and silent and loving, he is being bad, mouthy, and abusive!
Something is wrong with this picture. Do I just have to stand here and
take it? Peacemaker is in our job description, isn't it? This is one of the
earliest revelations to me.

You Can Speak

You can speak. When we see our man doing the wrong thing, we should
pray, and then we can possibly speak—once, if we feel it's the time and
place to speak. We should never be doing anything unless we feel it's what
God would have us do. Our husband, of course, tells us we are nuts and
to mind our own business, etc. Now what? Possibly you spoke too soon.
Therefore, you may need to repent and pray again, "God you see what he
said. I can't talk to him. You will have to deal with him. I can't." From
then on, we deal with God. (Later, if He tells us to speak again, we may.)
We don't grumble at the man. Every time a thought comes about your
husband (boss, husband, friend), refuse to entertain it. It's the accuser of
the brethren, not God, whispering worries and accusations concerning
our loved ones. *"What if he's not 'of the brethren'?"* The enemy wants to
destroy the marriages of all Christians, of all people.

In Christian circles we have given wives the mistaken idea that they
must remain silent and suffer mutely through whatever their husbands
say or do. In 1 Peter 3:1 it says, *"Likewise, ye wives, be in subjection to
your own husbands; that if any obey not the Word, they also may without
the Word be won by the conversation of the wives; while they behold your
chaste conversation with fear."* So you can speak.

Let's try a more modern version from the New Living Translation: *"In the same way, you wives must accept the authority of your husbands, even those who refuse to accept the Good News. Your godly lives will speak to him better than any words. He will be won over by watching your pure, godly behavior."* "If any obey not the word" means isn't saved, or isn't obedient to God.

Since the Bible means nothing to him, God wants our lives lived before this man to be a living epistle. Just as people knew there was something special about Jesus, your husband should see there is something special about you. God wants your mouth and your actions to agree. You will have to seek God each day, but this is not really any different than any Christian must do. Learning to walk as Jesus walked. He did not remain silent and you don't have to either. Jesus said, "I do what my Father gives me to do." and this included the words He spoke. We too must be able to say this concerning the things we do and say. We must learn to speak what God gives us to speak, when God tells us to speak, and to whom God tells us to speak. This is the key to your actions.

The problem is we are speaking without the anointing on what we are saying. We are into our own works. Our words are our works. If you have spoken it once and your husband has not received it, then it was not anointed. God can, at any time, bring what you said back to his remembrance. If He hasn't, then it's not the right time. If it's not the right time, then why are you saying it? Why should you insist on making it the time? You shouldn't, and if you do, then you are in error. It's sin to continue to do things when they are not anointed. Timing is very important in your Christian walk and learning it is crucial. It's one of the basic principles of obedience. You are not obedient if you out of God's timing.

You should repent if you are rushing God. That was the sin of Judas. Imagine that, being like Judas in his sin. Ask God to forgive you for being impatient and doing your own thing. You might need to apologize to your husband, but don't do this without checking with God first or until you can do it without telling him again what you've been trying to say unsuccessfully thus far. If, or when, you say you're sorry, don't go into detail about what God has revealed to you. Your husband is not ready for all that right now. He may never be, because his problems are different than yours. Your revelation is not for anyone but you unless God specifically shows you to share it with another person. And even then, He must chose the time and place.

Too often, what we are saying is not very wise or loving. That's why it's not anointed. It takes time to be wise and loving, time for God to do a work in us. That's why I say don't be too quick to speak. Too often what we say just hurts and convinces those we love how dumb and off base we are. Since our speaking may make things worse and not better, I say better not to speak at all until you are sure. And the only way to be sure is to know God and what He sounds like when He speaks in that still, small voice. *"My sheep know My voice"* (John 10:3–4).

My question to you is, Are you changing? Are you learning to forgive your husband? To forgive yourself? Your parents? Friends? Neighbors? Are you learning to love more people? And to love them better? Are you letting God show you others as He sees them? (He loves them.) Are you beginning to use your mouth creatively and not negatively? Your husband changing is not the whole answer. You have things God wants to change, too. God wants you to become more like Jesus and He will use your husband to perfect you.

Over the years Lamar has come to see he doesn't want to fight. He never intended to lose. He wanted to fight and win. And since he wasn't winning very much, he decided he didn't like fighting anymore. Works for me.

Fighting is hard to do in a way that doesn't hurt the participants. When you have someone who grew up in a dysfunctional family, they can't always think this far. If he is too stubborn or immature (or you are) to want peace or to apply some minimal standards of conduct to his actions, then he is too dysfunctional or immature to fight properly. It takes some convincing to establish that you should have a modicum of civility. These people can't see that you need to go in another room to discuss things privately or that it needs to be done respectfully. With

Lamar it was no holds barred, and it just wasn't possible for me to get that rancorous. Nothing is worth that much to me. Even if they agree to fight fair, when it comes down to it, they lose it and go back to their old destructive ways.

It takes time to undo old patterns and make new ones. It doesn't help when we react in kind, doing pretty much what they are. We need to back off and rethink things. Let some time and God show the other and ourselves something we hadn't thought of. If you can't control yourself, and he can't control himself, nothing will be accomplished by "talking." That's where a lot of couples are; backed off and not talking. Sad. This is when counseling could really help, when the couple can't seem to get things resolved properly.

When God sent me back to work with Lamar in his insurance business, I determined that we should not argue in front of the girl we had working for us. "How can we ask her to go home with a headache or her stomach tied in knots every day? No job is worth that," I insisted and he agreed. So, now what? We decided to go into the conference room across the hall every time we got into a "discussion." This worked quite well. Actually, much of our "fighting" came about because he was trying to get her on his side and then I would counter...you get the idea. If she hadn't been there, there wouldn't have been a discussion. But since she was, we would excuse ourselves to talk it out by ourselves, thus cutting out much of the debate. I knew we were getting somewhere when one day we were about to excuse ourselves Lamar asked, "Do you think we could do this here?" I assured him I could if he could. He understood it had to be civil. What a victory! We rarely went into the conference room after that.

There are books and counselors that can teach you how to fight: give each one a certain length of time and don't accuse; say "I feel...," etc. It's good to learn these things if you don't know them by now. Respect and proper decorum must reign in your home. *Nothing* gives you or your spouse the right to be out of control, abusive, or cruel. Very often it's the woman that can't control her tongue and pushes him too far. This is as much sin as what he does.

If your discussions are too bad and not for the kids ears, go to the car. Or ask them to go play outside for a while, get a babysitter, or put it off for a while. You simply cannot have these fights in front of the children. Learn to talk low and go to the bedroom. Make your husband really listen. You really listen. When I have something important to say, I get calmer and quieter. We must be respectful in our relationships even if others are not.

I understand things can be devastating and you want to scream and carry on, but this is a luxury we do not have as parents. It really doesn't help. After you have screamed and yelled, you still have to go on sensibly. Why not stay sensible? There is a right way and a wrong way to fight. You simply must have some rules or some help if you aren't doing very well. You need to sit down and try to talk things out without interference. And you may have to do it with a third person such as your pastor or a counselor. When we don't have peace, we need wisdom to get it.

> *Oh Lord, I don't know if I can challenge the sin in my home. I've tried. It's too ingrained. It upsets them too much when I do. You are going to have to help me. A step at a time, Lord, a step at a time. I'll try. I'll be like Esther: if I die, I die. And I know You won't let that happen. She lived and became the queen and got the big house. Help me get the victory for me and my family. I pray this in the precious name of Jesus. Amen.*

Don't make decisions when you are down or too soon in the process of finding out the truth. There is no need to rush to judgment. I eventually found out I was very much a part of the problem and that we didn't understand Lamar's problems at all. Give God time. So often, He has not even be able to begin even after many, many years of marriage. Don't determine to set up camp at the offense or the mess. Determine to get through it and get healing for everyone involved. "No, devil, you don't get the husband."

TWENTY-NINE

No, it's by the grace of Lord Jesus that we believe and are saved, in the same way as they are [the Gentiles].

—ACTS 15:11

Saved

ONCE A WOMAN HAS received the peace of God through Jesus, she just naturally wants everyone to know this peace. And the first place she looks is right next to her: her husband. The question millions of women have asked at one time or other is, "How do I get my husband saved?" You don't! But God will. It's by the grace of God that any of us are saved and it will be by this same grace that your husband will be saved. Don't ever think His grace is not enough.

Your job is to report to God every day, not to set the agenda and decide what to do and how it will be done. That's God's job. Your job is to see to the renewing of your own mind and to be obedient to what the Lord shows you to do. It might include doing something that will help in your husband's eventual "salvation," but don't let waiting for that keep you from doing what you should be doing today. Report for duty every day and leave your husband in His capable hands.

In Acts 11: 14 Peter tells the story of how he was sent to Cornelius, a gentile, and preached to him the message that hitherto was exclusive to the Jews: *"Send to Joppa for Simon Peter. He will bring you a message through which you and all your household will be saved."* It worked for Cornelius and it will work for you. I believe in household salvation. The people in Cornelius' home were not only saved, but Spirit-filled. So, don't be put off if your husband is not "saved" yet. It's just a matter of time. I feel we have precedence for believing in household salvation and that your husband will express his salvation before he dies, hopefully more than just a few days or hours before. It would be nice to enjoy some time together as believers.

I have my theories on why heathen men chase and marry Christian women. One is, if he gets a Christian woman to marry him, it's like saying he's OK with God, which we, of course, know is not true. You can fool a woman for a while, but you can't fool her forever, and you can't fool God at all. Or, it's like saying to her that her Christianity isn't real or she wouldn't even date him, let alone marry him. Once married, everything changes and it doesn't get better. Any Christian woman who would marry a non-Christian is asking for trouble and gets it. If she wasn't up to doing the right thing before she got married, she probably won't be after. But I do believe eventually she will come around, and he will, too.

I do not feel a woman can never speak on spiritual things to her husband. She can and she should, but only when it's God inspired. Too much of our talking is nagging, cajoling, and manipulating and not only unproductive, but hurts our case and that is what Peter is talking about. However, some women are too silent. I try to say what will get Lamar to thinking in the right way. There was a time between his "deliverance" and his "baptism" when he made fun of "tongues." He would talk in a foolish sounding foreign language and say, "I can do that." When I told Mom Brooks what he was saying, she quoted the scripture about blaspheming the Holy Spirit being the one thing that was unforgivable and said he was in very dangerous territory. The next time he did it, I said the same thing to him. The look on his face told it all. He never did it again and was spirit-filled shortly thereafter. I think that's why it was so special when he sounded so authentic, like a Jew preaching; because it wasn't his foolish sounding language.

I needed to say what I did. A wife needs to say these things. The scripture is just saying Lamar will be "won" as much by my life lived before him as what I was saying. Don't you know he saw the joy I had? He had to have seen a big difference in my life, from almost suicidal to joyful and peaceful about so many things. It's a shame when a woman doesn't say the needed thing at the appointed time.

THE SALVATION AND MATURATION OF YOUR HUSBAND

The following are a few suggestions that are good whether your husband is saved or not. There are carnal Christians, wilderness Christians, backslidden Christians, and unsaved "Christians" that we think are saved; they're the ones we know aren't, but they think they are. Then there are the people going through a dry spell or depression. It's not easy to tell the difference because we can't know their heart. I just don't go there. I don't try to decide if someone is or is not "saved." That's for God to know.

Let's face it: mountaintop experiences don't last forever, so we need to be prepared for the valleys. We must minister to our loved ones continually throughout their lifetime and these are some suggestions. Even the mountain climber needs some help and encouragement.

PRAYER

Prayer is essential. Not fluffy prayers, but intercessory prayer that takes our authority over the situation. If we are the only one that knows God, then we are the in the situation and we have every right to exercise that authority. A heathen has no spiritual authority. They may have authority in the natural, and we have to cooperate as much as possible if they are in authority over us, but they are not the spiritual authority. However, I would not tell him or her that.

Why did Jesus not experience the time lapse we do? Because He didn't experience the faith lapse we do! We are not beggars. If we have to beg God, something is wrong. Why are we begging God to do what He has already done? Jesus said, "It's finished." We just need to figure out what "it" includes, and I think it includes everything good we want or need. "It" includes our salvation and our family's, healing, prosperity, deliverance, and peace, just for starters. God called Himself "I AM" and He meant He is the great "I Am everything My people need." It's all been provided. It's now up to us to claim it, receive it in faith, and see how God appropriates it to our lives.

Just as there is a time lapse between when you pray for healing in your body and actually see it, there is a time lapse between when you pray for your husband and actually experience his salvation. You have prayed haven't you? Well, then start thanking Him for it. If you haven't really prayed, or haven't prayed in faith, then do it now. Remember, we aren't beggars. We aren't begging God to do it.

If you are sick, you should know your healing was accomplished two thousand years ago and will manifest itself some time after you pray. Well, know that about your husband's salvation and maturation, too. Just keep watching for the day you see it. God already sees it. And indeed you will.

"For the unbelieving husband [trustless man] is made acceptable [hallowed in] to God by being united to his wife, and the unbelieving wife [trustless woman] is made acceptable [hallowed (made holy or sacred) in] to God by being united to the Christian husband [man]" (1 Cor. 7:14, GNB).

In this passage the King James version tells us the unbelieving husband is "sanctified" by the believing wife. Sanctified means set aside as holy. Set aside from what? From the world, the negative spirit in the world. And not just sets aside, but set aside *as holy*! You set him apart from the enemy of your souls until that time when he understands and receives Jesus personally. Sounds good to me! Good enough to help me carry on while I wait.

An unsaved husband is just a very large unconverted area in our lives. Yet, that doesn't mean it won't be converted, and it doesn't mean God isn't working on it. It just means today it's still as of yet unconverted. I do what I can to cooperate with God to correct any area of my life, and I will cooperate with what He does with Lamar. That's all I can do. But I don't let it worry me.

You may wonder about your husband's free will. How free is it? Is he blinded by the devil? That isn't a free will. That's bondage. We aren't as free as we think we are. A great deal of his will is dictated by the enemy. So why can't it be dictated by you and God? All we want is for God to do His thing just as the devil is doing his. And when He does, your husband will bow his knee.

Do you remember my story where I tell how hopeless I thought Lamar was? He was a pretty tough case, but we have a tougher God, by far. You can't look at the reality of your tough case very long without panicking and living in fear and doubt. And taking your joy. It will be like a person watching a kettle to boil or for their ride to come. It seems like an eternity. No. Set your eyes on Jesus and no matter how long the wait, it will be glorious.

We are women of faith, not fear, and our prayers should reflect it. But, for goodness sake, don't make this the central prayer concern every time you approach God. Assume He is working on it and praise Him for it and then move on. There is a world out there that needs your prayers.

> *I thank You, God, that my husband is saved, sanctified, and Spirit-filled. I praise You for working on my behalf in this matter. Lord give him a hunger for Your Word and for the things of God. I thank You that he is the wonderful man he is. I ask You Lord to heal his hurts and the things of the past. Help him to see I forgive him and You do, too. Amen.*

CREATE

I create the fruit of your lips.

—ISAIAH 58:19

This is a promise just like the ones concerning being born again. Think about what God creating what you speak could mean to your life. If you can speak it in faith, He will make it come to pass. I don't know about you, but when I heard this, it revolutionized my life. I have a lot of things I know God wants to happen and I can agree by speaking it forth.

"My husband is a godly man. He loves the things of God. He loves to go to church and be with the people of God…" Whatever the devil reminds you you aren't seeing, claim. Remember: Faith is the reality of what is hoped for, the proof of what is not seen (Hebrews 11:1). See with eyes of faith what you don't see with your eyes of flesh. Thank God for the things you don't see. Refuse to see anything else no matter what proof the devil dangles in your face. "I don't see that devil; I see a man serving the Lord." Create the husband with your mouth that you want to see.

Put the burden of your husband's salvation back on God's shoulders where it belongs. He tells us to give Him our burdens and take up His, for His are light (Matthew 11:30). Then report for duty every day and be sure you do your part by taking up His.

STAND

The Bible says, *"Having done all, stand"* (Eph. 5:13). Be sure you have done all and then stand. And if something comes up, deal with it, but continue standing. We serve a big, powerful God. If you don't think your God is well able to bring your husband to the saving knowledge of Jesus Christ, you don't have a big enough concept of God! It's not that God can't do it. It's that God can't do it without your faith allowing Him to do it. The problem may be that you don't have confidence in you doing it, or your husband or God doing it for you. It's not going to be you or your husband that does it. The Bible says (now listen to this and believe it; God is speaking, not me): *"He [God] who has begun a good work* [and that includes getting you saved; you are a good work He has begun] *is faithful to finish it."* You have a promise that your husband will manifest his salvation one day! Your husband is part of that good work He has begun in you! (You and your husband are one.) Believe it! Don't you *ever* fear or doubt again. Tell the devil to get away from you with that nonsense that your husband might not ever be saved. There is no way that he won't be saved. You have a promise. Stand on it.

LIVE THE LIFE

One thing I had to realize was that this was not a bad thing. This waiting; Lamar being a mess. In fact, it was a blessing to me. It made me the mature, powerful, faith-filled, obedient Christian I am. If Lamar had been wonderful and on fire the whole time, there is no telling where I might be today spiritually. I might be a carnal Christian for all we know, or worse, not even a Christian at all. Our problems and my frustration with Lamar forced me to get answers and made me who I am today. And I like who I am a lot better than who I was.

I'd like to think I'd be just as mature if things had been different, but I don't know that. It really doesn't matter because that wasn't my choice anyhow. I had what I had and did what I had to do and it blessed me. Praise God! (And you have what you have and have to do what you have to do and praise God.)

Desiring your husband to be saved or more mature as a Christian will force you to live the life before him and keep you going back to God for help and comfort. What a blessing. You and the Lord will get to be such good friends. Can you really regret this time together? Do you really wish you had your husband as your closest friend instead of Him? "Why can't I have them both?" You can. But the truth is every dynamic changes things and you don't know what the dynamic of him being an on fire Christian would do to your life. I know we think it would be wonderful, but often, the sad truth is that we squander what we receive. Do you know for sure that he wouldn't have squandered it? Or you? We just don't know these things. We have to trust God.

I do know one thing; our problems force us to get closer to God. What problems would you have preferred if it hadn't been this one? Health? Financial? Family? Maybe you've had some of them, too. Life is hard. I experienced the loss of our home, business, and then my little girl. I understand completely the piling on of problems. The Bible says there's enough evil in the day (Ephesians 5:16). We are in a battle, not in heaven on earth.

I don't understand the timing. You will just have to keep going to God and being sure you are not the hold-up. Yes, it's true. We often sabotage our own ballgame. *Oh, Lord! Say it isn't so!*

BIND THE DEVIL

For the salvation of a loved one, bind the enemy from working in their life and ask God to take the blinders from his or her eyes. Pray that "he comes to himself" as the prodigal son did. Also, pray a hedge of thorns around him for all ungodly relationships.

You need to take your authority over the enemy. You can, you know. Just as God created the world with His words, you must use your words to control spiritual entities. "Satan, I bind you from interfering in this matter. Spirit of revenge, I bind you and send you to the dry places." Name any spirit that you feel is working in the matter and even "companion demons." The Bible says "Greater is He (God) that is in you than he that is in the world" (1 John 4:4). That means we can speak to them and God will back us up. Remember to use the name of Jesus when you do it. We continue to suffer because we do not take the authority we have in these matters.

"What if he doesn't leave?" There are such things as strongholds. Certain things are not going to be done in a day. It takes walking out your deliverance. But we can begin the work this day and continue it day by day. We have to leave the timing to God, but we are often the hold-up. Continuing sin, bitterness, unforgiveness, disobedience, etc., will cut the effectiveness of your prayers. Satan knows when he has a right to continue. He doesn't play games with his own mind like we do. He may be evil, but he's not dumb. Well, he is kinda dumb. It's really dumb to think you can be God. But, we try it. We are our favorite idol.

SOW THE WORD

One very important thing to do is to sow the Word in your home. If your family won't read the Bible for themselves and you do (you do don't you?), then it's up to you to tell them what scriptures fit their life situations. One little remark, the bulk of which is a scripture, is all that is needed and it needs to be said in love and concern. You are not saying it for any other reason than you love them and want the best for them. You assume they forgot or didn't know and will be glad to be reminded. Once is all that is necessary. The Word sticks in there when everything else has long since passed.

I remember the time I wrote a letter to a friend and it made her so mad she threw it in the trash. She complained later that the letter talked to her from the trash. She finally thought, "I might as well get it out; I can't throw it away." You can't throw away something that is anointed. If God gives it to you, it will be anointed. It may not appear to be when you first say it, but it will hang in there. I have had many people speak back to me my own words as their own, not realizing where it came from. In their mind it came straight from God Himself. Do you think I am going to say otherwise? "He must increase, but I must decrease" (John 3:30). Remember, I said "one little remark." Harping is not helpful!

Lamar didn't think I was all that wise in those early years. He was a skeptic for a long time even as a Christian. He didn't have the faith for the things I had faith for. He just didn't feel it was necessary. I figured if God cared, He cared about the little things. And He does. God was faithful to me and Lamar saw it. Now he doesn't fight my faith any more. Why look foolish? But, boy did I look foolish for a while, until I was redeemed. You must be willing to look foolish as you claim something in faith.

I always seemed to have a scripture concerning something we were dealing with, almost like a motto. Eventually I share it with Lamar and it becomes his motto, too. But, I don't share too early. You have to wait until it's time. When the time is right, they just grab onto it like a thirsty man getting a drink of water.

I really believe many husbands are not won to the Lord either because the wives do not receive wisdom from God (because we are not looking for it), or we do not pass it on once we have received it. In other words, we just allow the garbage to continue. On the other hand, we think it's our job to beat our husband over the head with a scripture we pick out as relevant. I question whether God actually gave it to us or if we just assume we should. This happened with one of my sons. The scripture I was thinking was not from God and He told me so.

We should tell our husband some of what God says to us, but he certainly isn't ready for it all. Once said, leave it with him. If it's anointed, it will do its work. Isaiah 55:11 says the Word will not return void (unproductive). Since this is true, why do we have to add our emphasis? Say it gently, sweetly, and let the Word have the impact not your voice or attitude. Why should we be the bad guy all the time?

INTELLECTUAL STIMULATION

I honestly believe that many men, and women too, have the mistaken idea that Christianity will not meet their criteria for being provable scientifically. Christians seem like a gullible bunch at best, fanatics at worst, whereas they are skeptics. Knowing this, it's important that you make sure the people, the churches, and the ministries you are associated with and ask your husband to grace with his presence, make sense. Christianity does make sense. It makes a lot of sense. But sometimes we misrepresent it. That's why Billy Graham has been so successful, because he connects the dots until the person can do nothing else but receive what Jesus did for him, or her, on the cross. Kenneth Hagin Sr. was another one that sounded so believable.

Be sure whenever you have any Christian ministry on when your husband is hearing it, too, that it's something that stimulates his interest and doesn't "turn him off". The worst thing you can do is make him listen to a bunch of emotional yelling. Do not insult anyone's intelligence by trying to make them "give their life to Jesus" until they are truly convinced that they are a sinner separated from God in need of a Savior. This is a job for the Holy Spirit and no simple woman. Do your best to be a wise godly woman and try to answer his questions, but beyond that, leave it to the Lord to do or someone He sends. Do not panic. He got you saved didn't He?

NORMALCY

It's also important that we appear normal. I know the Bible says we are peculiar people, but that doesn't mean we have to be weird. We should separate ourselves from the world, but Jesus said that He was not going to take us out of the world (John 17). We must be a part of the world, the salt; the source of God's life and light to this world. Yes, we are fanatics, but we are wives and mothers, sisters, employees, and friends, too. We are in the real world, a very vital part. Don't destroy your effectiveness by being too aggressive, mouthy, or dumb. Be wise as Jesus is wise. I wish I could tell you what that means in your life. You will have to ask Him to help you. He knows.

The Bible tells us to do things decently and in order (1 Corinthians 14:40). That sounds to me that God is saying use common sense. On one hand we say reasoning started all this trouble and then we say to reason. Which is it? We do have to use our brains. We use our brains to figure out what God is saying to us or think, "What would Jesus do?" Jesus walked a very special walk, but He never appeared "weird" and neither should we.

Step by step, God led us out of the mess we were in. I maintain I fed Lamar the Word when he wouldn't read it; Lamar maintains he knew the Word; that what I did that was helpful was stand. I think it was both. One thing I must say, I didn't beat him over the head with the Word and that is probably why the standing seems significant to him. I know that God had me standing on the Word. You can stand all you want, but if you aren't standing on the Word and know what you are standing on and why, you won't stand long enough to get the victory. People die standing. It's not just the standing that wins the victory, but standing on the right thing. It's the combination of the two: my part and God's part; and yes, three: Lamar's part, too.

I became close friends with a girl with a very problematic husband. It was hard to know where to begin. As I talked with her, I became aware of how hard his heart was toward anything she said. "How do I soften his heart?" she asked. Good question. This is in response to that question and may be a little redundant, but I feel it's good enough to include:

PLOW THE SOIL

If we take the scripture of the sower seriously, we should look upon our loved ones as soil. *"Oh, my. When we look at some of them, they sure do look rocky and hard. There is no way anything is going to sprout there."* Well, that's just fear and unbelief talking. We can do our part to plow it. How's that?

Prayer has been mentioned and it's an assumed. We must never fail to assume the essentials. I have been watching Rev. Dutch Sheets tape on the watchman. We have been put in place as a watchman for our homes and familys, our places of business, our cities, and nation, etc. Some have special anointings for special assignments, but many are assumed, such as wife and mother. I cannot go into all that is involved in prayer right now. Hopefully you know the essentials, like praying in Jesus' name and reminding God of the scripture that applies, etc. Take your authority in the situation and God will back you up.

FASTING

Fasting is always good. I mention fasting other places, but I need to be sure you know it's definitely on the list. I drink liquids, especially lots of water, and even nutritional shakes if I am not able to take a day off and am still very busy. The point of a fast is not to run myself down. Be sure not to add food back too quickly. Take your time when you are breaking a fast. In fact, you need to find out a little more about it so you can do it right.

One of the hardest things we will ever do is bring our body into submission. I don't know that the battles will ever end. Christians often refer to our body as "the flesh." Because of spiritual bondages, sometimes, it's literally impossible to break them without a spiritual intervention. Fasting is one way we do this. Fasting does not move the hand of God, it brings our body into submission to our spirit and we are more open to receive from God. I never have been one to fast, but recently it has been a great blessing. As Jesus said, some things are done only by fasting and prayer. Sometimes it's your only answer to the demonic hold over you or a loved one.

If you feel led to fast, there is a right way and a wrong way. If you are not up on the rights and wrongs, a pastor will be able to help you.

A Hedge of Thorns

Sow a hedge of thorns around ungodly relationships, even if they are family members. Do this every time you pray for them, daily. They can be reunited after they get saved. If it's an ungodly mother, you don't need her to have any influence over him, or a brother, etc. (But don't tell him you are praying this way!) Pray it and keep praying it. They will get so sick of their ungodly friends and family they won't have anybody to do anything with but go to church with you, or watch something on TV that gets them saved while you are at church. I know it works.

Forgiveness

Forgiveness is so important. They need to feel your love and acceptance in spite of their sin. They know you don't agree with what they do, but it sure is nice to know you still care. Don't be the bad guy or the heavy in their life. They have enough of those. God has given me an unnatural love for everyone, especially those who have hurt me. "Forgive them Father for they know not what they do." If Jesus can say it, I can, too.

Allow Ministry to Happen

I like to put on a good television show or radio program that might minister to Lamar, but I do not keep it on when it will just irritate and he can't listen anyhow. I wait until the proper time. I do feel I should get some of the choices when we watch television. It's not good to give him his way all the time. Your family must not be allowed to be selfish. And when I get my turn, it's usually something religious. Often, I just have Lamar check it and he is just as interested as I am. Right now we have bad reception of the local Christian channel, so I don't bother. But, Lamar knows I want it and he is making preparations to improve that channel. These things take time. There is also the radio and tapes. Since Lamar has phenomenal hearing, I am quick to turn whatever I am listening to off if it will not have a chance to minister. If there is something especially good, I will tell Lamar I want him to listen to it and he cooperates. Of course, he is a Christian. With non-Christians you only have a few chances where they will cooperate, so make them good.

LAUGHTER

I really must put laughter in here. Keep it light. My goodness, if your salvation doesn't give you joy, you don't have much of what God wants to pour out on you. Your joy is your strength. If you feel weak, it's because you are not doing what you need to be joyful. Obedience brings joy. As you do what He tells you to do and see what it produces, you will have joy. At first you are scared and have trepidations, but if you will obey, you will be redeemed and how sweet it is.

He is the God of the laughter movement. What a cleansing. Make your home a place of joy, peace, and laughter even in his heaviness. Don't be cruel and laugh at him (at least not very often), but help him see the humor in life. Give God your burdens so you can laugh again.

"But, Midge, you don't know what I'm going through!" No, I don't. I do know I lost a little girl and still managed to keep laughter in our home. Would my continual weeping have helped? No, the day had to come that I put that behind me, at least temporarily, and enjoyed the day with my three precious boys. Sure, I cried again. But, I laughed even more. And in the end, I laughed in the devil's face. And I'm still laughing. Don't tell me you can't laugh. I've been there. And I know what's possible after you've been to hell and back. If you aren't laughing then the game isn't over. God will redeem.

WHAT ELSE?

The unexpected. Always expect the unexpected. It's not going to happen like you think it will, so quit trying to anticipate how it will happen. Just relax and enjoy the life you have. God's going to work it out. Believe that. He loves him more than you do. He will surprise you if you are busy doing what He gives you to do. If you aren't, then there is no great surprise. It's just all tedious and a never-ending wait. Your joy is in what you do in obedience to God. If you have no joy, you figure it out.

GET MINISTRY FOR YOURSELF

You don't have to wait for your husband to go to a meeting with you. You need ministry for yourself. You need healing, peace, and the power of God in your life and you find this where people have gathered together that are hungry for more of God. Go to meetings or anointed ministry where the power of God is moving. Be sure it's a legitimate Christian ministry. There are a lot of fakes out there. If something they say or do is not scriptural, that is your clue. I don't want to scare you. God will guide. Ask mature Christian friends if you have doubts. There is a main stream of Christians, and you need to stay in the main stream. God is big enough to have a large group of followers. When we are in Alabama we go to a very small church, but they are a part of the main stream. You will see some wonderful and marvelous things and maybe something new, but nothing out of the main. Beware of something too different.

It's OK if they laugh or fall down or run or dance. They are all OK, but if it's too weird, quietly leave and find a group that isn't so weird—although, I guess some would call tongues weird and at times they were not mainstream, and Martin Luther was the heretic. "Snake handlers" are Christians and I agree God will protect us, but I don't think we should tempt these things. God doesn't protect us in our foolishness. The point of the gospel is not to handle a snake. But, you could do worse going to the local bar. So, I guess you will just have to let God sort the wheat from the tares for you. You must trust your inner spirit man and the Holy Spirit to guide you.

Do they lift up the name of Jesus? Do they love Him and want to serve Him? Are their lives changing in positive ways in their everyday life? Have they stopped cussing and fighting? Are they becoming better people because of what they have experienced spiritually? Talk with Christians you know are walking the walk. The answers to these and other questions should tell you whether you should be involved or not. But remember, sometimes it's our preconceived notions that is scaring us and not the Holy Spirit warning us at all. Sometimes what seems like God is really just our inner nervousness about things that are different. It's sometimes hard to know His peace from our peace.

But go. We can't be kept from good ministry because of the bad. We need powerful ministry and must go to where others bring their anointing. An amalgamation of Spirit-filled believers gathering together to worship the Lord and hear good preaching. I'm ready to load up right now. And what fellowship. It's glorious. And life changing. I don't know where I would be if I hadn't stepped out and gotten the ministry I so desperately needed. Need your life changed? Have a life changing experience.

Jesus says where two or three are gathered together in His name, there He is also. If Jesus is there, you don't just have a multiplication of power but unlimited power. The weak link will be you and your limiting mind. If the job isn't getting done, there is a reason. Be sure it's not you.

I don't know how your husband will come to the saving knowledge of Jesus Christ. I just know God is working on it. It's up to you to be sensitive to the timings and do what God would have you do. Work on yourself and your own maturity. Keep yourself so full of joy that the condition of your spouse doesn't pull you down. Salvation is the beginning not the end. In the next chapter I go on to share the path we continued on to where we are today: happy and free. Let's pray:

> *Dear heavenly Father, I lift up this whole situation to You. You know how much I desire for my husband to be saved. I've prayed and prayed to no avail. All I can do now is give the burden of it to You and report for duty. I know as I give You my burdens,*

You will take up mine. And You said Yours are light. I guess I haven't been carrying Yours because what I've been carrying has gotten very heavy indeed. I praise You for coming into my life. I know that is the beginning of my husband being redeemed, for we are truly one. Help me not to panic and pick up the load again. I just praise You that we have begun and we are where we are with me knowing You personally. I bind Satan from working in our lives and ask You God to put a hedge of thorns around any ungodly relationships that either of us have. I ask You to bring godly friends and mentors into our lives and help me to be the wife he needs to bring him on to maturity. Help me to say what You would have me say and stifle where I need to stifle. I pray all this is the precious name of Jesus.

Have you heard of reaping and sowing? We reap what we sow is a basic concept of life. What do you want to reap? Souls—the souls of your family and friends. Therefore, if you want to reap souls, what should you sow? Souls. Sow to somebody else's son or daughter, husband or wife and God will work on yours. If you don't sow souls, I just don't see how you can reap any. And I just don't see how you know God very well. If His heart beats for souls and yours beats for cars and clothes and looking good and a nice house, etc., I just don't see how He is really living in you. God in you will provide for a home and clothes and a car, etc., but it will be incidental to the bigger plan, which is souls.

POSSIBLE DRAWBACKS TO SALVATION

By understanding the drawbacks in your husband's mind to yielding to everything that is being said and done on his behalf, you can hopefully counteract them as God gives you wisdom (and patience).

1. Blaming God

I have to say one of the greatest drawbacks to getting our husbands to submit to God is because he is so hurt and frustrated in life and blames God for a lot of it. He knows if he was God, he would do things a lot differently. Also, and this is a big ticket item, many women haven't really improved by becoming a Christian and, in fact, just added this new stricter morality. The last thing he wants to do is "come to Jesus." That brings us to:

2. Blaming you

Wives are the source of a lot of a man's frustration and bitterness. Your husband may want to punish you. He certainly isn't going to do something you so desperately want if it means giving you the least little bit of satisfaction. Anyhow, he doesn't think it will do any good. So, what's all the fuss?

If yours is an adversarial relationship rather than a love relationship, you need to work on that. I know he makes it almost impossible, but what is so important that it's worth more than his soul? Your house? Your dog? Yes, your kids are. But, God wouldn't make that the choice. We can yield a lot even where the kids are concerned. I have found in hindsight that a great deal of my defense of my kids was not helpful and not in their best interest. They learned to manipulate the situation.

I don't think God will really require you give up your home. If you do, I believe He will eventually restore a better home to you. One you love even more. I'm standing in faith in this right now. I yielded a beloved barn/cabin about eight years ago and am just now seeing something better rise in its place. I am saying that in faith because they are putting the walls up as we speak. For a long time the thought of The Barn and the reality of no longer having it sent me into a fetal position, but even then I reminded myself and the devil, I did it in faith. If it was wrong, I had the best of motives. And I truly believe that I will be redeemed eventually. I have the lodge now and it's great!

I find most women love the Lord but have no concept of giving Him all the choices in their lives. They have to live in a certain house, with certain stuff, have this dog or no dog, eat at a certain time, and certain things, etc. The husband's choice is to like it or lump it. And I guess that's God's choice, too. And then the woman wonders why her man balks when he finally has a choice and the power to grant what she wants is in his hand. There is no give and take in the relationship. So far the give has been mainly on his part and not very much. Well, I take that back. She used to give. In fact, she gave until it hurt and now she refuses to give any more. So, they both do their thing and get more and more hurt and frustrated.

3. Blaming others

Heaven knows there is enough blame to go around. The victim status appeals to some people. It's especially bad when the one that hurt them was supposed to be a Christian. Deliver us from hypocrites.

My father was gospel hardened by his mother. He had hard feelings toward his parents, but would not talk about it. The truth is he really didn't want to live the Christian life. He was a teenager and wanted to do things God says not to do and then blamed the hypocrites. The Bible says the ones that diligently seek God will find Him. Diligently means over the hypocrites. When a person lets someone stand between himself and God, there's a reason for it.

We can, with God's help, help them to understand, even with all the problems, we are blessed.

4. Blaming himself

This may be the hardest of all: being too hard on himself.

It's all too typical that someone has heard the plan of salvation all his or her life, possibly even had godly parents who trained him in the way he should go, but never got saved. Or, was saved as a youngster, but has long since backslid. As the years rock on, people get more and more panicked about his soul. Oh, how they wish he would come to know the Lord. Everyone extols his virtue, but knows God cannot have sin in His presence so, every once in a while, they really get serious. Sickness or problems in his life will prompt renewed efforts to get him to go to church, but he won't have anything to do with it. He won't even listen. If he does listen or even attend church, there doesn't seem to be any response. It's sad.

Sometimes the person may even curse and have a bad outlook to the point that everyone around him thinks he is hopeless. Their hearts ache in despair for his soul. Usually this brings on more preaching, all to no avail. Let me say something that may help you.

First, you need to realize this person is well aware of their sin. In fact, it's ever before him; he just doesn't let you know that. He is not stupid. He knows there's a pretty good chance there is a hell and he may go there. Some actually believe and know full well they are going to hell. Others figure they aren't that bad and if others make it, they will, too. Certainly going to church and outward religiosity isn't the criteria, if there is a God at all, or so they theorize.

I had a friend's husband ask me, "What kind of sappy God would let me go to heaven?" This came out when he was drinking. I asked him, "What kind of a sappy God would send His Son to Cavalry for you?" It sounds sacrilegious, but I felt he needed the same shock value given back to him that he was giving me. We approach these people preaching conviction, trying to convince them how awful their sins are and how doomed they are and they are already convinced. "They may be convinced, but they sure don't act it. Their reaction is anything but humble." And that's true. If they are going to hell and have faced this fact, they can lie, cuss, yell, or act haughty at all the preachy people and it won't cost them anything. What can they lose? They've already lost and accepted it. But they can at least not give you or the others the satisfaction of rubbing their nose in it. They will die and go to hell on their terms, not yours.

And deep inside they feel a lot of these preachy, self-righteous people will be there with them. Then again, maybe God will see the good in them and they will make it. Who knows? They've really been humble in their own mind because they at least didn't think they had a right to make it. They dream of a twilight zone switcheroo—them in heaven and the preachers in hell. What a glorious thought that is. And furthermore, Jesus seemed to agree with them. Look how He came against the religious of his time. "See, even Jesus agrees with me."

When you find yourself in the presence of such a person, you need to be aware of the problem: their sin is so big, they can't see the cross.

They can't grasp the reality of what Jesus did and the phenomenal grace of God. What you are dealing with is actually pride. Watch to see how God leads and if He wants to use you. Maybe you are to tell someone else the problem and they will do the work. The "work" is to make Jesus and His work on the Cross real to them. Make Jesus bigger than their sin. Stop making their sin so big. They are overwhelmed with it already and you keep adding to it. Instead, help them get their proportions right. Their sin was just a small part of the work Jesus did. Not even one whole drop of His blood was needed to pay their debt because His blood is so precious. They are such a nothing compared to Him that their sin was easily covered.

So Your Husband Just Got Saved

Many women live for the day their husband gets saved, and rightfully so. There is a special relationship between a man and a woman when they are not only husband and wife but brother and sister in the Lord. However, we have a mistaken idea what it will be like. No one really knows what will happen next, but I can give you a few clues.

First, I want to tell you that your responsibility will be greater to hold your tongue and continue to wait just like you did to gain his salvation. "Wait for what?" you ask. His finishing. Too often we think we will be a part of God's finishing of our husband and we will, but not the way we think. It will be our weaknesses, the things that frustrate him about us, not our great strengths and wisdom, that God will use most of the time. It will be as he goes to God with his hurts and frustrations that he will get the victory in his life, just like it has been for us.

I am not saying you will never be used, but don't count on it. He will use your grace, your forgiveness, and your inner beauty most. If you have already mentioned something to your husband and he didn't respond, then evidently it's not anointed. God will have to handle things in your husband's life to help him see. He is blind and your words may not be enough to help him see. Your husband can't receive from you right now, at least not much. He wants to be your hero and criticism gets in the way of this goal. He is probably in very bad shape from years of being unsaved and under conviction. He needs to hear positive things, loving things, supportive things. Your biggest job right now is just as it has been, to hold your tongue and be in prayer and listen for what God is telling you. There are many things about yourself and your husband you don't know right now and God is having to take all things into consideration. It will not be like you think, so don't get a mind set on anything. Learn to flow with the Spirit. Be still and know that He is God.

If we are older in the Lord, our husband's salvation doesn't knock us out of the place of being more mature in Christ and we should be honored as such. A baby Christian should naturally be anxious to learn all he or she can, looking to the more mature for help and guidance. This is in the best of all worlds. We don't live there, so don't get upset when it doesn't happen. Now that your husband is saved, he will be making decisions concerning spiritual things. It takes a wise, mature Christian to handle this delicate job: turning over a leadership position to someone, especially someone new. It needs to be done very respectfully, never making him feel like the child. A new Christian will challenge our walk and mature faster than we think. All those years of negative experiences while serving the devil suddenly recompute and mature him in a positive way. A ten year old that is recently born again will not mature as fast as a forty year old new convert. We need to back off and let him and God work out their relationship unencumbered as much as possible. We are usually more of a hindrance than a help.

Give your husband some space—a lot of space. It takes time and maturity for someone (your husband) to see the need for honoring you for standing in the gap for so long and right now he may be a little touchy about taking on this important position in the family as spiritual head. *Wow!* He may be a bit nervy about it all, as well he should be.

Being a godly woman doesn't mean that you are holier than thou. Keep a light touch on your spirituality. Wives have the delicate problem of a man's ego. He doesn't want to appear needy or childish. Just as he won't ask for directions to get somewhere, he won't ask for them for spiritual direction either, especially from his wife. Therefore, we must feed him the Word and spiritual truths (a discernment, a principle, a word) in a backhanded manner. Not as one speaking from on high, but as one equal to another, acting as if he knew it and you were just reiterating it.

What we feel is God is actually only one facet of God. It's not helpful when I am dogmatic and think I have the mind of God on a matter and Lamar doesn't. God's mind is much bigger than mine. Backing off is always preferable. Staying open is, too. Your husband may just be right. Just as your children are right sometimes. Don't end up with egg on your face. He has a right to be wrong sometimes, too. He needs to see we are with him in this very crucial time as he works out his new relationship with the Lord. Don't talk so much or yell so loudly he can't hear Someone else. Men are especially bad to back off and let us have it (his authority) rather than listen to us. You simply must not get between your man and your God.

It's a glorious day, the day your husband is saved, and it does make life all that much easier. But life is never easy. So, don't get your hopes up and romanticize any part of life. We have an enemy of our soul and our family and we will have to face him—the devil—everyday. Rejoice knowing the next challenge will be in God's hands and not yours.

THIRTY

**As a bird that wanders from her nest, so is a
man that wanders from his place.**

—Proverbs 27:8

Finding My Place

I WAS RAISED WITH ALL boys and naturally thought of myself as one of them. This frustrated Lamar to no end. He wanted to do man things and thought I should do women things. I looked feminine enough; he didn't know I was a tomboy. The beautiful thing about being a tomboy is you get the best things of both worlds. I could play dolls or cowboys.

I had a great childhood. Life was a parade and my parents didn't rain on it much. They made us responsible, but didn't stifle us, the roots and wings concept. When I met Lamar, he loved my free-spirited approach to life but soon wanted to clip my wings—big time. Lamar had a lot of rules in his head, whereas I tended to be more nonchalant. I could see I needed to back off and let him make certain decisions. We couldn't both be the boss and it certainly wasn't going to be me. He was too determined, but it's hard when the other person is so dysfunctional, and gone a lot, not to make the decisions.

It took me a long time to see that, although I was almost a doormat, that I was not as submitted as I thought I was. Submission is not being subservient to the other person. It's choosing to cooperate with another person's decisions. Every once in a while Lamar would say to me, "You need to learn your place." Having a caustic mouth, even though I didn't use it that much, I said, "Ya, me and the blacks have always had a problem with that." Lamar was not bigoted, but he was raised in the South and understood my point. I didn't appreciate being treated like a second-class citizen.

In those days Lamar was the typical male-chauvinist pig. He opened the doors for me and was a gentleman. This was the good side. The bad side was when he verbally put me down and acted like my feelings didn't matter. But I don't mean to make it sound like it was all Lamar's fault, because it wasn't. We make the mistake of blaming our husbands and putting our problems on them when much of it is our fault. I should have respected Lamar's down time with his friends. I was just so needy that I didn't have the capacity to leave him alone. I needed fellowship, nurturing, adult companionship, my husband's time and attention, and I wasn't getting it. We were living in the South where I was an "outsider"— a Northern, Catholic, city girl, etc. It just seemed so natural to get it from him and his friends. They never seemed to mind. It was Lamar that minded. If I felt excluded before a remark, I felt a lot worse after, and he usually said it in front of them.

God would have filled the empty places, but I didn't know that. If Lamar had been living as a Christian, he could have helped me. As it was, we were both needy and not doing very well with each other. I couldn't fill him up and he couldn't fill me up. I didn't think I had a "religion" problem. As far as I was concerned there was nothing wrong with my religion. I wasn't looking for answers and it would be years before I realized how puny my answers were.

OUT OF PLACE

Lamar used to have terrible sinus infections. In fact, we moved to Florida partly because of them, and he still got them, just like I knew he would. I kept telling him he needed to stand for his healing. That would just make him mad, but he was so sick I couldn't help it. Then I got a cold and couldn't seem to shake it. I prayed but to no avail. "God, what's wrong? Why am I not being healed?" The answer came quickly, "You have inserted yourself between Me and Lamar." I repented right away because I didn't want to be sick. "If he dies of sinus trouble, I'm not saying anything,"

I thought to myself. I was healed and he was healed right after me. "I decided I was sick and tired of being sick and tired," he said. Just what I wanted to hear for years. He hasn't been bothered with them since. Being out of your place brings chastisement and stops the blessings.

Finding your place is not a place of dishonor for you. Whatever and wherever your place is, it's a place of honor. I should qualify that I am not advocating you necessarily get in the place man has for you. I am talking about the place God has for you. Sometime it's the same place, but not always. You will be honored eventually if you are faithful there. He has promised, "They will rise up and call you blessed." If you are a mother, that is your place. If you are a wife, then your place is to be what you need to be in that role, depending upon the situation.

However, not every mother or wife is able to physically care for the needs of her husband or children because of decisions made that drive a wedge between them. Others may usurp our place, and we must respect our loved one's right to make these choices even if we disagree with them. We may fight what is happening, but it's not always possible to change things. Our place may be to love them from afar, to pray and fight the spiritual battle. I have prayed for many years for a loved one that did not want to hear what I had to say. I would rather be close and loving, but that is not always possible. We can always be loving; we can't always be close. In these times, I lean on God for help. It helps.

Not only do you need to stay in your place, but you need to keep others in their place, too. If God sends a mentor or spiritual mother or father into your life, don't make him or her a buddy. Not that you can't be friends, but don't get too familiar. And if you have a spiritual daughter, don't try to make her a spiritual sister. Be appropriate with your relationships and you will help both you and them. If you have already made this mistake, quickly repent and begin to be appropriate. This is why I do not refer to my pastor by his first name. He deserves respect and putting "Pastor" in front of his name makes the proper delineation. You may have to refer to your husband as "Mr." or by his title in public to give him the proper respect. And expect the proper respect for yourself, too.

"How Do I Get in My Place?"

First, you have to find it. And before you can find what it is, you need to figure out what it's not. Kind of like a sculptor sculpting a bird removes all the stone that isn't part of the bird. Most of us don't know what that is. Let me give you a clue: it's not your husband's part or God's. Or anyone else's. These parts need to be expunged from your repertoire.

Everyone involved in a situation or relationship has his or her area of responsibility. I have mine. Lamar has his. And God has His. We must always be aware of what is our responsibility and what is theirs. I can't shirk mine, and I mustn't usurp theirs. The problem is, if we are not in our place, we are probably in someone else's and that's not good. If we are in someone else's, we are keeping them from being in theirs and we are not in our own. Didn't your mother ever tell you, you can't be two places at once?

What we should be doing goes lacking and we probably aren't doing a very good job at theirs either. God doesn't equip us to do someone else's job, but He does equip us and hold us responsible for ours—all of them. Have you considered how long that list is? Why would you want to take on someone else's?

> When I am not in my place,
> I am in the wrong place.
> That makes me no better
> Than my husband
> When he's not in his place.

I Don't Do Windows

Years ago I was talking to a woman that cleaned homes. This was before I could even think of getting help. My house left a lot to be desired, but it would have to stay that way. I was interested in how much it cost and what she did, even if I couldn't image ever having someone help. I mentioned windows and she said adamantly, "I don't do windows." She knew exactly what she did and what she did not do. No way was she going to do something that wasn't agreed upon before hand and she was not going to agree to do windows. I asked how do they get their windows done and she said, "They have to get somebody else to do them."

I was impressed. So impressed that when God was dealing with me about Lamar, He was able to bring this to mind to help me see what I was responsible for and what I was not responsible for. He told me I was out of my place, "Back off. Leave Lamar to Me." When someone told me what I should do about Lamar, I blurted out, "I don't do husbands." It became a guiding principle in my life: I don't do husbands. God does. After I had turned Lamar over to God, when Satan came to me and pointed out what Lamar was doing wrong, I said, "You have come to the wrong person. I don't do Lamar. You'll have to talk to God." I do what God gives me to do today and so should you: your daily chores, take care of the kids, visit a sick neighbor, pray for people, pay your bills, etc. God is such a big God, certainly He can take care of one little husband.

God also told me: "You don't chip on stone; I do." (I knew He made the Ten Commandments on stone tablets. This is why we must read our Bible, so we have a frame of reference for Him to speak to us.) Lamar was so stubborn it was like he had a cement block for a head, and I knew what He meant.

People are always encouraging me to "keep Lamar in line." Golly! There's a scary thought. Me keeping Lamar Vice in line, indeed! No human being could ever do that. His father tried and it is what we now call abuse. It only made him more determined. No, I'm good, but I'm not that good. I'm tough, but I'm not that tough. And I am quick to tell them, "No. I don't do that. I gave him to God and He does it. What I couldn't do in fifteen years, God did in two weeks!" And we have a good laugh because most people, even though they admire Lamar, know he is a piece of work. Any time I want to impress people on how real God is in my life, all I have to say is, "I'm married to Lamar Vice, you know!" You can just see as the realization of this sweeps over their face and they shake their head in agreement: I must be very close to God, indeed.

It's Not My Job to Change or "Finish" Lamar

Once you figure out your husband is wrong and God is not pleased, the natural thing to do is to try to encourage him to do the right thing and that's fine. There is nothing wrong with a word fitly spoken. The problem is it becomes many words and not very fitly spoken, a barrage of words battering him over the head. Somewhere you got out of your place again. It's really bad when you get in God's place. Why would you do that? Because you don't trust God. And the only way to correct it is to back off and give God time. Since God asks you to submit and cooperate as much as you can, and since God has said He will take care of the authorities that get it wrong, I say: "Not my job."

Me controlling Lamar or Lamar controlling me or any of us controlling anyone else is God's job. And if you do God's job, you will only make a mess of things and cost yourself a lot of time and pain because God won't be working on them while you are. You have put yourself in a chastising mode. Pray about things and give them to God. Learn your place and stay there. Trust God and take your hands off. You can't change your husband. Only God can.

The Weight

I hated what our problems did to my family and sympathized with what my kids were going through. What mother wouldn't? After years of trying to help the situation to no avail, God gave me the picture of a huge weight over Lamar's head coming down on him. It should have weighed him down, but I was standing next to him with my hands over his head holding the load for him. It was very awkward, at best. God let me know He was the one allowing the weight to come on him and I was in the way. Here I thought I was helping. Boy, did I repent in a hurry and get out of the way. Let them work it out.

God was using "the weight" to accomplish something in Lamar and I was preventing it. (The weight is a problem in our lives: financial, personal, medical, legal, etc., that brings pressure to bear on us.) Men need to feel the pressure to bring out the best in them. God created them with broad shoulders and strong backs to carry the load, just like He created women to bear the children. Let's get out of the way and let them do their job. It makes strong men out of them, men of character. I love it!

We can help people and should help people. We just have to be careful not to take on their burden. They are supposed to cast their burden on Him, just as we are, and take up His. How can they do this if we are in the way and the burden never gets to them? The truth is, even with all our help, it still bothers them and weighs them down, just not enough to give it to God. And that's the worst part. We are preventing the very thing we want most: our loved one and God working things out in their life. The best way we can help people is to bring the gospel to them. Instead of being part of the problem, we need to be part of the solution and sometimes that means standing aside.

The Boy in the Convenience Store

During the years I struggled with how to relate properly to Lamar, God gave me the vision of a boy working in a convenience store. The boy was supposed to load the drink machines, take out the trash, and anything else that needed to be done. He would do what he was told, but sometimes think better of it and do what he thought best. The Lord asked me, "Who is in authority?" "The owner, of course," I replied. "No, the boy is," was the answer. "Why the boy?" I asked. "Because he is making the final decision as to what is done, when, and how."

In case you didn't catch the implication, God was telling me that I was like the boy. Even when I did what I was told, I did it because I thought it was the right thing to do. I was making the final decision not Lamar. Just like the boy, I was in authority. He had usurped the owner's authority just as I had usurped Lamar's. Even if I went along with him rather than make him mad, that was not acceptable. I should have gone along because Lamar said it.

This give and take continued with the Lord until He revealed that "the owner has a right to proper feedback from his decisions, which he isn't getting now. He needs to know if something doesn't work. He will think it's working because the boy doesn't tell him he hasn't done it the owner's way. The feedback is arbitrary and confusing."

The boss or a husband, any leader, has the right to proper feedback. And this has to include failures. Lamar stands accountable to God for his family and what happens in his home. He needs the proper feedback to make proper decisions. If the information he receives is twisted by the people involved and gives him the wrong reading, it can be extremely harmful. And isn't this what the enemy wants? He wants us to think things are fine and we won't suffer the consequences. If the leader is wrong, it's all the more important that he understand he is and how it happened. Our manipulating the situation just makes things worse in the long run even if we temporarily make them better.

What can we do? The boy can and should explain to the owner, as I can my husband, that he has a problem with what he has been asked to do. See if he will agree to change it. That way the boss will know that a different plan was in effect and they will both see if it worked. If he doesn't agree, then the boy will have to yield and do it his way. Discussing things is not harmful. Sneaking or rebelling is. That's why we do things we shouldn't in silence. Silence is usually a good thing, but it has its limits. We manage to turn good things into bad things all the time.

Sneaking Around to Do Good

I don't remember how God started dealing with me concerning the error of not telling Lamar some of the things I was doing. Mind you, it was not anything bad. And I certainly wasn't doing anything sinful. In fact, it was usually something good like helping a friend. I knew Lamar wouldn't agree with some things, but I thought he was selfish, and maybe he was. I'm sure that was part of it, but part of it was because he worked hard for what he had and felt other people should do the same. And he's not wrong about that.

People just don't do as well when there is no relationship between how hard they work and what they have. Lamar has no problem with helping those who really need help through no fault of their own, but he wants to be convinced. Since our definitions and standards on who deserved help were different, rather than risk being turned down, I just didn't ask! Then I felt guilty about hiding things. I wasn't raised that way, and I hated that I was starting at this late date. I also knew what is hidden is brought to the light at very inopportune times. I didn't want to look like a thief when I wasn't one. Here I was trying to bless people and had to worry about Lamar finding out about it.

There was just something that didn't ring true, but it irritated me because Lamar was such a problem. Be very careful when you do something that you cannot tell your husband about (or pastor or best friend or mother, etc). I understand there are circumstances that are so dire a woman cannot tell her husband and that is why I say, you and God must work these things out. Some men cannot be trusted with all of the truth. A good example would be a woman in a Muslim country that is trying to escape with her children. She does not have to be honest in order to escape persecution and abuse. Generally though, we should not be sneaking around, even to do good. I really believe God will protect us from having to lie. We just won't have to say anything.

SILVER

Let me tell you about Jerry and Ann. They invited us to come for lunch after church. Our kids were good friends, and we always enjoyed each other's company. Their home was a "fixer upper" and Jerry was not good at this kind of work. He did his best. They were living meagerly in spite of the fact that he had a good job. We hadn't known them long, so I didn't know why they were struggling so. It was obvious there wasn't money for furniture or clothes. Her dishes and silverware were deplorable. Lamar had just given me a new set of stainless steel silverware even though my old set was still quite good. When we got home I asked him if I could give her my old set. "Heavens no!" he exclaimed. "We may need it." I was mortified, but had been convicted of not sneaking any more, so I had to go along with him. It sure didn't sit well with me, though.

A few days later Ann and I were talking and she told me one reason things were so tight was because they had invested in silver and the bottom had dropped out of the silver market. Their entire investment was lost. I asked her why they invested in silver, and she said because they had been advised to make investments and somehow they felt silver would be a good one. And that's why they were in the dilapidated house they were in; because it was an investment. There were two houses on the property and they rented the other. At this point both houses were more of a liability than anything because they both needed a lot of repairs. And they had to put the renters first because they couldn't ask people to live in something unsafe or unhealthy. I was mortified again. It just never dawned on me to put my family through this for investments. They were learning some hard lessons during this time and they would need them soon. Within the year, this wonderful family went on the mission field.

I was learning a very hard lesson, too. Lamar was right. Two people with that amount of education and wherewithal should be able to have decent silverware. And if they don't, then maybe they need to figure out why and let God tell them what they are doing wrong. For me to put myself in the middle of all this is for me to get out of my place. Then I would be the one cruisin' for a bruisin'. Do you see how one person makes choices that another person would never consider doing? It never would have dawned on me to invest my money if my family was so deprived. The Bible says to do things decently and in order. I, other the other hand, made other dumb choices. So God has to deal with each of us to help us see the error of our ways.

Since we are talking about sneaking around to do good, I should point out women aren't the only ones that sneak around to do good. Men do it, too. Our husbands are not necessarily afraid but they don't want to face our reaction, so they resort to sneaking around, too, and it's often not to pursue another woman. It's just that they see things differently than we do (the masculine mind as opposed to the feminine mind) and decide to do what they feel is best and neglect to tell us. It seems easier at the time, but it really isn't. I have learned to have my say (not screaming and having a fit either) and then allow Lamar the freedom to do his thing. If he fails, he learns a lesson and I help him clean up the mess. I won't say there is no embarrassment on his part, but I try to keep it contained. And because I do, he learns a lot and includes me in just about everything now.

Why do we insert ourselves where it's not our place to be, when it's not ours to do? (Sin number two again.) One reason is to stop the garbage. Another is because we want our husband or leader to confront some of the garbage and when he doesn't, we get frustrated. Things rock on getting worse and worse and we get more and more frustrated. Why doesn't he deal with it? I'm not saying we are necessarily wrong; we are just wrong in many of the things we do in an attempt to correct things. We often don't realize how much he has done. We are assuming he hasn't done enough. The truth is we don't hear and see everything he does. Furthermore, I don't know that we are the best judge of how much is enough. He may have said something, but it didn't do any good. He realizes it's going to take time and God's anointing. These problem situations are not always solved with a few well-placed words to a boss, or anyone else. In fact, a few well-placed words at the wrong time and in the wrong way aren't well placed at all. And your husband or boss, etc., knows this. So, when he won't say what we think needs to be said, we get in the flesh and eventually "pop off." This is the worse thing we could do because all heck breaks loose. And the damage is irreversible and it all falls on your head not his. Of course, you will be blaming him and that doesn't help at all. Even if we are right and something does need to be said, it's not ours to say. When it is, I just bet you will be fishtailing just like he is. It's not easy to confront people. It takes love and wisdom to do it properly. There is a proper time and way to do it. That is why we pray for a watch on our lips and why the Bible says the tongue is the unruly member.

Benny Hinn once said that the Lord told him:

What is done in the Spirit, I will bless,
What is done in the flesh, I will curse.

Ponder that a minute. Maybe even write it in big letters and attach it to your fridge or somewhere it will catch your eye once in a while, especially if you are prone to get in the flesh. Just think, all those actions are cursed. It's something we need to repeat until it gets in our brain and stays there. This means the changes you desire in your husband and family must be done by the Spirit, not your flesh.

What is your proper place? No, not that of a victim or a shrew. My place, your place, is the same as Jesus' place: where the Father wants us to be. More than anything, our place is in Jesus. And we get out of this place more than any other. We get into our own works and not His. It seems to take God so long and we are in a hurry to get our family fixed (saved, healed, and delivered, etc.). We end up out of our place. The good thing about Jesus is we can run back when we have messed things up again. He forgives an unlimited amount. I know He does because He asks me to forgive an unlimited amount.

We not only have to find our place in our lives and in Jesus, but in a local body of_believers. This is very important. The church is God's instrument here on this earth. You cannot be careless in this area. Your maturation and the deliverance of your family depend on you being obedient in this area.

Our final place is that mansion He has prepared for us. I love a big house. I love to rattle around in the rooms. I'm glad it's going to have some age on it when I get there. I love the nooks and crannies of old homes. But, it won't have problem plumbing or electricity like this one I have down here has. It will be up-to-date and functional. Oh glorious day, the day we graduate to a better place. I understand some people never feel they "fit." They feel "different" all their lives. So, if I tell them to find their place, they don't know what that means. If your childhood left you wondering where you fit in, just know you feel much like the rest of us. We don't feel like we fit in either. The truth is we are all "different." You must fight these feelings of unworthiness. They are a lie from the pits of hell. Learning your place is thinking rightly about yourself and then expecting others to start treating you that way. Learn what God thinks about you and forget what you think about yourself. God thinks you are very special, the apple of His eye.

And when you are in your place, at peace with yourself and your God and eventually with others, you will be in a place of favor. It's in this place that you will find an open heaven. Blessings will flow into your life and your family. Oh, there will continue to be problems, sometimes unbelievable challenges to your faith and everything you hold dear, but it will be like being in the eye of the storm because you are in Him. An unexplainable peace will envelope you.

> *Oh, dear Father, to find my place in You; to rest in knowing no matter what falls around me, that You and I are OK. Help me not to struggle so much and go where I should not go and try to be what You never created me to be and want what You never meant for me to have. Help me be happy in the place You created me to be in and not to take anyone else's place, leaving mine wanting. Oh, God, I struggle so to make things right around me and no one seems to co-operate. It just seems logical to help them and push them and even do myself what they should be doing. And I try to keep up my part, too, but it's too much. I see that now. I see that I am not allowing You to do Your thing because I am so busy doing mine. I'm going to try to back off and let You... but I get so tired of waiting. Why does it take so long? I guess it's because I'm not seeing what I need to see. You are probably waiting for me to see something. Oh, God help me see. Help me, Holy Spirit. Comfort me. Teach me. Guide me. Hold my hand as I traverse these pitfalls in my path each day. And most of all I pray for my husband, that he comes to more and more lean on You, see You in his life, and love You like I do. And my children, of course my children...*

Now, walk upright before the Lord, and if and when you slip and fall, run back to His waiting arms and tell Him you're sorry. You are in a wonderful place—a place to bless yourself and others. Don't try so hard to get out of it. Try harder to abide in Him more. Remember, you are just a branch. And a branch doesn't do much but pass on needed water and nutrients. Pass on the Word and Jesus and the Holy Spirit. Pass on everything you know, a little at a time. They can't stand much all at once.

Knowing your place is a part of being "chosen."

THIRTY-ONE

Love is very patient and kind, never jealous or envious, never boastful
or proud, never haughty or selfish or rude. Love does not demand
its own way. It is not irritable or touchy. It does not hold grudges
and will hardly even notice when others do it wrong. It is never glad
about injustice, but rejoices whenever truth wins out. If you love
someone you will be loyal to him no matter what the cost. You will
always believe in him, always expect the best of him, and always
stand your ground in defending him. All the special gifts and powers
from God will someday come to an end, but love goes on forever."

—1 Corinthians 13:1–7, tlb

Love Endures

LOVE HOPES ALL THINGS, endures all things" (1 Cor. 13:7, kjv). When
we are having problems in a relationship, especially if it goes on
for years, we think we are enduring, hoping. And we may be, but
are we believing? That's a lot harder. How do we believe in someone when
we don't believe in him? When they have given us no reason to believe
anything but the worst. Well, we are asked to believe in God whether we
feel like it or not. There are times when we are very disappointed that He
has not come through for us. He is watching us twist in the wind with all
the power of the universe at His disposal and doing nothing. The scripture that comes to mind is, "I believe, help Thou my unbelief." We have
to believe in spite of what we see or think.

Bigots, abusers, all sorts of criminal minds can be retuned. Not all,
but many are not hopeless. Tell them they will be in jail and lose all the
privileges they now enjoy and they somehow manage to recompute their
computer brain. A Jewish man brought into his home a terrorist who had

spent time in jail for shooting him. Every holiday possible, he had the man to dinner with his family. After a few months, the man had a totally different opinion of the Jewish people and the hatred he had been taught to believe. If we can believe for a terrorist, why can't we believe for our loved ones? Or maybe you don't believe for the terrorists. Shame on you. You need a bigger picture of your God.

Love is sometimes translated charity. This is helpful when you don't feel you can love. At least you can be charitable. That is love.

Another scripture that I feel is helpful is Luke 23:34, *"Father, forgive them; for they know not what they do."* Jesus said this after they chose for Him to be the one to be put to death instead of Barabbas. If a person doesn't really know what they are doing, it's easier to give them the benefit of the doubt. But we don't feel this is the case. They know what they are doing. Yes, they do know, but as with Jesus, they don't really appreciate the significance of it. The scripture is telling us to believe in them in spite of what they have done and what they are doing. Believe that somewhere in them is the capacity to get it right, to care, to change, to love, to forgive, to repent, to reconcile, to finally appreciate.

We aren't asked to believe they are doing the right thing when they aren't. It's asking us to believe they will "come to themselves" like the prodigal. We get into trouble when we begin to ascribe motives to the person in light of his or her actions. If you notice, the Bible tells what people did, not what their motive was. If it's a principle in the Bible, it needs to be a principle in our lives. Don't ascribe motives. Even if it's obvious, just don't say it. You may be wrong. You can say someone stole something if you know they did; you just can't say why they stole it. That is a heart issue.

"Come to himself" has a bit of a ring to it. I needed to come to myself, too. As the years went by, I somehow lost myself. I think most women do, and men, too. And they don't even know it. What do you do when you lose yourself? What you always have to do when you're in a mess: go back to your Father's loving arms. Ask Him what He remembers of who you were. Let Him tell you the best part of who you were and should become.

Lead me back, Jesus, back to the cross,
Back to what You created when you first molded me.
Lead me back to a person I have never known;
To the wonderful creation You envisioned from the beginning.

BLACK HAT/WHITE HAT

For years I worked at keeping the family together. Lamar would threaten me with divorce while inside I seethed. "If I ever say the word, you'll have one." I knew he didn't mean it, but I did. I never did speak the word, although I didn't have much hope for the marriage.

There was more than one time that it almost came to divorce, but I could never quite do it. I just knew it wouldn't solve our problems. Lamar would not have been a good divorced husband. His whole life would have been spent finding out what I was doing, who I was dating, and turning the boys against me. I didn't need that and neither did the boys. And he certainly wouldn't have cooperated with child support. I had more control over the situation in the home than I did out of it. So I stayed. But I didn't just stay; I turned to the One that was giving me answers. I learned who I was in Christ. I won't say it was easy, but it wasn't that hard most of the time. As I changed, Lamar changed. He was healed as I was healed. No, they aren't all hopeless. We just think they are.

Sometimes it's the woman in a marriage that threatens and the man that silently seethes. It doesn't make much difference; either way the marriage is in trouble. The difference is who is shocked when the spouse moves out. Lamar would have come home to an empty house. But I never quite got to that point. Not because it wasn't bad, but just because it's so hard on the kids. I knew I had to pray about it and, being the honest person I am, (God knows the truth, so we might as well be honest) I prayed it like I saw it:

Dear God, I see Lamar as selfish, self-centered, egotistical, mean, stupid... (it went on, but you get the idea). I see myself as patient, long-suffering, gentle, forgiving, giving, ...(you get the idea). In other words, I see myself as having the white hat and Lamar with the black hat; but if you don't see it this way, I want the truth. I want to stand in the truth.

And I think I told Him how hopeless it was.

But if You don't agree, I want you to show me.

What a pitiful prayer. But it's one that God can answer because it does ask for the truth. The Bible tells us to ask for wisdom and that's what I was doing. Boy, did I get an answer. Or should I say the answer began. I don't know that it has ever stopped. God began showing me things I did that hurt Lamar. He put the black hat on me and the white hat on him. I wanted the truth and the truth is, in spite of all I did to keep my marriage together, what I was doing wasn't helping.

If you feel like you are standing in the truth, you probably are, as far as you know it. God seldom tells me I'm wrong. Did that mean I have the truth? Yes, but... But, what? I hate these buts. What He does after I pray about something is give me a greater truth. That's what you need—more truth. He never told me that Lamar wasn't selfish and inconsiderate or that I wasn't being long-suffering and patient. He let me see oh so many things I wasn't seeing at the time, things about me and things about Lamar, things that until I saw them would continue to bind him and hinder our relationship. And God couldn't show me these things until I was ready.

What Time Is It?

Timing is everything. Obedience is linked with timing. God may want us to do something or say something, but not when we think it should be said or done. *"In the fullness of time..."* (Gal. 4:4). Jesus came in the fullness of time. My revelations came in the fullness of time, when I was ready. I had to be saved, Lamar had to be rededicated, and I had to be seeking and mature enough to be trusted with what He was about to show me—and show me He did.

It took ten years to get to this point. Amazing. It could have been shortened if Lamar had been more cooperative or if I had been more open. I don't think it had to take ten years, nor do I think Dadra had to die, but things are what they are and there is no use saying "what if?" We didn't, but thank God we finally did.

What did God finally show me? That Lamar had come out of his childhood emotionally scarred, and although he spoke highly of his family and childhood, there were some problems that were still affecting his life. The main one being that he had never bonded with his father. He was sickly and small for his age until he had his appendix out at age nine. He was the third son in a family of five at a time when money was scarce and times were hard. He was picked on and beat up for years by the kids that lived in the projects next to their farm because he wasn't one of them. During his football years, he and the coach had their problems and that made things hard for him. Lamar had a lot of good friends, but life was not easy for him. It was a constant fight and he tends to be easily depressed and a loner. Depression in a boy tends to take the form of bitterness and anger. They appear to be sullen much of the time or to keep to themselves, withdraw. To defuse his anger and frustration, Lamar would go fishing and hunting in the woods around the house. His family had about twenty acres and farmed part of it, which meant much of the work fell to Lamar. His oldest brother was in high school when they moved out of the city. The two younger kids weren't old enough to help and his father worked full time. That meant Lamar and the brother just older than him had to clear land, bring in large amounts of water because they had no running water in the house, dig long ditches for the water lines, bring in fire wood (they had no central heat, only one small gas heater), tend a huge garden, take care of the animals, go to school, and do all the other things a teenager does, like being a football player. He was given very little time to play because his father didn't see the need for it. So, as often as he could,

Lamar slipped off to his best friends next door and was whopped for it later. He was hit too hard and too much, which made him very tough and determined. It's great for playing football and being a Quartermaster in the Navy, but it isn't good for a marriage.

Lamar never hit me, but he was verbally abusive. Not because he meant to be, but to get me to cooperate. Rather than defend myself, I simply withdrew emotionally, putting myself in a protective bubble. That way he couldn't hurt me any more. That was fine until God put the black hat on me and helped me see the worst thing for Lamar was to have an unresponsive wife. He needed a wife that was emotionally attached. I protested, "But God, it's so painful." As usual God made His statement and then let me figure out why. What happened when I withdrew emotionally was to force Lamar to do more to get a response from me. Therefore, my solution made things worse not better. Say it's not so. That's what our answers, our gut level responses, do. They make things worse. This was the beginning of a vicious cycle.

It was bad and got a whole lot worse in the ten years before I was saved. Then it took a few more to reveal this to me. You are talking a lot of pain. Just because I realized I had to be more responsive doesn't mean it was easy. Protected is easy. Being in an emotional bubble is easy. Being vulnerable and open is hard. I remember the first day I let my feelings show. I began to cry in response to something Lamar said. He was shocked, "What's wrong with you?" I repeated what he said, and it was obvious anyone would be hurt by it. "Well, it never hurt you before," he retorted. After a few minutes he came over and took me in his arms. He really didn't want to hurt me. He just wanted a response. Well, he got one from then on. I didn't become shrill or ugly because as a Christian my responses have to be within acceptable limits. If I was doing this in obedience to God, I had to do it lovingly, but I can't say I did a very good job of it.

God helped me see He didn't expect me to do it perfectly right off the bat. These things take some getting used to for both of us. This was the first step in slowing down our vicious cycle. I will tell you more as we go on. You may think of some of your own gut level reactions and see how they have hurt, not helped, your marriage. Make a list. These things are very important because they must be changed. You must repent of them and ask God to help you change them. This isn't about me and my error; it's about you and your error. I know it's easy to read mine, but that's not the point. The point is to help you see yours.

Healing a marriage is a process. To get better, you have to identify the problems. I know you think you know the problem—him, but it's really more involved than that. There are many things that need to be revealed. Even though the things that are revealed are not usually good in themselves, having them revealed can lead to good. Nothing will change in your life or marriage until you become honest with yourself and he can be honest with himself. Then, maybe, someday, you can be honest with each other. The truth will set you both free. It will be called your testimony after you get the victory.

People usually care more than we think they do. And to make it worse, we ascribe to them feelings and attitudes they don't have. Only too often, things are the complete opposite of what we think they are. How can we relate to people properly if we are misreading them so badly? Our whole relationship is based on an error. All those assumptions and errors in my brain for all those years, and in the neighbor kids and Lamar's coach. It's a wonder we ever healed.

Feelings that go under the radar screen. We all have 'em. Black hat? White hat? What hat do you have on? What hat does he have on? Maybe we shouldn't be so sure we know. Maybe we should identify the black one on ourselves and the white one on his head since we already know the other.

> *God! I have lost myself! Where did I go—that spontaneous girl who loved the wonder of life? I didn't mean to lose her. Surely You Who know all things, knows where she is and can find her for me and send her back. What You created was special, and You meant for me to be the mature version of her. I'm sorry for*

whatever I did to send her away. Surely I yielded to something I shouldn't have. Help me to find her and when I do, to put up proper boundaries so I won't lose her again. Because truly, if she is who You meant me to be, then she is the best one for everyone else, too. To be the blessing You want me to be, it will be in finding and being her. I praise You, Father, now for doing it, for I know You will work in me Your good pleasure. In Jesus name I pray. Oh yes, and I forgive anyone who hurt her and made her cry and run off! Amen!

Thirty-two

Edith

W HEN YOUR WORLD IS crashing down around you and no one seems to understand because you don't have the heart to tell them, and even if you did, it wouldn't help; when all seems to be so hopeless, what do you do then? I know it's tempting to throw up your hands and give up. Jesus had such a time in His life just before He went to the cross. I know that doesn't give you much comfort right now, but it should. If Jesus chose to go to the cross, knowing what He would suffer, out of love for people that would someday appreciate Him, for those who never would, for those who would spit on Him, that is the example we must follow—not serving ourselves and our own wants and wishes, not even our own needs sometimes. We must abandon ourselves as Esther did, and Mary, and Sarah, and maybe our mother or grand-mother. And if you don't have a mother or a grandmother, then use me. I, too, had to abandon everything and yield myself to Him. And so I must tell you to keep walking, and as you keep walking, standing for what you know is right and true, you will be redeemed. Maybe not today, maybe not tomorrow, but you will be redeemed and many of those with you. That is the important thing: those around you.

When loneliness is a problem, the solution is to reach out to others; become involved in life; become a servant. Do what your hands find to do. Whatever you can do along the way; loving things that God would have you do (Ecclesiastes 9:10).

Archbishop Fulton J. Sheen told of being lonely early in his ministry when he had moved to a new city, studying for his ordination. He went out in the poor neighborhoods and found a young widower with a large family in desperate need of help. Even though he had very little, he did what he could for the next few years while he continued his studies. The day of his "verbals" for his ordination he ran into the man and asked what he was doing there. The man said he and his family had been praying the whole day for him. He said he was never lonely again. You know a priest, if anyone, struggles with loneliness. What a beautiful story of how such a special man overcame his.

Generally, as Christians, our job is to serve. This goes for everybody because God wants everybody to receive Jesus and be like Him. In His own words, Jesus said he who wants to be ruler over many must be servant of many.

> *You know that the rulers of the Gentiles lord it over them, and their high officials exercise authority over them. Not so with you. Instead, whoever wants to become great among you must be your servant, and whoever wants to be first must be your slave; just as the Son of Man did not come to be served, but to serve, and to give his life as a ransom for many.*
> —MATTHEW 20:25, NAS

He came and served and even died in the process. He is our example of a proper authority figure, serving and dying. Sounds good to me—Lamar serving and dying for me and the kids. And since we have authority in our home, too, and since we are called to lead at some point, I guess we should be serving and dying, too. What's good for the goose is good for the gander. Jesus was not exempting followers.

Serving was the big thing in those days. They had slaves. Jesus was now including the leadership. He was saying we must all serve. The greater you are, the more you serve. He didn't get rid of slavery by condemning it as much as He as He got rid of it by adding everybody to their ranks. It should be a competition of serving the most instead of who is going to get to be the leader or sit with Him in heavenly places. If you are going to be anything in the next life, you'd better serve in this one, and that includes people that aren't very lovable—especially those you want to win to Christ.

THE SERVANT SPIRIT

How do you properly serve? Being a servant is emptying yourself. Before you can properly serve another person, you must empty out your opinion, your attitude, your agenda. Then, you must take on their wishes as you would your own and help them do things the way they want them done. Boy, that's hard. Getting an opinion and an attitude comes so naturally. Not that you will never think again. We must never empty out God, the Word, or our regenerated spirit. It's not that we will never have an attitude or an opinion again, but we are busy trying to please, not man but God. An opinion is not really needed at this point. We are always open to anything God would have to say or do. In fact, we assume God is speaking through the other person, especially if they are in authority until we know differently, as shown to us in the Bible. This is the true servant spirit.

If we do get something from God, then we must pray about it until He shows us to act on it. Let's take Moses as an example. The Jews were in Egypt and at first things were fine, but eventually, they went bad. So bad, they were made slaves. It got even worse to the point they were going to kill all the infants under two years of age. I'm sure Moses' mother would have liked to be able to comply with the wishes of the leadership, but they had overstepped their bounds. She had to place her baby in a small floating container and allow him to be found by the Egyptian princess. There comes a time when God gives us a plan in the midst of our serving. In fact, she continued to serve. She was asked to be the "wet nurse" to the baby by the Pharaoh's daughter who found Moses in the weeds. This wasn't just an immediate answer, but a lifetime of serving for the whole family. We can't always deliver ourselves or our family in a short period of time. We must walk it out day by day. It's amazing what God calls our family to do. We are just a small part of the plan, but an important part. This was her son, but he was sent to deliver God's people. Our job as a mother is not just to embrace our children, but to figure out their calling and do everything in our power to see he or she is able to fulfill it.

If you have been put smack dab in the middle of an ungodly family or community or country, take that as a sign that you should be a part of delivering not just you and your immediate family, but the whole kittenkaboodle. Day by day, situation by situation, take your problems (challenges) to God in prayer and ask Him for a plan. Walk in love and forgiveness, grace and mercy, and be the main player in their deliverance if you have to be. I know God will send you an Aaron and others to help eventually, but if you start out alone, then walk it alone for as long as it takes until someone comes to the Lord. Believe me, that day it will be worth it all. And from then on, it will be all downhill.

My Mentor

Edith Bunker from *All In The Family* is such a good example of what we should do in the face of a difficult situation. The older I get, the wiser I think Edith is. Edith was the scatterbrained, middle-aged housewife of Archie, her grumpy, factory worker husband. Their daughter, Sally, and son-in-law, Meathead, live with them. Archie is the resident "conservative" and the kids are your typical liberals. It's the American political and ideological debate in a half-hour comedy. It's not as far off base as it might appear.

Archie is a bigot. He's also a hypocrite who espouses some Christian principles. You must bear in mind the writers are liberals, so they are going to paint Archie in the worst possible light and the kids in the best. Edith seems to be the best part of them both. Archie is small minded, mean spirited, ignorant, and selfish, with a low tolerance level. Sounds like a lot of "Christians" I know. The thing that makes it all work is that they aren't above poking fun at the liberals, too.

What Archie really hates is laziness and the mindset that coddles people because he has the same general attitude toward his son-in-law as he has toward the blacks. He's an equal-opportunity bigot. The show is so good because it's such a good mix of good and bad in everybody. Everybody but Edith that is. Well, she does have her faults, but she is so guileless, we don't blame her.

Archie is forever telling Edith to stifle, in spite of the fact that she doesn't say that much. It's just that she says the wrong thing at the wrong time in Archie's mind. Kind of like a child says the wrong thing at the wrong time, even though it isn't wrong. It's actually right on target and that means it hits Archie square between the eyes. She does stifle and I think it's because everybody is smarter than her. The Bible says keep your mouth shut and you won't show your ignorance (Proverbs 17:28). In the end, all the talkers prove how dumb they are while Edith just has to stand there and be redeemed. Everybody thinks they are so smart, but Edith is wise. If she can live with Archie and make it (have peace and joy), she must be doing something right. Don't all men seem like Archie sometimes?

Another thing to Edith's credit is, she appreciates Archie for what he is and does. He is a good man, a good father, and a good provider. He gets up every day and goes to the factory and does it with a good attitude, and he does it for them. He doesn't lie, cheat, or steal. He loves her and has dedicated his life to her, a fact that isn't lost on her. She feels privileged to have him for her husband. She doesn't major on his bad side; in fact she doesn't even seem to see it and appreciates all that he does do.

Edith keeps such a sweet spirit and thinks the best of everyone; people are a little better in her presence. She improves everyone, and the situation. She is so giving and encouraging. She is a doer. She cooks the meals, cleans the house, serves their needs, and doesn't expect anything in return. It's her pleasure to do it. This is why Archie's stinginess confuses her. She knows him as a giving person because he gives so much to her and their daughter. If he doesn't seem to be giving right now, she must not understand something. You can see her try to understand the negatives. She rarely does, but if she does, it makes her very sad for them; for the one who is being selfish. She is sad for the sinner. She hates the sin, never the sinner.

I understand that you may not be Edith. I'm not Edith either and find it very hard to stifle myself. I'm not dumb and don't have that working for me. I can't turn off my brain. But I don't think God wants us to be dumb or He would have created us that way.

The truth is, God expects us to have her better qualities. The Bible speaks of the mouth being the unruly member. God expects us to have respect for our husbands and to be cooperative. And He expects us to think the best of him and edify him. We are to be longsuffering and not keep a count of wrongs. Read the love chapter, 1 Corinthians 13. Archie and Edith agree on a lot. They disagree a lot, too. Archie is not all wrong. Edith would give away the house. People would use her good nature and generosity and in the end, she would have nothing if Archie didn't defend her and set her straight. It's not right to give to everyone. The truth is many people are in the mess they are in because they were foolish and brought it on themselves. Edith, without Archie to stop her, would rescue everyone. She would be a potential enabler if it weren't for Archie.

I don't want you to agree with Archie if he's wrong. That is no help. How can we change if neither of us see the problem, if we are both in error? We can't. One of us does need to see. But, seeing doesn't mean we do some things. We cannot "get in the flesh." That just makes things worse, like Moses smoting the rock. No, we must remain in check and say and do what God would have us say and do; what Jesus would say and do.

I was a lot like Edith, but I didn't do as well as she does. I had an opinion and an attitude. I guess you could say I was smarter. But was I? It didn't get me very far. Lamar is very determined in his mind, and I had to back off. Being a peacemaker, I couldn't allow my home to be under a cloud of heaviness all the time. I would have to give in most of the time. And because I did, I have come to see Lamar is not always wrong. And when he has been wrong, he has come to see that, too, as Archie does quite often. But men don't admit it. They get silent about this time. This is good to know so you will say nothing too. You don't have to.

"Edith is exactly what I feel I am now and what I don't want to be." That's a sign you are taking the Edith concept too far. Edith is able to carry it off because she is Edith and it comes so naturally. Her simplicity works to her favor. If you don't have that going for you, which is not a bad thing, then you have to learn to move on from this and add some new

techniques that will work with the Edith concept, and not keep you in bondage, but not take you into error either.

"But I am nothing like Edith." I'm not saying you have to be Edith; I'm just saying you should understand Edith's good qualities and try to emulate them.

You may be more like Maude. Remember her? A Maude can be a Christian. She just needs to let God clean up her act just like He does the rest of us. She can still be a can-do woman. Maude is very smart and knows what she is talking about and people listen. We need people like her. It's just that when you are a woman like that, you must understand being smart isn't the same thing as being wise. "Because the foolishness of God is wiser than men; and the weakness of God is stronger than the strength of men" (1 Cor. 1:25). Maude may think giving to her local church ten percent of her income is ludicrous, whereas Edith gives knowing God will bless her and bless her He does. Maude is smart; Edith is wise. But Maude has a certain amount of wisdom, too.

It was Maude that ended up divorced. As smart as she is and as dumb as Edith is, Edith's marriage worked and Archie was actually the better pick. Sometimes we're not as smart as we think we are. And maybe that's why Maude got so strong and mouthy. Maybe if she would have been wiser, she wouldn't have to be so strong and mouthy, fighting everyone's battles. In a comparison, I have to take Edith over Maude.

I'm as much of a softy as anyone, but God constrains me. I know He loves them more than I do and I must place them in His hands and trust Him. He won't let me down. He won't let them down.

Edith is so cooperative. If Archie tells her to do something, she does it. There's a concept. No argument; she just does it. She doesn't always agree, but she tries to comply. Sometimes she needs help with this because what she is asked to do doesn't compute with what she thinks she should do and she can't bring the two together. She has certain rules in her head and when what Archie asks her to do breaks one, she gets confused, not angry—never angry. She might even cry, but she is still trying to reconcile the order with her head. Usually though, she doesn't get her head involved. Boy! There's a real nugget of wisdom. Don't rethink everything.

Edith is so respectful of Archie. There is a principle for successful relationships. Edith is respectful of everybody, and the truth is, so is God. He is never disrespectful. Archie has a problem respecting some people. (He is a respecter of persons. God and Edith are not.) Archie only respects people that "deserve" respect. The Bible says to give honor to whom honor is due, but we are to give respect to all men (women included.) Archie is a little mixed up there.

It's Not Ours to Reason Why, But to Do or Die

I learned this with my dad. He should have been an engineer or inventor. He was always figuring out how to do things better and easier. He made an electric clothes washer before one was ever marketed. Daddy was always telling you to do something that didn't make sense. I learned not to ask questions and just do what he said. Why? Because I could trust him. That is a very important ingredient for submission. Some people want submission and never prove themselves to be trustworthy. We still submit, but with reservations.

Also, Daddy was good to explain stuff. You could ask questions. And a curious little girl can ask a million questions. Lamar was another matter. He hated my questions. To him questions meant criticism. I wasn't saying he was wrong. I just wanted to know why he was doing what he was doing. That would tick him off and he would yell at me. That would hurt my feelings, and I would say something back or cry, escalating things. It seems like anytime we were doing anything, Lamar was mad and yelling.

What I didn't understand at the time was that Lamar wasn't all that sure of what he was doing. He was a young man trying to do something he really wasn't skilled at. He was trying to figure it out and didn't have all that many answers. My questions just made him all the more insecure and often pointed out a problem. Even if he had a pretty good idea of what he was doing, he couldn't express it and certainly didn't feel he needed to have the problems pointed out. So he yelled and I stifled as much as I could.

One important concept I must stress, even though I make this point every once in a while is: keep it light. That's one thing Edith doesn't seem to have is a sense of humor. But she doesn't get "down" either. We women are so bad to get negative, allowing our homes and relationships to be "heavy." It's a killer. No matter how bad he is, you must not let him know it's getting you that far down. Find something in your life to be up about. Just be sure it's not an ungodly thing. Too often when God is about to defend us, we do something dumb (sinful). Now God has two people to chastise: your husband and you. Maybe that is why you are in the mess you are in. You are in a chastising mode.

Many Christians who think they are so wonderful and godly, aren't all that wonderful or godly at all. They are manipulative, controlling, and vengeful. Check your own life. I know he is a mess, but how about you? Remember, the candle of the Lord is in your heart too observing the condition there. Two wrongs don't make a right.

Many Christians that think they are saved, aren't saved at all any more than they are a car because they are in a garage. I hate to be the bearer of bad news, but it's possible to be a "wilderness" Christian or a carnal Christian. How do we know what someone is? Check the fruit. I know people say we shouldn't be judgmental but we can be fruit inspectors. Jesus cursed the fig tree for having none. It's easy to put on the outward trappings of Christianity. Buying religious jewelry and wearing witnessing pins is not the hard part. I would say, if it takes too much to get someone to witness, they don't have enough. Our love for Jesus should spontaneously spill out. If it's not, I question that the person has the real thing or enough of the real thing.

When we think of Edith, we do not think of a talkative woman or a gossip. Not that being talkative is a sin, but it sure makes it easy to get into sin. We think of a responsive woman not an initiator, except when it was necessary, as in the case of something pertaining to Gloria, or something she knew was wrong and needed to be said. How she responded verbally was very much a part of who she was.

When speaking about "the tongue," the unruly member, I feel we need to differentiate between the types of women we have in regard to how they use their mouth. Some women are not talkative and have a great deal of discipline naturally. They are good listeners and are often told things that people don't usually tell anyone because they know they can be trusted with their deepest secrets. This is not always an easy gift: to carry the burden of another person's heart.

This woman's challenge is to say what needs to be said, when it needs to be said. It's hard for her to express herself. We could call hers the sin of omission. She takes pride in the fact that she doesn't talk much or gossip. It is a good thing, but we need to be careful, because everyone has their challenges and it's just as wrong not to speak when you should as to speak when you shouldn't. Her tongue is an unruly member, too. Not something to take pride in.

Help. Father, I don't know if I can be like Edith. I do have a brain and it tells me all the things my husband is doing wrong. I wish I could be like her sometimes. I wish I could just see the good and not the bad. Oh, what luxury. Help me to forgive him and move on and learn to serve, serve without opinions, to do what Jesus did so wonderfully. I pray this in His name. Amen.

THIRTY-THREE

She watches over the activities of her household and is never idle.
—PROVERBS 31:27

Ruth

WOMEN ARE SUCH HELPFUL people. We want to help the people we love. Life is not easy and when we see our husbands weighed down with the cares of the world, it's only natural to try to help out. The only problem is the more we help, the more he seems to cause. We do without, so he buys a new boat. We're like a juggler with too many balls in the air and the balls keep coming. Why can't he see what he's doing wrong? We get frazzled and hostile but keep going, like the Energizer Bunny. Pretty soon everything comes crashing down and accusations fly. "I tried to tell you." "I never asked you to...." We've all done it.

Bad authority brings pain and sorrow. I can't deny this fact. If you are on the path with a transgressor, you will naturally suffer loss and lack because the scripture says the way of the transgressor is hard (Proverbs 13:15). However, in spite of it, God will be faithful. You won't go hungry. He will provide. You must believe this and stand in your day of trial, fighting the good fight of faith. You are not there to be trampled under foot. You are there to pray and intercede; to bring life, God's life, into the situation, to help turn the situation around, to get the victory. Don't weary or run. Stick in there and see it through.

Why are there people going hungry all over the world because of corrupt leaders? Why isn't God providing for them? There are two reasons for this:

1. The first group of hungry people are not Christians. His seed will not be begging bread (Psalm 27:35). The "whosoever" applies to whosoever shall come will be saved. They must come first. God hears man's cries and answers by trying to bring him to the knowledge of salvation. "But they don't all hear." That is a problem.

2. The second group are Christians: Christian martyrs. So, how can we claim the scripture that His seed won't be begging bread if He does, in fact, let some starve? I have to admit Christians do suffer and die for the cause. The Bible even admits some will be killed for the gospel's sake. We can't deny the truth, but even in this, He is faithful. It's not up to us to determine how He will spend our lives. Hopefully, you won't be a martyr. Maybe I shouldn't say that. What greater privilege? If He chooses for you to be a martyr, His grace will be sufficient. I doubt that Stephen is complaining. If you aren't a martyr, but just suffering terribly, you must ask yourself (your spirit man that is listening to the Holy Spirit) why you are going through this? What is to be accomplished by your suffering? Your own humbling? The power of your forgiveness and intercession for another?

It is very important that we realize the mess the world is in, our nation, cities, and families, is a result of our rebellion toward God and our refusal to submit to His authority. We have used our liberty to go our own way and abandon Him, the One who has blessed us with life and all the good things we have. This is why repentance must come first. You are not reconciled with God without it.

THE STORY OF RUTH

One day a friend insisted I come to a women's morning Bible Study where they would be studying Ruth. The Catholic Church had a study on Ruth when I attended, so I didn't feel I needed to do it again. Then my friend said, "I just feel the Lord has something special for you." How could I turn that down? During the refreshment time I got in a "discussion" (a fancy word for argument) with one of the ladies concerning the financial problem Lamar and I were in at the time. She thought I was not standing in faith and I felt I was. It wasn't my fault we hadn't seen the victory. I couldn't produce the result. God was going to have to do that. All I could do was stand—after I had done all I knew to do.

I guess some of the women felt I was standing negatively because I was admitting things were still bad. It's difficult to tell it like it is and yet speak positively. I pointed out to the lady doing most of the talking that she was standing for the healing of her son's ear and it hadn't happened yet. What was the difference? Christians are so bad to jump on someone else's "faith." I know she meant well, but it came across as condemnation to me. I guess she thought I was some novice that needed help. I did need encouragement in my standing just as she did for her son's ear.

In the car going home I was having a mental battle, but not with the faith issue. My real struggle was with the submission concept—the point of the study on Ruth. I felt I was submitted, but it wasn't working. Not only wasn't it working, but my spirit was getting other things, uncooperative rumblings, that weren't sitting well in my mind or with my husband. And, I'm sorry to say, I didn't know the Scriptures well enough to take the battle to the Word to sort out. What I did know was getting all mixed up in my mind and I needed help.

"I appreciate the story of Ruth," I said to God, remembering the movie I had seen a few years earlier. It was a simple narrated, black-and-white movie with no speaking parts. It went on for a few weeks so we could have discussion after each segment. I honestly don't remember what was said. The typical stuff, I'm sure: how good submission is, etc. "But that is not what I'm getting," I countered to the empty van, hoping He was in it. "I want to do the right thing, but what is right?" Astoundingly God answered my question with a question: "Why did Ruth submit to Naomi?" I thought, "That's a good question," assuming I would have to go home and look it up for myself. "Because she knew the character of

Naomi," came into my spirit. Wow! I was shocked that I got the answer so I pulled the van over to write it down. Sometime these thoughts leave and you can never get them back quite the same. You need to write them down immediately. They are so profound they are easily lost. Not finding a pen, I had to write it in lipstick. I sat there laughing and crying and praising the Lord. And then pondered what it meant: because she knew the character of Naomi.

I knew from the story that Naomi was a godly woman, a Jewess, and Ruth didn't come from a country that knew the one true God, Yahweh, like the Jews did. (Not every god people call God is the true and living God.) Naomi, her husband, and sons had gone to a foreign land because of a drought and her sons married local women, Ruth and Orpah. While they were there Naomi's husband died, and ten years later, her sons died. So, she decided to return home, assuming the wives would stay with their families, but Ruth wanted to go with her. I love the passage "…and your God shall be my God" (Ruth 1:16). If you don't have a god or if your god isn't a very good one, take mine. He's wonderful. I welcome anyone to have a relationship with Jesus, for He is truly God, a God that understands your suffering and infirmities. There was nothing in the story negative about Naomi, and their life together proved that out.

God was saying He doesn't expect me to submit to ungodliness. Ruth submitted to Naomi "because she knew the character of Naomi." I must submit, but it has its reservations. I, we, should be respectful and keep in mind the power someone has over us to fire us from our job or destroy our family, etc., but we do have the right not to submit, just as Ruth could have if Naomi had been an ungodly woman or asked her to do something immoral.

If the leader is not submitted to God, it's all the more important for the follower to be. If the authority is not listening to God, God is hindered but not limited. If you are His and stand clean before Him, then He will work things out on your behalf. I'm not saying they will seem good right now, or that you won't suffer loss, but in the end you will see how He has worked it to your good. Joseph is good example. He went through being sold into slavery, jail, and years of deprivation, but in the end he triumphed. However, the point isn't all that he went through or the victory; the point is that he delivered his family from starvation. The point of what you go through should be the deliverance of your family, not the chastisement to get you to do the right thing.

RITA

This reminds me of the story of a friend, a young mother I knew in our early years in Florida. I think the reason I thought of this one is because her husband was such a thug—a blue-collar worker that had everyone's respect because of how tough he was. She lived in the trailer next to a friend with two boys that we took to church. The three of us would sit in the yard and watch the kids play. One day she called me very upset. Her husband had come home for lunch as usual, but this day had pretended to leave only to sneak back and listen to what went on when he was not there. It was a hot day and the windows were open. She had tried to put the kids down for their nap, and he felt she was too hard on them. She was a mouthy mother, but she was definitely not abusive. Evidently he was raised in abuse and did not want it to happen to his kids. I can understand that, and she probably did sound over the top, but it's hard to get kids to take their nap. He told her she couldn't yell at them or spank them. By the time she called, she was at her wits end because she couldn't get them to cooperate. Her two big tools were taken away from her: that she could make them take a nap and that she was the boss. She assured me she was not abusive. Our mutual friend conferred.

She wanted to know what she could do. I told her to go in and tell the kids she was sorry she yelled at them and she was going to try to do better, but they needed to take their nap and if they didn't, they would be disciplined. She was to remind them that when Daddy is home, he is in charge, and when he is not here, she is. She was concerned this might not work because he didn't discipline them. I told her that is when the next phase of the plan comes in to play. I knew she read a lot and he watched television. I told her to clean up after supper and be sure anything she valued was put safely away. Then, retire to the bedroom to read as usual. It should seem like a very normal day. The kids will no doubt get rowdier and rowdier as their father lies on the couch. I gave her specific orders: "Do not say anything or in any way discipline the kids or try to get them to behave. I don't care what they do. It's not yours to deal with. I can guarantee, he won't last long. In fact, time it. I'd like to know how long it takes."

She called me the next day laughing. Sure enough, he lasted about an hour. It took the kids that long to really get brave. He apologized profusely and reinstated her authority. I love it. They won't sit there long while their house is being torn up. If he does, he's really got it bad. And if he starts disciplining that is good, too. So far it had been up to her. We don't have to run everything and would be better off backing off, letting him deal with more of this stuff. We must know what is ours and what is his to run. Do you see how getting even negative feedback helps a man make the right decision? We too often keep it from them, and we are wrong. When we do the right thing, he will do the right thing. It takes a little more thought and it does take disciplining ourselves, but it will work. All our talking bears little fruit. If we can think of other ways to convince our loved ones what they are doing is not really for the best, and to do what we suggest, we will be a lot better off. That's why we sometimes have to back off and let life or God show them some things.

There are two reasons why a person in authority would hurt you: 1) You are wrong. A person in authority shouldn't hurt anyone, but it isn't always possible not to if someone is doing something wrong. A policeman can't always keep from hurting an out-of-control person. This is one of the purposes of authority: to keep people in line so there will be order and safety in our communities. 2) He is wrong. This is when we are most concerned. We don't have a problem with number one, or shouldn't. Number two is another matter when the authority is wrong. Actually there is a third possibility that fits in here and that is when the authority figure is right, but reacting wrong, which is typical. This is when we too often think he is totally wrong and that's not true. We are wrong, too. The most common occurrence is we are both wrong.

The Rebellious Wife

I was counseling a friend whose parents were on the verge of divorce. I thought the father was the problem because he seemed so angry and out of control much of the time. As we talked about a recent incident she stopped me, "You don't understand, Midge, my mother has always been rebellious." She knew what her mother had done to provoke him. I left that day with something new to ponder.

For some background: her mother would say she didn't have to submit to what he was asking because what he was asking her to do was dumb and she wasn't going to do it. Isn't it amazing how dumb someone gets after we marry him? They were always butting heads and because she wouldn't yield, it ended with him exploding and leaving so he wouldn't do something he would regret. Since he can't hit her, and she holds most of the cards (sex, the house, the kids, the money, etc), all he could do was throw things and leave in a huff.

Fight, flight, or fume, that's their choice. "Just let her have it," is what many men say as they back off and let her do her thing, and then hold her responsible when it doesn't turn out. It's not their fault. But that means they are falling into the trap Adam fell into of shirking his responsibility. Sounds like a path we don't want to go down, but many women already have. Many women wear the pants in their family far too often. Some wear them all the time. And feel they have a right to. And he feels he has a right to stand off and let her do it.

It may sound like a plan if he is so dumb, but let me warn you, it leaves a bad taste in his mouth. It's OK if he sees that she is right, but nobody can agree all the time and when the disagreement comes and you do what you feel is best against his better judgment, you have bigger problems than that thing you are disagreeing about. One has to yield, and if it's the wife and he is wrong, he will come to see it. God will see to that.

It's a good thing when a man sees he's wrong. He probably won't ever think she is right because things will turn out the way she wants them and that isn't usually the way he wants them. So, even if she is right in her eyes, she won't be right in his. And he is more important than she realizes. God has to have an answer when the authority is wrong. Here's one:

THE HEART OF THE KING

The Bible admonishes us to pray for those in authority and do right (1 Tim. 2:2), and then God will turn his heart toward the people. It says in Proverbs 21:1, *"The king's heart is in the hand of the Lord, as the rivers of water: He turneth it whithersoever he will."*

This scripture had a major impact on me. I knew "king" meant whoever is in authority, so I read it as Lamar. Lamar's heart is in the hand of the Lord. That was an ominous thought because it was hardened at the time. In other words, I can blame God if Lamar's heart is hardened. That was something to ponder. Why would God harden Lamar's heart toward me? It must be to do a work in me. I shouldn't blame him. It was hard to face the fact that God had ought against me or wanted to do a work in me, not to make me bitter, but to make me better.

Why was Pharaoh's heart hardened again and again? Why didn't He just harden it once, have one plague and then let the people go? In the story, Pharaoh would say they could leave only to harden his heart and change his mind. Every time he did, God sent plagues until it took the lives of their first born sons. That is as bad as it gets. Why? As a judgment on the Pharaoh and the Egyptians, God allows certain things so that the judgment will be all the greater. He doesn't want us to get off the hook so easy. The person is so manipulative and evil that God wants it to ring out far and wide and for a long time what happened to him or her. I may be angry, but when I see God continuing to harden a person's heart, I shudder at the final cost. I'm not as tough as God. But then I don't understand like He does either. He sees it all. He knows how long He has tried to get them to do the right thing. Our "softness" just makes things worse.

Evidently free will has its limits. There was a point when he no longer had a choice. His heart was hardened. Read the story for yourself (Exod. 8). We must remember this was after many years and many choices. God doesn't start out hardening hearts, but He ends up that way. It's good to know. We just have to get the flow going in the right direction (the softening). If we do right, then God won't have to harden hearts.

There comes a time when someone is past repentance and you will never hear the first indication of regret. That's what a reprobate mind is: the absence of a normal conscience. There is no use feeling too sorry for someone that stubborn. But I have to say; it takes God to do what He has to do. He is a merciful God and I assume if God has brought someone to me, he or she is still salvageable. But then again, it could have been the devil and God allowed it.

God has promised to raise up a standard. *"Where evil abounds, grace does much more abound"* (Rom. 5:20, author's paraphrase).

Dear heavenly Father, evil is abounding in my world. If ever I needed grace, it's now. Please raise up a standard in my defense to meet the enemy. I claim it now. I'm sorry I didn't even know to claim it until now. I just assumed You would do it, but then You don't work on assumptions. I do. And help me to remember every time I need more grace than usual. I know if there is a problem, it's not Your fault. Help me to figure out what is the problem and how to cooperate best so You and I can solve it together. I thank You and praise You for the victory already won. I pray this in the precious name of Jesus. Amen.

The depth of your hunger is the length of your reach for God.

THIRTY-FOUR

**For the eyes of the Lord are on the righteous and his ears are attentive
to their prayer, but the face of the Lord is against those who do evil.**

—1 PETER 3:12

Men Who Won't Lead

MEN NOT LEADING AND women not following is typical. Lamar needs me as much as I need him. If I don't follow, he isn't leading. A person walking alone is a walker not a leader. Submission is a choice. I can choose to follow Lamar or I can choose not to follow Lamar and I've been tempted a time or two. In fact I refused a few times, and he had to rethink where he was going, but that is rare. Generally, I follow.

He needs to pray and be sure of God's direction. I am never to lead on my own when Lamar is in the position of leader. I am a confirming witness or a questioning voice. We do have a right, in fact a responsibility, to speak up when we feel a leader is making a mistake. We do not have the right to keep speaking and speaking. We do have the right to stand.

Men are too often either domineering or weak and women are either weak or domineering. Neither is right. Being domineering is not leading. It's abuse, plain and simple. Being weak is not following. It's being a victim, and we are not victims. The question for women is, How, as a wife, do I follow? And how do I lead as a mother? Notice the following comes before the leading. The question for the man is how do I follow? Although he is the leader, he must first follow those God puts in authority over him. By the time your husband gets to you, he should have twenty years of practice. I guess it's a good thing if he starts out leading just one other person: someone who loves him dearly and wants desperately for him to succeed. You should be a big encouragement to him.

Marriage should be a partnership, with the two people coming together as equals. There are scriptures that tell us to submit one to another and that is right. I do feel a husband should wait until the wife agrees before going ahead with most things, especially big things, because he doesn't need someone with an attitude working with him. However, there are times when a couple can't wait and someone has to yield. God is saying the wife should do it, although, again, the husband would do well to consider being the one to yield. In my experience, when I don't insist, Lamar rethinks things and I do, too, and we inevitably come to the right decision. I can't say it's always my way or always his way is that right. It's not good when one yields only to get to say "I told you so." When we yield, it should be with the spirit that we want his way to work. And it just may.

The truth is many husbands don't have anyone following, and that's sad—sad that he stands alone in what he feels led to do. I'm not talking about standing by him in his sin. That is another matter. For that, I excuse myself and refuse to be a part, but that seldom happens. Usually it's not blatant sin we are asked to help with, just foolish choices. Lamar knew even when I disagreed that I would cooperate with what he felt led to do. Like the saying, "I don't agree with what you are saying, but I will fight for your right to say it." I may not agree, but I respect his right to do it and will do my best on his behalf.

I don't want to be a rebel. If I do not do what Lamar asks, I want to be right in my refusal. I don't want God to have a problem with me when I refuse. I want Him to get after Lamar, not me, and not both of us. I want to be innocent. I want Him to say, "Well done thou good and faithful daughter," not "Depart from Me, I never knew you."

DENY SELF/SELF-WILL

From page 13 of Watchman Nee's *Spiritual Authority*: "For authority to be expressed there must be subjection (submission). If there is to be subjection, self needs to be excluded; but according to one's self-life, subjection in not possible. This is only possible when one lives in the Spirit. It's the highest expression of God's will."[1] Say this again and be sure you understand it because as it tells us, it's the highest expression of God's will. That is really saying something. What is the highest expression of His will? Subjection: the act of being subjected; being under the power of another. Submit: to place under or yield to authority. They sound the same to me. We use *submit* and Watchman Nee used *subjection*.

Nee is saying for a person to come under subjection or submission, a person must deny his own opinions. We have to cooperate with the other person's plans and work toward that end instead of our own. It's one thing to yield important choices if we agree; it's another to yield important choices if we don't agree. In order to do that, we have to know we can trust God to work on our behalf and we know that because we have already experienced God working in our lives and trust Him to continue to do so.

Your "flesh," your brain and body, will fight against denying your wants, needs, desires, and opinions with every fiber of its being. Don't you know this is true. If you want to stop at a nice restaurant and your husband doesn't, if you care very much at all, you are going to say something to convince him. It's just human nature. We want what we want when we want it. And even if we are yielding, there comes a time when we reach our limit. Now I'm not saying there should never be a limit, but it better be dictated by your spirit and that is what Nee is saying. This, denying what you want for another, is only possible when one lives in the Spirit.

A friend was bemoaning the fact that his step-children were such non-productive, wasteful young people in spite of everything he and his second wife had done to help them. He is not a Christian and despite years of witnessing by me and many others has never submitted himself to the Lord. In other words, he has been in rebellion to God the entire time he has been a stepfather, sowing rebellion and yet surprised when the crop comes in. Amazing!

Of course he doesn't see himself as a rebel. He sees himself as a good husband, provider, and father. He is a good man by man's standards. But, he isn't good. He is in rebellion. He is living his life as he thinks he should, not the way God wants it. Who knows, maybe submitted to God, his first marriage would not have broken up. His whole life would have been vastly different if God had been in control. Even if it didn't change much at all, which I don't believe, but let's say it didn't for the sake of the discussion, he still should have lived that way. Nothing justifies turning our back on God.

The situation with the step-father is typical. I really didn't understand how pervasive rebellion is until God made me aware of assaults against authority. Like Watchman Nee said in his book, "As God's servants, the first thing we should meet is authority. To touch authority is as practical as touching salvation, but it's a deeper lesson. Before we can work for God (before you can witness, minister or do anything for the Lord) we must be overturned by His authority. (Note he says overturned, in other words, it more than an "overhaul" of our brain and body. It turns everything upside down.) Our entire relationship with God is regulated by whether or not we have met authority. If we have, then we shall encounter authority everywhere, and being thus restrained by God we can begin to be used by Him."[2] Being thus restrained against doing our own thing (not responding as we normally would), only then can we begin to be used by Him.

The only problem is God doesn't come to us in the form of Jesus, He comes in the form of our husband, our boss, our father or mother who restrain us all the time and we resent it. We do not think of it as God, but that is the whole point. Once we have truly met God and understand His authority in our lives, we will begin to see where His authority exists in the men and women with whom we come in contact. And, being restrained by Him, we submit. If we don't, then we are not in right relationship with God. This being the case, we must pray and get things right with Him first before you or I will be right with our fellow man. I understand problems arise with those in authority, and we will get to that. First, let me lay the foundation. Then we will deal with the problems.

RESPONDING TO BAD AUTHORITY

"The greatest of God's demands on man is not for him to bear the cross, to serve, make offerings, or deny himself. The greatest demand is for him to obey."[3] As in the words of the prophet Samuel, "Obedience is better than sacrifice" (1 Sam. 15:22). God doesn't want your sacrifice; He wants your obedience. I won't say it will never require a sacrifice; it did for Jesus, but that is not the deciding factor. Obedience fulfills it all: love, faith, mercy, forgiveness, and so on.

If you told people they could be saved by giving to the poor and helping them daily, the poor would be in short supply. Everyone would be fighting over who was going to do for them. People want to work for their salvation. Coming humbly; now that's hard. God will accept your sacrifice *only* if it is what He asked you to do, not if it's your own idea.

How should we act in response to bad authority? In other words, what is the follower's responsibility when we are faced with a bad authority figure? I've already mentioned a few. Now I want to list some of the things we as followers do wrong. *Most of what we do wrong is through words*—words of unbelief, manipulation, or revenge; words that bring strife, confusion, and pain; or just plain unnecessary words, unanointed words, words we are responsible for. "If anyone is never at fault in what he says, he is a perfect man [mature], able to keep his whole body in check" (James 3:1, NIV). This is not a complete list.

DON'T LOOK AT THE MAN

The most common error people make in regard to their authority figure is to look at the man and not the position. The man may not look all that special. That doesn't mean that he doesn't carry any authority. Moses is a good example of the least likely to lead a people. God called Moses into a position of authority in spite of the fact Israel already had priests and leaders. Moses was a stutterer, but he was called just the same. His speech was so bad God agreed to send Aaron to speak for him, even though God had assured Moses He would correct the problem (Exod. 4:12). Moses didn't trust God to do it and insisted on help.

Don't you know it (doing what God told him to do) caused a problem when he got to town and started doing what God told him to do. Naturally, some of the people and leaders resented him, especially a man called Korah. Korah exemplifies a common mistake people make: he saw the man and not the position. If he would have checked with God, He would have told him that, yes, Moses has been called to do this. In fact, it was pretty obvious with all the miracles he was performing and the things he was saying that he was God's man.

Korah wasn't necessarily saying Moses didn't hear from God, he was just saying he did, too. He wanted his place in the sun, but God didn't call Korah to do it. He should have recognized Moses' calling and backed off. Just because God used you before doesn't mean He will use you this time. Recognize who God has called and don't get caught up in age, idiosyncrasies, education, background, past, family connections, money, etc. Is he the man God has called to be in this position or isn't he? Did He call you to that position? Probably not. Once someone is in that position, don't look at the man, look at the position and respect it.

DISRESPECT

Our husband does something wrong and we try to explain things to him. The only problem is we too often do it in a way that is disrespectful. Your husband is not a naughty little boy or your oldest child, and he shouldn't be talked to as such. He picks up on disrespect and resents it. Even if he does make mistakes and acts childish sometimes, he is not to be talked down to or talked about unseemly. That doesn't mean you cannot seek the counsel of a mature Christian or a friend who can keep a confidence. It just means that you need to use wisdom in how and with whom you discuss your husband and his faults. He should not be the brunt of cruel jokes or fodder for the neighborhood or church gossip machine. We make a big mistake when we assume, because our husband is not acting right, that gives us the right to say things we shouldn't be saying. It doesn't, especially to the kids.

Many women speak disparagingly about Daddy to their children. If you must say something about what their father has done or is doing, do it respectfully. We do have to be honest because daddies make mistakes and do hurtful things. We need to say what Jesus would say to the child, not what our hurts and frustrations say. You should approach your husband like you would a boss, deferring to him where appropriate, and when you disagree, saying it in a way that doesn't insult him or hurt him unnecessarily. We won't be able to avoid conflict all the time, so we must know how to approach them properly when there is a problem. *"Anger and sin not"* (Eph. 4:26).

CONTRADICTING HIM

I was with a couple recently and it seemed like everything one of them said, the other contradicted. It's really a form of disrespect. And yes, there is a great deal of disrespect in this home. The kids are unruly. They bad-mouth each other a lot. Not the guy so much because he really isn't the type to fight much. He'd rather back off. And if you do manage to get him started look out, it won't be pretty. Come to think of it, he does torment the kids a lot, and his wife. He's supposedly playing around, but it really isn't fun. It's really quite destructive.

If someone says something you disagree with, don't be too quick to say something and when you do, say it nicely. You may be wrong. Of course, some people fight so vehemently they will never know they are wrong because the other person decides it isn't worth it.

HAVING A BAD ATTITUDE OR BEING UNCOOPERATIVE

Watch your attitude. Keep a sweet spirit about you. I know life is hard and your husband probably isn't helping, but a bad attitude only makes things worse. Be as cooperative as possible—as possible as God knows is possible. And I don't mean to have a strict religious spirit. I mean like

457

Sarah had when she was even cooperative with his lies; that kind of cooperation. Men need a woman to keep their lives light and tolerable, a bad attitude and being uncooperative does just the opposite. It makes you the bad guy, just when you wish he would see that he is.

Bait and Switch

To salve our hurts, many wives go out and spend money. It doesn't solve anything and just makes things worse. Our husband sees how bad we are instead of how bad he is. You went from victim to victimizer when you ran up your credit card debt.

How we react to a leader tells more about us than it does him. It takes maturity to react properly. As Christians we need to mature and respond correctly to imperfect leadership because, the fact is, on this earth you will always have imperfect leadership. Two wrongs don't make a right. Too often that is exactly what we have: two wrongs.

Becoming Too Familiar (Not Respecting His Position)

Just because you know someone quite well and know their foibles, doesn't diminish their authority in God's eyes. This is especially hard for a wife. Remember when women used to call their husbands "Mister"? It brought home how much they respected him. Sarah called Abraham, Lord. We may not call our husband Mister or Lord, but we need to have the same respect.

The best example of this is Jesus in His hometown. The scripture says He couldn't do many miracles there. (See Mark 6:5.) If it happened to Jesus, it can happen to any man. I understand your husband isn't Jesus, but I also understand there are ladies out there that would be glad to have him and may treat him in a way where he would act a lot better. I remember complaining to a friend about Lamar only to have her chide, "Well, give him to me then." I had forgotten she had no one to complain about and Lamar looked pretty good to her. We both laughed, but it woke me up.

MURMURING (TURNING PEOPLE AGAINST THE LEADER)

"Miriam and Aaron began to talk against Moses because of his Cushite wife, for he had married a Cushite" (Num. 12:1). Another word for talking against someone is murmuring or reviling. It's one of the first things we do when we have a problem with our leader. And it's wrong. You are allowed to disagree, but you are not allowed to spread hate and discontent. Just as it was up to God to tell Moses what he was doing wrong, it's up to Him to tell our leader what he or she is doing wrong. We can't always prevent disaster and loss, much as we would like to. Sometimes we just have to stand back and let things happen. Moses was already married. It was too late. All their talk was not going to change anything but make things worse. Be sure what you say helps and doesn't hurt.

God's chosen people were always murmuring, and it did not bode well with Him. It has not gained any ground since then.

LEAVING

Running is typically the wrong thing to do—not always, but usually. We want to get out and may even succeed in getting ourselves out, but by doing so we miss everything God had planned for us, for our good. Yes, it's a difficult situation, but that doesn't mean God is not in it. We need to allow it to do its work until God gets us out, *if* He gets us out. He may decide to make it better with us there. Getting ourselves out just means God will have to set up another set of circumstances to accomplish the same thing. Why make Him bother. It just takes precious time. Stay and learn what He wants you to learn. And quit begging for Him to get you out the whole time. Pray for wisdom, for joy in the midst of it all, peace that passes all understanding, and the ability to be longsuffering in silence.

Sometimes God will show you to leave, and you need to obey. You don't always know the next step. You just know to leave, and usually in leaving the next step will be obvious, then the next and the next. He doesn't give us what we need until we need it. We just have to walk in faith. This is why it's important that you are walking it on a daily basis so when really difficult circumstances come up you know the voice of God.

Blaming God

When someone experiences abuse, an untimely loss, or something especially devastating, they often get angry at God. He could have prevented it and that is true. However, because we have free will in this life, He limits His interventions. God is involved, but it's hard to figure out why He makes the decisions He does. We want answers and He doesn't seem to feel responsible for giving them, which hurts us even more. But He does understand how hard these times are and grieves with us. When we are angry at God, it's a form of murmuring and murmuring is a form of unbelief. We are accusing God of things we should not accuse Him of: that He doesn't care, that He doesn't love us, that He loves someone else more than He does us, that He is punishing us through this loss or abuse, none of which is true. We are allowed to be angry, upset, and confused, but when we start accusing God of things and attitudes He is not guilty of, then we have gone too far. Grieve and even be angry, the Bible says we are allowed to be angry, but it tells us to sin not.

> *God, I just don't understand why You allowed this to happen. I thought You loved my family the way it was. I just can't see my life the way it's going to be now. I can't imagine going on without my little girl/the career I had planned/(put in your situation), but it looks like I don't have a choice. Oh, God, how can I go on? I know You say You will be enough but I don't see how, the hole is so big. The pain is so great. Only You can fill it. Help me not try to fill it with anything else. I'm so devastated. You will have to carry me for quite a while. Help me, Jesus.*

HARMING THE AUTHORITY FIGURE

David is good example of how to deal with a bad authority. After Saul was disobedient, God took away his anointing as king and gave it to David. David may have been anointed by God to be king, but he didn't sit on the throne for twenty more years. Don't you know that was hard. He didn't even get to go off and do what he wanted to do until that day. He had to be in the court and the king's palace regularly. David had to sing to King Saul to bring peace to the king's tormented soul. He married his daughter, and he had his grandchildren. This was not an easy twenty years. Saul chased David around and tried to kill him for years. Big thrill being anointed to be the next king. Why didn't God kill Saul first? I guess because He wanted to develop some character in David. Saul might have done better if he had gone through more before he ascended the throne.

It's never in your best interest to make the king (your husband) your enemy. Remember, the king is anyone that is in authority. We all get to be king in our own mind. Don't do anything to harm the leaders in your life and don't rejoice when harm comes to them. That's bad, too.

PROMOTING YOURSELF

Promoting yourself is doing in the flesh what God wanted to do by the Spirit. Hard as submission is, you really don't want to get ahead by your own doing. God knows how hard it is.

David had plenty of chances to kill Saul, but then he would have been "touching" God's chosen. God is the one that had Samuel anoint David to be king. Therefore, it was not up to David to secure the throne for himself. It was God's job to complete what He had begun. David had to endure years of being chased and mistreated by King Saul. If David had not endured it properly, he would have been no better than Saul. David respected authority even when it had turned ugly. That doesn't mean he didn't protect himself and run for cover, but he didn't retaliate.

There was a point after David had been king for years that his son was plotting to take the throne away from him. The people around David wanted him to defend himself. David, in his wisdom, tells them he didn't make himself king and he refuses to keep himself there. God will have to do it (2 Sam. 15:26; 16:12). Who in the Bible tried to promote him or herself? Certainly not Moses. He is an example of God promoting someone. Abraham is another and Mary, the mother of Jesus. They are all reluctant leaders. Lucifer, Cain, Joseph's brothers, Korah, Haman, and Judas are all self-promoters. Do you really want to put your name on this list?

MANIPULATING

Manipulation is worse than you might think it is. It's the sin of witchcraft. And it comes in many forms. I didn't think of myself as manipulative. I'm a straightforward person, or so I thought until God convicted me of it. How do women manipulate? With our looks, our bodies, our attitude, by being sweet, caring, doing nice things for people. Oh, we have our way. It just isn't His way. It's not so much what we do, but why we do it. We do it because we don't believe God can give us favor, or work things out for us—unbelief again.

WHOSE CAR IS IT ANYWAY?

A Christian friend was sharing an incident that happened with her son. He is backslidden and had called her for the first time in months. What it came down to was she had promised him a car someday and he was calling to take her up on it. She had just been given a car that she didn't really need due to a death in the family and he wanted it. I'm expecting her to lovingly say, "Hon, I love you very much and intend someday to give you a car, but I am not giving it to you now. You must be living a responsible life so that I can trust you to take care of it and right now you are not." Much to my surprise, she didn't. She made some phone calls to look into the matter and in the process upset another family member, which upset the whole family. It was a fiasco.

She was manipulating him. She is upset because her son manipulates and we now know where he gets it from. She claimed it was her husband, which is probably true. It's really bad when both parents teach you to manipulate. If being his mother leads her to do things that are harmful to him, I question her effectiveness as a mother. If we want things to change in our families, it has to start with us. We want them to stop manipulating, but won't stop ourselves. Amazing.

WITHDRAWING LOVE OR AFFECTION

One thing I did wrong that a lot of women do wrong was withdraw my love from Lamar. "But God, he doesn't deserve love," I argued. "Everyone deserves loves," God informed me. I was wrong again. How often am I wrong? Too often. Those that are the most unlovable need it the most. I never intended to use sex against Lamar, but I'm sure it seemed that way because I was so hurt (and turned off). It all gets tangled up.

God was able to show me that my gut level reactions were wrong. Protecting ourselves in ungodly ways is wrong. The Bible says not to defend yourself as most people do. If they force you to give them your coat, give them your cloak, also (Matt. 5:40). It was the law that they had to give up their cloak if the were asked. We are so quick to put up a defense; we don't give God a chance to defend us. He wants the clean to stand before Him so He can defend them. Don't get down and dirty, fighting the fight your way. Learn His ways and fight clean (1 Pet. 3:12).

Each of us will answer individually for our own actions. We can't use the excuse that it's someone else's fault that I am not doing right. No, it's our own fault. Anyone at any time can get right with God. And when you are right with God, He will bless you, defend you, deliver you, redeem you, and restore you. Don't worry so much about your authority figure. Let God do that. And let Him be the One to straighten him out. God is up to the job.

> *Lord, I do want to be a good follower. Help me to yield when I should yield and stand when I should stand, not being ugly or resentful, but respectful and graceful. Give me Your love for the people over me, especially my husband. Most of all give me*

wisdom, the wisdom to know what You would have me do. And give me strength of character, too, and mercy. Help me to be merciful, as you are merciful; not weak or whiney, but strong in You. I pray this in the precious name of Jesus. Amen.

THIRTY-FIVE

Then God the Eternal made a deep sleep to fall upon the man; while he slept, he took one of his ribs, closing up the flesh in its place; the rib he had taken from the man God the Eternal shaped into a woman, and brought her to the man. Then said the man, This, this at last, is bone of my bones, and flesh of my own flesh: this shall be called wo-man for from man was she taken. Both of them, the man and his wife, were naked, but they felt no shame.

—GENESIS 2:21

What God Did Not Intend

W E'VE COME A LONG way from "bone of my bones and flesh of my flesh." He's become a bully and she has lost herself. Where does that leave the kids? Sitting there stunned looking like deer in your headlights. This is definitely not what God intended. Now what? That's a very good question.

Years ago, Lamar and I were in a ministry where one of associates was a real problem, especially for the secretary. He had to use her office at night for counseling sessions and would leave it in a mess. When she arrived the next day, she couldn't find anything and even had to clean up spills that he had made the night before. She was at her wits end. Sometimes her notes were missing and she worried that she might forget something and often did. It kept her in a constant state of turmoil that began to affect her health. She begged him to be more careful, to no avail.

She worried about being fired because she couldn't afford to be out of work for even a few days. I couldn't convince her he was not to be feared because he was only an associate. She was doing a good job and had no reason to fear for her job except that she worried about how bad all this was making her look to the leader.

It was a terrible experience I wouldn't wish on anyone. But a rich one as far as life lessons go. I cried out daily, hourly, minute by minute, "Help me, God. Help me understand." It's at this point most people start praying for God to get them out, but I couldn't because I knew how much it meant to Lamar. It was his dream. I know it's tempting to run, but not helpful in the long run. No, once committed to a thing, we need to walk it out. I call it walking out your miracle. There is something to be said for being forced to stay because of the kids, financial concerns, reputation, or something else. It makes us try harder to make it work. That means we pray harder, listen better, and do what we are told.

I came to see what the man was doing was really a power play. He couldn't do it with people like Lamar and me, but he could to a power-less secretary. She, of course, did not want anything to do with it. She just wanted to do her job, get paid, and go home. Wives don't want to be in a power play, either. Most people don't. We just want to be happy, or relatively so. Why did he have to be so uncooperative?

Unbeknown to us, he was offered the chance to do something that appealed to him even more than our project. He desperately wanted to jump at the chance, but knew it wasn't feasible at the time. What he didn't understand is that God won't let your only chance to fulfill your dream come at the expense of another's. If something is wrong, we can't pursue it until it's right. If God is in a dream, He will help you fulfill it and you won't have to torment your secretary or break your word. That is the enemy seeing what he can rob you of and rob he did. Actually, if he had calmed down and worked harder at making the ministry a success, he could have moved on when it was time and looked back with pride at what he accomplished instead of with regret.

Outwardly he was mild mannered, peaceful, and logical, what we would call passive. And that was my clue when a TV show had a segment on the passive-aggressive male. It was him. They were describing the situation as if they had been there. These people appear to be very passive, but what they do has the affect of aggression. If allowed to go on, it tears at the very fabric of the venture until it literally consumes it, or it consumes the relationship.

What little power these people have, they use to stall projects and make everyone wait on them. They use their "passivity" aggressively. Do you understand how this works? A piece of a project depends on them and they know it, so they don't do their part. They never say they aren't doing it. To the contrary, they act cooperative and concerned. They just don't manage to get it done when it's needed. Everybody gets in a mess, upsetting the whole project and the people with it. He has power because the people care.

The secretary cared. She needed the job. We always had other options. Silly me thought the point of all this was to get the ministry established. It was the weirdest thing I had ever experienced. He was such a nice guy, people couldn't believe he was working against our succeeding. We couldn't believe it either. We kept trying to reason it out when it was not reasonable. In the end, he used our niceness, our naiveté, against us.

I tell this story because I feel so many problem marriages suffer from these same perverse power plays. Power plays that one spouse usually tries desperately to avoid. We give and give and give until there's no more to give and our spouse is still not satisfied. He or she takes and takes and takes until we get upset. But evidently that's the point. To get us upset. He is an angry, powerless person that hurts and wants others to hurt as bad as he does. He desperately needs to feel powerful and often the only place he can do that is at home with someone smaller and weaker than he is. Or maybe, he just wants to control everything. Maybe he is spoiled and wants his way all the time. Lots of dumb things.

This is not a gender thing. Maybe that's why some women are always late. To prove to him she has power. Or to hurt and frustrate him as much as she is hurt and frustrated. If this is you, you are doing yourself a grave disservice. It will not help your relationship and will do more damage than you can imagine. Manipulation is the sin of witchcraft.

One big reason we get into sick relationships is because one of us just

LET THE OLDER WOMEN TEACH

has to have the other. We put up with stuff we shouldn't. We kid ourselves. It's really quite sick. But for some reason we fall for it. When one person wants the relationship more than the other does, this gives the power in the relationship to the other person who doesn't care as much, skewing the relationship in their favor. This leads us to our first principle: the one who cares the least has the power in the relationship. Or maybe, the one that perceives the other cares less doesn't have the power in the relationship. Perception is everything.

PRINCIPLE #1: THE ONE WHO CARES THE LEAST HAS THE POWER IN THE RELATIONSHIP

The rule is set in stone but the relationship isn't. Eventually in every marriage some adjustments are made. The power can shift any time when the one that cared the most quits caring so much. That happens when he or she finally gets tired of the way he or she is being treated; when he or she decides it's not worth it and begins to make waves that will affect everyone involved. It's at this point that we will see new dynamics emerge. Most couples are able to make the adjustment and, over time, work out a new more balanced approach. But some relationships have an inflexible spouse that refuses to budge. They may give in, but when things don't get better, they will eventually carry through on their threats. Neither can stop indefinitely the change that is "perking" in the dissatisfied spouse, but they can change the outcome. The problem is the unyielding spouse may hear the words, but they do not understand how important it is that they begin to make needed changes. Eventually it's too late. It's at this point that the unyielding one wakes up and faces reality and is finally willing to cooperate. But the other is no longer willing or able to wait—he or she is now the unyielding spouse. What they hated so much, they have become. It's over and that's a shame, because I really do feel, at this point it's salvageable. I believe most marriages could be saved.

When a man is not able to lead his family, he doesn't take it lightly. He tries different ways to adjust. Some acquiesce, but these men resent it. So, he may look OK on the outside, but on the inside, it's not good. Other men dig in their heels and some get down right abusive.

PRINCIPLE #2: THE FEAR OF LOSS MAKES US PUT UP WITH THINGS AND DO THINGS WE ORDINARILY WOULDN'T

Fear is one of the most important factors dictating what people do. Try to figure out what your husband fears and it will help you understand why he is reacting the way he is. Fear is often manifested in anger. Now, do it for yourself: your fears. Look at what makes you angry and ask yourself why? What do you fear might happen?

Fear and unbelief go together. And anger is right there with them. In the story of Samson and Delilah, Samson did not tell the secret of his strength until he feared losing her. Knowing that he had been fooled by her twice before, why would he be so foolish to tell her his secret knowing that she was helping his enemies? Unbelief! He didn't really believe he would lose his strength. He thought his natural strength was enough, but soon found out it wasn't. He needed the anointing God was willing to give him. *"Pride leadeth the way to destruction"* (Prov. 16:18).

Marriage is a relationship and relationships need to be negotiated on an almost item by item basis. If one is not willing or able to do this, eventually they will need a judge and lawyers to do it for them.

Samson and Delilah did everything wrong. There is so much in their story that we could go into. The lies, the manipulations—all things we experience in our relationships. I am going to have to just pick out a few things and zero in on them. The first thing I see is how vulnerable Samson is. In fact, this is where his anger stems from. He trusts people and they do him dirty; but he's making some bad decisions, too. He is his own worst enemy and that just makes him angrier. Doesn't that sound familiar?

WE ARE THE MOMMIES

Let's face it: men are vulnerable, especially a man who can't control himself. He is at the mercy of the source of his satisfaction. It starts with his mommy and continues with Gramma, teachers, girlfriends, etc. All these women hold power over a man. Women rule the food, the money, their time, toys, play, and the choices. Everything a boy holds dear is meted out, or isn't meted out, by a woman. An absent mother has the most power of all.

Raging hormones do not lessen the problem. He is all the more vulnerable once sex is at a woman's discretion. Will he never be in a position where he holds the power? Yes, he will, when the hormones perk through his body. There is a God! (And a devil.) He suddenly became very desirable by the other sex. Some more than others.

Even if it's in the form of love, it's still power. Love is the ultimate power. Do you know how much a little boy idolizes his mother? And his daddy doesn't make him feel any better. Just the fact that Mommy loves Daddy and yields to him makes it all the worse. Daddy is a fearful figure to a small boy, even if the rest of us know he is a teddy bear. Many fathers are especially hard on their boys, especially their firstborn. If these relationships are non-existent or problematic, the fact that he cares so much still gives them power.

When we don't realize how powerless a man feels, we don't realize how much it means to him to be powerful in his own special way: physical prowess, good looks, money, position, influence, sex, personality, intellect, ability to put things together or fix things, bad boy antics, whatever. This is why it's so important that he is admired: so he has influence, most importantly with the woman he loves.

Very early on a man tries to figure out what a woman wants and sets out to give it to her. He wants to be her hero. Pleasing you is the one thing he wants in life. Samsons are really quite a catch and quite charming especially when you are a goal. The only problem is, once he has reached this goal, he moves on to the next one.

Don't make the mistake of thinking he will sound needy or vulnerable. The one thing he doesn't do is let on he is afraid of losing you. Samson has many secrets, not just the secret of his strength but of his vulnerability, his sexual appetite, his need for love and relationship. He is a needy man, but you will never know it. This is principle number one for a Samson:

SAMSON'S PRINCIPLE #1: DON'T LET PEOPLE KNOW YOUR TRUE FEELINGS

I was reading a book in which the author admitted how wimpy he is with his wife in order to keep the peace. He lost his first wife to divorce and doesn't want to lose another. And we thought we were the only ones. I'm all for peace, but it gets a bit ridiculous. How long can he stifle? How will his dissatisfaction reveal itself? This should be a warning to any woman whose husband never makes waves. Things may be fine, but then again, they may not be. Look for telltale signs of his dissatisfaction, that he is stifling. Don't be too sure your husband is as convinced of things as he says he is. Dishonesty is an open door to the enemy. A stifling man is not an improvement over a stifling woman.

The basis of this relationship is fraudulent. They may have started out with a great and wonderful love, but it's being chipped away, and yet, neither of them recognizes the danger. That's the real problem. Even if it's obvious something is wrong, they won't deal with it because he can't or won't confront her. Even if he did, it wouldn't do any good. He will be met with resistance, so why bother. And so they rock on until something forces the issue: the kids or finances or whatever.

A well-known playboy and a television talk-show host complained that men have made themselves to be something they aren't just to relate to women. Not that he's into relating. He's into you-know-what. He sees guys marrying to have "it" available. Too many men have been emasculated by their women. There is such a thing as manliness. If you don't know what that is, get the book by Harvey C. Mansfield. Manliness is a good thing; those wonderful qualities we associate with a good man. The male ego is not necessarily a bad thing. It's a necessary part of the male psyche.

Most things we fight about are superficial, but not insignificant. Let me tell a story that will help explain what I mean:

After Mom and Dad moved to Florida, Dad needed a shed for his lawnmower and yard tools. He wanted to build a garage at the end of the driveway, a natural place for one. Mom said no. And when my mom said no it meant, "By God, there won't be a shed there come hell or high water." She said it would mar her view. But her view was out the front toward the tiny lake across the street, and out the back to the yard, not out this side to the grove. In fact, they sold the grove a few years later for apartments to be built. Mom put up a blind of bushes and flowers and was fine with it.

Dad should have had a structure he could use and enjoy. As it was, he had to make do, storing his stuff under the house and in a lean to thing that to me was an even worse eye sore. It would have meant more to him than the view did to her and her eyes would have gotten used to it just like they did the apartments. She could have dressed up the building just as she created the blind. It irked Dad all the years they lived there, having to make all the adjustments knowing it was unnecessary. These kinds of things marred their marriage for years. He always admired me for being so cooperative with Lamar. Dad loved Mom, but it was in spite of these things.

My mother, my friend's mom, and women like them are doing exactly what they shouldn't do. In my mother's defense, she loved father dearly and was usually very supportive of him. It was a mixed bag, which most marriages are. Most women feel they give a lot, and I'm sure they do. Can't we have anything our way? Yes, we can and should. But it's how we have it that is important. Instead of being so insistent, we need to try to work it out to both of our satisfaction. And if we can't, we need to yield if at all possible (1 Cor. 6:7). Better to suffer loss than to be a bad witness.

I do not believe in giving in to the flesh. What my father wanted was not a fleshly thing. It was as reasonable request to make his job easier, to make the property worth more and look better. In this case, Dad should not have given in to Mom. He resented it and it hurt their relationship. Here she loved him dearly, but evidently not enough.

What made it even worse was Dad couldn't build a garage in Erie, Pennsylvania, when we lived there all those years because of easement requirements and the next door neighbor would not sign off on them. He was in rerun hell and this time it was Mom's fault. Don't you know the devil knows just how to get you. "The heart of the king is in the hand of the Lord" scripture comes to mind. Why would God harden the neighbor's heart and Mom's? Maybe because he wasn't attending church, or tithing, etc. He wasn't in covenant. He didn't have favor. Some of these things are our own fault, not our wife or husband's. In the end, God puts it back on us. But we don't see that and blame them.

So, in the end it was his own fault, but maybe if Mom would have given Dad what he wanted, maybe God would have softened Dad's heart and they could have gotten together spiritually and gone to church together as a family all those years. So, God puts it back on her too. If something's wrong in our lives, it always comes back on us. Not that the other isn't wrong, but that we are wrong, too.

This having "ought" against someone is a very important point. One reason we don't give our hurts to God and get past them is because we don't want to be grateful for anything the person does for us. If we forgive, we have to appreciate what they do that is good, and we don't want to appreciate anything about them. We like having them "owe" us. We can take what they give us as our due, not something to be thankful for. If a man makes mistakes and hurts his wife in some way, then from then on anything he does is put on the other side of the scale to balance out the offenses. And I can almost guarantee that he will never do enough to balance out the scales. There will always be a new offense.

The reason I understand this principle is because God convicted me of being ungrateful and helped me to see that I had ought against Lamar. Been there; done that.

"What should a husband do about a rebellious wife?" popped into my head that day as I left my friend's home. I cleared my mind and repeated the question, "How does a man deal with rebellion in his wife?" In the early years, when they are both sweet and loving, most men try to talk to their wives and resolve the problem that way. When this doesn't work, which it so often doesn't, he resorts to other things, most of which are ungodly, to which she reacts in kind, each round escalating until he loses his temper and does something dumb. All this adds up to years of fighting, which is what my friend had lived with her whole childhood. Her parents separated many times over the years only to realize they did love each other and would get back together again. There must be a better way.

The world looks on and sees his family in disarray. It makes him look bad, not only in our eyes, but in God's. He feels responsible for the mess. In fact, it's even scriptural. Although they were Christians and active in church, he would never take a position of leadership because of what it says in Titus 1:6, "If any be blameless..." She was fine with that because she felt he wasn't where he needed to be spiritually to be in leadership. And he probably wasn't. He felt awful about what he did and even though he repented, he never really got the victory.

Now the issues in their marriage are more serious than just hurting them and their children, which is bad enough. Their marriage issues have robbed them of their ministry and their witness in the community. But what's so bad is that they are both saying they are the victim and the other is the bad guy. They aren't taking responsibility for their part in the mess. And they think God is going to be satisfied with all this licking of the wounds? I don't think so. He tells us over and over again to overcome. Neither one is an overcomer.

What should a man do?

A man must do what Moses did with his rebellious people: throw himself prostrate before the Lord and let Him take care of them (Deut. 9), not smote the rock and abuse them verbally. (See Numbers 20.) And just like God deals with a rebellious man, He will deal with a rebellious woman. And it isn't pretty. You do not want it to be you. What choice did Moses have? He couldn't force the people to submit. God had to do that.

A man can't force his wife to submit. And who knows? God might tell him she's right, to repent and get the speck out of his own eye before he tries to get it out of hers, to study the Bible and show himself approved and to become the best husband she could ever have and the best father, employee, citizen, etc. If he keeps going to God, He will transform him into the image of Jesus. That should keep him busy for a while, and in the meantime God will do a work in her. Sounds like a plan to me. Actually, it sounds like the same thing I've been telling the wives.

However, there are some things he is called to do and he must do them. She may balk and cry, but eventually she should come around. A husband should have the confidence that God will redeem him in due time, giving God time to speak to her just like He spoke to Joseph about Mary's unexpected pregnancy. However, he should be very careful, if things aren't right, before he proceeds. If he is doing God's thing, then God can defend and anoint it. This is true for wives, too. I've watched Him do it for me time and time again. God is not into strife and confusion. We don't fight our battles. God does.

It's hard to reverse these controlling tendencies. It doesn't matter which one is being overbearing; it's still wrong. A control freak backed into a corner is not really the answer. We need the control freak at peace about yielding control. It's really a trust issue. That's why you must draw closer to God for answers. You can trust Him. But first you need to get to know Him.

People mature and change, that's inevitable. It's the inability to allow the proper change to take place that is the problem, refusing to change the dance. So many spouses try again and again to force their partner to change with no success. Finally, they feel they have no choice but to end it. This time they *really* mean it. Well, they meant it the last time, but this time is different. It's over in their head and their heart. Something has died within and they see no hope of resurrecting it. The sad part is this is the first time their partner really understands and would be willing to change.

No amount of begging will put the marriage back together, which is a shame because now is really the first time they could finally begin. And that is sad; that when it's finally workable on the one side, it's no longer workable on the other. Even if the dissatisfied spouse never leaves, they might as well because the marriage is dead emotionally. At this point the person feels numb, apathetic; they just want out. It's never going to change, so why not accept it and move on. If things are never going to change, what's the point? And I understand these feelings, but I don't believe things are never going to change. I serve a powerful God, capable of resurrecting the dead. We are supposed to die to ourselves so He can live through us, die to our opinion and our agenda so we can be a channel of His love. I know you don't have the love you need and neither does he; that's why you should go to the Source of love and get all you need—for him and for yourself.

No, you probably don't need a divorce any more than I did. You need the resurrection power of the Lord. Having done all, stand. Stand praising God. Stand vulnerable, confused, and seeking.

Dear God, I have to admit I haven't always done what my husband wanted me to do. I did what I thought was best, and it has caused trouble between us. Forgive me for doing this. I really didn't understand that it was more important that I obey my husband than my own mind. It's so hard to go against what I know is best and do what I think is wrong. I just don't know if I can do that. I understand I don't have to do anything morally wrong or harmful, but even just something I think is dumb is hard to do. You will have to help me, especially to not be ugly and say "I told you so" if he fails. I want to do the right thing. It's just that this is so hard. Please help me. I can't seem to ask You to help me enough. I know it will have to come from You. I pray this in Jesus' precious name. Amen.

THIRTY-SIX

The Perfect Wife

IF YOU ASKED MY friend Tracy, she would tell you what a great wife she has been over the years. She is great looking, has a great figure and personality. She keeps a nice house, can decorate professionally, and did at one time. She is a gourmet cook, a great gardener, a good athlete, a good mother, and can land a good job if she wants to. Furthermore, she is great in bed. (I'll have to take her word for that.) If she's so great, then how has she managed to lose two husbands and is working on losing a third?

All of her friends are astonished. "She just picks bad men" is all they can come up with. I disagree. I don't think she is as perfect as she and everyone else thinks she is. I think her inability to see what she was doing wrong is what did her in. Her faults are sinking her, and her denial keeps her locked into the problems. *"Pride leadeth the way to destruction"* (Prov. 16:18).

I don't want to tear anyone down, especially a friend. But, I'm not really tearing her down; I am looking at what we can learn from her failures. I know Tracy and she does want to help people.

Tracy had two problem areas that I feel bothered her husbands. The first one was that she spent too much money. Because of it they have to work very hard, long hours and resent it. When I mentioned it in an attempt to help her in her marriage, she would point out he spent money foolishly, too. Which was true. I'm sure he was frustrated with himself, but she was compounding the problem and wasn't willing to cooperate. I have to admit, he was chintzy. She would have been better served if she had out-chintzed him for a while, gone without, helped him to see she was on his side. (If you're not willing to do this, at least understand why he has an attitude and isn't very responsive. You can't have your new shoes and a kiss. Take one or the other. The cost of the shoes is his affection. Sadly, many women choose the shoes and then wonder why he's unresponsive.)

It's not the money, even when it is the money. It's the principle of the thing. It's not taking into consideration what is important to him. It's his inability to able to control his household, his woman. Men don't want to yell. They want a simple request to be taken seriously—seriously means we do it. I really believe if she had been economical and helped him be economical without nagging, she would have eventually been free to spend what she wanted to. Money problems are really spiritual problems: faith problems, fear problems, sin problems. You won't fully solve money problems by being chintzy yourself. Being cooperative is really a stop-gap measure that will help us to "win" him. Like the scripture says, *he will be won, if not by the Word, by her cooperative nature* (1 Pet. 3:1).

The second thing was that she has kept up her friendship with her ex. She sees no reason why they should quit being friends. Well, I'm not saying you have to quit speaking, but you don't have to keep up phone contact and frequent his business, etc. She insisted it was innocent, but it looked bad on her part, especially since the divorce was not her idea. Her husband never let on he was jealous, but I know it bothered him. She wanted it to bother him because he acted like he didn't care. She wanted him to be jealous so maybe he would be more demonstrative. It didn't work. It just made him resent her.

She did hurt him. Now they were both hurt. Hurting your husband and making him bitter will not improve your marriage. It won't even give you that much satisfaction. You become no better than your husband when you sin too. God now has two people to chasten instead of just one. The Bible says God's eyes search for the innocent to protect. First Peter 3:12 tells us:

For the eyes of the Lord are over the righteous, and his ears are open unto their prayers: but the face of the Lord is against them that do evil and who is he that will harm you, if ye be followers of that which is good? But and if ye suffer for righteousness' sake, happy are ye and be not afraid of their terror, neither be trouble; But sanctify the Lord God in your ears and be ready always to give an answer to every man that asketh you a reason of the hope that is in you with meekness and fear. Having a good conscience: that whereas they speak evil of you, as of evil doers, they may be ashamed that falsely accuse your good conversation in Christ. For it's better, if the will of God be so, that ye suffer for well doing than for evil doing.

The eyes of the Lord watch over the righteous (we are righteous through Jesus), but if we do evil, then He is against you. He asks, "Who is he that will harm you?" Could anyone harm you? Yes, they could, but He tells you not to be afraid if you suffer for righteousness' sake. It makes all the difference in the world why you are suffering. Yes, missionaries suffer and even die. They do it for gospel. He wants us to be willing to suffer for the gospel, not because we sin or are foolish. She needs to quit this ploy immediately and apologize, admitting that she was just doing it because she was hurt, assuring him that she really does love him and hates that they are having problems, but that she won't do it any more.

However, there are times it's better not to apologize and just do the right thing. Words, any words you speak, will just re-open the wounds. Actions speak louder than words. Stop what you are doing wrong and start doing the right thing just to see if you can do it. It's bad if you say you are going to do something and then don't do it. And, let's face it, so far you haven't been able to do it. Maybe you need to become accountable to a friend or pastor as you go through this process, especially when there are other people involved that you seem to be unable to separate from emotionally. After your husband notices the improvement, then you can share your resolve to make things better.

After Tracy had the first two problems and dealt with them incorrectly, she ended up with a third: her mouth; and a fourth: he quit caring as much. The more she did in reaction to what he did in reaction to her, the worse things got. When she irritated him and would not cooperate, he withdrew. Most people don't understand unconditional love and do not give it in marriage. She was wrong and he wanted her to know it. So, he withdrew his love and to a huggy, physically expressive woman, this is devastating. All because she wouldn't rein in her spending and quit playing games.

Instead of asking herself why he was angry and do something about it, she decided to be sexier, more desirable, and more playful. This just irritated him all the more. If he was upset to begin with, it was worse when she disallowed his feelings. Not to mention the fact that things weren't going to change any time soon. Nothing he said did any good. Whether he was right or not isn't the point. If he thought he was right, that was enough for him.

Not wanting to go through all this or to talk about it, he pulled away further and further. He worked longer hours and was more unavailable, knowing full well this would really get her. A wife, perfect as she may think she is, can't win at this game. All for a bunch of stuff. Women and our stuff. Nothing is worth this much to me.

Some women choose to do just the opposite, and they are the ones that withdraw. That doesn't work either. It just increases the gulf between them.

Once a couple gets to this point, it's really hard to go back because neither is willing to give up their hurt or their position. What they do from now on just makes things worse. You can pretty much guess what problem number five was: another woman. I don't think he was naturally a "run around," but he was vulnerable and so was someone else. There are women everywhere that find other women's husbands very desirable and are more than willing to cooperate. At this point nobody is in control of themselves or the situation. Come on in devil and take my man, my marriage, my life.

One thing Tracy did succeed at was in making him look bad. I guess that is some consolation if you are into keeping up a front. Some people are, you know. I myself prefer a happy, intact family. And sometimes that means humbling myself, not so much to my husband as to my God. Not that I am against being humble to my husband, but if I humble myself before God, I will do whatever else needs to be done and maybe I won't have to be so humble everywhere else. Believe me, this was a very humbling experience for this couple. I really believe this marriage was a workable situation.

If your husband has hurts and frustrations, face them head on. Try to work on areas he finds repulsive or problematic. We can be better housekeepers and make the children behave. It may take some doing on our part, getting help to learn how to do what we need to do in a better way. We can learn. We can change. He is not asking something that other women don't manage to do or that we should not be capable of doing. If we can't do it because we have a compulsion, then we need to work on that. We are upset with him because he can't control his compulsions. Let's show him how by controlling ours first. A good woman is a challenge to a man to be a better man.

Your husband wants you to be all you can be. He's just not saying it very well. What he is saying is probably making things worse, and he probably hasn't contributed very much. Let's quit making excuses and be all we can be in spite of the people who love us. Let's be the woman not only our husband needs us to be, but who God wants us to be. God wants our house clean and our kids well behaved. He also wants us to have a great sex life with our husband and to be beautiful inside and out. God made something beautiful when He made you, and He wants your life to reflect this beauty.

Let's look at things early. Ask yourself, "Is there something bothering him?" Of course there is. There is always something bothering the people we live with. What doesn't your husband like about you or your life together? Don't groan. List them. It won't be as painful as you may think. Here is a partial list. Put them in order of importance to him.

1. Is it a messy house? I know you have your reasons. Don't get defensive; just answer the question. We'll talk later.

2. Is it where you live or something about his physical surroundings?

3. Are the meals in your home satisfying his needs? Nutritious? Are they special?

4. Is your sex life fulfilling? Is it special?

5. Is it the way the kids act? Or maybe that the "kids thing" has been a disappointment? (It's not as easy as we thought either.) It's not as easy as it seemed when you were making them. Maybe he didn't even want to do the kid thing. Maybe it's your thing.

6. Is it his job? Maybe his job is a mess and a dead end at that. Maybe his dreams and vision has been put off indefinitely. Hope deferred makes the heart sick.

7. Is it that he is getting older and life's possibilities may be slipping away?

8. Is it the family problems? Maybe your family or his is a pain in the neck and he's tired of it. Are you preferring your family over his?

9. Is it money? Financial problems?

10. Do you have basic spiritual differences?

11. Is it health problems or other issues? You may not even know he has health problems.

12. Does he have a problem with your friends?

13. Is it your appearance? Or your attitude toward your appearance?

14. Is it the way you spend your time?

15. Is it your job or lack of a job?

16. Is it your mouth? Personality problems?

17. How about your attitude toward him? Toward life in general? Something specific?

18. Is it jealousy? Yours or his.

19. Is it your way or the highway? (You're too controlling?)

20. _____ (fill in the blank)

If it's all of these things don't panic. I've had them all! OK, let's go down the list: (Remember, whatever is your biggest problem is your number one.)

1. The messy house. Why this first you ask? Because it occurs more than we realize. And it was my problem. And because so many men feel it's a problem. Bad housekeeping is not something you can just turn over a new leaf and solve. It's something you need God's help to change. It's spiritual as well as mental and physical. All three must be dealt with.

Don't get an attitude; just do it. Put a Christian praise tape on and get the kids in gear and just do what needs to be done. That's what Nanny 911 does. She gets a plan, then works her plan and makes it fun.

2. Where you live or his physical surroundings. Some things are a real downer to men (and women). I understand there are a lot of these things we can't help, but at least we can acknowledge them and help as much as we can to make it as good as it can be. Very often a man feels stuck in a place because we won't cooperate and move. Or if we do cooperate, he won't ever hear the end of it. It's not worth the emotional price.

3. Meals. I think this is one of the most neglected areas in so many women's repertoire. A man doesn't expect anything fancy, but he does expect a decent meal. Convenience store food and stuff that you grab on the way home do not satisfy the soul like a home cooked meal. And they are too often not good for you or your family.

4. His sex life is a very important area. (It really is number one.) And, I'm not saying it's all your fault. Men are often the source of their own frustrations. They still tend to blame us. *"That woman you gave me...."* still happens today. You must begin the improvement in this area. I know

I have changed a lot over the years and Lamar has, too. We must meet the changes head on and deal with them. Be willing to help him be sexually fulfilled.

5. The children? That's a whole 'nother book. You simply cannot have unruly children for years and have them turn out right. Start now to make them the citizens you want them to be tomorrow. Get help to get it together.

6. His job? So many men work their job simply to pay the bills and that's a shame. I don't know what you can do to change this, but at least appreciate him and try to make the rest of his life as fulfilled as possible. And if you can in any way help him fulfill his dreams, do so. Lamar and I had a lot of skimpy years, but eventually it paid off. Each failure was a lesson that helped him the next time.

7. He's getting older. Life is slipping away. A recent study said forty-four is the least happy time for most men (and about the same for women) which is a shame. I think it's not just because of all the pressures on their time, but because they are having to face the fact that some things will never be. But this isn't necessarily true. There's a lot of life left after forty-four. We need to see this as the time to reevaluate things and figure out what is really important. God knew the pressures and possibilities. He knew it would never happen. My goodness, few of the men in the Bible did much before they were elderly by our standards. God still has a plan for the rest of your lives.

8. In-laws: This is a hard one, though they are all hard. A critical spirit can make you see things in a negative way, so it becomes your own worst enemy in this situation. It took me years to see things differently and to realize Mrs. Vice didn't have as much influence in the family as I thought she did. Now that I am a mother-in-law, it ain't as easy as it seemed. Back off a little, but not all the way. I have to say, today's attitudes make it a lot harder. We used to be a lot more respectful and not so quick to speak, though my daughters-in-laws don't have this problem. Be sweet, be forgiving, be merciful, and check your love walk. It's in these situations that you prove how mature you are as a Christian. My in-laws made me

a better person, and I was greatly blessed by them. Being an in-law is a ministry, and not an easy one at that.

Some men don't want their wives to be around her family and that isn't right. You can keep it in proper balance, but you cannot give in to a compulsive attitude just to keep the peace. If there are deeper issues, they must be dealt with or they will just keep getting worse. The problem is an outward manifestation of something deeper, and you need to find out what it's. Is it you? Is it him? Or is it both of you?

For many years I went to the Vice's even though it was hard. A lot of women would have refused. Then for two years I did refuse to go and found that didn't work either. Later I wondered why I put up with it, but realized I had probably made the best decision by going all those years. It was awfully hard and many woman wouldn't have put up with it, but it did give the kids a wonderful experience and a memory bank to draw on. Hindsight is so much better than foresight. No, I'm not sorry I sacrificed my feelings for them to know and love their grandparents.

9. Money? This is a fruit of a lot of things. Get them right and your finances will be fine. Remember *"the prosperity of the fool will destroy him."* God won't prosper you until you are wise. He won't because He loves you. Read the area on finances in this book and get other help, too.

10. Basic spiritual differences? Believe in God to reach him and let your light so shine for him to appreciate. In reaching your husband, you will become a mature Christian.

11. Health issues. Maybe things have been extremely difficult and he was physically, mentally, emotionally, or spiritually down to begin with. It's hard to be up when you don't feel well. Maybe he needs help with diet and exercise. You probably do, too. Do it together. Lamar had thyroid and gall bladder problems for years and we never knew it. It's so important that we get our numbers run (see a doctor).

12. Friends? This is almost always a bone of contention. He has a problem with some of your friends, and you have a problem with his. The truth is some people are not a true friend and we need to stay away

from them. It just takes time for this to be revealed. Then again, maybe our spouse is being unrealistic and we need to let him know we are not giving up some relationships. Ask other friends, hopefully mature Christians, what they think. It's a spiritual problem more than anything. Some friendships should be ended, some put in their place, and some encouraged. It's just nice when all three of us (you, your spouse, and God) agree and then you do it.

13. Appearance? You need to love yourself and accept your body—even love it. I understand you are probably disappointed with body parts, but your body is about more than parts and perfection. Your body is to serve your needs as you live your life. We should try to keep our weight down and exercise, not only for health, but to look good. But just because you're not the weight you would like to be, that doesn't mean you shouldn't love your body. You are harder on yourself than anyone else is and that isn't right. Feeling bad about yourself is not optional. The truth is your body is very, very special.

14. The way you spend your time? Your husband should have a lot to say about how you spend your time, just as he should listen to what you say about how he spends his time. If you are not considering his viewpoint, nor he yours, you need to start and so does he, but you can only control yourself.

15. Your job? Or lack of one? There are times when the man is wrong to ask a woman to work when she shouldn't, etc., but even then, it may be a good idea to cooperate and let him see the results. I would not sabotage it. These areas of contentions should not be.

16. Your mouth/ personality problems. The tongue is the unruly member. Learn to bridle yours or you will never be the mature Christian God means for you to be. It's not about other people; it's about you and your testimony. Back off and learn to let God run the show. Personality problems? Deal with your problems head on instead of running from them. Get some joy in your life. There is no reason to be down all the time—no reason other than unbelief, and that's sin. If you know Jesus, you should have joy and peace and all those good fruit.

17. Attitude. Attitude is everything, just like obedience is, because attitude affects obedience. I can't say enough about being grateful and merciful and magnanimous. Get a good devotional and read your Bible and abide in Him, and eventually He will change a bad attitude into a good one. None of us are all that great, just filthy rags cleaned by the blood of the Lamb.

18. Jealousy. This is a bad one. If he's the jealous one, just keep showing him how much you love him by the little things you do and be sure you don't act like you think other guys are special. It's a spirit and he may need deliverance, or you may. Bind it and pray about other spirits that are binding you.

19. Control issues. Trust is your issue. Not trusting God to work through your husband and other people and situations. The more you walk with Him and push things over on Him, the more you will see Him working on your behalf. You have either what you grab and hang onto or what He provides. The choice is yours.

A controlling spirit and attitude is sin, and you need to face it. I understand you are smarter and can do things better than anyone else, but God expects us to let less capable people have a turn at the bat to hone their skills. If they never get to practice when they are not good at something, when will they ever get good? You need to repent, and repent again and again until you quit. They may be bad, but you're worse. You are keeping God from using and blessing you.

20. Gee, I just wish I knew what you put here. I guess you will just have to put words in my mouth.

See, wasn't that easy? Seriously, please read and study areas where you need help. As I got busy changing me, somehow everyone around me got better. I bought a daily meditation devotional for the dysfunctional to give to a friend. The only thing I remember is: "My addiction takes so much of my time, I don't have time for the cure." Sad but true. Take the time back.

We should always assume our husband loves us. Love believes all things. That's 1 Corinthians 13 again. To men, just being there is proof enough; requiring more is an insult. (See "A Rose" at the end of this chapter.) Enjoy the free things, the lovely things and think on these things. (See Philippians 4:8.)

He could be one of those guys that is stingy. What then? Appreciate this attribute (frugalness). Enjoy what you do have. Try to work within his boundaries if at all possible and if not, ask God to soften his heart and if necessary, insist on some things. A husband must provide legitimate needs. But most of all remember you are dealing with a spirit. Bind it, send it to the dry places, release liberality in your husband, bind fear and unbelief, loose favor, speak creatively over him: "My husband has a generous heart and spirit, my husband loves to do things for me and give me things, my husband doesn't worry about money, etc."

Then walk in joy with what you have, but on some points set up boundaries. If he is lazy or spending on himself and neglecting the family, that is not acceptable. If it's too bad, professional help must be initiated.

I counsel Christian women all the time who aren't getting the victory. Why? Because they are not taking every thought into captivity. It only takes me a few minutes to discover error in her thinking and speaking. Within a few minutes I am shaking my head disagreeing with something this precious Christian is saying. I love her. I wish she were right, but she's not; and I have to tell her. Since I can't actually talk with you, you are going to have to try to do what I would do: see your error.

One couple in the process of getting a divorce was fighting over who would get what. She had jewelry, none of which he had given her. He had hidden her nicest piece because he didn't want her to sell it before the divorce settlement. She was frantic because she didn't know what happened to it. Naturally, she was livid. It was obvious she resented that she had had to buy it for herself, and he returned her venom. When you get to this point, you have already lost a lot more than a bracelet. I guess she figured it was all she had left, and she didn't want to lose that, too. And who could blame her?

Right here I see red flags that it's a shame she didn't see that it's not bad to buy jewelry for yourself. I do it all the time—nothing expensive, but then I never was one to want expensive jewelry. It's not who buys the jewelry that is important; it's our expectation of who should buy it. If to her it's a proof of his love or that he cares and he doesn't buy it, then it becomes a problem—unrealistic expectations. To him, it never was proof that he loved her. The proof that he loved her was in the fact that he married her.

This woman could be a very attractive woman without the jewelry, but she isn't attractive at all because of the bitterness she exudes. Whining is not pretty. Even if people understand she has been neglected and victimized, they still see a very unattractive woman. But she has great jewelry.

I can speak on this subject because there was a time when Lamar intended to buy me a very nice ring after we finally got past the financial crisis. One Sunday he got the mail that was on the foyer floor by the front door and saw that I had made a monthly pledge to a certain charity. He was upset that I had done it without consulting him. Well, I had gone to the meeting and he hadn't, and since I knew we could afford it, I didn't think it would be a problem. Well, it was. You know the "it's the principle of the thing" concept. Then I got upset because I had heard this for too long, and we never seemed to get around to "discussing it;" and therefore, we never got around to giving, which I felt was a cop-out and a problem to God.

Isn't it funny how this garbage gets started Sunday morning just before church? It really bothered me. It was a good cause and he knew it. The more I thought about getting an expensive ring, the more I didn't want it. Every time I looked at the ring, instead of admiring it, I would think, "Ya, you have a beautiful ring, but others don't have the gospel." The ring would be a symbol, not of love, but of selfishness. And so I blurted out, "Don't bother to get me a ring because if I can't give to spread the gospel, I sure can't afford an expensive ring."

Lamar was stunned, but eventually decided, "Well, we'll see about this," with the intention of getting me the ring assuming I would melt at the sight of it. But try as he might, it never worked out. Lamar, a former jewelry store owner and manager, is a discriminating buyer. He wasn't going to buy just anything or pay just any price. It wasn't anointed.

Every once in a while he would mention it to somebody and the women would think I was so foolish until I told them the story. "Every time I looked at the ring I'd think, 'Ya, I have this nice ring, but somebody doesn't have the gospel,' and it would be a symbol of sadness not pleasure to me. No, I don't want jewelry or any gift if it isn't a reminder of something special." Some understood and some didn't. But I do think it was a good message. Eventually, it was anointed, and yes, I have the ring today and we continue to give to the spreading of the gospel.

I understand how much this woman ached for her husband's love and affection and the pain had gone on for years. She may find a better husband, but he won't fulfill her needs completely either. We have to be full and complete without the jewelry, without his help in the kitchen, without whatever it is that matters so much (for him to listen and to care). The truth is she has a hole in the middle of her soul that only God can fill, and no matter how much her husband tries, it won't ever be enough. I'm assuming he tried a little. They usually do in their feeble way. Some try in a big way and still fail. We are all bottomless pits.

And so we turn on our husbands one remark at a time, one dig at a time, for what he did or didn't do. We see ourselves as a victim of his insensitivity. Men are obtuse creatures. And maybe he does need professional help. Maybe he won't ever change, no matter what you do. But getting a root of bitterness doesn't help. Reaching out for things that will never satisfy is not the answer either. That's what losing my daughter taught me: there were no good answers for me—not another man, not a nicer house, nothing. I didn't know I could know God personally, face to face, at the time.

We must remember adultery is a sin against God. Therefore, it's God who must defend Himself and guide them to repentance. When we insert ourselves in the middle of this, we stop the process and we become the enemy. Look to your own sin; I'm sure you can find some if you look hard enough. And when you find it, be sure to fully grieve over what it means to those you love.

Maybe you are tired of thinking of what you've done wrong. Maybe that's all you do: beat up on yourself. "It's time someone thinks about what hurts me and what they've done wrong. I'm the only one trying to change here. He's had it good. I've been a good wife." And I'm sure that's true. Tracy was a good wife; that wasn't her problem. I'm sure she did lots of wonderful things and was very thoughtful. That's not the point. The point is he wasn't in charge like he felt he should be. His life was out of his control. We don't submit to sin, but we must be very careful and prayerful in how we proceed. We can give in too little or too much. I'm not saying the man is right; I'm just saying we can't be wrong.

> *Oh, God, I don't want to defend myself when what I am doing is indefensible. I want to be right, not in my eyes, but in Yours. I want You to say, "Well, done thou faithful daughter." Not so I can lord it over anybody, but just because it's the way things should be: right. Right in Your eyes. And then I would truly have peace and joy and victory. Oh, blessed victory.*

A Rose by Any Other Name

Many marriages are marred by the gift-giving problem: she remembers and he forgets. She says (in her heart), *"You're here; now prove to me you love me."* The man says (in his heart), *"I'm here; that proves that I love you."*

She's waiting for her rose and never realizes—he's the rose. He has given her his most precious possession—himself, his time, his energy, everything. What more can he give?

Well, she has a few ideas. And because he hasn't given her tokens of his love, she gets hurt, and hurt feelings lead to ungratefulness. She eventually approaches him with ingratitude. She's hurt and unhappy, and he feels frustrated because he's living with an ungrateful wife and there's something within him that resents that and balks at all this tokenism. Enough is enough!

So the two of them are at a standoff. How sad, sad that both have given so much (their lives) and end up with so little. How dare we approach our mate with ingratitude. I know he has faults. I know he leaves a lot to be desired, but ingratitude is the last thing he needs. Appreciate what he has given. Even if its not enough, it's still a lot. And let's face it, they are losing an endless battle. There will probably always be something left undone that will keep you dissatisfied. We must stop looking at what's not been done and appreciate what has been done. The song "Count your blessings, count them one by one." should be our theme song when we approach our husbands.

I need to add a scriptural base to all this: Romans 14:5 says, *"One man esteemeth one day above another: another esteemeth every day alike. Let every man be fully persuaded in his own mind. He that regardeth the day, regardeth it unto the Lord; an he that regardeth not the day, to the Lord he doth not regard it."* Verse 13 says, *"Let us not therefore judge one another any more: but judge this rather, that no man but a stumblingblock or an occasion to fall in his brother's way."*

Satan is the accuser of the brethren, and when we ask for more and become the accuser, saying he hasn't done enough, do you see whose side you are on? When we free our husband from all this, I bet his mind will be more able to think of things on his own. Lamar was terrible about remembering when we were first married, and I never said much about it. I made a joke of it because I'm not much of a rememberer either, and do you know, he's gotten very good at it and I'm still forgetful. Recently I realized I had done very little for him for Father's Day and he did nice things for me for Mother's Day. Now it's time for me to get better. And I know I will. We should all appreciate each other each day for what we do, not what we don't do—both lists are awfully long—which one do you want to dwell on?

THIRTY-SEVEN

**My little children, let us not love in word or
in tongue, but in deed and in truth.**

—1 JOHN 3:18

Bad Choices

WHEN WE RESPOND INCORRECTLY to our mate, or if he or she wants from us things they should not ask or that we cannot provide, one of us ends up with bad choices. What does a woman do when her husband doesn't nurture her or meet her basic emotional needs? What does a man do when his wife will not satisfy him sexually? If she doesn't even try? I mean in the normal way, of course, not some perversion. I know it doesn't seem like much of an answer, but we must take these hurts and frustrations to God. To take them anywhere else is to make them worse.

There is a God-shaped vacuum in each of us and it takes the shape of our unfulfilled needs. We must invite Him to come in and fill this area of our life. I guarantee He can and will. He will fulfill you while you wait for others to get their act together, and He will be whatever you need Him to be. That is why He called Himself "I AM" to Moses when he was to speak to the sons of Israel (Exod. 3:14).

I had a friend years ago, Sybil, that was grossly overweight. She was a big church worker and everyone loved her, but it was like she was disabled. Her husband and kids had to do much of the housework and fetch stuff for her. She couldn't go certain places or sit just anywhere. It was always a factor in everything she did. She was originally very tiny, only five feet tall and one hundred pounds.

Sybil had a very difficult childhood as the oldest and only girl. Her mother was a perfectionist and worked long hours. All of the housekeeping and babysitting fell to Sybil. I feel her weight gave her presence; it made her feel safe. Obesity can be a safe place or a power play. It dealt a fatal blow to their sex life.

Housekeeping can be a power play, too. Anything that a man cares about. But, it's counter-productive to take advantage of your power in this way. It backfires. Sometimes excess weight and bad housekeeping are a result of being shut down emotionally. All of these reasons are spiritual at their core. And they all force the people in their home into bad choices.

Sybil would say, "I can't lose weight. I have tried every diet in the world and it just doesn't come off." We've all been there with some habit we struggle with. I have picked weight because it's so common, but I don't want to limit our discussion to weight. There are many addictions and compulsions that hurt a marriage: overspending, jealousy, gossip, negativism, victimhood, the lottery, Elvis, collecting of some kind, pornography, etc. Compulsion: when you have to have something no matter what it does to your marriage or your loved ones. It takes money from their needs, time, and, most of all, a big part of you. But you can't help it. That's a compulsion. It's bigger than love.

Did you say you can't lose weight or enjoy a sexual relationship? Whatever your problem, here's the piece for you.

"I Can't"

We all know what it's like to have habits we can't break. We eat when we want to diet. We eat foods we shouldn't eat, drink what we shouldn't drink, talk when we shouldn't talk, can't talk when we need to, etc. If you are a Christian very long, you will hear wonderful testimonies of how the Lord has set someone free from drugs, alcohol, cigarettes, cursing, shyness, etc. They give God all the glory and tell you again and again that the Lord did it, and rightfully so. They will often say, "When I quit trying and gave up, then God did it."

You also get the reverse of this: people telling you God won't do it all. You've got to help: the "you've got to pull yourself up by your bootstraps" concept. And there is a great deal of truth in it: God won't do it all. We should pull ourselves up by our bootstraps. When life knocks us down, after a time of recouping and wound licking, we need to get up, brush ourselves off, and keep on keeping on. But there are times when willpower won't do it. Whatever has us in its clutches is stronger than we are.

This self-made man attitude is reverse of the gospel. God is the power in my life. *Where I am weak, He is strong* (2 Cor. 13:9). Our part is saying the prayer, staying away from evil, listening, watching, and receiving. If it's in our power, goodness, or perfection alone, it won't get done.

Some people will tell you to just name it and claim it. Most of us have been around the "good confession" mountain. Confess the positive things you need and then lean on Jesus. I believe He is my strength and my mouth better agree. I believe this. And if my mouth doesn't agree, then I surely won't receive. But we can't force God to do everything we say. There are factors we don't understand. We set ourselves up for disappointment when we don't leave the choices with Him. We just have to be sure it's God's choice and not the devil's. Too many of us accept things God didn't put on us and would remove if we realized it was the devil doing it and asked Him.

People are too often living their own lives their own way, instead of letting Him live His life through them. Since I am doing His thing, His way, then He will sustain me as I do it. I get into the flow instead of asking Him to bless my flow. His flow is better. When it's my flow and I get in a mess and ask Him to help me, He might not answer because it's my flow. So, I stay in His flow and He answers.

Most of the time when someone says "I can't," it's not an "I can't" situation at all. There are some things in life you can't change. When my little girl was fatally hit by a car, that was something I had to accept.

Nothing would change the fact. I could deal with it with the help of God or I could do other things to salve the gaping wound, but I couldn't change the fact: she was not coming back. My life has been enriched by what came out of that experience, but it was hard. I chose to turn to God, and because I did, all that I have today is a result of the relationship that developed.

A person with a habit that leaves them powerless truly feels they can't change it. They've tried so hard for so long that to them it's impossible. It is of utmost importance, when we face a difficult situation, that we realize we are facing something that *can* be changed and thank God for that fact. Then, instead of being defeated, we will be empowered to move ahead with everything in us determined to claim our victory. We will speak victory and grab onto the tools we need to win: the Word and the promises that God has given us, the faith that believes what we *don't* see, the righteousness we have in Jesus, the name of Jesus, and the blood of Jesus. We are not powerless. We have the power of the universe at our disposal waiting for us to speak. Speak it forth and go forth and win that victory. Can you honestly say a hunk of meat or a little white stick of leaves (a cigarette) can win over you, when you and God are working together? I don't think so.

This should give you some encouragement, maybe enough to be open to the possibility that it isn't impossible, and by being open, begin the process of healing. Your "I can't" is a lie. The devil is wrong. Well, partially wrong, like he was with Eve. It's true you can't, but God can.

When we say we can't, the Bible gives us the answer:

> *Since we have united with him in his death, we will also be raised as he was. Our old sinful selves were crucified with Christ so that sin might lose its power in our lives. We are no longer slaves to sin. For when we died with Christ we were set free from the power of sin. And since we died with Christ, we know we will also share his new life. We are sure of this because Christ rose from the dead, and he will never die again. Death no longer*

has any power over him. He died once to defeat sin, and now
he lives for the glory of God. So you should consider yourselves
dead to sin and able to live for the glory of God through Christ
Jesus.

—ROMANS 6:5

Death no longer reigns in me. Talk about a happy person. I am a brand new creation. Throw off that old Midge and take on the new. Praise God that it was possible. I may still have to fight to walk in it, but it now abides in me. I'm not the same. My desire is for Him and to be obedient to what He would have me do, and it's not just me that feels this way. Every Christian has the same experience.

But then I saw myself fail. There are things that I don't have power over. What about them? Paul admits he is failing, too. Sound familiar?

It seems to be a fact of life that when I want to do what is right, I
inevitably do what is wrong. I love God's law with all my heart.
But there is another law at work within me that is at war with
my mind. This law wins the fight and makes me a slave to the
sin that is still within me. Oh, what a miserable person I am.
Who will free me from this life that is dominated by sin? Thank
God. The answer is Jesus Christ our Lord. So you see how it's: In
my mind I really want to obey God's law, (we are no longer so
happy in our sin) but because of my sinful nature I am a slave
to sin.

—ROMANS 7:21–24, NLT

Paul has the same problem we do. Every Christian does. The cords have been cut, now you just have to learn new habits. But the old ones come so naturally. Like an elephant that has been tied to a stake all of its life that has been freed, we have to understand that what freedom means. Romans 8 begins the victory. You really need to read and study it.

There is now no condemnation for them that are found in Him (Rom. 8:1). I don't want to put condemnation on you. Your husband should love you in spite of your size or your problem. He's not perfect either. But this is not the point. The point is, whatever your problem is, you should pray about it and really seek for answers. If God doesn't supernaturally deliver you, then you must do what you can to get your act together and get some help. There are doctors, counselors, support groups, work-out rooms, Christian diet groups, twelve-step programs, organizational professionals, etc. There is an agenda that God has in mind to turn your life around, and it may include something or someone outside of the church. (However, it will not include anything unscriptural. The devil will always try to sabotage you, so don't be naïve.)

Do you want your marriage healed or a hunk of meat? Esau lost his inheritance over it. What is important to you? Really important? We say we love our children, but I wonder, when we do the things we do. Sybil's children were ridiculed for years because of her size. If they are the important thing, then let's do what is best for them and that is for their parents to be healthy, to live a long life, and to be fulfilled in their marriage, both of them. If it takes losing weight, then you must do it.

The definition of an addiction is when love is not enough. In spite of how much you love someone, you know that if you do _____ [go into Internet porno sites, see the other man or woman, smoke that cigarette, or drink that drink, etc.), you jeopardize everything and you still do it: that is an addiction. You eat, drink, gamble, see your lover, or work too long, knowing it will get you in trouble and very likely cause your loved one to leave, but you still eat, drink, gamble, see your lover, or work too long anyway: you are addicted and that has become your god. You have broken the first commandment. Alcoholism is not how often you drink or how much or if you can cut down or quit for a while. That is not the definition of alcoholism. It's when a person drinks at some point, knowing if they are caught, it will cost them everything or something very precious. The compulsive has cycles of procrastination, fulfilling the desire, regret, turning over a new leaf, and then procrastinating again. They have to have the procrastination. Sybil did it even as she studied the Bible. Adulterers do, too.

Weight is terribly hard to lose, but with God, it's possible. It will even be a blessing as you work out your weight problem with Him. I don't care how much you have to lose, it's possible. Go online or to Weight Watchers. Start somehow. Smoking? Do the same. God will help you and be in it with you. Lamar quit and he was your typical three-pack-a-day salesman. A man? Men? Your marriage? Lack of a sexual drive? You can get the victory over your problem. Yes, you need a miracle, and yes, you will get it. The Bible says He will do exceedingly abundantly (Eph. 3:20), and I believe it's just the thing for those "I can't" times in your life. I had a real "I can't" time in my life and God totally turned that around. I'm so blessed. I'm the lucky one. And that's saying a lot. I believe your "I can't" situation will be turned around, too, and you won't regret it so much when you get through it. You will be saying how lucky you are.

Some people have already lost what is precious to them. Drinking and their buddies is all they have left. So, why fight it? The addiction continues to rob from them. There *is* more they can lose. Their health, their apartment, their job, their liver. It's amazing how far down a person can go.

It might be the wife that "falls" and it might not be an affair. It could be gambling, home shopping network, soap operas, etc. It's not unusual for both spouses to be addicted and to more than one thing. Demons travel in groups. Yes, we are dealing with demonic activity. If it's not God, who do you think it is? You, all by yourself? No, it's too insidious for that.

Don't do this alone, without some Christian input. After prayer, see what God brings into your life. You definitely need to talk with a mature Christian and see if they can help. Start walking and He will adjust your steps. Stay in your mess and He has nothing to adjust.

FORGIVING MYSELF

If there is ever an "I can't" situation, it's when we have really hurt someone. I think many of our relationship issues and addictions come from not being able to face a terrible guilt in our past. Yes, it happened to me, more than once.

A few years ago I was involved in a traffic accident that was my fault. It's a wonder someone didn't get killed. Although the other couple was injured, to what degree I honestly don't know because of privacy rights and legal issues. I do know that it never went to court. You can imagine how mortified I was. I'm not used to hurting someone like this, and it haunted me every waking hour for a long time.

I was going through an intersection that I have gone through for years, but the opposite way of what I was used to. My mind read it that I had the right of way when I didn't. There was construction signs that made it all the more confusing. I realized I had made a mistake just before the intersection, but there was no time to stop without stopping in the middle, which would have been worse. All I could pray was, "Jesus, help!" And He did because we didn't die.

After weeks of praying, repenting, and seeking God, I finally got peace. This is what I finally came to understand: I believe in something bigger than happenstance. I have to go to God and ask why me? And they will, too. I will never be perfect. That's why Jesus came, because I wouldn't be. And I have to trust Him to fill in the gap where I have failed and redeem what I can't. Redemption isn't just for eternal life, it's for now. For whatever reason things happened the way they did, I have to go to God and this couple will have to, too. And if what happened brings them closer to God, then that's a good thing. If they weren't ready to die and this helped them see that and be open to the gospel, that's a good thing. If good came out of my daughter's death, then good can come out of this, for them and for me. I had to give it to God to work it all out. I couldn't. At least it had happened with a person who would pray. I could do more than a lot of people could do. I could talk to almighty God on their behalf, and so I did. I prayed that God would send Christians to witness to them and that they would come to know Jesus in a personal way. Who knows? Maybe He already has. I'm still praying for them. And I just believe when I get to heaven, I'll meet them.

One good thing that came out of it was they finally put a light at that intersection. They had too many accidents there just like mine. The officer asked me, "Would you have had this accident if there had been a light?" And I said, "I certainly would not." We call it "Midge's light" when we pass by.

I share this story to help you if you are haunted by things you have done, failures in your life. We all make mistakes, big ones. We hurt people we love and strangers, too. After we have asked God to forgive us, we need to ask them to forgive us and make restitution as much as possible. Then, for their sakes as well as our own, we must allow God to forgive us and forgive ourselves. Trust Him to work in the other people's lives to make it OK and not just OK, but really great. God is not a God of just enough. He's a God of abundance, of too much. And I know He will be that God to not only you, but the people you care about and pray for.

What would I have done to get my little girl back? Anything in my power! "Name it! I'll do it or die trying." I would have given anything for the chance to change things, no matter how hard. Anything! You, on the other hand, may have a situation that *can* be changed and you are saying, "I can't"? You need to be as determined as I would be. See things for what they really are! The truth is losing weight is not an "I can't" situation. Neither is having a good sex life. You can do whatever God has called you to do. Let's start the journey to victory. Instead of defeating ourselves by repeating the lies of the enemy, repeat what Paul says: "*I can do all things through Christ who strengthens me*" (Phil. 4:13).

You can say, "But, I can't do it," and you will be right. You are the prophet of your own life. Or you can say, "By God, I'll do it," and you will be right. Why not be right by succeeding rather than failing? The only way you will do it is by God. As long as you say, "I can't," you can't. When you start saying, "It'll be hard, but I'm going to do it," you will do it. The battle is in your mind first. If you lose it there, you will lose it everywhere.

You must determine in your mind, "If Midge can do it, and other women can do it, then I can do it." If you don't do it for yourself, do it for others. Maybe you don't love yourself enough. Then love somebody else enough. Sacrifice yourself for your loved ones. I didn't do this for me. I did this for my kids. I had no answers. So, I did what was best for them. And in sacrificing myself, I did the best thing for all of us.

I feel sorry for anyone that doesn't love enough to get through their fears and doubts. Tell the enemy to "Shut up." We all have trepidations when we start out. You are in good company. The difference isn't the fear and doubt. The difference is going beyond it to victory. God appreciates when we go beyond, when we go on in spite of our fears. It's called faith.

I just wonder, if you can't win here, when will you win? If you think this one is hard, look around and you will find people facing things much harder. Could you win facing their enemy? I had to get the victory over the loss of my little girl and my marital problems. More recently my son went into acute renal failure. I was talking to a young man his age whose wife had run off with another man. Is kidney failure harder? I don't think so. They both will take a miracle. And we know what it takes to get your miracle: faith, obedience, walking out our miracle.

God isn't running the big roulette wheel in the sky with all of us down here wondering when He will shine upon us and plunk down what we are so desperately begging for. It isn't that way at all. We are in a battle and the victory goes to those who do what it takes to win it. You have an enemy that knows the rules and as soon as you let him know you know them too, he will check you out. This is why becoming a Christian brings on a flood of problems just as you are beginning to get solutions. God in His grace and mercy gets us through these problems with our child-like faith. But just as we are getting wiser and more formidable, so is our enemy. New level/new devil. And God allows it. Just as a mother hen must watch as her chicks peck their way out of the shell, He can't interfere prematurely. It would cripple us. Do you want to be mature or crippled? Then face this devil and face him down. The battle isn't over until you sing. And you might as well sing all the way through. Sing the praises of the Lord for He is worthy of our praise.

If my son is going to get a new kidney a year after he is diagnosed, why can't I rejoice now? Why wring my hands and ruin all the days in-between? This isn't happening to hurt my son, but to make him better. I really believe that. When he comes out of this, he will be a brand new person, with a brand new appreciation of his Father God. And so will his wife and daughters. It will build their faith, too. And so I rejoice today and everyday because the victory is mine.

Sure there was the day I was there when he came home from work looking so dark and worn. No mother wants to see her child's vibrancy sucked from him day after day as he gets worse and worse. I wanted to tell him to quit his job, we'll work it out somehow. But I knew that wasn't best, either. So many answers that weren't answers. I walked away from his home saying, "If I weren't a woman of faith right now, I'd be panicked." And I started to laugh, a laugh that could only come from my spirit.

The inability to deny ourselves something is often a result of being already so denied. A child whose parents have divorced is already so deprived that he or she cannot deprive him or herself any further. So they eat the candy bar. The only way to not be so deprived is to allow God to fill you up so that you no longer have empty places or wounds to lick. Allow Him to heal you and you can put _____(chocolate or whatever else) in its proper place. If chocolate is not your problem, figure out what is and put that in the blank. We carry these hurts into adult-hood and still have an empty place we stuff with things that won't ever satisfy.

How was Sybil denied? She had a terrible childhood and has little contact with her family. They lived clear across the country. Her husband travels in his business and is gone a great deal of the time. She had the children, and that helped. In fact, it's probably what has kept them together, although he loved her a lot and did not want out of the relationship.

She filled her days with church activities, but that has its limits in fulfilling a person, too. It wasn't so much what she didn't have, as much as it was what she did have. She had something controlling her life. She hated it and yet was powerless to change it. So, she justified it. Year in and year out she ran from the truth. Even her relationship with the Lord wasn't enough, because she wasn't allowing Him into all areas of her life. She was keeping Him at arms length, too, and that's what really hurt. But she didn't go there, either.

Things get away from us and the task looks impossible, but do what you can do and He will do the rest. While He's working on you and your problem, He will be working on your husband and his problems. If you aren't working on yours and He succeeds at his, you will be behind, and just remember, it's one step at a time. If you are not taking yours, your husband doesn't have to take his. You are the one holding up the parade.

More than the sex, I think Sybil regrets that her husband has never given his life to the Lord. They have never shared the most important relationship in her life. It never seemed to occur to her that she was not a very good witness for the overcoming power of God in a life. Did it not ever occur to her that his salvation was tied to her witness, and her witness was tied to her obedience, and her obedience was tied to her victory over her weight? God is very real in her life and has sustained her through it all, but God wants so much more. We miss God's best when we hang onto what we should give up.

> *Dear heavenly Father, I don't want anything that I do to stand between You and my husband or children. I am so sorry for all that I have done that has been a stumbling block to them. Forgive me, Lord, and help me to resolve these issues so they can not only forgive me but we can walk free of what binds us. Help me to know what I need to do to begin this work in me. I praise you, Lord, for what you have done so far. Help me to keep walking forward and to claim a healing for not only myself but my family. I pray this all in the precious name of Jesus.*

God has a divine order and you must get in it with your family. You may not be able to hurry your husband, but you sure can move up the time of your own victory. Being open to what He has to tell you will hurry up the process considerably. "Show me Lord what I don't see about myself."

THIRTY-EIGHT

A wise person has great power.

—PROVERBS 24:5

The Marriage Disintegrates

WHEN I TOLD THE story of our secretary in chapter 35, "What God Did Not Intend," the point wasn't for her to gain power over him. The goal was mutual respect. Today, when the woman begins to make threats, especially in America where divorce gives her the house, the kids, and big chunk of his salary, the power shifts in her favor. A smart woman, much as she might be tempted, will not take it. A smart woman knows she is powerful and doesn't need his. We start from a position of strength, but we move in love, grace, and gentleness. A wise woman never flaunts her position. It's so unattractive.

Men relate differently than women. He has family and friends, but it's different. If a woman meets someone, within a few minutes we know if they are married, have kids, and what they do for a living. A man meets someone and he doesn't know any of these things after spending an afternoon together playing golf. And then there are his friends. If he does have any, they are usually too close. They spend time together that should be devoted to the family and they do things married men shouldn't do: drink, gamble, play pool, run around, race cars, womanize, for starters. He gives more of himself, his time, and his money than he should, which brings her to feel the need to break up his friendships, and that doesn't play very well in the relationship no matter how it comes down.

Although they aren't usually as bad as his, he finds her friends threatening, too. This is one reason why a Samson will try to cut his wife off from her emotional support. He can be very jealous, often for no reason. It's not so much that he wants her all to himself, he is just afraid she prefers them to him and will soon realize she doesn't need him. He's the odd man out, or so he thinks; therefore he starts early to sabotage her relationships, which precipitates a problem for her. She didn't have a problem until he started acting so irrationally. He becomes so paranoid she starts questioning the wisdom of their relationship. Things go from bad to worse to intolerable.

Lamar never felt the need for many close friends. He worked in the public and that was enough "togetherness" for him—all the more reason why he needed our relationship to be a good one. When it wasn't, he felt very lonely indeed. And yes, he did try to come between me and my friends. I knew if I had a new friend, it wouldn't be long before she said, "I don't know why, but Lamar doesn't like me," and I would have to have the "he does it to all my friends" talk with her. This is one of the benefits of having the victory: I can now have girlfriends.

Because a woman is an emotional, sexual being, her husband's actions are a real turn-off just when he needs her to prove her love for him. What better way than sexually? He desperately needs to see she still finds him desirable. Well, he was until he acted so badly in front of her family and friends. She becomes increasingly resistant to his overtures of affection, and he doesn't react well to her cold shoulder. It's no longer about sex, if it ever was. Even if a woman sees the foolishness of cutting him off sexually and cooperates to some extent, it's not the same and he knows it. And it will never be the same, ever. Which really isn't as bad as you might think because it wasn't as good as you thought it was. It was a façade. And the façade is crumbling fast. Why regret it when what you end up with can be so much better? But it will take a miracle.

To make it through, it will take at least one taking every thought into captivity and matching it to the Word. She must fight the tendency to allow herself to be isolated, to get a victim mentality, or to become too independent. Any wrong way of thinking will be harmful to her and their relationship. It's so hard to know how to handle these marriages.

When a husband is overly controlling or abusive, his wife naturally begins to consider her options. If she has kids and no source of support, that is a big roadblock and he knows it. This type of man I call a Samson, will work to put her in a position where she has no options. That's why he sabotages her relationships and her attempts to lose weight or get an education, etc. When he makes positive changes impossible, she gives up. She lets herself go, gains weight, watches too much television, and generally has a bad attitude. She may just seem a little quieter than usual or withdrawn. Some women aren't mouthy and reactionary. Everyone around her notices the change and it's not good.

This is when the criticism hits a new level. Not only from her husband, who does it to keep her in line, but from friends and family too (in the form of encouragement to make changes, of course). And even if she doesn't say it, she agrees. She knows she's not doing what she should. She's not being the wife or mother she should be, but they don't understand how hard he has made it. They think she should just put him in his place and do what she has to do. Make him the enemy and fight him. But she doesn't have it in her. They don't realize how strong he is, that no matter what she does, he'll find her and make her pay. What they are telling her to do won't work for her. She loves him and knows he loves her and anyhow, she has kids to worry about. She can't make it on her own. As much as family might want to help, that wouldn't work either. At this point there are no good answers and so she withdraws, eats her bonbons, and allows things to rock on. At least she and the kids have a roof over their heads. In case you didn't recognize it: this is depression.

She is an accident waiting to happen. Everything everyone does just makes things worse. Drugs and alcohol, inappropriate sexual relationships, or something is going to step into the void. If she does get a job, more education, or lose weight, we will find that as she feels better about herself, he feels worse, not about her, but about the relationship. His worst fears are being realized. He is trying to clutch onto something he could never hold, and she is pulling away from what she doesn't really want to leave. The more determined he is, the more determined she is, and yet neither wants the result of their struggle: the split-up of their marriage. The biggest problem is that neither sees the problem. It isn't that they don't love each other, the problem is they are misreading what the other is doing and why. Perception is the problem. He thinks she doesn't love him and she thinks he doesn't love her. It's not about love, it's about fear: his fear of losing her.

It's about now that many divorces happen, however, they are not the solution. They are just another mess upon a mess. This woman doesn't need a divorce, she needs to begin to walk scripturally, to see the lies for the lies they are and quit being the victim and having a pity party. We are not poor little beaten-down creatures. We are children of the most high God, and we need to begin to act like it, not by getting even or bitter or angry, but by walking in love, creating the world we want to see, and living.

Much as he might like to believe you when you tell him you would never leave, his insecurity speaks louder than anything you or anyone else might say. The problem isn't with you; the problem is with him, with his thinking. If he thinks there is a problem and he reacts as if there is a problem, there is a problem. If there isn't one now, he will make one very soon. Perception is reality. That's why your moves to be independent and to be able to get along without him only make things worse.

You are blessed and highly favored. Claim it, and claim it for him, too (Luke 1:28). If we're losing right now, the game isn't over. Don't allow what the enemy is saying through anyone—you, your husband, parents, friends, etc.—to stand. Put a hedge around them and speak what you want to see, constantly. Go through your home taking your authority over the demons that are attempting to get a toehold there or that already have. Send them to the dry places, but just know, they will try to ride back in on the coattails of the people that come and go, at least until they reject them, and that will take a while.

Reject the victimhood being foisted on you, your husband, and your family. You can't be the child of an awesome God and be a victim. It just doesn't compute.

DOUBLE-MINDED MAN

The last time Lamar and I came close to divorce was after we moved to Florida. I had been a Christian for over five years by then, so it wasn't because we weren't saved and committed. Things had gotten so bad I thought I better tell our oldest son his father and I "may not make it." His response, "After all this?" It kind of shocked me. Wasn't Grant as tired of it as I was? He always had been in the past. All I could come up with was now that he was about to leave (he was in high school), he would like to be able to come home to one home instead of two. After all, we were his family. Good or bad, it was home and he didn't want to lose it now. Since we had come this far, he probably figured we should be able to work things out and we should. But the truth is Christians don't always do the right thing. I wish it weren't so, but it is. And I'm not saying which one is in the wrong because I don't know. But if I talk with you very long, I can usually figure out a few things you're both doing wrong. (And you could probably point out a few mistakes I'm making, too.) It did something to me to have to stand alone.

As I prayed, it was revealed to me that I really wanted out of this marriage. I couldn't believe it. That meant I was a double-minded man. I thought I was the good guy and God was challenging me on it. Here I was thinking I was the one holding my marriage together when the truth was there was a place in me that wanted out. It would feel good to be out of the stress and start over. Who can blame me for wanting out? But when I thought of the mess divorce would cause, especially for the boys—me dating, Lamar dating, remarriage for both of us—I sure didn't want that. I didn't want another man. But let's be honest. I knew me and I knew eventually I would get "involved." I realized I was not the good guy at all. I was as much of the problem as Lamar. I repented immediately of being double-minded and for my part in our problems. I prayed for a renewed marriage, a healed one, and became single-minded in my desire for Lamar and I to be together and happy. That would take a miracle. Finally, I was in line to get it.

> *A fool's mouth is his undoing, and his lips are a snare to his soul.*
>
> —PROVERBS 18:7

A modern-day Samson makes an enemy of the woman he tries to control. The trouble begins when she realizes how bad things really are when she has had enough. As long as she is controlled by the lies and manipulations, everything seems fine or at least good enough to stay together. But when she finally wakes up, that's when all hell breaks loose, literally. This is why it's so important that you not only wake up, but have your spiritual side awakened, too, and not only awakened but mature. This is why I advise a woman should stay in the home if her husband is not physically abusing her so she can fight the spiritual battle and he is not panicked about her being gone.

HE PRECIPITATES THE FIGHTS

You many wonder why if he doesn't want to lose you, why does he cause so many fights? It's simple: fear, anger, sin; dumb reasons that make no sense. He's trying to gain back some power if only by weakening you or ways that might help you get power. At best, these men are double-minded, wanting the best for their wives but not wanting to lose her. There's that awful word again—double-minded. If they are single-minded, it's on holding onto her. He never expected her to succeed. If it looks like your husband is sabotaging you all the time, he probably is. He is not doing it because he doesn't love you; he is doing it because he does.

You must have the truth in your head and heart to counteract it: the truth of God's Word. Review often the things He has done to begin to bring you out of your mess. Keep your testimony current. But most of all, read your Bible. While all this strife and confusion is going on, it's of utmost importance that you know who you are in Christ: *You are forgiven. You are esteemed. You are loved. You are important. You are the apple of*

God's eye (Psalm 17:8). God has a plan for your life. You are an important part of many plans. Nobody can do what He needs you to do.

Sometimes our husband is doing something awful like being involved with Internet pornography, having an affair, or failing in business and he is afraid if we find out, we will leave. I cannot stress strongly enough the need for you to get to the root of your husband's problems, be they sexual, mental, emotional, physical, or spiritual. Until you know the depth of the problem, nothing you do to try to solve it will work because he will continue to try to hide the truth from you because he doesn't want to lose you. So instead of being honest, he turns it around on you and tries to make you look bad: like your problems are your all fault when they are really his. It's not that he doesn't love you; it's that things are a bigger mess than you can imagine and that's why you need, not only help to find out what the real problem is, but once you find it, you need the wisdom and love of God to handle it properly. You must be controlled by the Holy Spirit and not by your emotions.

He is scared and his fear has turned inward. It may seem like he doesn't love you, but that's not true. There is a place in him that loves you dearly and cares a great deal. Don't assume he doesn't love you; assume he does. If he tells you his love for you has died, and more than likely he will, God can give him a new love for you, a better one.

I don't want you to think these men pick losers. Delilah was not a loser. She had her flaws; that was part of her allure, but she was not a loser. I don't think Lamar picked me because no one else would have me, but I do think he saw in me a person that was not only sweet and gentle, but also a person who was dumb. He could manipulate me because of my natural peacemaking tendencies, and he liked the way I looked. They pick us because they see in us a potential enabler, or because we are so smitten. If we love them that much, they figure they will get their way and we won't leave. When we aren't so smitten (dumb, codependent, nice, enabling), they begin to worry.

Just because someone is good-looking or especially sharp doesn't mean he knows it in his heart. He may even know it in his head, but things happened in his past that told him he wasn't good enough, especially sharp, or worthy of love. Many top performers, people like Cary Grant, no matter how much they are loved and fawned over, still have feelings of inadequacy that they find impossible to shake. When they get into a relationship that takes advantage of this side of their psyche, it's very easy for them to succumb to abuse. Physical, verbal, and emotional abuse are not uncommon among even the best known and loved actresses.

The problem is his low self-esteem. You might wonder why Samson might have had low self esteem. Think about it. There was no one more important in the world than Samson at the time. Shouldn't that have been enough? Think of how "wanted" he was. His parents yearned for a baby for years. Once they got him, he was loved and nurtured for years. The answer is not in nurturing. Don't get me wrong, nurturing and parenting is crucial, but it cannot make up for a break in our relationship with God. What sin does to us cannot be counteracted by anything else. In spite of his looks, money, power, and charisma, as long as unrestrained appetites drive him, Samson will not see himself as worthy or desirable enough. His low self-esteem or self-image comes out of his sinfulness. He knows what he is: he's a fraud. He fears the day he is exposed. But he needn't worry about being exposed by someone else. The same devil that makes him do what he does, will also make him expose the dirty deed.

All men fear being exposed as the fraud they know they are. This fraud "thing" is more important than we realize. I wish I could explain it like John Eldredge does in *Wild At Heart*. He says, "This is every man's fear: to be exposed to be an imposter, and not really a man."[1]

America today seems to think a good self-image will be enough. If Samson's bad self-image was a problem, then a good self-image should be the answer. Right? Wrong! A good self-image is wonderful, but it's not enough. It doesn't overcome the affects of sin. You can't good attitude yourself out of your sin. If you are living in sin, you know it and it affects the way you think about yourself. Period. There is only one way to deal with this problem. Since it's God that made the rules, only God can help you when you have broken one. Samson went to Him, and I'm sure he felt better in spite of everything coming down around him. I myself would like to get the victory just a tad sooner and live to enjoy it.

My New Self-Image

I had been hearing quite a bit about self-image, people encouraging the listener to have one. So, I prayed about it and pondered the subject. I asked myself what is this thing, this "self-image" that I am supposed to get? Well, self is a problematic word to a Christian. We are fearfully and wonderfully made, but we are told to be careful how full of self we are. Right off the bat I had trepidations, but I was committed to figuring this out.

An image is a likeness. It's not the real thing; it looks like the real thing. We are made in the image of God, but we are real. Fake things are not usually good. Better to have the real thing. I may be made in the image of God, but I didn't know about being an image of myself. So far it wasn't that encouraging, but I moved on.

So I visualize me getting an image or cut-out of myself and propping it up. Now what? Since I'm supposed to have a good one and it's a rather plain flat cardboard thing, I feature a pile of pretty jewels and baubles that I can paste on this "image," each stone representing something good. I pick one up and think about something good about me that it could represent: my personality. I have such an open, welcoming personality, it will make my image look a lot better. I get ready to stick it on my image. Then I hear an inner voice: "Welcoming personality indeed. You're so pushy and opinionated and mouthy. You call that a nice personality? You're just a nuisance and irritating." The voice is so harsh and critical I drop the gem, shaken to the core.

I eventually gather myself and decide if I'm going to do this, I better try again. I pick up another bauble and think about what it could represent: "My sense of humor. Yes, that's it." I start to stick that one on when I hear, "Your sense of humor? You have the most warped sense of humor I have ever seen. Are you kidding me? You're just weird." Rebuked again. I wonder about another, let's see....If I even begin to think of one, it's immediately counteracted with the other opinion. In panic I pray, "God, how can I have a good self-image if even my good points aren't good?"

This is when God helped me see that's why He sent Jesus, because I do have faults and I do fail. Big time. Even my good points are good because He made them. Only He can deliver me and heal me and anoint and soften the heart of my enemies. I have to take even my gifts to God to redeem and help me channel them. There is nothing more powerful than our gifts to pull us off course, causing us get the big head and leading us down the road to destruction. As long as we have unconfessed sin in our lives, we will have a self-image problem.

There is the possibility that your husband doesn't care, that he has been spoiled or not bonded properly and cannot relate normally. This is why it's so important to understand a person's childhood. But even after you know all of that, there will still be unknowns that only God knows and that's why you need to keep in close contact with Him, so He can show you things when you are ready to hear them. That's why we're working on you.

Trying to make sense out of sinful behavior when it makes no sense is a lesson in futility. I am trying to help you understand that a controlling, dysfunctional guy has ways of thinking that you do not possess. There are things you can do, but matching his irrational behavior with rational behavior is not the answer. You need godly wisdom. I'm not saying you won't ever be rational, but do in it context of what God reveals to you.

A vicious cycle has begun that a man cannot break without help, and yet he fights every attempt anyone makes on his behalf. This is what makes it so difficult to turn around, so self-defeating, self-perpetuating. Moreover, just as the enemy is convincing our husband of some pretty dumb stuff, he is convincing us of stuff just as dumb (we're not good enough, pretty enough, smart enough, etc.). And just as he thinks it makes a lot of sense, we think our garbage makes a lot of sense, too. It's not so much that we are wrong because the truth is we can't be pretty "enough" or thin "enough" because it isn't about being pretty or thin. If we succeed in making ourselves beautiful or thin, then it will be something else. Because he needs an excuse so that it's your fault and not his. He can't stand to face the fact that the problem is in him. The worst thing in his mind is for you to succeed in getting thin, beautiful, educated, self-supporting, etc., because then you will leave. It's our assumptions that are wrong, and because they are wrong, our perspective and approach are wrong. That makes us wrong.

Sometimes we have "issues" because the sin in other people's lives has adversely affected us. We don't always know why we have a self-image problem or that we have the problem. It's not our sin; it's their *their* sin. In this next story, I don't know how this girl ended up the way she did. I just know she did with a poor self-image.

How Do I Look?

How you look is more important than your comfort. You simply cannot look like a tramp or a clown, a homeless person, a teeny-bopper, or like you just got out of bed. It isn't an option. It's "missing the mark," which is what sin is. God cares how you dress and look and what people think. And so do your loved ones.

Don't wear tapered pants; they just make your butt look big. Don't line your lips. You never see the make-up artists do it. Watch your "bling." A little goes a long way. Don't use your body as a display case for a piece of art. Just because a piece of cloth is lovely, doesn't mean it will do anything for you. Frame it and put it on your wall.

Watch your florals and how short your skirt is. Remember, driers shrink clothes. Don't wear something if it's too tight, and for goodness sakes, don't wear baggy stuff, either. Neither makes you look thinner. Give yourself a shape even if you don't think you have much of one. Covering up doesn't work. It just makes you look like a bigger blob. Update your look at least every ten years. If you are forty, at least dress like you are thirty and not thirteen. It just makes you the brunt of the joke for you to look so ridiculous. Yes, men do look beyond the clothes and fall in love, but they still wish she dressed and looked as good as she could.

I am appalled at how women dress and put on their makeup. If your husband is not happy about something about your appearance, correct it. At least do what you can. Men are usually a good judge of what looks good on their woman. Most of these men (that love outrageously dressed women) would love it if she would change her look. Then again, some men are clueless about fashion and what looks good.

ANOTHER OPTION

Because weight is so hard to lose, the new fad is stomach stapling or bypass surgery. They are coming to find out it's not the wonderful answer they thought it was. It has its limitations and drawbacks that need to be considered. You can shrink your stomach on your own with probably not as much pain.

Have you watched any of the extreme make-over shows? I'd be interested in a follow-up program one, two, and five years later. On one show, a girl had very spaced-out teeth and a complexion problem among other things. They fixed it all. She looked like an entirely different person and yet some of the things that made her special like her big dimples were still there. She did look great at the end, a little like Sandra Bullock. Everyone was thrilled. But the look on her husband's face was the most telling of all. Such apprehension. He seemed like a real sweet guy, but I don't know that either of them was ready for this.

It's good that she thinks so much better of herself, but that is just outward beauty. She's going to need wisdom on how to handle the changes this will bring to her family. I just don't know that she will have this kind of help or know how to get it for herself. The last thing she said was she was going to be changing diapers and doing the dishes. You know her baby thought she was beautiful the way she was. And her husband saw something special, too. She really was beautiful before. Everybody seemed to know it, but her. Will she be satisfied with what she had before? Will it do something to her head to have all this attention? So far she's been a loving, giving wife and mother; has she now become self-absorbed? All this attention is pretty heady stuff. I pray for them, because they are going to need it.

In a marriage there more dynamics at work. Some men are not secure enough to have a woman who is so beautiful and outgoing. All of a sudden everything revolves around her, not him and the kids; the dynamics have changed. She is like a bird out of a cage and he's the cage. The "cage" is his castle, and he wants his queen happy there, not running hither and fro with a "new life."

If he married her for the way she was and she changes so completely, where does that leave him? These problems must be taken into consideration. We shouldn't have to stop our healing and maturity to satisfy their needs, but we can't ignore them either. This is one reason why fast change is not necessarily the best way because he needs time to adjust, and you do, too. You need time to change in ways that will help you sustain the change.

It amazes me how many people don't do the work they need on their teeth. It makes such a difference. I know it costs a lot of money, but I have found most dentists will work with you. I would rather have nice looking teeth than new clothes or a new car. Get dental insurance or just pay as you go.

Most women don't really need breast implants. A little plastic surgery is all they need and working out with weights and losing some weight. A dermatologist is usually covered for some or all of it under major medical. It's actually doable without *Extreme Makeover* coming to our rescue. Let's rescue ourselves.

Start with a mini-makeover of hair and make-up. It's amazing what we can do for a few dollars. I am shocked at how many women don't have their hair done and don't wear make-up. No wonder they think they look so bad. I do too when my hair isn't done and I have no make-up on. I think of myself as Rembrandt and my face as my canvas, but I keep a very light touch. Nothing worse than too much make-up. Watch these shows and listen to what people are telling you. Take a little good advice once in a while.

Did you know that your body believes your face? If you force yourself to smile, your body will respond positively. Force yourself to do what you think you can't do and you will find everything will get in line behind your decision.

If nobody ever comes to you and offers you a complete make-over, can you be satisfied with yourself? I hope so. It's really what's inside that matters. If these women had never had the makeover, they could still have come to see how precious they were to God. He wants you to be whole so much so that He will do it for you as you yield yourself and your needs to Him. Before you can bring wholeness to your marriage, you must bring wholeness to yourself. Since Jesus said everything we need was finished when He was dying on the Cross, then all we need to do is receive it (Him). I hope you have already received, but if you haven't, please stop and do it now.

> *Dear God, I so desperately want to be whole again. Maybe I never have been whole. Maybe I don't even know what it is. Come into my inner being, Lord, with Your healing power and infuse me with love, a love that I can pour out on the hurting around me. Take out any bitterness or unforgiveness and give me the grace to walk through this mess I call my life in a way that is helpful and not hurtful. I want to stop the devastation from coming down the generations any further. I want the pain to stop with me. I want everything You have for me. I need Your Holy Spirit in my life. Help me to live in a way that doesn't inhibit Your power in me. Forgive me for the controlling and manipulating I have done and help me to see it in the future so I can stop doing what harms your plans for my family and myself. Oh God. I need You so much. I love You so much, for only You have seen*

from the beginning and understand. I praise You for Your grace that has covered me thus far. In Jesus name I pray. Amen.

Now I'd like to include this very special letter I wrote to Lamar one day in the midst of our mess.

My Beloved,

I am writing this to say I'm sorry. Forgive me for making you feel guilty for your actions of late. The Bible tells me not to give place to my flesh and I didn't obey. I was hurt and frustrated, but I shouldn't have given in to it. I was wrong and I came against you wrongly. I agreed with Satan, but I didn't see it at the time. The Bible says there is now no condemnation for them that are in Christ Jesus. I know you received Jesus as your Savior and gave your life to God and you are His now. The Bible also says when God has begun a good work, He is faithful to finish it. I believe this and I had no right to act otherwise. How could I doubt God? You are His. And He is faithful. He will work out our problems. And yet, I panicked and acted in unbelief, as if God wouldn't or couldn't finish the job. He can and He will.

Our family—you and I—was bought by a price. We are not up for bids any more. Satan can't come and "decide" he wants us. There's a No Sale sign on us. The sign doesn't say the house is perfect; it just says it's been sold. I don't know how much of a bargain God got but it's a buyer beware philosophy here.

I think God knew the house had termites and a leaky roof when He bought it. I think God wanted this location in spite of our condition. I just have to believe God is up to the repair job no matter how it looks now as we look at the rubble. I don't think we should panic every time Satan pulls out a bad board and agree the job is impossible. I think every time he shows us a bad board we should praise God that He sent a Carpenter. Sure you still do things you shouldn't. God knows we are human. He's not surprised by out failures. That's why He's a Father to us. That is why Jesus has to EVER intercede for us. That is why He says not to worry about tomorrow because there is enough evil in today. God is not kidding Himself. He knows the battle we face. He didn't save us because we could do it ourselves. He saved us because He saw how much we needed it. Why would He save us and then leave us to drown in it all? He hasn't. He will take us through. Through the finances, the liquor, the drugs, the family problems, whatever. And your deliverance, when it comes, will be to God's glory because you and I will know He did it, not you. You will testify to God's glory in this.

There is now no condemnation to them which are in Christ Jesus, who walk not after the flesh, but after the Spirit. For the law of the Spirit of life in Christ Jesus hath made me free from the law of sin and death. For what the law could not do, in that it was weak through the flesh, God sending his own Son in the likeness of sinful flesh, and for sin, condemned sin in the flesh: that the righteousness of the law might be fulfilled in us, who walk not after the flesh, but after the Spirit.

—ROMANS 8:1–4, GNB

Before Paul wrote this, he wrote:

We know that the law is spiritual; but I am a mortal man, sold as a slave to sin. I do not understand what I do; for I don't do what I would like to do, but instead I do what I hate. Since what I do is what I don't want to do, this shows that I agree that the Law is right. So, I am not really the one who does this thing; rather it is the sin that lives in me. I know that good does not live in me—that is, in my human nature. For even though the desire to do good is in me, I am not able to do it. I don't do the

*good I want to do; instead, I do the evil that I do not want to do.
If I do what I don't want to do, this means that I am no longer
the one who does it; instead, it is the sin that lives in me.*

—ROMANS 7:14–20, GNB

*You and I are proof of our human frailty. God is going to show
us His Omnipotence. We are the clay; He is the potter. Is the clay
guilty? Does it chastise itself? Of course not. Clay just lies there;
not the potter.*

*Does the person who fires gold get upset with each firing?
Does he regret having to do it? No. He knows it has to be done
and he plans for it. Hotter and hotter, each firing skims off a
different form of dross. He isn't upset. He doesn't say "Darn.
Look at all that dross." Dross isn't a surprise to Him. It's a part
of the process. God is not surprised by any of this. He knew it
would take time to win the victories, to renew our minds and
to heal our deep inner hurts. He loves us and He's not going
anywhere. He's waiting to make His move. His timing is perfect.
It just seems like a long time to us.*

*We are the sheep of His pasture and He is the Good Shep-
herd. He will find us when we wander off. He will bring us home
and put oil on our wounds and pull the briars out of our wool.
He will carry us until He's taken care of us and we are ready to
return to the fold. We are the sheep of His Pasture. Sometimes
I forget this.*

*I love you. I forgive you and hope you forgive me. The Bible
tells us to edify each other. I am human and I need edifying too.
I'm not a Super Mom. I need God to help me and comfort me
and I need God to minister to me through you. God's arms are
your arms in my life. I need a shoulder to cry on and a hand to
take mine. Even when you've failed, I still need you. I don't want
the gap to grow wider because of our failures. I want us to put
these things behind us. Forget the bad and hold onto each other
as God does whatever He's going to do.*

God won't ever let us go. Why should we fear and worry and fret? Do we think His hand is shortened or His ear deaf? God will restore the years that the locust has eaten. We are very blessed. We've already been to our lowest point and we will not go back to it again. We will win this battle. I stand believing only this. I shall prevail. You shall prevail. I will believe nothing less!

I love you,

Your other half

THIRTY-NINE

God shall send forth his mercy and his truth.
—PSALM 57:3, MOFFATT

Believing a Lie

MOST DYSFUNCTIONAL MARRIAGES START out very happy with the best of intentions on both parts. Things go awry somewhere along the line, but the potential was there all along. Our first assignment is to understand what it was that the enemy was able to use so effectively against us. Unbelief, manipulations, strife, confusion, and ignorance of the Word are all root problems, but what was your open door? What was his open door?

One day God spoke the word *scrupulous* to me. I knew what He meant: be scrupulously honest about everything. I was surprised He said it because I'm a very honest person. Evidently there was something I wasn't being honest about. Now it was just a matter of figuring out what. Since the truth sets me free and I want to be free, then I need to be scrupulously honest. Every little mis-thought defeats you.

Honesty is very important in our relationships, but very hard to come by. Before a person can be honest with others, they have to be honest with themselves. That's the really hard part.

I had an acquaintance years ago who dearly loved her husband. He was the sweetest guy. They never had children. After years of going the medical route, they decided to adopt. She was thrilled because it looked so promising. Then, all of a sudden, he backed off. She was sad but accepted his decision, assuming someday he would come around. He never did. What she didn't know, his best friend changed her husband's mind. When he went by to tell him the good news about the plans to adopt, the friend rained all over his parade. But he never told his wife because he didn't want her to hold it against him. He just started talking like he had reservations about it and put it off.

Years later one of his family members inadvertently made reference to it assuming she knew. She was devastated. What hurt the most was that he put his friends' opinion over hers, and then to not even tell her made it worse. Here she thought she and her husband had an especially close relationship and shared everything, but they hadn't shared one of the most important decisions in their lives.

This happens quite often in a relationship. We just never know when something influences the other person, and it seems like the greater the impact the more likely they are to keep it from us. It's the beginning of a chasm that grows ever wider until something bridges the gap, a gap we didn't even know existed. We know things have changed, but we don't know why. When we finally find out, we feel betrayed, like our whole relationship was a lie, and to a certain extent it was. There will always be a certain amount of "privacy" that every person keeps, but when it involves your partner, he or she has a right to know.

I had this happen in one of my closest relationships. Evidently she was having misgivings about a project we were involved in, but didn't tell me. Coming from an alcoholic family, she isn't good with putting things out there. By the time it came out, it was all over. All our time, money, and effort were for naught. I was devastated because it was going so well. It wasn't the project that was failing; it was something inside her that no longer had peace.

I had no input in the decisions that were made, even though I was heavily invested in the venture. It would've been nice if we could have discussed it after I learned she had changed her mind. She had heard from God. As far as she was concerned, we just needed to move on. Which would have been fine, but I wasn't getting confirmation that her decision was from God. I was getting that her decision was wrong. It was the enemy making a bid to rob us of our blessing. It's especially hard when two Christians feel they are hearing from God and what they are hearing is so different. This is when it's especially important to talk, and also wait. It isn't God that rushes us when things aren't right. It's the enemy.

How do we know what is God and what is "the enemy"? The Bible says His sheep know His voice. But what if there are two sheep and they are getting something different? That is when I feel you need to back off and pray. If it's God, He will not have you keep it from the significant other person in the project. If it's God, He will speak to the other, like He did Joseph for Mary. He will not tell you to do something that will hurt or harm the person or make you break a promise or your word to them. In other words, if it's God, He will go through the proper process to bring the other person around.

If the person is not a Christian, maybe we shouldn't have given our word and made promises. But once we have, I just don't see Him asking us to break our word. God keeps His Word and expects us to, too. How you get out of a project is as important as how you get into it, and the devil will try to get you to rush any time he can.

God can do things in a hurry, but He doesn't rush us when there is confusion. Usually we are being pushed by "the enemy" prematurely when there are things in the way that need to be considered. I never want anyone to go against what they feel God has said to them. But if it's God, He doesn't mind you being sure. Sometimes this "being sure" (waiting) has the feel of torment when you talk with the person, but Christians will usually see it as "not having peace."

Christians are big on being led by their inner man to do things and that is wonderful when it is in obedience to the still small voice within. Yes, His sheep know His voice, but what about sheep in denial or playing games? There are things that warp our ability to hear properly. That's why we have the Word, but then we fight using the Word.

It must be scriptural. The problem was, my friend had her scriptures and I had mine. She had her counselors and I had mine, and they didn't agree. The Bible tells us there is safety in a multitude of counselors. The problem was the counselors weren't getting together. Nobody was getting together to discuss this.

This feeling led thing is not easy. You really have to be right with the Lord, and too often we don't even know that we aren't. That's why denial is so dangerous.

Even Jesus didn't always feel led to do something, like when His mother asked Him to perform His first miracle. Sometimes what God wants us to do is totally against every fiber of our being, and we have to fight tooth and nail to get past all this and do it. And many fail. They can't get past it, or they don't even try. They think it's Satan and tell him to "get thee behind me."

My friend wants us to go back to the way things were before all this happened, but that isn't possible. My brain has totally recomputed. Where there was trust, there is now doubt. All of a sudden I'm a skeptic, the worst possible thing to be when I should be loving and supporting. I am now a person in grief. I have lost something very precious to me: the faith I had in a person I loved and trusted. And the longer I have to stifle, the longer it will be before we are in a good place in our relationship.

It's as if I can't heal. As long as she doesn't acknowledge what this has meant to me, as long as she doesn't grieve, too, I can't seem to give it up. I'm sure she is grieving because it was hard for her to regroup, but she is grieving more for what it did to her and her family than what it did to me and my family. If she had cared, really cared, she would have come to me and talked about it. Christians talk a lot about loving someone, and then do things that hurt them deeply and don't even acknowledge it. It reminds me of when Jesus said, "They know not what they do." How could they not know? They just asked for Barabbas and not Him. They knew He was innocent. They knew, but they didn't "know." And, like Jesus, I have had to say, "Forgive them." But I don't feel any different. But forgiving isn't a feeling; it's an act. So now I just have to keep standing on this decision (to forgive) and wait for the feelings to line up with it.

I never had Lamar cheat on me, so I never had to deal with the issue of trust with him, although he wouldn't always tell the whole truth about things. You know how guys do so we won't get upset about something. So there was a little mistrust there, but not anything like an affair. I can now understand why these women can't heal. You go on. You find a place of peace, but you are emotionally estranged from that person. This is why accountability is so important. And as long as she is not committed to being honest, there is no accountability. Right now, I know if we were in another situation and she started getting doubts, she would do it again.

When I recomputed, I suddenly realized this wasn't the first time she had kept something important from me. In fact, it hadn't just happened once, it had happened a few times and over very important matters. It's the way she handles all her big problems, and I am supposedly her best friend, the one who could have helped her so her problems would not have been nearly as big or gone on for as long as they did. But she wanted to keep up a good front. Well, her front eventually falls. Can't she see that? I inevitably find out. Why not tell me early enough to help?.

And then the problem is, once we make our decision as she did, we look at everything to justify our decision, so we never rethink what we have done because we are so sure it was God and we were right.

I call what this friendship has become: a shallow invalid relationship. Shallow because it never was allowed to get very deep, although I didn't know that. Invalid because we aren't being honest. I can do shallow. I just don't like doing it. But as I do shallow I am praying and standing and binding the devil and praying a hedge of thorns around any ungodly relationships, and that includes Christians. Yes, I can stifle, but when I do, I am also very offensive in fighting the good fight of faith. Don't let the smile on my face fool you. I am very proactive, just proactive in very quiet, loving ways—kind of like Jesus.

We can at any time change a valid relationship into an invalid one or vise-versa. At the moment we, or that person, decides to start hiding the truth and feel that for some reason the truth would be too hurtful or destructive, we, or they, have begun down a path that in the end will destroy the relationship unless somehow the secret is exposed. Early is better than late. It just seems so much worse if you have been lied to for twenty years rather than for a week. This is why we must be truth seekers. It just never dawned on me this person would be anything but honest with me or would not allow me some input into the decision. And I know many husbands and wives feel this way—stunned. How do I get back to where we were? I've somehow lost my way. As I have walked this painful journey, I have finally gotten my eyes off of myself and my own pain and realized the pain she is in. And what is so awful is that it's all so self-perpetuating. The dysfunctional ways of coping she was taught as a child have become a way of life, and this very way of dealing with things keeps her from bringing about the changes she so desperately needs so she can heal. She keeps herself in her own bondage.

And for a while, I didn't care. Since stifling was so hard and the relationship now so painful and we are all so busy, it's easy to not see each other. It's hard to make the effort to seek out someone with whom we have "issues." And so, I didn't. And then I watched a Christian TV show. The pastor gave a scripture and told what it meant and said God didn't mean for us to withdraw from our family members. Busted! "OK, God, help me see how to handle this new initiative. Because I know I will need You to help me when I go."

I did go, and we had a very good visit. She understands how I felt and that this is an area she needs to work on. She has promised to stop keeping things I need to know from me and to be more honest with other people, too. Praise God!

WILLIAM C. MOYERS

Bill Moyers' son, William C. Moyers, wrote in his book, *Broken: My Story of Addiction and Redemption*, how hard it was to face that he had a problem with drugs and alcohol.[1] The first "incident" came on the heels of William being so caring when his parents brought their youngest son home from the hospital. Later, after William had a chance to go out, they got a call from the police; William was in their custody! Imagine how shocked they were to hear their wonderful oldest son was in trouble. It just didn't make sense—not William.

His mother told how out of character it was. But William now admits it was very indicative of what was going on internally. This was his character.

He was able to be something on the outside that he wasn't on the inside. They felt he was so special, but he didn't feel that way. He felt he didn't deserve what he had; he was a fraud. Does this sound familiar?

Much of his feeling of unworthiness comes from the absence of his father in the very earliest years of his life. Bill was absent because he became involved with LBJ's bid for the presidency in 1960. JFK made him deputy director of the Peace Corps during that very significant era. It was something a journalist couldn't turn down, or he felt he couldn't. But a child's emotional development can't wait, and they can't understand the significance of it all. He or she is so egocentric they think everything is their fault. They cannot compute it any other way. William was wonderful and worthy of love and attention, but never quite convinced himself. And all along he looked like he was doing so well.

William said for years when he was told in counseling he needed to surrender, he rejected it because he felt surrender was a form of giving up, of being a coward, something that just wasn't acceptable in his home. They were can-do people. You don't give up. You fight. You make it happen. But he wasn't able to fight this the toughest of enemies: drugs and alcohol. There are others just as tough: adultery, manipulation, control, fear, unbelief, etc., but I don't know that they are any tougher. And isn't this the attitude most of us have: pull yourself up by your bootstraps. If you cared enough, you would do it.

William was asked how he was able to hide his addictions (and it was a lot) and be an award-winning journalist. He just shook his head as he thought about how much of his energy it did take.[1] We cannot imagine how much these people put into hiding what is going on inside. That's why I say try to understand what is on the inside, so that your husband can put all that energy into being well. They don't want us to find out what they are hiding, but they desperately need us to find out what they are hiding. That's why we need to be ready when we do find out. It's not helpful for the spouse to be a raving idiot when the truth comes out. Upset, yes. Strong, yes. But not overly reactionary. Be able to start doing what needs to be done: get them into counseling and forcing them to be accountable. Stopping the lies is the first step.

The problem with lying to others is that eventually the person believes it, too. They may know what they have done wrong, but they start blaming others for much of it and much of it may have started out the other person's fault. William was a victim of his father's negligence. It's just what he did with it. Billy Graham's son Franklin took his father's absences wrong, too, until he finally took them to the Lord. It is a very common problem. Who doesn't lick their wounds instead of asking God to put His balm on them, at least for a while?

WHEN YOUR LOVED ONE BELIEVES A LIE

Sometimes when we are dealing with a loved one, we come to the shocking realization they believe a lie. Your whole relationship is tainted by what they think and it's not even true. When you speak to them about it, amazing as it may be, you can't convince him or her otherwise. I remember when Lamar accused me of turning the boys against him. My goodness, I was the one doing everything possible to improve their relationships. To be accused otherwise was devastating; however, nothing I said at the moment would change his mind. "At the moment" being the operative phrase.

If it were true, you could ask for forgiveness. But when it's not true, it's hard to know what to do. It's a lie from the enemy, a spiritual problem, that only spiritual weapons: prayer, Scripture, discernment, etc., will overcome. Sound familiar? It takes a great deal of self-discipline and prayer not to do the wrong thing, not to get into your own works. Your own works in this case are the words you might speak trying to convince him or her of the truth (as you see it). It's not so much that what you are saying is wrong; it's that it's not anointed for some reason. Unanointed words are the problem. How do you get them anointed? Intercession, obedience, patience, timing, favor. Jesus said some things are accomplished only by prayer and fasting (Matt. 17:21). So, we need to add fasting to the list.

WHEN YOU BELIEVE A LIE

A wife doesn't want to face the fact that her marriage is disintegrating before her eyes. Or a husband doesn't want to admit he is having an affair or is addicted to alcohol or drugs or sex or pornography. We don't look at the truth because then we will have to deal with it, and right now we don't have the capacity to deal with it.

I understand how hard it is, but it is an error the enemy has foisted upon us. I don't agree that you and God facing a situation will not be enough. When we act in fear, we are assuming everything we see right now is all we have or will have, and that is simply not true. God has many answers and sources we can't possibly know. Things never turn out the way we think they will. We have to face the truth and let Him guide us through the minefield. However, having said all this, we do have to wait for God's leading in these difficult situations. He will sometimes tell us to be still and stand for a while longer. That is why you need to strengthen your relationship with Him, so you will know when to stand and when to move. It's not your call; it's His, and you need to be able to know when it comes or doesn't come.

And while you stand, be sure that other people know what you are going through. They will possibly know better than you when enough is enough or how to handle these difficult situations. The worse thing we can do is withdraw and allow the problem person to be our only source or adult contact. Keep a journal, if only to someday document what God has brought you through. Just be sure to write in code in case it's found by the wrong person—or keep it at the office. Tell a friend where it is on your computer, etc.

When someone you love believes a lie, it's bad, but when you believe it, that's as bad as it gets. It's bad for you, but worse for them. You are drowning in a sea of lies. Your husband needs for you to stand for the truth no matter what he believes.

When you believe a lie, what happens is your loved one has to maintain the lie. In other words, he or she can't afford to admit the truth. And until they admit the truth, they can't repent. Therefore, maintaining the lie locks them into their sin away from God. Think of it. Their love for you and your love for them keeps them from getting things right and going to heaven. If you love them, then you must stand on the truth for the sake of their eternal soul. Remember, they will never die. It's just a matter of where they go.

How Long Is Forever?

I realize I cannot imagine how long eternity is or what hell would be like, but I feel I had a very small taste and it was enough for me to want to avoid it. When we lost our little girl in that tragic accident words can never express the horror in our lives that began that day. I was living far from my family and friends. I literally had no one. Lamar's family was worse than having no one. All they knew was bickering and fighting. I was plunged instantly into a living hell. It lasted four years, almost to the day. It seemed like an eternity. Every day seemed to have no end. Every hour, every minute, there was no relief. It's the last thought you think at night and the first thought in the morning.

I tried to handle it well for the boys' sake. I did everything I knew to do. All these things help, but only the tiniest bit. After I was "good" for a long time, I thought, "Why doesn't it get better? Is there no relief?" No, there is no relief. I don't care if you cry, pitch a fit, tear up a room, or tell people off. When you get done, nothing has changed. You just have a mess to clean up, people to apologize to or avoid, and none of that matters. Only one thing matters and that you will never change.

I feel like I lived an eternal hell and it was only four years. I can't imagine an eternity of it. Now I have to say that I was wrong. It did change. I didn't change the fact, but I did change what it did to me. And that's why I believe in miracles. I can believe for an arm to grow out. That is how great my healing was. Nothing is impossible for my God, nothing but those things we cover with fear, doubt, and denial; and I don't have them any more.

Imagine if it's your ignorance, your denial, you believing a lie that causes your loved one to suffer eternal damnation. If your love causes you to play games and believe lies and not face the truth no matter how bad it is, if your love is soft and pliable where it should be strong and steadfast, then that is what will happen unless the Lord intervenes. And we don't want it to have to be that way, where we don't claim the blessing for our loved ones, where we are part of the problem.

When you finally get to the point that you don't believe the lies any longer, you are finally ready to begin. That's right, begin. You don't even begin until you are standing in the truth. Then, once seen, you keep it to yourself for a while. Having something revealed to you means you pray about it. Seeing the truth does not mean that you tell it, yet. Action comes as the Lord puts on your heart that you must do something. This is not the time to get into your own works. Your husband is probably not ready for the truth yet. All this takes time, knowing what time it is.

Face the ugly truth—whatever that is, whether it is about yourself, your husband, or your child. Just be sure you are facing all of it: your sin, your unbelief, your denial, your bad attitude, that you don't love him any more, that you have been manipulative, selfish, mouthy, etc. Then talk to God about what you've discovered. There is a positive side of truth and it's God and what He has done for us, the wonderful story of redemption. It has been for my marriage (a positive) and it can be for yours. We must balance the negative with the positive in order to be able to stand it and not get depressed. That is why you must immerse yourself in Scripture, godly friends and counsel, Christian books and tapes, and a good church. Don't weary now.

Once you have repented and given it to God, if it comes up after that, it's not the ugly truth any more. It's a lie from the pits of hell. God has forgiven and forgotten. He has put it in the sea of forgetfulness. If somebody reminds you of it, he is lying because it doesn't exist any more. The real truth is God can't see or hear it and you shouldn't either.

In the meantime, before your husband or others understand the forgiveness you have received, you have every right to maintain the truth in the face of him believing a lie. However, it's probably best if you don't dwell on it. Of course this is after you have given him ample opportunity to express himself. He does deserve a hearing. He doesn't have the right to continue to harass you once you have determined he is lying, unless something new is being presented like an apology or proof he is not, in fact, lying.

"God has forgiven me, you said you forgive me (or I asked you to forgive me) and I have forgiven myself. God has put it in the sea of forgetfulness never to be heard from again. I want you to leave it there, too." Or, if it's concerning his sin, "God has forgiven you; I have forgiven you; and now you need to receive that forgiveness. God has covered it with the blood of Jesus so that He can't see it anymore and I can't either. As far as we are concerned, it doesn't exist anymore. I want you to say you forgive yourself." Make him say the words, and include anyone else he or she hasn't forgiven. Lead him through a prayer saying, "I forgive myself and anyone who has hurt me. I ask you now Lord to help me feel that forgiveness. I want to be free of this. It's hurting my life and my family. I understand it's counterproductive."

If the truth is you want your husband to hurt as bad as you do, then you are causing a lot of your own problems. But you won't admit that. That would make you as bad as him. As long as a marriage has two people trying to hurt the other, there will be no way to stop the degradation of not only your marriage, but also your own personal health. You need to remember the scripture, *"Vengeance is mine sayeth the Lord"* (Rom. 12:19). To try to get back at him is a form of revenge and it's His, not yours to do.

In our destructive years, I would say to myself, "He doesn't deserve love." And he didn't! But then a psychologist on television said, "Everyone deserves love! In fact, the most unlovely need it the most." There went my excuse! That was Lamar: needing love desperately and driving it away with everything he said and did. He tried to make it up to me, but I was too devastated. There came a point where nothing helped.

To get out of the chastising mode you are now in, you will have to admit that you are a big part of the problem and give up hurting him.

It's called repentance: turning and going in a different direction. Furthermore, you will have to tell him you are sorry and make restitution. And if there are others you have hurt in the process of hurting him (your children, his parents, etc.), you are going to have to tell them you are sorry, and again, if there is any restitution that needs to be made on your part, you need to do it; but not until you can do it in a way that doesn't accuse him or others or tries to illicit an apology from them or to get them to admit they were wrong. "I am sorry, but you really hurt me" is *not* the way to apologize. "I am sorry I had a bad attitude/was hateful/ uncooperative/vengeful/mouthy/disrespectful/etc. Please forgive me for anything I have done to hurt you." This is the thing you must do. They may have done something terrible to you, but if you did the wrong thing in response, you are wrong, too. You have to make your part right. You cannot make them make their part right. However, you can tell them you forgive them. "I forgive you and I hope you will forgive me." That is proper if they did things to hurt you, even if they don't admit it. Even if you feel justified for doing it, it was still wrong. Two wrongs don't make a right. This way they know they are released. It's now between them and God. Leave it there.

It's probably not the right time to approach anybody other than God. As long as you are willing and will be obedient when God says to do something further, you are right with Him. You may never be right in people's eyes again. That choice is in them, not you. Just pray for them. There are no prayers stronger than those of a victim for an abuser.

If you feel you have been wrongly accused, you can still say, "I am sorry if I offended you (hurt you, etc.)," and not be giving in on what you believe was their part in what happened. We can be sorry if they got offended even if they had no right to be, but don't say that. Do not go back over any of it. "I hope we can all forget this and go on. I really do value your friendship and the time we spend together." Never speak of it again unless the truth has been revealed to them and they are coming to you as you came to them earlier.

It's a good idea to keep this visit short so that you won't be tempted to go back over it and they won't be either. Give God time to help you all recompute. I was extremely hurt by a relative. I forgave her, but never got the victory in my heart. One day I saw things from her point of view and suddenly realized she had no idea how hurt I was or what she had done to me. It was hard to believe, but what she did came so easily to her that she really didn't see it. I was carrying this terrible burden and she was fine. Some people are ditzy or obtuse. Why work ourselves up over such a person?

Being the defensive mechanism it is, your mind thinks up other reasons to justify what you are doing to hurt him, acceptable reasons. Acceptable to you, games to everyone else. The ironic part is your husband may not have the capacity to hurt as much as you, no matter what you do. Does anyone? You are camped at the problem. Hurting him just makes him worse. You are hurting your whole family and keeping everyone from moving forward and that is the truth. Face it. You have a black hat on, too. Join the club.

One day in the middle of a very frustrating problem in my spirit I seemed to get the words, "I don't need your opinion." I came to see my opinion was costing Him precious time because He couldn't get to the problem until He worked on me. I was standing in the way of my own answer. Time was being wasted and yet I was frustrated at Him. Needless to say I repented immediately and determined to quit being so opinionated. If it's my opinion and not His, it's garbage.

It will take a deep work of the Holy Spirit to help a man understand he must forgive himself, that we all make mistakes, that his wife and family can be healed, etc. There is a lot to be accomplished before a husband or wife can simply face the truth. It's not as easy as it looks. It would make things so much simpler, but he can't see that. There are steps to be taken between here and there. Loving steps that the Holy Spirit will gently guide him through, and simultaneously, steps she will need to go through, too. We must stand in love during this time knowing that some day, we will be redeemed in his eyes, knowing this day can be a good day. We don't have to wait for our eventual redemption to have joy. We live by faith and our faith tells us He will take care of this. You can enjoy today knowing the day will come that your loved one will be free to face the truth, and in facing the truth, he will be truly free.

The thing that will help him the most is to see you healed. If he doesn't carry the weight of your wounds, then maybe he can begin to have hope. It will make the reality of God's love and forgiveness all the more real to him. If he sees you have peace and joy, it will do something to him, something words can't adequately express. Since the problems are so deep, we need the ministry to be deep. The reality of God in your life is one of those deep things. It's the way to crumble walls and build bridges. Allow God to do a work in you, and before you know it, the work in your husband will be done. He will be won, not only by your silence, but by your radiance.

I understand that you mean well and want to see him come to the freedom he can have if he accepts the grace of God, but somehow the message comes across as accusatory and condemning. That is why God encourages you to win him with your silence. Because it's so hard for husbands to receive our words—anyone but us. This doesn't mean you have to go along with the lie or stifle forever. You can speak. In fact, I would say many women don't speak when they should. Just be sure you are being led by the Lord.

You Can't Trust Your Own Mind

We knew a man whose life was destroyed by alcohol, drugs, and women. The few times I talked with him, it was obvious his thinking was way out of line. It was all lies. We had been good friends for years, so I felt I could talk with him openly, "Right now, Don, you cannot trust your own mind. You have to say to yourself, 'If my wife, my kids, and the people that love me all think the same thing, I have to believe them.' There are some times we cannot believe our own minds. The mind is a marvelous thing but it's not perfect and sometimes we must trust others to tell us the truth." He didn't listen because his mind was already too darkened. I'm sure he knew what I was saying was true, but he was too trapped to reach out. I don't know when he went too far or played the games too long, but he had and it cost him everything. I wept at his funeral. Such a waste. The family still suffers from his lies, lies now in their minds. The cycle continues. Only Jesus can break it. Oh, Lord Jesus, please break it for them, especially his grandchildren.

Your assignment is to make a list of things you have to have. And if God didn't say it's a rule, then start breaking them. Drink water. Let your child get dirty. Leave the dishes for a change. Turn off the TV. Stay away from the computer. Let your husband pick out your outfit and for goodness sake, let him tell you how to do your hair and make-up.

When Wives Believe the Lies

At one time Lamar and I were helping a young man in business. We came to see that, although he loved the Lord and had a desire to serve Him, he was really quite rebellious. He wasn't rebellious acting. In fact, he was quite charismatic and acted like he was cooperating. We would meet and agree on things only to find out things had changed. They weren't changed much, just enough to scuttle the project. It happened again and again, but he wasn't all that concerned. Why should he be? It wasn't his money that was funding the projects. We were supposed to be in charge but literally had no control over anything.

What was happening was bad enough, but what made it even worse was his wife couldn't see the problem either. She saw him as the victim. I do believe we all need someone who believes in us and supports us, but I don't know how helpful it is when the wife can't see the truth, when she believes the lie. She could have helped lead him out of his rebellion, but not if she can't see it.

On one hand we have the wife that sees only the negative and never seems to edify, and on the other we have the wife that sees only the positive and never challenges the error. Could we have some balance here? It sure would help their marriages. Where do you fall on the continuum with your husband?

THE BIGGEST LIE OF ALL

I read an article in a magazine of a husband and father that did not come home one night. His car was found with blood in it, but not his body. His family never knew if he was killed or he abandoned them. It was a mother's worst nightmare. A nightmare that was not to end any time soon. She soon found their thriving business was deeply in debt and had to be salvaged, leaving huge balances to be paid. The only job she was qualified for was minimum wage. The large insurance policy he thought would help them pay their bills did not pay off for years because there was no proof he had died. She was forced to declare bankruptcy, which further ruined her credit. And these are just the financial considerations.

Raising three little girls without a father is very difficult. They lost their home and most of their friends with it. Everything the girls knew and counted on was swept away in a few short months. After fighting for years to keep her family afloat, the mother was diagnosed with cancer, and, after a long illness, died much too young. Her sister took over and raised the girls, which was a good thing.

At some point the aunt found out the girls' father was alive. He was contacted and confronted with what he had done. He apologized but it did not satisfy the girls. The hurt was too deep. He was taken to court for back childcare to help with the girls' schooling. The father cooperated and tried to do what he could to make up for their loss. Two of the girls refused to speak to him after the first meeting. The oldest has continued a relationship, although it's strained.

The big question is why? Why did he do it? He claims he did it because he thought they would be better off without him. He had made such a mess of things that he felt that the insurance and other people helping were preferable to anything he might be able to do. Of course nobody believes him, especially not the girls. To them it doesn't make sense. Why didn't he love them enough to stay and help them instead of running away?

It's not about love. It's about perception. His perception said he was worthless and they would be better off without him. So, he sacrificed his happiness for their sake. That in his mind was love to him.

Nothing he says will ever be enough. He never dreamed the insurance would not pay off. All his assumptions were wrong and the family paid a dear price for his mistakes. He can never look sorry enough or grovel enough to pay for their pain. The man can't do what they need him to do. Only God can, but only if He is allowed to do it, and right now I don't see that happening.

One reason they don't believe him is because he is remarried and is raising her two children as his own. It appears as if he has happily moved on, but I don't think that's true. He never intended to "move on." He didn't think this far ahead when he was faking his death. He knew he would have to get a job, but the last thing on his mind was worrying about being alone. It just never dawned on him that he would make a new life for himself with a wife or kids, that eventually he would get involved with the people in his new life, and yes, someone would think he was a good catch and he would find it hard not to reciprocate. He is a needy person, needing love and encouragement. He's a sponge and this new love is his refreshing. He never ever thought he could love again or be happy again.

He believed a lie, and they believe a lie. They believe there is an answer: that he can do enough to satisfy them. They believe he didn't love them; that he didn't care. The sad thing is that their lie keeps them from moving on and having a relationship with their father today and maybe bringing healing to them all. They are so hung up on their pain, they can't see his. I call this the biggest lie because abandoning your family like this must surely be the biggest lie. However, the biggest lie of all is that he cannot be forgiven. He can. He may never be forgiven by his daughters, but he can be forgiven by God.

His selfish act has done its final terrible deed and stolen not only their childhood, their relationship with a loving father, and much of their adult happiness, but their relationship with God, too. That is the saddest thing of all. How far such selfishness and unforgiveness reach into our future and hurts those we love the most. The man is not worth their contempt. He is to be pitied, and yes, forgiven, if not for his sake, for their own.

You can be free of the lies. You may be adversely affected by them for a while, but once you know the truth, they are limited in how they can affect you. You don't have to wait for him to be free before you can be free. That's the wonderful thing about truth. There is freedom today, even though he still has areas that are bound. You will be so glad for what has been healed; it will sustain you while you wait for others to be healed.

Remember, you are not a victim. You may be in a mess, but you are not powerless while you are walking out your miracle. God is raising up a standard to meet the evil in your life. None of this is going to overtake and sink you. This is going to make you better. What the devil meant for bad, God will use for good. Believe it and cling to it. He is the one that has to bring about the powers of the universe so that you win. That to me is awesome. This lie is really not the biggy you think it is. Our God is the biggy. And someday the truth will reign and you will be redeemed. Today, you have to be satisfied with what you have and know.

> *Oh, God, to have life and life more abundantly. Help me to see when I get into sowing death into our lives. I never intended to. I thought it was expressing my opinion. But now I realize my opinion doesn't always agree with Yours, and even if I'm not wrong, I'm not right in the way I do it or when. Help me Lord to do it Your way—the right way. I really do want to. I pray this in Jesus name because He is the only One through whom my victory will come. Amen. And Amen.*

FORTY

**So when they continued asking him, he lifted up
himself, and said unto them, "He that is without sin
among you, let him first cast a stone at her."**
—JOHN 8:7

The Darkest Hour

A WOMAN'S JOB IS TO bring life into the home, not just the new life of a child, but life itself—joy, light, laughter, a lifting of spirits. And oh how difficult that is in the world we serve! I think of the wonderful black mommas that had to do that in the slave camps knowing their lives were anything but joyful. Think of the women like Corrie Ten Boom in the concentration camps that have to speak, if not joy, at least love and wisdom, the wisdom of persistence and forgiveness, the wisdom of going on in spite of it all. We will survive. Somehow at least some of us will survive, and when you do, you keep yourself true to your family character. Don't let them pull you down with their hatred. Good will eventually triumph. We must stay on the side of good. We will be redeemed. In God's time, we will be redeemed.

And then there is the opposite of this: the toxic person, the one who succumbs to the hatred, jealousy, and fear, the walking dead of this world. We all have a certain amount of the toxic within. If you don't have it when you are young, given to you by the world you live in at an early age, you inevitably get it along the way. Mine came late, at about the age of thirty. I was one of the lucky ones. It's wonderful to be spared the sad realities of this world for so long. But when it hit, it hit with a vengeance, and I was never the same. But that's just as well. I had to grow up sometime. After I was saved a while, God took me to Proverbs and wouldn't let me out because He did not want me naïve. I don't want you naïve either. It doesn't help our loved ones for us to be naïve, and it certainly doesn't bode well for us to be toxic.

The woman is not the only one that should bring life to the family. The man is the other half of the equation. If a man brings death into the home, toxic thinking that pollutes their home, it's awfully hard for her to overcome. Hard but not impossible.

> I can do all things through Christ who strengthenth me.
> —PHILIPPIANS 4:13

That's why John said in 1 John 4:4, "*Ye are of God, little children, and have over come them: because greater is He that is in me than he that is in the world.*" Love wins. Be loving, not weak—loving.

THE TOXIC HUSBAND

"How do you turn a toxic husband into a healthy one?" Good question. The first step is assessing the problem. In Ezekiel 3, God tells them that judgment must start at the church. That's me, that's you looking at ourselves and being honest about where we are toxic.

A man needs a lot of encouragement. He doesn't do well with criticism. This becomes a problem when he knows what a turkey he is and he knows you know it too. It's especially bad if his childhood has predisposed him to feeling bad about himself or to be undisciplined in the important areas of life like keeping a job, being faithful, paying the bills, being a good husband and father, etc. The question is how do we challenge the garbage and encourage him at the same time?

I'll never forget the response of an ex-husband when he was told that he should have encouraged his ex more when they were married. He tried, but there are some things that just seem to bounce off when the person is convinced otherwise, and those things are often the encouragement he or she so desperately needs. Saying nice things and complimenting her didn't work because she knew how lucky she was to have the husband

and family she had, despite how empty she felt. We have to help our loved ones come to terms with what they aren't saying, to help them to forgive themselves and understand we are all turkeys.

I've spoken a great deal about what you need to be and do. The following is a review of what I have felt is important when facing our marriage problems.

1. You must be trustworthy.
2. You must be godly.
3. You must seek to know the truth.
4. You must face the truth and walk in it.
5. You must unconditionally love him (or her).
6. He must know you are trustworthy; that you will never betray him.
7. He must know your love is unconditional.
8. You must speak the truth in love
9. You must be willing to do things in God's time, not yours.
10. You must not expect perfection of yourself or others and forgive all imperfections.

THE MOST TOXIC OF ALL

There are times in our lives when after we've brought in the professionals, the doctors, the lawyers, the authorities, it isn't enough. That's what I want to talk about now. To do it, I have to talk about some pretty bad cases. Hindsight is so much clearer, but rather than look at our past and glean from it, I want to look at somebody else's and hopefully it will help us avoid what came upon them.

Oprah had a guest whose husband tried to kill her on three separate occasions. It's a miracle she's alive. He was never physically abusive, although he became very controlling and verbally abusive. They had been high school sweethearts. Everyone thought they had the perfect marriage, proving that it's hard to know who is going to go off the deep end at some point.

A different show told of a husband who succeeded in killing his wife after almost killing her "accidentally" a few times. He, too, was never physically abusive. Both couples had children. It's important to understand that a person can at some point become a person you do not know. Take the signs seriously.

The woman on Oprah that lived, filed for divorce. This meant he would be forced out of the home, separating him from his kids. The courts would now decide how things would go in the most significant area of his life. She had everything on her side. He had nothing. Not the laws, not the facts, nothing, and he knew it. He had lost everything. But most of all, he had lost control. And to a control freak, that is unacceptable.

The world was very dark indeed, and it didn't get any better as the weeks went by. The more he tried to talk to his wife and the more he saw she meant business, the more he saw her as the problem. The woman of his dreams was now his enemy. The more he mulled it over unable to see any way out, the more panicked he became. The more reactionary he acted, the more she was determined to get him out of their lives. I don't know how long it took, but eventually he decided he had to get her out of their lives if he was going to see his kids.

Hopelessness is the critical factor in these tragic situations. Yes, we have power and we have everyone on our side when he is acting out, but that power must be tempered with grace. The person must not lose hope, the hope of a better day, and to them a better day will never exist if they can't see their kids. And right now a better day to him will include you. Separating the two in his mind is not easy. I know I wasn't ready to do it because I knew Lamar would not make a good divorced husband. Healing, hard as it is, is often easier. It doesn't seem possible, but right now if things are awful, nothing seems possible.

I think it's important to look back and see when things changed. There was a point in time when everything shifted and we very likely didn't even know it. And very likely it's linked to things in his childhood. So often a person thinks things will be different when he or she marries, and when it isn't and it gets worse, that's when they lose all hope.

I have said over and over again being a Christian makes a difference, but so many Christians are Christians in name only. They don't forgive others; they don't forgive themselves. They murmur and play the victim role or are in denial or controlling, whatever. And then they wonder why things don't change. This is why I say over and over again it must begin with you, because as long as he sees you talking the talk and not walking the walk, he won't change. He's bound and you're not helping cut his fetters.

It is of utmost importance that our husband sees God's love and grace in us. We must challenge the garbage early, not in a reactionary way, but lovingly, but not be too dogmatically righteous—"religious." And further-more, it is important that we understand what is within the normal range of aberrant behavior and what is outside.

Remind him those that have been forgiven much, love much. Take him to the Bible and make him read it for himself, maybe more than once. Ask him if he believes it? Make him say he does. Ask him if he thinks someone like Tex Watson, the convicted killer of actress Sharon Tate and six other people, can make it to heaven. If he says no, then that's your answer. He has an error in his thinking that Jesus didn't pay for all sin, just certain sin, which is preposterous. Help him see no matter what he does, Jesus forgives him. There is no pit so deep that the love of God can't reach. Encourage him to start thanking and praising the Lord. Make him or her list the things he or she is thankful for. Enumerate them. Write them down together. Help him to see how blessed he is. Of course, he will know he doesn't deserve it, so you will have to remind him none of us deserve what we get. Point out people that have more: Donald Trump for instance. Does he deserve what he has? No! It just makes him more responsible.

The basis of all this is fear; lack of faith; lies of the enemy telling him God won't help and nothing will change things, they will only get worse. What we have to do is to help him see the enemy is a liar. Begin in small ways because that's all he can handle right now. Here is an example: Lamar has had a lot things recently he's been struggling to get done. Nothing was working out and what had worked out had quit. Then we lost a new little device for the computer that allows you to use your e-mail even in the car. We finally traced it back to the hotel. That was the worse place to lose it. The room had been cleaned and possibly re-rented already.

Lamar was already tired and down, so this really hit him hard. He gave it up. In his mind it was gone. When I countered positively, he just came back at me explaining the reality of the situation. I insisted, "I don't live there. In reality, I have favor. God can give me favor." And He did. The man at the hotel called to say they found it and were sending it.

When I tell you to "lighten up," I'm not kidding. Problem people need to see that you aren't being pulled down with their misery. Get the victory in these small situations and it will go a long way toward changing the big ones.

We are acquainted with depression. If anyone needs the Lord, it's a Melancholy. Lamar now at least recognizes when he is cycling into a low point and doesn't let himself give into it like he used to. I have a son that is a melancholy personality, too. Knowing the Lord has made all the difference in his life. If you have one or are one, you need to learn more about it. There are some wonderful books explaining the four personality types: Sanguine, Choleric, Melancholy, and Phlegmatic. I don't see how a mother can understand her children and all their idiosyncrasies without knowing how their personality type affects her family dynamics. We can't blame a person because they are depressed. It would be easier if we could. It's so hard to watch as your loved one slips away from reality, and words don't seem to make any difference. Most of the couples I have spoken of tried counseling and even medication. That just proves how hard it is. If you are finding it hard, then don't feel so bad. Join the club with the rest of us that are struggling to get answers.

I don't want to give you the impression that I think all the help can come spiritually alone. Sometimes there are imbalances that need to be diagnosed. We do need to seek professional help to do evaluations and run tests, but we must never allow that to be the last word. A close relative was diagnosed with bipolar disease and put on medication. She hated how she felt. I guess this is why these people won't stay on their meds, but that just means they need to be adjusted. Getting the victory is work, and not just work in one area. The more you both learn, the more you can help them, and the more they understand that they aren't the only one. That alone helps. She has been able to be healed by disciplining herself in her Christian walk, but it didn't happen in a day. It took years. And it's still going on. God has led her through the pitfalls, but she has had to listen and not turn to the right or the left and when she gets off the path, to get right back on.

A wonderful Christian woman took her in after a terrible marriage and divorce, insisting that my loved one stay in the Word, attend church, and do what she told her to do. One area she mentioned was her mentor's insistence that she stop being so isolated. Do not allow a depressed person to isolate themselves or be alienated from the significant people in their lives, just as God showed me to not be gone so much when Lamar was going through it. We need to help them get their mind off of themselves.

Another important component to their healing is exercise. Get them moving. And to get them moving, you must move with them. Some people can afford to hire help and get them to a gym, but most of us have to be their personal trainer. Someone said that celery has a calming affect, so I decided to try it. I cut up some celery sticks and put them on the kitchen table with some little salt decanters. Sure enough the boys and their father ate them up and things were a lot calmer that day. It worked. You would think I'd have celery on the table all the time, but after I proved it to myself, that was enough. My family laughs about some of the things I do.

Physical things do make a difference, and so does good nutrition, exercise, light in the room, getting out in nature, having a friend come by, opening a window. Do something to make a positive change. Get somebody who is big enough or has the wherewithal to help you insist the person cooperate. Change their diet, but don't take away all their carbs, just some if they are overweight. We are too nice sometimes and allow things to go on that we shouldn't.

WHAT WERE YOU THINKING WHEN YOU DID THIS?

I was struck by how these people talked about a numbness. Everyone is trying to figure out what they were thinking, what their feelings were at the time, when the truth is they are almost in a stupor. They were totally disconnected from their feelings. And once disconnected, it was as if some power took over, as if it wasn't even them doing it.

One family that had a son that had spells of anger explained, "He got this *look*." They know it's almost supernatural, but they don't want to call it demonic, although they know it must be because he was so mean. It is demonic! The person is not under their own control. When you are not under your own control and you haven't put yourself in God's control (and this lasts only as long as you are obedient and challenging error), then you are under the devil's control. We hate to think we are dealing with the devil, but that's exactly who we are dealing with. If that person has given themselves over to these awful thoughts, they are not in control. And when they are not in control, you aren't in control either. There is spiritual help available, but you must seek it out.

Those of us that know the person is going through a difficult time must be watchful and not trust them to their own devices. They cannot be left alone. This reminds me of one of my best friends' husband who tried to commit suicide. She had taken him to a mental hospital because he was so depressed. The hospital for some reason, refused to keep him in spite of how bad he was. His family determined they couldn't accept this answer and that Monday she should go until they got an acceptable answer.

Monday morning she needed to get ready and didn't think taking a shower would be a problem. She told him she was going to take her bath and would be right back to help him get ready. When she got back, he was still sitting on the bed. He said, "You're going to be so upset with me," and then revealed to her that he had stabbed himself multiple times. Miraculously, he did not hit a vital organ. In all this, God was faithful.

The saddest part is that he easily could have been treated with medication. It isn't always best to spare our loved one the horror of what they bring upon themselves. It's just a shame that we have to go through it with them. But that's what love does. God hasn't chosen to remove Himself from all this, so why should we? We're not better than God. In the end, her husband is much better and they are enjoying their retirement years together, dancing up a storm no less. She was a professional dancer in her younger years and has kept it up over the years and he has now joined her. They teach at home and on cruise ships.

How do we give the hopeless hope? The real question is, "How do we get them to enlarge their capacity for grace?" They are hopeless because they are looking inward, and it's very dark indeed. They are their only source, and they know they are tapped out. My advice is usually to get the person help spiritually, but often he or she is a Christian, and not just a nominal Christian either. This lets us know any time we entertain wrong thoughts we can quickly be led down the wrong path.

THE ELDER

An elder at a church we were visiting admitted that he had been tormented for months and had been tempted to backslide. He had not quit attending church, although his attendance had definitely slipped, but he had back-slidden in his head and heart. That is where backsliding starts. Look for the carelessness. How does this happen that a godly man who has walked with the Lord for years, is suddenly tempted to give up. Yes, we can blame "the enemy," and surely he has his part in it all, but we have some responsibility, too. The Bible over and over again tells us we can overcome. In fact, we are commanded to overcome. So, why wasn't this man overcoming? Because he wasn't doing what it would take to overcome.

When we need an answer like this, we should ask ourselves what Scripture tells us about overcoming. I like to look at Jesus first: how did Jesus overcome when the enemy came to him? Since the Bible says there is enough evil in the day, even Jesus had to deal with it daily. When the enemy came, Jesus immediately recognized there was a problem: "If you are the Son of God…" "If," indeed! Jesus doesn't have to prove anything to anyone. This would have challenged a regular guy's ego, and he would have immediately turned the stone into bread and then been sorry for it, or turned the devil into a stone. However, it wasn't the time for that either. That would have been a real mess. No, Jesus did the proper thing. He knew this wasn't the voice of anyone connected with His Father, and if it wasn't connected to His Father, then why would He do what it said?

Notice He did not wait for a second thought to come as He pondered the first. Nor did he think, "That remark doesn't deserve an answer." No, He answered the lie with the truth, and this is what we must do. He met it not with emotion, anger, or even a good mental argument. He met the first thought with Scripture and cast it down. The Bible tells us to take every thought into "captivity" (2 Cor. 10:5). This is exactly what we must do. It is harder to reject two thoughts than one. It soon becomes twenty, and before we know it, a whole mind-set, a strong-hold.

This isn't easy because that first thought will not be something we don't agree with. It will be something we do agree with. That is what makes it so powerful. Jesus is the Son of God. If it were wrong, it would be easy to cast aside. But no, it's only too true or at least it sounds that way. Just one little two letter word made it wrong: *if!*

The enemy isn't dumb. He doesn't say, "He (your husband or your God) doesn't care!" when your husband or your God has just proven his/ His love for you. No, he waits until they haven't done what you feel you so desperately need. Then he says, "See! He doesn't care!" And you believe it. Oh how hard it is to cast down the very thought that you were thinking yourself. At this point, if you are mature, if you have taken seriously 1 Corinthians 13 when it tells you love endures all things, hopes all things, etc. you will dig deep to rehearse ways your husband or your God has shown you that he/He does in fact care. If you can't remember the salvation of your soul or a recent healing, how about: *"Those He loves He chastises"* (Heb. 12:6)?

The second thought appeals to Jesus' feelings. He was weary. How good it would feel to have the angels minister to His needs and carry Him where He wanted to go. This is why it is so easy to get involved with other women or to overeat, whatever will soothe your weary body, whatever will answer the immediate problem. Lastly, the enemy tries to get Jesus to turn from His Father. This is what the enemy, and everyone else you are involved with, will try to get you to do: turn from God, lick your wounds, believe you aren't important to Him or good enough or special enough. You might not think you would ever do that, but then neither did Peter. It's awfully easy. Are you always obedient? When you aren't, you have turned from your Father, God. And this is true of your husband, too. If he is not obedient to the Word or has turned off his inner spirit man, he has turned from God, and we have every right to talk about it. Sometimes it's good to admit to him how you have come to see your error so that in the process you can help him see his.

I believe it is possible to read the "signs" properly. Why can't we see the warning signals and take them seriously early instead of after the fact, hearing about all the things everyone overlooked, even the professionals, although often the professionals aren't hearing what they need to know. Let's not overlook the signs. Every word and every action is important. There is no such thing as an idle word. It is a window into the heart, and if the heart has become this darkened, we need to know it and face it. Yes, we want to hope for a better day, but we need to deal with reality and if reality isn't good, it isn't going to get better without a lot of help.

TRUST BUT VERIFY

There was a time in our convenience store that money was missing out of the cash register. The money taken in on gas purchases did not add up to what was delivered by enough that it was noticeable. We quickly figured out the likely suspect, but couldn't just accuse her of it. We needed proof. Lamar and I had to take turns taking the figures on the pumps and subbing the cash register a few times during the day, especially at the beginning and end of her shift, and yet make it seem very natural. It was so hard for me to not be honest, but it had to be done, for her sake as much as ours. If she was innocent, she would have come through just fine and we could move on to the next theory. Sadly, she failed. The register told it all.

When I went to her house to talk with her, she wouldn't even tell me if she counted her money when she got it from the previous shift. Her mother was mortified that we would even accuse her. I explained that right now I am just trying to get answers. Her refusal to talk with me told it all. It was really sad because we were good friends. I guess I'm funny, but if my child is stealing, I want to know it.

One of the morals of this story is that catching them red handed doesn't guarantee they will admit to what they have done.

We don't always have to set a trap. The evidence is right there in front of us if we would just see it. The following example is not about violence or abusing someone or even sin, but an example of seeing what's right there in front of our face. I'm thankful I don't have a violent example. It's an example of recognizing a problem early.

The first time my son's wife came to our home, she stayed in his room most of the time while he took care of things for the anniversary party we were having. I was so busy, I didn't think about her not being with the rest of us. The second time was Thanksgiving and for some reason she did not join us then either. When I asked my son later when she ate that day, he said they stopped for a salad on the way home. It just seemed odd to me that she didn't join us and eat something. Shyness would explain it, but I felt it had something to do with food. A red flag went up in my mind. Anorexics notoriously don't like to be around food.

When I realized this, I had a little talk with my son because everything I had observed reinforced that "we" had a problem. I told him, "I think your fiancé has an eating disorder. I don't know how it will manifest itself, just be watchful of the signs and if it's going too far. Pray about it, bind the spirits, and expect God to do something." It took a few years to get the victory, but she finally did. What meant the most to me was when she told me that she couldn't have made it without my son. He has been so supportive and loving. These things are not accomplished in a day, but they will be accomplished, if we pick up on them early enough.

Sometimes we are wrong. If we jump in with accusations too soon, it just makes us look foolish. Keep your suspicions to yourself for a while, and then maybe bring in someone you know you can trust to help in dealing with the situation. But be careful because sometimes it's the one you trust that is making the other look guilty. We've had that happen. We had money missing once in a business and it looked like it was the teenager on the afternoon shift. Lamar did the counting this time and figured out the money was missing between when the first shift counted out and the second shift came in. There was only one person that had access to the money at that point: the cook. We never would have believed it was her, a sweet old lady and a "Christian" at that.

This is why it is very important that we stay open to receive thoughts and vibes and not always react right away. Pray and ask God for answers. I do think it's possible to restore these people, but it will take the Holy Spirit to do it. However, I keep it in mind when they have access to any money. Is not fair to tempt a weak person with the object of their weakness. (This is why we must be very careful who we bring into our homes or leave with our husband or kids alone.)

COUNSELING

You need to go to counseling with your husband, at least the first few times. Counseling is only as good as the truth that comes out, and he will do everything in his power to hide it. You provide the other side. After he starts going alone, any problematic behavior should be reported in detail to the counselor. Never take his word on what the counselor says when you aren't there. You need to go every once in a while to be sure it's on track, but not all the time because then he will never open up. He has a right to have some secrets from you while he is trying to deal with his dark side. There are just some things you don't want to hear.

People with abuse problems or destructive behaviors need to be accountable. They need someone they can confide in and need to understand this is the only way they will get better: by challenging the garbage in their own head. Until they "own" their behavior, they can't change it. A mother on Dr. Phil's show knew she was on her son too much and too verbal, but not verbally abusive. Until it was proven to her in living color video tapes, she did not know she did it. She said she was very careful not to be because she had been trained in that area and knew how destructive it was. Only when she finally saw the tape was he able to begin the process it would take to heal their relationship.

Dr. Phil pointed out there could be a lot of things that changed her son's ability to do his school work. He could have a physical problem that is chemical in nature. He needs to be tested to rule out certain things. Her yelling at him was not helping anyone, least of all the child. Why had this child suddenly changed? The same goes for our husbands. We may know what they are doing, but we have to be very careful when we start assuming why they are doing it.

This is my prayer for you:

> *Dear God, I lift up this marriage that needs Your touch. Only You can turn it around and make it something beautiful again. I bind every hindering spirit that would try to tear asunder this couple. I ask You to help them first see there is hope and then to have faith for the fullness of all that You want them to have and be. I pray this in the precious name of Your Son, Jesus.*

Be sure you have prayed and taken your authority over the situation.

FORTY-ONE

Fidelity

IN MY *research bible* the word *fidelity* is translated "trust." In Proverbs 31 the first thing the king's mother mentions regarding a virtuous women is that her husband does safely trust in her. Faithfulness and fidelity are not just about not having an affair. It is trust in every area of the marriage. I may talk about adultery but many couples are as deeply wounded by other things as they would be by adultery: verbal abuse, emotional detachment, food addiction, inordinate spending, pornography, Internet sex, etc. This chapter is about them all.

I understand we want to be the one that fills up our mate's head and heart so much that these things won't happen, but that isn't possible as long as his mind is darkened. I do feel his heart will inevitably be the thing that gets him out of it and his love will be what forces him to get help, but that is a ways down the line. He has to see the need first and to see it he has to see a lot of hurt people. I wish it weren't so, but it is. It's a very painful process and you are in the middle of it. No one is more pained than the compulsive: the adulterer, the gambler, alcoholic, druggy, Internet porn seeker, etc. You must see this as an enemy you both must fight, rather than he is the enemy and you must fight him. I want you to have enough sympathy to fight, but not so much that you do not insist he do what he needs to do that only he can do.

I heard a wonderful testimony on *Life Today* with James Robison. A man had an addiction to pornography in his late teens and told his fiancé before they married. They prayed about it and she assumed that would be enough. He hoped so, too. When he saw it wasn't, he was too embarrassed to tell her. It caused him to withdraw emotionally from her and the kids, but she never knew the reason. He tried to get the victory on his own but things only got worse. He was so overcome with guilt at what he had done on a business trip that he dissolved in tears right there in the airport and told her everything. They got a room and spent the night talking and crying. She was determined the enemy was not going to destroy her family, including her husband. They attended a good church and were able to get good godly counsel on a continuing basis. They also felt a tape series of Dr. Robison really helped them. As a result of dealing with their problem head-on, the wife testified that he was a new man and I'm sure she will say she's a new person herself. What really struck me was how her eyes just shined as she told what a privilege it has been to be a part of this whole process—seeing her husband come forth from death into life.

I need to make the point here that no matter how close a couple is, there will always be places we keep private, and that is as it should be, within limits. As in the case of someone like my friend who never got to adopt a child or William C. Moyers, the relationship starts out with their need to keep too much private. Compulsive people lie and keep secrets; that's why we don't know they are compulsive. These secrets eventually come out. Our job is to help the compulsives in our lives see they can be delivered and redeemed from this thing that torments them.

A NICE NEW HOUSE

When we first moved to Florida, we lived in a small cement block house. It originally had two bedrooms and a one-car carport that was later converted into three tiny rooms. We put the back two together for Grant and Lamar used the front room for an office because it had an outside door. When Lamar got another office, we fixed it up for Matt, which thrilled him greatly.

The house was a real fixer-upper. We desperately wanted out. I knew financially we needed to wait, but not Lamar. He was sure we were ready and started looking. Some of the houses were really nice with a pool and a lot of other amenities. Two of them were taken off the market after we decided to make a bid on them. That's really hard once you have started dreaming of living there. Women are so quick to move in mentally and start decorating, at least I am.

I determined not to do that again, not to get ahead of things emotionally. But you know how that is, you look and talk to the people and things progress. You really do have to figure out how you will live in the house if you want to live there. Pretty soon you are arranging furniture in your head and making plans.

We found an especially nice home with a pool right outside the den/kitchen area. It was great and not too expensive. We kept going back looking at it as Lamar tried to make a deal. We were getting close. Lamar was ready give in to get it. So, he made the final call. As they talked, I could tell it was not going to go through. Lamar wrote the reason on a piece of paper. "He's going to sell it to his son." I was devastated. Why did he put it on the market?

As Lamar continued to talk to the man, I turned to God, "Why, God, why?" He quickly answered, "I didn't ask you to do it." I knew He was right because I had a burden that it wasn't time, but Lamar had insisted. That didn't matter. I knew and had gone against my inner witness. At that moment God made a connection in my mind and I don't even understand how because what was revealed has never been a part of our life, or my thinking at all. He revealed to me that this is what happens in an adulterous situation. The people open themselves up to know intimately and become involved emotionally with someone they have no business getting involved with. The person may be a wonderful person and have wonderful attributes apart from this moral lapse. They haven't had time to figure out each other's bad points. They don't have the struggles that a married couple does, dealing with kids, bills, etc. Maybe these two are better suited to each other. That isn't the point. One or both have prior commitments. It's not the time or the place to make a choice. And it certainly isn't appropriate to have sex with someone with no intention of committing to a relationship. Who said commitment was the criteria for a sexual relationship? Not God. No, we should wait until we are in covenant, and you can't do that when you are already in covenant (marriage).

Quit Lusting for What You Cannot Have

I understand that you haven't made many of the choices that have influenced your life profoundly: your parents, your temperament, the times and environment, etc. I don't want you to think you are to blame for a bad childhood. Heavens no! God grieves over what you have suffered. I just want you to understand what others have started you have no doubt continued. No, you aren't to blame for much of what happened in your childhood, but you are responsible for your responses and you are becoming more and more responsible. That's why the garbage has to stop as soon as possible.

Adultery and lust are not just sexual terms. God uses these words when He sees us as adulterous (Matt. 12:39; 16:4), when we allow another relationship to take precedence over His, when we lust after the things of the world instead of seeking diligently after Him. It was very appropriate that God linked the house experience to adultery. Lamar and I were committing a form of adultery by going off and finding a house we couldn't have, tempting ourselves when it wasn't the right time. If we had succeeded, we would have lost it because shortly thereafter we went through the worst financial disaster of our lives. I thanked God daily for my $93 house payment.

We lust after people and things we should not have. We are an adulterous people. It's something we will have to deal with all our lives. Only as we learn to walk in the spirit and yield to the spirit will we spare ourselves from these terrible cycles of pain and grace, pain and grace. It's part of the maturing process. And then, once you have learned, you have been prepared to share what you have learned with others. It's called your testimony. It must be fresh and constantly changing and it must be shared.

I think we need to have more sympathy for the adulterer, the alcoholic, the drug addict, the homosexual, anyone whose life is beyond their control. There is no way we can truly understand the struggles they face and the devastation that it has caused their life. They did not ask to have this problem. By the time they realized they had the problem, it was too late. They were hooked.

Most adulterers and compulsives are actually very sweet people, they are just weak in this one area or maybe by now two or three areas. No doubt they have prayed and begged God to help them, to take this terrible thing from them and have been very disappointed that He has not been there for them. They honestly don't think there is an answer for them. If someone gives a testimony how God has come through for them, that is just further proof that they aren't worthy and God has judged them and found them wanting.

We must be realistic and understand no one who has such a problem solves it immediately. These things take time. It is unrealistic to think his willpower alone is going to hold him in check, or that he will never fall again. The plan has to include some changes that will reinforce him in staying away from temptation and adding to his life something more powerful. Jesus, yes, but also plans to make life exciting and pleasurable in a new way. Jesus never meant to do it alone. He wants to be the beginning of a new life. It's our job to walk out the miracle.

When a man has an inordinate desire for women, he usually meets his wife in the process of pursuing women. He learns to be charming and attentive even though his goal is not honorable. Sometimes he gets caught when he didn't mean to (she gets pregnant), but it's just as likely that he gets caught by falling in love, in spite of the fact that he tries desperately not to. He really does love his wife. Because his need for love and admiration is so great, how can he help but fall in love? So much so that he thinks, for her, he can be faithful. In the back of his mind he fears that he won't be able to carry it off, but marries anyhow, hoping to somehow keep his inordinate desire in check. Now that's real love. He has to be really crazy about a woman to marry her in spite of the gorilla in the closet.

These men really do love their wives. They just don't face their weakness and what it will take to stand. He hopes their love (and a good sex life) will be enough. He thinks she's the answer to his problem. Then again, he may not know he has a problem. His parents may have been strict enough or other things may have kept his tendencies in check up until that fateful moment when he yields to something sinister within. He doesn't understand he has an addiction or what an addiction is: when love is not enough. The addiction is bigger than their love. To counterbalance his own guilt, he needs to be able to blame his wife for his failure. If she hadn't made him mad, hurt his feelings, shut him out, refused to satisfy his sexual needs, etc., he wouldn't have fallen. It's her fault, or so he convinces himself.

This begins an escalation of their problems. He is hooked and he knows it. He can't forgive her and restore their relationship. He needs the offense. It's his excuse. He doesn't admit it to himself and instead tells himself it won't happen again, but the temptation is still there and the reasons for his weakness are too. It would be best if he came clean and began the healing process now but very few face it this soon. They hide it in the hopes they can deal with it, but he can't. It has to get big enough for him, his wife, and the world to see. Everything changed that fateful day, but she won't know for a long time, and maybe it's just as well.

Once he has slipped, it does something to him. He knows he can never go back to the wonderful world of innocence, to the days when he hadn't yet fallen. There is a new reality in his life and he must go into the hiding mode. Oh, what tangled webs we weave when first we practice to deceive. I am speaking generally; the details differ from one couple to another and from one compulsion to another. It's not just adulterers that sneak. Food addicts, gamblers, etc., all have this in common. It's not always the guy that has the problem. She may be the one running up the credit cards, or drinking too much, maybe even having an affair and hiding the truth from her husband. He or she now has another agenda: to hide the compulsion they cannot control.

At this point he isn't really thinking clearly. There is no telling what he will start doing to cover up his guilt. If we think their marriage was a mess before, we haven't seen anything yet. Well, let me take that back.

The marriage may actually seem better. He may begin to cooperate and do the things she has been asking him to do. He may shower her with love and try to make up for it that way. Or he may start being critical and verbally abusive so that when it's discovered, her guilt will diffuse some of his, or so he thinks. I don't know what form it will take, but things will change and she will react to the changes until the fateful day she finds out. And she will find out. The same devil that makes him do it, will expose him.

It's important to understand this is not the worst day. You already had that day a long time ago, maybe even before you met. It's really best that it is out in the open where you can deal with it. But most people don't see it that way and instead of dealing with the deeper issues, take very shallow steps to make things seem better. That is why it happens again. Or they start the divorce proceedings and go down that awful road. One bad choice after another.

The Bible says in Hebrews 11:6, *"For he that cometh to God must believe that he is, and that he is a rewarder of them that diligently seek him."* This is what *diligently* means. Through all our hurt and confusion we keep struggling to understand, to reach Him. To be honest, I don't know if at this point we can expect either of them to do any differently. Until you find Him, I don't know that any answer you give to try to solve your problems will be a good one. It will just be another diversion keeping you from Him.

We have to go through this time of searching, groping, contending, and even making mistakes. It will keep you occupied, and at a time like this that means a lot, but really you will just be marking time or making things worse. Marking time at a time like this is making things worse. Just as I went down that terrible road with things getting continually worse, I didn't have the capacity to do better. I didn't understand. I wasn't ready. It takes a readiness. We really shouldn't beat ourselves up for these wrong decisions. How could I understand when I didn't understand?

The wife naturally makes him the bad guy and he accepts it because he feels so guilty. He is guilty. And because he does love her, he tries to make it up to her, vowing to never let it happen again. She hopes and prays it won't happen again, but we're talking a weak human against a spirit that controls him. He's no match for his compulsion and falls again. She wants to forgive and believe him, but each time he falls it gets harder until she can't forgive any more and becomes more and more hurt, angry, and bitter.

I need to point out here; the couple usually doesn't get good counsel, if any. Even if they do get good counsel, one or both of them isn't ready. They can't seem to do what the counselor asks of them.

The spiritual answers don't seem real to him and he is loath to pursue them consistently. He doesn't surround himself with people that will help him through this difficult period, nor does he add new activities to replace the old compulsive ones. And she doesn't do the work on herself either. Some do and that's wonderful, but others, for whatever reason aren't ready yet.

She desperately needs something to salve her wounded soul. She finds it impossible to deny herself the things that temporarily make her feel better, like food or drink, or maybe she returns the hurt by spending an inordinate amount of money, or some other foolish thing thus putting herself at fault in her husband's mind, and other people's, too. Talk about two wrongs not making a right. By this time the husband is in such a mess, he feels there's no way out. They are headed for divorce. They both hate it because there are kids involved, but they are powerless to stop it or so they think. Perception is reality. He's tried and she's tried. What else can they do?

I question whether they have really tried at all. It's not about just forgiving, although that is a start. She feels she has forgiven umpteen times and it didn't help. And it's not about giving up the woman, although that's a start too. No, it's about becoming new creations in Christ. Getting a new brain, new emotions, new responses, new everything. God makes all things new. And He does it by first helping you see how pitiful you are. By bringing you to a point where you don't want to resurrect the old you. Once you have finally died to yourself, you are finally ready to begin. A lot of people feel they are really beaten down, but they aren't as beaten down as they think. They still make excuses and play their games.

Until you say, "*Oh, woe is me, I am a man of unclean lips,*" you aren't humbled enough.

I have seen many people come to church and "get saved" at a time of crisis, but then they never become faithful and don't really latch on, setting a time for prayer and Bible study. They mean to, but everything takes precedence. They don't realize how crucial it is to get a foundation as quickly as possible. If you don't have the opportunity of a fellowship group, there are tapes and TV programs to supplement beyond your own study and what you learn at church. Whatever you do, you must do it day in and day out, dropping old habits and old haunts for new ones. You must change your daily routine to include good teaching and good Christian friends.

It's not as much about *not* doing something as it's about becoming something, being predestined to be conformed into the image of Jesus Christ (Rom. 8:29). The Bible not only tells the thief to steal no more, but to give (Eph. 4:28). It's one thing to stop stealing, but to give out of what is mine? Now that's hard if you were a thief and thought you had a right to everybody else's stuff. But, it's also needful. Then his attitude will really be changed. When we ask someone to stop doing what is a negative, we must ask them to do an appropriate positive. He must minister out; help others who have a need.

It is in adding to your life, not just denying your cravings, your "tendencies." Yes, you do have to drop what you are doing, but only to pick up what He is giving you. The point isn't to deny yourself; the point is to add a fulfilling new life with joy and laughter and good times together. Christianity isn't the absence of sin, although we are trying. It is the presence of all good things. It's now just a matter of figuring out what God would have you (both of you) add to your life. But be careful. We don't want this new thing to be a compulsion, either.

It's like finding a precious lost coin. You are studying and seeking to find that one revelation, that one key that will unlock the answer, your answer. There are many answers out there and they are all good. But they aren't all your answer. You may latch on to other answers, but you won't have real peace about it. You may feel better, but you won't have that *yes* inside that you will have when your inner spirit knows this is the one. This is what you were missing! And then you will know what you must do. And it won't be just one answer. It will be a progression of answers that as you follow them, will lead you to where you need to go, you getting your answers, and your husband getting his, and both of you healing a little at a time. And if he refuses to get his answers and to progress, your progressing will help him anyway, not nearly as much, but some. And eventually, I believe, your progress will at some point help him to latch on and begin seeking his answers for himself.

And as you get these revelations inside, it has to manifest itself on the outside. Faith inevitably shows itself through the works that result from it. Our struggle is not just to get better inside, but to get better outside, too. And I don't just mean your physical body. I mean your house will be cleaner, your bills will be paid, your children healthier and happier. We fight the good fight of faith for results.

God, everything stands in ruins around me. If You don't help me, nothing and no one else can restore my world. I guess what stands in ruin is the world I have built. All I can say is "help!" I need a revelation, or to at least the first one of many. I want the process to finally begin. I give you permission to reveal to me what I need to see; the error in my thinking; the third beyond my thinking and my husband's. I'm tired of being right in my own eyes; I want to be right in Your eyes, and in my husband's. I thank You for it in the name above all other names, Jesus. Amen.

FORTY-TWO

Do not let kindness and truth leave you; Bind them around your neck, Write them on the tablet of your heart.

—PROVERBS 3:3

Now What?

THE FIRST THING YOU must do is pray. This doesn't mean you will do nothing but pray, but I can't guarantee you will like what you are asked to do. In fact, the exact opposite. Most of the things you are asked to do by God will go against every fiber of your being, especially if you have been raised in a dysfunctional home. Because your responses up until now haven't been good. Before you do something or say something, you need to know it's what God would have you say or do and not what you worked up in your own mind. Much of our waiting is not because God is withholding from us or because our spouse will not cooperate. We are waiting because we are in the refining process.

The second thing you should do is back off, if you haven't already. We are usually too aggressive in the wrong way and at the wrong time. And then you should have a plan; a plan for accountability, a plan for restoration, a plan for normalcy, a plan to live again, to laugh and enjoy each other.

When you can't do what you should be doing, when you aren't in control of your own actions, I recommend fasting. I have talked about this before, and I am always amazed that people don't fast when they know things are in a big mess. How bad does it have to get before you get in gear and do a deeper work than just begging God? Remember, we don't fast to force God to do something. We fast to do something in ourselves.

Do not fast without finding out more about it. You must drink plenty of fluids and discontinue the fast if there are any signs of physical problems. I don't recommend fasting over three days unless you are sure you heard from God and it's OK with your doctor. God would never go against doctor's orders. Once you start adding food back, do it slowly and conservatively, avoiding spicy foods.

A TIME TO REFLECT AND PRAY

In the case of adultery, a couple might consider being celibate for a short period of time to be sure he has not contracted some disease and to give her time to heal. The offender will need to get tested to be sure there is no sexually transmitted disease.

It's a good idea not to be in a big hurry and to go through a dating process so the feelings have a chance to come back if at all possible. The Bible says a couple can stop for a time of prayer (1 Cor. 7:5). It would be nice if they could begin to be physically nurturing in other ways before they continue on to have sex. He should understand her need to be held and feel a bond that doesn't involve sex. However, she must understand it's hard for him to be physical and not to be sexual.

I don't believe in withholding sex because you are having problems. Sex is not a reward for good behavior. Sex is something a man needs, and a woman does, too. Therefore, if we are married, it's up to us to participate in the act. It's really not optional. Our body is our husband's as well as our own, like it or not. I understand he has hurt her beyond words, but he is hurting, too. He needs to know he is loved and accepted and there is hope of healing. This is how we begin, by being physically responsive. I wouldn't go beyond a couple of weeks of abstinence.

After you have had a time of prayer and reflection, you need to make needed changes in your life. Act on what you feel God has said or would say you should do. Don't set up camp around your problems. Embrace life and what you do have, not what you don't have or have lost. Yes, grieve and have a time of sorrow, but after that time of sorrow, get up and fix your face and face your world again.

If you are the one that committed adultery, everything that I say to the guys goes for you, too. The biggest problem a woman faces is his ego and his inability to let go of the offense. You cannot fall into this trap even if he does. You are forgiven. It is now in the sea of forgetfulness. You are a new creation in Christ and the apple of God's eye. If anyone tries to tell you differently—including your husband—they are liars and agreeing with the father of lies. All people sin. It is pride for one person to think their sin is better than another's. Pride is really bad.

Make verbal changes. Verbally change how you speak to him, to yourself, about him, about yourself. Make decisions on what you will say, what you won't say and to whom, and discuss it with him and whoever else is necessary. But don't keep secrets from everybody. Some people need to know and you need to agree on who those people are. To walk in the truth, the truth must be known. Right now, since you don't yet have the victory and therefore no testimony, all you can do is speak positively. Speak what you want to see.

Stop all incorrect speaking. Listen to every word out of your mouth. I would even tape it or write down some of it. Make a journal of how you are speaking and your general attitude when you are with your husband and your children. If you can't do it, have them do it. Pull a Dr. Phil and set up a camera and then review it later privately. Most people don't realize how bad they sound and act.

COUNSELING

Counseling is imperative. The offender must agree to be accountable. They must agree to counseling and mentoring. Healing cannot be left to chance or to the offender.

A spouse that "slips" should want to be held accountable. They need someone, a counselor or pastor that is connected to God to guide them because this is a journey not a one-time shot. Yes, they are forgiven immediately, but developing new patterns take some time. Old patterns got them in the mess. If they don't start new ones, they will be in a mess again. And since they can't be watched all the time, they need someone that can deal with these complex issues and guide them on a regular basis.

You must counsel together some of the time. This keeps things honest. The counselor needs to hear the other side once in a while. I went to a "how-to counsel" class and the moderator said he would not counsel a couple if both wouldn't agree to come in *and* if both did not agree Christian principles are the basis of their lives. If he can't get them to agree on the fundamentals, then he has no basis on which to proceed.

If he is the offender, I warn you that he'll try to come back with just the promise of getting counseling and not actually doing it. He should already be in counseling when he comes back. He should be committed to the counseling and doing what is necessary on his own, just as you should be doing the same. And he needs to understand when he stops the counseling, he must leave the home. He cannot stay without this help to get better. If he has a problem with the counselor, speak to him and try to understand the problem. If you feel it's the counselor, then it's OK to change. But usually, it's the person not the counselor. If you have to get a new one, don't allow him to stop going to counseling. Go with him when he starts to complain.

If you are the offender, you must be committed to counseling and to being held accountable as well.

Healing is the only way to deal with this problem properly. Sadly, some men are not ready to go through this process yet. For some reason the pain, embarrassment, and humiliation is not enough yet, and we must respect their right not to begin. That is when it's hard: when he is happy in his sin. At least we can make our decisions in this light (start legal proceedings, etc.). It's almost harder when the man says he wants to change, but doesn't mean it. He's just saying what we want to hear, and when we have let down our guard, he will revert to his old games. It's hard to know the difference. They sound so sincere. How do we know? We really don't. It's in his attitude toward the counseling that we get our clues. Being together must include positive steps toward healing, and counseling and accountability are essential.

The problem with most counseling and the reason it takes so long is because the professional is talking to a person in denial and who isn't facing the truth. It is in talking with them over a period of time that finally the truth comes out in some little snippet that gives the counselor a clue and he or she follows up on it.

Lamar and I knew a couple about to counsel with the pastor and I said to Lamar, "I wish they would take me." I knew the truth wouldn't come out because they didn't know the truth. They played their games and were absolutely convinced they were the wounded party. This is why friends and relatives can be so helpful. They can tell you the truth, if you will listen. That pastor recommended divorce. And they had two young children. Their marriage was not that bad. There was no reason for them to divorce except the pastor just heard one whiney side.

In a book for alcoholics, they told how most alcoholics succeed for a few years and then fall back into it because they get careless. They quit doing what has made them successful and think they can be around it and not have it bother them.

Like that wonderful old philosopher Pogo said, "I have met the enemy, and he is us."

Unfaithfulness is a recipe for pain and failure. No matter how we have hurt each other or been hurt, God has provided an answer: forgiveness for everyone involved. He intended a beautiful, special relationship, and we can still have it, but now it takes a lot more to get it and keep it. It doesn't come cheap and it doesn't come easy, but at least it can come. In time, in prayer, it can come. A good long-term marriage is worth the fight of faith it takes to claim it. Allow me to pray for you:

> *Dear heavenly Father, I pray for my friend. You know her family and You know her needs. I don't. I ask You to touch her in a special way, right now and give her a hunger for Your Word. Help her to use her mouth creatively and create her family by the words she speaks. Help her to stop all negative speaking, and I ask You to put a watch on her lips and a hedge around*

any words that sow unbelief and strife and death to her loved ones. You love her more that I ever could and You know her better than I ever could. I ask You now to give her wisdom and discernment in her situation. Bring mature Christians into her life, a spiritual mother and father, brothers and sisters in Christ, to lead and guide her in the way she should go. But more than that I ask You to send the Comforter and Teacher, the Holy Spirit, to her and pour her out a blessing she will not be able to contain. Let it spill out on everyone around her. And let it take the form of joy and peace and, yes, even laughter. Give her a spirit of laughter that will carry her through the dark days. May she be a blessing to all she meets. In Jesus name I pray, Amen. And God, I pray this for the woman in the example in particular. Do a special work in her life and lead her out of the hell she is in. Amen.

I have to assume there were many things that caused the adultery to happen and just as many things that can be accomplished by walking out the healing process. We need to understand that not just the husband has "issues," but the wife has them, too. I am not the victim of my husband. I am a child of the most high God and no weapon formed against me shall prosper. And by "me" I mean me and my husband, because we are one.

Let's do a movie.

WHEN LADIES MEET

When Ladies Meet is one of our wonderful old black and white movies, made in 1933. Myrna Loy, an author, is involved with her publisher. She is working on her latest book about a woman involved in an affair who wants to talk with the wife. The publisher, her lover, doesn't like the last chapter and doesn't feel the wife has been properly fleshed out. They decide to steal away to a friend's home in the country to work on it.

Myrna has a male friend who really likes her but isn't getting anywhere because she's stuck on the publisher. He is friends with the publisher's wife and after a round of golf talks the wife into taking a ride in the country with him. When he finds Myrna at the friend's home, he talks the wife into pretending to be his date to make Myrna jealous. He has an idea the sordid mess might come out and expose the husband and break up the affair to his advantage.

Myrna and the wife become fast friends and talk into the night. Just as the wife is beginning to suspect something, her husband rushes into the room not knowing she is there. Immediately the wife knows he is having an affair with Myrna, but no one says anything. The wife goes to her room and gets ready to leave even though it's 2 a.m. Because of her fondness for Myrna, she no longer wants to stand in the way of this special relationship. Myrna realizes her affair with the publisher isn't really that special, and she decides to dump him. The husband/lover realizes his goose is cooked when he sees he has lost his wife.

The point of the movie is the "other" woman can be very special, but their relationship really isn't. He is special, too, but he has a problem, a problem she would have with him if she were the wife. Any woman would. Anyone that marries him will get a very special man with a problem. But he does love his wife. And, because they have kids and a life, it really would be best if he got over his roving eye and settled down for once and for all. Not all these men aren't worth having. Many very special men have had this problem and realized how destructive and foolish it was. They stopped and went on to a very special marriage. There is life and love after an affair, a very special love.

The other woman is a deceived woman, deceived by her own mind and emotions as much as by him. He is deceived by his mind and emotions. Don't you be deceived, too, by your mind and emotions. He does love you. It's just that he got all mixed up and didn't know how weak he was. He's like the prodigal of which it's said later, "he came to himself." Pray that your husband comes back to himself, to the man God created him to be, not so you can have him back but just so things will be right with him.

FORTY-THREE

**And be kind and compassionate to one another, forgiving
one another, just as God also forgave you in Christ.**

—EPHESIANS 4:32

The Worst Choice: Unforgiveness

RATHER THAN TELL YOU to forgive and forget, which we both know will someday be necessary, I feel it would be helpful for you to look at life and what has happened through the eyes of the other person. You have to get out of your brain for a minute and look from another vantage point. It's important for you to understand that by the time the affair happened, the two people involved very likely did not have a choice. The choice was made a long time ago, and it may have been made by someone else, parents (the father was an adulterer, abusive, neglectful, spoiled him), alcohol, etc. There really wasn't a choice that fateful day. They were already set up for a fall by factors, many of which they had no control over. Sin starts in the heart and mind long before we see the result of it.

I don't know why some people are predisposed to alcoholism and others to adultery. All I know is some people are and they aren't astute enough to know it. It's true, if a person never takes a drink, they never have to face the problem of alcoholism. If they are never alone with a woman, they will never fall into adultery, but in this day and age our society is awash in alcohol and sexual promiscuity. Is it any wonder some drown? And when they do, whose fault is it? The alcoholic or adulterer bears much of the responsibility and it will be their battle to fight and their cross to bear, but the rest of us aren't always innocent. Maybe what we are doing to our kids or others is predisposing them to do something they shouldn't. We need to help the fallen instead of giving them the fatal blow. It's such a difficult process to come out of deep-rooted sin; it can only be done with the help of people that have traveled the road before us. If we forgive and "get over" whatever it is, then we sometimes feel that lets them off the hook and they don't deserve to be let off the hook. They need to pay for what they did. But they are paying for what they did. Their lives are full of the payment of the sin and will be for the rest of their lives. They will never escape this. It's one thing to be the victim, and it's another to be the perpetrator. Remember how hard it was for me to deal with the accident I caused, and I didn't think I hurt the people that bad. And I could justify some of it because they weren't wearing their seat belts. But it was still my fault. Think of hurting loved ones over and over again. That's enough to make you want to run or drink or numb your brain some way. This is why it's so important that we never forget we all sin. None of us are worthy of casting the first stone.

"My husband had an affair (committed a crime, lost our life savings, etc.) and I just can't seem to get over it." One reason why you may not be able to move on is because you may not be able to forgive, not that you haven't tried. You pray to forgive him, but you still feel the bitterness and anger rise up and you know you haven't really forgiven him. So, you pray again and repent of your bitterness and anger and ask God to help you only to have it rise up again and again. You want to forgive, but can't until you finally concede.

You are not understanding forgiveness. Forgiveness is not a feeling; it's an act of our will. Freeing the person, not from their sin, but from you so you can turn them over to God. I'm assuming you prayed a prayer releasing them and giving it all to God. This begins the process. You have done the right thing by praying about it and even repenting for your feelings. This is a lot like a healing you so desperately want but never seems to come. You aren't healed when it finally manifests itself in your body. You were healed when Jesus took His stripes. He said it was finished when He died on the cross. Everything you needed was accomplished. We can't make the actual manifestation come about. God has to do that. All we can do is the praying and the receiving and the thanking and the waiting. You walk a path to the manifestation of your healing, just as you will walk this path to the feeling of forgiveness for your husband or anyone else that has hurt you.

After you have prayed the prayer for your healing, you should continue to thank God and do what you are able to do. When the "proof" that you are not actually healed hits you in the face, it's a lie. And you can tell the devil it is. Do you remember my story in chapter 12 of being healed of allergies? I kept saying, "Satan, you're a liar." I must have said it thirty-five times that day. I certainly didn't look like I won that battle, but I did. That was the last time I had an allergy attack. You pray for help in areas that are still troubling you, but you accept the fact that you are healed and your body will eventually come in line. We walk in faith, not in sight. And so it's with forgiveness. We have forgiven him, and when bitterness rises up or hurt or anger over the past, we just remind the enemy and ourselves that we already did that and we don't have to do it again. We keep telling the devil to get away from us, we have forgiven him already. It's a done deal. And we have forgiven ourselves, etc.

Now the forgetting is a different thing. By forgetting we do not mean that our husband doesn't have to be accountable or that we can't make changes in light of what he has done. He is weak in this area, and we mustn't be foolish and go back to letting down our guard. But once we have made the proper adjustments, we should give it to God and quit entertaining thoughts that are linked to the past. God's memory is perfect; ours is not. When the enemy comes and reminds you of your past or your husband's, both of which have been put away as far as the east is from the west, you can say, "What are you talking about? That doesn't exist anymore." You can forgive and you can forget. It just takes time and discipline. Eventually, it will become a reality.

Any time there has been an offense, a sin against another person, there must be healing that includes repentance, grief, reconciliation, and restoration. When we, the offended party, say we won't or we can't coop-erate with this progression, for whatever reason, healing is stopped at that point. The offender can only do so much on their own and they can get the victory if they have done all they can do. You are the one that stays in the offense. If you don't forgive, God says He can't forgive you (Matt. 6:15).

You are the person that holds your own world in your hands. You are the one that decides if today you have joy or sorrow and bitterness. Another person may bring sorrow and pain to you, but you are the one that keeps it and turns it into bitterness.

I know sorrow and bitterness because my marriage had become a place of sorrow and bitterness much too soon. Even though I knew our marriage was in trouble, I got pregnant anyway because I didn't want Grant to be raised alone. Dadra was born two years almost to the day after Grant.

The name Dadra was taken from the Swedish name Deidre, but I changed the spelling because I liked the sound of the long A better. The middle name I took from Lamar: Marra. His mother had doubled the r's; so, I named her Dadra Marra Vice. After she was gone and I had become a Christian, I came across a book of names and discovered Deidre meant sorrow, a tragic Swedish figure. It was as if someone punched me in the stomach. A while later, when I was reading the Old Testament, I came across the name Mara in Ruth 1:29: *"'Don't call me Naomi,' she told them. 'Call me Mara, because the almighty has made my life very bitter.'"* I was stunned! I would have never named her Marra had I known. My precious daughter was named Sorrow and Bitterness! Words cannot express how I felt at that moment.

The truth is, and you know me and my search for truth, Dadra was conceived in sorrow and bitterness. Therefore, the name is not inappropriate. I just would have never done it if I had known. But isn't that the point? God brings things around in ways we can't predict—the ironies of life. He is there in them somewhere. It was saying He knew long before I knew.

I understand sorrow and bitterness and would grieve with you if I had a chance. That's why I'm am writing this book, in the hope that you can get past your sorrow and bitterness, as I got past mine. You can do it. You can forgive, not for him, but for you, for those you love. And in forgiving him, you will free not only him but yourself. It's time to move on. If he never understands, changes, or repents, it's not yours to worry about. You must worry about you and what it will take to get *you* healthy. And what makes you healthy will make those around you healthier. If he's included in the bunch, so be it. If he chooses not to be, that's going to have to be OK too.

Now I am asking you to say the words that you forgive him, the other woman, anyone else involved, and you forgive yourself and you forgive God. Say a prayer that will release you from this garbage heap you have been camped at for too long. You do not owe this one more minute of your time. I had to come to the place where I quit being a victim; where death had robbed me as much as it was going to rob me. I was going to laugh again and enjoy life again and do whatever made me happy and what made Lamar happy and the boys! And you must, too. There's a world out there that needs you healthy and whole and until you get there, people will continue to hurt.

LIFE LESSONS

I know we don't like to think we draw to ourselves the lessons we need to learn, but I think we do. I wouldn't take this too far because children and the innocent aren't to blame for their abuse, but generally, we seem to keep going around the same mountains until we finally learn the lesson of the mountain. I don't mean to say that you brought the affair on yourself or whatever has come upon you and devastated you. We live in an evil world and you are one of its targets. However, you will experience only certain evils. Your enemy is good at choosing what will devastate you the most, what it will take to take you down and keep you there. It won't be easy to get pass it, but it is possible, and when you do, you will be a whole new person and your enemy won't bother to send that one your way again.

Both spouses in any tragic situation should allow themselves to grieve.

Just as a person must do certain things after a physical death, so must you (or the wounded one), and even the perpetrator do certain things. I learned after the death of my little girl that I had to fight emotionally to not be sucked in by my grief. It's a discipline of the mind. Just as an alcoholic must live one day at a time, so must the bereaved. If you look back, you will either remember the good things or maybe you will start rethinking things and looking for clues, although a little bit of this is probably helpful so you will be wiser from here on in, much more than that will be counterproductive. No, don't look back even to remember the good times, at least not too much, because it will just make you regret that you won't have them again. And don't assume you won't because you really don't know what you will have, but it will never be the same again.

And you can't look forward because that will just remind you of what will never be. No, you must live in the moment. And that's really how all of us should live—one day at a time, one moment at a time.

"One day at time, sweet Jesus, that's all I'm asking of you. Help me today; show me the way; one day at a time." I've sung it for years to help me stay on course. We should never assume God doesn't have wonderful plans for our lives. So, why should we ever look forward with regret? You serve the most high God, the Creator of the universe, and He loves you with an everlasting love. How dare anyone tell you things won't be stupendous!

You must say, like Scarlet O'Hara in *Gone With the Wind*, "I'll think about that tomorrow." And then you stop these thoughts from tormenting you. And when you finally can't do it, steal away for a while and yell at God and tell Him what a raw deal you think you got. Let it all out until you can't yell anymore, and then pray and read the Word, whatever it takes until you are ready to face the world again.

People thought I did such a good job handling Dadra's death. I don't feel I did a good job. If I did, it was just because I did whatever I had to do in private. I made time for my grief. And I put the boys' welfare ahead of my own.

You do get to a point when you can't cry any more. There are some things you can't do, like Christmas parades were for me. So, I didn't go to Christmas parades. I got somebody to take the boys or we just didn't go. Know your limits and try to work within them, or allow God to give you the grace to expand them. These things expand our capacity for grace and that's a good thing.

We talk about going around the mountain again. When we take on the offense, and it warps and colors our life, the only way to rectify the situation is to go back to the place of the offense and do it right this time. This is why we keep going around the same mountain. The movie *50 First Dates*, starring Drew Barrymore and Adam Sandler, is a good example. She suffers a head injury and can't remember past the day before the accident, so she keeps living that next day again and again. He falls in love with her, well, I won't ruin it for you, but the movie helps us see it's possible to live continually in the moment and life can be good.

"But I tried to do the right thing for so long I wearied at it and that's why I failed," some would say. And I'm sure that's true. We have to continue to throw ourselves on God's loving arms even when we don't understand what went wrong. There is a timing in the things that happen, a readiness, evidently something wasn't in place yet. Possibly you weren't as close or as dedicated to the Lord as you thought you were. Possibly you were a double-minded man—part of you wanting the Lord, but part of you wanting other things. Something was wrong, and I have to assume it was you, your partner, or something else and not God, and you should assume that too. And I believe, if you continue to go back and seek God, eventually you will understand.

Just think, I prayed for ten years before I got saved. God heard my prayers, but the answer was not to give me what I wanted, but to lead me to salvation. Reconnection with Him had to happen first. He had to allow things to get worse in order for this to happen. He was hearing me, but I didn't understand what the first step was, so I wasn't taking it.

No wonder things didn't get better during that time. How could I receive answers if my receiver wasn't even hooked up? And then after it's hooked up, we still have difficulty comprehending what God is trying to tell us. Our denial system can be so strong! It's a wonder He gets through what He does. Lamar didn't even know he was abused for years. Each of these needed revelations took time. That is why it's so important we are open to what He would like to say to us.

When things are so hard, it's a sign we are doing all the work. The Bible tells us to take up His burden for it's light and to give Him ours, for it's heavy. You evidently were carrying the wrong burden, doing too much of it yourself. Remember, you didn't make the rules and it's not up to you to uphold them, to judge others when they break them, or to bring redemption to them. Your job is to edify, encourage, be a channel of love, wisdom, discernment, encouragement, joy, and peace; in other words, a channel for God to flow through to others, especially the hurting and downtrodden. We are to have joy in the midst of the storm, peace that passes all understanding. If you don't, then you moved away from the spigot. Move back quickly and don't blame your husband for the lack of it. Circumstances do not dictate our joy or peace. God does.

You have an agenda, too, and you need to figure out what it is. Could you really want out of this marriage? Maybe you didn't love him as much as you thought you did. Maybe you aren't as innocent as you think you are. Maybe it's time to start facing the truth and getting real with God. He already knows.

We have seen what sexual brokenness can do to a nation. Adultery is a terrible thing, as are any lies or manipulations—any betrayal. We are so hurt we don't want him to even touch us, let alone go further. Many wives feel being deeply hurt gives them the right to deny their husband sex on a permanent basis because she is so hurt and cannot function sexually feeling the way she does. She stops having sex with him for many reasons: because she can't respond, to punish him, but also as a practical consideration in the case of adultery. There are sexually transmitted diseases that kill, so this makes a lot of sense because she doesn't know if he has a disease. They need to have a time to be sure the affair is over and that he is disease free and to heal emotionally.

But it really doesn't make a lot of sense in the long run not to make love because a man does need sex. It's a tangible way to show him he is forgiven and you can move on. The proof is in the pudding and if there is no pudding, there is no proof. If there is no proof, has the healing begun yet? Probably not. Why not? Because you are an emotional sexual being and your emotions are totally torn up. You can't get past your own hurt and don't care what it's doing to him. You want him to hurt as bad as you do, and I just bet he already does. If a wife denies her husband sexually, she assumes he will continue to fulfill his sexual needs elsewhere and that is fine with her. If she hasn't thought that far, I have to ask, Why not? It sounds like denial to me. Just because she doesn't care if she ever has sex again, he does. Since he does, the logical thing is to consider how he is going to satisfy this powerful human desire. Does she really want him going elsewhere? I understand the anger and the desire to punish and withhold is very strong. I also know, in this day and age of disease, it's tempting to do it on that basis alone. I would go along on that basis, but I feel withholding sex has the potential of more problems than it answers.

What does the husband find so alluring about other women? Is it about his manhood or his ego? Something in his head needs to be figured out and satisfied some other way. Check out John Eldredge's *Wild at Heart* for some good insights into the male psyche.

First, to choose not to have a physical, sexual, relationship means there will never be a resolution to the problem. You have allowed a door to remain open through which the devil will go in and out of your lives at will. And once in, he goes anywhere he chooses. Your family is in the mess it's in because the enemy has had an open door. We need to figure out where and close it or you will just go from this mess to another.

Second, I am assuming others will eventually know and that makes your family a bad witness to others and a source of embarrassment and ridicule.

Third, you are keeping the "broken" person (your husband and possibly you) in a continual state of brokenness. Why is it that we don't have God's idea? Adultery is not God's idea, but neither is this. "But this keeps the family together." Yes, but, it keeps the family in a continual state of hurt and frustration; hardly a good lesson to come from parents.

And finally, because it's unscriptural. That says it all. The others are good enough in themselves, and do it for the children if you must, but it's really better to do it because you love God and you know He loves you and wants the best for your life. Hopefully someday you can do it because you love your husband, too.

I was reading one of those wonderful "Can This Marriage Be Saved?" articles. A counselor was trying to help a couple who had been married about eighteen years, and although very much in love when they married, had not had much of a relationship for the last ten years. What really struck me was that the woman did not assume her husband was having sex somewhere else. How naïve can we be? He was quite a flirt and an outgoing person beloved by many. And she thinks he is just being charming? Amazing!

The estrangement started out slowly. Problems arose and for some reason they weren't dealt with properly. The vicious cycle got going good and a wall went up between them. He actually used his flirting to hurt her. At some point it went beyond flirting, and although that would have hurt her even more, he couldn't quite bring himself to take advantage to that extent. He probably was so mad and frustrated at the time it didn't matter until after the fact and then he came to his senses and realized what he had done. So, maybe he didn't really want to hurt her at all, just manipulate her into cooperating. Well, that didn't work. Instead of reacting and solving the problem, she went into denial and stifled her feelings all these years. And he's been making do.

They love their kids. They are the center of their world (do you see a clue here?) and no one has any idea how bad things are. They would love to divorce but hate to for the kids sake. A good enough reason to do everything possible to make this work. Why have they waited so long? Because it worked for them on some level maybe? She got to avoid sex and he got to go elsewhere. There was only one problem: the kids. And the fact that this wasn't a solution at all. It was running and God is not into avoidance as a solution. You can run, but you can't hide.

First, let me say, divorce will not be easier if the parents wait until the children are grown. I don't have the statistics, but divorce, especially for kids who have been raised in pseudo-happiness, will be devastating. They think they are important, but they are about to find out their world really revolves around the needs of their parents. There is no good time to get divorced. But I do have to admit, it's probably better to wait.

If a person finds their mate so problematic that they cannot remain in the marriage, is it really right to leave their children with this problematic person without their help to cope with what is so bad? How can anyone in good conscience do this to their kids? I understand kids have a right to grow up without all the fighting and stress. Then, quit fighting. I understand some situations do require separation and divorce, but not as many as we have now.

I read about another couple that experienced an extended affair. When the husband returned "for all the right reasons," they weren't ready to relate on an intimate level. They were both too wounded to respond. He came back for the kids' sake and because he knew it was the right thing to do. She agreed because it was an answer to prayer. She stood for the healing of her marriage, but the reality wasn't anything like she hoped it would be. There is a time lapse between when we do what is right and have the feelings that go along with it.

It was one thing to come back together for the kids' sake and another thing to make the marriage work. "What do we do now?" They had to make an effort to do what couples do that have loving feelings for each other. They had to make time for each other and plan dates. It takes time to be romantic and loving. So, they made the effort to do what came so naturally to other couples. And eventually, the feelings came. But it must be understood: they were doing many other things to heal their marriage including working on their own "issues." Don't you know they had to stifle during those first "dates" so as not to ruin it for the other? But you can't stifle forever. That's why you must be doing other things day by day: reading your Word, talking to mature Christians, attending church and Bible Study, going to counseling, listening to praise and worship music, etc.

As they went through the healing process, the husband was surprised the hold the other woman still had over him emotionally. Even though he had left the other woman a long time before he came back home, he still had very deep feelings for her. It took months of Bible study, prayer, and the help of a Spirit-filled mentor to break this hold over his mind and emotions. He came to see it was actually bondage and not love at all. He didn't know it at the time, but he was not a good judge of what love is. The affair felt like love. He thought he finally had the real thing. It wasn't until he saw what it was doing to the kids, hers and his, that he realized something was terribly wrong and he couldn't continue on this path. He learned not to trust anything but the Word. We must have something more trustworthy than our feelings.

A proper conclusion of his attempt to do the right thing would not have been possible if he or his wife had judged their actions by their feelings. It wouldn't have been done by logic either, because it didn't make sense to go back to a failed marriage. Counselors even agreed that his wife was not good for him. His brain is what got him in trouble in the first place and it wouldn't get him out. He had to have a scriptural basis for everything he did. Then, and only then, would he have the help and power of God in what he did.

"Why would the counselors recommend he leave his wife? Weren't they Christians?" Yes they were. They saw things in his wife that were troubling and they thought the "other woman" was a godly woman. The wife wasn't where she should be spiritually and when push came to shove, it was hard for the counselors to choose her. They were looking at the outward signs, but the inward signs weren't good either. The marriage had broken down to such an extent they felt it was hopeless. They might as well move on. She was the only one that couldn't accept it; she and maybe one or two of her friends.

Sometimes you do need to accept it. I can't say God will put every marriage back together. And it sure didn't look like He would this one. Although she continued to pray and stand for her marriage, she was forced to deal with reality. And the reality was he was gone. She had to begin to do what she had to do as a woman living alone. She also accepted the fact that she couldn't change or control her husband. The only one she could change was herself. And for a control freak, that was quite an accomplishment. She determined to work on herself and that is when everything began to change, but it didn't look like it for a long time.

Of course she had to forgive the woman, but not just forgive, pray for her. This is just step one. We think if we forgive, then it's time to stop the whole thing and get what we want. It's the later things we learn that are the richest. Keep on walking and seeing what He wants you to do next. Let God do His perfect work in you. I call it walking out your miracle.

Please don't think you are immune to falling. Sin's tentacles are no doubt wrapped around you in some fashion and go into the inner recesses of your being. Just because you were not the perpetrator of this sin doesn't mean you were not reached with its decaying influence. This wife found there was a lot of work to be done in her life long before the husband returned and long after. In fact, there was work to be done long before her husband entered the picture. As the adult child of an alcoholic father, she was an accident waiting to happen. God helped her to see that she was too controlling and he was wrong to give into her. That's the Jezebel and Ahab spirits. If you have this problem, it would do you well to do a study in the Word on this subject for yourself with the help of other people either at church or even a good book or tapes. This couple continues to minister together to bring healing to not just those who have experienced adultery, but to anyone who needs to forgive. Today they are both free.

THE JEZEBEL SPIRIT IS NOT MERELY SEXUAL, NOR IS IT A GENDER

The spirit of Jezebel is a controlling spirit. God doesn't want us to be controlling. This is going further than doing the right thing.

The Jezebel spirit seems to attract the Ahab spirit. The Ahab person gives other people their way because they don't have the strength of character to do the right thing. Ahab appeases and appeases until it's too late. These spirits take up residence in people and cause them to act out in ways that are destructive to themselves and others. There are no good answers once evil has its toehold. No good answer except one: obedience. What is right doesn't come easy.

> *Oh, God, for a greater good to come to pass in spite of the affair. (Or whatever it was that he did.) I was so hurt, I assumed it was all his fault and I was a victim of forces I had no control over. I can see now I had a part to play in our downfall and I can have a part to play in our healing. Help me to walk it out. Help me to be a part of his healing process as well as my own. I want to stand in the truth. I give You the right to show me when I am wrong. I am tired of being the last one to see things the way they are. I see a lot, but it's what I haven't seen that has hurt us. Help me to see what You want me to see. And help me to love as You would have me love. Help me to love myself so I can properly love others. I bind Satan from blinding our eyes and lying to us any longer… (continue praying)*

FORTY-FOUR

All you have to do to be selfish is to wake up in the morning.
—KEITH MOORE

He Cares

WHEN A WOMAN WITH deep marital problems asked her husband what he wanted, he replied "to be king of my castle." In other words, he wants to call the shots in his own home. Sounds a lot like what God wants. The only problem is she doesn't agree with many of the shots he is calling. That is a problem. She mentioned that he is too lenient with their children. That is bad. Then she mentioned that he tried to get her to cut down on her long distance phone calls, which is understandable, but she refused. Why? Because her marriage is such a mess and she and her husband were already so emotionally divorced that she needed some emotional support. Been there, done that. But, it doesn't help to run up your bills and make your husband mad. I wonder how many of these things there are. Little things that she refuses to do? How many things in their home aren't the way he wants them to be?

She is trying to solve her problems the wrong way and it's causing the rift to grow. What does a woman do when a man is emotionally divorcing himself from her? That's a hard one because often it's a woman who can least cope with it. She needs to be close to her husband, but her dysfunction (or his dysfunction) causes her to push him away.

The first thing I would say is this: your husband is not the enemy. We tend to get into the "I'm right/you're wrong" posture and that is not helpful. I'm not saying he's not wrong and you aren't right. It's just not helpful to square off this way. Most things are not right vs. wrong issues, but rather of preference.

One of the most harebrained ideas women get is "my husband doesn't care." This is simply not true. He may do dumb things and be terribly selfish and self-centered but he really does care. He may have gotten to the point that he thinks he doesn't care, but that doesn't make it so. The fact that he is so upset means that he does care. If he's still there, he cares. I have to admit some people are so dysfunctional they seem to be selfish all the way to the core. I'm going to assume you don't have one of these, but it's yours to know, although when the devil is getting them, they all seem this way. So far, most of the guys I've seen are not as bad as the wife thinks he is.

Your husband cares more than you think. It may not look that way, but that's why he is acting so badly. He may be threatening you with divorce. Lamar did—daily. But he didn't mean it and I knew that. He was just trying to get me to see things his way. I hated it for the boys, but I wouldn't have hated it for myself. By this time I wanted out.

Lamar's thinking was all messed up, and he wasn't making much sense. His gut level reactions were as bad as mine. That is why we can't think this thing out logically. It isn't logical. I took care of the boys and generally kept the boat afloat. Lamar worked and provided. He did love us, but like I used to say, "If this is love, I'd hate to see hate." I stopped telling him I loved him because I find it hard to lie; and to be honest, I didn't think I did love him.

When Love Dies

One night as we were getting ready for bed, I said something that hurt Lamar deeply. I can't even remember what it was. We were going to bed still fussing about something (by this time we were Christians) and he said, "You have done it now. You have killed my love for you. I will never again feel the same toward you." I was so upset with him, I really didn't care, but I can't imagine what I said was that bad. I was probably just being honest and said it like I saw it. I'm not a vindictive person.

As I lay in bed, suddenly I realized I had never lived with Lamar without his love. It makes a difference when you are angry if the person loves you or not. The reality of such a loss washed over me. I knew talking to Lamar wouldn't help. All I could do was pray about it. I repented of what I had done. I hadn't meant to hurt him. Then it dawned on me: Lamar knows God. God can give him His love. God could restore the love and a better love. I asked God to give Lamar His love for me and with that had a peaceful night's sleep. I know the Bible says not to let the sun go down on your wrath, but at this point I figured it would just make things worse if I tried to apologize. I needed to give God time to help him get over it. Anyhow, he could go to the same place I went and I guess he did because I never noticed a difference. It just keeps getting better. If the love has died in your marriage, ask God to bring it back.

During the time when things aren't all that good, it's a good idea to look at the positives. I don't think we realize how hard it is for our husband to see us discontented and upset all the time. So many homes have a heaviness hanging over them all the time. It really isn't conducive to resolving your problems. It makes a man want to run away, stay away, maybe even drink, or worse. It makes him think poorly of himself, yet he feels powerless to change it. He feels he's tried and for some reason it has failed; either he can't do what you want or he feels he will never be able to satisfy you.

It's really not scriptural to be this way. The Bible talks about the peace that passes all understanding; joy coming out of the ashes of mourning. Faith is seeing what your physical eyes can't see right now. If you are unhappy, it's because you are allowing what is in front of your face to dictate your responses. "You see a defeated man, devil? I see a victorious man on fire and serving the Lord." You must fight this battle in your mind before you can fight it anywhere else. In fact, it will always be in your mind. And as you win it in yours, you will win it for others, too.

Men want to be our heroes. They long to be admired. I know there doesn't seem to be much to admire at times, but we must. They are really very sensitive and easily hurt. One day I read an article on Lamar's personality type and it told some of the bad things he was: domineering, controlling, etc., and then it went on to say he was sensitive and touchy.

He's mean to me and then touchy when I am mean back. And yes, I have to deal with it. I have to be careful with this toughie I'm married to not to bruise him. It's tempting to jump all over him when he's so thick-headed, but it is counterproductive.

He really does want to please. He goes out of his way to do something nice and sometimes it is so inappropriate. It's so tempting to be *honest*! And I need to be, but sometimes he can't take much more. He's had a rough day and now is not the time. If I do speak harshly, it just takes him all the longer to get over it. Lamar's been known to get physically ill from what I say. It opens his spirit and he comes down with a cold or the flu or whatever is "going around." I'm serious. Sickness comes in through an open spirit first. Just think back and you will usually see what upset you or him just prior to an illness. I'm telling you: it is not worth it. Bring your mouth into submission when approaching your husband—actually, anybody. The Bible says the tongue is the unruly member. Who is it the most unruly toward? Your husband. And whose next? Your children!

WHAT DO YOU AGREE ON?

Instead of thinking about all the things you disagree about, you need to start thinking about what you agree on. You agree on more than you think. After you have accepted the fact that you agree more than you realized, you need to make a list of these things. Most people agree they want a decent home, a car and certain physical comforts, to pay their bills. If they have children, they want them to be nurtured, disciplined, well provided for, etc. They want friends, to be well thought of in the community, have a certain amount of privacy, and so on. You may both agree on some other things like football games, motorcycles, physical fitness, etc. You had something in common when you were dating; refresh your memory on what it was. Hopefully it was more than sex. If he committed to marriage, there must have been more. Look at what you agree on and build on that instead of majoring on what you disagree about.

Major on the Majors

After you have listed the ways you agree, major on them. Try to do it in a way that agrees with your husband. Sometimes we agree only to disagree about how it should be accomplished. Ask yourself if you can be more agreeable about the way you go about things. Even if we feel we will never agree with our spouse, that doesn't mean we have to fight for our way. We can let some things go. People have the right to be wrong and we need to respect it. They have a right to fail. And they have the right to fail without us saying anything (or at least not much). Sometimes we don't agree today but we will tomorrow, *after one of us sees the light*. Not saying anything brings you a lot closer to being appreciated by him and probably God. The Bible speaks well of our silence.

We do need to sit down and discuss things, but it's not easy because we are so busy and so hacked out. I want to find out where my husband is coming from and what his intentions are. Sometimes this is not possible. It would be counter-productive. If this is the case, don't push it. Watch and pray and see what your husband does, God does, or "life" does. In other words, stand. *"And having done all, to stand"* (Eph. 6:13). Now is not always the best time to talk.

Timing is everything. And we are prone to get ahead God. .We have to respect a person's right *not* to talk about things, although there comes a point when we have to and only you can know when that is. Putting things off may not be the best idea. Pray. Get good counsel. Don't try to do everything alone. And if you get counsel, but it doesn't seem quite right, get more. Eventually you will know what is right if you stay tender in your spirit. It's almost always the enemy that rushes us, trying to get us to do something too soon. If the rush to "talk" becomes a tormenting thought, it's not God.

On the other hand, if you feel led to say something, go ahead and say it. Have a monologue; tell it like it is (lovingly), take a stand and do what you feel you must do. Why make a discussion out of a statement? "This isn't working for me, hon. I feel...." Tell him how you feel, but don't accuse or blame him. Speak in love as you pray and get God's mind and pass on what you have come to understand. Just be sure it is God and not your self-righteousness.

The point is I have something I feel led to say and I say it. "Feeling led" being the operative words. How do we know if it is God, our own mind, or "the enemy"? This takes experience: hearing, checking it with the Word, your inner witness, and seeing the outcome a few times—walking it out until you know. If the person isn't up for a discussion, I drop the subject. It isn't time and it won't be anointed. I have to stay tender to the Holy Spirit. I'm not doing my thing. I'm trying to help Him do His, staying open and continuing as normally as possible. And enjoying what I do have in the relationship.

What Time Is It?
It Is Very Important We Know What Time It Is, and I Don't Mean According to Your Watch

I was watching an Oprah show where the men were telling how they changed their approach to their kids after watching an earlier show. They thought they were doing enough by bringing home a paycheck until other men shared how involved they were in their families. It really does help for guys to be around godly, vulnerable, Christian men instead of the dumb rubes they seem to gravitate to. Recomputing is great when it comes as a result of wise counsel. But we can't force them to the wise counsel. It has to be his idea. It will come when he gets tired of all the dumb counsel he's been getting. You may not think it's sinking in, but it is. You will be the last one he tells when it's getting old. Watch and wait.

I love Luke 2:19, *"But Mary kept all these things and pondered them in her heart"* (KJV). If you think of it, Mary didn't say much that we are aware of, but she was a powerful figure in Jesus' life. Her power didn't come from what she said; it came from who she was: the chosen vessel. You are a chosen vessel, the vessel through which God wants to pour His love, deliverance, and healing to your husband.

We really do need to hold things in our heart and our cards close to our chest. Even when you have unmet needs and burdens and want to give your loved one some advice and pull him in the direction you think he should go, it is still better to wait and listen. The Bible speaks about a word "fitly" spoken. I'm not saying you will never get to say what is on your heart. I am saying sit and have a simple conversation and see where it goes. Let your husband or God lead the discussion where they would have it go. You will probably find out something that will force you to totally recompute. And even that recomputing will not be written in stone. We recompute to recompute again. Life is a continual recomputing and upgrading. You will have to learn all new skills again and again.

JACKIE

Jackie attended our church for a while. She sat up front all by herself anxious to soak up the teaching and anointing. She would ask for prayer for her unsaved husband and advice on a problem, many a result of living with his parents. Her husband was trying to save for the day they could buy their own home, or so he said, but both of them spent money foolishly, putting off that prospect until who knows when. She could have helped, but when you are so frustrated, you make a lot of foolish decisions. She loved her job and did not talk like she was going to quit very soon. The mother-in-law was their free baby sitter.

It was the weekends that caused the most problems because they had no privacy. During the week, it didn't matter. They could have made arrangements to get off by themselves, but that costs money and he didn't want to spend it, although he did go drinking with his buddies and that's not free. He left Jackie with the mother-in-law for long periods of time, which caused them to butt heads about the kids, the house, food, etc. The longer this went on, the more resentful of her husband and her mother-in-law Jackie became. The worse it got, the more she complained, making herself the bad guy and putting his mother in the middle.

I'm sure the mother didn't want to be in the middle, but she put herself there and deserved what she was getting because she should have known better than get between a man and his wife. The mess she was in was the natural consequence of her own error: hanging on to her boy when she should have cut him loose. Why didn't she? Because she loved having the grandkids around. Some women can't give up their mother role they love it so much. I can understand that, but we have to fight these tendencies. It leads us to hurt our children and cripple them as adults. Here she was trying to be a blessing and ending up the bad guy.

I really do think he didn't want to spend money, but the pull to drink and be with his buddies was stronger than his good intentions. Then, having created a bad situation at home, he avoided it at all cost. I should also explain her new spirituality wasn't helping. When she started going to church and did a complete turnabout in her life, this created a rift between them and the worse things got at home, the more she wanted to be at church. She prayed for him and tried to witness to no avail. That just made things worse. The more he rejected her, the closer she drew to us. We became her friends and family. And God, she drew closer to Him, too.

Finally, she told her husband enough is enough. She was taking her part of the money, the kids, and getting a place. He could come or not; it was up to him. But if he did come, be prepared to give up his drinking buddies and change his ways. She had had it with all of that, too. He didn't move out with her and was very uncooperative for a while but finally came to realize he missed all she meant to him. He missed his kids, too. He went to church and got saved and that really made a big difference. She was sweet and loving and tolerant for a long time (three or four years) but finally something had to give. In the end, she saw he really did agree with her about it all, and the relationship with the mother is better now. She still keeps the kids a lot.

Sometimes you just have to agree to disagree and go your separate ways until something is resolved. I don't like to recommend it because you start building your lives apart from each other. No telling what the enemy will do then. Be sure *you* aren't getting into sin, too. Just because he is, doesn't give you a right to. God's eye is watching for the *righteous* to defend (1 Pet. 3:12).

It is better if both give a little and tolerate what each isn't really thrilled about to build a life together. If he refuses to give up his drinking and his buddies, and you certainly can't give up your new found Jesus, although you may be able to give a little on when you go to church and how often, you might allow things to rock on as long as he is not spending too much money or worse. If you are doing your thing and he is doing his thing, it can work for a while as you get stronger in the Lord. Don't be too quick to make changes until you feel God is showing you to or until your husband insists.

Be sure you are praying a hedge of thorns around his ungodly relation-ships. Anyone that takes him away from you and the Lord is ungodly. Yes, even a mother! The hedge of thorns makes him and his friends become aggravated with each other until they finally split up. Just be sure you aren't a thorn, too.

Jackie was in prayer about how to handle things and instead of forcing a move, stayed on and continued to grow in her relationship with the Lord (and save the needed funds to make the move). There really wasn't any hurry. It was the enemy trying to get her to rush before she was ready and the time was right. *Timing is so very important.* It is tied into obedi-ence. It seems like God never speaks or you can't hear, but neither is true. He does speak and you can hear. Just get quiet. He's there. You just have to recognize Him. Since He searches your inner parts and knows what you think, why don't you search your inner parts and find out what He sees. Meet inside yourself. It's awesome.

It is very important steps are taken to secure his income from going down the tubes with the buddies. One episode with a lost paycheck is enough to take measures to see that it doesn't happen again. Direct deposit is nice. Don't neglect the practical things as you take care of the spiritual. You still have to be some earthly good to your family. I disagree that a person can be too heavenly minded to be any earthly good. Jesus was a very practical person and did not have His head in the clouds and yet no one was more heavenly minded.

That's just a cop out. However, if you have done everything you feel you should do and you still suffer the loss of a paycheck or a large amount of money, throw yourself on the mercy of the Lord again and remind Him He is your Source and you are depending on Him. We are limited in what we can do and after that it's the Lord's to do. He's my defender, protector, advocate, provider, interior decorator, dietician, nutritionist, social secretary, etc. He is everything I need Him to be.

I should point out, the more "spiritual" you become, the more irritated the unsaved will become with you. The spirit in him doesn't like the Spirit in you and it will take some time for this to come to a head. (He is under conviction and it's not pretty.) Your husband will tell you withdrawing from God will make it better between the two of you, but withdrawing from God never does anything but make things worse. You don't have to be so obvious about your spiritual hunger and growth, but you must maintain it, and it will spill out. He may be upset, but you cannot deny it. If something has to give, it must be him and the devils controlling him. Now is not the time to back up. Now is the time to fight all the harder *spiritually*, not verbally by fighting with him! You will find a list of your weapons in Ephesians 6.

In the process of all your fighting, no doubt one or both of you will say your relationship can't continue the way it is. You don't want to see the relationship end, but you don't have very good choices right now and can't seem to stop the deterioration. Nothing is the way you want it. You don't want a divorce but you can't stand the marriage. Now what?

Coming to a point of crisis is not necessarily bad. You can't just keep deteriorating. At some point each of you will have to decide if you want to do what it takes to make the marriage work. For many the answer will be no, but that doesn't mean the answer will stay no. Sometimes the person has to live where he or she thinks the grass is greener for a while to figure out it isn't greener at all. I just don't receive that your husband is going to choose to leave and stay gone. If he does, it's not a good sign. He may be like Lamar and never really leave. Let's not worry about all this right now and get *your* head on straight.

Your thinking has got you to this point, so something must be wrong with your thinking. He is not the only one that needs help in this area. We have to get you turned around, or even if he makes some positive moves, you won't be able to sustain them. I have known of men to come home only to leave again because nothing had changed and we don't want this to happen to you.

I understand things look impossible right now. Right now is not the time to look at how impossible it is. We serve an impossibly powerful God. He will do whatever it takes to get your husband to cooperate. It won't be easy; just know that God is up to the job and He will help you so that you are up to the job too.

I must reiterate, it is not God that brings the bad things upon your husband to turn his thinking around. It will be you or your husband that has opened the door because one or both of you has stepped out of God's protection and God is allowing some of it.

One incident happened to Lamar when he was backslidden. He was returning home from Miami on a single engine plane when they encountered a terrible storm. One tiny engine against the forces of nature. He thought for sure they weren't going to make it. He was as white as a sheet when he disembarked the plane. Do I need to tell you he went to church that Sunday? He didn't have to get right at church. He got right 30,000 feet up!

IF YOU DO TODAY WHAT GOD WOULD HAVE YOU DO, TOMORROW WILL TAKE CARE OF ITSELF

I understand we think things will never change, but they do change. They change all the time, sometimes to the better and sometimes to the worst. I remember the day they changed to for the worst for me: the day I missed the "express" bus to Florida and had to take the "local" that stopped at every Podunk little station along the way. It came in only two hours later, but it was a hundred wake-up stops and me with a little boy that woke up too. I sat there amazed, not just that I had missed my bus, but my life was no longer charmed. It just seemed all my life I had made things in the nick of time. I always pulled it out and things turned out OK. And for some reason I knew this time wasn't just a fluke. That this would be the way things would be for a long time. That's why, when I finally could hear from God and we had a relationship and He started showing me things and I was obedient to this voice within, that it was such a special life changing thing. Now I wasn't just "charmed," I was anointed and that's so much better. Things did change, and not just for the better but beyond what we ever dreamed possible.

Maybe you don't feel charmed or anointed. Maybe you feel relieved that you are saved and life is better, but charmed? That's a bit much. I think my life is that way because I pray about it and expect it. I pray about a good parking place. I pray about God opening up a new line for me. I watch for the anointing. But always remember, I will witness at the drop of a hat. I try to be very obedient. So, God is not helping me as much as He is helping us. We are a team. My time is His time and He cares about it. He and I are living this life of mine together; why shouldn't He open a new line for us? He's God! He's charmed and He's in me! So, I'm charmed, or I should say, anointed. The Bible says you have not because you ask not. Begin to ask (and in asking, expecting) and then watch. We miss so many blessings. According to your faith, so let it be done to you.

This walk with God is exciting even if it isn't easy. You have to get out of your comfort zone. And that is why we must be walking in the power of the Holy Spirit, because we do need a power greater than our own. It's all in this wonderful relationship we now have with God, our Father, Jesus, and Holy Spirit. Abide in Him and the circumstances in your life *have* to change.

PROVERBS

There are two scriptures I think we should end on. The first is Proverbs 14:1: *"Every wise woman builds her house, but a foolish one tears it down with her own hands."* It should probably say "with her own mouth." If your house falls down around you, you probably had a lot to do with it.

Please consider your ways and make today the day you begin to say and do something differently.

The second is Proverbs 31. Every once in a while Lamar would decide we needed to study Proverbs 31. He seemed to be hinting that I wasn't measuring up. Heaven knows I didn't need the Bible to tell me that. I was trying about as hard as I could and didn't see how I could do much more. Oh, to be like that special woman, worthy of her family rising up and calling her blessed. Then one day God asked me to read Proverbs 31 and He and I would read it together. I had trepidations, but didn't need to. The point is *not* to compare. That is a perversion of the scripture. Most of us don't have servants. We don't have to rise in the middle of the night and purple isn't our color. No, the point is do we do what it takes to nurture and take care of our family's needs.

As I began to read, God seemed to say "Slow down! Go back! Ponder what you just read. Consider what that means." What does it mean to be more precious than a ruby? God walks on gold and has precious stones inset all around Him in heaven. To Him they are common. He was saying I was anything but common. I was His child, for heaven's sake. What a special time as God told me how special I am to Him. No condemnation; no comparing me to anyone else; just Him and me reading the Word. A woman is very special to God. Don't ever let anyone make you think you are not. He loves you with an everlasting love. And if you were the only one that needed it, He would have come and died for you and you alone. He wants you with Him forever and ever. He loves you. Don't *ever* doubt that. He really doesn't like doubt.

Proverbs 31 is *the* woman's chapter, so we really need to ponder it. Let's you and me read verses 10–31 of this very special chapter together.

- *"A wife of noble character who can find?"* By seeking truth, living in obedience, and staying close to God, you can have a noble character. Your character is very important in your marriage and to your kids. It is primary.

- *"She is worth far more than rubies."* In case you didn't know it, rubies are more precious than diamonds. You are more precious than *the* most precious gem. You are priceless. Jesus was our price. Don't *ever* talk poorly about yourself. It reflects poorly on Him. You were made in the image of God and that alone makes you more special than you can ever imagine.

- *"Her husband has full confidence in her."* Trust is just about the most important thing in a marriage. Just as you want to trust him and that is of utmost importance to you, it is to him, too. How often we do things that destroy this trust and what is even worse, don't even acknowledge it. No wonder they stand off and take a defensive stance.

- *"She brings him good, not harm all the days of her life."* Think of how many of us bring harm to our husbands in spite of all we try to do right. I know I did! I'm just thankful that I was able to figure it out and stop a lot of it. Thank God it was all finally redeemed.

- *"She selects wool and flax."* Well, I don't think this is necessary; we have such wonderful new fabrics! The point is to make good choices for our home and business.

- *"And works with eager hands."* Heaven knows most of us work diligently to provide and care for our families. I know I'm worn out doing it. But love it and wouldn't have it any other way. When someone says, "I don't want to put you out." I think, I want to be put out. I love having friends and family here.

- *"She is like the merchant ships bringing her food from afar."* Well, maybe just from the local grocery store. But, hey, we are willing to do what it takes. Some women have to carry huge water bottles on their heads for miles and miles. Now that's a good woman. How many groceries have you toted in? Lots? I know I have.

- *"She gets up while it is still dark."* I've been known to get up before dark and you probably have, too. If we don't once in a while, I wonder if we are engaged in life properly.

- *"She provides food for her family and portions for her servant girls."* Like I said: she totes in the groceries, and cooks them! Gee, I missed out on the servant part. Today we call them employees, if we are lucky enough to be an employer. God expects some of us to even have help doing what we have to do and we have to provide for them properly.

- *"She considers a field and buys it."* Did you hear that? No shy thing here. I guess this will put to rest that God is a male chauvinist pig. I don't do the buying, but I do help in the decision making and that is very important. Lamar values my opinion, sometimes more than his own.

- *"Out of her earnings she plants a vineyard."* Well, some of us may need to do something else with our money. The point is she will reinvest her earnings.

- *"She sets about her work vigorously."* Just a busy little bee, that's me!

- *"Her arms are strong for her tasks."* Yes, and I built up some muscles, too, but if you don't have any, I don't think that was the point. To be what our husband needs us to be is the important thing. Joni Eareckson Tada is a blessing without strong arms or legs. But she sure does accomplish a lot.

- *"She sees that her trading is profitable."* It's not easy to be an entrepreneur. A good woman is wise enough to properly assess the costs and challenges of a business before she makes that commitment. It didn't come up for me because Lamar was so busy doing his thing with me his right hand man.

- *"And her lamp does not go out at night."* God is really into having oil in your lamp! Spiritual oil.

- *"She opens her arms to the poor and extends her hands to the needy."* God wants us to help others and a godly woman will do this. If you aren't already, you need to start. When God says something twice, it means it's really important! The Bible says in James 1:27, *"Pure religion ... is this, to visit the fatherless and widows in their affliction, and to keep himself unspotted from the world"* (KJV).

- *"Her husband is respected at the city gate."* I made a big point of this with Lamar. I felt he wasn't doing enough to influence the community and he is a wonderful, wise, godly man and he should be at the city gate, or in our case, the city council, determining the laws that are passed in our city. He was on the zoning board for a few years, but has since left because he is so busy. Now he just tries to be helpful in the local church.

- *"Where he takes his seat among the elders of the land."* Our husbands, fathers, and sons should be in leadership in our communities. We have no one to blame but ourselves if our land is in a mess.

- *"She makes linen garments and sells them."* Anyone that says God is against a woman working doesn't know their Bible. God wants us involved; we just have to be sure it is in the proper context of our lives as a whole. Nothing should harm our kids! But it is. Too much is harming our kids today.

- *"And supplies the merchants with sashes."* Whatever. I, myself, was an office manager. I'm sure that counts.

Lamar didn't need me to make sashes. Someday I will surely hear it preached—the significance of sashes. That's what I love about the Bible. It's so rich.

- *"She is clothed with strength and dignity."* Inner strength is more important than outer strength; however, we should be as physically fit as possible. Don't just do the inner beauty thing. That's a cop out. Be as strong physically as you can be. I have always been very active and feel it is an important part of life. Dignity is *very* important. A man does not want his woman to embarrass him. He wants to be able to be proud of her and God does, too. Your reputation is very important. It is possible to make a new one.

- *"She can laugh at the days to come."* Laughter is very important today, tomorrow, and all the days we have. Laugh at the devil when he comes to call. Joy is the proof we believe what God says. This indicates the bad days to come, good or bad, our faith is in the Lord to see us safely through.

- *"She speaks with wisdom."* This is not always easy, so speak along scriptural lines and you won't make a mistake. That requires that you study and know what it is saying! I am really into watching what we say. We are the prophets of our own lives *and* our family's. The opposite is just as true: don't speak foolishness!

- *"And does not eat the bread of idleness."* Put down that bon-bon and step away from the couch! This is not a suggestion! It is a command! Repent if you have not followed it!

- *"Her children arise and call her blessed."* Amen. It's about time! I'm exhausted. (But girl, you shouldn't be. Maybe you've done more than your part! Don't be an enabler! The Bible says we are to lay down our heavy burden and take up His light burden. So why are we so tired? Maybe we picked ours back up and now have them both!)

- *"Her husband also, and he praises her."* It's music to my ears. When that wonderful day came I was shocked, it came so early. I really thought I would have to wait until I was on my deathbed. How sweet it is! Yes, Lamar finally praised me as a Proverbs 31 woman!

- *"Many women do noble things."* Yes, women all over the world care for their families and do it in a way that requires a great deal more work on their part than what I do. I am not better than them!

- *"But you surpass them all."* Only because I know the Lord. Only through Him!

- *"Charm is deceptive, and beauty is fleeting."* I don't know about the charm thing, but I tried desperately to stop beauty from fleeting to no avail. Our choice is to get older or die and I choose to stay and hope for the inner beauty thing to kick in enough to overcome the lost outer beauty.

- *"But a woman who fears the Lord is to be praised."* There it is! The crux of the whole thing! Do you *really* fear the Lord? Or are you still doing your own thing much of the time? If you don't fear the Lord, you won't be praised.

- *"Give her the reward she has earned."* We have to earn the accolades we receive. They don't just come without us lifting our finger. Sure, it is Him that gives the increase, but only as we do our part. And that's the hard part, but it is a blessing. He gives it to me daily, new blessings every morning, more than I can contain.

- *"And let her works bring her praise at the city gate."* Eventually what I do is noticed, but more than what I do: what He anoints. I'm anointed! And because I am anointed, I am blessed. These blessings bring me accolades and that's OK too because I turn them back on Him. Because I know if there is any good in me, it's because of Him in me. It's all in Him! Praise God forevermore.

And so there it is: a trip through Proverbs 31, something like he did it that day. I hope you liked it better this way. You must do it again someday with Him. It will seem like you never read it before. You would do well to model your life after this chapter:

1. Be of noble character
2. Be trustworthy
3. Be good
4. Be discriminating
5. Be a provider
6. Be a hard worker
7. Be generous
8. Be watchful
9. Be involved
10. Be strong
11. Be confident
12. Be joyful and laugh easily.

Dear God! How can I ever be all these things?! It sounds like a sick joke! Only through You, Lord. Only through You!

Let's go to the movies! I'll treat.

ENCHANTED

My new favorite movie is *Enchanted*, starring Amy Adams, Patrick Dempsy, and James Marsden. I've seen it twice at the theaters just to get my husband to see it once. There are just some things you want your husband to experience so he will understand what you're thinking and talking about. And there are some movies that need to be seen on the big screen. I'm not quite an animation come to life, but almost. I *am* from another place, a place of goodness and joy. A place where there is no sickness or poverty. Well, now that I think of it, there was an evil queen in Andalasia, but so far she hadn't shown it very much, only to manipulate her stepson Edward's life! Gee, that doesn't speak well of mothers that are manipulating their children's or husband's lives, does it?

Giselle, the main character, lives in the animated kingdom of Andalasia, engaged to the wonderful Prince Edward. On her way to her wedding, she is captured and in the process sent tumbling down a tube to New York City of all places. She immediately meets a lawyer, Robert, and his very special daughter, Morgan, who save her from falling off a large sign. She may be made of flesh now, but she seems to have maintained some of her special powers. She can whip up a new dress in a snap. She is a can-do woman.

Giselle doesn't seem to have the ability to comprehend bad things. That's the way God originally created us. Only knowing good. So, when we are redeemed, I feel we should go back to that state of mind. "Love doesn't last forever" is the male character's big saying, and she simply cannot agree. Marriage is forever. Divorce? I don't think so. It just doesn't compute. I'm sure sickness wouldn't have fit into her mindset either.

Her greatest desire is to help people. Sounds like what God had in mind to me. She was so sad when she saw what a mess the place was in. No problem; she and a few of her "friends" could get it done. Robert, of course, is always trying to rein her in. Again, sounds like Lamar and me.

I love the way she bursts out in song and dance. I am a dancer. I still have my tap shoes. The grandgirls get exasperated because they can just use a word and get me started on a song. Lamar is always having to tell me to tone it down. I love it when he leaves so I can finally cut loose. And sometimes he comes right back and walks back in the middle of my biggest moment.

I've been known to sing Christmas carols in July. Why does Christmas have to be just one day? She brings such joy into everyone's life. She lifts their spirits. That is what a woman should do. We are from another place, a better place. And we know things these poor beaten down humans don't know. We know we can win. We simply cannot compute life any other way. Not that we are naïve, but that there is a greater truth: love. God's love. Jesus living in and through me.

Too simplistic? Well, it is all very simple. God is good and the devil is bad. What don't you understand about that? God wants to bless you and the devil wants to stop Him. God gave us dominion and the devil took it away and Jesus got it back for us. God wants obedience, and we want our own way. God will help us, and we have the right to choose.

No, I'm not Edith after all. I'm Giselle. And Lamar is Prince Edward. Well, actually now he is King Edward because his mother, the queen, (and an especially nice queen, definitely not an evil one) passed on. My question to you is who are you? The wonderful thing about Jesus, the Father and the Holy Spirit is if you are the mean queen, you can go ahead and die (to yourself) and be reborn as a princess and eventually become the nice queen when your husband becomes king. The choice again is yours. God wants you to be a princess or a queen and your husband does, too. How can you lose with these two on your side? You can't. The Word says, "I can do all things through Christ who strengthenth me."

If you are a godly woman, things are bound to change for you and in your favor. In fact, we have been promised favor. God has promised people will rise up and call us blessed. And the gospel tells us we can begin our walk in righteousness at any time. It's never too late. Today is the only day you have to begin the changes.

I hope you have gleaned something out of my stories as Lamar and I have come to a point of a special, wonderful love. Not because we are so special, but because He is. Our story is like that of the woman at the well, told in John 4:7–39, who Jesus told if she drank of living water she would never thirst again. We found the source of love, and our love has never run out since. Oh, precious love that flows from His throne above and waters the flowers of our garden when we are as barren as they are. Oh, precious love that makes all things new, that resurrects dead relationships. Oh, precious love that soothes my battered soul when I have done all I can do and only made things worse. Oh, precious love that plans the answer when I don't even know there is a problem. Oh, precious love that picks me up when everyone else has kicked me and left me to die. Oh, precious love that never leaves me even when I deserve what I get. Oh, precious, unfathomable love that gives me joy and peace when all around me stands in ruin. Oh, precious love that makes me laugh when I should be crying. Oh, precious love that reveals to me how very, very much He loves me in spite of myself, and that He does hold me in high esteem; that He cared enough to search for me and find me in that terrible pit I was in; that love that said, "My daughter is lost! Come, help me find my daughter! I will not rest until she is found!" And to that love I say, "Abba, Father! Precious Daddy! I love You, too! With the only (imperfect) love I can muster. I really do!"

This is the love I want for you. Abide in Him. Be His child, and He will be your Abba Father. What I have is available to anyone, just like it was for anyone that day that the woman touched the hem of His garment. God loves for us to seek Him out, to include Him in our day, to invite Him, and to remind Him of what He has promised us. He wants a very active, loving relationship with you more than you will ever know.

And now it's time to leave it with you. Maybe some day on the earth we will meet and have a special time together. But if we don't, we have all eternity to hang out together and see all those precious ones we have sent on ahead. There will be streets of gold and wonderful jewel tones everywhere, and most of all there will be Jesus and His wonderful Father, our wonderful Father; and the Holy Spirit, our wonderful Teacher and Comforter, the one who has spoken for us and been so faithful here. Our tears will be wiped away and joy will fill our days, and we will be eternally grateful and filled with the wonderful splendor that only God and the angels know now. Oh, glorious day when we finally see Him face to face!

So, we must part temporarily. And I say to you what I would tell my sons when they left the house, "Be sweet."

Love,

Midge

SERVE GOD, SERVE PEOPLE, AND SERVE GREAT FOOD!

Notes

Chapter 2

My Personal Search for Truth

1. "I Have Met the Enemy and He Is Us," *I Go Pogo*, http://www.igopogo.com/final_authority.htm (accessed March 17, 2008).

Chapter 3

The Search for My Personal Truth

1. Please note that if you are experiencing physical or verbal abuse, your relationship needs professional intervention, and fast. It will only escalate if you allow it to go on. God will help you walk through this, too, and just remember that it's not your fault that you are being abused. Quit hiding the truth and seek help; secrecy works in their favor, not yours. You must reach out for the abuser's sake as well as your own, but be very careful. Don't be naïve about the dangers of rocking the boat. An intervention is often a good way to get them into the process and bring about their healing, but it takes a group of professionals and the proper planning.

Chapter 5

What God Intended

1. John Holmes, *The Farmer's Dog* (London: Popular Dogs Co. Ltd., 1960).

2. Watchman Nee, *The Spiritual Man*, vol. 2 (Anaheim, CA: Living Stream Ministry), 7–9.

CHAPTER 6

MY DARK HOUR

1. Benny Hinn, *The Anointing* (Nashville, TN: Thomas Nelson, Inc., 1992), 23.

CHAPTER 7

AUTHORITY

1. Watchman Nee, *Spiritual Authority* (Richmond, VA: Christian Fellowship Publishers, 1972), 24.

CHAPTER 8

MAN AND WO MAN

1. Jack Serra, *Marketplace, Marriage, and Revival*, 129–130.
2. Helen B. Andelin, *Fascinating Womanhood* (New York, NY: Bantam, 2007).

CHAPTER 14

ONE MIND

1. Diana and John Hagee, *What Every Man Wants in a Woman/What Every Woman Wants in a Man* (Lake Mary, FL: Charisma House, 2005).

CHAPTER 16

WHY MEN RUN

1. Will Rogers quote accessed at http://www.greenwayparks.com/index. php/greenway-parks-history/the-early-years.html (September 11, 2008).

CHAPTER 19

TO BE CONTENT

1. Quote from Clarence Thomas, *My Grandfather's Son: A Memoir* (New York, NY: Harper Perennial, 2008), accessed at http://www. claremont.org/publications/crb/id.1564/article_detail.asp (September 11, 2008).

CHAPTER 24

BARE MINIMUMS

1. Virginia M. Axline, *Dibs in Search of Self* (New York, NY: Ballantine Books, 1986).

CHAPTER 25

SABOTAGING THE PLAN

1. William Shakespeare quote accessed at www.BrainyQuote.com (September 10, 2008).

CHAPTER 34

FOLLOWERS

1. Nee, 34.
2. Ibid.
3. Ibid., 13.

CHAPTER 38

THE MARRIAGE DISINTEGRATES

1. John Eldredge, *Wild at Heart* (Nashville, TN: Thomas Nelson, 2006).

CHAPTER 39

BELIEVING A LIE

1. William Cope Moyers and Katherine Ketcham, *Broken: My Story of Addiction and Redemption* (New York: Viking, 2006).

To Contact the Author

GRAMMAMIDGE@HOTMAIL.COM

www.lettheolderwomenteach.com